The Real World Entrepreneur

Field Guide

GROWING YOUR OWN BUSINESS

David H. Bangs, Jr. and Linda Pinson

D1370353

Upstart
Publishing Company®
A Kaplan Professional Company

▼▼▼▼▼▼▼▼▼▼▼▼▼▼▼▼▼▼▼▼▼▼▼▼▼▼

To Clare, Lily
and Nick

▼▼▼▼▼

This publication is designed to provide accurate and authoritative information in regard to the subject matter covered. It is sold with the understanding that the publisher is not engaged in rendering legal, accounting, or other professional service. If legal advice or other expert assistance is required, the services of a competent professional person should be sought.

Editorial Director: Cynthia A. Zigmund
Acquisitions Editor: Robin Nominelli
Managing Editor: Jack Kiburz
Interior Design: Lucy Jenkins
Cover Design: Scott Rattray, Rattray Design
Typesetting: Eliot House Productions

Published by Upstart Publishing Company®, a Kaplan Professional Company

Printed in the United States of America
99 00 01 10 9 8 7 6 5 4 3 2 1

Library of Congress Cataloging-in-Publication Data
Bangs, David H.
    The real world entrepreneur field guide: growing your own business/David H. Bangs, Jr. and Linda Pinson.
        p.   cm.
    Includes index.
    ISBN 1-57410-113-7 (pbk.)
    1. New business enterprises—Handbooks, manuals, etc. 2. Small business—Handbooks, manuals, etc. 3. Entrepreneurship.
    I. Pinson, Linda. II. Title.
    HD62.5.B362   1999   98-31848
    658.02'2—dc21   CIP

Upstart books are available at special quantity discounts to use as premiums and sales promotions, or for use in educational programs. For more information, please call Upstart at 800-621-9621, ext. 4529, or write to Upstart Publishing Company, 155 N. Wacker Drive, Chicago, IL 60606-1719.

Module 2   START-UP BASICS   41

Module 3   THE BUSINESS PLAN   **97**

Module 8 CREATING AND MANAGING GROWTH **503**

LIST OF FIGURES

Personal Workshops

CASE STUDIES

Introduction: Welcome to the Real World

*H*ello, and welcome to the beginning of a very exciting time in your life! No less than Columbus or Neil Armstrong, you are setting out on a voyage of discovery and exploration. And this book you're holding is your map, your chart, your field guide—the tool that will help you get from where you are, through mysterious and unknown regions to where you want to be. Thanks for deciding to bring us along for the ride.

THE BOOK THAT ISN'T A BOOK

What you're holding in your hands is no ordinary book. In fact, we hesitate to call it a *book* at all. The folks at Upstart Publishing pretty much know what a book is, and this collection of pages bound together flies in the face of a lot of the things we've come to expect of a book. So welcome to the future, and to the book that isn't, strictly speaking, a book.

Why isn't it a book? Well, traditionally a textbook locks you in to a particular model. It starts with Chapter 1, which is a general chapter about the subject, and proceeds to subsequent chapters in a neat, straight line. From Chapter 1, you go to Chapter 2. When you're done there, you are off to Chapter 3, and so on. Each chapter builds on material taught in the chapter before, layering information on top of information until you end up with a big, layered pile of comprehension that you can either stand on top of to survey the world, or be buried under. That's the old model.

LET'S GO SURFING

Today, we live in the age of the Internet, in an age of instant access to detailed information on very specific topics, chosen and ordered and arranged by users to fit their personal needs. People surf the World Wide Web, picking up scattered bits of connected information to construct something meaningful for themselves. *For themselves*—that's the key phrase. Modern technologies increasingly put the power to construct knowledge in the hands of end-users. Information isn't given to people any more: now they go and get it for themselves.

Which brings us back to this book. Even though we've numbered the chapters from 1 to 26, and you *can* read them in that order if you want, it's not necessary. The chapters follow the logical order of a conventional small business start-up. But we know, from long years of experience, that while small businesses are a lot of things, conventional is rarely among their characteristics. So we aren't being too picky about how you read this book. Not because we don't care, but because we think the best judge of what you need to know is you (and your instructor). The chapters are clearly titled, so you can tell what they're about. And they're grouped by general subject matter into eight business development modules. The same rule goes for the modules, too: you can read them forwards, backwards, or inside-out...it's up to you. Why? Because the chapters in this book have been "de-linked"; that is, they are freestanding and independent of one another (sort of like an entrepreneur). Your instructor will decide how to work you through them.

See Also . . .

► 2. The Economics of Small Business

► 3. The Personal Side: What Kind of Business Is Best for You?

► 13. Creating an Identity and Choosing a Name

► 16. Customer Service and Sales

► 17. Developing a Web Presence

► 18. Forms of Organization

A NEW, INNOVATIVE WAY TO LEARN

Your instructor may want to follow a business development model, in which case you'll go from Chapter 1 straight through to the end. Or he or she may want you to follow a business-plan focus, in which the chapter order will be based on the general structure of a business plan. If a big-picture, little-picture model is preferred, you'll start with the broadest topics and work your way down an inverted pyramid to the specifics. Your instructor may also have some other model in mind. The point is, you won't be at a disadvantage if you read the chapter on naming your business before you read the one on the small business economy.

But just in case you're worried about missing something, you'll find a navigation map at the beginning of each chapter. This is similar to the site maps you'll find on Web sites that illustrate how pages relate to each other and show you where you've been. Our navigation maps illustrate your position in the structure of this book, and show you which other chapters include relevant, related content that could help build or reinforce your understanding of the subject matter. It's up to you whether to refer to those chapters, of course, but the maps help you anticipate the level and breadth of comprehension required. Here, at left, is a sample map from Chapter 22, *Home-Based Business Issues*. The map clearly indicates which chapters are especially relevant to the subject of home-based business.

IF IT'S NOT A BOOK, THEN WHAT IS IT?

OK, we know the title of this book is a mouthful, but it describes exactly what you're looking at. Let's consider that hefty title in its separate parts to figure out what this book is—and isn't—about.

The Real World... This book is not about business theory, or pure economics, or fundamentals of accounting. It's not about making you feel good about yourself, or promising that your business will grow into a market-dominating behemoth in 12 months. It's about the *real world*: the world where you have to think about things before you do them; where every decision has consequences; where, sometimes, good ideas are ignored and promising businesses fail. Of course, it's also the world of risk and opportunity and excitement and potential; the world where a man or a woman armed with an idea and good business skills can create a new business that builds jobs, brightens futures, improves the world—and may put some money back into his or her pocket. That's the real world.

Entrepreneur... This book is not for people who automatically start with Chapter 1 just because the publisher printed the book that way. This book is for people who look at the contents, find what they want, and go there; people who don't waste time with what they don't need; people who have an idea and do something about it. That is, it's for entrepreneurs like you.

Field Guide. This book is like a tool that a geologist might take to a dig, or a bird-watcher to the woods, or a botanist to the bog. A field guide is used by professionals and amateurs to identify objects in their natural environment. For instance, an ornithologist might carry a field guide to help identify various species of birds. Traditionally, field guides are organized by characteristics such as color, size, location, or behaviors. No one would try to use a field guide to identify a mineral by starting on page one and reading straight through to the end, hoping that somewhere along the way they'd find what they were looking for. Rather, they would open the guide to the relevant class of distinguishing characteristics. Same thing with this book. It's designed to be used by entrepreneurs not just in the classroom, before you get started with your business, but "in the field"—out in the real world, to be opened up and consulted as needed. Mark it up, make it your own: its information is specific, and concrete and based on experience and insight. It isn't just a pretty theory.

NAVIGATING IN *THE REAL WORLD ENTREPRENEUR*

One of the biggest pitfalls for entrepreneurs starting new businesses is they fail to see the forest for the trees. They get so bogged down in the details of day-to-day nuts-and-bolts operation issues that they lose track of their business vision, their family life, and their sense of personal direction. Their skills and strengths are so scattered and subdivided among thousands of nagging details that they have nothing left for the big picture.

At the same time, many entrepreneurs have the opposite problem: they fail to see the *trees* for the *forest*. That is, they are so focused on the big picture that they ignore the vitally important operational details. While they're gazing into the glowing future, the floor is falling out from under their feet.

When we wrote this book, we decided that our primary objective had to be to help entrepreneurs chart a safe course between these extremes. We want you to see the forest, the trees, the flowers, the bunny rabbits—and the bears, too. We want you to see and enjoy the whole thing.

This whole book is based on four practical steps we call LEAP™. Through these steps you will not only learn how to run a business, but how to think like a businessperson. The four steps that form the LEAP™ learning process are:

1. *L*earn (collect information).
2. *E*xplore (analyze the information in detail, and see how it's used by others).
3. *A*pply (test the information's usefulness to a relevant situation).
4. *P*roduce (use the information in improving your day-to-day business development activities).

LEAP™ is designed to give entrepreneurs what they so desperately want: results. The four-part system engages you to understand ("learn") a new concept. That concept is illustrated through "exploration" of its parts, of issues it raises, and of others' experience. Next, you "apply" the concept through exercises, such as personal workshops, self-evaluation exercises, or case study roundtable discussions. Finally, you "produce" the end result in your business: a business plan, marketing strategy, cash flow analysis, pro forma, etc.

The LEAP™ process is embedded throughout the book: it is the framework on which the book is built. You won't find a special section called Learn or Explore—you'll just do it. That's a reflection of the real world, too. In the real world, you often won't find clearly labeled step-by-step instructions.

CHAPTER FEATURES

All the chapters in this book have several special features. The features are designed to make this a more interesting, more effective learning tool. The features are found throughout the text, many accompanied by easily identifiable icons. Here's a brief overview of the features you will find:

Mission Statement

Each chapter opens with a LEAP™ analysis of its content. The Mission Statement essentially tells you what the chapter will focus on, and what you can expect to learn.

Key Terms

Each chapter also starts off with a list of key terms. Sometimes, these are vocabulary terms that will be used in the chapter; other times, they are business jargon you need to know.

First Person

Who knows more about the real world challenges faced by entrepreneurs than other entrepreneurs who've been there? The First Person features of this book provide readers with real life war stories from people who share their advice, success stories, and hard knocks. The authors (painfully) recognize that people tend to listen more carefully to this kind of first-person information than to all the expert advice they can give. As a result, real people have been given a place to explain, advise, and sometimes warn readers about their real world experiences.

URLinks

"URL" is web-ese for *uniform resource locater*, and it means an Internet site's Web address. Throughout this book, we've included the URLs of useful, interesting, and relevant Web sites you can visit for more information about particular topics. Following the URLinks will take you to corporate home pages, on-line entrepreneurial workshops, commercial product sites and state, national, and even international government agencies.

Personal Workshop

Over 50 personal workshops have been included here. These are forms, checklists, self-evaluation exercises, or other tasks that give you a hands-on, interactive experience of the information you're studying.

& Taxes

We all know that there are only two things certain in life, and one of them is taxes. The "&Taxes" feature clues you in to the tax issues raised by certain topics. This is not tax advice—and you should always consult a competent tax attorney or accountant before you make any tax decisions—but this feature lets you know that an issue exists, so you can deal with it in an informed manner.

Liability Alert

Entrepreneurs are exposed to lawsuits in many situations, especially employment, contracts, and organizational matters. The Liability Alert gives you some general information about issues of law and liability. These features are not intended to be legal advice, of course (you should see your attorney if you have any questions). Like the &Taxes feature, however, the Liability Alerts provide a heads-up for the small business person.

Case Study

Case studies are included at the end of each chapter. These are detailed scenarios based on actual small business situations that highlight the chapter's main topics. These tend to be long and often contain a lot of information. As you read them, look for issues on which the chapter focused.

Case Study Roundtable

Following each case study, you will find a Case Study Roundtable. In this discussion-style feature, characters from the case study elaborate on their experiences and pose questions to you. Here, you are the expert, and get the opportunity to apply what you've learned to someone else's problem. The "discussion" is kept focused and directed by "Discussion Points" that guide you along the right path.

Some roundtables also include an additional feature, called "Back to the Table." Here, people from case studies in other chapters join your discussion and ask you to apply your newfound understanding to their situation. If you've already met them and read their case study, you can answer the questions right away. If you haven't been there yet, you can read their case study as additional reinforcement.

Chapter Briefcase

The Chapter Briefcase is a quick summary of the chapter's main points. If you need to study or review, the Briefcase is a good place to jog your memory. If you're looking for information in the real world, the Briefcase will remind you what you need to know.

Real World Video

Bringing the *Field Guide* to life is a robust video that explores the excitement and challenges of business ownership through personal stories of entrepreneurs. At the end of each video clip, contributing authors David H. "Andy" Bangs, Jr. and Linda Pinson offer expert commentary and advice. *The Real World Entrepreneur Video* icon will prompt you to cue up the video to a specific clip number and view a real world entrepreneur in action.

The video is ideal for group (classroom) or self-study and can be ordered directly from Upstart Publishing by calling 800-235-8866.

LET'S GET STARTED!

Now you know why this book isn't strictly a book. The de-linked chapters, the Navigation Maps, the LEAP structure, the icon-based features—it's the closest thing to a Web site that we could offer you without actually putting this book online (maybe next edition). So go ahead: surf away, jump in anywhere. Already know about business names and locations? Start with forms of organization or financing. We've given you the information, and the tools to apply it to your business. From here, it's up to you: you are responsible for your own decisions. Welcome to the real world.

ACKNOWLEDGMENTS

*Thank me no thanks, proud me
no prouds*

—William Shakespeare,
Romeo and Juliet, iii, 5

*I*n Greek mythology, there's a story about Athena, the daughter of Zeus, who sprang full-grown (and wearing armor) from her father's forehead. That is *not* how *The Real World Entrepreneur Field Guide* happened. This book is the end result of a lot of hard work and many valuable contributions from experts in both business and education. Whether by suggesting the direction the book should take, or reviewing the manuscript or video, these individuals provided vital professional guidance and real world expertise from which we all benefit. The diversity and quality of *The Real World* team should give you confidence about having chosen this book.

REVIEWERS

Our reviewers committed to hours of reading, analyzing, and commenting on the first draft manuscript. This book is built on the foundation of their feedback. To each of them, thank you for your many ideas and suggestions.

Fred Aiello, University of Southern Maine Small Business Development Center
Brian Burwell, University of Southern Maine Small Business Development Center

Bruce Davis, Weber State University
Chuck Davis, University of Southern Maine Small Business Development Center
Cathie Elliott, Western State College
John Entwistle, University of Southern Maine Small Business Development Center
Fred Kiesner, Loyola Marymount University
Mary Lou Lockerby, College of DuPage
Richard Lorentz, University of Wisconsin-Eau Claire
David Miller, Bloomington Indiana Small Business Development Center
Charles Toftoy, George Washington University
Henry J. Turner, Minority Business Assistance Center Small Business Development Center
Larry Wacholtz, Belmont University
John Wallace, Marshall University

REAL WORLD ENTREPRENEUR VIDEO

Hattie Bryant, creator of the public television show *Small Business 2000*, is an example of excellence in small business. Hattie and her partners at Quin Matthews Films were complete professionals, and always thought about our needs. Thanks to them, *The Real World Entrepreneur Field Guide* literally comes alive. A special thanks to Stewart Mayer for his eye for detail in editing.

CUSTOMERS AND FRIENDS OF UPSTART

We surveyed many people for perspectives on entrepreneurial training—what's being done, what needs to be done, and how a new, comprehensive training system from Upstart could serve the needs of students and trainers more effectively. Whether they answered a questionnaire, talked with us on the phone, or responded to a fax, their observations, opinions, and input were vital and appreciated components of the development process.

Nick Adams, Indiana Small Business Development Center
Rayanna Anderson, Missouri Small Business Development Center
Aaron Armendariz, El Paso Community College Small Business Development Center
Joann Ard, Wichita State University Small Business Development Center
Elise Ashby, Friendship House Small Business Development Sub-Center
Anne Bayless, Temple University Small Business Development Center
John Baker, Louisiana Small Business Development Center
Craig Bean, Northwest Texas Small Business Development Center
Lucy Betcher, University of Southern Mississippi Small Business Development Center
Debby Blatzer, Moraine Valley Community College
Randee Brady, University of Kansas Small Business Development Center
Jim Brazell, University of South Carolina Small Business Development Center

Tanya Brockett, Central Virginia Small Business Development Center
Dione Cahillane, University of Pittsburgh Small Business Development Center
Virginia Campbell, Missouri Small Business Development Center
Kathy Carrico, Nevada Small Business Development Center
Paula Carter, Springfield Missouri Small Business Development Center
Steve Carter, Iowa State University Small Business Development Center
Bonnie Chavez, Santa Barbara College
John Ciccarelli, Massachusetts Small Business Development Center
Mary Collins, New Hampshire Small Business Development Center
Mary Copps, Idaho State University Small Business Development Center
Linda Darraugh, Chicago Women's Business Development Center
Scott Daugherty, North Carolina Small Business Technology Development Center
Bruce Davis, Weber State University
Don Davis, Central Missouri State University Small Business Development
    Center
Vince Decker, Longwood Virginia Small Business Development Center
Jeff Dee, St. Louis University Small Business Development Center
Janice Donaldson, University of North Florida Small Business Development
    Center
Robert Ebberson, New Hampshire Small Business Development Center
Mark Enstrom, Illinois Department of Commerce and Community Affairs
Kim Esteran, Maricopa Community College Small Business Development Center
David Gay, College of DuPage Small Business Development Center
Peter George, New York Small Business Development Center
Linda Gerardo, Missouri Small Business Development Center
Verna Goatley, Bellarmine College Small Business Development Center
Dennis Gruell, Connecticut Small Business Development Center
Ronald Hall, Michigan Small Business Development Center
Barbara Harmony, Mansfield Adult Education
Joseph Harper, Houston Community College
Dwane M. Heintz, Wyoming Small Business Development Center
Lorraine Hendrickson, Eastern Michigan University
Jose Hernandez, Howard University Small Business Development Center
James Heyliger, Queens New York Small Business Development Center
Greg Higgins, Wharton Business School Small Business Development Center
Michael Hollbrook, Clark University (Massachusetts) Small Business
    Development Center
Leonard Holler, Wyoming Small Business Development Center
Janet Holloway, Kentucky Small Business Development Center
Irene Hurst, University of South Florida Small Business Development Center
Douglas Jobling, Rhode Island Small Business Development Center
William Joubert, Southeastern Louisiana University Small Business Development
    Center
Erica Kauten, University of Wisconsin, Extension Small Business Development
    Center
Walter Kearns, North Dakota Small Business Development Center
Ram Kesavan, University of Detroit Mercy Small Business Development Center

Donald Kilpinski, Vermont Small Business Development Center

Barrie Kirk, Midlands Technical College

Janice Kitchen, New Hampshire Office of Economic Initiatives

Dan Klingman, Washburn University Small Business Development Center

Ralph Kloser, Montana Small Business Development Center

John Lenti, South Carolina Small Business Development Center

Neil Lerner, University of Wisconsin-Madison Small Business Development Center

Todd Madson, Iowa Small Business Development Center

Betsy D. Mallon, St. Francis (Pennsylvania) Small Business Development Center

Donna Maupin, Kentucky Small Business Development Center

Robert McKinley, UTSA South Texas Border Small Business Development Center

Jane McNamee, UTSA South Texas Border Small Business Development Center

Denise Mikulski, Joliet Junior College

Laura Miller, Pittsburg State University (Kansas) Small Business Development Center

Deric Mims, Crestar Bank Business Information Center

William Minnis, Indiana State University

Jeff Mitchell, Illinois Small Business Development Center Network

Gillian Murphy, San Joaquin Delta College Small Business Development Center

Judi Nielsen, Iowa State University Business Development Center

Bill Nunnally, Brookdale Community College

Georgette Peterson, Galveston County Small Business Development Center

Jane Peterson, Springfield Missouri Small Business Development Center

William Pfaff, Delaware Technical and Community College Small Business Development Center

JoAnn Powell, City of Bryan, Texas

Pam Pyeatt, Missouri Small Business Development Center

Daniel Regelski, Florida Gulf Coast University Small Business Development Center

Lowell Salter, University of North Florida

Joseph Schwartz, SUNY Farmington Small Business Development Center

John Scott, U.S. Small Business Administration, Las Vegas Nevada Region

Jeff Seifried, Aurora Colorado Small Business Development Center

Deb Shough, Northwest Missouri Small Business Development Center

Deleski Smith, Lansing Community College Small Business Development Center

Anna Steele, LCRA Small Business Development Center

Kathy Stittleburg, University of Wisconsin, Extension Small Business Development Center

Sharon Stratton, West Virginia Small Business Development Center

Max Summers, Missouri Small Business Development Center

Kim Takaki, Colorado Small Business Development Center

Steve Thrash, Indiana Small Business Development Center Network

Elaine Tweedy, University of Scranton Small Business Development Center

Michael Varderlip, University of Mississippi Small Business Development Center

Mark Weaver, University of Alabama

Ronald B. Westbrook, East Central Community College
William Wetzel, University of New Hampshire
Robert Wilburn, Virgina Small Business Development Center
Diane Wirth, Maryland Small Business Development Center
Bonnie J. Winnett, Zanesville-Muskingum Small Business Development Center
Bryan Ziegler, Buena Vista University

PATTING OURSELVES ON THE BACK

Finally, special thanks are due to Carol Luitjens for her vision and support throughout this project. Evan Butterfield and Lucy Jenkins of Dearborn, along with Dana Anderson, Sandra Holzbach, Jack Kiburz, Robin Nominelli, and Cynthia Zigmund at Upstart, all spent more time and energy than was strictly within their job descriptions to make this book a standard of excellence.

AND FINALLY...

No book is really finished until it is opened up and used. The research, writing, production and marketing of a book are vital steps in its life, but no step is more important than the last one: being read. If no one buys it, if no one reads it, then none of the rest of the steps in the process, no matter how excellent and well-intentioned, make much difference. So to those instructors who have adopted this book for use in their classrooms: Thank you! And to the students (and non-students) who have bought this book and are reading it now: Thank you!

Remember as you read this book that even though the two people listed on the cover would, by themselves, be more than sufficient, you are actually hearing the voices and benefiting from the expertise of about 125 different professionals. The entrepreneur may be a "lone wolf" in the marketplace, but you're hardly alone here. All of us hope this book makes your real world adventure a positive and profitable one.

A Complete History of
The Real World Entrepreneur Field Guide

▼▼▼▼▼▼

*If I have seen further it is by standing on
the shoulders of Giants.*

—*Sir Isaac Newton*

HOW THIS BOOK WAS BORN

The Real World Entrepreneur Field Guide is a pretty big book, and its development was an enormous undertaking. First, we talked with our customers and friends to find out what they liked (and didn't like) about the entrepreneurial training materials they were currently using, and what wasn't there that they'd really like to find. With their observations in mind, we looked at our existing product line and realized that much of what people wanted had already been created. Problem was, it had been created by different authors, for different audiences, at different times, and in different ways. The Upstart "database" was broken up into a number of (excellent) products that each concentrated on a single limited issue in small business development: the business plan, strategic thinking, accounting, marketing—each with its own separate book. We could clearly see that the wheel had already been invented; it was up to us to turn that rolling stone into a steel-belted radial. And so that collected material became the foundation of our vision: a single, all-inclusive guide to starting, managing, and running a small business in the real world.

We wrote this book, basically, by standing on the shoulders of giants: the proven work of carefully selected professionals—along with a lot of completely new material. Like the development of a small business itself, this book relies on both time-tested ideas and new and visionary innovations.

▼▼▼▼▼▼▼▼▼▼▼▼▼▼▼▼▼▼▼▼▼▼▼▼▼

Once we had what we thought was a good book, we went back to our friends and customers. Based on their comments, we tweaked and rewrote and edited the manuscript. We kept asking more questions and generally making pests of ourselves until we felt that we had a superior product that we could be proud of. Once we were satisfied, a bunch of other people worked very hard to take what we'd produced (over a thousand sheets of paper and several floppy disks) and turn it into something readable. And here it is. Welcome to *The Real World*. Enjoy.

THE REAL WORLD ENTREPRENEUR FIELD GUIDE: DEVELOPMENT AND SOURCES

About the Writer

Evan M. Butterfield. An experienced writer of adult learning products, Evan took on the job of creating a single, cohesive book based on several very different Upstart titles. During his tenure at Dearborn, Evan has written more than 25 publications on subjects ranging from real estate law to economics, marketing, and small business management. He has an MA in English from the University of Illinois at Urbana and a JD from DePaul University College of Law. A certified instructional designer/developer, Evan has 10 years of experience teaching college and workplace writing courses. Currently Online Education Product Manager at Dearborn Financial Publishing, Evan has published several articles on Web-based training and has been a featured speaker at seminars, conferences, and government regulatory hearings.

About the Consulting Editors

David H. "Andy" Bangs, Jr. Regarded as a leading expert in the field of small business management, Andy founded Upstart Publishing in 1977. His credentials come from over 30 years of small business management experience. *The Business Planning Guide*, now in its 8th edition, is a blockbuster, with more than one half million copies in circulation. Andy has written several other small business titles, including *The Market Planning Guide, 5th Edition, The Start Up Guide, 3rd Edition, Launching Your Home-Based Business*, and others. He is nationally known as a small business speaker and consultant.

Linda Pinson. Entrepreneur, author of six business books, and developer of a robust business plan software program, *Automate Your Business Plan*, Linda is a model woman business owner. Her best-selling book, *Anatomy of a Business Plan* (now in revision for its 4th Edition), received the 1994 Ben Franklin Award for Best Business Book of the Year. In 1989, her publishing company, Out of Your Mind...and Into the Marketplace™ was named Small Press Publisher of the Year. In addition to educating entrepreneurs through her books and software, Linda is a frequent media guest expert and a nationally recognized speaker on small business issues.

Upstart's Greatest Hits

The Real World Entrepreneur Field Guide includes adapted material originally published by the following authors:

David H. Bangs
The Business Planning Guide
The Market Planning Guide
The Start Up Guide

Marilyn Batey
Human Resources: Mastering Your Small Business

John de Young
Cases in Small Business Management

Fred Fry
Strategic Planning for the New and Small Business

James N. Holly (Biography provided in Appendix C)
Total Quality Management: Mastering Your Small Business

Sheri Moore Humphrey
Business and the Legal System: Mastering Your Small Business

Jerry Jinnett
Anatomy of a Business Plan
Keeping the Books
Steps to Small Business Start Up
Target Marketing

Kevin D. Mathews
Business and the Legal System: Mastering Your Small Business

Scott Minter
Business and the Legal System: Mastering Your Small Business

Linda Pinson
Anatomy of a Business Plan
Keeping the Books
Steps to Small Business Start Up
Target Marketing

Jill A. Rossiter, Management Education Institute
(Biography provided in Appendix C)
Human Resources: Mastering Your Small Business
Total Quality Management: Mastering Your Small Business

Fred Safer
Business and the Legal System: Mastering Your Small Business

John R. Sosey
Business and the Legal System: Mastering Your Small Business

Susan Stites, Management Allegories (Biography provided in Appendix C)
Human Resources: Mastering Your Small Business

Charles Stoner
Strategic Planning for the New and Small Business

Stephen R. Tumbush
Business and the Legal System: Mastering Your Small Business

WOULD I START MY OWN BUSINESS AGAIN? YOU BET I WOULD!

Starting a business is an exhilarating experience. You can't imagine how much you will learn about yourself, other people, and business when you jump into the entrepreneurial life.

I have only two regrets. The first is that I didn't strike out on my own earlier. I was in my mid-30s when I founded Upstart with $3,000. Looking back, I had all of the necessary skills when I was in my early 20s but I didn't have the motivation. The notion of being an entrepreneur simply never crossed my mind. Think of the years I wasted working for other people!

The second is that I didn't realize that it takes no more effort, intelligence, and risk to build a big business than a small one. The upside potential of a fast-growing business is much greater than for a small steady business, and the downside risk no greater. (You can go just as broke with a small venture as a large one.) A major venture capital firm in New York City approached me in 1986. After months of talk they said they were willing to fund Upstart to the tune of $2–3 million to get in early on electronic publishing. I panicked. Now I know that it would have been fun and maybe I'd have made more money. Or maybe not. Money is nice, but it is hardly what drives me. The thrill comes in making a business grow, serving more customers, trying out new ways to deliver value to them, and watching your employees grow and develop. Try it. You'll like it. The worst that can happen is that you'll lose some money, and money can always be replaced. Your time cannot.

—Andy Bangs, Author, Sailor, Entrepreneur

AH... THE AMERICAN DREAM

*O*wn your own business, make lots of dollars, do the work you want to when you want to, and conduct lots of your business on the golf course. I can certainly say that I have lived the American Dream, but not all of the parameters turned out to be the ones I envisioned. True, I own my business and I have made lots of dollars. I have also spent lots of dollars. I do the work I want to do, but I worked far more hours than the law should allow. And the only business I conduct on the golf course is the business of smelling the roses. But, what an adventure it has been!

The greatest thing about entrepreneurship is that I have been allowed to be me. I have learned much about life through the world of business: that a focus on excellence and ethics comes first and success will follow, and that real growth is gained through the formation of strategic alliances.

I, like all entrepreneurs (and other folks) have things I would have done differently. I would have started earlier, risked more, and shared more responsibility with others. But my road here has been my own and I could do no better than to wish that those of you who read this book will eventually reap as many rewards as I have.

Educate yourself and *climb your mountain. The view from the summit is great!*

I wish you success.

—Linda Pinson

Adapted with permission from
Small Business 2000, the
series on public television.

INTRODUCTION TO ENTREPRENEURSHIP

Bill Tobin (Stamford, Connecticut)
PC Flowers and Gifts
www.pcflowers.com

"*A*n entrepreneur to me is sort of like a dog with a bone. He doesn't drop it until there's not a scrap of meat left on it. He stays with it. He is focused, he is myopic, he is tenacious, whereas people that just try to be entrepreneurial are merely skipping and jumping and spreading themselves thin. An entrepreneur is absolutely driven and cannot sleep, cannot eat, cannot do anything until he accomplishes that goal.

I meet guys all the time in large corporations who tell me they want to go out on their own, and about 90 percent of them shouldn't. A guy who is used to working for someone else says, "Well, I've made $50,000 this year. I'd be willing to go out on my own for $40,000." No, an entrepreneur is willing to go out on his own for nothing, with no income possibility for the next couple of years, risking everything he has instead of saying, "This is for my kids' college. This is for this. This is for that." You've got to take all those marbles and put them up on the table. Set a little aside, keep a little back, but most of it must go on the table for your next venture or to get the penetration you need for your current venture. An entrepreneur is truly one of the biggest gamblers in the world, but he gambles in an area where he controls the odds, as opposed to the house controlling the odds. *"*

Chapter 1

ENTREPRENEURSHIP, SMALL BUSINESS, AND YOU

▼▼▼▼▼

*A man who carries a cat by the tail
learns something
he can learn in no other way.*

—*Mark Twain*

MISSION STATEMENT

In this chapter, you will

*L*EARN how the entrepreneurial process fits with your goals and the start of your business.

*E*XPLORE the characteristics of entrepreneurs and their businesses.

*A*PPLY your understanding to the start-up case study roundtable discussion.

*P*RODUCE an analysis of your business and your personal character to help determine your suitability for the world of small business.

KEY TERMS

entrepreneur	risk	Small Business
entrepreneurship	small business	Administration (SBA)
innovation		vision

WHAT IT MEANS TO BE "ENTREPRENEURIAL"

This is a book for people who consider themselves "entrepreneurs." That's why we called it *The Real World Entrepreneur*. But what do we mean by that? We happen to think that anyone who has the courage to stop working for someone else and give up that regular paycheck and comfortable benefits package is an entrepreneur. There's only one way to really learn how to be entrepreneurial, and that's to take the risk and do what you want to do. Like Mark Twain said: there's only one way to learn the truth about carrying a cat by the tail—and there's only one way to learn the truth about being an entrepreneur. (Of course, being an entrepreneur usually has better results than picking up a cat by the tail—for both entrepreneurs and cats—but there are, as you'll find out, a few similarities, too!)

For some, the financial stakes may be six or seven or eight figures; for others, it may be only a few thousand dollars. But the difference is only one of quantity, not quality. For all of them, the risk of personal failure is real and frightening and potentially disastrous: it's just a matter of scale. When a billionaire loses everything on an entrepreneurial gamble, it makes a big splash. When someone sinks her life's savings into a home-based basket business that fails, the splash is smaller. In both cases, though, the owners are equally broke. Risk is a great leveler.

Small Business: The American Way

The history of the modern American business economy is a history of entrepreneurship. From Henry Ford's "better idea" to Steve Jobs and Steve Wozniak who started Apple Computers in their garage and launched a cultural revolution; or little start-ups called Microsoft and Starbuck's. In recent years, we've watched tiny companies grow almost overnight into international powerhouses, fed by the power of the Internet, like Yahoo, the successful Web search engine started by Jerry Yang and David Filo (who became billionaires in less than four years) and Amazon.com, whose founder, Jeff Bezos, became a billionaire before his 35th birthday.

 URLinks
http://microsoft.com/mscorp/
http://www.research.apple.com/extras/history/default.html
http://www.amazon.com

Obviously, not every start-up grows into world dominance, but the lesson is clear: courage to pursue risk, innovation, and persistence—the essential elements of entrepreneurship—*can* lead to success. Without those essential elements, a venture *will* fail.

But how important is small business to the American (and global) economy? Consider this, from Section 2 of the Small Business Act:

> The essence of the American economic system of private enterprise is free competition. Only through full and free competition can free markets, free entry into business, and opportunities for the expression and growth of personal initiative and individual judgment be assured. The preservation and expansion of such competition is basic not only to the economic well-being but to the security of this Nation. Such security and well-being cannot be realized unless the actual and potential capacity of small business is encouraged and developed.

Entrepreneur Defined

Entrepreneurs are innovative in their approach to problems. They may try several ways to arrive at a solution, and won't be discouraged when one method fails. They just take the next approach. In your circumstance, you may have said, "I can do this better," or "I can be happier and achieve greater independence," or something along that line, which has led you to buy this book or take this class. You are beginning to act like an entrepreneur: we applaud you.

There are several definitions of entrepreneur. Let's look at how some experts define the "E" word.

The entrepreneurial hero. The word *entrepreneur* derives from the medieval French word *entreprenour*, or "one who manages, undertakes or controls." Originally, it was used to refer to a person who was a leader in a battle, a champion.

Bill Tobin, the quintessential entrepreneur, shares his personal definition of an entrepreneur.

FIRST PERSON

At various points in each chapter, you will read the real world comments of small business developers just like you. Many of them recall how their businesses grew and prospered; others reflect on their mistakes and failures. They are printed here to reinforce what we're telling you. Sometimes, people listen more closely to the voices of those who've "been there, done that, got the T-shirt," than they do to recognized experts in the field, such as your humble authors. That's OK with us: we've been there, too.

Ladjke C., New York, New York: For the past 20 years, my home country was in complete collapse; the economy, the society, the politics were all a disaster. There were three different rebel groups and the government, all fighting with each other. The ones who really suffered were the regular people. When I emigrated to the United States it was to work in R&D at a big chemical company. I became a citizen as soon as I could; it was so much better here in every way. But I felt bad when I thought about my friends and family back home, like I should do something: things were getting worse there. So I left the chemical company and started a glass company of my own. My people are famous for their crystal work, and I was able to bring over many of my relatives and friends to work for me. I was their immigration sponsor, and the work was something no American could do, because it was native craft. They got green cards, and all of the first group to come over are now citizens. I've expanded, and have been able to bring more people into the business, both immigrants and native-borns. We've even started to get into international business. We pay taxes, we vote, we generate jobs and business, and we are saving some of my fellow countrymen from the old country. We have gotten great gifts here and from the old country, but I think we're also giving a lot back to both.

The entrepreneurial visionary/risk-taker. Howard Stevenson and the entrepreneurship faculty at Harvard Business School have defined entrepreneurship as "the pursuit of opportunity beyond the resources one currently controls" (Stevenson and Gumpert, 1985).

FIRST PERSON

Shirley A., Rosemont, Illinois: In 1973, at least around here, girls just didn't do yardwork. Well, I thought that's just too bad, because there were no babysitting jobs and I'm just no good at cleaning houses. But I mowed our lawn at home, and kept after the hedge, and I loved that. So that year, when I was 12, I got started in "business." I mowed our neighbor's lawn, and trimmed their bushes, and then the other neighbors liked what they saw and asked me to do theirs. Some of the boys were really mad, and made my life pretty miserable, but I kept going. I got my sister in on it for a while, and then a couple of my friends two summers later. By the time I graduated high school, I could see that I had a regular business going. So I made my parents mad when I decided not to go to college, but instead took some business courses locally and kept pursuing the lawncare thing. Today, my company is the only all-female yardcare business in the region, and folks love us. "YardMaids" has about a hundred employees now, ranging in age from retired women who specialize in flower gardens to teenagers who love running the bigger equipment. So from my dad's lawnmower (which I still keep on display out in the lobby), we've grown to the point that we're giving the big boys a run for their money.

The entrepreneurial innovator. According to Peter Drucker (1985), "Innovation is the specific function of entrepreneurship." Arthur Koestler (1990) explored "bisociation," the ability to relate two seemingly unrelated things to produce that "ah ha!" sensation in the marketplace.

FIRST PERSON

Randy P., Columbus, Ohio: How did I get started? It was pretty sudden, really. One day I was trying to hang a picture on the wall in my apartment, and I just couldn't hit the stud. I live in a newer building that has metal wall frames, and after I'd pounded about twenty holes in the living room wall, I went down to my son's room and got the big magnet out of his science kit, and it stuck to the wall right where I wanted the nail to be. I hit on an idea: a nail/picture hanger that was magnetized, so it would "stick" to metal studs. I tried it first at home, using that same science kit to magnetize some picture hangers and nails, and it worked! People said, "That's kinda stupid, Randy," and told me about the little electronic studfinder gadgets, but I went ahead with my idea. It was a cheap, quick solution that didn't require that the homeowner or renter go out and buy some gizmo they'd need maybe twice in their lives. I got a patent on it, trademarked the name "Smart Hanger," and went into business. At first, it was a real sideline, almost no more than a hobby. But then I started getting more actively involved in marketing, and linked up with some building management organizations. They loved the idea of minimizing random wall holes. We haven't taken the world by storm yet, but I was able to retire from my job to do this full time and no one's repossessed my car yet!

The proactive entrepreneur. Entrepreneurial researcher Raymond Smilor (1997) defines an entrepreneur as a person who

- pursues opportunity,
- acts with a passion for a purpose,
- lives proactively,
- builds teams, and
- enjoys the journey to create lasting value.

Isn't it great to be known as a "heroic, visionary, innovative, proactive risk-taker"? We also find words like determination, optimism, persistence, drive, creativity, charisma, and independence used to describe the entrepreneur.

Before you get too full of yourself, though, there's more. After further research and talk with entrepreneurship educators, researchers and small business consultants, we came to the conclusion that the "E" word works best to describe a process more than a person.

In the real world there are varying degrees of entrepreneurship. You'll find, through your business life, that some of your decisions will be more entrepreneurial than others. Depending upon the market, your business cycle, your personal and family responsibilities, and other variables, you may be averse to risk some days, and open to it others. You may continue on in the "business as usual" way for years, until you strike upon an innovative idea and take a risk that you deem worth trying.

For example, a specialty food producer, software developer, clothing manufacturer, corner grocery store owner, restaurateur, and family dentist may all be entrepreneurs of some sort. But some people may argue that the clothing manufacturer is more accurately characterized as a home-based microbusiness. Others may fail to see the entrepreneurial aspects of being a dentist. And someone may point out that the grocery store owner inherited the business from her parents (with little of her own risk). We maintain, though, that as your own boss, you have the opportunity to take on risk and innovation and act as entrepreneurially as you wish! The initial start-up decision is an entrepreneurial act, and it's up to you to see that the E-ball keeps rolling. Who knows—maybe in five years the clothing manufacturer will have started a fashion trend, leading to more orders, a new facility outside the home and several employees. The dentist may find an innovative way to market new procedures. And the grocer may have expanded into a multiple location franchisor or developed a highly profitable specialty foods niche.

Generally speaking, an **entrepreneur** *acts innovatively and assumes risk to start and build a business.* We think it's very important to discuss how you (the entrepreneur) and your planned business fit into the entrepreneurial process. That's what this chapter is all about. If you've already looked through our *Field Guide*, you've discovered that we'll delve into the nuts and bolts of small business start-up and management. It's our job first to help you understand the concept of entrepreneurship. It's your job to continue to think entrepreneurially. Then, we'll help you leverage your risk by teaching and showing you how to be effective in your venture. It's up to you to take this knowledge and ultimately apply it to your business.

Incidentally, this is a pretty good illustration of how the LEAP process—the instructional design approach on which we've based this book—works. There are two steps in LEAP that depend on us (the Learn and Explore parts, where we present information to you) and two parts that depend on you (the Apply and Produce steps, where you take what you've learned and do something with it). Back and forth, throughout this *Field Guide*. You'll get used to it; just when you think you're in for a longwinded discussion of some topic, we'll plop it back in your lap.

Entrepreneurial Researcher Raymond Smilor, in the preface of *Entrepreneurship 2000*, made an interesting observation of entrepreneurs:

Entrepreneurs are usually referred to as risk-takers. But I don't think this is quite accurate, if we mean by that the gambler who is willing to bet everything on one roll of the dice and then prays that it comes up seven or eleven. A better analogy would be the chess player, who may make a bold move, but also understands the parameters of the game and anticipates the possible countermoves. In this sense, the entrepreneur prefers the odds to be stacked in his or her favor. More importantly, the entrepreneur seeks to secure those odds by acquiring superior knowledge or a key advantage about the domain in which the risk is taking place.

In *The Real World Entrepreneur*, we will attempt to help you acquire superior knowledge and a key advantage!

Throughout this book, you will be presented with many Personal Workshops. These are questionnaires, self-tests, or other exercises to help you apply your skills, understanding, and experiences to the real world development of your business. The first Personal Workshop will help you determine what makes you entrepreneurial.

DEVELOPING YOUR OWN BUSINESS

There are advantages to developing your own business. Generally, it costs less up front to start a business than to buy one, and you can make use of your creative talents by developing something unique. You can address unexplored markets. You are free to

PERSONAL WORKSHOP 1
Being Your Own Entrepreneur

▼ By now you probably realize that there are as many definitions of an entrepreneur as there are entrepreneurs. So, we suggest you form your own, personal definition of entrepreneur. Use the chart below to construct your own three-word definition by choosing a word from each of the three columns. Once you've made two or three of these definitions (for instance, "creative, self-confident, problem-solver") you'll have as good a personal definition of entrepreneur as any.

adventurous	enthusiastic	business-builder
aggressive	extroverted	delegator
creative	innovative	organizer
flexible	resourceful	problem-solver
goal-oriented	responsive	risk-taker
realistic	self-confident	visionary

▼ Now that you've come up with a few short definitions, ask yourself the hard question: do these characteristics describe *me*?

choose your own location and develop your own management style and policies. You will not be buying the problems and flaws of an existing business.

Most people who start their own businesses are good at what they do. They have used their talents and creativity to develop something unique. They manufacture or sell a good product or they provide a useful service. But a successful entrepreneur has to provide a good product or service and understand how a business works.

There are certain inherent risks in developing your own business. Normally, you have to start from scratch. You are responsible for choosing a legal structure, a location, and a recordkeeping system. You must get licenses and permits. You develop your customer base, your management and organizational systems, and your marketing plan. At times, this can seem overwhelming. The purpose of this book is to take the mystery out of business start-up. You will see that a business starts and develops in a

PERSONAL WORKSHOP 2
Pros and Cons of Developing My Own Business

▼ Fill in this checklist to indicate your feelings concerning the advantages of starting your own business: is each statement important or not important to you?

The **advantages** of developing my own business are:

	Important	*Not Important*
I can use my talents and strengths.	____	____
I can address new markets.	____	____
I can choose my own location.	____	____
I can develop my own business style.	____	____
I can develop my own policies.	____	____
I can spend days doing what I enjoy.	____	____
I have the freedom to fail.	____	____

▼ Fill in this checklist to indicate your feelings concerning the risks of starting your own business: difficult or easy?

Starting my own business can be overwhelming because I need to…

	Difficult	*Easy*
develop a customer base	____	____
develop a management system	____	____
develop a marketing plan	____	____
develop an organizational system	____	____
manage a recordkeeping system	____	____
meet legal requirements	____	____

logical order. Understanding how a business works is one way to increase your chances for success.

WHAT IS A "SMALL BUSINESS"?

There are a variety of definitions of a "small" business. The **Small Business Administration (SBA)** has different definitions depending on the industry. In establishing standards, the SBA considers such economic characteristics of each industry as degree of competition, average firm size, start-up costs and entry barriers, technological changes, competition from other industries, growth trends, historical activity, and any factors unique to the industry. In some cases, a business can be quite large and still be within the SBA's definition.

According to 3(a)(1) of the federal Small Business Act, a small business is one that

- is independently owned and operated
- is not dominant in its field, *or*
- is an agricultural enterprise that earns less than $500,000.

If your business concept fits these basic requirements, chances are you've got an official "small business."

A precise definition of *small* is stressed only when government programs are considered. For example, government procurement programs have requirements to ensure that certain percentages of government contracts go to small businesses. Similarly, funding sources that include state or federal involvement are often reserved for small businesses. In these cases, it is important to know when a business is considered small. While the formal designation of small business is industry specific, one conclusion is clear: most businesses in the United States are small businesses.

In reality, most business owners never give explicit attention to any of these definitions. They simply see themselves as being small-businesspersons. Ultimately, if an owner thinks the business is small, it probably is!

HOW DO I GET STARTED...AND SHOULD I?

People start businesses for many reasons. When people were asked in a recent survey, "What is the major reason why you might want to start a business for yourself?," over 50 percent responded, "To be my own boss." Other reasons in order of responses included "To earn lots of money," "To overcome a challenge," and "To build something for my family."

Starting a business takes courage, creativity, business savvy, money and hard work. And there can be a fine line at times between failure and success. In the same survey, the general public was asked, "What is the major reason you might *not* want to start a business for yourself?" and 37 percent considered age or family situation the major reason. Other reasons in order of responses included, "Problems with managing the business," "Lack of energy/time/skills/ideas," and "It is too risky."

The most any book, class, or small business counselor can do is to show you directions, pose questions, and suggest ways to arrive at the answers. You have to provide the detailed answers, and in the process will learn a lot about whether or not you should be in business for yourself.

This is particularly important for those of you who have suddenly found yourself unemployed due to downsizing, outsourcing, RIFing (reduction in force), corporate re-engineering, or any of the other euphemisms for unanticipated early retirement. The lure of self-employment is strong but the very qualities which made you successful in a larger business or organization may work against you.

FIRST PERSON

 Jim H., Witchita, Kansas: I once started a business with a high-level banker, a highly intelligent and skilled man with years of banking experience. The small business world was utterly foreign to him, full of uncertainties (such as an irregular pay-check!) and duties that he hadn't had to perform before: running the copier, sweeping the floor, calling slow-paying accounts, and hardest of all, selling a product to a reluctant market. He missed the benefits and status and power of his banking job. He missed the socializing too, the long lunches with other executives, the meetings with interesting and powerful clients. He lasted less than a year before scurrying back to a comfort-

---

PERSONAL WORKSHOP 3
Six Key Questions
▼ ▼ ▼ ▼ ▼

▼ Ask yourself these six key questions about your new business venture. These questions represent the core concerns you need to address now and throughout the life of your business. Don't worry if you can't answer each one specifically right now: just keep reading, keep asking these questions, and listen to your market. You'll figure it out.

1. What kind of business is this?

2. What is my industry?

3. What are my products and services?

4. Who are my customers?

5. Who are my competitors?

6. What is special or distinctive about my business?

able institutional position. In that world he is very effective. He wasn't able to make the transition to the alien and uncertain world of small business. This is no reflection on him; it is simply the way small business affected him. I couldn't last a month in his world. He at least lasted ten months in mine.

Before beginning the process of starting a business, ask yourself some tough questions to determine your ability to own and operate a business. Business ownership is an important part of the American dream, but it is not right for everyone. Qualities that make a difference between success and failure include perseverance, emotional and physical stamina, courage to ride out tight times, ability to make decisions with incomplete information, communication skills, and willingness to take limited (not careless) risks. *Not everyone has these qualities.* There's no shame in taking a good, close look at yourself, your abilities, and your business idea and saying, "Self-employment is not for me."

For example, the ability to follow instructions flawlessly is useless if you have no instructions. High technical abilities in a limited area, such as corporate finance, are not readily transferred to a small business, where more general skills are needed. Few people in a Fortune 1,000 company get to see the "big picture," which includes the competitive, economic, political, environmental, social, and strategic environments the business operates in.

In a small business you have to do it all: finance, marketing, personnel, sales, public relations, and on and on. You won't have corporate services to rely on, there is no one "down the hall" you can go to for a quick answer. It isn't that you cannot transfer your skills and experience. The small business world is just so different from the corporate world that a lot of un-learning has to take place before you can move forward: you have to give up the old, habitual way of doing things and adapt yourself to new challenges.

Making the Jump

The conflict between the structures and practices of big versus small businesses can be overcome, of course. Many people have made the jump successfully. But it takes time. As more people make the shift from working in big organizations to starting and running their own business, those who make haste slowly will come out ahead. Take your time. Business habits and expectations that took years to develop don't go away overnight.

You don't need to be a genius to have a profitable start-up. You do need common sense, and should be willing to face and accept your own limitations. Successful businesspeople seek out and follow the best advice they can. Refusal to seek out and follow such advice is a good way to guarantee failure and is not evidence of strength of character. Outside advisers help you make decisions based on facts (not wishful thinking), provide a reality check, and give you insights that help you run your business better. Some helpful advisers include:

- Service Corps of Retired Executives (SCORE), 800-634-0245
- Small Business Development Centers (SBDCs)

- Accountants
- Attorneys
- Suppliers
- Other small business owners

 URLinks

http://www.score.org/
http://www10.geocities.com/WallStreet/2172/sbdcnet.htm
http://www.sba.gov/hotlist/sbdc.html

These advisers are particularly helpful in the pre-start-up phase, because you probably don't know what questions to ask.

At the end of each chapter of this book, you will find a lengthy case study that details the evolution, operation, and development of an actual small business. Much of the focus of the case study will be on the subject matter of its chapter, but each one includes a wealth of detail on all aspects of operating a small business venture. As you read each case study, look for the facts that were covered in the chapter you've just read. At the same time, see how what you've learned in other chapters can be applied.

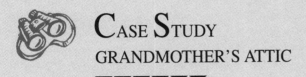

CASE STUDY
GRANDMOTHER'S ATTIC

*L*ess than a year ago, Latonya Ellis and Kate Petrakis opened Grandmother's Attic Heirloom Dresses, a small shop specializing in custom replicas of women's dresses and children's clothing from the late 1800s and early 1900s. Latonya and Kate had grown up together in the same small town in South Carolina, and shared an interest in fancy clothing, especially the "heirloom" items that had been passed down to them from their grandmothers. Over the years, they occasionally discussed going into some sort of vintage clothing business together. However, as they grew older, they found themselves entering the business world along separate paths.

Prior to opening Grandmother's Attic with Kate, Latonya had 15 years experience working in a neighboring town as part-owner of a wholesale business that produced custom heirloom dresses for retail institutions located all along the East Coast. Latonya's job within the wholesale organization was to design the patterns for the dresses. For a variety of personal reasons, Latonya decided to sell her share of the business to her partner, who did not ask her to sign an agreement not to compete. After some thought, Latonya felt that she would like to try her hand in the retail market.

Kate, too, had experience in the clothing business, although hers was not as extensive as Latonya's. After working as a clerk in several retail stores, Kate briefly entered the world of small business start-up when she opened a business specializing in women's ready-to-wear. Though her business had only limited success, and closed within two years, Kate had been bitten by the entrepreneurial bug, and jumped at the idea when her old friend Latonya called her and proposed a partnership in a new retail heirloom dress business.

CONTINUED ▶

FIGURE
1.1

The Six Myths of Business Ownership

Business ownership is surrounded by myths. Don't fall for the following, which represent the six most common—and most dangerously wrong—reasons for starting a new venture.

Myth	Reality
"I can bootstrap it."	Probably not! Undercapitalization (too little money invested in the business) is the biggest cause of small business failure. While you may indeed be able to bootstrap a small business, why take the risk when you can calculate the amount of capital investment needed to make your venture succeed? This cash reserve makes you sleep better, helps avoid panicky decisions, and gives you the breathing room you need.
"I can start living off the business immediately."	Forget it! Most business owners find that it takes between six months and a year before their business can pay them a decent wage. Early expenses always outrun early revenues. For this reason alone, consider starting your business as a part-time or weekend venture if possible, or be prepared to live on savings (or have another income supporting you) until your business can afford to pay you. Home-based companies are a great way to start, as you can minimize your cash needs. This kind of bootstrapping is highly recommended, but of course doesn't fit all businesses.
"I'll be my own boss."	Not likely! The business and its customers will be your boss and keep you occupied 60 or more hours a week. Your other bosses include employees, vendors, bankers and investors.

FIGURE
1.1
The Six Myths of Business Ownership, continued

Myth	*Reality*
"I'll get rich overnight."	You won't! The get-rich-quick stories are either bogus (the many years of preparation are hidden) or so unusual that your chances of winning the lottery are higher. Small businesses are a great way to build wealth, but it takes time. David Birch, the eminent small business researcher, notes that more than a third of businesses that grow significantly don't do so until they've been active for ten or more years.
"I have nothing to lose: I'll incorporate and use other people's money."	In a word: Hogwash! The "corporate shield" only exists in rare cases where the business is strongly capitalized and big enough to make creditors (suppliers, bankers, investors) rest easy. Start-ups seldom meet these criteria. The same applies to using OPM (Other People's Money). In spite of all the books and articles urging you to borrow your way to wealth, it isn't that easy to find OPM. More important, it seldom makes business sense to take on debt if you can avoid it.
"It takes money to make money."	This one's a half-truth. Good business ideas attract money. Bad ones don't, and shouldn't. There are businesses where the hurdle to entry is so high that substantial capital is needed. Printing, for example, and most manufacturing businesses call for such great investments in machinery, plant, and equipment that for all intents and purposes it does take money to make money. Many businesses don't have such high barriers to entry. Service businesses, some retail businesses, and some wholesale or distribution businesses fit this low capital criterion. If you lack capital, you should try to find such a business. People have made fortunes in all kinds of businesses.

They decided to locate the business in a town about 30 miles from their own because it had a much larger year-round population and a state university that would bring in additional customer traffic. The town was also located on a transportation route. Latonya and Kate found an affordable, 600-square-foot boutique in an appropriately old-fashioned building on a busy street just two blocks off the highway and not far from the university campus. They signed a one-year lease on November 1 and hurried to have their official opening two weeks later, in time for the Christmas shopping season. Each partner invested about $25,000 of her own money in the new operation. The shop was set up to emphasize the main focus of their business—made-to-order heirloom dresses—but Kate and Latonya thought it would be wise also to rent formal wear and include a limited line of contemporary classic clothing targeted mainly to women. Grandmother's Attic was ready for business.

Unfortunately, the timing of the opening did not result in the sales that the partners had anticipated. Latonya and Kate discovered that most of the women who came into the shop had already bought dresses for the holiday season. Rental income from the formal wear was also disappointing: total sales for the period ending December 31 were only $2,500. Moreover, Latonya and Kate discovered that the boutique was just too small: the fitting room was cramped, workspace was inadequate, and the showroom area had almost no space for the effective display of some of the more elaborate heirloom dresses.

Fortunately for Grandmother's Attic, a store just up the street went out of business at about that same time. This location seemed to meet all of their needs: the building had space for a large cutting room, a display room for the rental garments, a room for the ready-to-wear and accessories (hair bows, earrings, hosiery, handbags, and belts), and a room for the proper display of the heirloom dresses. Even better, the store had other rooms that would allow for future expansion. It was closer to the college campus, and across the street from a busy shopping center. Although it was a more modern building, it blended well with its quaint neighbors in the historic district.

The building turned out to be for sale at a reasonable price. Although neither Latonya nor Kate had planned to invest more of their savings, they decided to buy it. Two factors entered into their decision: First, their landlord agreed to release them from their lease because she knew she could rerent the space for more money; and second, Latonya and Kate were able to arrange for a tanning shop to rent an area at the new location for $250 a month. A tanning shop, they figured, would bring in a steady income as well as additional customer traffic. By February, the partners had secured a 15-year mortgage and were able to move their business to its new location.

Today, both partners act as salespersons and Kate does the bookkeeping. However, in many ways, the business is heavily dependent on Latonya, who designs and cuts out all the made-to-order dresses. Latonya does this freehand, basing her designs on old photos and catalogs, and has developed no patterns for anyone to follow. The business faced a major crisis when Latonya was injured in a traffic accident and was unable to work for several weeks. Luckily, no special rush orders came in during that time. Latonya plans to make patterns in the future for others to follow, but hasn't had enough free time.

One of the characteristics of the heirloom dresses is hemstitching, which can be done only by hand or on older sewing machines. Grandmother's Attic was recently able to buy one of these older machines, which has helped in speeding up production, but so far only Latonya knows how to operate it. Still, the process is slow. Latonya cuts out the dress pieces, and does all the hemstitching and lace gathering before she turns over the garment to a seamstress for completion. Grandmother's Attic currently uses four seamstresses who work from their homes and are paid for each completed garment. Since a neighboring town has two sewing factories, Grandmother's Attic has a large pool of competent and enthusiastic seamstresses to draw on.

All of the heirloom dresses in Grandmother's Attic are made of the finest imported cotton and lace. Though they are replicas of earlier fashions, the dresses' overall high quality ensures that they can be passed down from generation to generation and eventually become authentic family heirlooms. Demographically, Latonya and Kate feel their customers are primarily mothers with young children (through junior high school). The shop is popular among young girls who need pageant and debut dresses, and professional

CONTINUED ▶

women with above average incomes who need striking dresses for special formal occasions. Neither Latonya nor Kate has any notion of how large their geographic market may be, though they feel they could successfully attract customers from larger towns, each more than an hour's drive away.

The partners plan to expand their line to include custom-made sun dresses for children by next summer. Latonya figures she will have the extra time since summer is usually a downtime for the heirloom dresses and gown rentals. Latonya also believes that she will be able to expand her offerings of custom clothing for little boys since already 5 percent of Grandmother's Attic's business is in this area. Grandmother's Attic also does alterations on demand and offers custom shoe dyeing. The rental formal wear business remains slow, and the line of casualwear the partners decided to carry as "insurance" generates very modest returns.

Though Latonya and Kate are optimistic about the future, they admit they have no real sense of direction for their business nor a good feel for what their monthly sales and operating costs will be. At present, their business decisions are dictated by the demands of day-to-day. The partners are also faced with a credit problem: they have not been in business long enough to establish credit lines with their suppliers. All orders are paid on a C.O.D. basis, which results in many small orders at higher prices.

Another problem that Latonya and Kate realize they have to overcome is that each heirloom dress takes two weeks to produce. The result has been that Grandmother's Attic must turn away orders whenever business picks up. For example, the partners had to cut off orders for Easter at the beginning of March because Latonya and her four seamstresses had more work than they could handle. Latonya and Kate agree that it is better to turn away business than to fail to deliver a made-to-order dress on schedule and risk being stuck with a product they would probably not be able to sell. Nevertheless, it hurts whenever they have to say "no" to a customer who's ready to pay.

Partly because of the constant time crunch, and partly because of the cash flow issue, Grandmother's Attic has done very little in the way of promoting itself. Latonya and Kate placed a few ads in local newspapers when they first opened, and another when they moved to the new location. A local restaurant displays their fliers. They tried advertising for a month on a local radio station, but were not sure that the results were worth the considerable expense. They have relied on word of mouth and are reluctant to advertise for fear of generating greater demand than they can meet.

Markup on all products in the store is 100 percent—costs are simply doubled to determine selling price. They figure the cost of each heirloom dress is 60 percent materials and 40 percent labor. Rental prices for the gowns are $100 per night for the long gowns and $50-$75 per night for the shorter gowns. These prices are competitive with other rental stores in the area (though there are currently no other rental stores in the immediate vicinity). The dresses cost between $300 and $700 each and can be rented 7 to 10 times before they need to be replaced. Grandmother's Attic is able to sell these outdated dresses for approximately 10 percent of their original cost. Latonya and Kate have not factored dry cleaning expenses into their rental prices.

The partners estimate utility costs run about $130 a month. Mortgage payments are $578, and employees' salaries are approximately $1,100. Neither Latonya nor Kate is drawing a salary, and both are, in fact, plowing all money from sales back into the business.

When Latonya and Kate opened Grandmother's Attic, their goal was to show a $10,000 profit by the end of their first year and to double that by the end of the second. They did not set a five-year goal, believing that it would depend on the direction that the business took after the first year or two. At times, they voice regrets about having invested their savings in the purchase of their current location, though they agree it is ideal for their business. They feel that they should have put more money into the business itself rather than a building. Recently, they've begun talking about expanding into retail mail order as an easy way to increase revenues. ▼

Case Study Roundtable

▼▼▼▼▼▼

Following each case study in this book, you are invited to participate in a round-table "discussion" with the main characters in the case study. They have come to you (and your colleagues or classmates) with specific questions about how you can apply your expertise (what you've learned in the chapter) to their particular problems. After each question, you're provided with some guiding discussion points to focus your thoughts.

Kate: Since this business is in its very early stages—it's only been six months, even though it seems like a lot longer—what would you suggest as our next step?

Discussion Points

- Were Latonya and Kate prepared to enter this business venture? What lessons have you learned from this case to help you when you start your own business?
- How would you advise Latonya and Kate regarding the promotion of their business?
- What issues should Latonya and Kate consider as they decide whether or not to get into retail mail order? Explain what you would recommend they do.

Latonya: OK, I admit it: I'm a perfectionist and a control freak. I like doing all the designing and cutting and everything myself, and I'm not sure I'll ever find the time to do pattern papers. But our whole success hangs on quality in every detail, and there's only one way to be sure of that, right?

Discussion Points

- How would you suggest that the partners handle the problems associated with the heirloom dress line's dependence on a single person?
- How does a small business with limited resources balance what Latonya refers to as "quality in every detail" with the increasing demands of a growing customer base?

BACK TO THE TABLE
Latonya and Kate

In many instances, the characters from one chapter's case study will reappear in other chapters: they'll come "Back to the Table." There, they will ask you to review their case study, and apply another chapter's content to their facts.

Latonya and Kate will be back to get your advice about

- how to handle their credit issues (Chapter 12).
- how to develop a customer service policy (Chapter 14).
- how to promote their business (Chapter 15).

CHAPTER BRIEFCASE
▼ ▼ ▼ ▼ ▼

- The word **entrepreneur** means different things to different people. Generally speaking, an entrepreneur acts innovatively and assumes risk to start and build a business. A person may act more or less entrepreneurially at certain times depending upon the stage of the business and the person's individual or family responsibilities.
- There are advantages to developing your own business. There are certain inherent risks in developing your own business.
- The **Small Business Administration (SBA)** has different definitions of small business depending on the industry. Basically, a *small business* is one which is independently owned and operated, not dominant in its field, or an agricultural enterprise that earns less than $500,000.
- A precise definition of *small* is stressed only when government programs are considered. In reality, most business owners never give explicit attention to any of these definitions. They simply see themselves as being small-businesspersons. Ultimately, if an owner thinks the business is small, it probably is!
- Business ownership is an important part of the American dream, but it is not right for everyone.

▲ ▲ ▲ ▲ ▲ ▲

REFERENCES

Drucker, P. *Entrepreneurship and Innovation: Practice and Principles*. New York: HarperBusiness, 1985.

Koestler, A. *The Act of Creation*. New York: Viking, 1990.

Smilor, R. *Entrepreneurship 2000*. Chicago: Upstart Publishing, 1997.

Stevenson, H., and D. Gumpert. The heart of entrepreneurship. Cambridge, Mass.: *Harvard Business Review* (March-April, 1985).

Walstad, W. *Entrepreneurship and Small Business in the United States*. Kansas City, Mo.: Ewing Marion Kauffman Foundation, 1994.

Chapter 2

THE ECONOMICS OF SMALL BUSINESS

▼▼▼▼▼

Trade is a social act. Whoever undertakes to sell any description of goods to the public, does what affects the interest of other persons, and of society in general; and thus his conduct, in principle, comes within the jurisdiction of society.

—*John Stuart Mill*, On Liberty

MISSION STATEMENT

In this chapter, you will

*L*EARN about the basic operations of supply and demand in an economy, the factors that govern those forces, and the way goods are bought and sold.

*E*XPLORE the importance of small business to the economy, and of macroeconomic factors to your own small business, as well as how goods and services move through various channels of distribution in the marketplace.

*A*PPLY your economic understanding to a start-up case study.

*P*RODUCE a supply-and-demand analysis for your product or service, and an analysis of your business's actual or potential distribution system.

KEY TERMS

catalogs	e-commerce	net exports
consignment	elasticity	net migration
demand	infrastructure	point of equilibrium
demographics	inventory control	population diversity
direct sales	investment mobility	supply
distribution	JIT distribution	supporting facilities
diversion	mail order	wholesaler
diversity	natural increase	

INTRODUCTION TO THE SMALL BUSINESS ECONOMY

There are over 24 million businesses in the United States. The past five years saw a record-breaking number of new businesses start up, a phenomenon that suggests that the 21st century may well be experienced as the century of the entrepreneur. Between 1982 and 1998, nearly 25 million new businesses were started up, almost all of which (over 99 percent) met the Small Business Administration's (SBA) industry-based size requirements for small business status. Two-thirds of those new businesses operate full-time. In the four-year period between 1992 and 1996, small businesses in the United States (those with fewer than 500 employees) created nearly 12 million new jobs. At the same time, businesses with more than 500 employees actually lost more than 6 million jobs.

There's a downside, though: according to SBA statistics, one out of seven start-up businesses fails. There were 790,000 new incorporations in 1996, and over 840,000 new firms. That same year, there were 850,000 failures (business closures) of which 125,000 ended in bankruptcy (closure while owing debts). The small business economy is clearly vibrant, and experiences a great deal of churn: new businesses come and go in rapid succession.

URLinks
http://www.sbaonline.sba.gov/
http://www.doc.gov/eda/
http://www.mbda.gov/

Small businesses...
- provide virtually all of the net new jobs in the United States.
- represent over 99 percent of all employers.
- provide almost half of the nation's sales receipts.
- account for nearly two-thirds of the nation's annual technological innovations.
- account for one-third of high technology jobs.

WHY STUDY ECONOMIC THEORY?

We all know that real world small business developers have very little time for theory. What today's entrepreneur wants is hands-on action, concrete experiences and no-nonsense advice from people who've been there and back. However, even the real world operates in the context of certain recognized "theoretical" forces that a lot of people depend on for very real results. Whole books could be (and many have been) written about economics. No doubt you've read a few. You may have studied economics in high school or college classes.

In this chapter, though, let's take a step back from the mechanics of starting your business and consider the big picture issues: the economic concepts that will make, or break, your new venture. Understand the fundamentals of macroeconomic forces that make the modern market economies of the world run, and you will find your business successfully interwoven into that vast, interdependent system. Fail to understand these "theoretical" forces, and your very real world business will be left in the dust.

URLinks
http://www.frbsf.org/econedu/indx.eced.html

SUPPLY AND DEMAND

Supply and demand are the two principal economic forces that drive an open market. *The function of any marketplace is to provide a setting in which supply and demand can operate to establish price.* First, we'll consider supply factors and demand factors separately. Note that some of the same factors define both forces, although in different ways. Then, we'll look at how they interact to create a dynamic marketplace.

The operation of supply and demand in the market is how prices for goods and services are set. Essentially, when supply increases and demand remains stable, prices go down; when demand increases and supply remains stable, prices go up. Greater supply means producers need to attract more buyers, so they lower prices. Greater demand means producers can raise their prices, because eager consumers will compete for the product.

Supply

Supply refers to the amount of any given product available in the marketplace. Supply can refer to scented candles, real estate agents, doctors, refrigerators, or recreational vehicles. Supply is dictated by a wide range of factors, including government policies, prices of raw materials, and the accuracy of buyers' and manufacturers' projections of demand.

Supply curve. A supply curve is a distinctive portrait of supply of a particular product or service, indicating the quantity that would be supplied at various prices. When the supply schedule is plotted on a graph with price on the vertical axis and quantity on the horizontal axis, the line that joins the points slopes upward to the right. This is the characteristic direction of the supply curve (see Figure 2.1).

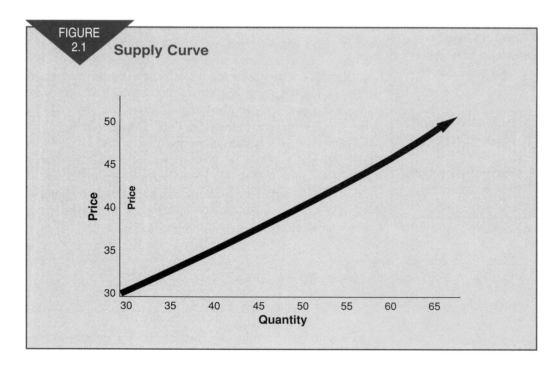

FIGURE 2.1

Supply Curve

If the number of products or services offered at each price increases, the whole supply curve shifts to the right (see Figure 2.2).

Similarly, if the number decreases, the curve shifts to the left (see Figure 2.3).

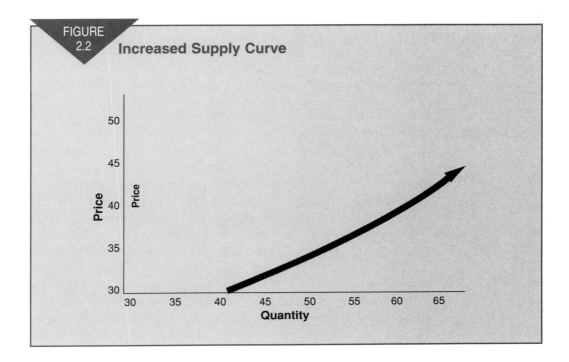

FIGURE 2.2 **Increased Supply Curve**

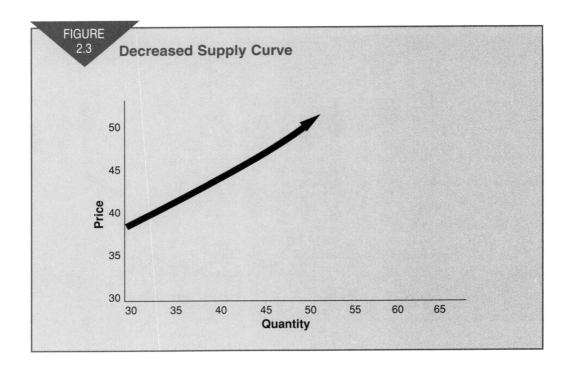

FIGURE 2.3 **Decreased Supply Curve**

Note that the use of the vertical axis for independent variable (price) and horizontal for dependent (demand) is the reverse of most graphs. However, this is the conventional practice for displaying both supply and demand curves.

Demand

Demand refers to the amount of goods or services people are willing and able to buy at a given price. Demand is dependent on a single factor: *affordability*. Unless this factor is present, demand has no way of manifesting itself. Other factors that tend to affect the demand side of the market include population, demographics, and employment and wage levels, as shown in Figure 2.4.

Population. Although the total population of the country continues to rise, the demand for products or services increases faster in some areas than others. For instance, the population of northern industrial states is declining, while that of southern and western states rises. Products and services that are considered necessities in some parts of the country are viewed as frivolous extravagances in others. Where there is demand for products and services, the supply will be dictated by the local population. Obviously, the number of people living in a community will determine how many doctors, lawyers, and cellular phones are needed. In some locations, growth has ceased altogether or the population has declined. This may be due to economic changes (such as plant or military base closings), social concerns (such as the quality of schools or a desire for more open space), or population changes (such as population shifts from colder to warmer climates). The result can be a drop in demand for products and services in one area, matched by a correspondingly increased demand elsewhere.

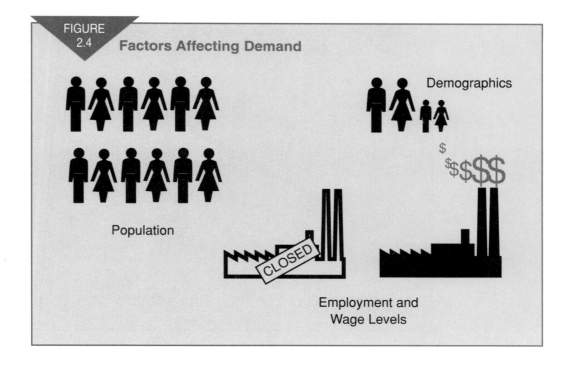

FIGURE 2.4   Factors Affecting Demand

Demographics

Population

Employment and Wage Levels

The two basic components of population as a consideration of market economics are **net migration** (the number of people coming into an area divided by the number of people who leave) and **natural increase** (the number of births divided by the number of deaths). These factors can be measured on a neighborhood, community, state, or national level, depending on the scope of the economic investigation. It is important to remember, however, that although increased population figures may indicate a *potential* demand, they may not reflect *actual* demand.

Demographics. **Demographics** describe a population. As we've mentioned, the population of a community is a major factor in determining the quantity and type of products and services available there. Family size, the ratio of adults to children, the ages of children, the number of retirees, family income, lifestyle, and the growing number of both single-parent and "empty-nester" households are all demographic factors that contribute to the amount and type of products and services needed.

Employment and wage levels. Decisions about whether to buy and how much to spend are closely related to income. When job opportunities are scarce or wage levels low, demand usually drops. Thousands of markets for goods and services might, in fact, be affected drastically by a single major employer moving to or leaving a particular area.

Measuring Demand

A **demand curve** is a graphic display of demand for a particular product or service. When this is plotted on a graph with price on the vertical axis and quantity on the

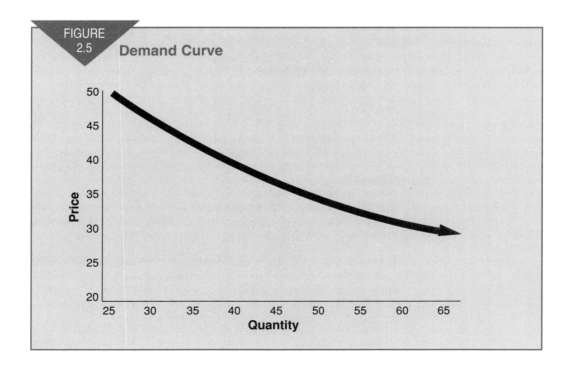

FIGURE 2.5 **Demand Curve**

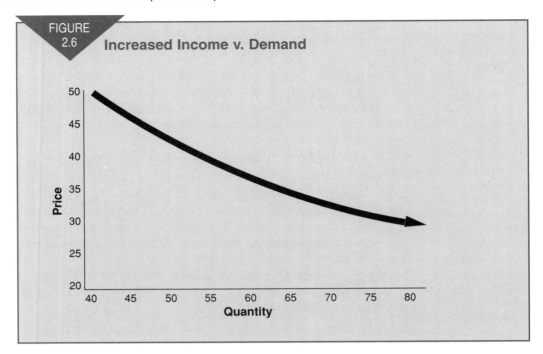

FIGURE 2.6

Increased Income v. Demand

horizontal axis, the line that joins the points slopes downward to the right. This is the characteristic direction of the demand curve (see Figure 2.5).

Again, note that the use of the vertical axis for independent variable (price) and horizontal for dependent (demand) is the reverse of most graphs. However, this is the conventional practice for displaying both supply and demand curves.

The curve's slope is determined by the degree to which price affects demand. This reflects the elasticity of demand. When price has a relatively small effect (such as with necessities), the curve will be close to vertical. When price has a strong effect on demand (as with luxury items), the curve will be closer to horizontal.

Changes in income. If the disposable income of the average household increases, the quantity of various products desired at each price will go up and the demand curve will shift to the right (see Figure 2.6). If disposable income decreases, the quantity of various products demanded at each price will go down and the demand curve will shift to the left.

Equilibrium

The primary objective in any market-driven economy is to reach the stage at which supply and demand are in balance. This is referred to as the **point of equilibrium** (see Figure 2.7). When a market is *in equilibrium*, it is balanced: enough product is provided to meet the exact demand for that product and the price is satisfactory to both producers and consumers.

On a supply and demand chart, a line drawn from the point of equilibrium to the vertical axis (price) indicates the equilibrium price. Similarly, a line drawn to the horizontal axis (supply or demand) indicates the equilibrium quantity. Figure 2.7 shows the point of equilibrium for our candle store example. For the shopkeeper, a price of $40 for

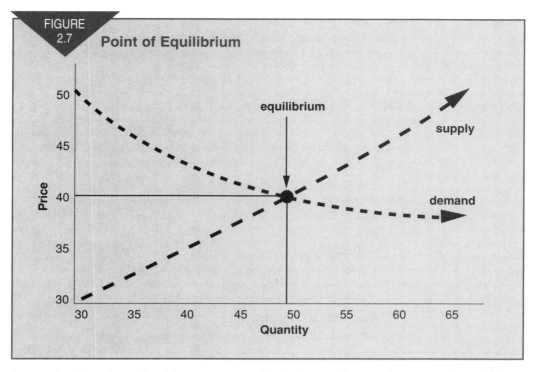

FIGURE 2.7 **Point of Equilibrium**

just under 50 units will achieve an acceptable balance. That is, the point of equilibrium for this one product in this shop at this point in time is roughly $.80.

Elasticity

The interrelationship between demand and price is referred to as **elasticity**. Luxury items such as electronics tend to have a high elasticity, since demand can increase significantly with a significant decrease in price. On the other hand, a lowering of the price of necessities, where demand is fairly constant, will produce little increase (other than some possible hoarding). In other words, the demand for many basic products is relatively inelastic.

FIRST PERSON

Maria J., Phoenix, Arizona: "Supply and demand" always seemed to me like some sort of college thing that I wouldn't have to worry about once the Econ 101 final was over. But this year, I started a small business selling hydroponic organic produce to specialty food stores all over the region. I had no idea how popular the product was going to be, and my initial prices were low. But my product caught on very quickly—the local pride element, and the popularity of organics, I think, were the driving forces—and the stores wanted more of my vegetables. I was able to raise my prices substantially, and plow the profits back into better facilities. A few months ago, though, a national chain of organic grocery stores set up two stores in the metro area, and all of a sudden there was no shortage of fresh organic produce. I still have the "local origin" edge in marketing, and I think my hydroponic vegetables are better than the dirt-grown ones they truck in from other states, but I had to adjust my price when the demand fell and the supply of what people think are similar products rose. My company's still doing great, though, and we have a couple of niches where we're safe and profitable. It just goes to show that all this econ stuff actually happens in real life!

LOCAL ECONOMIC STRENGTH

In economics, one must always look at the **macro** (big picture) issues as well as the **micro** (localized picture) ones when considering factors that influence demand. International events and local conditions can both have a serious impact on the real estate sector. Some of the macro- and micro-factors that may affect the health of the community include net exports, population diversity, infrastructure, mobility of investment, and taxes.

Net exports. If a community produces more than it consumes, it is in an excellent state of economic health. A community that consumes more than it produces (that is, its imports exceed its exports) is putting itself in a risky economic position.

Population diversity. Like a healthy investment portfolio, a healthy economy will not have all its economic eggs in one basket. Towns that exist solely for the employees of the local mill, factory, or military base are extremely vulnerable. In recent years, the closing of numerous military bases across the country sent many local economies into collapse. This was particularly true where the community had become wholly dependent on business generated by the base and had failed to diversify its economy.

Infrastructure. Community amenities that have a tendency to enhance value include:

- *Educational opportunities*—public and private schools, colleges and universities
- *Public transportation*—bus and train transportation within a community and between neighboring communities
- *Streets, highways, and freeways*—well-maintained roads and bridges
- *Utilities*—sufficient water, sewerage, gas, and electricity capacity to meet expanding requirements
- *Sports, cultural, and recreational facilities*—important for residents as well as attracting out of town visitors for special events

Investment mobility. Local investment may be discouraged if rates of return or risk levels are more favorable in other areas. Nations with rising incidents of terrorism and cities with increasing crime rates often suffer when wary investors divert their investments to safer places.

Taxes. As the federal government continues to experiment with capital gains, depreciation, allowable investment expenses, passive income definitions, and other tax policies, demand can be stimulated or stifled in the process. Recent tax laws have sought to encourage home ownership by providing incentives through tax reforms. Investment property is particularly vulnerable to shifts in tax policy.

THE COMMERCIAL DISTRIBUTION SYSTEM

Distribution is a major component of the business economy: it's how goods and services flow through the marketplace from producer to consumer. Under that definition, of course, distribution essentially *is* the economy. In a sense, the two are inextricably linked together.

The distribution process has been compared to a pipeline or channel. Information, orders, products, services, and payments flow from consumer to product manufacturer or service provider and back again. More accurately, the distribution process is an intricate and delicately balanced interconnected web that connects forests, fields and quarries to factories and forges; manufacturers of screws, bolts, staples, and buttons with makers of steel, lumber, glass, and fabrics. Everything that's made is made as a result of the interaction of literally hundreds of hands, in a process with thousands of steps, each reliant on the other. And it all flows through the web toward the center: your business and, ultimately, the consumer.

When you think about it this way, the operation of the commercial distribution system is mind-boggling. In order for this most elaborate of all human systems to work smoothly and effectively the full cooperation and understanding of each participant is required. When cooperation fails—a union calls a strike or a company tries to seize monopoly power—the effects ripple out all across the webwork, and affect every part.

CHANNELS OF DISTRIBUTION

If you are a manufacturer of a product, you may wish to develop a flow chart to examine the channels available for distribution of your goods. Figure 2.8 illustrates various means of product distribution.

Each of the sales channels illustrated in Figure 2.8 requires some sort of distribution. Figure 2.9 shows the principal delivery methods involved.

As you can see, distribution involves sales and delivery. As a participant in the real world economy, you must analyze how an order is placed and how a product is delivered. For example, if you sell directly to the customer or to a retail outlet, you will be responsible for order fulfillment and shipping. If you sell through a manufacturer's representative, you may ship to a warehouse for consolidation of your order with others. All of these factors involve costs, because they involve other people who are operating their businesses for a profit, just like you. You see, the classic image of the small business operator functioning in the market as a kind of "lone wolf" is a myth: to do business in the modern economy, and to participate in the market, you have to link your business with many others.

The result of this distribution link has a clear impact on your business: it is important to look at all of the costs involved in your sales and delivery systems in order to choose the most cost-effective channels. This information will also be important when you determine a selling price for your product or service.

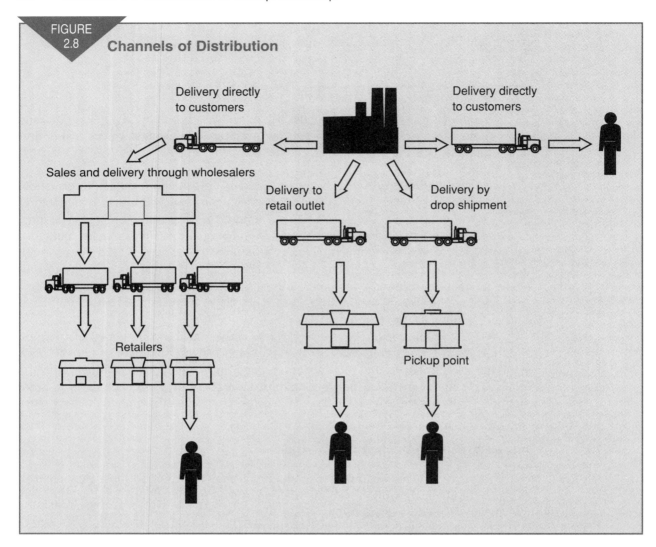

FIGURE 2.8 Channels of Distribution

Direct Sales

Direct sales to the consumer can be made in a number of ways, including door-to-door representation, display booths at fairs, trade shows, and mall events, or through mail, e-mail, Internet, or phone order. The seller solicits the order directly, on a one-on-one basis (that's why it's called "direct sales"). This method allows the business owner or a company representative to meet and communicate with the consumer and gather information useful to future marketing. Delivery can be made at the time of sale, or later by personal delivery or shipment by common carrier.

Mail order. A unique way of doing business is selling through mail order. Orders are generated through the mail with catalogs, brochures, telephone solicitations, and other advertising methods. The customer sends the order and payment through the mail; the product is returned to the customer through the mail or other shipping method. This is a popular sales and distribution method for small manufacturing companies to use

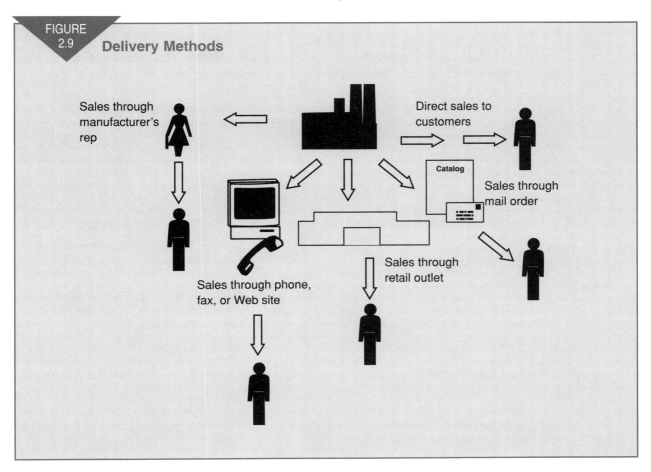

FIGURE 2.9 Delivery Methods

before they've generated sufficient capital to acquire their own space. Many home-based businesses also rely on mail order selling, because there's no requirement to have a store. But be warned: the cost of producing and mailing promotional materials can add up quickly, and can end up being enormous, especially when selling direct to consumers.

FIRST PERSON

Kevin S., Chicago, Illinois: At our publishing company, we gave direct mail a shot a few years ago. What we found was that a typical $20 book would need to be repackaged and sold for about $150 just to cover the costs of direct mail marketing! Needless to say, few of our customers would find that an attractive product to buy.

Catalogs. A popular tool for marketing and distributing products are catalogs, and their popularity has increased over time as people's lives become busier and leisure time too rare to spend going to stores. You may choose to develop your own catalog, or pay a fee (or a percentage of your sales) to have your product or service included in an established catalog. Review relevant catalogs and see if your product would be appropriate for addition to their current product line. If your market analysis indicates that your customers purchase by mail, contact the catalog company regarding sale of your product or service through its catalog.

What happens when you join an established catalog? The catalog company may submit a purchase order and you will ship merchandise directly to them for resale to customers. Alternatively, the company may submit copies of customer purchase orders and ask that you ship the merchandise to the customer yourself. In the first case, you are responsible for delivering the products to the catalog company. In the second case, you are responsible for filling and shipping individual orders. If you are involved in drop shipment (direct delivery) of goods, clarify who is responsible for collection of sales tax and shipping charges.

A company involved in mail order must be aware of the postal regulations that affect mail order, the different tax laws in each state into which mail is delivered, and the Federal Trade Commission rules. For example, the FTC requires that delivery on all mail orders be made within 30 days. If you will be using mail order, contact the FTC and the Interstate Commerce Commission for shipping rules.

E-commerce. Electronic commerce is a new but rapidly growing form of sales and distribution. Instead of mailing out paper catalogs, distributors create electronic virtual catalogs on their Web sites. Customers can select items they wish to order, adding them to their "shopping basket"—a program that simply keeps track of a customer's ordering activity. When they're ready to order, customers key in information about themselves in an interactive order form screen. Encryption software keeps the customer's credit card information secure as it is transferred via modem (that is, using phone lines) from their computer to yours. From there, the distribution follows traditional means. (At least until technology makes it possible to send cookies, books, and furniture through phone lines!)

One of the most visible e-commerce companies today is Amazon.com, the online bookseller. Amazon.com, in fact, is nothing more than a distribution channel. The books on its virtual shelves are not collected in one place, like a traditional bookstore, but are in warehouses, storage facilities, and even bookstores all over the United States. When a customer places an order, the order is filled by searching Amazon.com's vast database of cooperating warehouses and suppliers for the book's location. The book is shipped under the Amazon.com name from wherever it is found. In a sense, Amazon.com is, as its advertising claims, the world's largest bookstore, because its bookshelves cover the nation. Other booksellers, such as Barnes & Noble and Borders, have followed Amazon.com's lead into the world of the virtual bookstore.

Amazon.com is an example of the enormous potential of e-commerce to overcome the limitations of space and time, and free businesses to engage in more aggressive, widespread, and diversified commercial activities through the "storefront" of the Internet.

 URLinks
http://www.toolkit.cch.com/text/P02_3431.stm
http://www.amazon.com

Resellers

Resellers are the wholesalers and the retailers. They are the people we call the **middlemen**, because they operate in the middle, between the product supplier and the customer. If you sell your product through a retail store, you may represent yourself and sell directly to the retail outlet for a wholesale price plus shipping and handling. The store will submit a **purchase order** through the mail or by phone. You will fill that order by direct delivery or common carrier shipment.

Consignment

Some stores will take products on **consignment**. This is the typical selling arrangement in the arts and crafts field. The consignment arrangement provides a good way for the product producer (the **consignor**) and a store owner (the **consignee**) to introduce a new product and to test market a price. This is, in fact, the way that many small businesses that produce products for consumer purchase first enter the market.

When an item is sold, the store will give you the proceeds—after deducting a consignment fee, or percentage of the sale price. Essentially, a consignment system lets you use shelf space in someone else's store to display your merchandise, saving you the expense of acquiring and maintaining a physical market presence. You also "rent" the use of their sales staff.

However, there are some disadvantages to this method of selling. In a consignment arrangement:

- The consignee agrees to display the item for sale but is not responsible for theft or damage. The consignor assumes all the risk.
- The consignee provides only the physical space, with no guarantees of what will happen in that space. There is no guarantee of the product's safety and security, and no guarantee that any effort will be made to sell the product.
- You may find your inventory tied up for long periods of time, which could lead to cash flow problems.
- Consigned goods remain the property of the manufacturer until they are sold to the customer by the retail store. However, if the shop should file for bankruptcy, your goods may be seized and be subject to the claims of creditors. The law regarding consignment varies from state to state.

Because of the risks involved, consignment may not be a desirable alternative. However, if consignment is the normal method of sale for your product, limit your risks. Research the reputation of the store by contacting other individuals who have dealt with it on a consignment basis. Limit the type and quantity of items you offer on consignment, so you don't tie up your inventory in a sales conduit over which you have no control. Require a consignment agreement that clearly establishes the rights and responsibilities of the parties, as well as the timing of payments. Visit the store often to check on the manner in which your merchandise is promoted, displayed, and maintained.

FIRST PERSON

Fiona Y., Stamford, Connecticut: I've found with my ceramics that shop owners are more enthusiastic about selling merchandise they've already paid for—their regular shelf stock. While that's certainly understandable, it doesn't help you make money. The stores I use to distribute my stuff are great, and very cooperative, but I still can't help feeling that my products are not as aggressively marketed as the "regular" ones. In most of the stores I don't get the prime visibility spots like the window, the front shelves, or near the register. A couple of the stores sell greeting cards and mass-produced gift items, and they have what they call the "Local Artisans' Corner"—they might as well put up a big sign that says "Amateur Junk," which my items most definitely are not. But an outlet's an outlet, and I get at least some sales from them. The stores whose merchandise is 100 percent consignment are the best, though, because you're really attracting customers who are looking for locally produced craftworks. And they place items more fairly, too.

Representatives

Another selling and distribution method is the use of a manufacturer's or sales **representative**. A manufacturer's rep will handle your product and represent it to the retailer through trade show exposure or direct sales contact. Sales reps usually carry a line of related but non-competitive products. They cover specific territories, usually work strictly on commission, and receive a percentage of the wholesale price. You must furnish the sales materials: price lists, brochures, sample sets. You must also have a written contract specifying the territory, terms of sale, allowance for returned merchandise, commission percentage, and terms of contract.

Manufacturers' reps can be important members of your marketing team. They are an excellent source of information for learning about new trends in your field because their ideas are based on the demands they observe firsthand in the marketplace. Let the rep know when you have developed or are considering a new product or design: they can informally test market receptiveness.

Wholesalers

Wholesalers serve as a distributive link between the producer and the retailer or user. They purchase goods from manufacturers for their own account and resell those goods to other businesses such as retailers, other manufacturers, or end users. Wholesalers are also called *distributors* or *jobbers*. They carry stock in large amounts and redistribute it in small quantities. Note the difference between a wholesaler and a consignee: the wholesaler purchases and resells the goods; the consignee typically does not own the goods on consignment.

For example, a manufacturer may want to sell a new product in stores across the nation. Rather than contacting individual retailers and delivering each order, the manufacturer can locate a few distributors who have branches or access to those retailers. The costs of individual delivery, contact of retailers, storage, and handling can be reduced. Since manufacturers are concerned with the need to have their products carried by those retail stores in which consumers expect to find such items, the broad market coverage manufacturers need can be provided by a wholesaler.

Wholesalers offer additional services as well. Some extend credit, offer advice on store locations, and give information on how to package and display goods. Many provide promotional materials and notify customers of new products coming into the market.

The most important function of a wholesaler-distributor is **inventory control**. Inventory control is working within the practical limits of space, money, personnel, and time. When a customer places an order, it is expected to be filled in a short time. The entire wholesale operation revolves around serving customers economically, efficiently, and effectively. It is important to work closely with your wholesaler and to keep the lines of communication open.

Wholesalers generally are paid a percentage of sales, offer co-op promotional opportunities for a fee, and maintain a returns account, which provides a small cash reserve for refunds. Payment schedules may vary. Review all contracts to determine when you will be paid and who will pay shipping charges.

DISTRIBUTION OF SERVICES

Distribution is a process of sales and delivery. It's easy to think of a *product* being distributed, but services are distributed, too, even though they can't be put in a box and sent somewhere in a truck. Unlike products that are produced, sold, and then used, services are often sold first, then produced and used at the same time. Simultaneous production and use creates unique considerations regarding sales and delivery. The following are the three main service distribution channels, which may be used singly or in some combination:

1. Service performed at the customer's location.
2. Service performed at a business location.
3. Service performed through a communication link.

Services performed at a customer's location require the use of business transportation in the form of a delivery van, repair truck, or other vehicle. The cost of these vehicles as well as the necessary supplies, assistant's salaries, and other incidental costs must be considered when determining the hourly rate you will charge for your service.

The service may be performed at your business location. The customer comes to your shop, for example, with an item needing repair: a tooth to be filled, a lamp to be rewired, clothing to be cleaned, a lawsuit to be filed. Everything the service-provider needs to perform the service is probably located at the business location.

An example of a service performed through a communication link would be airline reservations made by phone, with the tickets being delivered by Federal Express or the postal service. E-commerce transactions are communications-based systems, too.

Combinations of these channels occur when, for instance, a broken watch is mailed to the repair shop and picked up later by the customer. A manuscript can be transmitted via computer modem to a desktop publisher for editing and final formatting before printing. With advances in electronic and computer technology, most service businesses find that they are using a combination of delivery systems in order to reach their customers.

Choose sales and delivery methods based on what is acceptable to your target market. How do they expect to order and receive your product or service? Consider all of the costs involved in the methods you will use. When starting out with a new idea and a new business, you may find it more cost-effective to operate on a "do-it-yourself" basis. You may wish to deal directly with retailers and customers and provide your own warehousing in a small, self-storage location. You may wish to provide your service in the customer's home or through a shop set up as a home-based business. Your decision will also take into account your market, your image, your cash flow, and your location.

CASE STUDY
PULASKI'S SOUPS

*I*n 1930, when the Great Depression hit, Doris Pulaski had three children and was in desperate need of money. Before the depression she and her husband, Teddy, were wealthy, and material things were never discussed. But Teddy lost everything in the depression and died prematurely. Doris worked odd jobs to try to make ends meet. One day she struck upon the idea of selling her homemade soup to earn money. People who used to come to dinner at her home had always raved about her unique soups. Several of her guests had even suggested to Teddy that he buy a soup company to market her soups, but he never took the suggestions seriously.

Doris decided to make soup in her kitchen and sell it. However, she lacked sufficient funds to purchase Mason jars for preserving the soup once it was prepared. Although Doris was a proud woman, she did get up enough nerve to ask an old friend, Marty Rouget, for a $1,000 loan. He agreed to loan her the money and asked if he could do more for her. She assured him that she would be all right. She wanted to succeed on her own and felt that if her children got to know hard times they could face even more difficult times in the future. Marty said he would check in on her from time to time to see how she was doing.

So, Doris started making soups. In the beginning, she concentrated on just four kinds: New England clam chowder, chicken noodle, tomato, and vegetable. She went to all the stores in the neighborhood and asked them to sell her products. Most of the stores refused, but Doris was determined and kept trying. Eventually, a few stores stocked the soup and it sold well. At the end of the first year Doris's sales reached $3,000, which was a lot of money in those

days. She did not make much of a profit, probably not more than $300 after all the expenses. However, Doris felt she was going to make it. She continued to work as a part-time maid and seamstress. Somehow she was able to manage, and she even was able to send her son, Derek, to the prep school in Duluth, Minnesota, where her husband had gone years ago. The costs were high, but Derek managed to get a scholarship that paid for 50 percent of the tuition. He was an excellent student who delivered newspapers every morning to earn extra money. He had 200 people on his route and brought in $2 per week.

As the years went by, Doris's business grew rapidly. Stores that had once rejected her products were now begging for them, and she was producing soup as fast as she could. However, she was running out of space. She wanted to pack her soup in cans and get herself a nice label so people could identify her products more easily. Her sales had exceeded the $200,000 mark, and she estimated she was earning about $20,000 a year.

Marty had come around often over the years, and was always very helpful. He understood her dilemma, and found a plant that could be converted to a canning factory for a small sum. Doris was excited, but she told Marty she wanted no "hand-outs." He laughed and told her he intended to become her business partner. On that basis she agreed to work with him. Doris took over the plant and Marty hired the employees needed to put the operation into working order. When they finally discussed costs, Marty stated that he felt one-third of the ownership would take care of his cash outlays. He offered to provide her the rest of the working capital on a loan basis. Doris shook hands with him and the new plant was under way.

CONTINUED ▶

As time rolled on, Derek graduated from the university and Doris's two daughters, Marilyn and Leah, soon followed. All of them majored in business and were very intelligent. Doris managed the production line, and she turned over the marketing end of the business to Derek. He originally kept things as they were, but gradually made some minor adjustments. He was careful not to upset the success of the business.

It was obvious that no other brand in the region could compete with Pulaski's Soups, as the line was now called. Doris had added 11 other kinds, and they were all successful. She had plans for adding more when suddenly she suffered a stroke. She fought hard to overcome its effects, but she was paralyzed on the right side. Although she was mobile to a small degree, she was of little use to the business.

So responsibility fell to the children to keep the business running. Leah took over her mother's production management position. Marilyn, who had majored in finance and management, eventually took over the general management of the company. At the time of Doris's stroke, the company had reached sales of $25 million and future prospects still looked bright.

Derek proposed they think about expansion to other areas of the country. There were people interested in carrying the soups outside the region, but transportation and handling costs put the price of the soups out of reach for the average consumer. Derek needed some advice on how to proceed.

Marilyn, however, was investigating the possibility of adding new product lines to complement their present line. She felt that since they would be going into the same stores and selling to the same wholesalers, it would cost nothing more to offer additional products to each outlet. However, she didn't know whether to pack the additional products on the premises under the present brand name, or to buy a company with a name that might be a target for a takeover.

There was yet a third possibility for expansion. Presently, the plant was not being utilized 24 hours a day, operating only about 10 hours a day with at least 12 hours of free time available for use. Derek had been approached by other companies who wanted Pulaski's to pack for them under their own private label using any soup left after completing packaging of the soup. He had rejected these offers because he didn't want his mother's soups to end up in competitors' cans to be sold at a cheaper price. Yet, he knew he could make money that way. ▼

CASE STUDY ROUNDTABLE

▼ ▼ ▼ ▼ ▼ ▼

Marilyn: What about the big picture here? I mean, do you think what Mom did is still doable? Is it still possible to start a business in a little kitchen and develop it into a large empire?

Discussion Points

- How was Doris able to take an ordinary product and make it special and salable?
- What entrepreneurial characteristics (Chapter 1) did Doris display that made her a success after being thrown into poverty?
- Explain how the fundamental principles of supply and demand relate to the successful development of Pulaski's Soups.

Derek: How can I distribute Pulaski's products to other areas? What kinds of arrangements might make that possible?

Discussion Points

- Should Pulaski's consider packaging products for other firms who want their products under their own labels? How could this arrangement be profitable? How would this affect demand for Pulaski's Soups?

- If distribution is a challenge, how might Pulaski's Soups explore alternative distribution systems? Which ones do they currently use? Which ones might they explore?

CHAPTER BRIEFCASE

▼▼▼▼▼▼

- There are over 24 million business in the United States. In the four-year period between 1992 and 1996, small businesses in the United States (those with fewer than 500 employees) created nearly 12 million new jobs. At the same time, businesses with more than 500 employees actually lost more than 6 million jobs.

- Supply refers to the amount of any given product available in the marketplace. Demand refers to the amount of goods or services people are willing and able to buy at a given price. Supply is dictated by a wide range of factors, including government policies, prices of raw materials, and the accuracy of buyers and manufacturers to project demand. Factors that tend to affect the demand side of the market include population, demographics, and employment and wage levels.

- The primary objective in any market driven economy is to reach the stage at which supply and demand are in balance. This is referred to as the point of equilibrium. When a market is in equilibrium, it is balanced: enough product is provided to meet the exact demand for that product, and the price is satisfactory to both producers and consumers.

- Goods and services flow through the economic system through distribution channels. These include direct sales, resale, wholesalers, and representatives.

▲▲▲▲▲▲

PERSONAL WORKSHOP 4
Measuring Supply and Demand in Your Business
▼ ▼ ▼ ▼ ▼

▼ Think objectively about your new product or service, and about the market you are about to enter. Then use this simple form to evaluate the approximate relationship of supply and demand as they apply to your business. (We've included an example, to show you how this works...)

Business Name: __Bob's Mosquitoes__

Product or Service: __Provider of bulk mosquitoes to consumers__

Special Market Conditions: __Seasonal (summer only)__

The **SUPPLY** of my product or service		The **DEMAND** for my product or service	
high 5	X	high 5	
4		4	
3		3	
2		2	
1		1	
low 0		low 0	X

Analysis:
When supply is greater than demand, prices will be low. To compete, I'll need to offer lower prices than my competitors and/or attract more buyers.

Business Name: _____

Product or Service:_____

Special Market Conditions: _____

The **SUPPLY** of my product or service		The **DEMAND** for my product or service	
high 5		high 5	
4		4	
3		3	
2		2	
1		1	
low 0		low 0	

Analysis:

START-UP BASICS

Lori Davis (Detroit, Michigan)
Knitz & Pieces
with Hattie Bryant
Creator of *Small Business 2000*

Adapted with permission from
Small Business 2000, the
series on public television.

"*L*ori: The first thing I did was contact the SBA about information on how to make a business plan.

Hattie: So you did that on a Monday morning?

Lori: It was kind of like, 'Okay, what do I have to do? I want to do this business, you know.' And so I went the next week, and I contacted them. They sent me this package, and I pull it out. That's the first time I just went, 'Oh my God, I can't do this,' they wanted so much information. I was really overwhelmed by it. But I just broke it down step by step and, you know, I spent a lot of time in the library, spent a lot of time on the phone calling people. And people are really great. You call them up and you're like, "Well, I need to know how much it would cost for me to have signs," and you have to figure out what size your signs are gonna be, what you want on them... You need all that information. ...It took me three months from the day I got fired to finish my business plan. "

Chapter 3

THE PERSONAL SIDE: WHAT KIND OF BUSINESS IS BEST FOR YOU?

▼▼▼▼▼

Lack of money is no obstacle. Lack of an idea is an obstacle.

—*Ken Hakuta (inventor of Wacky Wallwalkers and author of* How to Create Your Own Fad and Make a Million Dollars)

MISSION STATEMENT

In this chapter, you will

*L*EARN how your new venture may impact your home and family life, and how to find new business ideas that suit your skills, experience, and interests.

*E*XPLORE the strengths and weaknesses of your business idea and identify your distinctive competencies.

*A*PPLY your understanding to your financial goals, and how they relate to your business idea.

*P*RODUCE a clear visualization of your business idea, and a strategy for achieving success.

KEY TERMS

commitment	interests	skills
distinctive competency	personal qualities	support

INTRODUCTION TO THE PERSONAL SIDE

This chapter is about you. It's about getting yourself organized and the considerations and planning that have to be addressed before you can get down to actually starting up a business. We'll begin close to home, by addressing how your new venture may affect your family and create unexpected challenges in your personal life. From there, we'll turn to the formal planning process: what it means and how to go about doing the most effective pre-start-up planning possible. Finally, we'll examine the bigger context in which your planning takes place: how to deal with the ever-changing real world and how to minimize the risks inherent in any new venture.

YOUR FAMILY AND PERSONAL LIFE

Starting a business affects every facet of your life. There are always loose ends to tie up, work to do, and bills to pay. The result is that your family and social life will suffer. While this is usually a problem only until the business settles into a routine, it is grave enough to make many enterprises fail. A supportive family and understanding friends go a long way to making your business a success.

Don't underestimate the emotional ups and downs inherent in a start-up. They are unexpected and often severe. You'll find that periods of elation and excitement are followed by panic when accounts receivable are slow to turn into cash, or a supplier pulls out, or your biggest customer decides to trade elsewhere. If you are not used to the fluctuating fortunes of small business life, be aware. This is a problem that you will have to learn to live with. Corporate refugees find this especially tough to swallow.

Make sure you consider how your new venture will affect four vital aspects of your personal life: (1) income, (2) hours, (3) support, and (4) commitment. Starting your business should be a positive and exciting experience. Negative motivations don't last. Positive motivations do, which is why it is so important that you place your personal goals ahead of your business goals. Your business should serve your goals.

Lori Davis from Knitz and Pieces tells why she started her retail store, how she decided on the business name and location, and shares issues related to being a woman-owned enterprise.

Income

Unless you are able to retain your full-time job and start your business as a part-time enterprise, your income will suffer. Start-up businesses don't usually provide a decent salary to the owner right away. If you can, save some money to plug this gap. A second income (a supportive spouse, in many cases) can also make a big difference.

Hours

Start-ups devour time. In the first few months of a business, when everything is new and shortcuts haven't been discovered, you'll literally live your business. You'll think about it all the time, whether at the office or not. Your time will not be your own. One of the biggest problems newcomers to small business ownership face is that they can't forget the business at 5 PM and go home. They lug the business with them. So will you. And when you bring your business home (home business operators never leave the office), you bring it to your family, too.

Some businesses are more limiting than others. A retail or hospitality business demands that the owner be there all the time. The hours are long, the rewards high, but it may not be a good choice for a person who places a premium on family or community activities.

Support Level

Wholehearted support from family and friends helps you avoid burnout. People who take an intelligent interest in your business can provide you with objective advice and criticism. To get this kind of support, keep them informed from the start. Don't keep everything to yourself. If you are worried, tell them. If you are uncertain, tell them.

The loneliness that goes with small business ownership is self-induced. Somehow the myth of the rugged individual who never shows the least sign of doubt or fear has become mixed up with being the owner. Don't buy the myth. Your family and friends have a sizable emotional investment in you and your business. Let them help, and they will. Give them a return on their investment and all of you benefit. They will understand the demands of your business better, which in turn defuses their concerns about the amount of time, effort, and worry you put into your start-up.

A shaky marriage or other relationship is never improved by starting a business (or buying one). Don't expect to lose yourself in your start-up and magically come out of it with a better marriage.

Commitment

Many entrepreneurs find that the lack of time for family, community, and personal activities (hobbies, sports, reading, and so on) is the highest price they pay for business ownership. During the start-up period this price is reasonable. Later, when the business is actually going, it becomes a leading cause of burnout. At this point, make sure you have a clear picture of what your commitments will be, how long they'll take to fulfill, and what sacrifices (if any) you'll have to make.

FIRST PERSON

David S., Tuscaloosa, Alabama: More years ago than I'd like to think about, I was an intelligent and industrious high school physics teacher. But unlike my obviously fulfilled colleagues, I felt particularly restricted and unfulfilled as a teacher and longed for a greater sense of freedom and independence. The logical choice: start my own business. I was committed to working hard to make this career change a success. In exploring my entrepreneurial options, I was driven by a strong desire to do hands-on work and not be confined to the rigors and structure of a 9-to-5 job. Because I loved and appreciated motorcycles and motorcycle racing and was a pretty good backyard mechanic, I decided to open a motorcycle repair shop.

Eighteen months later, after exhausting my family's savings and enduring a regular regimen of 70-hour workweeks, I recognized that the business was doomed and filed for bankruptcy.

Looking back, I understand now that my business decisions were spontaneous and unplanned. In the beginning, I reacted to my need for independence, without ever really thinking about my business prospects. I didn't ask important questions about the actual demand for the proposed service. I relied on personal opinion, feeling, and emotion, and was just too optimistic about market potential.

I never performed a competitive analysis. Sure, I knew the names of my major competitors, but I just had no feel for the size of their businesses, the markets they tried to reach, or their success. My repair shop was geared to the hard-core, serious motorcyclist. Unfortunately, this was the same segment of the market that two competitors had already targeted and were serving. So then I decided to go for the weekend rider

PERSONAL WORKSHOP 5
Visualizing Your Business

▾ Have you ever said to yourself, "I can see myself running that business?"

▾ Picture yourself in a business of your own. You might be making pottery, setting up a factory to produce salsa, distributing wooden furniture, running a fancy restaurant, or helping someone solve an interior design problem. Let your imagination loose.

▾ Make your vision come alive. Talk about it, write about it, or draw it. What are you wearing? What are you doing? Are you in front of customers? Working alone? Working at home? Do you need a computer, a store, or a bulldozer?

▾ You'll want to come back to this image again and again. It will probably change, maybe completely, as your ideas take firmer shape. But for now, just try to imagine what it will be like in your own business.

who didn't know much about motorcycles. I knew the competition was from dealers, who have the reputation for poor service and high prices. I positioned myself as the low-cost, high-quality alternative to the dealership. Trouble was, there just weren't enough motorcycle riders in the area. Again, I just didn't read my market.

DETERMINING YOUR FINANCIAL POSITION

Financial risks are measurable. You can look at your personal finances and make a good estimate of how much you are willing (or able) to put at risk in your business. Personal financial statements (such as a balance sheet and income statement) will be needed to support credit applications.

Three Important Questions

This may seem like early days yet for filling out personal financial statements. After all, you've just made the decision to forge ahead on your own, you've just had your business idea, and you've barely even thought about what to call your new company. But this is a critical time for you, and you must have straight, supportable answers to three very important questions.

1. *How much money do I need to put into the business?* The answer will come from many sources: cash and conversion of assets into cash (selling stocks or that extra car, for instance) can provide some start-up money. You may be able to get the balance of what you need by using your assets to support a bank loan.
2. *What is my bottom-line living budget?* In other words, you need to figure out pretty accurately how much money you need in order for you to make ends meet. Not how you'd *like* to live, but how you can live, at least for a while. We're talking food, clothing, shelter, and other basics here. You may have to put off the vacation cruise, or buy groceries in bulk from the supermarket rather than from the fancy little food boutique you prefer. Your mortgage company may applaud your entrepreneurial courage, but it still wants that check once a month.
3. *Will my business generate enough money to meet my personal and business needs?* That is, how much reliable income can you count on from all sources? If the answer to this question isn't at least the same as the answer to Question 2, then you really need to re-examine your plans—or find some way to lower your expenses. Sometimes, a part-time job or a working spouse (or both) can make all the difference. But you have to know what the numbers are if you're going to make the best decision.

PERSONAL GOALS

The financial goals you set for your business are clearly very important to its success—and your lifestyle. But equally important to your decision about going into business are your own personal goals.

Ask yourself this question: *What would I like to be doing five years from now?* In five years, you might want to open another store, or retire to the Bahamas with your pile

PERSONAL WORKSHOP 6
Preparing a Personal Financial Statement

▼ Personal financial statements are familiar territory for you. You had to fill out a personal financial statement the last time you applied for a credit card. They are easy to fill out, if you just proceed patiently, line by line. Complete this personal financial statement for yourself, to help you answer those three vital questions.

INCOME

▼ Look carefully at your current income, the income that you are used to living on. Your total income will probably go down somewhat during the first year of your business—but it may go down more than you expect if a significant part of your current income is in the form of bonuses and commissions.

Annual Income	Amount ($)
Salary	
Bonuses and commissions	
Rental income	
Interest income	
Dividend income	
Capital gains	
Partnership income	
Other investment income	
Other income (list)	
Total Income	

▼ Relying on a new business as your major source of income is dangerous. It is highly unlikely that your new business will be able to support you in its early stages.

EXPENDITURES

▼ Your current expenditures reflect your current income level. As income goes down, some expenses go down too—income taxes, both state and federal, for example, are based on what you actually earn. Look at this list carefully to see where you can whittle unnecessary expenses, and also look at those expenses which may go up. If you have benefited from employer-paid health insurance, will you now have to seek new coverage? At what cost to you?

Annual Expenditures	Amount ($)
Home mortgage/rental payments	
Taxes	
State/federal income	
Real estate	
Other	
Insurance	
Health	
Homeowners	
Car	
Life	
Car payments	
Other loan payments	
Telephone	
Gas/electric utilities	
Waste disposal	
Alimony/child support	
Educational expenses	
Medical/dental expenses	
Car expense	
Food	
At home	
Away from home	
Clothing	
Household operations/supplies	
Recreation and entertainment	
Savings and investments	
Cash contributions	
Other expenses	
Total Expenditures	

▼ Expenditures (cash going out) are easier to control than income. If you expect your income to drop you will have to cut expenditures to make ends meet. Bankers will look closely at your personal expenses when making lending decisions. They won't be interested in financing a lifestyle based on more income than the business (plus other income sources) can generate.

ASSETS

▼ Some assets can be used as collateral for loans or can be put into the business as part of your capital investment. Chairs, desks, and bookcases, for example, can be used as office furniture; shop equipment from a hobby can be put to work making a product. This will vary from one business to another. Be as specific as you can with your list of personal property and "other assets."

Assets	Amount ($)
Cash in the bank	
(including money market accounts and CDs)	
Readily marketable securities	
Non-readily marketable securities	
Accounts and notes receivable	
Net cash surrender value of life insurance	
Residential real estate	
Real estate investments	
Personal property	
(Including automobile)	
Other assets (list:)	
A: Total Assets	

LIABILITIES

▼ A list of your liabilities (what you owe) helps assess the strength of your collateral position. Assets you own free and clear are more likely to be acceptable to your banker than assets encumbered with debt. Note that some debts might be put on a different payment schedule, which in turn could lower your expenditures to a more comfortable level.

Liabilities	Amount($)
Notes payable to the bank	
Secured	
Unsecured	
Notes payable to others	
Secured	
Unsecured	
Accounts payable	
(including credit cards)	
Margin accounts	
Notes due: partnership	
Taxes payable	
Mortgage debt	
Life insurance loans	
Other liabilities (list)	
B: Total Liabilities	
(A – B): Net Worth	
	$

▼ Your net worth, what's left after subtracting liabilities from assets, will be a factor in credit decisions. A negative net worth is not a good way to start off in business: it means you owe more than you own, which, in turn, may scare off suppliers as well as bankers.

PERSONAL WORKSHOP 7
Personal Goals

▼ Write down your personal goals for the next year and the next five years. Don't take a lot of time thinking about this. You can return to this workshop later and make changes. If you write down your goals you'll not only think about them more, you'll also take them more seriously.

▼ Think of these goals as a work in progress. You'll develop other goals and interests and modify some of your initial goals. This first look gives you a basis on which to build.

My Five-Year Goals	Financial
	Family and friends
	Social and community
	Health and fitness
	Personal development
Goals for Next Year	Financial
	Family and friends
	Social and community
	Health and fitness
	Personal development

of money, or manage a rapidly growing company, or devote your time to research. Whatever you want is OK. That's your goal. Use the five-year test to help you think about not only what you're doing now, but *why* you're doing it. If you have a goal to work toward—that expansion, that hammock on the beach, those hundred employees—the day-to-day frustrations of small business life will be easier to handle.

The five-year horizon will also help you define some benchmarks and plan how you will reach them. Maybe you want to spend more time with your family, or do community work. That's fine, too. The ability to pursue such non-business goals through your own business is one of the most profoundly satisfying motivators imaginable.

LOWERING THE RISKS OF A START-UP

Let's review some of the proven ways to lower the inherent risks of starting a business.

Get experience. Experience in management and in the type of business you plan to start is not the only way to learn, but it is still the best teacher. Combine experience with course work, study, and participation in trade groups, and you have an almost unbeatable start towards business success.

Plan ahead. The action orientation many entrepreneurs pride themselves on has to be tempered with foresight and careful planning. A written business plan is inexpensive insurance. It will help you focus on the important parts of your business, use your resources wisely and consistently, and save a lot of trouble.

Enlist your family's support. Even though you're not devoting 24 hours seven days a week to your business, your family will think you are. If your family understands and is willing to provide the emotional support you'll need during the start-up period, your chances improve dramatically. The impact of uncertain income, demands on your time and attention that will preoccupy you 24 hours a day for months at a stretch, and the sheer anxiety of being the responsible owner of a small business put strains on the best relationships.

Be prepared to become tired and discouraged—and still persevere. It goes with the territory. Stamina is important. So is persistence, because when things get tough (and they will) it's very easy to give up. Experts like to talk about the "five-yard-line phenomenon," in which a business owner presses on against huge odds, gets discouraged, and quits or makes a dumb mistake when the goal line is within reach. Starting a business from scratch is hard. You (and you alone) have to provide the impetus to get things going and keep them going. You don't have the built-in momentum that an existing business has. The consistent inpouring of energy can become draining, but you have to do it.

Use *facts* to substantiate your insights and hunches before acting on them. Decisions based on facts are far more likely to be good decisions than those based on whim. Your business is too important to risk on the consequences of a lot of hasty decisions. An idea that still seems sound after you sleep on it is probably a good idea. Remember the old clichés, "Haste makes waste" and "Look before you leap"? They apply to business.

Follow your strengths and interests. They will sustain your enthusiasm. If you like selling, but hate bookkeeping, hire a bookkeeper so you can do what you like to do. After all, one reason to go into business is to be able to exercise your favorite skills and interests. Listen to yourself (never easy, but always necessary) and be honest. If you don't like being in charge, or being responsible, or taking risks, don't try to start a business.

At the risk of sounding negative, don't be *too proud* to quit. If your idea doesn't feel right, don't press on just because you don't want to quit. You may be able to modify the start-up plan, or switch to another business, or overcome whatever doesn't feel right. That's fine. There's a big difference between being persistent and being pigheaded. If the idea continues to raise more doubts and worries, it may not be the right idea for you, or the right time to pursue it. Be prepared to abandon your business idea if the facts tell you it makes sense to do so. Part of the value of planning is that it reveals warning signals.

There are no road maps to a successful start-up. There are no shortcuts, either. However, if you pay attention to your personal goals and desires, make sure your business goals reflect them, and proceed carefully, you will greatly increase your chances for success.

GOOD BUSINESS IDEAS: THE NEED FOR VISION

One of the many definitions of an entrepreneur is a visionary. You will easily recognize the entrepreneurs in the following list. All of them had a vision for a new product, service, or method of distribution. They all started with little money and small staffs, but buoyed by an idea and a vision, they built economic empires that we take for granted today.

- Walt Disney (Disney Studios; Disneyland; Disney World)
- Ted Turner (Cable News Network; Turner Network Television; Turner Entertainment; Atlanta Braves)
- Richard Branson (Virgin Records)
- Bill Gates (Microsoft)
- Ray Kroc (McDonalds)
- Sam Walton (Wal-Mart; Sam's Club)
- Steve Jobs (Apple Computers)
- Bill Hewlett and David Packard (Hewlett-Packard Computers)
- Jerry Greenfield and Ben Cohen (Ben & Jerry's Ice Cream)
- Wally Amos (Famous Amos Cookies)
- Orville Redenbacher (Orville Redenbacher's Popcorn)
- Paul Galvin (Motorola)
- John Johnson (Johnson Publications)
- Michael Dell (Dell Computers)

URLinks
http://www.disney.com/Business_Info/index.html
http://tnt.turner.com/index.html
http://www.virgin.com/richard_branson.html
http://microsoft.com/mscorp/
http://www.mcdonalds.com/corporate/history/index.html
http://www.wal-mart.com/community/mrh/history.html
http://www.research.apple.com/extras/history/default.html
http://www.hp.com/abouthp/history.htm
http://www.benjerry.com/scoop/freeconehistory.html
http://www.mot.com/General/Timeline/timeln24.html
http://www.us.dell.com/corporate/access/dellstory/index.htm
http://www.ltbn.com/HallofFame_1.htm
http://www.horatioalger.com/

These entrepreneurs all had a vision for a new product, service, or method of distribution. Their vision represented a glimpse of some desirable and possible future for the business. These entrepreneurs' vision became the unifying force for their respective organizations.

Some of these entrepreneurs overcame significant hardships to pursue their vision. In addition to possessing drive and a commitment to hard work, they each had the ability to identify a need and fill it. They all had the ability to focus on the market and to marshal resources necessary to launch and expand their venture.

Vision and dedication are necessary ingredients for a successful small business. As the business environment becomes more and more complex, it is necessary to focus on the future to continue to meet the needs of an ever-changing customer. Vision is the precursor to planning. The owner's vision is translated through the strategic planning process into a mission, objectives, and carefully designed strategies.

EXPLORING BUSINESS IDEAS

Ideas for new businesses come from many sources. Primarily, though, they come from three general areas: 1) what you like, 2) what you know, and 3) what you can do.

Do What You Like

You may want to turn a hobby, volunteer experience, leisure activity, or personal interest into a business. You could develop a line of specialty foods, do event planning, give golf lessons, or develop an antique locating and refinishing service. As we've already seen, liking what you do is a vital part of a successful start-up. If you have an existing enthusiasm for something, your interest will carry over and help energize your business effort.

Do What You Know

Almost any specialized knowledge or skill can be turned into a business. You can develop a newspaper column, write a book, present workshops, and conduct seminars on your area of expertise. An understanding of the Internet can lead to a business of designing, monitoring, and updating home pages. This same knowledge can be used to retrieve information useful to other businesses. You can prepare demographic studies, databases, market surveys, and information resource lists.

Do What You Can Do

Many new businesses are started by individuals who use existing skills from their salaried jobs. Accountants, payroll administrators, technical writers, and computer specialists are examples of employees who have marketable skills that can be developed into service businesses. As companies downsize and outsource, new opportunities arise for entrepreneurs. You can put to work equipment and technology you already have. Desktop publishing, video recording of weddings, and photography of children's sports events are examples of businesses that make use of equipment you may already own and be proficient in using.

On the other hand, you may wish to explore an idea or area that is new to you. Take classes, apprentice, or work in an area dealing with your new field of interest.

Building a Better Mousetrap

An inventive entrepreneur can develop a new product or improve an existing one. Now is the time for the old adage, "find a need and fill it." New products are usually spawned out of the imagination. If you can't think of something new, it is well to remember that many existing products can be improved upon. Any task or responsibility that people don't like to do or don't have time to do for themselves can be the basis for a service business. House cleaning, home repairs, gardening, proofreading, gift purchasing, and furniture refinishing may fill needs in your business community.

Figure 3.1 offers a step-by-step process for developing a good small business idea.

FIGURE
3.1   **Seven Areas to Explore for Business Ideas**

1. Continuing your current career, but in business for yourself.

2. Turning a hobby or other leisure activity into a business.

3. Selling your expertise.

4. Using equipment you already own to start a new business.

5. Providing needed services to individuals and businesses.

6. Taking classes or working at a job to learn about a new field of interest.

7. Developing a new product or an improvement to an existing one.

IDENTIFYING SKILLS, INTERESTS, AND PERSONAL QUALITIES

Regardless of where your business idea comes from, you must step back and take an objective look at what lies ahead. Business ownership is not for everyone and not all business ideas are viable. Most entrepreneurs are not adequately prepared to go into business. While they have the motivation and desire for business ownership, many have not taken the time to properly investigate and research their abilities and their business ideas.

A careful evaluation of your skills, interests, and personal qualities can help you determine the business for which you are best suited. **Skills** are abilities to use one's knowledge proficiently. **Interests** are those things you enjoy doing and that bring you pleasure. **Personal qualities** are the traits and characteristics that make you unique. Do you have a mechanical ability? You might consider a repair service. Are you interested in arts and crafts? You can turn what has been a hobby into a full-scale business. Do you enjoy working with other people? If so, you could consider tutoring or teaching.

When you have an idea for a type of business, take classes to learn all that you can about your chosen field. Find a job in your field of interest and get hands-on experience. Community colleges and the Small Business Development Centers in your area will offer or can direct you to workshops and classes on business topics such as record-keeping, marketing, financing, and business planning.

 URLinks
http://www10.geocities.com/WallStreet/2172/sbdcnet.htm

Just as you looked at your strengths and weaknesses as a business owner, you must look at the strengths and weaknesses of your business idea. Do this *before* you quit your job, invest your money, or spend your time in starting the new business. When you have decided on a business, answer the following questions:

- Do you have the **skills** needed to run this business?
- Do you know what **help** you will need and where you will find that help?
- Do you have the **time** required to learn what you need to know?
- Can you afford the **money** needed to hire staff or to pay consultants?
- Are you genuinely **interested** in this particular business?
- Are you **committed** to the business's success?
- Are you willing to devote the time needed to **develop** a successful business?
- Does this business fill an unmet **need**?
- Is there a sufficient consumer **demand** to support your business?
- Can you effectively **compete** in the marketplace?
- Will you be able to understand your business **financial statements** such as cash flow, profit and loss, and balance sheet?
- Are you developing a **business plan** that you can use throughout the life of your business?

To be the owner of a successful business venture, you must be able to answer "yes" to all of these questions. Research business ideas and see how they fit with your personality and background. Use the worksheets at the end of this chapter. Look at your skills, interests, and personal qualities in an objective manner. Look at your strengths and weaknesses. Plan ways of overcoming your weaknesses. If this involves taking classes or hiring consultants or employees, calculate both the cost and the time involved. You may wish to delay the start of your business until you have gained the knowledge and help you need.

Who Am I and What Am I Doing Here?

So you have a good idea, and have thought carefully about your own entrepreneurial abilities. The next step is to think about how you, with your skills and abilities, can use your wonderful idea to achieve success in the business world.

There are four basic questions you should ask yourself.

1. What kind of business will this be?
2. How am I going to run it?
3. Why will this business succeed?
4. How could it fail?

Deciding what your business is—and what it will be in five years—are the most important decisions you have to make.

Any business will be involved in more than one activity, so your judgment of what the central activity is (or what the central activities are) is crucial. Your entire planning effort is based on your perception of what business you are in. If you make a serious error at this point, your chances of success will be sharply diminished. So be sure to think this decision through.

Knowing exactly what your business does and how it operates enables you to plan effectively for profits. This means you must be able to clearly identify the goals of your business at the beginning of your planning. Once the goals are clear, then you can start figuring out ways to make a profit. As the business progresses, the question of how to make profits must be continuously asked and answered. Making profits is what business is about. Even non-profit organizations must have revenues that exceed expenses to survive.

Focus is the aim. The tighter your focus, the less time and money you'll waste, and time is exactly equal to money: if you're spending time spinning your wheels for lack of focus, you're not making money. If you know what business you are really in, you'll concentrate your efforts and use your resources efficiently.

A FINAL NOTE

Perhaps no activity more fully symbolizes the American dream than being a small business owner. Taking charge, exercising personal creativity and independence, risking substantial personal funds, working long hours, and planning competitive business strategies are all part of the challenge and excitement that lure one into the world of small business. But the dream of owning and operating a small business can quickly turn into a nightmare of devastating frustrations if the firm's performance lags behind

PERSONAL WORKSHOP 8
Entrepreneur's Assessment Workshop
▼ ▼ ▼ ▼ ▼ ▼

▼ The Personal Workshop on the following pages has been provided to help you analyze your skills, interests, and personal qualities and determine types of businesses for which you may be suited. Keep this worksheet within easy reach and fill it out as you go through your day's activities. You may have everyday skills, interests, and personal qualities that could be enhanced and utilized for business purposes. Analysis of your skills may have indicated areas in which you will need help. You don't have to be an expert to start a business, but you must have a realistic understanding of your strengths and weaknesses. No business owner knows everything!

▼ Take some time to fill out this assessment worksheet. It will help you analyze your particular entrepreneurial strengths and abilities, and help focus your energies in positive, concrete, and constructive directions. Even better, it won't take long to do.

▼ Here's how it works. In the first three columns, list your skills, interests, and personal qualities. Don't be shy, and don't limit your list to what you think are "business-related" items. If you love to paint watercolor seascapes, put that down on the list. Be specific: *Skills* include being organized, being a good writer or speaker, and using computers. *Interests* include hobbies and leisure activities as well as building a business. *Personal qualities* are the things that make you who you are: gregarious, self-confident, hard-working, decisive—whatever makes you tick. List your qualities as if you were analyzing someone else.

▼ When you have completed the first three columns of the worksheet, you are ready to tackle the fourth column, business possibilities. In part, this column is filled out by evaluating and combining the other three. For example, if one of your interests is dining out and you have writing skills, you could write and publish a local dining guide. If you are interested in collecting music boxes, skilled in mechanical repairs, and proficient at working with the public, you can provide a music box service combining repairs and sales. Extra emphasis should be placed on the area of "interest." You will be spending a great deal of time in your business pursuit and you might as well enjoy it. The ability to do well at your business may prove to be rewarding while the business is new, but if you do not like your work, it soon becomes a drudgery. Instead of looking forward to beginning your business day, you will be searching for ways to escape to more interesting occupations.

▼ Next, be critical and merciless: what strengths and weaknesses do you bring to make each business idea a reality? How do your skills, interests, and qualities apply in a positive or a negative way? Again, don't be nice: this is where hard-edged, objective analysis is vital. Here is where you make the distinction between what you want to do and what you can do: an important distinction if you're going to build success. If you identify an area in which you will need help, don't panic: remember that expertise can be learned or bought. You can compensate for weaknesses by taking classes, hiring staff, or using consultants.

▼ Finally, what are you going to do about it? What specific actions can you take to make each idea a reality, to build on each strength and compensate for any weakness? How do you improve your existing skills, pursue your current interests, and at the same time evolve into an entrepreneur? List specific actions, as well as how much they'll cost and how much of your time you'll need to invest.

Entrepreneur's Assessment Worksheet

Personal Data		Business Ideas	Personal Data+ Business Ideas		Action Plan		
Skills	Interests	Qualities		Strengths	Challenges	Action	Cost	Time

original projections and expectations. Although small firms make up over 99 percent of all United States businesses and employ almost 50 percent of the private United States workforce, successful small business ventures are the exception rather than the rule. Of the new small businesses started each year, many will struggle and some will fail within the first five years. These casualties ignite deep and pervasive economic and social consequences. Perhaps more important, however, are the crushed hopes and ravaged fortunes of the strong-willed persons who fought to build their fledgling operations into viable competitive entities—and lost.

Although small businesses encounter difficulties for numerous reasons, certain consistent themes persist. Some companies are victims of unfortunate and largely unpredictable environmental and competitive occurrences. Some simply miss their market completely. However, the vast majority of small firms fall prey to their managers' own lack of foresight. These managers fail because they do not properly analyze and evaluate their relative competitive strengths. They fail because they are out of touch with their market and do not perceive shifting consumer tastes and preferences. They fail because they lack a clear blueprint of necessary goals and support activities and therefore encounter costly duplications, overlaps, and internal inefficiencies. In short, these businesses fail because their owners and managers are unable or unwilling to focus on one of the prime determinants of business success—strategic planning.

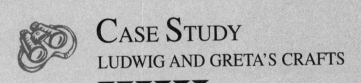

CASE STUDY
LUDWIG AND GRETA'S CRAFTS

Ludwig Helmholtz and Greta Lehmann were close friends. Ludwig was a civil engineer, and Greta was a controller for a paint manufacturer. However, both were also very involved with their respective hobbies. Ludwig was a genius at building scale models of trains, doll houses, European mansions, castles, and boats. From time to time people would come to his workshop and ask to buy some of his work. Ludwig was always hesitant to sell anything because his creations were very important to him. However, because he was running out of space and because some of the people were offering what he considered ridiculously high prices, he decided to start selling a few of them. One model of a famous castle sold for more than $10,000! Greta made beautiful pottery, sculpted candles, and costume jewelry. People would sometimes venture over to her workshop and see what she was doing. Because of her unique talents, she found that her products were in demand. However, like Ludwig, she was hesitant to get into business commercially.

She often remarked that her hobby took her away from the real world and transported her to another dimension where she was happy.

Both Ludwig and Greta were pleased with the results of the past year; Ludwig had sold about $40,000 of his scale models and Greta $23,000 of her artwork. Ludwig was 61 years old and Greta was 52. Neither of them was married. They often wondered if perhaps there might be a chance of going into business someday on a full-time basis, but both were hesitant.

Ludwig suggested that they merge their activities but remain at home in their respective workshops until they developed an intelligent plan for expansion. For the time being, both would prefer to pursue their craft careers on a part-time basis. They agreed that what they need to do is to find some way of marketing their products so that they can move from part-time to full-time occupations.

Both Ludwig and Greta were unsure how much to charge for their products. Ludwig estimated that the

CONTINUED ▶

model of the castle in Liechtenstein cost him approximately $5,000 for travel and hotel expenses and another $4,000 for materials. He said that it took him more than four months to complete the model on a part-time basis, some days spending one hour on it and perhaps more on the following day. When he sold it, $10,000 seemed like a lot of money: in light of how much he calculated it had cost him to create, he realized his profit was not all that impressive. In the future he and Greta agreed to keep accurate records on how much time and labor they put into each project.

Clients kept coming to their workshops, and from time to time purchased their products. However, neither had come up with a marketing plan which would include both a pricing and promotion strategy. Both of them wondered what they should charge for requested projects. For example, one client wanted an exact replica of Windsor Castle, and Ludwig did not know how to approach the question of price or costs. Greta had been requested to do unusual pottery pieces, including everything from face masks of famous people to surrealistic art based on fantasies. Greta also was unable to come up with prices and labor figures. ▼

CASE STUDY ROUNDTABLE

▼▼▼▼▼▼

Ludwig: Let's get right to the point: Do you think that Greta and I should quit our jobs now and work on our crafts on a full-time basis?

Discussion Questions

- Are Ludwig and Greta prepared to enter the commercial field?
- Can they make as much money as they do in their present positions, or should they wait for retirement and then devote their time to their hobbies?

Greta: What we really need to know is, what do we have to do to turn a hobby into a business?

Discussion Questions

- Should Ludwig and Greta develop a short-term plan?
- How can they determine whether or not there is a sufficient market for their products?
- Is there any difference between their individual hobbies with respect to potential sales and profits?

BACK TO THE TABLE
Ludwig and Greta

Later, Ludwig and Greta will be back to get your advice about:

- The financial feasibility of their planned start-up (Chapter 4)
- How they can determine whether a market exists for their crafts (Chapter 4)

- How they can relate their hobbies to actual sales and profits (Chapter 4)
- How a strategic plan could help them make sound decisions (Chapter 25)

▲▲▲▲▲▲

CHAPTER BRIEFCASE

▼▼▼▼▼▼

- A supportive family and understanding friends go a long way to making your business a success. Make sure you consider how your new venture will affect four vital aspects of your personal life: (1) income, (2) hours, (3) support, and (4) commitment.
- Especially in the early phases of starting up, you'll experience a lot of change, and have to make a lot of adjustments. Be flexible and willing to adjust, but don't change your basic strategic plan without strong reasons.
- Experience, planning, support, and realistic expectations will help you weather the challenges of the early phases of starting a new business venture.

▲▲▲▲▲▲

Chapter 4

DETERMINING THE FEASIBILITY OF YOUR BUSINESS IDEA

▼▼▼▼▼

I find that the harder I work, the more luck I seem to have.

—*Thomas Jefferson*

MISSION STATEMENT

In this chapter, you will

*L*EARN if there are customers to buy enough of what you are selling to make your business viable.

*E*XPLORE questions to gain information about your market, and processes for determining your financial potential.

*A*PPLY your understanding of feasibility to the case study.

*P*RODUCE information on your ideal customer, your competitors, and your products/services to create estimated start-up costs and an operating budget. Ultimately you will figure your breakeven point.

KEY TERMS

adaptability	green revolution	prospects
breakeven analysis	image	quality
breakeven point	market definition	reputation
competition	market feasibility	service
conceptual definition	study	technology
consumer orientation	niche	definition
distinctive	operating budget	technological
competencies	personnel	innovations
fixed costs	price	variable costs
flexibility	product definition	

64

INTRODUCTION TO DETERMINING THE FEASIBILITY OF YOUR BUSINESS

By now, you should have a pretty clear business idea. Now, you need to find the answers to two key questions:

1. Are there customers who want to buy what you'll be selling?
2. Will they buy enough to meet your financial obligations?

These are pretty big questions, and the answers are much more detailed than a simple "yes" or "no."

This chapter is the foundation for your business, and will require a great deal of work from you. But as you know, work isn't without its rewards, and can be fun. We hope you enjoy it. You'll be uncovering information that will ultimately determine whether your business can make it in the real world. Once you're through, however, you will be on the road to business start-up and growth.

First, we'll do a **market feasibility study**, which is the way you answer that first question about potential customers. Then, we'll determine the financial potential of your planned business: whether or not all those customers will pay enough for your product or service to keep you going. These are critical considerations. We actually think that although all the information in this book is important, this chapter more than any other is absolutely critical for start-ups. Before you can think of setting entry strategies and goals, writing your business plan, naming your business, and the multitude of other decisions you're about to make, you've got to determine your business potential.

MARKET FEASIBILITY

Are there customers who want what you'll be selling? To answer this question with any certainty, you need to ask (and answer) five more questions:

1. What business will you be in?
2. What trends are happening in your industry and around you?
3. Who will be your customers?
4. Who will be your competitors?
5. Why will people buy from you instead of your competitors?

Let's look at each of these questions in turn.

What Business Will You Be In?

There are lots of ways you could answer this question. A **product definition** lists the products or services you offer. A **technology definition** stresses your technological competencies. A **market definition** defines your business in terms of your current and

---

▼▼▼▼▼▼▼▼▼▼▼▼▼▼▼▼▼▼▼▼▼▼▼▼

PERSONAL WORKSHOP 9-A
Your Business
▼▼▼▼▼▼

▼ Now it's your turn to answer the question.

I am in the _____ business.

---

prospective customers. A **conceptual definition** gives a sense of what your business is all about, what it hopes to become, and how.

This question is the meat behind your mission statement, which is discussed in Chapter 7. Your mission statement helps you position yourself in the marketplace. The concept of positioning is critical to your promotional and advertising efforts, and to developing your business into what you want it to become.

What Trends Are Happening in Your Industry and around You?

Look around and see how you can capitalize on trends and innovations in the marketplace. Many wildly successful companies were created by finding new ways to package an existing product or service. How can you benefit from current trends? Here are just a few examples to get your imagination working.

Service and convenience. Customers want what they want now. We are used to picking up our cell phone, getting the information we need, and using it to manage our lives at incredibly fast paces. We get burgers and fries handed to us through our car window; groceries delivered to our door; books, fruit, and flower arrangements ordered via the Internet; and psychic advice from 900 phone lines.

Technological innovations. Rapid advances in technology now allow us to reach new markets and serve them expediently, in the comfort of our own home or office. Offices couldn't operate without fax machines, voice mail systems, and computer networks. People are looking to the Internet for fast answers and faster transactions. Adults and children alike are carrying pagers and cell phones for instant communication.

The green revolution. Heightened environmental awareness and ecological concerns create opportunities for new markets. Just coping with the paperwork and the flood of information concerning environmentally sensitive materials has made more than one fortune. And as environmental concerns grow, so will the opportunities to manage, reuse, and recycle more things that we currently toss into landfills. Maybe your business can alleviate social concerns over polluted air and the impact of endless traffic jams. Consumers are increasingly interested in environmentally-friendly products, from clothing to food: more major market opportunities.

An older population. An increasingly healthy older population is enjoying a more abundant lifestyle than in the past. They take more adventurous vacations, dine out more, and retire to upscale communities designed around their needs. There will also be increased healthcare needs to service this population as it continues to age.

International trade. Importing and exporting are increasingly becoming opportunities for small businesses of all kinds. The North American Free Trade Agreement (NAFTA) has opened up enormous opportunities for small businesses to engage in cross-border transactions with minimal government interference. Travel and language are no longer barriers to trade: English is effectively the global language, for both business and science. Air travel and allied freight services make moving people and things easy—and the Internet and other electronic pathways provide instantaneous communication and commercial opportunities worldwide. The possibilities for small businesses are staggering.

FIRST PERSON

Kim K., Boston, Massachusetts: I started the Son Won Karate Academy in 1980. There were three basic reasons for the decision to open the Academy. First, it seemed to be a good way to use my interest in karate and tae kwan do (I am a third-degree black belt). Second, it represented the opportunity to capitalize on the growing market I observed in the mid-sized American city where I live. Finally, it was important to me to somehow contribute to the survival of the cultural heritage I'd grown up with. My first students were tough, aggressive, macho types, like those who went to the four other karate academies in the area. Nearly all my students were adults.

By the early 1990s, the karate industry was booming and there were eight academies competing with each other for a piece of the relatively small pie. I looked at the karate world and could see certain clear changes. The focus of the sport was increasingly shifting to self-defense. Plus, nearly two-thirds of the people who were enrolling in karate classes were children, about a quarter of them were girls. Also, two-income parents were encouraging their children to take karate lessons, not only for self-defense but also for the exercise and discipline. It was also becoming increasingly trendy to be involved in "multicultural" activities. I hadn't thought of myself in "ethnic" terms before, but suddenly it made business sense!

So I made a change. I started promoting the academy as a center for building discipline and fitness in young minds and bodies. My newspaper ads pictured a boy and girl, and included a message on building self-discipline. All of this was in the context of a centuries-old Oriental tradition. I conducted free demonstrations at local school assemblies, where I could not only display the physical and mental benefits of the martial arts, but educate the students about my culture. I encouraged parents to stay and observe while their children took a free trial lesson, and stressed the carryover benefits of better social adjustment and better school performance.

By gearing my advertising and promotional policies to the demographic trends I observed in the industry, I created what some people might call a "distinctive competency" among the affluent parents in my market area. Whatever it's called, I developed a clear competitive edge over my rivals, who were left playing catch-up and fighting among themselves for the leftovers.

PERSONAL WORKSHOP 9-B
Trends

▼ How will your company address trends in the industry and around you?

Market Need	Trend	Your Product/Service

Who Will Be Your Customers?

You can't serve everyone. There used to be a store in New Hampshire that proudly boasted "We have everything for everyone!" Turned out they didn't. Not even the largest international corporation can claim everyone as their prospect.

Your aim is to know in detail what your customers want that your business can profitably provide them. When we discuss market research in Chapter 14, we'll talk more about your target markets and how to learn as much as possible about those people. For now, we need to focus on a specific group of people who will buy your products or service.

The important word here is *focus*. In the big picture, we're talking about your target market. But to bring it down to a more practical level, let's put faces on these people and determine precisely who they are.

The focus implied by this question suggests finding ways to limit your markets because you have only so many hours and so many dollars to find and satisfy your customers and prospects. Who is your ideal customer? Does he or she want a high-quality product or service (at a premium price)? Or does your customer look for the lowest-cost alternative?

FIRST PERSON

Christine H., Pensacola, Florida: I used to pay an arm and a leg for a haircut. My hairdresser kept a file on my various styles, cuts, coloring treatments, and permanents. During my shampoo, I would receive a fabulous head massage, which would put me into a state of tranquility, far away from my hectic executive lifestyle. A year ago, my husband and I decided to start a family, and I chose to start a home-based business at that time. There's more of a strain on our family budget as I get my

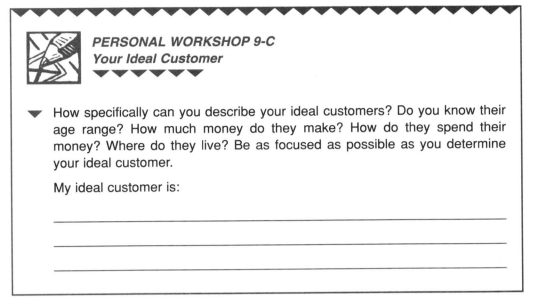

PERSONAL WORKSHOP 9-C
Your Ideal Customer

▼ How specifically can you describe your ideal customers? Do you know their age range? How much money do they make? How do they spend their money? Where do they live? Be as focused as possible as you determine your ideal customer.

My ideal customer is:

_____

_____

_____

business going, not to mention the division of time between my business and my (growing) family. I don't have the time or money for extravagant haircuts, which is fine—it's worth it for me. Now, I prefer a salon that offers me a quick in-and-out cut. My hairdressers change pretty regularly, but I don't mind. I've got a simple cut and can get a quick cut from just about anyone.

Who Will Be Your Competitors?

You can learn a lot from your competitors: What do they do better than you? In what ways do they drop the ball? How do they please their customers? What are their pricing policies? When and how do they advertise—and does their advertising work?

Your suppliers will have insights into what your competition is doing and what others in your line of business (in another city or state, for example) are doing. If you feel bold enough (or are in a start-up or transitional business) take a trip and visit businesses like yours. Small business owners will love to talk with you about their businesses if you

- aren't a direct competitor,
- make an appointment at their convenience, and
- let them know beforehand what you are going to ask.

A less intrusive way is to visit their Web sites.

Information is power. Most small business owners do not take the time to painstakingly assemble competitive information. There is nothing wrong or immoral about scouting the competition—athletes and armies do it all the time. So should you. This will give you a strong competitive edge.

PERSONAL WORKSHOP 9-D
Competitors
▼ ▼ ▼ ▼ ▼ ▼

▼ Answer the following questions about your competition.

▼ Who are your five nearest competitors?

_____

_____

_____

_____

_____

▼ How are their businesses—steady, increasing or decreasing?

_____

_____

▼ How are their operations similar or dissimilar to yours?

_____

_____

Why Will People Buy from You instead of Your Competitors?

Everything in your business revolves around your customers and **prospects** (people you plan to have as customers). Your product or service has to be tailored to their perceptions of what is worth buying. Your location and working hours have to fit their needs. Management and personnel have to be selected and trained with one goal in mind: satisfying the customers to encourage return business. Even the capital structure of the business revolves around the customer. If you can persuade your bankers, investors, and suppliers that you have a strong and stable customer base, you won't lack capital.

It sounds so simple: Put the customer first and the profits will follow. In practice, of course, it's much more difficult.

What you need to determine is what your business will do particularly well. This is sometimes referred to as determining your **distinctive competencies**. While we can't list all possibilities, Figure 4.1 notes nine of the more common areas of distinctive competence likely to be recognized by small business. Which ones will you strive for in your business?

Quality. A key area of competence and one that is of great importance to consumers is quality. If your aim is quality, you'll need to demand that your products or services meet certain standards. Those standards are initially defined by you, the owner, and by comparison to the competition. Ultimately, the customer will decide.

Service. Often hand-in-hand with quality, service aims to provide a level of care, concern, instruction, advice, and follow up (perhaps repairing any problems after the sale). Every business needs some level of service. However, you may come to realize that in your business some services are not profitable. Customers may prefer a more affordable price in lieu of special treatment or programs.

Location. A factor that often dictates a firm's success is location. Location may affect your company's visibility, likelihood of attracting customers, and competitive edge over businesses offering similar products or services.

Filling a special niche. Utilizing this important competence, your business may choose to enter an untapped market, provide unique services or products (and thus limit direct competition), or add aspects of novelty or originality to existing products. Such extensions and variations must be focused on real needs of some segment of the market. Providing a unique product that no one cares about or wants to purchase won't do you any good.

Flexibility and adaptability. A small business can focus on these particular strengths to gain a competitive edge over larger, more formalized, and rigid operations. For example, a small business may do custom work that a larger company may not be able to provide.

Consumer orientation. Because a small business is often less formal and in closer contact with its customers, it is better able to meet the shifting demands of its

---

FIGURE
4.1 **Areas of Distinctive Competence Commonly Recognized by Small Businesses**

Quality
Service
Location
Filling a special niche
Flexibility and adaptability
Strong consumer orientation
Reputation and image
Personnel
Price

customers. This is the whole idea of personalized service that is often promoted by smaller businesses.

Reputation and image. These important competencies may be a function of a number of other areas, yet your customers will often see the cumulative effect in a general or encompassing way.

Personnel. If you and your staff have extensive experience or knowledge, these factors are business strengths. For example, two hardware stores both have experienced, knowledgeable workers. One store, however, is primarily self-service. The second emphasizes personal interaction and help. Both stores possess personnel strengths, but only the second has transferred that strength into a distinctive competency.

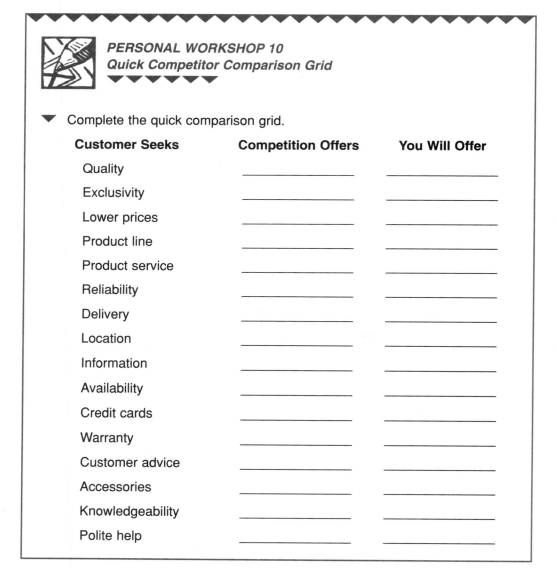

PERSONAL WORKSHOP 10
Quick Competitor Comparison Grid

▼ Complete the quick comparison grid.

Customer Seeks	Competition Offers	You Will Offer
Quality		
Exclusivity		
Lower prices		
Product line		
Product service		
Reliability		
Delivery		
Location		
Information		
Availability		
Credit cards		
Warranty		
Customer advice		
Accessories		
Knowledgeability		
Polite help		

Price. A powerful yet remarkably fragile competence, its potential as a competency may be significant if competitors are conservative and new entrants into the market are unlikely. However, if a competitor is willing or able to alter its existing price structure in return, this competency can be stripped of its value very quickly. Price is therefore often viewed as a rather short-term competency. On the other hand, price can be a long-term competitive advantage if your company has a better cost structure than your competitors: that is, if you can have lower prices with adequate profit margins.

Remember these nine areas are competencies only if customers perceive them as being valuable. Perception is often more important than reality. For example, you may feel that your company's customer service is superior to that of the immediate competition. However, if customers are unaware that your service is better, it is not a distinctive competency. It is at best an unexploited strength. A strength must be built or developed into a true area of distinctive competence. Effectively marketing the strength may be the bridge to creating a distinctive competency.

FINANCIAL POTENTIAL

Will your customers buy enough to meet your financial obligations?

To answer this question, you'll need to do a few things. First, you will need to figure how much money is required to open your doors. Do you need to rent or buy space? Purchase equipment and supplies? What about promotional items such as business cards and brochures? Then, you'll need to create an operating budget for your monthly and annual expenses. Once you have that information, you will determine your breakeven point, which will tell you how much you need to sell to keep your business afloat.

You can hold down some of your expenses by purchasing second-hand or borrowed equipment, renting space, and leasing equipment instead of purchasing. But the total amount will probably still be more than you expect.

The dangers of undercapitalization cannot be too strongly emphasized. Get the real figures. If they are manageable, great. If not, perhaps you can find ways to lower them. Don't go ahead until you are pretty sure that you can afford to go into business.

Importance of Accuracy

It's important to be accurate, descriptive, and use vendor sources rather than guesswork or estimates for start-up costs.

The process of going over start-up costs repeatedly, looking for economies and ways to lower those costs, is excellent practice for actually running your business. Careful cash management is one of those business skills that spells the difference between success and failure.

You will be very accurate in projecting start-up costs if you speak with vendors, check out catalogs and price lists, and look for actual prices. Don't guess! A businesslike list of assets will help you build credibility, especially if you can show that you have done everything you reasonably can to hold costs down.

Accuracy also pays off when you meet with your financial backer and explain why you need to borrow money for your start-up. The portion of your start-up costs that you put up yourself will show up as part of your investment in the business and can, on occasion, be used as collateral for a loan. Facts impress bankers. Guesses do not.

How do you know what it will cost to start a business? You can organize your start-up costs with the help of the forms in Personal Workshop 11.

What Is Your Operating Budget?

You don't have to become an accountant to understand and use a budget. In fact, you are already familiar with handling your personal finances. All your **operating budget** does is set down the expected amounts and timing of revenues and expenses in a standard form that can be used to strengthen your business decisions.

Your operating budget serves a variety of purposes. It helps you hold down spending, provides and supports financial self-discipline, and helps you set timelines and measurable goals. It gives you a scorecard, a way of seeing how well you are doing and whether or not you need to change some business behaviors. It is an indispensable tool for raising cash, whether from bankers, vendors, or investors. It provides a reality check: Will your business expenses outrun the business's ability to generate revenue?

The Appropriate Time Frame for Your Operating Budget

Operating budgets cover a period of time, usually a fiscal year (required for tax purposes) but are most useful if broken down to a monthly or even weekly basis.

Most businesses will find that a monthly budget is the most useful, as it allows enough time to smooth out some of the bumps, yet it is short enough to take timely action if you find something wrong (or going better than expected). Information that is 12 months old can arrive too late to be useful, especially during the early months of a start-up when reliable patterns haven't been established. Ask your SBDC or SCORE counselor, or other financial adviser for help.

BREAKEVEN ANALYSIS

Your breakeven point is defined as the level of sales at which you don't make a profit and don't suffer a loss. If you sell less than this level, you lose money; sell more and make a profit.

Breakeven analysis is a great reality check. If you know that you need sales of $200,000 to reach breakeven, but have estimated sales of $100,000, the breakeven analysis sends a clear and strong signal.

How to Compute a Basic Breakeven Point

The breakeven point can be expressed mathematically. The formula is:

Breakeven point (units) = Fixed costs ÷ Selling price − Unit variable cost

PERSONAL WORKSHOP 11
Estimated Start-Up Costs and Operating Budget
▼ ▼ ▼ ▼ ▼ ▼

▼ **Part 1: List of Furniture, Fixtures, and Equipment**

Leave out or add items to suit your business. Use separate sheets to list exactly what you need for each of the items below.	1 If you plan to pay cash in full, enter the full amount below and in column 3.	2 If you are going to pay by installments, enter the down payment plus installments for 3 months. Add the total to column 3.	3 **Total of Columns 1 and 2**
Counters			
Storage shelves, cabinets			
Display stands, shelves, tables			
Cash register			
Computers and software			
Communications equipment (phone systems, fax)			
Copiers			
Safe			
Window display fixtures			
Special lighting			
Outside signage			
Delivery equipment			
Other (specify)			
Total: Furniture, Fixtures, Equipment			

▼ **Part 2: Start-Up Costs You Only Have to Pay Once**

Item	Action	Costs for First 3 Months
Fixtures and equipment	Put the total from Part 1 here	
Decorating and remodeling	Speak with contractor	
Installation of fixtures and equipment	Talk to suppliers from whom you buy these	
Starting inventory	Ask suppliers	
Deposits for public utilities	Ask utility companies	
Legal and other professional fees	Ask lawyer, accountant, etc.	
Licenses and permits	Find out from city offices	
Advertising and promotion for opening	Estimate: ask ad agencies	
Accounts receivable	What you will need to buy more stock until credit customers pay	
Cash	For unexpected expenses, losses, special purchases, etc.	
Other (specify)	Make a separate list and enter total	
	Add up all the numbers in column 1	
Total Estimated Cash you Need to Start:		

▼ **Part 3: Operating Budget**

Item	Monthly Expenses Column 1	Annual Expenses Column 2
Salary of owner or manager		
All other salaries and wages		
Rent or mortgage		
Advertising		
Delivery expense		
Supplies/materials		
Telephone/fax		
Utilities		
Insurance		
Taxes (Social Security only)		
Interest		
Loan payments		
Maintenance		
Professional fees		
Miscellaneous		
Other (specify)		
Total Costs		

1. Calculate fixed costs: **Fixed costs** are those that stay the same no matter what the sales level is. They must be met even if you make no sales at all. Examples include overhead costs (rent, office and administrative costs, salaries, benefits, FICA, etc.), interest charges on term loans and mortgages, and "hidden costs" such as depreciation, amortization, and interest.
2. Estimate average selling price: For the purposes of this pre-start-up exercise, try to estimate an average selling price. Your price should reflect the net after any quantity or wholesale discounts based on your experience and competitive information. Determining your price structure and average selling price is a serious undertaking and an ongoing concern. The prices you set will ultimately convey your philosophies on value, quality, service, and market focus. Chapter 11 addresses pricing strategies in detail.

3. Calculate unit **variable costs**: These are the costs that will vary directly with sales. For example, as sales increase, so will the materials and supplies that are used to produce your products or services. The same is true with sales commissions. If you pay employees based on their sales generation, you will pay out more as their sales increase.
4. Calculate breakeven point: Plug the numbers into the formula.
5. Convert to dollars: Simply multiply your breakeven point by your estimated selling price.

Shortcomings of Breakeven Analysis

Since the breakeven point rests on the relationship between fixed and variable expenses, you have to have a pretty good idea of what these will be and a reasonably accurate sales forecast as well. In a start-up, this may look like a tall order, but remember you don't have to know everything—you just have to know where to find people who have the knowledge you need.

YOU MADE IT!

If you've gone through the material and personal workshops in this chapter thoroughly, you've gotten off to an excellent start in your business. What you've done in this chapter is as difficult as your business decisions will get. Other chapters may be more detail-intensive, or include more financial information, but none is as basic to your business success as this one. You have just built a solid foundation—the hardest and most critical part—and are now ready to get your business going.

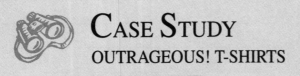

CASE STUDY
OUTRAGEOUS! T-SHIRTS

▼▼▼▼▼

*S*cott Hackett is a recent college graduate. He majored in marketing, but is not interested in working for an established company—he wants to start his own business. For several months, Scott has been looking for a low-risk venture he can start with minimal capital. He has come up with the idea of buying and selling T-shirts. While this business idea is certainly not new, Scott believes he has discovered a particularly profitable approach. He has a source from which he can purchase decals for 25 to 35 cents, and a supplier that can provide white or colored shirts for $3.00 each. With a $700 hot press, he can transfer the decals to the T-shirts in a workspace in his parents' garage. He estimates he can produce shirts with decals for a total cost of $3.50 each. Scott would then sell the T-shirts at a 100 percent markup—that is, $7.00 each—to retail shops on the boardwalks in Atlantic City, Ocean City, Wildwood, and Cape May, New Jersey. Scott feels that the retailers could sell the shirts for $10.95 or more. The trick, Scott realizes, is to get decals that are unique, daring, provocative, and outrageous, yet appealing.

Scott does not know the potential of this business, but he feels certain that he can make more money by using his marketing skills than he could by working at a pizza parlor or hamburger stand. He has about $1500 to invest and is eager to get started in time for summer. ▼

URLinks
http://www.bec.com.au/becarm/assess.htm
http://www.slu.edu/eweb/plan1.htm

 ## CASE STUDY ROUNDTABLE
▼▼▼▼▼▼

Scott: Now, I know you're thinking that this is a half-baked idea, and you're probably wondering why a young guy with a college degree wants to get into selling T-shirts on the boardwalk. But I'm smart enough to come to people who've been there for advice. So here I am: what's the advice?

Discussion Points

- Do you think Scott's idea for a T-shirt business is viable? Why or why not?
- How should Scott go about marketing his T-shirts? What kinds of stores might be interested in Scott's product?
- How outrageous do you think Scott's T-shirts should be? What kinds of images and messages do you think would attract attention and create a high demand for the shirts during the summer?
- What do you see as Scott's short- and long-term competencies in his niche market? How can he best exploit these advantages?

▲▲▲▲▲▲

 ## CHAPTER BRIEFCASE
▼▼▼▼▼▼

- The big question concerning feasibility of your market is, "Are there customers who want what you're selling?"
- The big question concerning the financial viability of a business is, "Will customers buy enough of your product to support your financial obligations?"
- You need to figure out what business you're in, the trends in your industry and around you, who your competitors are, and how you will differentiate yourself from them.
- It's important to write out your estimated start-up costs and create an operating budget so you know how much you will need to sell to break even.

 ▲▲▲▲▲▲

Chapter 5

SETTING GOALS FOR ENTERING THE MARKETPLACE

▼▼▼▼▼

If a man does not keep pace with his companions, perhaps it is because he hears a different drummer. Let him step to the music which he hears, however measured or far away.

—*Henry David Thoreau,* Walden

MISSION STATEMENT

In this chapter, you will:

*L*EARN how to differentiate your business from the rest of the market.
*E*XPLORE setting specific strategic goals for your business.
*A*PPLY your understanding to a case study scenario.
*P*RODUCE a reasonable target action plan for achieving your goals.

KEY TERMS

differentiation	horizon goals	segmentation
goal statement	near-term goals	target action plan
goals	strategy	target goals

INTRODUCTION TO ENTRY STRATEGIES

Chances are, your business will not be a monopoly. You will not be the only game in town; you will not control the marketplace. Chances are, your customers won't be your own personal property: they're a prize that others want to win, too. You will have competitors who may be just as good at what they do as you, who may make a product that does essentially the same thing as yours. They may even have been doing it longer, or making more of them, or offering lower prices or greater convenience. Your competitors may be bigger, or have the advantage of name recognition or traditional buying patterns in their favor.

So in the face of all of these challenges, what will make people want to come to you? What will set you apart?

▼▼▼▼▼▼▼▼▼▼▼▼▼▼▼▼▼▼▼▼▼

DIFFERENTIATION

Differentiation (also known as *positioning*) is arguably the most important of all small business marketing strategies. Your aim is to locate a market niche: a slice of the market that is big enough to be profitable, yet small enough to defend against other businesses. Your niche should be suited to your resources, interests, and abilities.

Some differentiating ideas will fit your start-up. Others won't. You should decide ahead of time how you want to position your business to influence your markets' perceptions of you. If you plan to sell on quality, you will go one way. If you decide to differentiate your business on grounds of convenience, price, durability, or simply newness itself, you have other options. You cannot follow all of them without hopelessly blurring your image and confusing your potential customers.

The following are some ways businesses differentiate their products and services:

- Accessibility
- Convenience
- Credentials
- Cultural identity
- Familiarity
- Financing options
- Method of production
- Native son or daughter

- Perceived value
- Price
- Product range
- Quality
- Reliability
- Service
- Specialization
- Warranty

As you become more familiar with your product or service, markets, and competition, you will begin to see other ways to differentiate your business. The important thing is to be careful and consistent. The image your business projects when it starts will be very hard to change later, if it can be changed at all. (See Figure 5.1 and Personal Workshop 12.)

SETTING YOUR ENTRY STRATEGY GOALS

Once you've developed your new business concept and distinguished its position in the marketplace, you need to methodically plan out your entry strategy. Life would be so much easier if a new business could just open its doors (or activate its Web site) and the customers would come running to buy its goods or services. But the real world marketplace doesn't work that way, and successful entrepreneurs know it. They also know that it's only by careful planning, analysis, and strategizing that a new business opportunity has any chance of success.

Benefits of Specific Goals

Suppose you and a friend are taking a leisurely drive around the city on a warm, lazy Sunday afternoon, and you discover that you have no idea where you are. Are you lost? The answer is no: you weren't going anywhere, so you aren't lost. Now suppose one of you suddenly says, "It's four o'clock! We were supposed to be at a meeting fifteen minutes ago!" Now, suddenly, as if by magic, you are lost.

FIGURE
5.1

Business Differentiation Worksheet

▼ Background: Carla has started a cottage industry business of producing and selling candles. Her "production plant" also serves as the retail store. Here is how Carla completed her Business Differentiation Worksheet.

Business Differentiation Worksheet

Name of Business: _____Carla's Candles_____

Characteristic	Pro	Con	Action
Convenience	x		nearness to new Regional Transit Center
Credentials	x		Candlemaker Certification by ASCM
Familiarity		x	(new to area)
Financing options			NA
Location		x	only handmade candles in 20 mile radius
Method of production	x		old-world quality; hand-dipped; natural dyes and scents
Perceived value	x		snob appeal
Price		x	more expensive than competitor; maybe perceived value?
Product range	x		wide range of styles and colors
Quality	x		handmade; durable
Reliability	x		hey, they're candles!
Selection	x		wide range of styles and colors
Service	x		knowledgeable staff, good phone advice, parties
Specialization	x		only Carla's candles, no mass-produced product
Warranty	x		guaranteed to burn at least 4 hours
Other			

PERSONAL WORKSHOP 12
Business Differentiation Worksheet

▼ Fill out this Business Differentiation Worksheet for your own business:

Business Differentiation Worksheet

Name of Business: _____

Characteristic	Pro	Con	Action
Convenience			
Credentials			
Familiarity			
Financing options			
Location			
Method of production			
Perceived value			
Price			
Product range			
Quality			
Reliability			
Selection			
Service			
Specialization			
Warranty			
Other			

That lazy Sunday afternoon drive was fine as long as the only "goal" was to have a good time. But once you needed to get somewhere, there suddenly was a problem. You looked around for landmarks or asked directions in order to find the way. The moral of our little story: Only if you have a specific goal to strive for do you take the actions necessary to achieve it. Fortune cookie stuff? Maybe. But it's also a fact of life for business.

Once a goal is set, performance can be measured in terms of that goal. A goal is simultaneously a planning tool and a control. It is a planning tool because it must precede the actual development of a plan. It is a control because it is a preset standard against which performance can be measured. If the goals have not been achieved, corrective steps may be taken to improve performance.

Goals are motivators, too. Achievable goals can become a rallying point for the entire company. Recently, the owner of a small manufacturing firm attributed her firm's ability to weather some tough economic and competitive times to the fact that the employees knew where the company was headed. They knew what the owners expected and had a good sense of what was likely to happen. She noted that sharing goals built a sense of identity. She was convinced that the open sharing of goals fostered a "we're in this together" spirit that helped the firm rebound from some bleak days.

Goal Statements

If goals are to have meaning and the process of goal setting is to work, certain basic rules, guidelines, or considerations must be noted. In general these rules apply to all types of goals. Nowhere is this more important than in drafting a formal statement of your personal and business goals.

First, a goal statement should be phrased in terms of *outcomes* or results rather than actions. That is, you should focus on the goal, not the series of tasks required to achieve the goal. There is a world of difference between saying, "This week I'll work on the budget," and "By the end of this week, the budget will be done."

Second, goal statements should be clear, specific, and to the extent possible, *quantifiable* or measurable. The clearer and more precise the goal, the greater the likelihood that it will be pursued and attained.

Third, effective goal statements should be challenging, yet *realistic*. Challenging goals are essential for growth-oriented businesses and growth-oriented people. Goals that are too simple or too easily reached cheat the business of its full potential. They can cause you (and your employees) to feel underutilized. When people don't feel they're working up to their potential, the result is declining morale and reduced job satisfaction. On the other hand, goals that are too lofty may quickly be perceived as unreasonable or unrealistic, and no one will even try to achieve them.

Finally, goals must be *communicated* throughout the organization. Regardless of the size of your business, and no matter how impressive a goal statement may be, its potential to influence behavior is lost if it isn't communicated. Many business owners interpret communication even more broadly and include their employees in the goal-setting process. This not only enhances the goals, it also becomes a key to motivation. The empowerment movement of recent years focuses on mutual understanding, involvement, and agreement between owners and employees with regard to goal setting. This is particularly important for small businesses, where the big corporation's fashionable "team-talk" is a day-to-day reality. In a small company, everyone's performance is vital to success. In business-speak, this is called *employee buy-in*. Buy-in is vital, especially when you have only a few employees. A clear understanding of the company's goals, and buy-in from all levels, goes a long way toward helping ensure success. The characteristics of good goals are summarized in Figure 5.2

FIRST PERSON

Tonya B., Bangor, Maine: I have a florist shop that is not a big operation—I have four full-time employees, two girls who come in on weekends to work the counter and help with orders in back, and my accountant. But when I started this business two years ago, I knew I had to have some kind of goal to strive for, other than just staying in business. So I had a breakfast meeting with my full-timers (there were three of them then) one Saturday before we opened. I sat them down and said, "We've been in business now for a couple of weeks, and we're doing great! But when I got the idea for this shop, I had a goal for it. Now that we've begun, I want you to tell me what you think of it, and whether we'll be able to achieve it." Well, we talked about the goal, about what was realistic, about how we could market the services we offered. They had good ideas, and I think they really liked that the owner wanted their input. I wrote down their ideas the next day, and created a new goal statement that actually included some of their best ones. I posted it in the back, and I think it really helps motivate people. I've heard the original employees telling the new ones about that goal statement on the wall, and how they helped write it.

Creating Goals: A Process Approach

Although setting viable goals is largely a judgmental process, based on your strengths and vision, it should not be done by the seat of your pants. In part, it is based on historical data. In part, it's dictated by the real world circumstances in which you find yourself (and these, of course, change all the time).

The focus of goals may change from time to time. Suppose, for example, that sales have increased as planned over the past several years, but costs have risen dramatically. The goal for the next period may focus on cost containment. Sales increases may still be encouraged, but the primary emphasis will be on reducing expenses per sales dollar.

Conflict among Goals

No business will have a single overriding goal. All groups, all businesses, all individuals, have multiple goals. Many of the goals are congruous, but some will be in conflict. For example, your goals to be a successful business owner sometimes conflict with your goals to be a successful parent. Conflicts among goals within a business can affect the strategy of the firm.

Mutually Exclusive Goals

When a business has multiple managers, they may have mutually exclusive goals. One manager's goal may be in conflict with another manager's goal, or a manager may have two goals that conflict with each other. In either case, the exclusivity means that

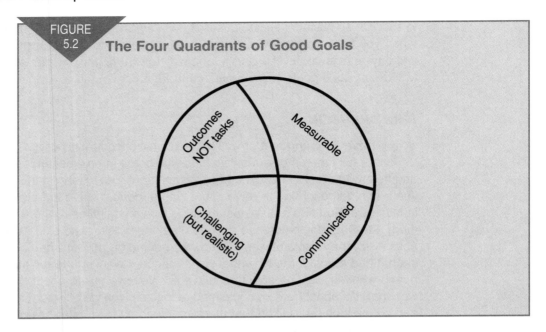

FIGURE 5.2   **The Four Quadrants of Good Goals**

one cannot be achieved without serious damage to the other. These goal conflicts must be resolved. One of the first orders of business for a multiply managed start-up is to establish a mutually agreeable system for resolving differences of opinion about important issues (like goals) as well as day-to-day details (like what color file folders to buy). This is not usually an issue for a start-up, but you should think proactively: there may well be a time when you have a staff of several managers.

Goal Priorities

Everyone establishes priorities for themselves. People can never attain all that they want to attain nor do all that they want to do. Somehow they learn to prioritize their lives and determine which of life's objectives are most important.

The same holds true for businesses. Businesses will have multiple opportunities and multiple goals, and it is difficult, if not impossible, to achieve all of them. It is necessary, then, to prioritize the company's goals. Owners may decide that the major emphasis this year will be on hiring new employees because the major emphasis last year was on expanding into a new area. Sales may have increased dramatically, and now personnel needs must be addressed. Although growth and expansion received first priority last year, they now must take second place to human resource considerations.

Setting priorities for your goals is particularly important in product development. If your firm has a number of products that could be marketed, you may decide that products A and B will receive attention next year, with products C, D, and E funded the following year. Similarly, you may budget to replace some of your old equipment this year and schedule the remainder for replacement two years from now. Your goals for your company should mesh with your goals for yourself (and your employees or partners), and everyone should understand how their personal goals contribute to the overall business goal.

FIRST PERSON

William T., Miami, Florida: Video Memories is the business I started a few years back. We take people's still photos and old home movies and put them on high-quality videotape with titles, music, and other effects. We're doing great now, but it was touch-and-go there during our first year, before we got organized. There are four main guys in my company: Tom is in charge of advertising—getting the word out about what we do and how well we do it; I run the business end of things, like finding financing, purchasing equipment, and paying the bills; and Jeff and Bryce are the technical guys—real artists with the conversions. Well, we thought we had it down pat, but it turned out that Tom was a heck of a lot better at marketing and promotion than we'd thought. He did this huge ad campaign about how we could "salvage your memories before it's too late," which made people think their photos of grandma were about to burst into flames or something. That was fine, but he promised one-day turnaround. You can guess what happened: I nearly lost Jeff and Bryce because they were so swamped, the machinery broke down from overuse, and the customers pitched fits. We got it straightened out, but it really drove home for us how important it is to be coordinated.

Goal Time Frames

Small businesses typically establish goals within three different time frames, as shown in Figure 5.3. These three time frames—horizon goals, near-term goals, and target goals—are interrelated and interdependent.

Horizon goals focus on accomplishments expected over the course of the business's planning horizon. The long-term nature of these goals means they involve relatively high

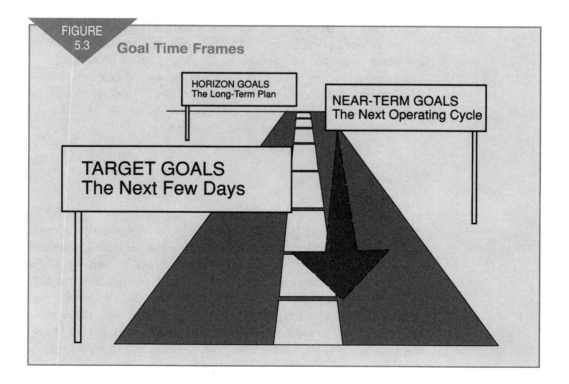

FIGURE 5.3 Goal Time Frames

HORIZON GOALS
The Long-Term Plan

NEAR-TERM GOALS
The Next Operating Cycle

TARGET GOALS
The Next Few Days

levels of uncertainty. Horizon goals therefore tend to be broader and less specific than other types of goals.

Near-term goals are established to define results or accomplishments expected within the firm's next operating cycle. That period may vary for different industries and companies. Normally, near-term goals deal with the next six months to a year.

From a planning perspective, horizon goals should be established before other goals. Often there is a strong temptation to think of the shorter-run, near-term goals as a starting point. If horizon goals are set first, however, the business must be analyzed with an eye on the distant future. All subsequent plans aim toward the long-term goal rather than being unduly constrained with meeting near-term profitability or sales targets. At the very least, horizon goals should be developed for sales dollars, market share, dollar profits, cash flow, and return on investment.

Near-term goals are the in-progress portion of horizon goals, the part of the horizon goals that can be achieved in a short period of time. For example, if the planning horizon for a manufacturing firm is five years and the horizon goal is to increase sales by 50 percent, then the near-term goal could logically be to increase sales by 10 percent over the next year. Similarly, if a restaurant manager has a three-year planning horizon and desires to have a new restaurant in place at the end of the three years, a near-term goal may be to accrue $10,000 in interest-bearing accessible funds by the middle of the current fiscal year.

Once horizon and near-term goals have been determined, the final goal-setting task is to segment the near-term goals into **target goals**. Target goals refer to very short-term goals that are quite specific as to time and measurability. Target goals may generate actions that must be completed in a few weeks or even a few days.

Suppose a real estate business has as one of its *horizon goals* to increase its market share for residential sales by 10 percent within five years. This goal may be segmented into the *near-term goal* of increasing market share by 1 percent in year one, 2 percent in each of years two, three, and four, and 3 percent in year five. *Target goals* are then developed to refine the near-term goals into smaller, more workable units: increasing home sales by 10 percent in the first quarter, increasing listings by 20 percent, increasing sales per broker by 5 percent, or any other goals that will ultimately lead to the first-year 1 percent increase in market share. Finally, *specific actions* are developed to achieve those target goals. (See Personal Workshop 13.)

The key to target goals is to make them

- specific,
- measurable, and
- attainable.

Once all the target goals are defined, reverse the process: check the target goals to ensure that they mesh with the larger or longer near-term goals. Some target goals will change monthly, some will change weekly, and very specific targets might change daily. Although target goals should be included in the strategic plan, they should be physically easy to remove (included in an appendix, for example), since the targets may change frequently. But it is still necessary to write down the target goals and related activities in order to communicate them, get commitment, and help direct employees.

Target Goals

Unfortunately, many small business owners develop goal statements that are so broad and ambiguous that they are merely platitudes. These dream-list approaches do little to provide a clear focus and direction for business activity or to offer meaningful indicators of business progress or necessary corrective actions. Moving incrementally from horizon to target goals forces owners to work through this potential goal stalemate and to produce a series of relevant and significant target goals.

Target Action Plans

Once a set of horizon, near-term, and target goals has been developed and communicated, many owners think that planning has been accomplished, that further refinement is unnecessary. These people will rarely see their goals reach fruition and will be understandably frustrated at having wasted so much time on the process. A target action plan forces you to move beyond this scenario. This target action plan itemizes a series of tasks to be prescribed and accomplished in meeting each target goal.

The first step in the target action plan is to restate the target goal in clear, precise, objective, results-oriented terms. In the Rabek Manufacturing example in Personal Workshop 13, the target goal is to develop an advertising specialty campaign within the next month. Note that this is part of a larger near-term goal to increase market share by 3 percent over the next year. Note also that even though the decision to use the advertising specialty approach had already been made, staff commitment to this approach has not been secured. With the target goal firmly in mind, a series of important action steps come into play, including determining any barriers that must be overcome, determining specific tasks that must be done, setting deadlines for completion, and identifying elements of feedback to use to assess results.

Barriers

Barriers are the obstacles or bottlenecks that must be overcome or circumvented before target goals can be reached. It is critical that you take the time to consider, in detail, the barriers that stand in the way of reaching your target goals. Barriers typically relate to human resources, financial resources, and time. There are three types of barriers: (1) insurmountable barriers, (2) barriers that can be overcome but only with a concerted redirection of effort toward the barrier, and (3) barriers that can be hurdled while enroute to the target goals.

The first type is a barrier or a series of barriers so overwhelming and significant that it is clear the target goal will never be attained. Suppose, for example, a company has a target goal of completing a marketing research project by the end of the month. If the two primary researchers on this project suddenly resign, the goal becomes unreachable. It is important to recognize an insurmountable goal early in the action process, before you waste important resources and become frustrated. When you hit an insurmountable barrier, you need to abandon your target goal and consider alternatives.

The second type of barrier must be resolved before target goals can be addressed. This kind of barrier forces the owner to abandon the target goal temporarily and focus

PERSONAL WORKSHOP 13
Action Planning Worksheet

▶ First, look at how Rabek Manufacturing developed its action plan, then fill out an Action Planning Worksheet for your own company.

Rabek Manufacturing, Inc. Action Plan

Goal		Deadline	Barriers	Action Tasks	Deadline	Feedback
Near-Term	Increase market share by 3%	12/31				
Target	Develop a new advertising specialty campaign	2/28	Staff attitudes—have never used advertising specialties before	Talk to staff about concept, get their input on message and form, gain their commitment	2/10	Informal comment and perceived commitment
			Will have to pull Jones off his present project to work on specialty campaign	Meet with Jones to explain need	2/14	
				Personal time to arrange report	2/18	
			Time in evaluating project	Meet with staff to present results and get go ahead	2/24	
				Delegate action phases to appropriate people	2/28	

Goal	Deadline	Barriers	Action Tasks	Deadline	Feedback
Near-Term					
Target					

on overcoming the barrier. For example, if a machine is not performing to specifications, the target goal must be set aside and energies directed toward repairing the machine or acquiring a new one. Only then can the original target goal be readdressed.

The third type of barrier is not as pervasive or overwhelming but still requires some element of sacrifice, in terms of either resources or time. Owners must be aware of these sacrifices and be open and responsive to addressing these difficulties and explaining likely benefits if the barriers are overcome.

Action Tasks

Action tasks are the specific tasks that must be completed if target goals are to be achieved. They are the final refinement in the process of segmenting goals into smaller, incremental units. These tasks are the most basic and narrowly defined.

Each necessary action task must be noted. (Some action tasks may focus on dealing with barriers.) Once action tasks have been prescribed, they must be arranged or prioritized into a logical sequence. The specificity of the actions depends on the owner's confidence in the employees. If employees are knowledgeable, dedicated, and innovative, action tasks are best stated in broad parameters, leaving it to the employees to determine specific activities. Conversely, if employees are new or unskilled, they may need more specific instruction and direction.

Deadlines

It is important to establish deadlines, or completion dates, for each task in the sequence. These deadlines must be real, not arbitrary, so that employees treat them seriously. Imposing an artificially early deadline only frustrates employees, who no doubt have a number of simultaneous responsibilities.

Deadlines should also be meaningful. Deadlines for the most critical tasks (those that if delayed will cause severe problems) should be set first. Deadlines for other tasks can then be assigned and prioritized accordingly.

Feedback

Some method of securing feedback should be determined in order to evaluate whether a task has been completed or is progressing as required. Feedback needs to give the owner a solid feel for the success of the task. Feedback regarding individual tasks may be easily identifiable, as when an employee obtains a contract, or may be more qualitative, such as favorable comments from customers or an apparent increase in the ratio between sales calls and sales dollars. Monitoring feedback forces the owner to concentrate on action tasks and evaluate efforts to meet each part of the action task sequence

URLinks
http://poe.acc.virginia.edu/~sms3k/weblioorg.htm

CASE STUDY
MELANIE'S BOOKSTORE

▼▼▼▼▼▼

*M*ark Selleck had always wanted to own his own business. Unfortunately, he never had been able to raise sufficient capital to fulfill his dream. After he completed high school, Mark worked for several companies doing odd jobs, but he couldn't seem to get promoted beyond clerk or cashier. His last job was with a successful gift shop, where he was in charge of receiving and shipping. He would check out the receiving inventory against the company purchase orders, noting any discrepancies. He also helped out as cashier when the store was busy.

Mark and his wife, Melanie, had two children. Mark was a good family man, always leaving work at 4 PM and returning home promptly every day. He would not work evenings or weekends, even though he needed the money. He valued the time he spent with his family, and he allowed nothing to interfere with that aspect of his life.

Mark had been with the gift shop two years when he heard about a new 20-store minimal opening about 50 miles from his home. There was a supermarket, a pharmacy, a savings and loan, a restaurant, a jewelry store, a sporting goods store, an optical center, and several other stores that complemented one another. He spoke to the mall manager, Fred Stokes, who informed him that they had one store left that would rent for $4,000 a month. The store was not fully renovated; it would be up to Mark to make it presentable. The manager went on to say that utilities were extra, and that maintenance was paid by all tenants on a proportionate basis. In addition, any increase in taxes or insurance would be passed on to the tenant. The normal terms were for the tenant to put up two months' rent as a security deposit and a one-month advance. This meant that Mark would have to come up with $12,000 when the lease was signed. The lease was for three years, and there would be a three-year option with the rental to be negotiated six months before the end of the three-year term. Mark told the manager that he would like to open up a bookstore. The manager gave him 30 days to make up his mind whether to rent space in the mall.

Mark went back to Melanie, excited about the prospect of the bookstore. He believed it would make a great deal of money. Mark made a list of publishers from which retail bookstores usually obtain their books. He wrote to the publishers explaining his intention to open a bookstore, and requested meetings with a sales representative to discuss prices, discounts, credit terms, return policies, and other essential matters. Mark contacted several existing bookstores and concluded that it would take about $25,000 for shelves, equipment, a sign, and other renovations. Around $20,000 would be needed for working capital and at least $100,000 for inventory. For rental deposits, insurance, and other items, he estimated an additional $22,000, for a total investment of $167,000.

Mark now had the basic information he needed. He and Melanie met with their parents to ask for help in raising capital. Mark's in-laws came up with $125,000. They obtained an equity loan of $75,000 (second mortgage) on their home and sold all their stock investments, which amounted to $50,000. Mark's parents came up with $69,000 which similarly included a $50,000 equity loan on their home, plus their entire life savings of $19,000. All together, then, Mark was able to raise a total of $194,000—$19,000 more than he needed. Mark agreed to make the mortgage payments on both mortgages for his parents and in-laws; he also agreed to pay $1,000 to each on a monthly basis until the other money was paid off. Both sets of parents stressed that they could not raise any more money and should Mark fail, they would be set back many years. Mark and Melanie assured their parents that they knew what they were doing and would work hard to make the business a big success.

Mark first secured the lease and opened up a bank account with the savings and loan located in the mall. He then talked to an accountant who set up a basic accounting system and obtained Mark's federal and state identification numbers. Mark got the name "Melanie's Bookstore" cleared with the County Clerk's office. The accountant offered her services for $250 a month, but Mark declined the offer. The accountant informed him that he had to pay sales taxes, federal

CONTINUED ▶

taxes, and social security taxes, and that all that paperwork was included in the $250. Mark still declined, however. He felt that Melanie could handle the financials, since she had studied bookkeeping in high school. In any case, Mark understood the importance of keeping expenses down. Besides, his business was "too simple," as he put it, to require outside help that would drain him monthly for services he could perform himself.

Before long, all the publishing representatives who had received Mark's letters began to make their calls. Mark requested the basic classics and told the representatives he intended to concentrate on current best-sellers. He estimated a gross profit range of 30 to 35 percent, with additional earnings coming from occasional special promotions. The sales representatives were all very cooperative and offered to help set Mark up when the books arrived. They agreed to take back books that did not sell, as long as it was within the prescribed period. They also agreed to grant him terms of 30 days after he had made a few purchases, assuming that his credit was satisfactory.

After about a month, the store was ready to open. Mark hired three people to work with him during the day and two people for the evening. Business began with a bang. The first week sales reached $15,000, and there always seemed to be people in the store. Sales soon tapered off, however, and Mark found that there were peaks and valleys. Some weeks sales were less than $5,000; other weeks, they climbed to $10,000 or even $15,000. In any case, Mark was extremely pleased with himself and his ability to manage his personnel. Initially, he stayed at the store until 5 PM, but as soon as he grew comfortable with his manager, he left promptly at 4 PM to be with his family.

The store had been open for about eight months when problems started to develop. Mark's cash position was $1,500, and some of the publishers were screaming for their money, which they stated was long overdue. When he added up all the monthly statements, Mark was surprised to learn that he owed the publishers over $80,000. To get them off his back, he went down to his friend in the savings and loan and asked for an $80,000 loan. The bank wanted a financial statement, so Mark drew one up himself, using the bank's financial statement form. Mark had no idea how much he owed, or exactly what his financial position was, but he managed to construct adequate documentation to secure the loan. He was able to pay off his publishers with the new cash infusion, and received a new supply of books. Now, with his inventory replenished, sales were up and he was bringing in larger daily cash receipts. But he found it necessary to withdraw more money each week to take care of his loan with the bank. Although he wasn't able to take care of his parents' or in-laws' mortgage payments or begin to make good on the other debts he owed them, he was confident that in a few months he would be able to do so. Everyone seemed to be satisfied with his story, and they encouraged him to keep on fighting.

A few months later, Mark's night manager quit unexpectedly, saying he had to rush off to Florida to care for his aging mother. In order to save money, Mark decided not to replace him. Then, several weeks later, Mark's daytime cashier informed him that she, too, had to leave immediately for personal reasons. On checking his bank statement, Mark noted that he was down to about $3,000. This was not enough to pay the rent, which was due in a few days, or to pay the employees. And then, where was he going to get the household money for the week? Fortunately, sales took an upward turn, enabling him to pay the rent and his employees and take $700 home for Melanie. But then came a visit from the State Tax Bureau, resulting in the confiscation of Mark's entire bank account because he had never paid any taxes he collected from retail sales. The tax authorities would not budge; they informed Mark that businesses are supposed to be financed by business owners, not by the consuming public.

Finally, Mark brought the accountant back into the business and asked her to draw up a financial statement. The accountant agreed to prepare a qualified statement that would not be certified. She emphasized that the balance sheet was only an estimate based on information she had received from Mark. As for Mark's bankrupt status, there could be many explanations.

Mark had been under the impression that he was doing well. Now, however, the situation looked bleak. He owed his parents and in-laws the money he had borrowed. He was also behind on his own mortgage, and he had $266,675 in business debts. To make matters worse, the mall manager came around and informed him that he would have to close shop, since he had defaulted on his lease. News traveled fast in the mall. The bank quickly demanded immediate repayment of the balance of its loan.

When the bank discovered that the statement Mark gave them for the loan was not only inaccurate, but largely fictionalized, they filed criminal charges against him for obtaining money under false pretenses. Mark and Melanie appealed to their parents to keep Mark out of jail. ▼

CASE STUDY ROUNDTABLE

▼ ▼ ▼ ▼ ▼ ▼

Mark: I know about the only advice anyone can give me now is to get a lawyer, and I've done that (although I don't have the foggiest idea how I'm going to pay him). But it all looked so right, and seemed so simple. The question I have for you is, what did I do wrong?

Discussion Points

- Was Mark prepared to go into business? What skills did he lack?
- What were the main reasons for Mark's failure? Explain in depth.
- How did Mark's personal and business goals conflict?
- What kind of goals, both horizon and long-term, could you have helped Mark set for his business in order to increase the likelihood of success?

Mark: I opened Melanie's Bookstore in an upscale suburb 30 miles outside of a major city. How could I have made the store stand out more from the others?

Discussion Points

- What do you see as Mark's competitive advantages?
- What were the environmental opportunities, and was he internally prepared for them?

BACK TO THE TABLE

Later (if he manages to stay out of jail) Mark will be back to get your advice about whether a business plan would have helped him avoid failure.

▲ ▲ ▲ ▲ ▲ ▲

CHAPTER BRIEFCASE

▼ ▼ ▼ ▼ ▼ ▼

- Differentiation, or positioning, is arguably the most important of all small business marketing strategies.
- A goal statement should be phrased in terms of outcomes rather than actions: focus on the goal, not on the series of tasks necessary to achieve it. The statement should be clear, specific and measurable. It should be challenging yet realistic, and communicated throughout your business. *Employee buy-in* is essential to achieving your business goal (even if there are just one or two employees).

- Setting priorities for your goals is especially important. Horizon goals focus on accomplishments expected over the long term. Near-term goals cover shorter planning periods. Target goals generate actions that must be completed in a few weeks or a few days. Action tasks are tasks that must be completed if target goals are to be achieved.

▲▲▲▲▲▲

Adapted with permission from
Small Business 2000, the
series on public television.

THE BUSINESS PLAN

Jill and Doug Smith
(Spokane, Washington)
Buckeye Beans
with Hattie Bryant
Creator of *Small Business 2000*

"*H*attie: You've got a mission statement to make people smile. But you've got a strategy to make that happen.

Doug: Well, the rest of the statement really deals with what we're interested in, and we call it the HEHE principle. And HEHE stands for humor, education, health, and the environment. And that's really the rest of our mission statement and what we want to do.

Jill: We're really niche marketers. That's really what we're about. We just happen to have a bean soup product. But we're looking for niche markets to sell it in, different channels of distribution and different places in the marketplace where we can take what we do well and put it out there, and make more people smile.

Doug: People buy a lot of our products because of an impulse. I mean, they see it, they go, 'Oh, that's great. I'll buy it.' After all, our products are, like Jill has said, just either beans in a bag or pasta in a bag. But we try to romance that product and add value to that simple product to the point that it's a very attractive, whimsical, fun thing. You're not just buying a soup, you're not just buying a pasta; you're buying a whole story, a whole image. "

THE BUSINESS PLAN

▼▼▼▼▼

It is not good enough for things to be planned—they still have to be done; for the intention to become a reality, energy has to be launched into operation.

—*Pir Vilayat Inayat Khan*

MISSION STATEMENT

In this chapter, you will:

*L*EARN about the important role a business plan plays in the life and success of your business.

*E*XPLORE the strengths and weaknesses of a business plan.

*A*PPLY your understanding to evaluate what makes a complete, organized, effective business plan.

*P*RODUCE an effective executive summary.

KEY TERMS

business plan	mission statement	statement of purpose
competition	organizational plan	target markets
executive summary	pro forma	

INTRODUCTION TO BUSINESS PLANNING

The business plan is a unique document, and this chapter has been designed specifically with this fact in mind. *But you must do the work.* A business plan won't do you any good if you don't thoroughly understand it. That level of understanding only comes from being involved from the very start. Your business plan is the tool you use to convert your "dream business" into an ongoing reality.

Lack of adequate planning is one of the principal reasons that most businesses fail. The importance of planning cannot be overemphasized. By taking an objective look at your business you can identify areas of weakness and strength, pinpoint needs you might otherwise overlook, spot opportunities early, and begin planning how you can best achieve your business goals. Your business plan also helps you see problems before they grow large, helps you identify their sources, and suggests ways to solve them. Your business plan will even help you avoid some problems altogether.

BUSINESS PLANNING: THE KEY TO YOUR SUCCESS

The best way to enhance your chances of success is to plan and follow through on your planning. For instance, if your proposed venture has weaknesses, the business plan will show you why. It may even help you avoid paying the high tuition of learning first-hand about business failure. It is far cheaper to abandon an ill-fated business at the start-up phase than to learn by experience what a business plan would have taught you.

There are three critical facts that demonstrate the importance of learning how to create a complete, effective business plan.

1. Most lenders and investors require a business plan.
2. Most businesses would operate more profitably with a business plan.
3. Most business owners do not know how to write a winning business plan.

Yet for all its undeniable importance, no task seems to cause more fear and dread than that of preparing a business plan. In fact, many new business owners will forge ahead without a formal plan, certain that a good idea, enthusiasm, and the desire to achieve their goals will be enough to ensure business success.

Unfortunately, there is a major flaw in this type of thinking. Most business owners are not proficient in all phases of their particular industries and, therefore, do not have enough knowledge to make the best decisions and see what changes will have to be implemented in the future. Business planning is the most effective way to overcome this deficiency and enable you to organize the making of business decisions into a logical process. Most business owners love their business, but hope to avoid anything that resembles paperwork.

You will soon learn that about 20 percent of your time as a business owner will be spent directly working with your product or service. The other 80 percent of the time you will be kept busy doing all of the managerial and miscellaneous chores that need to be done to keep your business functioning.

WHY WRITE A BUSINESS PLAN?

A business plan is a formal, written document that serves as a guide to your future, provides direction and focus, and helps you model your business and avoid problems. There are four main reasons for writing a business plan. What are they and why are they important enough to convince you to write one?

1. **The business plan helps define your business.** The process of putting a business plan together, including the research and thought you put in before

beginning to write it, forces you to take an objective, critical, unemotional look at your business project in its entirety.

2. **The business plan serves as a guide during the lifetime of your business.** This is the most important reason for writing a business plan. Writing a business plan will force you to consider everything that will come into play to make a success out of your business. It will also provide you with a means to periodically analyze what is happening in your business and give you a solid basis upon which to make decisions and implement changes. In short, it is the blueprint of your business and will serve to keep you on the right track. If you will spend the time to plan ahead, many pitfalls will be avoided and needless frustrations eliminated. You wouldn't take a long car trip without planning the route; you wouldn't canoe the Amazon without a map; why would you, even for a second, consider running a business without a plan?

3. **A business plan will be required for securing financing.** If you are planning to seek loan funds, you will be required to submit solid documentation in the form of a business plan. The days are gone when your local banker would extend a loan because you are a good, trustworthy person with an entrepreneurial idea that sounds great. The world is more complex, the economy is unforgiving and the banker has to have complete documentation that will justify your loan. Remember: a banker is the caretaker of his or her clients' money. If your business plan is realistic, and if you can offer documented evidence that you will be able to repay your loan plus interest, then the banker can make a case for lending you the funds you need.

4. **A solid business plan will help attract investors.** You may be looking for venture capitalists to invest in your business in return for a share of the profits. In today's market, they have many different investment opportunities from which to choose. If your business seems solid, promising, and supported by a clearheaded plan, your chances of attracting their attention are greatly improved. Your business plan will provide potential investors with detailed information on all aspects of the company's past and current operations and future projections. It will detail how their investment will be used to further the company's goals. Investors want to make money, and they want to know how their investment will improve the worth of your company. Your business plan will detail how the money will be used and how it will enhance the company's profitability. And for investors, more profits for you mean more profits for them.

Now that we've discussed the *why* of a business plan, let's turn to the *how*.

WRITING YOUR BUSINESS PLAN

Many business planning workshops focus heavily on why you should hire a professional planner (usually the company that's sponsoring the event). There is also a lot of hype in magazines and on the Internet claiming that you can install your business planning software and create a business plan in a few hours, with just a few simple keystrokes.

PERSONAL WORKSHOP 14
Why You Should and Should Not Write a Business Plan
▼ ▼ ▼ ▼ ▼

▼ Here are two checklists. Take a moment and read each one, checking off all the statements with which you agree. They should help you understand the significance of the business plan to your small business.

Checklist A: Why You Should Write a Business Plan

Check all that apply.

	I'd like my business to make more money.
	I could use a map and compass for the future.
	I would like to impress my lenders or investors with the financial soundness of my business.
	I am interested in setting realistic goals for my business.
	I would like to develop sound operating and financing plans.
	I believe it's important to communicate my goals and plans clearly.

Checklist B: Why You Should NOT Write a Business Plan

Check all that apply.

	I don't need one: my business will do just fine without formal documents.
	I have it all in my head, and I don't want to tell anyone else.
	I don't know how to begin, and I don't want to learn.
	I don't have enough time.
	I'm just not a numbers person.
	I'm just not a writer.
	I make more money than I really need, I'm immortal and I never make mistakes.

▼ When you're done, look at your results. If you're taking yourself and your business opportunities seriously, you should have checked off most, if not all, of the statements in Checklist A. If you did, you have a good attitude about creating a plan that will help build success for your business. If you checked any of the statements in Checklist B, you should probably rethink the whole entrepreneurial choice you've made, before you embarrass yourself in public.

The fact is that, in the real world, things are rarely accomplished simply. Writing a business plan requires many days (and possibly months, depending on the complexity of your business). But not only *can* you write it yourself, you *should*. If you do, you will know your business better before you finish.

Certainly, there's a lot of research to be done. Even if you hire a professional planner, you will be required to supply the information and statistics that will go into your business plan. What those self-promoting workshops don't tell you is that compiling the information—your part of the work—is about 80 percent of the job. The other 20 percent is simply a matter of knowing how to put the information together into a readable plan. Should you pay for that?

Much of the confusion seems to stem from the fact that most business owners do not know what elements to include or how to organize their information in a logical sequence. In writing a business plan, like putting together a child's bicycle, "some assembly is required." And like a bicycle, a business plan must not only have all the necessary parts in order to work the way it's supposed to, it must be put together in the right way. With a bicycle, you get an instruction booklet that tells you how to assemble a box of metal and rubber pieces into a shiny new bike. With a business plan, you get this chapter.

Like so many other things in life, writing a business plan is a process. It starts with you sitting down and thinking about what, exactly, you're doing.

THE PRELIMINARIES

You don't just sit down and start writing. There are several things you have to do before you get started. Some analysis and organization needs to be done if your business plan is going to be worthwhile. But don't reinvent the wheel. You already have a good start on the business from your work in the early stages of the start-up process, when you analyzed your strengths, skills, and abilities; observed the marketplace and your competitors; and set some short- and long-term goals.

Refine Your Mission Statement

The mission statement (discussed in Chapter 7) is a mini version of what your business plan, ultimately, will be. The mission statement is a "big picture" document; the business plan fills in the details.

In many ways, it's a good idea to write your mission statement after you've written your business plan. At that point, you'll have a very clear idea of exactly what your business will be like, what its strengths and limitations are, and how you'd like it to grow. On the other hand, writing a pre-plan mission statement during the earliest phases of your venture can help keep you focused as you lay out your plan. If you write a pre-plan mission statement, just know that it will change (perhaps dramatically) by the time your plan's complete. If you've drafted a pre-plan mission statement, look at it again. What does it say? What business are you going to be in? Why are you doing what you're doing? Keep working at your answer. It should change as your research progresses. Remember that your aim is to find ways to make your business stand out from others, including both direct and indirect competitors.

Check Out Your Competition

Competition is a fact of business life. If you have no competitors, you probably don't have a viable business idea, or haven't come to grips with what business you are really in. Some years ago, Theodore Levitt noted in a classic essay entitled "Marketing Myopia" that at some point in the early 1950s Hollywood decided that it was in the movie business, and that television was not competition. After losing billions of dollars of business to this newer medium over the years, however, Hollywood finally realized that it was in the entertainment business, not just movies, and began to compete successfully.

All businesses have competition. List your five closest direct competitors and begin to collect information on them. Clip copies of their advertisements, jot down notes on your observations of them, pay them visits as a customer.

But wait, you say: this is supposed to be *my* business plan, for *my* business. At this point, what do my competitors have to do with it? The fact is, your competitors will help you understand who you are. That is, you will, to a large extent, define your business by your competition. Most businesses operate within fairly tight parameters: all grocery stores carry more or less the same items; one hardware store is very much like another; lawyers are interchangeable. Within these limits of product, service, and distribution there are plenty of ways to set yourself apart. A grocery store might offer a particularly wide range of exotic and organic produce. A hardware store might have a strong automobile parts division. A lawyer might specialize in legal issues of interest to small businesses.

The better you know your competition, the better you will know your own strengths (and weaknesses). And the better you know yourself, the better you'll be able to compete. Start with the most direct competitors, but keep an eye out for indirect competition—those businesses that aren't obvious competitors. For example, retail stores have to contend with mail order competition. And some mail order firms have begun to open retail outlets in choice locations. If you can spot these trends early, you can compete.

But remember the lesson of the old westerns: there's always some young hothead coming into town looking to make his name against the established local gunfighter. As your business succeeds and grows, it will attract the attention of new competitors. Your competitor list will grow.

As you make your list, you'll gain insights into your own business. You'll find yourself plotting ways of heading off competitors at the pass, of anticipating their next move, of planning innovation. As you do that, you'll be working on your business plan. Start your list early, add to it as needed, and be prepared to receive disproportionate benefits from your research.

Define Your Target Markets

Defining target markets is another ongoing project. Don't do it once and expect to enjoy success. Your markets change. People move. Tastes change. Competition increases, especially in profitable markets. Products and services change, and what sold yesterday won't sell today.

Eventually, you will almost unconsciously redefine your markets. That takes experience, though, and to offset a lack of experience, be prepared to go through a lot of spadework.

Interview Prospective Customers

You can't beat prospective customers as a source of hot information. Ask yourself who might buy your goods and services, then interview them. People like to express their opinions; you need to listen to them. This information will help you define what your business will be. People buy what they want to buy, which is not necessarily what you plan to sell.

WRITING THE PLAN

Once you've done the groundwork, you're ready to get started putting pen to paper (or fingers to keyboard). The text of a business plan must be concise, yet must contain as much information as possible. This may sound like a contradiction, but you can solve the dilemma by using the **key word** approach. Write the following key words on a card and keep it in front of you while you are writing:

- Who
- What
- Where
- When

- Why
- How
- Unique

- Benefit to customer
- How much

Answer each question asked by the key words in one paragraph at the beginning of each section of your business plan. Then expand on that thesis statement by telling more about each item in the text that follows. Stress any uniqueness and benefit to the customer that may be relevant to the subject you're writing about. Keep in mind that the lender's (or investor's) time is limited, and that your plan is not the only one being reviewed. Often the first paragraph following a section heading will be the only one read. It's very important, then, to include as much pertinent and concise information as possible in that first paragraph. Don't assume, however, that only first paragraphs will be read: whether your lender or investor reads every word of your plan or not, you have to write it as if they will.

Figure 6.1 gives you the big picture: the conceptual three Cs of the business plan. Here's a more detailed overview: a sample outline, a sort of road map of what a complete business plan looks like.

In the following pages, we'll define, examine and explain each of these parts in turn.

The Cover Sheet

The cover sheet should contain the name, address, and telephone number of the business and the names, addresses, and telephone numbers of all owners or corporate officers. It should identify the preparer of the business plan, and when the plan was prepared or revised. Figure 6.2 is a sample cover sheet

The cover sheet should not be elaborate. It should be neat, attractive, and short. Use clearly legible type and a simple layout. Avoid fancy desktop publishing effects and colored paper: this is a serious document, and should look like the author takes it seriously. If the plan is to be used primarily as a financing proposal, use a separate cover

FIGURE
6.1
Outline of a Business Plan

▼ Cover Sheet: Name of business, names of principals, address and phone number

Statement of Purpose or Executive Summary

Table of Contents

▼ Section One: The Business
  A. Description of business
  B. Product/Service
  C. Market
  D. Location of business
  E. Competition
  F. Management
  G. Personnel
  H. Application and expected effect of loan (if needed)
  I. Summary

▼ Section Two: Financial Data
  A. Sources and Applications of Funding
  B. Capital Equipment List
  C. Balance Sheet
  D. Breakeven Analysis
  E. Income Projections (Profit and Loss Statements)
      1. Three-year summary
      2. Detail by month for first year
      3. Detail by quarter for second and third years
      4. Notes of explanation
  F. Cash Flow Projection
      1. Detail by month for first year
      2. Detail by quarter for second and third years
      3. Notes of explanation
  G. Deviation Analysis
  H. Historical Financial Reports for Existing Business
      1. Balance sheets for past three years
      2. Income statements for past three years
      3. Tax returns

▼ Section Three: Supporting Documents: Personal résumés, personal balance sheets, cost-of-living budget, credit reports, letters of reference, job descriptions, letters of intent, copies of leases, contracts, legal documents, and anything else relevant to the plan.

sheet for each bank or capital source you submit it to. Figure 6.3 is a sample cover sheet for a financing proposal.

FIGURE 6.2 **Sample Cover Sheet**

Wholesome Foods, INC.

123 Main Street

Orange, Florida 11111

111-111-1111

Business Proposal for Don Pendleton and Marie Tellini

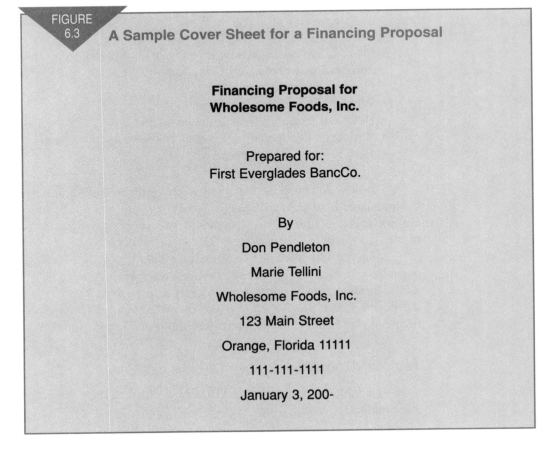

FIGURE 6.3 **A Sample Cover Sheet for a Financing Proposal**

**Financing Proposal for
Wholesome Foods, Inc.**

Prepared for:
First Everglades BancCo.

By

Don Pendleton

Marie Tellini

Wholesome Foods, Inc.

123 Main Street

Orange, Florida 11111

111-111-1111

January 3, 200-

Statement of Purpose

The statement of purpose is also known as the thesis statement or executive summary. Essentially, the statement of purpose summarizes your plan and states your objectives. Even though this is the first section of your plan, you should really write it last, after you have completed all the parts of the plan it summarizes. That way, you'll be sure your summary really tells people what your plan's about. If you are seeking loan funds or investment capital, it will list your capital needs, how you intend to use the money, the benefit of the loan funds to the business, and how you intend to repay the loan or return profits to the investor.

Your statement of purpose must be strong and persuasive as well as comprehensive. At the same time, it should also be extremely short: one or two pages at most, a few paragraphs at best. Remember that it's the first part of your plan a lender (or investor) will read, and in some cases it may be the only part they read. It's your chance to sell your business, or fail to sell it. Literally, effectiveness of your whole business plan depends on a strong statement of purpose. Those first few paragraphs often make all the difference between a needed infusion of capital and an apologetic handshake.

This first page of your plan should state your objectives as simply as possible. If the plan is for your sole use, the statement should be a brief description of how you intend to use the plan once it has been developed. For example: "This plan will be an operating and policy guide for Wholesome Foods, Inc."

If the plan is also to be used as a financing proposal, the statement of purpose becomes more complex. It should include responses to the following questions:

- Who is asking for money?
- What is the business structure (for example: sole proprietorship, partnership, corporation, Subchapter S corporation)?
- How much money is needed?
- What is the money needed for?
- How will the funds benefit the business?
- Why does this loan or investment make business sense?
- How will the funds be repaid?

The deal you propose—the loan or investment, its use and expected effects on the business, and how you will repay it—will be supported by the rest of your plan. If you are not seeking a loan, the plan should still support and justify the use of your own money (or the money of partners, friends, or family).

Keep the statement short and businesslike. It will usually be no longer than half a page, but can be longer if necessary. Use your own judgment.

The statement of purpose cannot be completed until you have calculated your capital needs. It can be written, but the exact amount needed won't be known until the financial projections have been worked through. (See Personal Workshop 15.)

Table of Contents

The table of contents should follow your statement of purpose, and reflect the three main sections of your plan:

PERSONAL WORKSHOP 15
Evaluate Your Statement of Purpose
▼ ▼ ▼ ▼ ▼

▼ Use this form to evaluate the effectiveness of your plan's statement of purpose.

0 = No　　　　　**1 = Somewhat or Mostly**　　　　**2 = Yes**

General Style	0	1	2
Motivates reader to continue: prioritizes substantive highlights of plan; uses lists and bullet points			
Content: covers all major items of plan			
Dynamic, effective writing style: clear, concise, complete sentences; short paragraphs; active language ("The business will realize a profit margin of eighteen percent" rather than "A profit margin of eighteen percent will be realized by the business"); avoids unnecessary jargon or thesaurus-style big words used only to impress			
Professional tone: Avoids slang, informal language			
Persuasiveness: Shows commitment and enthusiasm, logical presentation and effective language			
Length: Two pages or less			

Topic Coverage	0	1	2
Purpose			
Market analysis			
Company description			
Mission			
Marketing/sales strategy			
Competitive advantages			
Management team biographies			
Operations			
Financial strategy			
Long-term goals			
TOTAL			

Scoring:
23 to 32—Good Summary
15 to 22—Promising Summary (needs work)
Less than 15—Poor Summary (throw it out and try again)

1. the business
2. financial data
3. supporting documents

Having a table of contents will help the reader move smoothly from one section of the plan to another when verifying information.

For example, if a lender is reading financial information regarding advertising on a pro forma cash flow statement, he or she can use the table of contents to locate the advertising section for specifics on where you will be advertising and how the advertising dollars will be spent. The table of contents should also refer to the page in the supporting documents section that will contain advertising rate sheets backing up the advertising plan.

These basic sections may be broken down further if necessary. Since a business plan, even for a modest deal, can run to twenty or more pages, you want to help readers find their way to sections or subsections of particular interest. The statement of purpose states what your deal is. The table of contents makes it easy to find supporting material.

A format of this kind makes it easy to find the section of most interest to the reader at any given time. You will have to fill in the actual page numbers as you go along, but the table of contents also serves as a guide to writing and organizing your business plan.

The Organizational Plan

The first main section of your business plan should contain information about how your business is structured administratively. It should essentially provide a detailed definition of your operation, including the following points, as relevant:

- A description of your business
- Your legal structure
- Identification of your management and personnel
- Where you plan to locate
- How you will do your accounting
- What insurance you will have
- What security measures you will take to protect your inventory and information

The best way to understand the kinds of information you should include, and how it should be included, is by looking at an example. Figure 6.4 illustrates the organizational plan for a small wholesale/retail business.

The Marketing Plan

The second main section of your business plan defines your total market, with emphasis on your target market and your competition. The purpose of the marketing plan is to support the financial projections in section three of your business plan. You should describe how your product or service will be promoted and marketed, and its pricing. Here you will explain the reasons underlying your decisions about timing your

FIGURE
6.4

A Sample Organizational Plan

Description of Business

Wholesome Foods, Inc. is a fresh produce market specializing in selling certified organic fruits and vegetables to local retail and wholesale customers. At present, about 60 percent of sales are retail. Wholesome plans to concentrate more heavily on the wholesale trade (restaurants and grocery chains) in the future. Although margins are lower in the wholesale trade, profits are higher due to lower personnel costs and faster inventory turnover.

Wholesome began business in September 1991. The store is open seven days a week from 10:00 AM to 8:30 PM (6:00 PM in the winter) for retail business and from 6:30 AM to 8:30 PM year-round for wholesale.

The retail demand is seasonal and fluctuates according to weather. The quality of our produce is exceptional, and since Don Pendelton is a former farmer with many personal friends in the organic farm niche of the agribusiness industry, we do not anticipate trouble maintaining good relations with our suppliers. We have made a policy of paying premium prices in cash for the best, freshest produce.

Description of Management

Marie Tellini was born in Orange, Florida, and has lived there all her life. After graduating from local schools and serving in the United States Navy for three years, she became a self-employed carpenter, taking night courses in small business management and sales at the University of Western Florida, with the aim of owning and managing a retail store. She currently serves on the local zoning board. She and her husband (a medical technician) live in Orange with their two children.

Mr. Pendelton was born in Wisconsin, where his family ran an organic farm. He attended schools in Utah, Alaska, and Florida. He test-drove motorcycles for a year, then served as parts manager for Wheely Cycles, Inc. before joining the produce division of Tasty Foods as a packer in March 1989 in their East Melara, Florida, plant. While working for this large grocery chain, Mr. Pendelton became acquainted with local agricultural product suppliers, and found himself increasingly interested in the organic farmers throughout the region who followed the same practices, with many improvements, as his family in Wisconsin. In June 1991 he resigned as line foreman of the Vegetable Department to join Ms. Tellini in starting Wholesome. He is unmarried and lives in East Orange.

Both owners are healthy and energetic. They believe their energies complement each other and will help them make Wholesome a success. In particular, Mr. Pendelton knows all of the local farmers while Ms. Tellini is a well-known member of the community. Since Mr. Pendelton has had experience in cost control and line management, he will be responsible for the store and inventory control. Ms. Tellini will be primarily responsible for developing the wholesale business. They will set policies together. Personnel decisions will be made jointly.

Salaries will be $950/month for the first year to enable the business to pay off start-up costs. Ms. Tellini's husband earns enough to support their family; Mr. Pendelton's personal expenditures are low since he shares a house with five other men. In the second year they will earn $1,200/month, in the third year $1,500/month with any profits returned to the business.

FIGURE 6.4 **A Sample Organizational Plan, continued**

In order to augment their skills, they have enlisted the help of Twiste and Schout (CPAs); Dewey Cheatham & Howe (attorneys); and Halsey Johnson, a retired banker who will be on their advisory board. Other advisory board members are Andrew O'Bangfo, business consultant, University of Florida's Venture Incubator Division's Etienne LeBlanc, and Gene Brudleigh of OFF (Organic Farmers of Florida). This board will provide ongoing management review.

Description of Personnel

Wholesome will hire one part-time salesperson within six months to sell produce over the counter to the retail customers. He or she will be paid $4.00/hour for weekend work; no fringe benefits or overtime are anticipated. We will also employ, on an as-needed basis, one worker at $6.75/hour to help process produce for the wholesale trade. We think the counter help will be needed for 10 weeks during the summer and the other worker will be needed for about 20 hours/week for 16 weeks. (This should take care of the second summer as well. For the third year, we plan on two counter helpers plus a full-time summer employee.) In the second year, we'll add one full-time employee at $850/month, with a raise to $900/month in the third year.

No further employees are planned unless business grows more rapidly than we have forecast.

Application and Expected Effect of Loan or Investment

The $120,000 will be used as follows:

Purchase of Main Street property	$75,000
Equipment:	
Used Ford pickup with insulated body	3,885
Dayton compressor (used, serial #45-cah-990)	365
Sharp scrubber (used, Speedy model)	400
Renovations (see contractor's letter in Supporting Documents)	12,500
Working capital	12,000
Inventory	1,500
Cash reserve	14,350
Total:	$120,000

Wholesome can purchase the 123 Main Street property at a substantial savings under the terms of a lease/purchase agreement. An independent appraiser has calculated the value of the property, including leasehold improvements already done by Wholesome, at $135,000. The monthly payment for a 15-year mortgage ($75,000 at 11.5% interest) will be $875/month, a net increase of $325/month over the current rent. See the Financial Data section for the effect on the business.

The truck will be used to deliver merchandise to our wholesale customers, retard spoilage, and maintain the quality of the seafood.

The compressor will replace the one now used for the freezer and will lower electrical costs and provide a measure of insurance against loss of refrigeration. (We'll keep the old compressor as a spare.)

FIGURE 6.4 **A Sample Organizational Plan, continued**

The scrubber is necessary when dealing in organic produce, due to the natural fertilizers used and the surface pests resulting from nonpesticide growing.

The renovations are: a toilet and wash sink separate from the work area, and replacement of the current obsolete heating system, to reduce fuel expenses.

The working capital will enable Wholesome to meet current expenses, offset negative seasonal cash flow as shown in the Cash Flow Projection in the Financial Data section, and ensure the continued growth of the business.

The bank will hold the reserve as a line of credit. It will be used to take advantage of special opportunities or to meet emergencies.

Summary

Wholesome Foods, Inc. is an organic produce market serving retail and wholesale markets in and around Orange, Florida. Don Pendleton and Marie Tellini, the owners, are seeking $120,000 to purchase the 123 Main Street property, perform necessary renovations and improvements to the property, maintain a cash reserve, and provide adequate working capital for anticipated expansion of the business. This amount will be sufficient to finance transition through a planned expansion phase so the business can operate as an ongoing, profitable venture.

Careful analysis of the potential market shows an unfilled demand for exceptionally fresh organic fruit and vegetables. Ms. Tellini's local reputation will help secure a sizable portion of the wholesale market, while Mr. Pendleton's managerial experience assures that the entire operation will be carefully controlled. Ms. Tellini's current studies at University of West Florida will provide even more control over the projected growth of Wholesome and complement the advice of a thoughtfully selected advisory board.

The funds sought will result in a greater increase in fixed assets than may be shown, as Ms. Tellini will be performing much additional renovation and improvements herself. The additional reserve and working capital will enable Wholesome to increase its sales substantially while maintaining profitability.

market entry. If your location is tied to your marketing decisions, discuss that as well. You should also examine current industry trends, to create a context for your business decisions.

Your marketing plan is based on the realistic answers to three basic questions:

1. *What business am I in?* Work on your mission statement; it will help you position your business in the marketplace. What makes your business unique? What do you want your business to become? Your marketing plan is one of the tools you use to achieve that goal.

2. *What are my target markets?* You can't serve everyone. Even though McDonald's will tell you they've sold billions and billions, there are still a lot of people in the world who've never had a Big Mac, and a lot who've had hundreds. By careful market planning, you can target your market and ensure that

your marketing dollars are spent in the most efficient way possible: reaching the people who are most likely to be your paying customers.

3. *What do my customers buy?* The answer to this question is bigger than "widgets" or "handwoven baskets," or "legal services." The real question is, What *benefits* do your customers think they are receiving when they buy your product or service? Your marketing plan should be built around those benefits, because that's what the customer wants.

Financial Analysis

The third major section of your business plan translates the information from the first two sections of your plan into financial figures that can be used to more objectively analyze your business and make decisions about its profitability potential. In upcoming chapters, we'll look at how you construct the various elements of your financial plan, and the tools you'll need to create a plan. For now, however, it's enough for you to understand that you'll need to use those financial tools in writing your plan.

The financial documentation includes three basic components:

1. **Pro forma** (projected) financial statements
2. Actual (historical) statements
3. A financial statement analysis

The analysis section should include these specific documents:

- A summary pro forma cash flow statement
- Three-year income projection
- Break-even analysis
- Quarterly budget analysis
- Profit and loss (P&L) statement
- A balance sheet

If you are going to a lender or investor, you will also need a summary of financial needs, loan fund dispersal statement, and financial history.

Supporting Documents

This final section of your plan includes all the documents referred to in the plan itself. It provides the evidence necessary to support the statements, projections, and assumptions you made in the three main sections of your business plan.

This section should include:

- Owner/manager resumes
- Personal financial statements
- Articles of incorporation or partnership agreements
- Legal contracts
- Lease agreements
- Proprietary papers (copyrights, trademarks, and patents)

- Letters of reference
- Demographic documentation
- Any other materials that support the plan

REVISING YOUR BUSINESS PLAN

Writing a business plan does not mean that you can never vary from it, even if you carve it in stone. In fact, if your plan is going to be effective, either to the business or to a potential lender, it will be necessary for you to update it on a regular basis. Changes are constantly taking place in your industry, in technology, and with your customers. You, as the owner, must be aware of everything that is happening in relation to your business in particular and your industry in general. You must be prepared to take the necessary steps to stay ahead of your competition. Every quarter, you will want to look at what has happened in your business, make decisions about what you can do better and revise your plan to reflect the changes you want to implement.

PERSONAL WORKSHOP 16
Preparing Your Business Plan

▾ Use this worksheet to help organize your thoughts and data about your business as you prepare to write your own plan.

Company Description: Company name, type of business, location, and form of organization	
Mission Statement: a concise statement of your business's purpose	
Stage of Development: Is your company a start-up or ongoing business? When was it founded? How established in its market is it? Have sales activities begun?	
Products and Services: List the type of products or services you sell or plan to sell.	
Target Market(s): List the markets you intend to reach, and why you chose them. Summarize results of market research and analysis.	
Marketing and Sales Strategy: Briefly describe how you intend to reach your target market(s).	
Competitors: Describe your competition and how the market is divided.	

CONTINUED ▶

Competitive Advantages and Competencies: Explain why your company will be able to successfully compete. List important distinctions.	
Management: Describe the backgrounds and capabilities of you and your management team.	
Operations: Outline your locations, distributors, suppliers, production techniques, and other operational characteristics.	
Financials: Indicate your company's expected revenues and profits for the first three years.	
Long-Term Goals: Describe what your company will look like five years from now.	
Funds Sought: How much money do you need? What are your sources of financing? How will the money be used?	
Exit Strategy: How will lenders and investors get their money back? What financial protections can you offer them?	

 URLinks

http://www.business-plan.com/automate.html
http://bus.colorado.edu/centers/entrep/publications/purpose.htm
http://www.cbsc.org:4000/sbc-doc/intro_bp.html
http://www.azresource.com/busplan.htm
http://www.toolkit.cch.com/Text/P01_4500.stm
http://www.fascination.com/pub/bellis/bizplan.html
http://guide.infoseek.com/Topic/Business/Small_business/Start_a_business/
    Business_plan
http://www.toolkit.cch.com/Tools/buspln_m.stm

THE NEXT STEP

The remainder of this chapter is devoted to a detailed case study that includes a complete business plan. It's a longer case study than we've considered before, but we think one of the best ways to learn is by seeing how something is really done. As you go through the case study, ask yourself whether the entrepreneur is making the right decisions and putting together a useful plan. In the round table discussion, you'll be asked to analyze the business plan's effectiveness.

CASE STUDY
AMERICAN FURNITURE

▼▼▼▼▼▼

Dean Foley is 32 years old, married with two children. For more than 20 years, Dean has been a carpenter. He especially likes to design lawn and office furniture and is considered by many to be extremely talented. He has worked for various builders for the last 14 years, and he has done some work on his own on a part-time basis. Because he has been working full-time, he has never been able to generate more than $20,000 a year in sales from his own carpentry pursuits. Nevertheless, for a long time Dean has been harboring a dream of starting his own business.

He estimates that he has more than $50,000 in equipment, most of which he was given by his father, a retired carpenter. Dean has a home in the country on five acres with a separate workshop behind his house where he manufactures furniture. The house is worth $125,000, and carries a mortgage of $35,000. Both Dean and his wife, Jenny, have been saving money so that one day Dean can go into his own business. They have about $40,000 in the bank.

Recently, one of Dean's furniture clients, Anna Vlouscek, called him after her husband died. She wanted to know if Dean would be willing to quit his job and create furniture for her late husband's company, American Furniture, a mail-order business that George Vlouscek had run from his home for 13 years. The company sold office, home, and lawn furniture to the public, but did not manufacture it. Instead, Vlouscek made contacts with various carpenters and purchased furniture from them at wholesale prices. He would then incorporate the furniture into his own small but growing catalog under his own name. Over the years, sales had steadily increased and Vlouscek had always made a good profit. He developed a mailing list by purchasing names from mailing-list brokers from time to time. At the time of Vlouscek's death, the company had a growing client base of more than 7,000 names.

When she called, Anna Vlouscek also asked Dean if he would be interested in purchasing the company. Dean asked her how much she wanted for

the business, and she stated that if she sold the business outright, she would want about $350,000. However, if she could remain in the business, she would be willing to sell a 51 percent interest in it for $200,000 and retain the rest herself. Dean stated without hesitation that he was interested but he would like to contact a friend of his who was very knowledgeable about business.

Dean and Jenny were very excited and called their friend, Robert Saprahamin, who owned his own business. Saprahamin asked Dean many questions that he could not answer, but Dean insisted that Vlouscek's business was ideal for him since it consisted of woodworking. Saprahamin agreed to help and contacted his friend Martha Kearns, manager of the local branch of National Bank, and asked for an appointment. A meeting was set up, and Kearns indicated that the bank might be interested in the project providing the loan met all its criteria. First, the bank wanted to obtain financial statements, including a balance sheet, income statement, and tax statements for the last three years. National Bank also requested a business plan and gave Dean an outline of what the plan should cover. A personal financial statement and a résumé covering Dean's background, especially in the area of business, would also be necessary. Kearns informed Dean that the bank's credit committee would review the completed loan application to determine whether they would handle the loan themselves or put the loan through the Small Business Administration for a loan guarantee.

Dean met with Anna Vlouscek and informed her that he had gone to the bank and was now putting together all the papers necessary to obtain a loan. Dean stated he was not certain whether he would buy her out completely or come in as a 51 percent partner. Mrs. Vlouscek made it perfectly clear that either option was all right with her.

"One thing, though," she said, "I want to be certain that the business will be in good hands. I'd like to see a complete outline of what you plan to do with the

CONTINUED ▶

business, how you'd manage it, and what product line you'll be selling. George worked hard to build this business, and I won't let anyone ruin it, no matter how much they pay."

She also stated that she wanted the name American Furniture to remain intact, and the reputation of the company be continually positioned as a quality producer and an ethical firm in all respects. Dean informed her that he had to prepare a business plan for the bank and he'd give her a copy.

Dean then told her that the bank required financial statements about the business. In particular, Martha Kearns had requested the following information:

- A history of the business
- Aging of all payables
- Aging of all accounts receivable
- Copies of leases, if any
- Data concerning the total number of clients and the geographic area the business covers

Mrs. Vlouscek gave Dean the financial statements and told him she would have the other information in a few days.

Dean next talked the business over with his father, Ray, who said that he could offer Dean about $100,000 in financial backing if the business was as solid as Dean said. Ray's only condition was that he wanted to work for the business—retirement was getting boring. Dean thought this was an excellent idea: his father was a good administrator and understood the business. Dean's father said the money would be a gift to Dean's family. He also felt that it would be better to purchase the business outright rather than have Mrs. Vlouscek as a partner, and that the price could be negotiated somewhat.

Ray accompanied Dean when he went to pick up the rest of the financial information from Mrs. Vlouscek. At the meeting, Ray brought up the subject of the selling price, and at first Mrs. Vlouscek was quite adamant that it was not negotiable. Finally, after several hours of sometimes heated discussion, Mrs. Vlouscek agreed to accept $275,000. However, she would not agree to finance any part of the selling price. She wanted cash, and she wanted an acceptable business plan.

The following are the financial statements for American Furniture for the last three years.

Balance Sheets

	1999	1998	1997
Current Assets			
Cash in bank	$48,000	$36,000	$30,000
Accounts receivable	$50,000	$55,000	$58,000
Inventory	$15,000	$10,000	$12,000
Prepaid items	$5,000	$6,000	$9,000
Total Current Assets	$118,000	$107,000	$109,000
Fixed Assets			
Equipment (nonoffice)	$52,000	$56,000	$60,000
Equipment (office)	$13,000	$16,000	$19,000
Total Fixed Assets (net)	$65,000	$72,000	$79,000
Total Assets	**$183,000**	**$179,000**	**$188,000**
Current Liabilities			
Accounts payable	$32,000	$23,500	$31,000
Payroll taxes payable	$1,000	$1,500	$2,000
Total Current Liabilities	$33,000	$25,000	$33,000
Long-Term Liabilities			
Note payable	-0-	$15,000	$25,000
Total Liabilities	$33,000	$40,000	$58,000
Capital			
McGovern Capital	$150,000	$139,000	$130,000
Total Liabilities and Capital	**$183,000**	**$179,000**	**$188,000**

CONTINUED ▶

Notes: 1. Mr. Vlouscek had operated the business as a sole proprietorship and withdrew all the funds he could each year; however, he left some funds in the business so that it would grow at a gradual pace.

2. If the Foleys buy the business, the cash in the bank and prepaid items would belong to Mrs. Vlouscek. Dean would receive everything else.

Income Statements

	1999		1998		1997	
Sales (net)	$750,000	100%	$650,000	100%	$575,000	100%
Less: Cost of sales	$450,000	60%	$409,500	63%	$373,750	65%
Gross Profit	$300,000	40%	$240,500	37%	$201,250	35%
Expenses						
Payroll—customer service	36,000		18,000		15,000	
Payroll—office	30,000		15,000		14,000	
Payroll—other	10,000		8,000		6,000	
Payroll taxes 12%	9,120		4,920		4,200	
Advertising	30,000		28,000		25,000	
Auto expense	8,000		6,000		5,000	
Credit card expense	30,000		26,000		23,000	
Maintenance	5,000		5,000		4,000	
Legal and accounting	12,000		12,000		12,000	
Insurance	28,000		27,000		24,000	
Depreciation	7,000		7,000		7,000	
Postage (office)	3,500		3,000		2,800	
Contributions	1,500		1,200		600	
Utilities	9,600		9,000		8,900	
Rent	12,000		12,000		12,000	
Office expense	6,000		5,000		5,000	
Supplies	4,000		3,500		3,000	
Interest	600		1,200		1,500	
Travel and entertainment	2,000		2,100		1,500	
Misc. expense	1,500		1,300		1,000	
Total Expenses	$245,820	33%	$195,220	30%	$175,500	30.5%
Net Profit before Taxes	$54,180	7%	$45,280	7%	$25,750	4.5%

Analysis of Profits and Withdrawals

Net profit—business	$54,180	$45,280	$25,750
Rent charged by owner	$12,000	$12,000	$12,000
Salary—Vlouscek	$20,000	$18,000	$15,000
Total Owners Profit	$86,180	$75,280	$52,750

Notes: Gross sales price includes the cost of packing and shipping. Thus, the customer is paying for all the boxing and shipping costs. All shipments are made through United Parcel Service. Net sales do not include shipping and handling. Customer Service employees in 1999 consisted of two sales people, including Mrs. Vlouscek. They handled all incoming sales and when not busy made sales contacts to secure more business. Office personnel consisted of two people in 1999. Other personnel costs were for one person who performed other tasks on a part-time basis.

CONTINUED ▶

Dean now started completing the rest of the proposal. He looked at the other items pending and decided to work on the business plan, using the format that the bank had provided:

Outline of the Business Plan
Purpose of the Loan

Business Information
1. Description of business
2. Product/service offerings
3. Market information
4. Competition
5. Management
6. Personnel
7. Investment criteria
   a) Amount requested
   b) Use of the funds
   c) Other information

Financial Data
1. Income projections for three years
2. Cash flow projections for three years
3. Any notes to the income statement and cash budget
4. Pro forma statements for three years

Other Information Requested
1. Résumé containing management ability and experience in the field
2. Ability to obtain term life insurance in the event of disability or death for the amount of the loan
3. Personal financial statement
4. Any other information that will support the loan proposal and provide the bank with evidence of the ability of the borrower to repay the loan and be successful

Dean took the information he received from Mrs. Vlouscek and put together the following plan. (The plan that follows is exactly as Dean Foley prepared it for the bank; he did not obtain any assistance in writing the plan.)

Business Plan for the Bank

From: Dean Foley

Purpose of the Loan

I want to borrow money to buy out Mrs. Vlouscek. I need $175,000 to pay her off.

Business Information

1. The bussiness is making and selling furniture.
2. The products will be made out of wood and be sold to clients everywhere.
3. Their are markets all over the place. Everybody buys products made out of wood.
4. The only competition I know is Charlie Young who is always loosing money. The other man is Bernie Smith and he is smart but not as a carpenter. He should of been in the electircal field because he is good at that.
5. My father and me will run the business. Dad really knows his stuff and was retired and taught me the bussiness when I was a kid. He knows all about paper work.
6. Me and my father will make all the furniture we can and we intend to keep Mrs. Vlouscek.
7. We want the money to buy out Mrs. Vlouscek. We will use the money to do that. You can be sure that we will do a good job and that you're money will be taken care of.

Financial Data

1. We will make money in every year. We will make more money than Mrs. Vlouscek. So for three years we will not loose money but make about $100,000 bucks each year.
2. The cash will flow smoothly for more than three years. We dont accept to have any interuptions with cash flow. It will be like a fast moving streem.
3. I have no notes because I have not bought the bussiness yet.
4. All forms will be good for many years. We will give a statement with each piece of furniture that will give every customer 5 years guarantee.

CONTINUED ▶

Other Information Requested

1. I have been working for many years as a carpenter and I can do anything in the bussinesss. I learned first hand from my father.
2. I am in great shape and I know I can get a policy on my life. My grandfather lived until he was 94 years old.
3. I own my house. The house is worth more than $125,000 and I owe about $35,000. I also have $40,000 in a savings account.
4. You have my word and that of my father. I also swear on my kids and my relatives that I will make money. I dont believe in loosing money. I know I will be successful because I want to and I have wanted to be in bussiness like my father. My father's bussiness made a lot of money thanks to his hard work and know how. My father will be working with me to make sure my bussiness makes money too.

Thank you.
Sincerely,
Dean Foley

After Dean completed the business plan, he attached the other information the bank requested. He decided to use the documentation supplied by Mrs. Vlouscek and the company's accountant, reproduced here exactly as Dean attached them.

From Mrs. Vlouscek:

History of the Business

AMERICAN FURNITURE was established more than thirteen years ago by my husband, GEORG VLOUSCEK. At one time in his career he had been a carpenter and always felt that if he offered basic furniture to the consuming public, he could make a good living. He decided to start a home business offering a few products for the office and homes. He offered cocktail tables, bookshelves, picture frames, chairs, and special tables for office and home use and began to develop a small volume of business. He then purchased a few mailing lists from list brokers and immediately his sales started to grow. In addition, instead of continuing to send out single-sheet leaflets outlining the product line, he had a small ten-page catalog of furniture produced showing all the different product offerings. Eventually, he expanded the catalog to include lawn furniture. My husband never made any furniture himself but contracted with various carpenters who had the skills and equipment to produce quality furniture. He was always looking for new designs, and he was always pleasantly surprised with some of the products that his suppliers were able to manufacture over the years. Mr. Vlouscek began to develop a good name and reputation. He sold to some large department stores, and he backed up every product he sold. All the suppliers had to stand by the products he purchased from them, or he would drop them from his supplier list. He demanded perfection. The business has grown each year and has a great deal of potential. He intended to increase the mailing list and change the catalog to attract more consumer interest. However, he firmly believed that sticking to office, lawn, and the basic home furniture and not getting involved with complicated designs was the direction the company should follow. Unfortunately, my husband died, and his dream was not fully realized. However, the basic foundation stones are in place, and an aggressive and caring person could develop the AMERICAN FURNITURE into a big organization.

From the accountant's report:

Aging of Receivables and Payables

This information is presented in summary form.

CONTINUED ▶

Aging of Accounts Receivable

Total Accounts	Total	0 to 30 days	31 to 60 days	over 90
8	$50,000	$38,000	$10,000	$2,000

Note: All the accounts are mainly large department stores that buy in quantity.

Aging of Accounts Payable

Total Accounts	Total	0 to 30 days	31 to 60 days	over 90
5	$32,000	$32,000	-0-	-0-

Note: The company owes five suppliers the above amount, and each invoice is paid within the 30-day period. It has been the policy of the company to pay the suppliers of furniture as quickly as possible but never take more than 30 days.

Leases

The company has a lease with American Leasing Company, an entity owned by the Vlousceks. The annual rental is $12,000.

Client Database

The total number of clients in the database is 7,000. The active list is about 10 percent of the total. Included in the client base are some large department stores that purchase at list price minus 20 percent and which purchase a variety of products. Each of these large accounts has been credit-checked, and all are reputable. The large accounts represent about 10 percent of total sales. All the other clients purchase furniture using credit cards. The charge paid by the company for accepting credit cards is 4 percent of total net sales. It should be noted that prices offered do not include shipping and packing. This charge is passed on to the client, and the company incurs no expenses for this cost. The geographical area covered is the Northeast portion of the United States. The majority of businesses are located in Pennsylvania, New York, New Jersey, and Delaware.

After everything was completed, Dean decided to first show the proposal to his friend Robert Saprahamin and his father. Both men were very understanding and immediately picked up the many problems with the proposal. Saprahamin suggested that Dean visit one of the Small Business Development Centers in his area for advice on proper preparation of the entire loan package. Saprahamin pointed out that, even though Dean had many years of carpentry experience, he still had to convince the bank that he was equipped not just to manufacture furniture but to manage the whole business effectively. In addition to spelling and grammatical errors, Saprahamin also pointed out that he did not include the projections for sales or the cash budget in the financial information requested. Dean was somewhat confused but decided to do what he was told since both Saprahamin and his father knew much more than he did about business.

Dean contacted the local Small Business Development Center (SBDC) and was surprised to learn that there are over 900 SBDCs across the United States that assist small businesses without charge.

They are a partnership between the Small Business Administration (SBA) and a state-endorsed organization that serves as a host institution. In this case, the host institution was the local university. Dean spoke to a consultant at the SBDC who listened to the entire proposition and felt that she could assist Dean in preparing the loan package so that it would be acceptable to the bank. The consultant asked Dean to answer the following questions regarding the business proposal:

- Would the company's present personnel be retained in their present capacity?
- Would their compensation remain the same?
- Exactly what did the Foleys think their sales would be for each of the next three years? (The consultant wanted the sales for the first year broken down by month and for the next two years by quarters. She also wanted the expenses broken down by month for the first year and then quarterly for the next two years.)

CONTINUED ▶

- What percentage of the total projected sales would Dean and his father be producing in their shop?
- How much gross profit would they be making as a manufacturer?
- Would Dean retain all the present suppliers?
- How much capital was going to be invested into the business in working capital to keep the business operating? (The consultant pointed out that when Dean actually purchased the business, the cash and prepaid items would be kept by Mrs. Vlouscek. Dean would assume all other assets and payables.)
- Would the phone and other equipment purchased fit into the Foleys' present facility or would they have to expand their present facility?
- Would Mrs. Vlouscek remain in the business for a transition period of, say, 90 or 180 days and, if so, would she be compensated?
- What rent would Dean be charging for the rental of the facility in the back of his house? (The consultant suggested setting up a separate corporation to handle the rental and establishing a Subchapter S corporation for the new business using the existing name.)
- How did Dean plan to handle the company's

present furniture manufacturers, who would eventually discover that the Foleys were also producing furniture for the catalog?

Next, the consultant wanted Dean to furnish her with a complete résumé of his background, including personal data, educational background, and a summary of his experience in the carpentry business from the time he learned his craft up to his present-day activities. She also wanted a complete résumé from his father since he would be a major player in this company.

Finally, the consultant suggested that it might be a good idea for Dean to contact and use the Vlousceks' present accountant, who could provide continuity and knowledge that would be difficult to find with an accountant who was not familiar with this type of business.

Dean knew his work was cut out for him, and he did exactly what Ms. Schmidt, the SBDC consultant, recommended. He contacted the present accountant and told him what he needed in the way of financial data. Then he and his father sat down and decided to complete the next steps, along with the consultant and the Vlousceks' accountant. Together, they came up with the following:

Sales Projections

Sales for the first year after Dean takes over the business will be exactly the same as in 1999. Sales in the second year will be 20 percent higher than the first year, and sales for the third year will be 20 percent higher than the second year. Dean will be producing 20 percent of projected annual sales during the first year and 30 percent each of the second and third years. He will charge the same prices the company paid in 1999.

Collections

All sales will be collected in the same month the sale is made. This is possible because most sales are credit card sales. The large department stores also pay within the 30 day period.

Suppliers

Dean expects to retain all the present suppliers, although their volume might drop the first year.

Expenses

Expenses for the first year will be exactly the same as 1999. Expenses in the second and third years will be higher in the following categories: Customer Service will add one employee in the second year at a cost of $18,000, plus additional payroll taxes of 12 percent of the $18,000. Advertising costs will increase by $5,000, and insurance will be $5,000 higher. Auto expense, maintenance, postage, utilities, office expenses, supplies, travel, entertainment, and miscellaneous expenses will be 10 percent higher than in 1999.

Credit card expense is 4 percent of 90 percent of estimated net sales.

Interest expense on the bank loan will be at prime rate plus 2.25 percent. The interest expense will be 8.50 percent on $175,000, or $14,875 per annum. The loan will be a demand

CONTINUED ▶

loan, and only interest payments will be made quarterly. Assume that the loan will not be called during the three-year period.

Mrs. Vlouscek will remain with the company for six months, training Jenny Foley at no compensation. Jenny will receive the salary of $18,000 a year that Mrs. Vlouscek was receiving which was included in the year 1999.

Rent Expense

The Foleys will charge $12,000 annually for rent. The Foleys will set up a separate company to collect the rentals. Telephones and all equipment will be moved. Dean and Ray are presently expanding the existing facility.

Balance Sheet

Cash in Bank: The initial cash start-up for the new company will be $40,000.

Equipment: Dean will also be selling the new company his equipment valued at $50,000. The equipment will be depreciated over a ten-year period, or $5,000 per year. Dean will also be acquiring the equipment listed on the balance sheet of American Furniture of $52,000 and $13,000. Depreciation expense will continue to be $4,000 and $3,000 respectively or a total of $7,000 for purchased equipment.

Inventory: Inventory consists of some fast-moving stock that Vlouscek carried for some special clients. The amount of $15,000 will be a constant for all three years. It has already been included in the net sales projected as well as in cost of sales for each of the three years. Therefore, do not include this as a separate item.

Cash Advances and Retained Earnings and Form of Ownership

The company will be a Subchapter S corporation. Dean and Ray Foley will not be taking a salary during the first three years. Instead, they will take advances when needed and then deduct those amounts from their distributed profits at the end of each year.

All profits at the end of the year will be distributed on the basis of 50 percent to the stockholders with the other 50 percent remaining in the business. Because the company will elect to be an S corporation, taxes will have to be paid on the entire 100 percent of net profits, even though 50 percent is retained in the corporation. The Foleys feel that, by putting back 50 percent of profits, the company will be able to grow. The 50 percent distributed will take care of personal taxes and their advances.

Stock Ownership

Dean Foley will own 100 percent of the common stock. Dean will be the president. Ray Foley will not own stock but will receive 25 percent of the net profits. Ray will be the vice president in charge of administration and marketing, and he will also help in manufacturing when he gets time. Dean will spend most of his time in the shop. Jenny will be the secretary and treasurer and will take over the position of Mrs. Vlouscek after her six-month training period.

Investment Criteria

The total investment for the purchase of the business is as follows:

Agreed purchase price:	$275,000
Advance made by Ray Foley:	$100,000
Balance borrowed from bank:	$175,000

This loan will be obtained from the National Bank at 8.50 percent on a demand loan basis. Interest will be paid quarterly. Interest during the first three years will be 2.25 percent over prime. Assume that it will not exceed 8.5 percent per annum. The $175,000 will be used to complete the purchase of American Furniture.

CONTINUED ▶

The new company, American Furniture, Inc., will assume all the assets of the former company less cash and prepaid items, and it will assume all the liabilities. In addition, the new owners will be investing $40,000 into working capital and $50,000 worth of manufacturing equipment.

Market Information

The company has a customer database of 7,000 clients although only about 10 percent purchase each year. At some time most of the 7,000 will make some purchase. Use the database as your market and in your business plan determine how you can increase sales in the present base.

Competition

There are many carpenters but very few firms that are in the direct-mail business of selling office, lawn, and residential furniture.

Management

The father, Ray Foley, has the successful experience in the operation of a furniture business. Jenny and Dean will be learning as they go.

Personnel

The company will be taking over the same personnel that Vlouscek had working for him.

Insurance

Dean checked with his insurance agent and after his medical examination was approved for a $250,000 term life policy. He was also approved for accidental and disability.

Information for Résumés

Dean Foley: Dean Foley is 32 years old. He graduated from high school and attended vocational school for two years specializing in carpentry and designing. He started learning the carpentry business at the age of 12. He worked for his father and various builders for the last 20 years. Dean has assets of $225,000. This includes a house valued at $125,000, equipment at $50,000, $40,000 in a savings account, and $10,000 in a checking account. His only debt is a $35,000 mortgage against the house. Thus, Dean has a net worth of $190,000.

Ray Foley: Ray Foley is 60 years of age. He was in business for more than 40 years. He is an expert in cabinetmaking and is able to manufacture many other products. He operated a successful business and managed an employment force of six people. He is presently retired and has a net worth of $485,000. Included in his net worth is a home with no mortgage that has a market value of $250,000. He has no debts. He also has $10,000 in a money market account, $200,000 in mutual funds, and $25,000 in a checking account. Ray Foley graduated from high school. ▼

CASE STUDY ROUNDTABLE

▼ ▼ ▼ ▼ ▼

Dean: I've learned a lot in this process, mostly thanks to Ann, the consultant at the SBDC. Starting my own business is a lot more complicated than I ever thought it would be. But do you think that my original business plan was so bad? Everybody came down pretty hard on it, but I thought I should just tell the bank what I wanted to do. I guess just plain honesty's not enough these days, though.

Discussion Points

- Analyze the first business plan that Dean prepared. Explain why it would probably not have been accepted by the bank.
- Do you think Dean should present the final business plan in whole or part to Mrs. Vlouscek? Why or why not?
- Respond to Dean's statement that "I guess just plain honesty's not enough these days." Is he right?

Dean: OK, now that we've sat down and put all this information together, what's next?

Discussion Points

- How would you explain to Dean the elements he needs to communicate in his business plan?
- How do you think Dean and Ray might make their plan more professional?
- What presentation tips would you offer Dean and Ray to follow when they meet with their banker?
- Use the checklists in Personal Workshop 15 to help you analyze American Furniture's plan. Write a draft summary statement.

BACK TO THE TABLE
Mark Selleck

In Chapter 5, you met Mark Selleck, and learned about his disastrous experience opening Melanie's Bookstore. Mark has managed to keep out of jail, and he's trying to reconstruct what went wrong. *Based on what you now know, do you think a business plan would have helped Mark avoid failure? Why (or why not)?*

▲▲▲▲▲▲

Chapter Briefcase

▼▼▼▼▼▼

- Lack of adequate planning is one of the principal reasons that most businesses fail. A business plan helps you anticipate problems before they grow large and suggests ways to solve them.
- A business plan helps define your business, serves as a guide to the ongoing operation, is required for securing financing, and helps attract investors.
- The most important part of your business plan is the statement of purpose (also known as a thesis statement or executive summary). It states your objectives, describes your plan's highlights, and discusses your business's strengths and distinctiveness.

▲▲▲▲▲▲

Chapter 7

POSITIONING YOUR BUSINESS, INSIDE AND OUT

▼▼▼▼▼

Make no small plans: They have no magic to stir men's blood, and probably themselves will not be realized. Make big plans; Aim high in hope, and work, remembering that a noble, logical diagram once located will not die.

—Daniel H. Burnham, city architect

MISSION STATEMENT

In this chapter, you will

*L*EARN about the importance of a mission statement to the success of your new (and growing) business.

*E*XPLORE the best type of strategic position for your business, and how to evaluate a well-written mission statement.

*A*PPLY your understanding by evaluating actual mission statements.

*P*RODUCE an effective mission statement and develop a strategic position for your business that will put your mission statement into action.

KEY TERMS

developmental growth position

diversification position

expansive growth position

focused product/market position

mission statement

product innovation position

strategic position

SWOT

INTRODUCTION TO MISSION STATEMENTS AND POSITIONING YOUR BUSINESS

So far, it may seem like you're being asked to do a lot of brainwork, when what you want to do is follow your business vision. *Think about who you are and what you want to do*, you hear us say; *Make strategic plans and think about where you want to be tomorrow, next month, two years from now.* "But I just want to get started!" you say. "I want to get to work!" We'll get there together, and soon. But remember, successful businesses don't just spring up overnight. They take planning and thought and their start-up follows a step-by-step process of self-creation. So in the first few chapters you did some big-picture thinking, and some analysis of your goals.

On the other hand (ever notice how there's always that other hand out there somewhere?), entrepreneurs are successful in large part because they act quickly and decisively. Well, to some extent that's true: it's the rare successful entrepreneur who dithers and worries for weeks before coming to a decision. But, many would-be entrepreneurs have rushed headlong into the marketplace, only to hit a brick wall, hard. By carefully thinking about your business before it gets going, by analyzing its market entry strategy, and by knowing its strengths and weaknesses, you can put yourself into a position in which positive, quick, informed decisions can be made without disastrous results.

Key to that position is the development of a written mission statement.

MISSION STATEMENTS

Mission statements address the question "What business should this company be in?" This may or may not be the business that you are in. Your mission statement should answer these questions.

- Who is your market? (Or: Who are your customers?)
- What is your product or service—and what benefits do they provide your market?
- What is your special competence, strength, or competitive advantage?

Your mission statement should ideally be based on an objective analysis of the *internal* strengths and weaknesses of the business, as well as the opportunities and

PERSONAL WORKSHOP 17
Strengths, Weaknesses, Opportunities, Threats
▼ ▼ ▼ ▼ ▼ ▼

▼ Conduct an informal SWOT analysis of your business by "brainstorming" responses to each of the SWOT elements:

What are my business's...

Strengths	
Weaknesses	
Opportunities	
Threats	

threats *outside* in your commercial environment. Taken together, these four elements—Strengths, Weaknesses, Opportunities, and Threats—can be remembered by the acronym *SWOT*. This SWOT analysis helps keep you from being blindsided by changes in technology, regulation, competition, and so on, and should be part of your ongoing business life.

Some business owners tend to dismiss this part of the planning process. They tell themselves that they already know where the firm is headed. However, the two steps discussed in this chapter are among the most important in the strategic planning process. A firm's basic mission and its accompanying strategic positioning provide a focus. Without a mission statement, the company may flounder, headed in no particular direction. Without a strategic position, the firm may attempt a strategy that is not well grounded and does not translate well into specific actions.

What Is a Mission Statement?

A **mission statement** is a concise statement of the general nature and direction of the company. By carefully and clearly stating the basic aim, scope, and direction of the business, the mission statement becomes an outline of what the company will do and what it will be. Although the mission statement is purposely broad (it's your company's general mission, not a to-do list for the next week or so), it must offer a clear picture of the firm. Often, an elaborate-sounding, sweeping compilation of platitudes is offered as a mission statement. Such a statement fails to provide the precision and scope necessary to be useful as a meaningful planning tool. The owner should ask, "What separates us from other similar companies?" The answer to that question becomes a unique mission statement that is the basis for a definitive corporate strategy.

The Value of the Mission Statement

A written mission statement has two major benefits. First, it is a communication both inside and outside the firm. Often, employees complain that they never know what is happening. They don't know what the owner's plans are nor how they, the employees, fit within those plans. This makes it difficult for them to be committed and motivated workers. The mission statement helps clarify the firm's vision and the employees' role in it. It's also important that owners be able to clearly enunciate why the company exists.

The second major value is the commitment that the owner of the firm has to the mission once it is printed and publicized. It's like a New Year's resolution, but with higher stakes. If you make a resolution but tell no one, there is no particular incentive to keep it. But if you write it down, ponder it, type it up, post it on the refrigerator, tell your friends about it, maybe even wager that you will keep it, this public commitment means you can't break it without losing face (or maybe money). In the same way, the written mission statement commits the company to the stated strategy and philosophy and may result in equal commitment by others in and around the business.

Such a commitment in no way suggests that a company's mission is cast in stone, never to be altered. Mission statements, as representations of the firm's place in a dynamic environment, may change over time. However, these changes evolve as the firm assesses movements in its competitive situation. The mission statement provides a central focus and unifying drive for the business within its planning horizon.

Jill Smith from Buckeye Beans talks about her mission statement—"to make people smile"—her business philosophy, and the HEHE principle that reinforces the company's values.

URLinks
http://www.businessleader.com/blsep96/shared.html
http://www.washingtonpost.com/wp-srv/frompost/features/nov97/stories/hoax17.htm

THE PARTS OF A MISSION STATEMENT

The mission statement contains three major elements. Each should be given careful consideration. The first defines the nature of the business. The second expresses the business philosophy that drives the company. The third states the tangible actions that the company will take to act out its philosophy in the real world (see Figure 7.1). So you see, even something as supposedly "abstract" and "theoretical" as a mission statement is really a vital real world tool for entrepreneurs.

The Nature of the Business

The first element of the mission statement defines and clearly specifies the basic nature of the firm's business. Four different areas must be considered.

1. The *industry and product line* of the company and the *type of services* provided
2. The firm's *position in the distribution channel* (is the company a wholesaler, a manufacturer, a retailer, or a mail-order business?)
3. The *prime goals* of the firm (quality, breadth of product line, price, or service?)
4. The *target market* (who does the firm presently serve? who does it intend to serve in the near future?)

By telling explicitly what the firm is, the mission statement also tells implicitly what the firm is *not*. These limiting statements serve as a control to keep the general direction intact, like fences on either side of a highway.

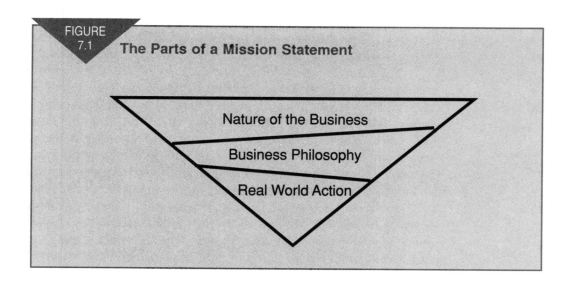

FIGURE 7.1 The Parts of a Mission Statement

Nature of the Business

Business Philosophy

Real World Action

FIRST PERSON

Tyrone D., Rochester, New York: I learned the importance of a mission statement the hard way. I decided to start a bicycle shop that sold and serviced bicycles. Simple enough, right? I had the space, I had the know-how, I had the tools. So I hung out a sign. A few months after I opened, though, along came the opportunity to add a line of mopeds. OK, I thought, mopeds are just bicycles with a little motor stuck on. So I added mopeds. Well, about six months later, the regional manager for Honda motorcycles stopped by. Seemed the local Honda dealer was retiring, and I had a once-in-a-lifetime opportunity to land a coveted Honda dealership. Suddenly, less than a year after I opened my little bike shop, now I had a bicycle/moped/motorcycle selling/servicing business. Then came snowmobiles. The line was a good one, and I couldn't say no. No, wait: I *could* have said no, but I *didn't*. After all, I thought, snowmobiles really have a lot in common with motorcycles—except they run primarily on skis instead of wheels. Within two years I'd added garden tractors, lawnmowers, snowblowers, and (this is true) I was seriously talking with the Winnebago people. My one-time bicycle shop became what a consultant might call a "highly diversified dealership for a number of marginally related products." I was out of control, and so was my business. I tried to do so much that I got overextended—in terms of time, energy, space, and money. The whole business, my perfectly good little bike shop, collapsed under the weight of all the other directions I was trying to go in at once. Now I understand that a well-written mission statement, one that was simple and clear that I could follow, would have allowed me to specialize in bicycles until I decided it was time to expand. If I'd done that, expansion would have been the result of market analysis, and I'd have been financially ready to take on more business. Without it, I lacked focus and just struck out in any direction that came along. Don't do that."

Many businesses, large and small, fail because of rapid, uncontrolled growth. For example, large businesses often acquire unrelated firms or start up new businesses in unrelated areas with the stated goal of broadening their earnings base or gaining a countercyclical business. Many of these same subsidiaries are later divested as the parent firm's executives decide to "return to the things we do best." Obviously, the corporation's management strayed from its basic mission and later realized its error.

The Basic Business Philosophy

The second major element of the mission statement is an expression of the business's management philosophy. A mission statement doesn't create an organization's culture, but it can help define the kind of culture the owner wants. Over the last dozen years, much has been written about "corporate culture" and its impact, power, and influence on the behavior and activities of large organizations. The concept of culture is equally important for the small firm. The mission statement should capture the owner's basic philosophy of how business will be conducted. In simplest terms, the mission statement should explain the core values that are most central and most critical to the business. The result is a value orientation that becomes an important guide for subsequent management action.

For example, a small manufacturer included in its mission statement the phrase, "We build quality into every product we produce." The owner wanted to convey clearly to all customers and potential customers that the business was committed to the highest level of quality assurance. The owner emphasized the significance of this theme by including the phrase as the company motto on its business letterhead.

In making a philosophical or cultural declaration, the mission statement may say a great deal about the firm. Will the firm be a risk taker? Will it be employee oriented? Will the firm be run on the highest ethical standards? Will it be an aggressive competitor? Will it be a pioneer or a follower, a me-too firm? The key is to include those items about which management feels strongly and omit those items about which it does not. For example, the mission statement may mention nothing about a promote-from-within policy, but instead discuss the strategy of hiring young managers with new ideas.

The Real World Action

Once you've defined the big picture issues—the nature of your business and the underlying business philosophy—you're ready to define what you're going to do with it. The final part of the mission statement is a definition of the concrete actions the company will take in order to "walk the talk"—that is, to achieve its company goals by acting on its philosophy.

Figure 7.2 is a mission statement for a small toy manufacturing company. The statement clearly lays out the nature of the firm as well as the tone or philosophy of the company. At the same time it does not give away any proprietary secrets. Figure 7.3 shows how the toy company's mission statement follows the basic forms we've

---

▼ FIGURE
7.2　**Joy's Toys Mission Statement**

Our Mission...

Joy's Toys produces a wide line of moderately priced educational toys for preschool and young school-age children. We service a four-state area surrounding Missouri and sell directly to schools or school district buying centers. Our first product priority is quality. We would rather lose a sale by being overpriced than sell low-quality merchandise. We offer quick and accessible service and repair on all merchandise we sell.

We care about children and view their education as the critical part of our task. Our toys are designed to enrich the child's educational experience. All design work is done in-house to assure responsive, innovative products.

In hiring sales representatives, we seek to attract former primary school teachers who are in tune with the needs and wants of children and who can identify with the concerns of parents. We exclusively promote from within.

FIGURE
7.3   **Analysis of Joy's Toys Mission Statement**

	The Nature of the Business
Joy's Toys produces a wide line of moderately priced educational toys for preschool and young school-age children. We service a four-state area surrounding Missouri and sell directly to schools or school district buying centers.	the **industry and product line** of the company the firm's **position in the distribution channel** the **target market**
Our first product priority is quality. We would rather lose a sale by being overpriced than sell low-quality merchandise.	the **prime goals** of the firm
We offer quick and accessible service and repair on all merchandise we sell.	the **type of services** provided
	The Basic Business Philosophy
We care about children and view their education as the critical part of our task. Our toys are designed to enrich the child's educational experience. All design work is done in-house to assure responsive, innovative products.	An expression of the business's management philosophy. The mission statement should capture the owner's basic philosophy of how business will be conducted.
	The Real World Action
In hiring sales representatives, we seek to attract former primary school teachers who are in tune with the needs and wants of children and who can identify with the concerns of parents. We exclusively promote from within.	How the company plans to "walk the talk."

FIGURE 7.4 **Sample Mission Statements**

Cascade Properties

Cascade Properties provides services for residential and commercial real estate sales. In addition, we have a property management firm that markets apartments, residential homes, office buildings, and commercial complexes. We are also involved in the environmental services area.

As the real estate industry continues to change, we will aggressively explore new market opportunities and continually educate our associates to provide outstanding service to our clients and customers.

Ben & Jerry's

Ben & Jerry's is dedicated to the creation and demonstration of a new corporate concept of linked prosperity. Our mission consists of three interrelated parts.

1. Product mission: to make, distribute, and sell the finest quality all natural ice cream and related products in a wide variety of innovative flavors made from Vermont dairy products.

2. Economic mission: to operate the company on a sound financial basis of profitable growth, increasing value for our shareholders, and creating career opportunities and financial rewards for our employees.

3. Social mission: to operate the company in a way that actively recognizes the central role that business plays in the structure of society by initiating innovative ways to improve the quality of life of a broad community: local, national, and international.

---

discussed here. Finally, Figure 7.4 shows examples of some other companies' mission statements.

In summary, the mission statement must do only two things, but it must do them well. First, it must set forth the direction of the business, thereby specifying what the business is and what it is not. Second, it must set forth the tone or culture of the business based on the owner's philosophy of how the business should be run.

POSITIONING YOUR COMPANY

The mission statement, if properly developed, defines the general direction of the business and indicates its management philosophy. Before more specific goals can be defined or strategies developed to achieve those goals, the business owner needs to determine the firm's strategic position.

PERSONAL WORKSHOP 18
Drafting Your Own Mission Statement

▼ Construct your own draft of a mission statement by filling in the blanks below. As you customize this "generic" mission statement, you will force yourself to think about the fundamental vision and purpose of your business.

_____ **[produces or provides]** _____
name of company   choose one   what you do

for _____. **Our geographic market is** _____
     general customer type   place

and our customers are _____. **Our first priority is** _____.
           specific customer type   priority

We are superior to our competitors because _____.
                         what, specifically, makes you superior

Our [product or service] is _____. **It is**
       choose one   product or service

exceptional because _____.
                 what, specifically, makes it exceptional

In providing our [product or service], our primary goal is _____.
             choose one   company goal

We will achieve this goal by _____.
             how, specifically, you will achieve your goal

A **strategic position** is a general indication of how the business will behave in its attempt to achieve its overall mission and secure a competitive advantage. It is management's overall plan of action for running the business in response to external opportunities and threats, based on awareness of its market, assessment of its strengths and weaknesses, and the business's set of distinctive competencies. The strategic position grows directly out of the final part of the mission statement: it develops the basic "real world action" theme.

Often, small businesses fail to give specific attention to a strategic position and instead emphasize short-term goals. In this situation, the firm's strategic position evolves as a reflection of past actions: it describes what the firm has done rather than defines what the business will do. Such a position fails to reinforce the sense of direction generated by the mission statement's vision.

First, we will address the focused product position, because it's really the starting point for new businesses. If your business is up and running, however, you'll want to consider the other alternative positions as well.

Focused Product Positioning

Undoubtedly, the best strategy for the start-up business is to concentrate its efforts on a particular product or service, or a single market. For example, an aluminum door manufacturer, automotive repair shop, or the family-style diner all (typically) focus on a specific product or market.

One of the biggest mistakes a new business owner makes is losing focus. The **focused product position** addresses this problem by demanding you do what you know well and do best. You can do yourself a big favor, at least initially, by limiting your involvement to areas where you have solid experience and understanding of the market. Focusing on a single product or market will allow you to concentrate on the nuances of that particular situation. You can orient and target your energies and give your business a better chance of getting—and staying—on top.

By using the focused product position, you can actually gain an edge over big business. Perhaps you can respond to the market's needs faster, or provide better, more personalized service. As a smaller business, you can be the quicker, more agile David to the powerful corporation's imposing but slower Goliath. You may also find that your focused product position can earn you a good living that would be a strain to the systems in place by the larger firms.

Once your business is up and running, you'll want to consider three other ways to grow: expansive growth positioning, developmental growth positioning, and product innovation positioning.

Expansive Growth Positioning

Are you ready to meet the challenges of expansion? A business that assumes an **expansive growth position** recognizes that there are opportunities to expand the company's scope of operations. An expansive growth position will generally take one of two forms: expansion of the primary location and expansion across geographic markets.

Expansion of the primary location.
This position may involve enlarging the company's present facility or relocating to a larger space. There is no attempt to alter current products or markets. In fact, the overall strength of the market and product acceptance requires expansion to exploit the excess demand. In other words, your business will do the same things it has always done, but on a bigger scale for greater returns. (See Figure 7.5.)

Geographic expansion.
In a second form of expansive growth, a business establishes additional facilities in promising new market areas. The multilocation approach is focused on new market areas, but not new or different target markets. The product remains unchanged, and the business still emphasizes the customer and product characteristics that have provided past success. New geographical markets for existing product lines are identified and tapped. In other words, the business will do the same things it has always done, but in more places and for greater returns. (See Figure 7.6.)

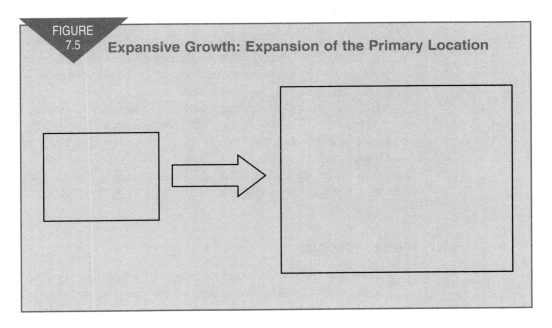

FIGURE 7.5 Expansive Growth: Expansion of the Primary Location

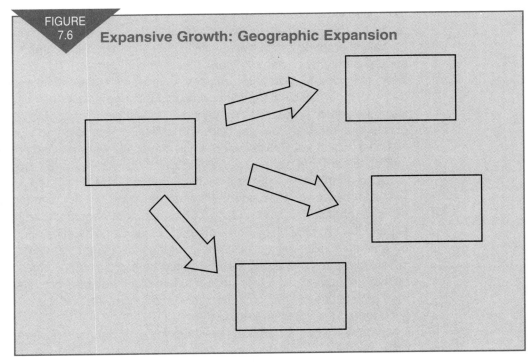

FIGURE 7.6 Expansive Growth: Geographic Expansion

Challenges of an Expansive Growth Position

An expansive growth position allows you to increase capacity and returns from additional business. It's critical that you first determine the market potential (will more customers buy more stuff?) and whether you can handle the increased work capacity.

Expanding always requires more human and financial resources. Misreading the demands or your markets could lead to an expensive outlay of capital and underutilized facilities: the classic "biting off more than you can chew." Unfortunately, it's much easier to spit out a big bite than it is to get out of a lease for more space than you really need.

You will need to determine whether you're ready to give up leadership and control. Expanding will probably mean delegating authority to staff members who may not be as committed as you, the owner. You will need to hire, train, and manage new people. Often, small business owners find it difficult to "hand off the baton," even when their business grows beyond their ability to manage it. You (or someone) will also need to monitor quality and production standards at the various facilities to be sure they meet your standards.

FIRST PERSON

Toni M., Tampa, Florida: I started TropicWeave Rug Cleaners in an exclusive section of Florida's Gulf Coast in the mid-1960s. Initially, my market analysis showed a promising opportunity. First, the market boasted extremely high income levels. Homes are quite large and expensive, and quality carpeting and rugs were common. Second, although there were a number of cleaning firms in the area, none had really established themselves as specializing in carpeting. TropicWeave's marketing campaign emphasized our expertise in cleaning expensive carpets and dealing with the special problems of natural fiber carpets in our climate. The upper-income customers were reluctant to trust their carpets to most of the existing operations, particularly because incorrect cleaning methods could damage or ruin their carpets. I had my crew trained extensively in cleaning methods and techniques, including those unique to high-grade and oriental carpets, and TropicWeave Rug Cleaners was licensed by the National Institute of Residential Rug Cleaners. We were the first and only cleaner in the market to earn that distinction. By distinguishing TropicWeave from the competitors and focusing on this single product position, the business prospered and grew.

Maybe we were too good! Within three years, the demand for TropicWeave's services far outstripped our capacity, both in terms of people and equipment. I decided to expand the physical plant, and eventually established satellite operations in a few nearby markets. This was no piecemeal expansion, though: it was carefully planned. I'd seen too many companies get so excited by a growing customer base that they sunk all their resources into expansions that just didn't pay off. I brought in experts, and created projections of how much demand would increase over a period of years. I carefully budgeted the costs and returns.

Once we had a clear idea of where the existing markets were, and where the new ones were likely to be, we carefully and slowly expanded to meet the demand. We hired more people and bought more equipment on a controlled schedule. If I do say so myself, we've done quite well.

Developmental Growth Positioning

A business that uses a **developmental growth position** decides to grow either by selling its existing product to new markets or new products to existing markets.

In market development, the business attempts to appeal to completely new market segments. Their characteristics or demographics are different from those of established markets. Product development stresses variations or improvements in the firm's primary products. The products are introduced to current customers in the hope that the positive image customers have of existing products will carry over. Existing products are not changed: Growth comes because the *same* customers buy both the existing products *and* the new products.

When selling existing product to new markets (market development), the characteristics or demographics are different than those in your current markets. You will need to consider the differences and promote your product accordingly. It may mean wording your promotions so they relate to your new market. If you decide to introduce new product to existing markets (product development), your hope is to achieve a better, more positive image. Since you already understand the nuances of this established market, you will stress the variations or improvements.

One of the key advantages of a developmental position is that the business maintains a high degree of consistency and stability. In product development, present customers (with assumed loyalty) are maintained and targeted while product variations are introduced. In market development, new market segments are tapped but products remain unchanged. (See Figure 7.7.)

Product Innovation Positioning

The distinction between product development and product innovation may be confusing. The two certainly have common elements. **Product development** seeks product variations and improvements, but *involves no overriding change in the fundamental product*. **Product innovation**, on the other hand, changes the existing product so fundamentally that a totally new or different product is created: Your customers shift away from the existing products to the newer ones. (See Figure 7.8.)

Although product innovations are generally assumed to be outgrowths of big businesses with well-supported research and development staffs, many contemporary product advances have come from small, entrepreneurial operations. Advances in computer hardware and software are common examples. And don't forget the Internet: where would the World Wide Web's phenomenal success be without those search engines built by bootstrap entrepreneurs? Small businesses—working intensively hands-on with a particular product every day—often generate astonishing product innovations.

An innovation position is very attractive as well because of the possibility it creates for generating huge returns. Introducing new services or products can bring big profits—at least until competitors recognize and respond to the new changes. However, significant risks are also present: Being on the "cutting edge" demands a careful and accurate reading of market trends and requires a timely and cost-effective response.

FIRST PERSON

Paula F., Chicago, Illinois: For seven years, we ran Cancroft Cabinetry, a family operation that specialized in building and renovating closets in customers' homes. We found that people's closets were storage nightmares, but we also found that much of the rest of their homes were disorganized disasters, too. Of course, it was because

FIGURE
7.7
Developmental Growth Position

For years a company sold square clocks with round faces to its market with good success. In adopting a developmental growth posture, it began offering to the same market round clocks with square faces.

Alternatively, the company could decide to start marketing its current style of clocks to a new market, in addition to its traditional one.

FIGURE
7.8 **Product Innovation Position**

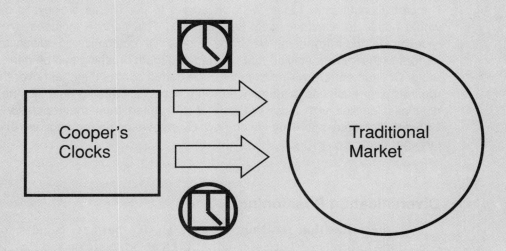

For years a company sold square clocks with round faces to its market with good success. In adopting a developmental growth posture, it began offering to the same market round clocks with square faces. This is an example of *product development.*

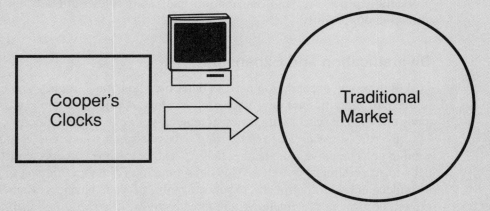

In response to changing market demands, the company decided to leverage its name recognition and quality reputation into a line of personal computers targeted to its loyal customer base. This is an example of *product innovation,* bringing a new product to a tradtional market.

so many other aspects of their lives were so frantic and full of too many activities. There's not much we can do, as basically carpenters, to deal with that part of their problem, but we do know storage and efficient use of space. So we changed our name to Cancroft Consultants. Today, we give advice to our clients on how to organize their whole house to eliminate daily time-wasters. This service includes everything from redesigning and rearranging wardrobe closets with customized modifications to adding mirrors to the shower stall so that shaving and tooth brushing can be done while showering. Consumers are willing to pay for the added control they gain over their time and routines. Our business is steadily growing, especially among dual-income, upper-middle-class families with kids. We sort of catapulted from the reputation we had as Cancroft Cabinetry into what we do now. By innovating on our past, we think we built a stronger company.

Diversification Positioning

A **diversification position** occurs when the business decides to expand its operations into related but essentially different products or services. Although an established core area of concentration may still command the bulk of the business energies, you may broaden your business horizons to include supporting, related products or services. For example, a belt manufacturer might diversify its operations beyond belts into manufacturing other leather goods as well. Similar raw materials, production processes, and distribution and retail sales outlets often make this an attractive opportunity.

Diversification and Expansion

Before you expand, you need to determine how much money you can realistically make by entering into new, uncharted territory. A rule of thumb is to only grow into areas that are consistent with, or complement, your existing operations.

Be sure some *logical relationship* exists between where you are and where you want to go. The move from leather belts to leather handbags seems realistic, but leather belts to scarves make no sense. This determination is often a function of your capacity to understand and control the expanded realm of your business. Remember: even if growth occurs out of something you already know, it is *still a new business!* It is very risky to expand beyond your depth of experience or demonstrated competence. We talked about this earlier: know your personal strengths and weaknesses, and know when to say no.

The Choice of Strategic Position

Small business owners must decide which positioning strategy is most appropriate for their own situation. Clear, obvious, straightforward answers are rare, and exceptions are common. However, certain considerations may help determine where each position is likely to produce success. The three key variables are shown in Figure 7.9.

Attractiveness. When choosing a strategic position, first consider the present and future *attractiveness* of your company's products and industry. Assessing "attractiveness" can be more complex than it sounds. At the most basic level, you must decide whether demand is stable or growing. Careful and thorough market analysis should provide enough information to decide if product and industry attractiveness is relatively strong or relatively weak. Of course, attractiveness must be assessed not only in the present, but projected over the firm's planning horizon.

Competitive strength. Through internal analysis, you must understand your business's strengths and potential in relation to your key competitors. This is especially important if one or more large businesses dominate the industry.

Owner's vision. Different entrepreneurs have different views of their businesses and what they would like them to become. Maybe you desire rapid growth and are willing to accept the risks in return for (potentially) high returns. Another person may be content to remain small and modestly successful. No variable is more basic, and it frequently defines and limits the choices of strategic position.

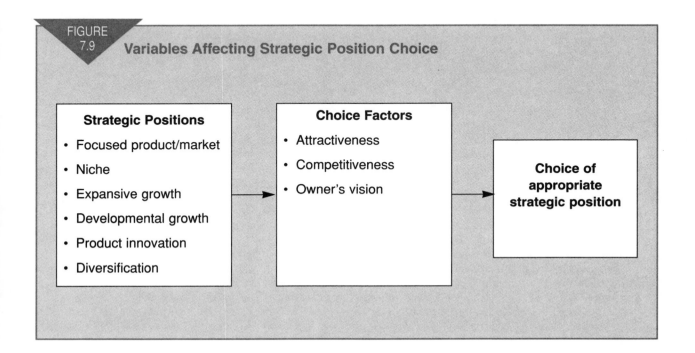

FIGURE 7.9 — Variables Affecting Strategic Position Choice

Strategic Positions
- Focused product/market
- Niche
- Expansive growth
- Developmental growth
- Product innovation
- Diversification

Choice Factors
- Attractiveness
- Competitiveness
- Owner's vision

Choice of appropriate strategic position

CASE STUDY
ARTHUR SANDBURG SELF-DEVELOPMENT SEMINARS

▼▼▼▼▼▼

*A*rthur Sandburg had been a vice president of marketing at a midsize high-tech company for 25 years and was earning a substantial salary. His home was worth over $200,000, and he had a summer home worth twice that. Arthur and his wife, Eleanor, were highly respected in Baltimore society. But when Arthur's company merged with a giant multinational firm, Arthur decided it was time to go out on his own and see if he could be successful in his own venture.

Arthur was a natural salesperson, and also had a unique capacity for rejuvenating salespeople who were suffering from burnout. He had conducted countless in-house motivational seminars, and Arthur was confident that he could go public with his talents: he could build a series of seminars based on successful selling and developing self-confidence.

Arthur knew he would have to refine his topics to make them attractive to diverse audiences, but he felt that with his background, experience, and distinguished bearing, his chances of success were excellent.

Arthur decided to test his idea in Baltimore to assess the market. He offered three seminars: How to Speak Effectively in Public; How to Be a Sensational Salesperson; and How to Develop Confidence in Yourself.

He charged $45 per seminar, or $100 for those who registered for all three. Arthur rented a 100-seat conference room in one of the local hotels, and placed advertisements in the local newspapers promoting the benefits of each seminar. He appeared on local television, promising that his seminars would help people learn the keys to self-confidence and how to be at ease under any conditions.

At first very few people responded to his ads and promotional appearances, but eventually more than 300 people wanted to take the confidence-building seminar. Only 35 people were interested in the others, though, so Arthur decided to cancel them. To handle the unexpectedly heavy response to the self-confidence seminar, he booked a larger room at the hotel. The new room cost $2,500, but provided the seating arrangement Arthur needed, screens for slides and a short movie, and a long table for refreshments.

On the night of the seminar Arthur greeted everyone at the door, welcoming them with a pleasant smile and a few comments about how pleased he was that they could come. Finally, Arthur took the stage, introduced himself, and asked each person to examine the folder that had been placed on each chair. Arthur began his presentation, sprinkling his comments with humorous anecdotes. He could see that some audience members were yawning, others were daydreaming, and some just looked confused. A few seemed interested, but remained silent.

During the break, Arthur circulated throughout the crowd to get feedback. Many people were pleased and liked what he said, but some were disappointed because they expected him to teach them individually how to be more confident. Arthur could see that there had to be some adjustments, but it was hard to make on-the-spot alterations to his carefully outlined program. During the break, about 90 people left, and the vacant chairs did not do much for Arthur's own confidence. During the second half of the evening's program, however, Arthur started using more specific examples and pinpointing typical problems. It seemed to work.

At the end of the seminar, Arthur thanked everyone for coming and said he would let them know of upcoming programs. Scorecards from the participants concerning their opinion of the seminar indicated that 20 percent thought the program was excellent; 25 percent thought it was good; and 40 percent thought it was only fair. Fifteen percent of the audience indicated that they had learned nothing, and thought the event was a waste of their time.

Arthur reviewed the entire seminar and felt that while it was a success financially (he cleared around $4,000 after expenses), something was missing. He didn't feel that he was headed in the right direction. He thought that groups of 300 kept him from close contact with the participants. If he had about 25 people maximum at a time he could do a terrific job. However, for that to work he would have to charge about $250 per seminar to make money—a figure too high for most people. Another possibility was that he could still handle 300 people, but break them down into smaller

CONTINUED ▶

groups after a basic presentation. However, this would mean hiring others to work with him. In any case, Arthur thought that the concept of selling seminars needed more refinement. Perhaps a different methodology would make them more successful, not only financially, but from the participants' point of view. Perhaps a series of topics could be repeated in different places for different audiences.

To assess his needs, Arthur decided to send a form letter to all the participants thanking them for coming and asking them for suggestions. The 100 responses he received were interesting. A considerable number suggested some type of entertainment be provided along with the seminar. Many said they started getting bored after about 45 minutes, and some entertainment would have stimulated their interest. Arthur was grateful for the comments, but confused. In his former organization, people were always interested. He had acted seriously with the poise a serious subject demanded. He certainly wasn't a comedian and he had no idea what type of entertainment he could use. However, he decided to make another attempt and give the public what it wanted.

A few months later, Arthur again announced on television and in the newspapers that he was offering the same seminar on building confidence. This time the television commercials included paid actors who appeared with him to give testimonials. After Arthur had made his statements about the wonders of the seminar, he referred the audience to two of his success stories.

Arthur rented the same hotel facilities and 310 people enrolled for the second seminar. This time Arthur gave a brief presentation and then introduced the paid actors to the group. They each told stories that Arthur had meticulously conceived, and they were received with warmth and enthusiasm. There were many questions but the actors were so well rehearsed and prepared that they fielded them with ease. Arthur returned to his presentation. Soon after, someone rushed up on the stage and took the microphone from him. Of course, this was all planned. The paid comedian told a few jokes about confidence and what it had done for him, then collapsed on the floor. There was much laughter and within 10 minutes the comedian left the stage. After that little interlude, Arthur went on with his presentation until breaktime.

This time the comments were good. However, several people recognized that the people he presented as proof that his technique worked were actors from the local playhouse, and they asked him to verify that fact. Arthur vehemently denied anything underhanded and said that they may perform at the local playhouse, but when they came to him they were in need of help, and help them he did. When the break was over Arthur went back to the center of the stage and proceeded with the last segment of his program. While there were no additional incidents involving the actors, Arthur was shaken: he realized that the whole evening could easily have come crashing down around him, and that he could have been labeled a fraud. In the end, he made only $2,000 on this seminar, because he had to pay the actors and give them a bonus for their excellent ad libs. The seminar business was not working out as he'd expected. ▼

Case Study Roundtable

▼ ▼ ▼ ▼ ▼

Arthur: I thought my seminars would be wildly successful; I even had plans for making videos and audio cassettes to distribute all over the country. Now, I don't know any more. After that near-disaster with the actors, I may just be too gun-shy. What do you think?

Discussion Points

- Do you think Arthur researched his market in depth? What else could he have done?

- How would a mission statement have helped him before he made the decision to go into business? What might he include in his mission statement?

- At the first seminar, Arthur greeted the guests as they arrived. Do you think it would have been better if someone else had met them, prepped the audience about the seminar, and finally presented Arthur to the group?

- After the first seminar, do you think Arthur should have quit, or should he have continued? Do you feel the results of the first seminar were encouraging?

- With respect to the second seminar, do you think Arthur was unethical in using two paid actors to convince his audience? What other methods could he have used? Do you think his attempt at entertainment could have been improved?

- Why did such an obviously intelligent and experienced business executive make the mistakes he did?

- How might Arthur benefit from determining his strategic position? What is his current position? Should he try a different one?

▲▲▲▲▲▲

CHAPTER BRIEFCASE

▼▼▼▼▼▼

- Your mission statement should ideally be based on an objective analysis of the internal strengths and weaknesses of your business, as well as the opportunities and threats within your commercial environment—known as a "SWOT" analysis.

- A mission statement is a concise statement of the general nature and direction of the company. By carefully and clearly stating the basic aim, scope, and direction of the business, the mission statement becomes an outline of what the company will do, and what it will be. A mission statement communicates with employees and customers, letting them know why your company exists. It also represents your commitment to growing the kind of company you envision.

- A mission statement is composed of three parts: (1) a definition of the nature of the business, (2) a statement of the business's fundamental philosophy, and (3) a strong statement of how that philosophy will be applied in the real world.

- A strategic position is a general indication of how the business will behave in its attempt to achieve its overall mission and secure a competitive advantage. There are a number of growth strategies suitable for different businesses at different phases of their development.

▲▲▲▲▲▲

Chapter 8

DEBT AND EQUITY FINANCING

▼▼▼▼▼

A banker is a fellow who lends you his umbrella when the sun is shining, but wants it back the minute it begins to rain.

—*Mark Twain*

MISSION STATEMENT

In this chapter, you will

*L*EARN about the various types of debt and equity, the role of debt and equity considerations in financing a business, the six "Cs" used by bankers to evaluate credit risk, and how to prepare a financing proposal to match your business needs.

*E*XPLORE the various sources of debt and equity financing.

*A*PPLY your understanding of financing issues to a case study.

*P*RODUCE a contact list of financing sources.

KEY TERMS

debt	line of credit	six "Cs"
equity	long-term financing	unsecured loan
financing proposal	mortgage	venture capitalist
intermediate-term financing	secured loan	
	short-term financing	

INTRODUCTION TO BASIC FINANCING CONCEPTS AND TERMS

When you are planning to open a new business (or expand your current operation), five very important questions arise relating to finance.

1. Do you **need** to borrow money?
2. If you need outside financing, **how much** do you need?

3. **When** do you need it?
4. What are the **sources** of funding available to meet your needs?
5. How much will it **cost**?

To make an intelligent decision on a timely basis, you will need to address all five of these questions. If you fail to do so, the lack of sufficient and ready capital can quickly lead to business failure.

Do You Need to Borrow Money?

The first step to answering this question is to ask yourself some more questions. The answers will help you make the right decision and realistically understand your financial needs. These questions will keep you from making costly errors that may ultimately bankrupt even the most potentially viable business.

To determine whether you will need outside financing, ask yourself:

- *Have you written a business plan?* If you haven't written one, do so. As we've already discussed, a business plan can help you make vital financial decisions based on achieving your desired business goals.
- *What are the risks?* Any venture has some built-in risk, even the surest "sure thing." Consumer preferences can change overnight: yesterday's must-have item is today's garage-sale special. Shops that were wildly popular a week ago now find customers staying away in droves. Suppliers can be unreliable, workers can be hard to find, the weather can be uncooperative—for any venture, the list of uncontrollables can be a long one. Know the risks, plot out the worst-case scenario, plan solutions, be prepared, and know what you are asking your lender to get into.
- *What are your own sources of available capital?* Make a list of all your current sources of cash: existing loans, capital reserve accounts, private savings, friendly relatives with deep pockets, whatever. Before you think about borrowing additional funds, know what you have now, and where it comes from.
- *Would you be willing to risk your own money on your venture?* If *you* are not willing to take a risk, don't expect someone else to. More to the point, why would anyone else want to take a risk on your business if you wouldn't? You've analyzed your current capital sources; now can you demonstrate your commitment to the venture in tangible terms by risking at least part of your own reserves?
- *Do you really need additional financing or do you just need to manage your present cash flow more effectively?* Again, everyone would like to have more money, but financing isn't free: why take on the cost of borrowing money if you can free up necessary capital just by changing your habits?
- *What do you need the money for?* Of course, everyone can find a use for more money. But if you want to convince a lender to extend a loan to your business, you need to have a clear, specific plan for how the money will be used. The lender's primary interest is not in the details of how you run your business—it is your lender, not your partner—but in when the borrowed money will generate sufficient revenues to repay the debt and interest owed. If you borrow, can

you realistically project increased revenues? If so, when will those increased revenues justify the debt?

How Much Do You Need and When Do You Need It?

If you have decided that you will need additional financing, you will then need to carefully assess your needs and determine not only the *amount* you need, but *when* you will need it. Many business owners overestimate or underestimate their capital requirements or do not time their financing to the best advantage. Either can lead to serious problems. Both together can spell disaster.

The first thing you need is a realistic business plan: one that you intend to follow as closely as possible. (Does this sound repetitious? Only because it's important.) The only way to look at every aspect of your business is through the planning process. It will force you to create an organizational plan and a marketing plan and combine them into projected financial statements with reliable figures that can be read and analyzed. Those projections give you an educated estimate of your financial needs and tell you when these needs will most likely occur. Your business plan will answer such financing-related questions as:

- *What are your most critical needs?* That is, of all the goals you have for your business, choose the one or two that are the most important to its overall success. Then analyze exactly what you need (and what it will cost) to achieve those vital goals.
- *If you need the money for immediate operating capital, how much will you need to operate your business until it becomes self-sustaining?* Many start-up businesses find it easy to forget this part. Getting things up and running is certainly important; no less important are the day-to-day costs of keeping your business going. Eventually, of course, revenue starts rolling in and the business pays for its own expenses (preferably with profits left over).
- *Does your market research show that expenditures for expansion, improvements, or additional assets will allow you to reach the target market that justifies purchasing the assets?* This is where the market research part of your business planning will help you. Your research should offer you an indication of how likely it is that your expansion or improvement will pay off in the form of increased business activity.
- *What are the most effective ways to reach your target market?* How much will it cost to advertise and market your business? Will the increased marketing be reflected in even higher increases in revenues? According to your analysis of industry trends, what are the best selling periods and when will you need financing in order to have the lead time to advertise for the best results?

What Are Your Sources of Funding?

Most of the cash required to start a business is provided by the business principals themselves. If more capital is required, you will need to tap into outside sources, which fall into two broad categories:

1. Debt financing (dollars borrowed)
2. Equity financing (ownership dollars injected into the business)

Debt versus Equity

When you go to your bank for a loan, you are seeking **debt** money, which you will repay over a period of time at an additional cost (interest). The money you invest in your business is ordinarily **equity**: that is, money that will not be repaid to you unless you sell a portion of your ownership. Debt financing doesn't lead to sharing ownership of your business with the financier. Equity financing does.

Control is another matter. Your banker may exert substantial control over your business through a legal loan document or through suggestions—but he or she doesn't own your business. Debt pays interest, usually for a finite time. Equity pays profits forever.

DEBT FINANCING

Debt is a loan, usually from a bank, that the lender expects you to repay at some determinate time. The lender will ordinarily receive a return for the use of the funds in the form of interest. The interest rate reflects the lender's perceived risk. The higher the perceived risk, the higher the rate. Your business plan must take into account the need to repay both principal and interest as agreed. This has far-reaching effects on your profits and cash flow, so borrow with care.

If you use bank debt, you may find yourself subject to loan agreements that effectively compel you to share decision-making with your creditors. For example, an agreement may limit the amount of debt you can incur relative to the net worth of the business, which can force you to find new equity money in order to grow.

Debt financing is generally obtained from one of two sources. It can come from either a non-professional source such as a friend, relative, customer, or colleague, or from a traditional lending institution such as a bank or commercial finance company.

Friends or relatives. Borrowing from a friend or relative is generally the most readily available source, especially when the capital requirements are smaller. This is frequently the least costly in terms of dollars—but it may prove to be the most costly in terms of personal relations if your repayment schedule is not timely or your venture does not work out. This alternative should be approached with great caution!

Traditional lending institutions. Banks, savings and loans, and commercial finance companies have long been the major sources of business financing, principally as short-term lenders offering demand loans, seasonal lines of credit, and single-purpose loans for fixed assets.

Almost all lending institutions are strict about collateral requirements and will require established businesses to provide one-third of the equity injection and start-ups up to fifty percent or more. Borrowers are required to have a business plan with adequate documentation demonstrating that you will be able to repay the loan with interest.

SBA guaranteed loans. The SBA guaranteed loan program is a secondary source of financing. This option comes into play after private lending options have been denied. The SBA offers a variety of loan programs to eligible small businesses that cannot borrow the amount needed on reasonable terms from conventional lenders.

Most of the SBA's business loans are made by private lenders and then guaranteed by the agency. Though it may not necessarily be easier to get approved for an SBA guaranteed loan, the guaranty will allow you to obtain a loan with a longer maturity at better repayment terms and interest rates.

SBA loan programs are generally intended to encourage long-term small business financing. As a rule, loan maturities (the length of time the borrower has to pay back the loan plus interest) are based on the borrower's ability to repay, the loan's purpose, and the nature of the assets financed, if any. However, the SBA has established maximum loan maturities:

- Real estate and equipment: 25 years (after any significant new construction or renovation is completed)
- Working capital: 7 years (unless a longer period is needed, up to 10 years)

Interest rates are always negotiated between the borrower and the lender. In the case of SBA-guaranteed loans, however, the interest rate may not exceed the set SBA maximum rates. The SBA's maximums are linked to the prime rate.

Interest rates for SBA-guaranteed loans may be either fixed or variable. Fixed rate loans may not exceed the prime rate plus 2.25 percent if the loan's maturity is less than seven years, and 2.75 percent if the maturity is seven years or more. When the amount of the loan is less than $25,000, the maximum interest rate may not exceed prime plus 4.25 percent for loans less than seven years (4.75 percent for loans of seven years or more). If the loan is for an amount between $25,000 and $50,000, the maximum rate is prime plus 3.25 percent for loans less than seven years (prime plus 3.75 percent for loans of seven years or more).

Variable rate SBA-guaranteed loans may be tied to either the lowest prime rate or the SBA optional peg rate. The SBA's optional peg rate is, basically, an average of rates paid by the federal government for loans with maturities similar to the average SBA loan. The optional peg rate is determined on a quarterly basis, and published in the Federal Register. The amount that will be added to this base rate is freely negotiated by the lender and the borrower, and an adjustment period is selected.

The SBA charges lenders a guaranty fee and a servicing fee for each approved loan. The lenders may pass these fees on to the borrower after the lender has paid them. The actual amount of the fee is based on the amount of the loan guaranty involved.

For instance, if the guaranty portion of the loan is $80,000 or less, the guaranty fee will be 2 percent of the guaranteed portion. If the loan amount is between $80,000 and $249,999, the fee will be 3 percent. For the next $250,000 of the guaranteed part of the loan, a guaranty fee of 3.5 percent will be charged. A 3.875 percent guaranty fee is applied to any amount of a loan that exceeds $500,000. In addition, the SBA charges a 0.5 percent annual service fee. This fee is applied to the outstanding balance of that part of the loan guaranteed by the SBA. The lender may not charge the borrower of an

SBA-guaranteed loan any processing fee, origination fee, application fee, points, brokerage fee, bonus points, or any other fees.

The following are some of the most popular SBA guaranteed loan programs available to small businesses.

- *SBA 7(a) Guaranteed Loan Program.* SBA will guarantee 85 to 90 percent of a loan up to $500,000. Usual minimum is $50,000.
- *SBA LowDoc Program.* A simple, fast loan program using a one-page form and expedited approval process. Can be used for existing business, purchase of a business, or start-up, for loans under $100,000.
- *SBA Fa$tTrack Program.* Offered as a pilot with a limited number of lenders. SBA will guarantee up to 50 percent of the loan. Maximum loan amount is $100,000. Lenders may use their existing documentation and procedures to make and service a loan that will be guaranteed by the SBA, without any additional forms or waiting periods prior to SBA approval.
- *Minority Pre-Qualification Pilot Loan Program (MPQ).* Intermediaries (such as Small Business Development Centers) work with minority businesses to help them develop effective loan application packages and secure loans. Intermediaries may charge a fee for their assistance. Businesses must be at least 51 percent owned and managed by a racial or ethnic minority person and must meet SBA 7(a) size standards and general eligibility criteria. The business and/or personal assets will be pledged when warranted. SBA will guarantee 80 percent of loans up to $100,000. Larger loans will be considered on a case by case basis. The same interest rate rules apply as in the 7(a) program.
- *Capline* (formerly known as Greenline). Eligibility and interest rate rules are the same as 7(a) guaranteed loans. Capline is designed for working capital. Collateral may include accounts receivable, inventory, and assignment of contract proceeds. SBA guarantees are the same as for other 7(a) programs, up to $750,000. Under the Capline program, SBA will provide small businesses with four types of working capital: (1) seasonal, (2) contract, (3) builder, and (4) asset based. The asset based lines are limited to $200,000.
- *504 Program.* Certified Development Programs (CDCs) are private/public sector non-profit corporations whose purpose is to contribute to the economic development of their areas of operation. They provide small businesses with 10 or 20 year financing for the acquisition of land, buildings, machinery, and equipment. To be eligible, the business must operate for profit. Net worth must not exceed $6 million and average net profit after tax must not exceed $2 million for the past two years. Financing is usually limited to land, buildings, heavy machinery and equipment. The maximum guarantee amount is generally $750,000 (although that amount may go up to $1,000,000 if the project meets certain public policy goals, such as business district revitalization, or expansion of export, or expansion of minority business).
- *International Trade Loan Program.* The SBA offers a loan program specifically designed for small businesses that are currently engaging in international trade, or planning to expand into the international market. The program is also available for small businesses that are adversely affected by competition from imports. The applying business must demonstrate that the loan proceeds will be

used to significantly expand or develop an existing or projected export market. If the business claims that it is adversely affected by foreign competition, it must demonstrate how the proceeds of the loan will be used to upgrade equipment or facilities, or otherwise to improve its competitive posture.

- *Pollution Control Loan Program.* This program is designed to provide eligible small businesses with loan guarantees for a specific purpose: to offset the costs involved in planning, designing, or installing a pollution control facility. To be eligible, the pollution control facility must effectively prevent, reduce, abate, or control any form of pollution. Recycling programs are included.

- *Women's Prequalification Pilot Loan Program.* These targeted SBA loan guaranty programs rely on intermediaries (usually Small Business Development Centers) to help prospective women borrowers develop effective loan application packages and secure loans. The program uses only nonprofit organizations as intermediaries. Intermediaries may charge applicants a fee for their assistance. Of course, the fees charged by for-profit intermediaries will tend to be higher than those charged by nonprofits.

  Participants' loan application packages receive expedited consideration from the SBA—a decision is usually made within three days. After the application is approved, the SBA provides the applicant with a prequalification letter that states the SBA's intent to guarantee the loan. The intermediary helps the borrower identify the lenders who offer the most competitive rates. The maximum amount for loans under the women's program is $250,000; under the minority program, it is generally the same (although other limits apply in certain areas). In both programs, the SBA will guarantee up to 80 percent of the loan amount.

- *MicroLoan Program.* Through this program the SBA makes very small loans available to small business borrowers. Under the MicroLoan program, the SBA makes funds available to nonprofit intermediaries, who in turn make loans to eligible borrowers. Loan amounts under this program range from $100 to a maximum of $25,000, with an average loan amount of $10,000. Loans may be for as long as six years, with rates no more than 4 percent over prime. The application-to-approval period is usually less than a week.

Lori Davis tells how she got an $80,000 start-up loan. And, you'll meet the banker who awarded her the loan.

TYPES OF BANK FINANCING

Bankers customarily divide loans into three general categories: (1) short-term, (2) intermediate, and (3) long-term debt. Risk, the odds against an expected happening in the future, is just one of the elements in a credit decision. From a banker's viewpoint, the higher the debt, the riskier the deal. Also, the longer the term, the riskier the deal.

Short-Term Financing

Short-term financing is usually provided through notes to be paid within one year, usually in one sum. These notes are repaid through inventory turn or by converting receivables to cash within the time frame of the note. **Short-term debt** is for short-term needs: seasonal inventory loans, short-run production or construction loans, and short-term liquidity problems. These are repaid from the returns on specific transactions or series of transactions in a short period of time. If these debts are financed over a longer time span, the result is almost always deepening debt and erosion of business assets. Even though your cash flow will look good by spreading the cost over a longer period, you would be violating a cardinal rule of borrowing: paying for a benefit after it has been exhausted. One reason bankers are hesitant to bail small businesses out of chronic trade debts is that those unpaid debts are evidence that the business is seriously mismanaged. Paying for a dead horse is bad business.

A **line of credit** is a short-term tool that works like a credit card. You arrange before the need arises to have a certain amount of credit to draw against; then you pay it off (or renew it). The main thing to avoid is paying for last year's short-term needs with new debt—it's bad enough for an individual but worse for a small business.

Intermediate-Term Financing

Intermediate-term debt is for needs that last between one and five years. The most common are equipment loans and working capital loans for businesses undergoing rapid growth. By converting debt to earnings, and then retaining a portion of the earnings as capital, it is possible to grow using debt money. Don't plan on this, though, as it requires a farsighted banker, considerable risk, and profits high enough to handle the added interest costs.

Intermediate-term financing ranges from one to five years and is usually repaid in fixed monthly payments or fixed principal payments plus interest. These loans are repaid from operating profits.

Long-Term Financing

Long-term financing is provided for periods longer than five years. The most common example is real estate financing, where repayment is made on a prearranged schedule over a long period of years. **Long-term debt** is for long-term needs: fixed assets that will be used and paid for over the long haul. To pay this kind of debt off too fast is a mistake unless you are extremely well capitalized, in which case check with your banker and accountant first. They'll tell you.

These loans may be secured or unsecured. A **secured loan** is backed by collateral (liens against your property, savings account, or Certificate of Deposit, or perhaps cosigned by someone with more assets) that would be applied to recover the loan in event of default.

An **unsecured loan** (sometimes called a *signature* or *character loan*) is one not backed by any collateral. These are almost always short-term loans available only to the most creditworthy individuals and companies. The loan is backed by your banker's faith in your character, capability, and capital.

Your banker will lend your business money if he or she feels comfortable with the risk. They are under no obligation to lend money to a business that doesn't fit their risk tolerance—a frequent source of anger to credit seekers. To help your banker decide in your favor, lower the risk by keeping a low debt-to-worth ratio (discussed in Chapter 11), have enough working capital to cover current liabilities, and match the financing request to your real needs. Note that from a banker's viewpoint, a loan should be repaid as soon as possible.

FIRST PERSON

Anne T., Houston, Texas: From a banker's perspective, it's really frustrating when you have to work with small business owners who don't understand the differences between various types of financing or the importance of those distinctions to the success or failure of a business. Many small business owners don't even try to understand how their proposal looks to the banker. I end up spending way too much time trying to educate people about things they should have thought of before they started out.

But uninformed owners don't just cause bankers trouble. The owners themselves can get in big trouble if they don't have a clear understanding from the beginning of how viable their proposal is. This understanding can help business owners avoid the biggest banker-related pitfalls. For instance, you may encounter the banker who won't say "no" to you (there really are such creatures!), either because he's your friend, or knows your family, or just likes to say yes to entrepreneurs, but can't or won't be able to provide adequate financing. Or there's the banker who gives the wrong loan for the wrong reasons. Either of these situations are doomed from the start.

Banks are not venture capitalists, risk takers, or gamblers. They shouldn't be. Their business is investing other people's money, and they have to be cautious. You really have to convince a bank that your business is a good investment.

MEET YOUR BANK

The primary source of money for most small businesses is a bank. Accordingly, entrepreneurs have to act carefully and selectively in choosing and nurturing a bank. Your relationship with your bank has to be based on factual information as well as some intangibles, but above all keep in mind that, as a rule, *banks do not like surprises*. Keep your bank informed about bad news as well as good, and about any major changes in the way you do business. Of course, this is more than just common courtesy: if the bank has made an investment in your business, it has the right to know what you're up to. Regardless of the motive for keeping your bank informed, the results will be worth the effort.

The Six "Cs"

Most bankers have been trained in the "Three Cs of Credit":

1. Character
2. Capacity
3. Capital

Character. This reflects the borrower's willingness to pay. A record of non-payment or a prior personal bankruptcy, for example, might cause a banker to view a person's character as too risky. Loans to small businesses are not commercial loans in the sense that they are made to individuals, not to businesses. Many bankers claim, in fact, that they never lend to small businesses, but rather are investing in the owner on the basis of knowing his or her character.

Ultimately, the owner will be responsible for repayment of loans. You will find that you have to sign personally as a guarantor of any bank loan your business secures. The kind of person you are has a lot to do with the kind of reception you will get at the local bank. If you have a reputation for being honest, straightforward, and responsible, you will probably get your loan application approved.

Character is fundamentally a personal factor. It includes many intangibles (integrity, for example—try to define it) but your personal track record provides a clue. This is why a full résumé has to be part of your financing proposal. Even if your banker has known you forever, include one anyway. Other bankers may not know you as well. Your education, experience, and history are important.

You'll probably have to sign personally for a loan while your business is small. Remember: when you're starting a business, you are your business. So a loan to your business isn't a transaction with some big faceless corporate entity; it's a loan to you. Self-marketing is an important part of your financing package.

Capacity. This refers to the amount of debt you can take on safely, and how much your business can bear. Remember that small business loans tend to be made on the basis of the individual's ability to support that debt rather than the strength of the business's cash flow. A careful cash flow projection will shift much of the burden to the business, but your banker will still look to you as the ultimate source of repayment. Your banker will ask for a personal financial statement as well as your business's balance sheet and cash flow in order to figure out how much you can afford to borrow. They are the experts, so listen to them. They don't want to burden you with too much debt because they want you to succeed.

Capital. You have to have at least as much at risk as the bank or other investors. This doesn't mean that your borrowing capacity is limited to what you can put in personally, but it does mean that you have to have some of your own cash (plus, in some cases, the cash investment from other investors). The "creative financing" deal is not generally appropriate for business owners who plan to succeed. Your banker may ask you to secure more capital before a loan can be granted. Permanent capital (including subordinated debt) provides a cushion for the business and gives your banker a sense of security about lending you money.

Three other "Cs" are also often cited:

4. Credit
5. Condition
6. Collateral

Credit. Your credit history is a key piece of the puzzle for your banker. How have you handled credit in the past? If you have paid your debts more or less on time, don't have a history of bankruptcy or creditor lawsuits, and have proven that you can use credit effectively, your banker will be somewhat eased. A good credit record seldom causes the banker to make a loan, but a bad record will cause him or her to deny credit.

Experience is a factor here: Your experience in a given business affects your banker's perception of your ability to successfully run this business. The benefits of capital are obvious: a well-capitalized business is inherently less risky than an under-capitalized business. Costs will be lower, for example, and a capital cushion makes for sounder decisions.

Condition. This refers to the state of the economy and of the business generally. If the economy in your area is rolling off a cliff, the risk of your deal will be magnified. Economic factors may be beyond your control but, once again, will affect your banker's decision. Your business idea might be poor today but wonderful tomorrow—and no banker would do you a favor by launching you into business at the wrong time. If times are tight, think carefully about a new venture (that doesn't mean not to pursue it, just to think it through carefully).

Collateral. This is useful as a means of tying you to the deal. Experience has shown that people who have their own assets on the line fight harder to make a deal work than people who are working with little of their own money at risk. Collateral also serves as a comfort factor for the banker. Bankers really don't want to seize your collateral—they have no desire to be secondhand equipment dealers or sell out your stocks and bonds. But they like to have some recourse just in case your business fails.

That's as it should be. Bankers are not in business to take risks or bet on a long shot. For that matter, neither should you. Most studies of successful business owners show a profile of moderate risk taking: not too conservative, but certainly not too eager to run unjustified risks.

Collateral is taken for two reasons: (1) security (reduction of perceived risk to the bank) and (2) commitment. Collateral represents a source of repayment in the worst case scenario (which reduces the risk of extending the credit in the first place). By putting up collateral, you show that you are at least as committed to the success of the venture as you expect the bank to be.

Fit the Financing to Your Need

Tell your banker what you need the money for, how it will be repaid, and why the deal makes good business sense. Your financing proposal does just that, and if based on your business plan and careful analysis, you should get the right financing. Remember: *Planning is the key to success.*

Your bank will match the financing with the reason for the financing. A good rule of thumb is never borrow short term to meet a long-term obligation, and never borrow long-term to cover a short term obligation.

Short term loans are used for short-term needs, such as inventory loans, with repayment to come from selling the inventory, which are usually 30 to 90 days. Short-term cash flow gaps are often covered by short-term notes secured by receivables. Chronic cash flow shortages reflect undercapitalization or poor cash management. Both are serious problems that your bank will want you to solve as soon as possible.

Your bank will suggest a line of credit to simplify paperwork if you will have occasion to borrow short term frequently. A line of credit works much the same as a credit card, except that you have to pay it off in full at least once a year.

Equipment loans are repaid from operating profits over a period not to exceed the life of the equipment. These are usually set up as term loans, with fixed payments made on a regular working basis, over one to seven years. Working capital loans are treated the same way.

Mortgages are long-term loans used to purchase real estate and may extend up to 15 years. In some cases long-term loans are used to purchase major equipment.

When projecting your cash flow (which we'll do in Chapter 9), you calculate two things that help determine the right financing mix for your business. The first, negative cash flows, both net cash flow and cumulative cash flow, indicate how much money you need and when you need it. The second, projected cash receipts, give you an idea of how you will generate money to repay the loan or make good the investment. If you don't arrange for enough financing (of whatever kind), your deal will be dead. If you borrow more than you can handle, your deal will be doomed. If you borrow at the wrong time, or for the wrong reasons, you aggravate the already high risks of being in business.

Earlier in this chapter, we heard a banker allude to the problem of lenders who can't say no but won't provide the right amount of financing. If you have thought through your business plan, you will know how much you need and when you'll need it. Make sure to get the right financing; less will only complicate matters. If your banker can give you good reasons to borrow less, pay attention—but think it through. Don't settle for enough money to get you into trouble but not enough to see you through.

Extending the Loan

Before a bank will consider making a loan to a small business venture, whether a start-up or an ongoing concern, it has to be satisfied with the answers to two key questions:

1. *Does this loan make sense for this business?* The owner's business plan must demonstrate convincingly that an infusion of capital will make the business stronger, more competitive, more efficient, and more profitable.
2. *How will the loan be repaid?* If things don't work out and the business should fail, the bank needs to know that there is a secondary repayment source; that the bank won't be left to write off a bad debt.

FIRST PERSON

Richard P., St. Louis, Missouri: My bank does a lot of work with small businesses. Some of them are start-ups, and some of them have been with us for many years. When my dad opened this institution, it was the first one in town that took entrepreneurs really seriously and understood their problems and needs. That was his vision. Some common misconceptions about banks are that they only will lend you money when you don't need it—that only businesses that are financially in great shape already and that show promising income projections can possibly qualify under the tough and stingy standards we set. I hear that we are "insensitive to start-ups" (whatever *that* means!) and have some sort of double standard for small businesses in general. I've heard people say that the banks just want to own your house and everything else. But here's the thing: unprepared applicants don't get the financing they think they deserve. And if people come in here with some sort of flea market mentality, expecting the bank to bargain down their loan requests, they ask for way too much in the first place, and destroy their credibility right off the bat. I've seen it happen, and it isn't very nice.

Ask your bank for help, explaining that your plans and your cash flow indicate your need for a loan. Put the bank on your team. Your bank is experienced in financial areas that you are not (most average local banks typically see 200 or more business loan applications each year); it has a vested interest in seeing you succeed. Banks always want their small business customers to become bigger businesses, because bigger businesses take out bigger loans, and make bigger deposits. And even if you don't become a "big business," the bank wants you to succeed for the simple reason that it wants you to be able to repay the loan.

Banks are not venture capitalists or charitable organizations. They make their profit by renting out their depositors' money. They can't make a profit if they don't get the money back, so they are conservative, and avoid risky ventures and long shots. Their fiduciary relationship to their depositors forbids them from such investments. And legally, they cannot lend into negative net worth businesses. If you are aware of your bank's concerns, you will be more likely to secure the kind of financing that will help your business grow profitably.

EQUITY FINANCING

Equity funds come from selling a portion of the business to yourself or another person. The amount you have to sell to acquire the needed funds reflects the amount of risk that the investor perceives. If your venture seems very risky, you may have to sell a substantial share. If it is not seen as very risky, you won't have to give up as much ownership. With outside equity, you don't have to repay the funds, but you give up a share of ownership and will have to share decision-making and profits. If the business grows to the point where you wish to sell out, the real cost of an equity investor can be far greater than interest on a loan.

If a company has a high percentage of debt to equity (what it owes compared to what it owns), the company will find it difficult to get debt financing and will probably need to seek equity investment for additional funds. What this means simply is that the company's owner will trade a certain percentage of the company for a specific amount of money. How much of the company will the owner have to "sacrifice" in exchange for needed capital? The exchange of equity for capital is based on supply and demand. In other words, the deal is made according to who has the best bargaining power.

Where does equity financing come from? As with debt capital, this type of capital can come from friends and relatives. But remember: mixing your friends or relatives and your business may not be a good idea.

Venture Capitalists

The **venture capitalist** is a risk taker and professional opportunity-seeker. Venture capitalists usually specialize in certain industries, and prefer newer companies that have demonstrated high growth potential: such companies usually offer higher-than-average profits to their shareholders. Venture capitalists' investments are sometimes made through businesses specializing in acting as "matchmakers."

The SBA licenses Small Business Investment Companies (SBICs) and Minority Enterprise Small Business Investment Companies (MSBICs). They make venture/risk investments by supplying equity capital and extending unsecured loans to small enterprises that meet their criteria.

As risk takers, venture capitalists are entitled to participate in the management of the business. If the company does not perform, they may become increasingly active in the decision making process.

Venture capitalists also require an exit strategy to be included in the company's business plan. This minimizes risk to the investor, providing a way out if there is a strong indicator that the business will fail to reach its profitability goals.

Angel programs. For smaller business owners, women, and minorities, there has been a growing trend toward the development of "angel" programs through business organizations and companies specializing in small business. Individuals and small companies that want to invest smaller amounts in promising business are linked with those companies and the two decide whether the loan will be made. Angel investing has been around for years. The establishment of organized programs is relatively new, but holds some promise for the future.

The tables in Figure 8.1 and 8.2 compare various sources of debt and equity financing.

YOUR FINANCING PROPOSAL

Assuming that you pass these rough sorting criteria, what comes next? Your business plan, tailored to the financer as a financing proposal, gains added credibility if you ask for the appropriate financing to fit your needs. You can research this ahead of time by involving your banker in your planning (never a bad idea anyway) and by asking your accountant.

In a very few situations, capital sources other than banks should be approached—venture capital firms or investment bankers, for example. If your deal is large enough and the anticipated payoff is sufficiently high (financing needs of over $1 million, with an anticipated payout rate greater than 40 percent annually are two rough measures), your banker and other advisors will steer you to the right people. Otherwise, don't waste your time or theirs. Only 5 percent of business financing deals ever get beyond the first screening, and only a handful of those get venture capital or go public. If your deal is attractive enough to warrant attention, you will want to tailor your proposal to the needs of your intended audience, a process well beyond the scope of this *Field Guide* and one that requires detailed knowledge of the players involved.

For those small business entrepreneurs with more modest deals, a banker is the first and most likely option. Your banker may refer you to a local venture capital club or other source of equity, but start with your banker. If you need more equity than you have available, check with your accountant and lawyer, who may be in touch with individuals who invest in local or startup deals. If you don't have a banker and an accountant, you surely will have no need for specialized financing.

FIGURE 8.1 **Sources of Debt Financing**

Source	Borrower Characteristics	Advantages	Disadvantages	Best For...	Worst For...
Banks and lending institutions	• Ability to repay collateral • Current income from business	• No profit-sharing • No obligation for ongoing relationship after repayment • Definite amount to repay	• Difficult for new businesses to secure • Personal assets at risk • Same financial obligation regardless of business performance	• Established companies that need funding for specific activities • Short-term cash-flow problems	• Ongoing operational expenses • New companies with inexperienced management
Family and friends	• Personal character • Relationships	• Easier to obtain than institutional loans • Definite amount to repay • No profit-sharing	• Can jeopardize personal relationships • Unsophisticated lender • Unsolicited advice and frequent questions	• Companies with no other lending option • Companies with secure future	• Risky businesses • Entrepreneurs with difficult family circumstances
Cash advance on personal credit cards	• Ability to repay	• Easy to obtain	• High interest rate • Limited loan amount • Risks personal credit	• Businesses requiring only small amounts of money for a limited time • Short-term cash-flow problems	• Ongoing, long-term financing

FIGURE 8.2 Sources of Equity Financing

Source	Borrower Characteristics	Advantages	Disadvantages	Best For...	Worst For...
Venture capital	• Business in area of interest • Growth potential • Experienced management	• Large sums available • Investor's expertise • Investor connections	• Difficult to locate and secure • Requires exit time-frame • May take substantial or controlling equity	• Potentially large companies • Sophisticated entrepreneurs	• Small or medium-sized businesses • Inexperienced entrepreneurs
Private investors and angels	• Good business opportunity • Better potential rewards than conventional investments	• Willing to fund small- and medium-sized businesses • Easier to secure than venture capital	• Sometimes unsophisticated investor • May take equity in company • May want involvement in decisions • Long term relationship • Expects quick return on investment	• Smaller companies • Sophisticated entrepreneurs	• Companies that require a long development time before profitability
Family and friends	• Personal character • Relationships	• Easier to obtain than institutional loans • Definite amount to repay • No profit-sharing	• Can jeopardize personal relationships • Unsophisticated lender • Unsolicited advice and frequent questions	• Companies with no other lending option • Companies with secure future	• Risky businesses • Entrepreneurs with difficult family circumstances

The difference between a business plan and a financing proposal is one of emphasis rather than design. The main function of your plan is to enable you to understand and master the complexities of your business, while the function of the financing proposal is to show your prospective backers that you not only know what you are doing but will also make their investment as risk-free as possible. Your business plan needs little alteration to become a first-rate financing proposal.

Although the greatest dollar amounts of credit for businesses of all sizes is trade credit (money owed to suppliers), your single most important financing source is your local bank. Such esoteric financing tools as factoring, warehouse loans, and the many forms of stocks, bonds, and debt instruments just don't apply to most businesses. If you need them, your banker will help you find the right professionals.

HOW MUCH WILL IT COST?

The cost of financing is usually related to the degree of risk involved. If the risk is high, so is the cost: it's simple market economics. Let's look at some of the possible sources of financing, from the least expensive to the most costly.

- *You.* The least expensive money to use is your own. The cost to you is whatever you would have made on your money by investing it in other sources (savings, money market accounts, bonds, retirement plans, or real estate, for instance). Many new business owners borrow heavily on their credit cards only to find themselves overwhelmed by astonishingly high interest rates. Credit cards are one of the most expensive sources of cash and have paved the road to bankruptcy court more than once. Don't get caught in this trap!
- *Friends and relatives.* The next lowest cost sources of money are friends and relatives who may charge you a lower interest rate. But don't forget that it may cost you in other ways.
- *Banks and other traditional lenders.* The third on the cost ladder is probably the traditional lender (such as banks and the SBA). This lender will want to know what the capital will be used for and will require that it be used for those specific needs. If the risk is too high, most conventional lenders cannot approve your loan because it would be a poor financial decision for the bank's investors. One default out of ten will undermine their whole program.
- *Outside lenders and venture capitalists.* Traditionally, the most expensive sources of money are the outside lender who charges a high interest rate because of the risk involved and the venture capitalist who requires a percentage of your business.

Calculating the Cost

Before you get financing, take time to understand the terms under which the loan will be made. What is the interest rate? How long do you have to repay the loan? When will payments begin and how much will they be? What are you putting up as collateral? If you have venture capital injected into the business, will you also be paying interest on that investment? What part of the payments can be written off as deductions?

Remember, principal repayments are not tax deductible. We'll look at the math of financing in Chapter 9.

The cost of any source of financing can and should be calculated before the financing is finalized. Again, go back to your business plan. Determine when the financing is needed, plug cash injection, repayment figures, and resulting income projections into your cash flow statement and check out the result. Will the financing make you more profitable and enable you to repay the lender or distribute profits to the venture capitalist?

FINDING ASSISTANCE

Your accountant and other financial advisors will have had experience with businesses like yours, and should be called on to help you make reasonable projections of profitability and expenses. Trade association publications sometimes run articles on how to forecast sales. If you can locate one of these, use it. What has worked for other people will work for you. Once you've been in business for a while, you can safely try your own methods. But not when you're starting out.

SBDC and SCORE counselors have forecasting experience. So do some bankers and consultants. Ask them. If they haven't done much forecasting, they won't be much help. Good forecasting takes experience.

Put Together an "Advisory Board"

Although most small business owners don't have a board of directors, most could benefit from an advisory board's objective oversight and advice. Successful business owners go to great lengths to get such boards together, and then heed the advice given.

Where would you find advisors? Ask people you think could help you. Most likely, they'll be flattered; the worst that could happen is that they'll say no. Try talking to the following:

- Business friends
- Former employers or supervisors
- Retired business people from your industry
- Professionals
- Business professors
- Investors
- Consultants
- Experts in your field

You don't necessarily need a whole boardroom full of experts. Even one outside advisor will be invaluable. You will benefit from their experience and contacts; they benefit from involvement with a growing business. Even a personal friend who can intelligently listen to you makes a good sounding board. Business success comes from common sense and diligence. Outside advisors will help you preserve both.

A Final Word

Securing financing for your company must be planned well in advance. The more immediate your need, the less likely you are to get the best terms. Don't ask your banker to give you a loan yesterday. Planning ahead for cash flow is one of the best means for determining if and when you will need a loan. It will also help you to determine how much you need.

When you plan for a loan, remember that you will not only have to show that your industry has good potential for profit. You will also have to present a strong case for your ability to manage your company through the period of debt. Financing is serious business for both you and the investor. Take time to plan carefully for your financial needs and your company will prosper and grow accordingly.

PERSONAL WORKSHOP 19
Financing Contact List

▼ It's time for you to begin making connections with financing sources. In Chapter 4, you prepared your estimated start-up costs. This information will be useful in figuring how much money you need. But, (unless you've skipped ahead to Module Four on financials) you're still not quite ready for meeting with a financing source. Right now, you should be thinking of whom you will contact and what you will say to them. If you think you may need a bank loan, do you know any bankers? If not, who will you contact to introduce you to one? Which friends and family might you approach? This list will come together as you figure out exactly how much money you need. For now, the best thing you can do is get the ball rolling so when your numbers are ready, your contacts will be lined up.

Contact	For What Type of Financing ?	Estimated Amount of Money

URLinks
http://www.equitysecurities.com/about_financing.htm
http://www.uacpa.org/smallbiz/financing/htm
http://www.kcilink.com:443/rbff/
http://www.sbaonline.sba.gov/financing/
http://www.nvca.org/
http://www.aaeg.org/
http://www.nasbic.org/

CASE STUDY
ANGELO BANDELO

▾▾▾▾▾

*A*ngelo Bandelo worked as a mechanic for 15 years. He was considered an excellent mechanic with an instinctive ability to fix and repair cars. Angelo also could do some body and fender work, but preferred the mechanical side of the business. Angelo never had the opportunity to go to college but he did take a few night courses. His grades were barely passing because of his inability to write well, but he felt he learned a great deal from his instructors. Angelo also attended a few seminars put on by various colleges and universities in conjunction with their small business development centers, and he also attended some seminars sponsored by the Small Business Administration. After more than a year of classes and seminars, Angelo felt he was ready to enter his own business.

Although Angelo lacked sufficient capital to go into a complete mechanical operation, he found two service stations that were available. Both service stations were operating, but from what he could determine from the owners, they were not making money. One was located on the main highway of the town, which was a suburb of Louisville, Kentucky. This station had been operated by several owners, each of whom eventually went out of business. Most of the major gasoline brands were represented within a radius of about two miles. Price competition was fierce.

When Angelo checked out the distributor prices and how much the service station earned per gallon, he found that on regular gasoline they were lucky to make a penny a gallon. The profit on unleaded and premium gas was slightly higher. The owner wanted to sell the property as well as the business, but agreed that he would lease the business to Angelo for 18 months after which time Angelo could purchase the building; otherwise, the current owner would have the option to sell the property to someone else. The location included an adequate building with a small office for the owner and a storage room for parts, batteries, and other items needed to handle quick service for clients. The service section had room for three bays where cars could be fixed or where other parts could be stored.

The owner of the station wanted $25,000 for the business plus the value of the inventory on a dollar-for-dollar basis. He would rent the entire site, which included approximately three acres, for a total of $3500 per month. He wanted the first and last month's rent in advance plus one month's rent as security. The owner, Ted Marcos, said that he purchased gasoline from all sources, including the major refineries and other independent dealers who would call and have a tank available at certain prices. The problem all gas station operators experienced, according to Marcos, was having sufficient cash on hand to buy tanks of gas cheaply when they were available. As long as Angelo maintained a solid cash position, he could make a nice profit and compete; if his cash position became tight, he would suffer. Marcos added, however, that distributors would extend credit terms, which would help even though the gas tank prices would be much higher.

The second gas station was off all the main highways, back in the interior of the city. The station had no competition and was located close to a small shopping mall. The gas prices were much higher

CONTINUED ▶

because of the lack of competition, and instead of making a penny on each gallon of regular gas, the owner made five cents per gallon. However, the volume certainly didn't compare to that of the other station. The site was smaller than the first station, but attractive. There was an office, a storage room, and two bays for repair work. In this operation, the owner also had a tow truck which added to his income. Since he was located in a residential area, he had developed a steady clientele, most of whom he knew.

The owner of the second station, Ray Stokes, sold a major brand of gasoline products that he purchased from the local distributor. He had six gas pumps and could have used a few more, especially when traffic was busy. Stokes wanted $250,000 for the site and the total operation. Angelo lacked the money to buy the location outright, but Stokes suggested he go to one of the local banks to see how much of a mortgage he could get on the building. Angelo contacted a local savings and loan association, and after appraising the location the representatives said they would come up with a mortgage of $175,000 for the property, which included two acres. Angelo had personal resources of $45,000. He was still short $30,000 of the purchase price, and he would need working capital to buy gasoline, parts, and accessories for the station. Angelo's wife, Maggie, contacted all her relatives to see if they would help Angelo get started. She only managed to scrape up $25,000 from them, however, and each of the relatives demanded a share of the business. The specifics of the profit sharing were not spelled out. Angelo went back to Stokes and told him the amount he had managed to raise. Stokes finally agreed to accept a second mortgage on the building and their personal guarantee for the $30,000. He wanted the amount paid off at the rate of $1,000 a month plus interest of 15 percent per year.

Now Angelo had two locations to consider. The first station could be purchased for $25,000 plus the stock, and he could rent for $3,500 per month. It was located on the main highway and promised tremendous volume compared with the little operation inside of town. However, the highway location produced very low profits in the face of intense competition. Angelo felt that his mechanical expertise would not be as useful in that high-volume, transient situation. He opted for the second location because it faced no competition and he could build up the business in other profitable areas, including repair.

Angelo assumed the business, and the major-brand distributor gave him all the cooperation he could to get him started. Business was not too brisk, but after a while Angelo got to know his customers. It was a small area and there was a limit to sales of gasoline and oil. He also found that he was losing out on some of the cheap purchases of gas due to his franchise agreement with the refinery and the distributor. He was making a greater profit than he would have made on the main highway, but his possibilities were limited. The stockholders wanted to know when they were going to get some profits. Angelo didn't know what to tell them or how to determine what they should get. To make matters worse, the twelve owners of the business were coming to the station and charging all the gasoline purchases and repairs to their accounts. When Angelo tried to collect, they told him to take the money they owed him out of profits. He called an accountant, who also was a customer, and asked him to take care of his books on a monthly basis. Perhaps he could determine an equitable distribution in accordance with the terms of the corporation. According to his accountant, Angelo was making just enough to take care of his loans and bills. He was only keeping $800 a month to live on. When he worked as a mechanic, he could count on $25,000 a year.

Angelo tried to determine what profit centers he should develop to make additional money. Possibilities included automatic car washing; used tires; used car rental for people having their cars fixed; the purchase of used cars for parts sales in the manner of a junk yard; major repairs such as transmissions; expansion of the muffler business; body and fender work; an emergency sales package that would take care of road repairs, tows, breakdowns, and other needs; upholstery work including seat covers; and complete air conditioning repairs. Although these areas would take some additional capital, Angelo thought he could handle some of them. However, he didn't know which ones would produce the greatest return on his investment.

Maggie's relatives were not likely to invest more money. In fact, seven of them wanted to withdraw their investments, totaling $20,000. Others were willing to remain and told Angelo to pay them what he could when he could. However, those who were willing to stay felt they should be able to continue to charge their purchases at the station.

The accountant informed Angelo that the total initial investment was $70,000 ($45,000 from Angelo and $25,000 from relatives). Based on those figures, Angelo owned 64.28 percent and his relatives 35.72 percent of the business. Angelo felt he had to come up with the $20,000 because Maggie and the family were fighting bitterly and were barely on speaking terms. ▼

CASE STUDY ROUNDTABLE

▼ ▼ ▼ ▼ ▼ ▼

Angelo: How am I going to pay back the $20,000? The banks have turned me down because I'm a new business. But this accountant, who also happens to be a customer, has offered me the entire amount of $25,000 to pay off all the stockholders. Trouble is, she wants 49 percent of the business in exchange. On the other hand, she promises not to make any purchases on credit, to take care of the books without charge, and to defer distribution of profits until the business becomes profitable. Should I accept her offer? If I don't, what other options do I have?

Discussion Points

- Is it a good idea to borrow money from relatives? What mistakes did Maggie make when she borrowed the money? How could they have been corrected at the time she accepted the money?
- Should Angelo partner with the accountant/investor? What are the risks and benefits of such a source of financing?
- Use the charts of financing sources in Figures 8.1 and 8.2 to discuss the pros and cons of each source in Angelo's case. Which sources are the most likely to be available to him?
- Suppose another person approaches Angelo and wants to purchase the business. He is willing to pay off the mortgage with the bank and the balance owed the former owner, as well as give Angelo and his relatives their entire investment back. Assume that Angelo's former employer wants him back as service manager. He would pay Angelo $30,000 a year plus a percentage of profits in the service department. Do you think Angelo should sell the business and go back to his old job?

BACK TO THE TABLE
Angelo Bandelo

Later, Angelo will be back to get your advice about how he

- can increase sales and profits (Chapter 11).
- can know if his prices are right (Chapter 11).
- can most effectively market his products in his current location (Chapter 15).

▲ ▲ ▲ ▲ ▲ ▲ ▲

CHAPTER BRIEFCASE

▼ ▼ ▼ ▼ ▼ ▼

- When you are planning to open a new business (or expand your current operation), five very important questions arise relating to finance.

1. Do you **need** to borrow money?
2. If you need outside financing, **how much** do you need?
3. **When** do you need it?
4. What are the **sources** of funding available to meet your needs?
5. How much will it **cost**?

To make an intelligent decision on a timely basis, you will need to address all five of these questions. If you fail to do so, the lack of sufficient and ready capital can quickly lead to business failure.

- If you have decided that you will need additional financing, you will then need to carefully assess your needs and determine not only the amount you need, but when you will need it. Many business owners overestimate or underestimate their capital requirements or do not time their financing to the best advantage. Either can lead to serious problems. Both together can spell disaster.

- Most of the cash required to start a business is provided by the business principals themselves. If more capital is required, you will need to tap into outside sources, which fall into two broad categories:

  1. Debt financing (dollars borrowed)
  2. Equity financing (ownership dollars injected into the business)

  When you go to your bank for a loan, you are seeking **debt** money, which you will repay over a period of time at an additional cost (interest). The money you invest in your business is ordinarily **equity**: that is, money that will not be repaid to you unless you sell a portion of your ownership. Debt financing doesn't lead to sharing ownership of your business with the financier. Equity financing does.

- Bankers customarily divide loans into three general categories: (1) short-term, (2) intermediate, and (3) long-term debt. Risk, the odds against an expected happening in the future, is just one of the elements in a credit decision. From a banker's viewpoint, the higher the debt, the riskier the deal. Also, the longer the term, the riskier the deal.

- The "Six Cs" of credit used by bankers in assessing whether to approve a loan are: (1) character, (2) capacity, (3) capital, (4) credit, (5) condition, and (6) collateral.

- Your bank will match the financing with the reason for the financing. A good rule of thumb is never borrow short term to meet a long-term obligation, and never borrow long term to cover a short-term obligation.

▲▲▲▲▲▲

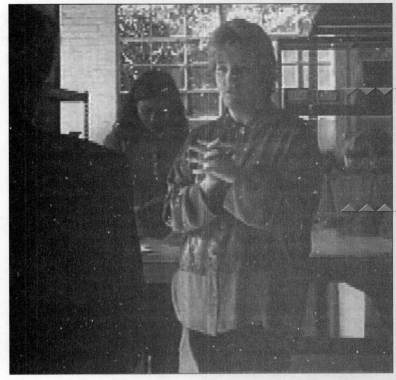

SMALL BUSINESS FINANCIALS

Laurie Snyder (Santa Monica, California)
Flap Happy
with Hattie Bryant
Creator of *Small Business 2000*

Adapted with permission from *Small Business 2000*, the series on public television.

" *L*aurie: We are very picky about who we actually give credit to. We are not afraid to say no to an order if the customer isn't willing to do things the way we need them to do it. We're extremely creative about the way we let people pay us. If someone does not have good credit, we take credit cards, we can have them prepay their order, we sometimes have them take it COD and we'll hold their check for 30 days, we have all kinds of ideas. And so that helps us get as many orders as possible.

Hattie: Than people who do similar work in a conventional way?

Laurie: Right. I made a decision about sales—my number one goal is not how much money there is in sales but how much the profit is. And in order to stay profitable, I have to very carefully pay attention to whom I sell to. If I sell to mass merchandisers, the specialty stores aren't going to want to buy our product anymore because they want something that's special and something that's unique. "

Chapter 9

RECORDKEEPING AND ACCOUNTING

▼▼▼▼▼

Q: How many kinds of accountants are there?

A: Three—Those who can count, and those who can't.

MISSION STATEMENT

In this chapter, you will

*L*EARN about the ways businesses keep vital records of their activities and track their day-to-day transactions in traditional accounting formats.

*E*XPLORE the structure, content, and application of a variety of recordkeeping forms and accounting methods.

*A*PPLY your understanding to a case study.

*P*RODUCE sample posts to help you transfer learned skills to your own business's recordkeeping needs.

KEY TERMS

accounts payable	debit	inventory
accounts receivable	double entry	journal
balance	general ledger	single entry
credit		

INTRODUCTION TO BOOKKEEPING AND ACCOUNTING

So why a joke? The quote that opens this chapter is the only intentional joke you'll find in this book. Why here? Because we know that bookkeeping and accounting are topics that many people find especially discouraging, and sometimes very daunting indeed. So we start with a joke, to sort of help you get the idea that bookkeeping and accounting are not particularly scary things.

▼▼▼▼▼▼▼▼▼▼▼▼▼▼▼▼▼▼▼▼▼▼▼▼

In fact, they're about organizing information and that's all. So when you find yourself feeling a case of numbers-phobia coming on, remember the joke: accounting is all about counting, bookkeeping is all about being organized, and you can do those two things easily. You've been counting since *Sesame Street*, and if you weren't able to get things organized, you wouldn't have gotten this far.

In this chapter you will learn about the general records that are used to track the daily transactions of your business. You will also be introduced to single- and double-entry accounting and you will learn how to develop a chart of accounts that is customized to your business.

The most common general records are:

- General journal
- Independent contractor record
- General ledger
- Payroll records
- Revenue and expense journal
- Mileage log
- Petty cash record
- Travel
- Inventory records
- Entertainment records
- Fixed assets log
- Customer records
- Accounts receivable
- Business checkbook
- Accounts payable

Keep your records as simple as possible. You will need to think about all the things that are relevant to your business and then determine the simplest way to have the information at your fingertips. We will discuss a variety of standard formats, but it is not absolutely essential that you use them exactly as they are presented here. Rather, you should feel free to customize them to meet your business's particular needs. There is no "one right way" to keep records: you should use whatever tools and methods let you keep track of useful information in an efficient, complete, and reliable way. The key here is organization!

USING STANDARD FORMATS

All of your records will be used to develop your financial statements. For this reason, it will be important to use forms that have been developed using an accepted format. The forms discussed in this section will provide you with records that are easy to use and interpret by you and anyone else who has occasion to retrieve information pertaining to your business. Remember, though, that it's important that you make these formats your own: use them in ways that will be most effective for you.

Single- and Double-Entry Systems

There are two basic bookkeeping methods:

1. Single entry
2. Double entry

In the past, only double-entry accounting was thought to be proper for businesses. However, it is now generally recognized that a single-entry system will adequately serve most smaller businesses. As the business grows and becomes more complex, it may then become more effective to move into double-entry accounting.

Single entry. This is a term referring to a recordkeeping system which uses only income and expense accounts. Its main requirement is a revenue and expense journal which you maintain on a daily basis for recording receipts and expenditures. You will also need to keep general records in which you record petty cash, fixed assets, accounts payable and receivable, inventory, mileage, travel and entertainment, and customer information. Single-entry recordkeeping is the easier of the two systems to understand and maintain. Even so, it can still be extremely effective and 100 percent verifiable.

Double entry. This is a bookkeeping and accounting method by which every transaction is recorded twice. (That's why it's called "double entry," but you probably figured that out already.) This method is based on the idea that every transaction has two sides. A sale, for example, is both a delivery of goods and a receipt of payment. Every delivery of goods is a deduction from inventory and an addition to income. On your balance sheet, the delivery of goods to your customer decreases your inventory and would be recorded as a credit (reduction of assets), while the payment to you for the goods purchased from you would be counted as a debit (increase of assets). You should note that the words debit and credit do not have the usual non-accounting connotation in this application.

The two halves of the double entry always have to be equal. They need to **balance**. Many small businesses use only the single-entry system, while larger businesses, especially partnerships and corporations, will need to set up their accounting with the double-entry system. A clear understanding of the double-entry system is necessary before using this method. A thorough study may be made using resources in your local library—or you may wish to have your accountant set it up for you.

In the following section, we will introduce some basic information on double-entry accounting. Unless your business is large or complex, you will not need to set up this type of system. Still, it's not a bad idea to know what it is you're not doing, and why you're not doing it. Later, as your business grows, you can add these elements. Talk to your accountant if you are in doubt.

Single-entry business note: You will not use a general journal or general ledger for single-entry recordkeeping. However, you may wish to familiarize yourself with the double-entry concept and then skip ahead to the section later in this chapter discussing a revenue and expense journal, where you will begin setting up your own recordkeeping.

DOUBLE-ENTRY ACCOUNTING

If you are a larger, more complex business and need double-entry accounting, the next few pages will give you a basic understanding and you can work with your accountant to tailor a system for your business.

Flow of Data in Double-Entry Accounting

After a transaction is completed, the initial record of that transaction, or of a group of similar transactions, is evidenced by a business document—a sales ticket, a check stub, or a cash register tape, for instance. On the basis of the evidence provided by that document, transactions are then entered in chronological order in the general journal. The amounts of the debits and the credits in the journal are then transferred to the accounts in the ledger. The flow of data from transaction to ledger may be diagrammed as follows:

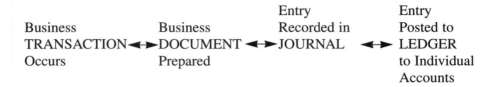

Numbering of Accounts

Double-entry accounting requires the numbering of accounts. These account numbers are used when recording transactions in the general journal and posting them to individual general ledger accounts. Two financial statements, the balance sheet and income statement, are compiled from information derived from the accounts in the general ledger. If you are using a double-entry system, it will be necessary for you to understand how to develop a *chart of accounts*.

Major Divisions of a Chart of Accounts

All accounts in the general ledger are separated into the following major divisions:

- Assets
- Liabilities
- Capital
- Revenue
- Expenses

Each division contains its own individual accounts that must be numbered. Although accounts in the ledger may be numbered consecutively like the pages of a book, the flexible system of indexing as described in the next section is preferable.

Setting Up a Chart of Accounts

To illustrate this concept, Figure 9.1 is a sample chart of accounts for a fictitious business. Each account has three digits. The first digit indicates the *major division of the ledger in which the account is placed*. Here is a "key" to the account numbers:

- 1 = assets
- 2 = liabilities
- 3 = capital
- 4 = revenues
- 5 = expenses

FIGURE
9.1   **Chart of Accounts for a Fictitious Business**

Balance Sheet Accounts

1. ASSETS

101 Cash

102 Accounts Receivable

104 Supplies

105 Prepaid Rent

108 Production Equipment

109 Accumulated Depreciation

2. LIABILITIES

201 Accounts Payable

202 Salaries Payable

3. CAPITAL

301 John Jones, Capital

302 John Jones, Drawing

303 Income Summary

Income Statement Accounts

4. REVENUES

401 Sales

402 Services Income

405 Interest Income

5. EXPENSES

501 Rent Expense

504 Supplies Expense

505 Salary Expense

509 Depreciation Expense

514 Misc. Expense

The second and third digits indicate the *position of the account within its division*. For example, in Figure 9.1, in account number 105 (prepaid rent), the 1 indicates that prepaid rent is an asset account and the 5 indicates that it is in the fifth position within that division. A numbering system of this type has the advantage of permitting the later insertion of new accounts into their proper sequence without disturbing other account numbers. Using the three-digit system accommodates up to 99 separate accounts under each division. For a large enterprise with a number of departments or branches, it is not unusual for each account number to have four or more digits.

Reminder to small businesses using single-entry accounting: The next two records, general journal and general ledger, are only for businesses that are going to set up double-entry accounting. Those using single-entry accounting, which will probably be most of you, will want to skip to the revenue and expense journal to begin setting up your recordkeeping system.

General Journal

As its name implies, the general journal is used to record all the types of transactions that a business has. The transactions are listed in chronological order—that is, in the order they occur. Each entry affects two accounts, one in which a debit is entered and one in which its corresponding credit is entered.

Recording transactions in the general journal requires a clear understanding of the terms "debit" and "credit." In Figure 9.1 we set up five categories. Increases and decreases in each of these accounts are represented by debits or credits as follows:

Asset (100) and Expense (500) Accounts
   Increases = debits
   Decreases = credits
Liability (200), Capital (300), and Revenue (400) Accounts
   Increases = credits
   Decreases = debits

To help you understand how transactions are recorded in the general journal, Figure 9.2 is a sample general journal page with entries for five transactions of a fictitious business. Each entry provides a written analysis of one transaction, showing which accounts and what amounts should be debited and credited. It is also very important to include the description for each entry.

On July 31st, ABC Company had the following five transactions:

1. Received payment for consulting, $1,900 in cash.
2   Sold inventory for $1,200 on credit.
3. Paid $154 to vendor on credit account.
4. Paid rent for August in amount of $725.
5. John Jones took an owner draw of $800.

General Ledger

We have just seen how transactions are recorded in the general journal. The next step in the flow of accounting data for double-entry accounting is to transfer or post these same transactions to individual accounts in the general ledger.

Using the chart of accounts developed for your business, each account will be kept on a printed form that has a heading and several columns. The forms used for the accounts are on separate sheets in a book or binder and together make up what is referred to as the general ledger. This is the master reference file for the accounting system because it provides a permanent, classified record of every financial aspect of the business's operations.

Several different forms are available for general ledger accounts. One of the best is the *balance ledger form*, because the balance of an account is always recorded after each entry is posted. This is the format that you see on the sample accounts in Figure 9.3.

FIGURE
9.2

Sample General Journal Page

General Journal   **Page 6**

Date	Description of Entry	Post Ref.	Debit	Credit
7/31	Cash	101	$1,900.00	
	Services	402		$1,900.00
	Consulting for J. Smith Co. paid with			
	their check no. 2546. My invoice 4302.			
7/31	Accounts Receivable	102	$1,200.00	
	Sales	401		$1,200.00
	Sold 100 books at 40% discount, on			
	credit, Net 90 to Norman Wholesale			
	Books. Invoice 4303			
7/31	Accounts Payable	201	$154.00	
	Cash	101		$154.00
	Paid Unique Office Supply, Invoice Nos.			
	3207 & 3541, Check 1294			
7/31	Rent Expense	501	$725.00	
	Cash	101		$725.00
	Paid Aug. rent to J.R. Properties			
	Check 1295			
7/31	John Johns, Drawing	302	$800.00	
	Cash	101		$800.00
	Owner draw. Check 1296			

FIGURE 9.3 **Sample General Ledger Accounts**

Here ABC Company's July 31st transactions are posted from the general journal (Figure 9.2) to individual accounts in the general ledger.

Account   Cash   Account No. 101

Date	Description of Entry	Post Ref.	Debit	Credit	Balance	DR. CR.
7/31	(1. Consulted for cash)	J6	$1,900.00		$1,900.00	DR
7/31	(3. Paid vendor on credit acct.)	J6		$154.00	$1,746.00	DR
7/31	(4. Paid August rent)	J6		$725.00	$1,021.00	DR
7/31	(5. John Jones, Owner Draw)	J6		$800.00	$221.00	DR

Account   John Johns Drawing   Account No. 302

Date	Description of Entry	Post Ref.	Debit	Credit	Balance	DR. CR.
7/31	(5. John Jones/Owner draw)	J6	$800.00		$800.00	DR

Account   Sales   Account No. 401

Date	Description of Entry	Post Ref.	Debit	Credit	Balance	DR. CR.
7/31	(2. Sold inventory for credit)	J6		$1,200.00	$1,200.00	CR

Account   Accounts Receivable   Account No. 102

Date	Description of Entry	Post Ref.	Debit	Credit	Balance	DR. CR.
7/31	(2. Sold inventory on credit)	J6	$1,200.00		$1,200.00	DR

Account   Services Income   Account No. 402

Date	Description of Entry	Post Ref.	Debit	Credit	Balance	DR. CR.
7/31	(1. Consulted for cash)	J6		$1,900.00	$1,900.00	CR

Account   Accounts Payable   Account No. 201

Date	Description of Entry	Post Ref.	Debit	Credit	Balance	DR. CR.
7/31	(3. Paid vendor on account)	J6	$154.00		$154.00	DR

Account   Rent Expense   Account No. 501

Date	Description of Entry	Post Ref.	Debit	Credit	Balance	DR. CR.
7/31	(4. Paid August rent)	J6	$725.00		$725.00	DR

Note: Descriptions are left blank on routine entries. The column is for special notations. We have used them to reference the transactions of ABC Company in order to help you see the flow of information from the transactions to the general journal and then to the ledger accounts. If your entries are posted correctly, the total debit and credit balances will always be equal.

Posting Entries from the General Journal to the General Ledger

The transfer of information data from the general journal to the general ledger is known as "posting." The procedure used in posting data from a general journal entry is to start with the first account listed in the entry—the account to be debited.

After the debit has been posted, you will need to post the corresponding credit for the same transaction to its appropriate ledger account. Locate the necessary account; the first transaction for ABC Company requires posting a debit to "Cash" (101) and a credit to "Service Income" (402). To post the credit, you will follow the same steps as posting the debit amount. Once this work is done, the posting process for the transaction is complete and the journal entry includes the numbers of the two ledger accounts that were posted.

Writing the journal page number in each ledger account and the ledger account number in the journal indicates that the entry has been posted and ensures against posting the same entry twice or not posting it at all. This use of referencing journal page numbers in the ledger accounts and ledger accounts numbers in the journal also provides a great cross-reference when you need to trace an entry or verify a transaction.

Trial Balance

The general ledger accounts are arranged beginning with asset accounts and ending with expense accounts. At the end of an accounting period, you or your accountant will list all of the balances of the general ledger accounts on a trial balance form. The debit and credit balances are added separately. When the Debit and Credit columns of the trial balance are equal, the accountant knows that the financial records are in balance and that a debit has been recorded for every credit.

Income Statement and Balance Sheet

When the trial balance shows that the general ledger is in balance, you or your accountant are ready to prepare the financial statements for the period. The accounts from the trial balance are adjusted for such items as expired prepaid expenses and depreciation, and the balances are transferred to another worksheet, the *adjusted trial balance form*. This form contains separate sections for adjusted trial balance, income statement, and balance sheet with a debit column and a credit column for each.

SINGLE-ENTRY ACCOUNTING

If you read the information on double-entry accounting, you learned that a business transaction occurs accompanied by some sort of document. Then the transaction is recorded in the general journal and the journal entry is posted to an individual general ledger account. This requires a thorough understanding of the concept of posting debits and credits, which is confusing at best to most business owners. In single-entry accounting, you will not need to develop a numbered chart of accounts. However, you should remember that there are five major divisions of transactions:

1. Assets
2. Liabilities

PERSONAL WORKSHOP 20
Practicing the Posting Process

▼ The following exercise will take you through the process of posting ABC Company's five transactions from the general journal to the general ledger.

To help you better understand the transfer of information from the general journal to the individual ledger accounts, we will follow the same five transactions that were recorded in the general journal in Figure 9.2.

Follow the posting of each of the five transactions through both its debit and credit entries to the corresponding individual accounts in the general ledger.

▼ Locate the corresponding accounts for each transaction in the general ledger and follow these six steps:

1. Enter transaction date in the Date column.

2. Describe the transaction being recorded.

3. Record the number of the journal page in the Posting Reference column. ("J6" is used for all the entries in the ledger since all are from page 6 of the Journal.)

4. Record the debit amount in the Debit column.

5. The balance of the account is computed and recorded in the Balance column.

6. In the last column enter the abbreviation "DR" (debit) or "CR" (credit) to indicate the type of balance.

7. Record the number of the ledger account (101 for "Cash") in the Posting Reference column of the General Journal.

After the debit has been posted for a transaction, post the corresponding credit for the same transaction to its appropriate ledger account. Locate the necessary account (the first transaction for ABC Company requires posting a debit to "Cash" (101) and a credit to "Service Income" (402)). To post the credit, follow the same steps as posting the debit amount.

General Journal

General Journal **Page 6**

Date	Description of Entry	Post Ref.	Debit	Credit

General Ledger Account

Account _____   **Account No.** _____

Date	Description of Entry	Post Ref.	Debit	Credit	Balance	DR. CR.

3. Capital
4. Revenues
5. Expenses

You will develop a better understanding of these divisions as you progress through the general records.

The beauty of single-entry recordkeeping is that it reduces the posting process to simply entering revenues and expenses on a single form and requires no formal accounting education. You are still required to keep those general records pertinent to your business (such as petty cash, accounts receivable and payable, fixed assets, travel and entertainment, inventory), but in a very simple and logical way that will still provide for perfect retrieval of needed tax and business analysis information.

With this method, the flow of accounting data will be as follows:

		Entry
Business	Business	Recorded in
TRANSACTION◄─►DOCUMENT ◄─►REVENUE & EXPENSE JOURNAL

Now you are ready to set up your recordkeeping system. We will take you one step at a time through the entire process. Begin by setting up a revenue and expense journal.

Revenue and Expense Journal

A revenue and expense journal is used to record the transactions of a business. They are recorded as revenues (income) and expenses. **Revenues** are the transactions for which monies are received. Equity deposits and loan funds are not revenues. **Expenses** are all transactions for which monies are paid out. Owner draws and principal payments on loans are not included.

To make your accounting more effective, you will need to have enough columns in the revenue and expense journal to cover major categories of income and expenses (or create two separate forms—one for revenues and one for expenses). If you have done your homework and figured out the categories of variable and fixed expenses that are common to your business, these divisions will serve as headings in your journal. Usually, a 12-column journal will suffice for most small businesses, but feel free to use more or less, as long as your report is clear and easy to interpret.

Avoiding Errors

The use of a revenue and expense journal is part of single-entry recordkeeping. However, each entry is recorded twice (not to be confused with posting debits and credits). If you will look at the sample form in Figure 9.4, the first two columns are headed "Revenue" and "Expense." Every transaction is entered in one of these two columns. The next groups of three and five columns are breakdowns of revenues and expenses. The entry is first recorded as a revenue or expense and then entered in its corresponding breakdown column. For example, an advertising expense of $100 would be entered under the heading "Expense" and also under the expense breakdown heading "Advertising." When the columns are totaled, the amount under "Expense" will equal

FIGURE
9.4

Revenue and Expense Journal

Check Number	Date	Transaction	Revenue	Expense	Sales	Sales Tax	Services	Inventory Purch.	Advert.	Freight	Office Supplies	Misc.
						Revenues					**Expenses**	
		Balance Forward	1,826.00	835.00	1,218.00	98.00	510.00	295.00	245.00	150.00	83.50	61.50
234	7/13	J.J. Advertising		450.00					450.00			
235	7/13	T & E Products		380.00				380.00				
236	7/16	Regal Stationers		92.50							92.50	
***	7/17	Deposit:	1,232.00									
		1. Sales (Taxable)			400.00	32.00						
		2. Sales (O.S.)			165.00	O.S.						
		3. Sales (Resale)			370.00	Resale						
		4. Services					265.00					
OK Bank	7/19	Bank Charges		23.40								(bank chg.) 23.40
237	7/19	Petty Cash Deposit		100.00								(petty cash) 100.00
		Totals	3,058.00	1,880.90	2,153.00	130.00	775.00	675.00	695.00	150.00	176.00	184.90

the sum of all expense breakdown columns. The "Revenue" total will equal the sum of all revenue breakdown columns. This serves as a check for accuracy and will save hours of searching your records for errors when attempting to balance your books.

Headings in the Revenue and Expense Journal

The column headings in the revenue and expense journal for any business will follow the same format. The first five columns headings are:

1. Check Number
2. Date
3. Transaction
4. Revenue
5. Expense

Remaining columns are used for individual categories of revenue and expense for which you most frequently write checks or receive income. The **revenue breakdown** columns will be divided by source (for instance, as authors and speakers, we have columns headed Book Sales, Software Sales, Sales Tax, and Seminar Fees). The **expense breakdown** columns reflect the categories for which you most frequently write checks (for instance, Inventory Purchases, Freight, Advertising, Office Supplies, and Vehicle Expenses).

The headings for the individual revenue and expense columns will vary from business to business. Every business is different and it may take some time to determine the categories that will best reflect the transactions of your particular venture. If you are coordinating your recordkeeping with a tax accountant, you might ask that person to help you develop your headings. The best rule of thumb is to devote a column to each type of expense for which you frequently write a check.

Miscellaneous Column

The last column in any revenue and expense journal should be Miscellaneous. This column serves as a catchall for any expense that does not fall under one of the main headings.

Say you write only one check every six months, in the amount of $500, for insurance. Record that transaction first under Expense and then under Miscellaneous with an explanation either under the Transaction column or in parentheses next to the amount in the Miscellaneous column, such as "$500 (insurance)." The explanation is a must. This will allow you to group infrequent expenses under one column and still be able to allocate them to the proper expense categories at the end of the month when you do a profit and loss (or income) statement.

Totals

Each column should be totaled at the bottom of each journal page. Remember to check accuracy. The sum of all revenue breakdown columns should equal the sum of the column headed Revenue and the sum of all expense breakdown columns should equal the sum of the column headed Expense. All totals are then transferred to the top of the next page and you continue to add them until you have completed a month. At the end of the month, the last page is totaled and checked. The breakdown revenue and expense totals are transferred to your profit and loss statement and a new month begins with a clean page and zero balances.

PETTY CASH RECORD

Petty cash refers to all the small business purchases made with cash or personal funds instead of a business check. These purchases may account for several thousand dollars by the end of the year. Failure to account for them can result in a false picture of your business and additional cost in income taxes. It is imperative that you keep an accurate record of all petty cash expenditures, that you have receipts on file, and that you record them in a manner that will enable you to categorize these expenses at the end of an accounting period.

FIRST PERSON

Carla S., Nashville, Tennessee: In my mind, the biggest purpose of keeping a formal accounting of your petty cash transactions is to provide information that will classify those expenses for income tax retrieval (and, sure, for general business analysis, too). When I worked at the IRS field office, any time we saw large miscellaneous deductions we were very suspicious. So though it may seem like a hassle, failing to be detailed in your petty cash accounting might very well single your return out for an IRS audit. While meticulous records are no guarantee against an audit, they certainly make it less painful if it happens.

Where Do Petty Cash Funds Come From?

In order to transfer cash into the petty cash fund, you must first draw a check and expense it to petty cash in the revenue and expense journal. That same amount is entered in the petty cash record as a deposit. When cash purchases are made, they are entered in the petty cash record under Expenses. When the balance gets low, another check is drawn to rebuild the fund. At the end of the tax year, you can let the balance run as a negative, write a final check in that amount and deposit it to petty cash to zero out the fund. The end result will be that you will have deposited an amount that is exactly equal to your petty cash expenditures for the year.

Petty Cash Format

Dividing your petty cash record into the following six categories will provide for individual purchases to be summarized, combined with expenses on the revenue and expense journal, and entered on the profit and loss statement.

1. Date of Transaction
2. Paid to Whom

FIGURE 9.5 **Sample Petty Cash Record**

Petty Cash   **Page 6**

Date	Paid to Whom	Expense Account Debited	Deposit	Amount of Expense	Balance
	Balance Forward →				$10.00
7/19	**Deposit (Check 237)		$100.00		$110.00
7/20	ACE Hardware	Maintenance		$12.36	$97.64
7/23	Regal Stationers	Office supplies		$20.00	$77.64
7/23	U.S. Postmaster	Postage		$19.80	$57.84
7/31	The Steak House	Meals		$63.75	($5.91)
8/1	**Deposit (Check 267)		$100.00		$94.09

Toward the end of the year, you can let the petty cash account run a minus balance. On December 31st, a check is written for the balance and the account is zeroed out.

The amount of cash spent during the year will be exactly equal to the amount deposited into the petty cash account from your checking account.

Note: 1. Save all receipts for cash purchases.
2. Exchange receipt for cash from petty cash drawer.
3. Use receipts to record expenses on petty cash form.
4. File receipts. You may need them for verification.
5. Be sure to record petty cash deposits.

3. Expense Account Debited
4. Deposit
5. Amount of Expense
6. Balance

In the sample petty cash record in Figure 9.5 you will see how deposits and expenses are recorded. If a cash expense also needs to be entered in another record (i.e., Inventory or Fixed Assets), do so at the same time to keep the record current and eliminate omissions.

FIRST PERSON

Ben K., Spokane, Washington: I think they call it the "KISS" accounting system: Keep It Simple, Stupid! I know it works for me. Your bookkeeping system should be simple enough for you or, even better, for one of your employees to keep up to date on a daily basis. Then you can do your weekly, monthly, quarterly, and yearly summaries more easily. Your checkbook and the cash register tapes are part of your bookkeeping system, too. But mostly, your method of bookkeeping should be suited to your specific needs.

INVENTORY RECORDS

The term *inventory* is used to designate merchandise held for sale in the normal course of business, and materials used in the process of production or held for such use.
Common kinds of inventory include:

- Merchandise or stock in trade
- Raw materials
- Work in process
- Finished products
- Supplies (that become a part of a product intended for sale)

The recording of inventories is used both as an internal control and as a means of retrieving information required for the computation of income tax. Inventory control in a retail business can help you to see such things as turnover time, high and low selling periods, and changes in buying trends. Periodic examinations of your inventory and its general flow may be the meat of your existence.

FIRST PERSON

Hugh L., Minneapolis, Minnesota: I know about the importance of inventory control—I nearly lost my restaurant because I didn't have it! Turned out some of my employees were carrying groceries out the back door at closing time, so even though the restaurant had plenty of business, at the end of the year our profits just didn't add up to much. I was pretty confused and disappointed, and just about closed the place. But I had my accountant carefully examine my records, and she found that I hadn't inventoried my stock properly. I set up a strict inventory control system, and that pretty much closed down the free food pantry. This year, the increase in profit saved the business.

Format for Inventory Records

Basic inventory records must contain information in the following five categories to be effective:

1. Date purchased
2. Item purchased (include stock number)
3. Purchase price (cost)
4. Date sold
5. Sale price

If your inventory is at all sizable, you will want some sort of point-of-sale (POS) inventory system. That means that when a product walks out the door, it's automatically deleted from inventory. POS systems are usually electronic and connected right to the cash registers. However, you can keep POS data in handwritten form if you keep it current and do it regularly.

On any given day, you need to know how long you have had each item, which items are selling repeatedly, and what time periods require the stocking of more inventory. Keep in mind that all businesses differ. Compile your inventory according to your specific needs. Be sure that it is divided in such a way as to provide quick reference. You can sort your inventory by using separate records for each company from which you make purchases. Another method might be to separate records by type of item. The important thing is to make your inventory work for you.

Valuing Inventory

To arrive at a dollar amount for your inventory, you will need a method for identifying and a basis for valuing the items in your inventory. Inventory valuation must clearly show income, and for that reason, you must use this same inventory practice from year to year.

Specific identification method. In some businesses, it is possible to keep track of inventory and identify the cost of each inventoried item by matching the item with its cost of acquisition. In other words, there is specific identification of merchandise and you can determine the exact cost of what is sold. There is no question as to which items remain in the inventory. Merchants who deal with items having a large unit cost or one-of-a-kind items may choose to keep track of inventory by this method. For instance, if you are an art dealer, you should have a pretty good idea which items are in your warehouse at any particular time.

FIFO and LIFO. For those businesses dealing with a large quantity of similar items, there must be a method for deciding which items are sold and which remain in inventory. In a FIFO (first in, first out) system, you assume that the items you purchased or produced first are the first sold. This method most closely parallels the actual flow of inventory. Most merchants will attempt to sell their oldest inventory items first and hopefully have the last items produced bought in current inventory. A FIFO system is particularly important for businesses dealing in perishable items.

LIFO (last in, first out), on the other hand, is a method that assumes that the items of inventory that you purchased or produced most recently are the first you sell. Specific IRS regulations apply to this method, and you must consult the tax rules to see if your business qualifies before electing this method.

The FIFO and LIFO methods produce different results in income depending on the trend of price levels of inventory items. In a period of rising prices, valuing your inventory by the LIFO method will result in a higher reported cost of goods sold, a lower closing inventory, and a lower reported net income. This is because it is assumed that you sold goods purchased at the higher price. Conversely, in a period of falling prices, the LIFO method would result in a lower reported cost of goods sold, a higher closing inventory, and a higher reported net income than the FIFO method.

Cost or market, whichever is lower. At inventory time, if your merchandise cannot be sold through usual trade channels for a price that is above its original cost, the current market price is determined and compared to your accepted costing method (FIFO, LIFO, or Specific Identification). The lower figure, either *cost* or *market,* is selected. This is especially useful for outdated inventory. If you use this method you must value each item in the inventory.

Whichever method you use, you must use it consistently!

The sample inventory record in Figure 9.6 uses the specific identification method of taking inventory. Remember, it is for inventory of products that differ from each other and can be individually accounted for as to purchase date, description, and cost. The sample inventory record in Figure 9.7 is for non-identifiable inventory.

ACCOUNTS RECEIVABLE

An accounts receivable record is used to keep track of money owed to your business as a result of extending credit to a customer who purchases your products or services. Some businesses deal in cash transactions only. In other words, the product or service is paid for at the time of the sale. If this is the case in your business, you will not need accounts receivable records. However, if you do extend credit, the amount owed to you by your credit customers will have to be collected in a timely manner to provide you with the cash needed for day-to-day operations. It will be essential to have detailed information about your transactions and to always know the balance owed to you for each invoice. This can be accomplished by setting up a separate accounts receivable record for each customer.

Format

In order to ensure that you have all the information needed to verify that customers are paying balances on time and that they are within credit limits, the form used will need to include these eight categories:

FIGURE 9.6 Sample Inventory Record: Identifiable Stock

Wholesaler: All Time Clock Company   Page 1

Purch. Date	Inventory Purchased		Purchase Price	Date Sold	Sale Price	Name of Buyer (opt)
	Stock #	Description				
9/23	25-72-D	Oak Gallery (25")	$352.00			
11/19	24-37-A	Desk Alarm (1)	$18.00	12/08	$28.50	N/A
		(2)	$18.00			
		(3)	$18.00			
2/21	26-18-C	"The Shelby" GF	$1,420.00	4/20	$1,865.00	J. Kirkland
3/19	25-67-D	Mahog. Regulator	$247.00			
5/4	26-18-C	"The Shelby" GF	$1,420.00			

Note: 1. Use this record for keeping track of identifiable goods purchased for resale. If your inventory is very large, it may be necessary to use some sort of **point-of-sale** inventory system.

2. Each page should deal with either (1) purchases in one category or (2) goods purchased from one wholesaler.

3. Use the name of the wholesaler or the category of the purchase as the heading.

FIGURE
9.7 **Sample Inventory Record: Non-Identifiable Stock**

Department/Category: Ski Hats/Headwear

Production or Purchase Date	Inventory Purchased or Manufactured		Number of Units	Unit Cost	Value on Date of Inventory	
	Stock #	Description			Value (Unit cost x Units on hand)	Date
1999						
2/5	07-43	Knitted Headbands	5,000	$2.50	0	1/99
3/25	19-12	Face Masks	3,000	$5.12	$450.80	1/99
4/14	19-10	Hat/Mask Combo	1,200	$7.00	$3,514.00	1/99
4/18	19-09	Hats, Multi-Colored	10,500	$4.00	$5,440.00	1/99
8/31	19-07	Goretex (w/bill)	10,000	$8.41	$50,460.00	1/99
Begin 2000						
2/1	19-12	Face Masks	2,500	$4.80		
2/28	19-09	Hats, Multi-Colored	10,300	$4.00		

Note: 1. This record is used for inventory of like items that are purchased or manufactured in bulk. It is a good idea to divide your records by department, category, or manufacturer.

2. Inventory these items by a physical count or by computer records. A physical inventory is required at the close of your tax year.

3. Inventory is valued according to rules that apply for **FIFO** or **LIFO**. Read the information in your tax guide carefully before determining inventory value. The selected method must be used consistently.

1. Invoice Date. This will tell you the date the transaction took place and enable you to age the invoice.
2. Invoice Number. Invoices are numbered and can be filed in order. If you need to refer to the invoice, the number makes it easy to retrieve.
3. Invoice Amount. This tells how much the customer owes for each invoice.
4. Terms. This details the time period allowed until the invoice is due; it also states if a discount applies (i.e., Net 30/2% Net 10 means the invoice is due in 30 days, but a 2 percent discount will be allowed if payment is made in 10 days).
5. Date Paid. This shows when the invoice was paid.
6. Amount Paid. This states whether the customer made a partial payment or paid the invoice in full.
7. Invoice Balance. This details what portion of the invoice is not paid.
8. Header Information. The customer's name, address, and phone number will tell you where to send statements and how to make contact.

At the end of a predetermined billing period, each open account will be sent a statement showing its invoice number, amounts, balance due, and preferably age of balances (over 30, 60, and 90 days). The statement should also include terms of payment. When the payment is received, it is recorded on the accounts receivable record. The total of all the outstanding accounts receivable balances is transferred to current assets when preparing a balance sheet for your business.

The form in Figure 9.8 illustrates a sample accounts receivable record.

ACCOUNTS PAYABLE

Those debts owed by your company to your creditors for goods purchased or services rendered fall into accounts payable. Having open account credit will allow your company to conduct more extensive operations and use your financial resources more effectively. If you are going to have a good credit record, the payment of these invoices must be timely and you will need an efficient system for keeping track of what you owe and when it should be paid. When your accounts payable are not numerous and you do not accumulate unpaid invoices by partial payments, you may wish to eliminate accounts payable records and use an accordion file divided into the days of the month. Invoices Payable may be directly filed under the date on which they should be paid, taking into account discounts available for early payment.

Format

If your accounts payable are stretched over a longer period, you will need to keep separate records for the creditors with whom you do business. The form used will need to include these eight categories:

1. Invoice Date. This will tell you when the transaction took place.
2. Invoice Number. If you need to refer to the actual invoice, the number makes it easy to retrieve. File unpaid invoices behind the record.

FIGURE
9.8 **Accounts Receivable Record**

Customer: T & E Movers

Address: 222 Handy Road

City/State/Zip: Winnemucca, NV 89502

Tel. No.: (702) 843-2222　　　　　　　　　　**Account No.:** 1016

Invoice Date	Invoice Number	Invoice Amount	Terms	Date Paid	Amount Paid	Invoice Balance
6/9	3528	$247.00	Net 30	7/2	$247.00	$0.00
7/14	4126	$340.00	Net 30	8/15	$340.00	$0.00
9/26	5476	$192.00	N30/2%10	10/2	$188.16	$0.00
10/3	5783	$211.00	N30/2%10	11/1	$109.00	$102.00
10/12	6074	$386.00	N30/2%10			$386.00

3. Invoice Amount. This tells the amount of the transaction.
4. Terms. This details the time period allowed until invoice is due; it also states if a discount applies (i.e., Net 30/2% Net 10 means the invoice is due in 30 days, but a 2 percent discount will be allowed if payment is made in 10 days).
5. Date Paid. This shows when you paid the invoice.
6. Amount Paid. This states whether you made a partial payment or paid the invoice in full.
7. Invoice Balance. This details what portion of the invoice is not paid.
8. Header Information. The creditor's name, address, and phone number will tell you where to send payments and how to make contact.

You will be billed regularly for the balance of your account, but the individual records will help you to know at a glance where you stand at any given time. They should be reviewed monthly and an attempt should be made to satisfy all your creditors. After the invoice is paid in full and the payment is recorded, mark the invoice paid and file with the rest of your receipts. At the end of your accounting period, the total of your accounts payable should be transferred to the current liabilities portion of the balance sheet.

Figure 9.9 illustrates a sample accounts payable record.

TRANSPORTATION, ENTERTAINMENT AND TRAVEL EXPENSES

If you plan to take advantage of legitimate income tax deductions available for certain transportation, entertainment, and travel expenses incurred as part of your business, you will have to prove your deductions with adequate records that will support your claim. Records required should be kept in an account book, diary, statement of expense, or similar record. *It is important that these expenses be recorded as they occur.* It is difficult to remember them accurately after the fact.

Transportation Expenses

These are the ordinary and necessary expenses of getting from one workplace to another in the course of your business (when you are not traveling away from home). They do include the cost of transportation by air, rail, bus, taxi, and the cost of driving and maintaining your car. They do not include transportation expenses between your home and your main or regular place of work, parking fees at your place of business, or expenses for personal use of your car.

Car Expenses

If you use your car for business purposes, you may be able to deduct car expenses. You generally can use one of these two methods to figure these expenses.

1. Actual expense. Includes all expenses for gas, oil, tolls, parking, lease or rental fees, depreciation, repairs, licenses, and insurance.

FIGURE
9.9   Accounts Payable Record

Customer: ___Charles Mfg.___

Address: ___1111 E. Trenton Road___

City/State/Zip: ___Tarington, NH 03928___

Tel. No.: ___(603) 827-5001___   **Account No.:** ___2072___

Invoice Date	Invoice Number	Invoice Amount	Terms	Date Paid	Amount Paid	Invoice Balance
2/16	10562	$1,500.00	Net 15	2/24	$1,500.00	$0.00
2/25	11473	$870.00	Net 30	2/18	$870.00	$0.00
3/17	12231	$3,200.00	N30/2%10	3/25	$3,136.00	$0.00
7/2	18420	$2,400.00	N30/2%10	8/1	$1,800.00	$600.00
8/15	19534	$2,600.00	N30/2%10			$2,600.00

2. Standard mileage rate. Instead of figuring actual expenses, you may choose to use the standard mileage rate, which means that you will receive a deduction of a specific amount of money per mile of business use of your car.

You are required to record business miles traveled during the year in a mileage log. A sample mileage log is shown in Figure 9.10.

Meals and Entertainment Expenses

You may be able to deduct business-related entertainment expenses you have incurred while entertaining a client, customer, or employee. The expense must be *ordinary* (common and accepted in your field of business) and *necessary* (helpful and appropriate for your business, but not necessarily indispensable). In addition, you must be able to show that these expenses are

- directly related to the active conduct of your trade or business, or
- associated with the active conduct of your trade or business.

Entertainment includes any activity generally considered to provide entertainment, amusement, or recreation. For example, entertaining business associates at night clubs; social, athletic, or sporting clubs; theaters; sporting events; on yachts; or on hunting, fishing, or vacation trips. Entertainment also may include satisfying personal, living, or family needs of individuals, such as providing food, a hotel suite, or a car to business customers or their families.

Entertainment does not include supper money you give your employees, a hotel room you keep for your employees while on business travel, or a car used in your business. However, if you provide the use of a hotel suite or a car to your employee who is on vacation, this is entertainment of the employee.

You may deduct only 50 percent of business-related meals and entertainment expenses. You must record these expenses with date, place of entertainment, business purpose, the name of the person entertained, and the amount spent.

Figure 9.11 illustrates a sample entertainment expense record.

Travel Expenses

Deductible travel expenses include those ordinary and necessary expenses you incur while traveling away from your home on business. As with entertainment expenses, it vital that you keep careful, current, and complete records of all expenses.

The following expenses can be deducted:

- Transportation fares between home and business destination.
- Taxi, commuter bus, and limousine fares between the airport and your hotel or temporary work site.
- Baggage and shipping costs, between regular and temporary work locations.
- Car expenses which include leasing expenses, actual expenses, or the standard mileage rate.

FIGURE
9.10

Mileage Log

Name: ___ABC Company (John Higgins)___

Dated: From _____November 1_____ **to** _____November 30_____

Date	City of Destination	Name or Other Designation	Business Purpose	Number of Miles
11/1	Orange, CA	ExCal, Inc.	Present proposal	67 miles
11/3	Cypress, CA	The Print Co.	p/u brochures	23 miles
11/4	Long Beach, CA	Wm. Long	Consultation	53 miles
11/7	Fullerton, CA	Bank of America	Loan meeting	17 miles
11/23	Los Angeles, CA	Moore Corp.	Consultation	143 miles
11/30	Los Angeles, CA	Moore Corp.	Consultation	140 miles
			Total Miles this Sheet	**443 miles**

Note: 1. A mileage record is required by the IRS to claim a mileage deduction. It is also used to determine the percentage of business use of a car.

2. Keep your mileage log in your vehicle and record your mileage as it occurs. It is very difficult to recall after the fact.

FIGURE 9.11 **Sample Entertainment Expense Record**

Name: ___John Higgins___

Dated: From ___November 1___ **to** ___November 30___

Date	Place of Entertainment	Business Purpose	Name of Person Entertained	Amount Spent
11/4	The 410 Club	Consulting	Wm. Long	$27.32
11/23	Seafood Chef	Consulting	Thomas Moore	$23.50
11/27	The Cannon Club	Staff dinner	Company employees	$384.00

Note: For more information on meals and entertainment, please refer to IRS Publication 463, *Travel, Entertainment, Gift, and Car Expenses*.

- Lodging, if a trip is overnight, or long enough to require rest to properly perform duties.
- Actual or standard meal allowance if business trip qualifies for lodging.
- Cleaning and laundry expenses while away from home overnight.
- Telephone expenses, which include fax and other communication devices.
- Tips related to any of the above services.
- Other business-related expenses connected with your travel (i.e., computer rental).

The following expenses, on the other hand, may not be deducted:

- That portion of travel, meals and lodging for your spouse or other non-business guest—unless there is a real business purpose for his or her presence.
- Investment travel (such as investment seminars or stockholders' meetings).
- Amounts you spend for travel to conduct a general search for, or preliminary investigation of, a new business.

The travel record in Figure 9.12 illustrates one way of keeping track of all the expenses you incur.

BUSINESS CHECKBOOK

Your business checkbook is not just a package of preprinted forms that represents your business bankroll. It is also the initial accounting record showing when, where, and what amount of money was dispersed. It also shows when, from what sources, and how much money was received by your company. This information is all kept on the recording space provided in your checkbook. In short, your business's checkbook is your front-line accounting system.

What Type of Checkbook Is Most Effective?

Don't get the same kind of pocket-size checkbook you use for your personal transactions. While perfectly suited to slip into your purse or jacket pocket for trips to the grocery store, this type of checkbook does not provide enough space for entering the kind of information you need to keep your business going. Some points to consider when selecting your business checkbook are:

- Size. A business-sized checkbook is best. There is a personal desk type with three standard size checks on each right-hand page and a register (recording) page of equal size on the left. Instead of one line of check register for each transaction, you will have room to record such things as invoice numbers and descriptions of purchases. You can divide amounts paid with one check into separate expenses. These and other notations will be invaluable when you do your weekly bookkeeping because you will not have to look for paperwork to supply missing information.

FIGURE 9.12 **Travel Expense Record**

| Date | Location | Expense Paid to | Meals | | | | | Hotel | Taxis, etc. | Automobile | | | Misc. Expense |
			Breakfast	Lunch	Dinner	Misc.				Gas	Parking	Tolls	
6/15	Phoenix, AZ	Mobil Gas				6.40			21.00			
6/15	Phoenix, AZ	Greentree Inn		12.50								
6/15	Chola, NM	Exxon							23.50			
6/15	Las Cruces, NM	Holiday Inn			27.00		49.00					
6/16	Las Cruces, NM	Exxon							19.00			
6/16	Taft, TX	Molly's Cafe		16.25								
6/16	Dallas, TX	Holiday Inn			18.75		54.00					
6/17	Dallas, TX	Expo Center								8.00		
6/17	Dallas, TX	Harvey's Eatery		21.00								
6/17	Dallas, TX	Holiday Inn			24.50		54.00					
6/18	Dallas, TX	Holiday Inn	9.50									(fax)
6/18	Dallas, TX	Expo Center		14.00						8.00		9.00
6/18	Dallas, TX	Holiday Inn			16.20		54.00					
6/19	Pokie, TX	Texaco							21.00			
6/19	Pokie, TX	Denny's		18.50								
6/19	Chola, NM	Holiday Inn			27.00		48.00					
6/20	Chola, NM	Holiday Inn	12.75									
6/20	Flagstaff, AZ	Texaco							22.00			
		Totals	22.25	83.25	113.45	6.40	259.00		106.50	16.00		9.00

Attach all receipts for meals, hotel, fares, auto, entertainment, etc. Details of your expenses can be noted on the receipts. File your travel record and your receipts in the same envelope. Label the envelope as to trip made. File all travel records together. When expenses are allocated, be sure not to double expense anything (i.e., gas cannot be used if you elect to use mileage as the basis for deducting your car expenses).

- Duplicate feature. Many business owners number among the ranks of those people who do not automatically record information when they write checks. To eliminate the frustration created by this unfortunate habit, banks can provide checkbooks made with carbonless copies underneath each check. If you fail to record a check at the time you write it, a copy will remain in your checkbook.
- Preprinted and numbered checks. Your checks should be preprinted with your business name, address, and telephone number. They should also be numbered. Some businesses will not even deal with you if you try to use personal checks or ones without preprinted information. Some vendors with which you wish to do business perceive personal checks as a possible danger signal and indicator of a lack of your credibility.

Balancing Your Checkbook

Once a month your bank will send you a statement of your account, showing a summary of your activity since the last statement date. It will list all deposits, check withdrawals, ATM activity, bank charges, and interest earned. You will need to reconcile it with your checkbook on a timely basis. This is one of those chores that is frequently ignored. The "later when I have more time" attitude results in undiscovered errors and overdrawn accounts. It is not difficult to balance your checkbook if you follow the steps outlined below.

Update Your Checkbook

Add:
- Interest earned
- Deposits not recorded
- Automatic credits unrecorded

Subtract:
- Service charges
- Checks not recorded
- Automatic debits unrecorded
- Payments not recorded

Mark Off:
- Amount of all checks paid against statement
- Amount of all deposits shown
- All ATM and electronic transactions that are recorded

List and Total:
- All deposits made and other credits not shown on the statement
- All outstanding checks not shown on current or previous statements

Balance:
- Enter statement balance as indicated
- Add the total deposits and other credits not shown on current or previous statements

- Subtract items outstanding
- Total

Your total should agree with your checkbook balance. If not, recheck your addition and subtraction in your checkbook. Check amounts in the checkbook against those in the statement. Look for uncashed checks from previous statements and be sure they are not still outstanding. Check the amount of the difference and see if it matches the amount on any of your checks. Be sure that you did not add a check when you should have subtracted. Be sure that you recorded and subtracted all ATM withdrawals in your checkbook.

URLinks

http://ewmdws003.ibm.net/smb/smbusapub.nsf/DetailContacts/862566130059C
ODC852566210066AB45?OpenDocument
http://www.techweb.com:3040/smallbiz/product1224a.html

CASE STUDY
GRUBER'S MATERIAL HANDLING SYSTEMS DESIGN, INC.

*E*ric Gruber was an engineer who specialized in material handling equipment, such as industrial cranes and sophisticated conveyer systems. Gruber had worked for Von Mag Handling Systems, Inc., in Memphis, Tennessee, for the past 19 years. Things were going well for Gruber when suddenly everyone in the organization was notified that the company was closing at the end of the week. Gruber and all the other employees were shocked. No one had seen this coming. Because he was 48 years old, Gruber saw all sorts of obstacles to seeking employment with another firm. Elsa, his wife, was also surprised, but reassured Eric that perhaps it was for the best. He had always talked about starting his own business. Maybe now was the time.

After several weeks Eric decided he would either start his own business or look for an existing business in the field of handling systems. He had several real estate agents and his banker looking for the right opportunity. Finally, after nine months of looking, an opportunity came up. The Cornell Materials

Handling Center was for sale, and could be purchased at the right price.

Cornell's handled casters, forklift trucks, industrial conveyers, hand trucks, dockboards, ladders, and other small products for materials handling. The firm did not design systems for industrial companies because it lacked the expertise and equipment to handle that aspect of the business. James Cornell, the owner, thought that he could have increased sales dramatically if he had had that systems-designing capability. As it was, Cornell concentrated on selling and servicing German-made forklifts and the other equipment. Cornell stated that he wanted to sell the business because his son had no interest in taking over. Cornell had been in the business for nearly 25 years and wanted to retire.

Cornell was asking $486,000 cash for the business. However, he would be willing to consider terms if the buyer was creditworthy. Eric asked him for some financial figures and Cornell gave him the following:

CONTINUED ▶

	1999	1998	1997
Sales	$1,750,000	$1,500,000	$1,350,000
Gross profit	315,000	270,000	216,000
Net after taxes	33,250	13,500	12,150

Balance sheet figures as of December 31, 1999, were as follows:

Cash	$ 21,500	Accounts Payable	$45,000
Accounts receivable	125,000	Notes payable bank (floor plan)	295,000
Notes receivable	20,000	Other current	$15,000
Inventory	395,000	Total current	$355,000
Other current	10,000	Stockholders' equity	286,500
Total current	571,500		
Fixed assets	$70,000	Total Liability and	
Total Assets	$641,500	Stockholders' Equity	$641,500

Eric asked his lawyer for advice. The lawyer suggested that he not buy the corporation itself, because of unknown contingent liabilities. Rather he should try to purchase just the assets he wanted and assume those liabilities. Under no circumstances should he buy the stock of the corporation. He could include the name of the corporation in the purchase if he wanted. Eric preferred to use his own name, for he had been in the trade for a number of years and was well known.

So Eric and Cornell negotiated the price of the business, and after hours of discussion, Cornell agreed to permit Eric to purchase assets and assume all the liabilities of the business for $350,000.

Finally, the closing came and Cornell delivered the lease approved by the landlord under the same conditions; only now the lease read Gruber's Material Handling Systems Designs, Inc. Cornell also delivered letters of intent from the manufacturers he represented, indicating that they would accept Eric as their dealer for the present. They reserved the right to make a change if they felt he was not acceptable. Eric's attorney protested this point, for he stated that the lines were vital to the success of the business. They needed more assurance. Cornell thought Eric would have absolutely no difficulty retaining the lines; he had experience and was taking over a competent personnel group. Cornell assured Eric that he would give him the cooperation he needed if there was any difficulty. He would not assume any liability, however, if any of the manufacturers failed to deliver their lines. Eric's attorney advised him that he should not accept the company on that basis, but Eric insisted that it would be all right. He felt that Cornell's cooperation was all he needed.

The sale went through, and the new balance sheet for Gruber's as of January 31, 2000, looked as follows:

Cash	$50,000	Accounts payable	$35,000
Accounts receivable	105,000	Notes payable (bank)	325,000
Notes receivable	25,000	Other current	10,000
Inventory (forklift truck)	325,000		
Inventory (other)	73,000		
Other current	10,000		
Total current	$588,000	Total current	$370,000
Fixed assets	70,000	Stockholders' equity	400,000
Intangible assets (goodwill)	$112,000	Total Liability and	
Total Assets	$770,000	Stockholders' Equity	$770,000

CONTINUED ▶

The bank had approved Eric for floor plan financing and gave him a line of credit up to $500,000 subject to review. However, the agreement included a proviso that inventory in stock for 90 days would have a curtailment charge of 10 percent which would have to be paid by Eric. There would be additional curtailments of 10 percent per month until the sixth month when the unit would have to be paid in full. Thus, if a forklift cost Eric $15,000 and it was in stock 90 days, he would have to pay $1,500 in 90 days, another 10 percent on the unpaid balance or $1,350, in 120 days, $1,215 in 150 days, and the balance of $10,935 at the end of 180 days. Thus, Eric would have to see that all stock moved quickly and make certain that the models ordered were popular. Otherwise, he could be stuck with high inventory costs.

Eric and Elsa took over the business, changed the name, advertised in all the newspapers, and sent out direct mail letters to all their clients. They advised them of the sale and described the new services the company would be able to offer in systems design engineering. The employees of the company settled down after a few weeks, except in the office where Elsa had replaced the office manager. Eric called together his sales, service, and parts managers. He told them that he had full confidence in their ability and expected them to perform their jobs as competently as they had for Cornell. He would devote most of his time to developing the engineering side of the business. This would eventually help all the other product areas increase their sales. He expected each manager to report any problems and the progress that was being made. He was clear with the sales manager that all trucks should move out as quickly as possible, since he didn't want to pay curtailment fees on trucks. Eric believed in delegating authority, and he would support his managers completely as long as they produced.

One day the bank called Eric and informed him that the corporate account was overdrawn. The bank had found it necessary to bounce his checks. Eric was stunned. He managed to scrape up sufficient money to handle the overdraft in the account, but the suppliers were nervous about his checks bouncing and threatened to put him on a COD basis.

Eric called in a respected accounting firm to bring the books up to date so he could get an immediate grasp of his financial position. Since his problem was cash flow, the accountants immediately worked up the following: an aging of accounts receivable; a breakdown of inventory into the units on floor plan; the units that were paid from the floor plan and which Eric owned, if any; the inventory of other stock; an aging of notes receivable; and an aging of accounts payable. Within a few days the accounting firm came up with the following data:

Aging of Accounts Receivable

Total	0-30 days	31-60 days	61 days and over
$210,000	$95,000	$40,000	$75,000

Aging of Notes Receivable

Total	0-30 days	31-60 days	61 days and over
$25,000	$ 15,000	$3,000	$7,000

Forklift Inventory

On floor plan with the bank	$275,000
Owned by the company (paid off)	125,000

Inventory of Other Stock

Total inventory of $125,000, up from the $73,000 amount when Eric took over the business. Thus, there was an increase of $52,000.

Accounts Payable

Total	0-30 days	31-60 days	61-90 days	91 days and over
$140,000	$35,000	$25,000	$30,000	$50,000

CONTINUED ▶

Contingent Liability (as a result of financing trucks with the bank on a with-recourse basis)

Fourteen trucks were financed with recourse and the aging of those trucks is as follows with respect to their payment:

Total	Current	30 days past due	60 days past due	90 days past due
14 trucks	5 trucks	1 truck	2 trucks	6 trucks

The trucks past due have a total balance owing on them of $84,000, which will have to be paid by the company if the accounts are not brought up to date. When Eric asked the sales manager why he had approved the financing on a with-recourse basis he was informed that, in spite of his objections, Elsa had approved of the sale because they stood to make a 3 percent interest rebate from the bank on each transaction. The sales procedure was to route all sales contracts through the office to be submitted to the bank. When Cornell owned the business, he rarely accepted a sale on a with-recourse contract. In addition to these problems, Eric had a payroll of $18,000 to make that week, and he didn't have the money in the bank to pay the employees.

When Eric compared how the business stood now with how it stood when he started as owner, he observed the following changes:

	Started	Now	Change
Cash	$50,000	1,000	-49,000
Accounts receivable	105,000	210,000	+105,000
Notes receivable	25,000	25,000	0
Inventory			
Trucks on floor plan	325,000	275,000	-50,000
Trucks owned by comp.	0	125,000	+125,000
Stock other products	73,000	125,000	+52,000
Accounts payable	35,000	140,000	+105,000

Eric couldn't understand how all this had happened in such a short time. His receivables were excessive, but sales had increased dramatically in all the departments. The sales manager was pushing very hard to sell the trucks he had to pay off, and while he was having difficulty selling some of them, he did have some possible deals working that might reduce the stock. Eric told him to sell the trucks they owned at any price to get some cash. The inventory of other products had increased because the parts manager felt that too many sales were being lost because of the lack of basic parts that Cornell never would agree to stock. He pointed to increased sales to prove that the additional inventory had paid off.

According to the accountant, the credit policy of the company was not uniform as it should be. Decisions were made by all of the managers without consultation and consensus. Credit policy was something Eric had not been involved with at his former place of employment, and he didn't understand sales or inventory procedures. He knew engineering and that was the only area that showed improvement.

At this point Eric had numerous designs underway. In several cases, they needed only a little more work before he could sell them to clients. He tallied up his back orders and had approximately $300,000 of engineering systems sales pending. These would be completed when the parts and materials he ordered arrived. The gross profit on these sales averaged 40 percent of the sales figure. But Eric knew he had to attend to other parts of the business immediately, and was at a loss as to where to begin. ▾

CASE STUDY ROUNDTABLE

▼ ▼ ▼ ▼ ▼

Eric: Look at my statements: There are many problems. What should I attend to first?

Discussion Points

- How would you suggest he handle each asset and liability?

Eric: Was there any way I could have foreseen the problems that developed? Maybe even prevented them?

- Is there any way better organization or recordkeeping would have helped Eric avoid the problems his business developed?

BACK TO THE TABLE
Cathy Dooley

Chapter 18 studies the problems faced by the four men who started Shamrock Automotive Service Center. Based on what you know now, how would you answer Cathy's question?

Cathy: I was so mad at the guys when I found out about the missing checks and the unreported spending! What's worse, at the end of the first month, we didn't have as much money as we'd expected, and some customers who were supposed to pay cash hadn't. No one could remember how much they'd spent of what the company owed to vendors. How could we have prevented all this?

▲ ▲ ▲ ▲ ▲ ▲

CHAPTER BRIEFCASE

▼ ▼ ▼ ▼ ▼

- All of your records will be used to develop your financial statements. For this reason, it is important to use forms created using an accepted format.
- There are two basic bookkeeping methods: single entry and double entry. In the past, only double-entry accounting was thought to be proper for businesses. However, *it is now generally recognized that a single-entry system will adequately serve most smaller businesses.* As the business grows and becomes more complex, it may then become more effective to move into double-entry accounting.

- Single entry refers to a recordkeeping system which uses only income and expense accounts. Double entry is a bookkeeping and accounting method by which every transaction is recorded twice. (That's why it's called "double entry.")

- Petty cash refers to all the small business purchases made with cash or personal funds instead of with a business check. These purchases may account for several thousand dollars by the end of the year. Failure to account for them can result in a false picture of your business and additional cost in income taxes.

- Your business checkbook is the initial accounting record showing when, where, and what amount of money was dispersed. It also shows when, from what sources, and how much money was received by your company. This information is all kept on the recording space provided in your checkbook. Your business's checkbook is your front-line accounting system.

▲▲▲▲▲▲

Chapter 10

BASIC FINANCIAL STATEMENTS

▼▼▼▼▼

Annual income twenty pounds, annual
expenditure nineteen six.
Result: Happiness.
Annual income twenty pounds, annual
expenditure twenty pounds ought and six.
Result: Misery.
—Wilkins Micawber (in Charles Dickens'
David Copperfield)

MISSION STATEMENT

In this chapter, you will

*L*EARN about the basic types of financial statements: the balance
sheet, income (profit and loss) statement, cash flow projections,
and how to forecast sales and expenses.

*E*XPLORE the real world use of financial accounting by connecting
financial statements with their underlying facts.

*A*PPLY your understanding to a detailed case study.

*P*RODUCE preliminary financial statements for your own business.

KEY TERMS

balance sheet	income statement	profit and loss (P&L)
cash flow	predictable	statement
projection	payments	scheduled payments
fixed expenses	pro forma	variable expenses

INTRODUCTION TO FINANCIAL STATEMENTS

For any business to be successful, it is vital that its owner be mind-
ful of preparing, maintaining, and understanding its financial statements.
A business may *appear* to be about its product or service, but in fact all
businesses are, one way or another, about money. It may sound cynical,
but the bottomline question for any business is: How do I get the money
out of my customer's pocket and into my bank account? Money is the

life's blood of your business, and its financial health is as important to its survival as physical health is to yours.

Before you start your business, it is essential that you have a competent accountant set up a system to give you adequate financial records. If you can't afford this, purchase an easy-to-use accounting software program, but be careful with that option: the financial accounting on which the success or failure of your small business depends should be handled by experts, not by an amateur (even yourself) armed with a generic number-cruncher. You can also visit your local SBDC office or SCORE chapter. They will most likely be able to help you get organized. The bottom line is this: If you don't understand the need for financial and accounting records, you don't have enough management experience to be starting a business. This is a common problem area for many small businesses.

You don't have to be a wizard to prepare, understand, and use your financial statements. The more technical aspects can be handled by your accountant or other financial advisors, or even by computer software. What's important is that the numbers come from your input and ideas.

The key financial documents—the balance sheet, income statement, and cash flow statement—form the basis of your financial policy and control procedures. From these documents, the deviation analysis is created and the break-even is fine tuned. Ultimately, your accounting system should be a working model of your business. All of these financial tools are important: *Financial control* means using the cash flow as a budget to hold down spending and the balance sheet to show the shifting balance between assets and liabilities. It spells the difference between making money and going broke.

The two most important financial statements are the income statement and the cash flow projection. The **income statement** (also called the profit and loss statement, or **P&L**) is designed to show how well the company's operations are being performed over time by subtracting expenses from sales to show a profit or loss. The **cash flow projection** is designed to show how well the company is managing its cash (liquidity) by subtracting disbursements (actual cash outlays) from cash received.

The balance between profitability and liquidity can be hard to maintain. Fast growth (with high profits) can deplete cash, causing illiquidity. Companies have been known to fail even while they are profitable. The role of projected income and cash flow statements is to help you spot these kinds of severe problems in time to do something to forestall them, such as raise new capital or arrange for the right kind of financing. Your banker will be helpful here; ask.

SALES AND EXPENSE FORECASTS

Forecasting Sales

Whether you've been in business for a while or are starting a business, your sales forecasts are the basis for most of your financial planning. You will use the sales forecast in both the projected profit and loss statement and in your cash flow projection. Express your sales forecasts in dollars, keeping in mind that units sold times price equals total sales. You may want to skip ahead to Chapter 11 on pricing strategies if you haven't yet determined your price structure.

PERSONAL WORKSHOP 21
Sales Forecasting
▼ ▼ ▼ ▼ ▼ ▼

▼ Test out the three-column approach to sales forecasting for your own business. If you have several products or services, group them into categories and arrive at a realistic unit price for each category.

Category	Worst Case	Most Likely Case	Best Case
Total:			

▼ It is important to remember that these figures are educated guesses at best, especially if your business is a start-up. That's OK. As your business progresses, your guesses will become more educated and more accurate. Try to err on the conservative side. If you estimate sales lower than they turn out to be, you'll be far better off than pitching your estimate too high. Why? Because many expenses are geared to the sales forecast, and everyone knows it's always easier to spend more than to cut back.

This step is usually seen as the single most difficult part of financial projections. In many ways, that's because it is. Projecting sales is more art than science; at its best it will be imprecise. Too many outside factors affect sales: economic conditions, competition, changes in consumer and business buying patterns, even the weather. But you still have to estimate the level of sales your business will work toward achieving.

One helpful technique to use involves breaking your goods and services into several lines, then applying a three-column form to arrive at a "most likely" figure. (See Personal Workshop 21.) Begin by assuming the worst. In the column headed Worst Case (or Low) put down the sales you expect if everything goes wrong—poor weather, loss of market share to a new competitor, new product competition that you can't match, and so on. Be gloomy. Assume your salespeople will be loutish, lazy, and surly.

Then (this is more fun) assume everything works out the way you'd wish. In the column headed Best Case (or High), put down your rosiest hopes. All your promotional efforts will succeed, markets will grow dynamically, your competition will stub their toes and slink away from the market, and your suppliers will be able to instantaneously fulfill your requirements.

Now look to the realistic scenario, where things work out in between the high and low estimates. The figures here will (usually) be more accurate than a one-time estimate can be, since more thought has gone into their preparation. Do this for the period you need to forecast.

Forecasting Expenses

Expenses fall into two categories: fixed and variable. **Fixed expenses** are those that remain constant whether business is lagging or booming. Examples include salaries, rent, and licenses. **Variable expenses** fluctuate depending on business activity, and include sales commissions, travel and entertainment, and freight charges. Figure 10.1 lists common fixed and variable expenses.

It is important to be systematic and thorough when you list your expenses. The expense that bleeds your business dry (makes it illiquid) is almost always one that was overlooked or seriously misjudged, and therefore unplanned. There are some expenses that cannot be foreseen, and the best way to allow for them is to be conservative in your estimates and document your assumptions.

Increased sales and increased expenses go together, but not in a smooth line—particularly in growing businesses. Expenses, both in absolute dollars and in management time, tend to rise in steps as a percentage of sales. A modest increase in sales may greatly increase profits, because it won't affect fixed expenses. But a major sales increase can actually result in lowered profits—and severely (if temporary) negative cash flow—if fixed expenses take an upwards leap.

If you expect a substantial increase in sales over the next budgeting period, try to figure out what this will mean in terms of the following:

- Operating margins. Will they remain stable? Go lower? Higher? Why?
- Fixed costs. New plant and equipment may be needed. What will happen to overhead and administrative expenses? Will new debt be needed?
- Profitability. What will the increase do? Will there be a lag? What about credit and collection expenses? Bad debt expense?

Variable costs rise and fall with sales levels, and can usually be forecast as a percentage of sales. Your own records, plus trade figures, will give you a realistic percentage range for each variable expense.

A few expenses are mixed. Take a conservative approach and treat these as fixed expenses, unless you have good reasons to link them more closely to sales.

FIRST PERSON

Judith R., Nashville, Tennessee: I would say the most important thing to do before you visit your banker is make sure that your balance sheet, your sales forecast, and your cash flow projection are all updated and documented. What you want is for your banker to take you seriously. That kind of credibility is a great asset, but it's hard to earn and easy to lose. Since your balance sheet and cash flow have been prepared on the basis of your research and plans for your business, you have to be the person to go talk with your banker. Bring your accountant if you want to, if it makes you more

FIGURE
10.1 **Fixed and Variable Expenses**

Fixed Expenses
- Salaries
- Payroll tax
- Benefits
- Rent
- Utilities
- Licenses and fees
- Insurance
- Advertising
- Legal and accounting
- Depreciation
- Interest
- Maintenance and cleaning

Variable Expenses
- Sales commission
- Sales tax
- Boxes, paper, etc.
- Travel
- Entertainment
- Freight, cartage
- Overtime
- Bad debt

Mixed Expenses
- Telephone
- Postage

This is not an exhaustive list. If you are undecided about which of your expenses are fixed and which are variable, check with your accountant.

Rule of thumb: Try to understate your expected sales and overstate expenses. It is better to exceed a conservative budget than to fall below optimistic projections. However, being too far under can also create problems, such as not having enough capital to finance growth. Be realistic; your budget is an extension of your forecasts.

comfortable, but you have to be ready to answer most of the questions yourself. The banker will really wonder if you don't know why you think such-and-such a sales level will be reached, or what you'll do if it's not.

THE INCOME STATEMENT

Income statements, also called profit and loss statements, complement balance sheets. The balance sheet gives a static picture of the company at a given point in time. The income statement provides a moving picture of the company during a particular period of time.

Financial statements that depict a future period are called **pro forma** or projected financial statements. They represent what the company is expected to look like financially, based on a set of assumptions about the economy, market growth, and other factors. Pro forma income statements will help you estimate income and expenses in the near to middle future. For most businesses, income projections covering one to three years are more than adequate. In some cases, a longer range projection may be necessary, but in general, the longer the projection, the less accurate it will be as a guide to action.

You don't need a crystal ball to make your projection. While no set of projections will be 100 percent accurate, experience and practice tend to make the projections more

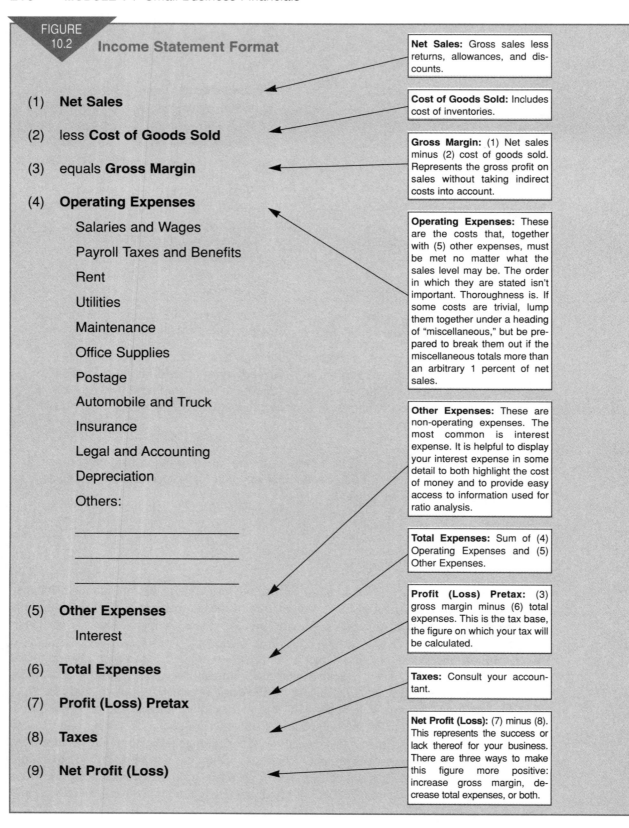

FIGURE 10.2

Income Statement Format

(1) **Net Sales**

(2) less **Cost of Goods Sold**

(3) equals **Gross Margin**

(4) **Operating Expenses**

    Salaries and Wages

    Payroll Taxes and Benefits

    Rent

    Utilities

    Maintenance

    Office Supplies

    Postage

    Automobile and Truck

    Insurance

    Legal and Accounting

    Depreciation

    Others:

    _____

    _____

    _____

(5) **Other Expenses**

    Interest

(6) **Total Expenses**

(7) **Profit (Loss) Pretax**

(8) **Taxes**

(9) **Net Profit (Loss)**

Net Sales: Gross sales less returns, allowances, and discounts.

Cost of Goods Sold: Includes cost of inventories.

Gross Margin: (1) Net sales minus (2) cost of goods sold. Represents the gross profit on sales without taking indirect costs into account.

Operating Expenses: These are the costs that, together with (5) other expenses, must be met no matter what the sales level may be. The order in which they are stated isn't important. Thoroughness is. If some costs are trivial, lump them together under a heading of "miscellaneous," but be prepared to break them out if the miscellaneous totals more than an arbitrary 1 percent of net sales.

Other Expenses: These are non-operating expenses. The most common is interest expense. It is helpful to display your interest expense in some detail to both highlight the cost of money and to provide easy access to information used for ratio analysis.

Total Expenses: Sum of (4) Operating Expenses and (5) Other Expenses.

Profit (Loss) Pretax: (3) gross margin minus (6) total expenses. This is the tax base, the figure on which your tax will be calculated.

Taxes: Consult your accountant.

Net Profit (Loss): (7) minus (8). This represents the success or lack thereof for your business. There are three ways to make this figure more positive: increase gross margin, decrease total expenses, or both.

precise. Even if your income projections are not accurate, they will provide you with a rough set of benchmarks to test your progress toward short-term goals. They become the basis for your budgets.

For the most useful projection, state your assumptions clearly. Do not put down numbers that you cannot rationally substantiate. Do not puff your gross sales projection to make the net profit positive. Give yourself conservative sales figures and pessimistic expense figures to make the success of your deal more probable. Be realistic. You want your projections to reflect the realities of your business.

Income statements and projections are standardized to facilitate comparison and analysis. They must be dated to indicate the period of time they cover and also contain notes to explain any unusual items such as windfall profits, litigation expenses and judgments, changes in depreciation schedules, and other material information. Any assumptions should be footnoted to help remind you how the numbers were originally justified and to help boost your learning curve when you review your projections before making new ones.

Figure 10.2 suggests a format for an income statement. The content may have to be modified to fit your particular operation, but do not change the basic form.

Remember: The purpose of financial statements and forecasts is to provide you with the maximum amount of useful information and guidance, not to dazzle a prospective investor.

PREPARING A PRO FORMA INCOME STATEMENT

Smaller businesses should make three-year projections for both planning purposes and loan proposals. The proper sequence (for both income and cash flow projections) is:

- A three-year summary
- First year projected by month. If the business doesn't break even in the first year, you might want to continue the monthly projections until it does.
- Years Two and Three by quarter

If you are already in business or are considering taking over an existing business, historical financial statements should be included for the two immediately previous years. Tax returns help to substantiate the validity of unaudited statements. Figures 10.3 through 10.6 are samples of the types of income projections you should make.

Explanation of Income Statement Projections

Let's go through the Wholesome Foods income statement projections in Figures 10.3 through 10.6 line by line to see

- how the figures on the projection were calculated and
- what assumptions were made.

Line 3. Sales include sales of produce and ancillary products such as seasonings, sauces, and dressings. In the future, some tourist items may be included.

FIGURE
10.3

Sample Income Projection: Three-Year Summary

Wholesome Foods, Inc.
Income Projection: Three-Year Summary

	A	B	C	D
		Year 1	Year 2	Year 3
1		Year 1	Year 2	Year 3
2				
3	Sales:			
4	Wholesale	$90,000	$265,000	$325,000
5	Retail	$126,000	$180,000	$210,000
6	**Total Sales**	**$216,000**	**$445,000**	**$535,000**
7				
8	*V Cost of Materials	$155,520	$320,400	$385,200
9	V Variable Labor	$2,800	$2,800	$7,520
10	Total Cost of Goods Sold	$158,320	$323,200	$392,720
11				
12	**Gross Margin**	**$57,680**	**$121,800**	**$142,280**
13				
14	Operating Expenses:			
15	F Utilities	$2,160	$2,640	$2,880
16	F Salaries	$22,800	$39,000	$46,800
17	V/F Payroll Taxes & Benefits	$2,850	$4,875	$5,850
18	F Advertising	$9,555	$11,125	$13,375
19	F Office Supplies	$300	$360	$480
20	F Insurance	$1,200	$3,800	$4,100
21	F Maintenance & Cleaning	$300	$360	$420
22	F Legal and Accounting	$1,500	$2,000	$2,500
23	V/F Delivery Expenses	$1,800	$8,900	$9,095
24	F Licenses	$115	$115	$115
25	V/F Boxes, Paper, etc.	$400	$800	$1,200
26	F Telephone	$1,020	$1,800	$2,400
27	F Depreciation	$7,700	$12,500	$12,500
28	F Miscellaneous	$480	$600	$720
29	F Rent	$1,650	$0	$0
30	Total Operating Expenses	$53,830	$88,875	$102,435
31				
32	Other Expenses:			
33	F Interest (Mortgage)	$6,258	$8,280	$8,052
34	F Interest (Term Loan)	$1,632	$3,189	$2,900
35	F Interest (Credit Line)	$500	$500	$500
36	Total Other Expenses	$8,390	$11,969	$11,452
37				
38	**Total Expenses**	**$62,220**	**$100,844**	**$113,887**
39				
40	**Net Profit (Loss) Pre-Tax**	**($4,540)**	**$20,956**	**$28,393**
41				
42	*V = Variable Cost, F = Fixed Cost			

FIGURE 10.4 Sample Income Projection: Year One by Month

Wholesome Foods, Inc.
Income Projection: Year One by Month

	A	B October	C November	D December	E January	F February	G March	H April	I May	J June	K July	L August	M September	N Total
1														
2														
3	Sales:													
4	Wholesale	$4,000	$4,000	$5,200	$5,600	$6,000	$7,000	$7,000	$8,400	$10,600	$11,300	$11,300	$9,600	$90,000
5	Retail	$9,730	$9,500	$9,500	$9,000	$8,400	$8,750	$10,300	$11,540	$12,165	$12,165	$12,475	$12,475	$126,000
6	Total Sales	$13,730	$13,500	$14,700	$14,600	$14,400	$15,750	$17,300	$19,940	$22,765	$23,465	$23,775	$22,075	$216,000
7	Cost of Goods Sold:													
8	Cost of Materials (a)	$9,886	$9,720	$10,584	$10,512	$10,368	$11,340	$12,456	$14,357	$16,391	$16,895	$17,118	$15,894	$155,520
9	Variable Labor	$0	$0	$0	$0	$0	$0	$0	$0	$604	$796	$796	$604	$2,800
10	Total Cost of Goods Sold	$9,886	$9,720	$10,584	$10,512	$10,368	$11,340	$12,456	$14,357	$16,995	$17,691	$17,914	$16,498	$158,320
11														
12	Gross Margin	$3,844	$3,780	$4,116	$4,088	$4,032	$4,410	$4,844	$5,583	$5,770	$5,774	$5,861	$5,577	$57,680
13														
14	Operating Expenses:													
15	Utilities	$160	$165	$180	$200	$200	$180	$170	$165	$185	$185	$185	$185	$2,160
16	Salaries	$1,900	$1,900	$1,900	$1,900	$1,900	$1,900	$1,900	$1,900	$1,900	$1,900	$1,900	$1,900	$22,800
17	Payroll Taxes	$238	$238	$238	$238	$238	$238	$238	$238	$238	$238	$238	$238	$2,850
18	Advertising	$450	$450	$450	$450	$450	$450	$4,605	$450	$450	$450	$450	$450	$9,555
19	Office Supplies	$25	$25	$25	$25	$25	$25	$25	$25	$25	$25	$25	$25	$300
20	Insurance	$70	$70	$70	$110	$110	$110	$110	$110	$110	$110	$110	$110	$1,200
21	Maintenance and Cleaning	$25	$25	$25	$25	$25	$25	$25	$25	$25	$25	$25	$25	$300
22	Legal and Accounting	$125	$125	$125	$125	$125	$125	$125	$125	$125	$125	$125	$125	$1,500
23	Delivery Expenses	$150	$150	$150	$150	$150	$150	$150	$150	$150	$150	$150	$150	$1,800
24	Licenses	$9	$9	$9	$9	$9	$10	$10	$10	$10	$10	$10	$10	$115
25	Boxes, Paper, etc.	$15	$15	$15	$15	$20	$35	$40	$45	$50	$50	$50	$50	$400
26	Telephone	$85	$85	$85	$85	$85	$85	$85	$85	$85	$85	$85	$85	$1,020
27	Depreciation	$0	$0	$0	$455	$460	$460	$1,050	$1,055	$1,055	$1,055	$1,055	$1,055	$7,700
28	Miscellaneous	$40	$40	$40	$40	$40	$40	$40	$40	$40	$40	$40	$40	$480
29	Rent	$550	$550	$550	$0	$0	$0	$0	$0	$0	$0	$0	$0	$1,650
30	Total Operating Expenses	$3,842	$3,847	$3,862	$3,827	$3,837	$3,833	$8,573	$4,423	$4,448	$4,448	$4,448	$4,448	$53,830
31														
32	Other Expenses													
33	Interest (Mortgage)	$0	$0	$0	$695	$695	$696	$695	$695	$696	$695	$695	$696	$6,258
34	Interest (Term Loan)	$0	$0	$0	$0	$0	$0	$272	$272	$272	$272	$272	$272	$1,632
35	Interest (Credit Line)	$0	$85	$85	$0	$0	$0	$0	$0	$165	$165	$0	$0	$500
36	Total Interest Expense	$0	$85	$85	$695	$695	$696	$967	$967	$1,133	$1,132	$967	$968	$8,390
37														
38	Total Expenses	$3,842	$3,932	$3,947	$4,522	$4,532	$4,529	$9,540	$5,390	$5,581	$5,580	$5,415	$5,416	$62,220
39														
40	Net Profit (Loss) Pre-Tax	$3	($152)	$170	($434)	($500)	($119)	($4,696)	$194	$190	$195	$447	$162	($4,540)
41														
42	Cumulative Profit (Loss)	$3	($149)	$21	($413)	($912)	($1,031)	($5,726)	($5,532)*	($5,343)	($5,148)	($4,701)	($4,540)	

*Low Point

FIGURE
10.5

Sample Income Projection: Year Two by Quarter

Wholesome Foods, Inc.
Income Projection: Year Two by Quarter

	A	B	C	D	E	F
1		1st Qtr	2nd Qtr	3rd Qtr	4th Qtr	Total
2						
3	Sales:					
4	Wholesale	$38,900	$54,800	$76,500	$94,800	$265,000
5	Retail	$41,000	$37,400	$48,600	$53,000	$180,000
6	**Total Sales**	**$79,900**	**$92,200**	**$125,100**	**$147,800**	**$445,000**
7						
8	Materials	$57,528	$66,384	$90,072	$106,416	$320,400
9	Variable Labor	$0	$0	$604	$2,196	$2,800
10	Total COGS	$57,528	$66,384	$90,676	$108,612	$323,200
11						
12	**Gross Margin**	**$22,372**	**$25,816**	**$34,424**	**$39,188**	**$121,800**
13						
14	Operating Expenses:					
15	Utilities	$660	$660	$660	$660	$2,640
16	Salaries	$9,750	$9,750	$9,750	$9,750	$39,000
17	Payroll Taxes	$1,219	$1,219	$1,219	$1,219	$4,875
18	Advertising	$1,998	$2,305	$3,128	$3,695	$11,125
19	Office Supplies	$90	$90	$90	$90	$360
20	Insurance	$950	$950	$950	$950	$3,800
21	Maintenance/Cleaning	$90	$90	$90	$90	$360
22	Legal and Accounting	$500	$500	$500	$500	$2,000
23	Delivery Expense	$1,598	$1,844	$2,502	$2,956	$8,900
24	Licenses	$25	$30	$30	$30	$115
25	Boxes, Paper, etc.	$150	$175	$225	$250	$800
26	Telephone	$450	$450	$450	$450	$1,800
27	Depreciation	$3,125	$3,125	$3,125	$3,125	$12,500
28	Miscellaneous	$150	$150	$150	$150	$600
29	Rent	$0	$0	$0	$0	$0
30	**Total Operating Expense**	**$20,754**	**$21,338**	**$22,868**	**$23,915**	**$88,875**
31						
32	Other Expense:					
33	Interest (Mortgage)	$2,070	$2,070	$2,070	$2,070	$8,280
34	Interest (Term Loan)	$798	$798	$797	$796	$3,189
35	Interest (Line of Credit)	$0	$0	$140	$360	$500
36	Total Other Expenses	$2,868	$2,868	$3,007	$3,226	$11,969
37						
38	**Total Expenses**	**$23,622**	**$24,206**	**$25,875**	**$27,141**	**$100,844**
39						
40	**Net Profit (Loss) Pre-Tax**	**($1,250)**	**$1,610**	**$8,549**	**$12,047**	**$20,956**

FIGURE
10.6

Sample Income Projection: Year Three by Quarter

Wholesome Foods, Inc.
Income Projection: Year Three by Quarter

	A	B	C	D	E	F
1		1st Qtr	2nd Qtr	3rd Qtr	4th Qtr	Total
2						
3	Sales:					
4	Wholesale	$58,750	$55,000	$97,500	$113,750	$325,000
5	Retail	$47,400	$43,600	$56,000	$63,000	$210,000
6	Total Sales	$106,150	$98,600	$153,500	$176,750	$535,000
7						
8	Cost of Materials	$76,428	$70,992	$110,520	$127,260	$385,200
9	Variable Labor	$0	$0	$1,622	$5,898	$7,520
10	Total COGS	$76,428	$70,992	$112,142	$133,158	$392,720
11						
12	Gross Margin	$29,722	$27,608	$41,358	$43,592	$142,280
13						
14	Operating Expenses:					
15	Utilities	$720	$720	$720	$720	$2,880
16	Salaries	$11,700	$11,700	$11,700	$11,700	$46,800
17	Payroll Taxes	$1,463	$1,463	$1,463	$1,463	$5,850
18	Advertising	$2,654	$2,465	$3,838	$4,419	$13,375
19	Office Supplies	$120	$120	$120	$120	$480
20	Insurance	$1,025	$1,025	$1,025	$1,025	$4,100
21	Maintenance/Cleaning	$105	$105	$105	$105	$420
22	Legal and Accounting	$625	$625	$625	$625	$2,500
23	Delivery Expenses	$1,805	$1,676	$2,610	$3,005	$9,095
24	Licenses	$25	$30	$30	$30	$115
25	Boxes, Paper, etc.	$200	$200	$350	$450	$1,200
26	Telephone	$600	$600	$600	$600	$2,400
27	Depreciation	$3,125	$3,125	$3,125	$3,125	$12,500
28	Miscellaneous	$180	$180	$180	$180	$720
29	Rent	$0	$0	$0	$0	$0
30	Total Operating Expense	$24,346	$24,034	$26,490	$27,566	$102,435
31						
32	Other Expenses					
33	Interest (Mortgage)	$2,013	$2,013	$2,013	$2,013	$8,052
34	Interest (Term Loan)	$725	$725	$725	$725	$2,900
35	Interest (Line of Credit)	$0	$0	$140	$360	$500
36	Total Other Expenses	$2,738	$2,738	$2,878	$3,098	$11,452
37						
38	Total Expenses	$27,084	$26,772	$29,368	$30,664	$113,887
39						
40	Net Profit Pre-Tax	$2,638	$836	$11,991	$12,928	$28,393

Lines 4 and 5, wholesale and retail sales. Wholesome plans to service the wholesale trade more extensively than shown here, although the trend has been built into the calculations. Due to a major marketing effort (see line 18, advertising), wholesale sales should increase to 60 percent of gross sales within two years. Retail sales are expected to be more volatile than the wholesale business, leveling off around $20,000 per month due to space restrictions. Volatility is seasonal, building from late March to a late summer peak. The increases shown in line 4 are based both on the greater number of restaurants open in the summer and the intense marketing efforts, planned for the winter months, to sell directly to the many restaurants that don't yet know Wholesome. Wholesale sales for September of the preceding year were $9,600, so these figures are perhaps more conservative than they need to be.

Wholesale sales in years two and three follow the same pattern as year one (seasonality) but start at $10,000 in October in year two as the result of advertising and marketing efforts, longer experience with the wholesale market, and greater exposure to the market. Year three is a bit more seasonal, reflecting a flattening out of the sales curve.

FIRST PERSON

Kyle R., Sioux Falls, South Dakota: How realistic should your projections be? I think it's better to be a little pessimistic, even though you want to be full of optimism. But the degree of pessimism you build into your projection is a matter of judgment, really. Some is good; too much can be bad, because it will distort a good game plan and make a realistic deal look too risky.

Line 6, total sales. The total of wholesale plus retail sales.

Line 8, cost of materials. Wholesome's inventory has an average cost of 68 percent of sales (including a start-up spoilage rate of 5 percent which has been reduced to under 1 percent of sales), and has been calculated as 72 percent of sales to allow for the fluctuation of prices during the winter.

Line 9, variable labor. In years one and two, two part-time summer helpers will be needed: a counter person at $4/hour for 16 hours/week for 10 weeks, and another at $6.75/hour for 20 hours/week for 16 weeks. In year three, two full-time counter helpers and a full-time worker will be needed for 10 and 16 weeks, respectively.

Line 10, cost of goods sold. The total of cost of materials plus variable labor.

Line 12, gross margin. The difference between total sales and cost of goods sold.

Line 14, operating expenses. These are (by and large) the fixed expenses, those that don't vary directly with sales levels. Keeping control of operating expenses is immensely important and easily overlooked, perhaps because so much emphasis is placed on generating sales. A profitable business needs to control costs and maintain (or increase) sales.

Line 15, utilities. Prorated by agreement with the utility companies, this expense goes from $165/month (year one) to $240 (year three). These figures may change as new equipment and better insulation are installed.

Line 16, salaries.

Year one:	$950/month each for Pendleton and Turilli
Year two:	$1,200/month each for Pendleton and Turilli
	$850/month for a full-time employee
Year three:	$1,500/month each for Pendleton and Turilli
	$900/month ($50/month raise) for employee

Salaries are lower than Wholesome would pay for a professional manager in order to preserve scarce capital (they are undercapitalized, and the salaries reflect "sweat equity"). As the business grows, they hope to take annual bonuses based on profits—after capital needs are met.

Line 17, payroll taxes and benefits. These amount to 12.5 percent of salaries. This is low; in many businesses fringe benefits alone are over 25 percent of salaries. In a small business, benefits are often skimpy.

Line 18, advertising. Wholesome's advertising consists of local newspaper and radio spots. This is an expense that Wholesome might profitably increase. They reason (correctly) that a consistent, though modest, campaign will be more productive than sporadic, intensive promotions. The advertising budget is 2.5 percent of total sales. In year one, a large one-time promotional blitz will be made in April to build off-season wholesale business.

Line 20, insurance. This includes liability, workers compensation, vehicle, and other normal forms of insurance. As the business can afford it, they will add key-man disability to the life insurance coverage. Year two reflects the increase in workers comp and the property insurance.

Line 21, maintenance and cleaning. This expense covers mainly supplies—a food business must meet stringent health codes.

Line 22, legal and accounting. This consists of retainers to their attorney and accountant, used to smooth out cash flow. Otherwise occasional large bills would distort monthly income projection figures, even though the use of these services is spread evenly over the year.

Line 23, delivery expenses. This reflects delivery of merchandise to restaurants and other markets. Year two: 2 percent of total sales; year three: 1.7 percent. As the wholesale business increases, route efficiency should also increase, causing delivery expenses as a percentage of sales to decrease.

Line 24, licenses. Includes all licenses required by state and local authorities.

Line 25, boxes, paper, etc. This consists of packaging supplies, which are a semi-fixed expense.

Line 26, telephone. This includes all phone use needed for sales, pricing, and contacting suppliers and markets.

Line 27, depreciation. Five-year, straight-line on equipment (beginning April, year one); 19-year straight-line on building (beginning January, year one). These are based on the assumption that 1/5 and 1/19 respectively will be "used up" in the normal course of doing business. Some businesses try to set this sum aside as a replacement fund.

Line 28, miscellaneous. This includes all operating expenses too small to be itemized.

Line 29, rent. These expenses are only applicable for three months in year one. They will be replaced by mortgage interest on the income statement. The principal payments show up on the cash flow projections as part of mortgage payments. (The mortgage payment of $876 per month includes both principal and interest. Principal payments on loans do not appear as income statement items.)

Line 30, total operating expenses. This is the sum of lines 15 through 29.

Line 32, other expenses. Non-operating costs are broken out to give them special prominence.

Line 33, interest (mortgage). $75,000 mortgage for 15 years at 11.5 percent. This is a normal term and interest rate for commercial buildings at this time. More than 15 years is rare.

Line 34, interest (term loan). $30,000 loan for seven years at 12.25 percent. Rule of thumb: The longer the term, the higher the risk to the bank—so the higher the interest rate to you.

Line 35, interest (credit line). Estimated use of line: average of $7,500 outstanding for six months a year at 13.5 percent. Lines of credit are not intended to replace permanent capital or long-term credit needs.

Line 36, total other expenses. This is the sum of lines 33 through 35.

Line 37, total expenses. This is the sum of total operating expenses and total interest expense.

Line 40, net profit (loss) pre-tax. This is the difference between gross margin and total expenses. On this statement (and the other projections) a tax liability should be imputed. It is not included in this example, because it will vary from one state to another and depend on the legal structure of your business. Make sure to check with your accountant to arrive at a true net profit (loss) figure. As one banker puts it, "There is no such thing as a pre-tax profit."

Wholesome does not expect to make much money for the first few years. This is no surprise for a business so thinly capitalized. Even if there were no debt at all, net profit would have been only $8,000 for the year, or less than 4 percent of sales.

This is a projection based on conservative figures. In their more optimistic moments, the owners hope to hold fixed costs to $4,500 per month, not the $5,200 projected, and increase sales 12.5 percent. Their budgeted net profit would be around $18,000, not the projected loss of $4,540. If their gross margin were to continue at 30 percent of sales, not the 28 percent projected, their net profit would be over $18,000, their "best case" assumption.

One item that should be mentioned again is rent. The cost of space appears on the cash flow as mortgage ($876/month). Another is loan amortization, which also appears on the cash flow as term loan ($534/month). These include interest and debt retirement, which are not expenses since they are capital improvements that will be written off as "depreciation expense" over the course of several years. It is important not to double-deduct expenses: Such a practice is not only illegal but also obscures the information about your business.

Information is the most important result of financial statements. Accurate, timely information helps you run your business.

THE BALANCE SHEET

A well-prepared balance sheet is mandatory. Your banker needs it. You need it. Your accountant or bookkeeping service will need it. A balance sheet, like the cash flow, is a tool to help you better manage your business. The balance sheet is often compared to a snapshot bearing a date: it shows what your company looks like at a given moment. The balance sheet weighs what you own (assets) against what you owe (liabilities). The difference between the assets and the liabilities is net worth (owner's equity), sometimes used in figuring the value of the business.

Some financing sources (banks or other investors) may want to see balance sheets projected for each quarter for the first year of operation and annually for the next two years. This would quickly show changes in debt, net worth, and the general condition of the business, and could be another helpful control document. You may wish to have a monthly balance sheet (easily done with a microcomputer-powered accounting system), but for many businesses, a year-end balance sheet is all that is required.

URLinks
http://www.edgeonline.com/main/bizbuilders/index.shtm
http://www.toolkit.cch.com/tools/tools.stm#DZ02
http://www.edgeonline.com/main/toolbox/pbalsht.shtml

Creating a Balance Sheet

The format of the balance sheet is governed by a simple rule: assets and liabilities are both listed in order of their immediacy. Those assets that are nearest to cash are listed ahead of those assets that are used to maintain the business (the so-called fixed assets). Those liabilities that are nearest to being due are listed ahead of long-term debt, and all liabilities are listed ahead of the permanent capital (invested capital) and owner's equity, which won't turn to cash until the business is sold. Figure 10.7 shows the basic layout of a balance sheet.

The format is standardized to facilitate analysis and comparison: do not deviate from it. Balance sheets for all companies, great and small, contain the same categories arranged in the same order. The difference is one of detail. Your balance sheet should be designed with your business information needs in mind. These will differ according to the kind of business you are in, the size of your business, and the amount of information your bookkeeping and accounting systems make available.

Filling in your balance sheet is easy once you know what all the terms mean. *No mathematics more complex than basic addition and subtraction is involved.* What you are trying to find out is how your business measures up against other businesses and how your assets and liabilities are distributed.

Depreciation and amortization are technicalities best left to your accountant. They affect asset values by writing their purchase and installation costs off as expenses over the expected life of the asset according to some rather arbitrary tax codes. Ask your accountant to help you.

If you need to provide more detail, do so—but remember to follow the standard format. If your balance sheet is assembled by an accountant, the accountant will specify whether it is done with or without an audit. If you do it yourself, it is without audit. The decision to use a certified public accountant (CPA) should be made carefully for tax and other legal reasons.

Figure 10.8 is a sample balance sheet for Wholesome Foods which is modestly detailed. No depreciation has been taken, for example, because the business has just started. The net worth section could have been more complex. The important thing to notice is that it provides a level of detail appropriate for the purposes of the principals, who own all of the stock.

THE CASH FLOW PROJECTION

The cash flow projection is the most important financial planning tool available to you. If you were limited to one financial statement (which fortunately is not the case), the cash flow projection would be the one to choose. For a new or growing business, the cash flow projection can make the difference between success and failure. For an ongoing business, it can make the difference between growth and stagnation.

FIRST PERSON

Lisa P., Torrance, California: I think of my cash flow budget as being like my checking account. I don't record my deposits until I've actually put the cash in (that would be my cash inflows). When I write a check, that money is gone (like my outflows). I've learned, through years of running my business, that it's all about *amount* and *timing*. I've learned to become disciplined not just about spending, but about *when* I

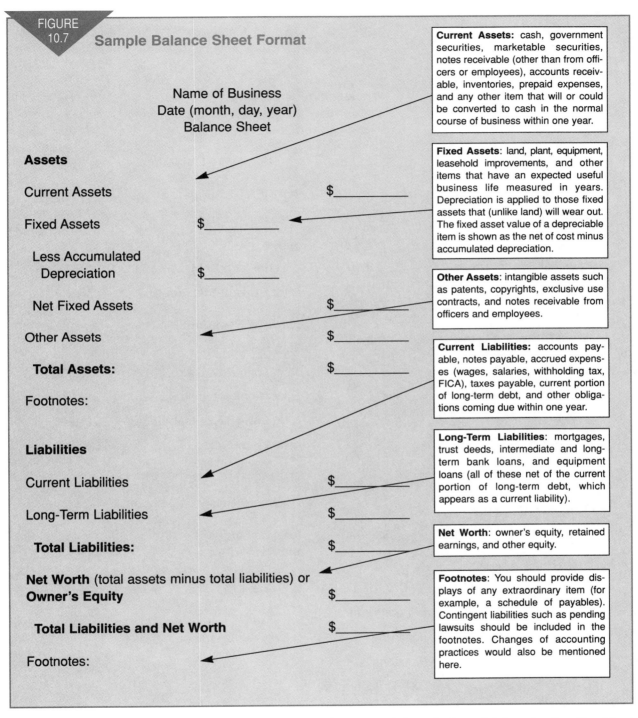

FIGURE 10.7 Sample Balance Sheet Format

Name of Business
Date (month, day, year)
Balance Sheet

Assets

Current Assets $_____

Fixed Assets $_____

   Less Accumulated
   Depreciation $_____

   Net Fixed Assets $_____

Other Assets $_____

  Total Assets: $_____

Footnotes:

Liabilities

Current Liabilities $_____

Long-Term Liabilities $_____

  Total Liabilities: $_____

Net Worth (total assets minus total liabilities) or
Owner's Equity $_____

  Total Liabilities and Net Worth $_____

Footnotes:

Current Assets: cash, government securities, marketable securities, notes receivable (other than from officers or employees), accounts receivable, inventories, prepaid expenses, and any other item that will or could be converted to cash in the normal course of business within one year.

Fixed Assets: land, plant, equipment, leasehold improvements, and other items that have an expected useful business life measured in years. Depreciation is applied to those fixed assets that (unlike land) will wear out. The fixed asset value of a depreciable item is shown as the net of cost minus accumulated depreciation.

Other Assets: intangible assets such as patents, copyrights, exclusive use contracts, and notes receivable from officers and employees.

Current Liabilities: accounts payable, notes payable, accrued expenses (wages, salaries, withholding tax, FICA), taxes payable, current portion of long-term debt, and other obligations coming due within one year.

Long-Term Liabilities: mortgages, trust deeds, intermediate and long-term bank loans, and equipment loans (all of these net of the current portion of long-term debt, which appears as a current liability).

Net Worth: owner's equity, retained earnings, and other equity.

Footnotes: You should provide displays of any extraordinary item (for example, a schedule of payables). Contingent liabilities such as pending lawsuits should be included in the footnotes. Changes of accounting practices would also be mentioned here.

spend money. When my business first started, I made the mistake of acting like I had money before it was in my pocket. I've learned through trial and error, cash comes in more slowly than I expect, and leaves a lot more rapidly.

FIGURE
10.8
Sample Balance Sheet

Wholesome Foods, Inc.
October 1,1998
Balance Sheet

Assets		Liabilities	
CURRENT ASSETS:		**CURRENT LIABILITIES:**	
Cash	$ 2,150	Accounts Payable	$ 8,077
Accounts Receivable (net)	1,700	Current Portion	
Merchandise Inventory	3,900	Long-Term Debt	1,440
Supplies	450	**Total Current Liabilities:**	**$9,517**
Pre-Paid Expenses	320	**LONG-TERM LIABILITIES:**	
Total Current Assets:	**$ 8,520**	Note Payable (a)	$ 535
FIXED ASSETS:		Bank Loan Payable (b)	1,360
Fixtures and Leasehold Improvements (d)	$13,265	Equity Loan Payable (c)	9,250
		Total Long-Term Liabilities:	**$11,145**
Building (freezer)	4,500	**Total Liabilities:**	**$20,662**
Equipment	3,115		
Trucks	6,500	**NET WORTH:**	
Total Fixed Assets:	**$27,380**	Owners' Equity	$15,238
Total Assets:	**$35,900**	**Total Liabilities and Net Worth:**	**$35,900**

ACCOUNTS PAYABLE DISPLAY:

Eldredge's Inc.	$ 3,700
Lesswing's	4,119
Paxstone	180
B&B Refrigeration	78
	$ 8,077

(a) Dave N. Hall for electrical work.
(b) Term loan secured by 1987 Jeep, 1992 Ford.
(c) First Everglades BanCo.
(d) Includes $10,000 in improvements since June.

PERSONAL WORKSHOP 22
Preparing Your Preliminary Balance Sheet
▾ ▾ ▾ ▾ ▾

▾ Use the following worksheet to create an outline of your balance sheet. The worksheet includes all the information you'll need to get started, in the format you will want to follow. The categories can, of course, be defined more precisely, and you should feel free to make the format fit the needs of your business. However, the order of the categories is important and you should follow it. They are arranged in order of decreasing liquidity (for assets) and decreasing immediacy (for liabilities). That is, they are arranged to reflect how quickly you can get your hands on the cash, and how soon you have to pay it out again.

Name of Business		
Date (month, day, year)		
	Balance Sheet	
	Assets	Liabilities
Cash, government securities, marketable securities, notes receivable (other than from officers or employees), accounts receivable, inventories, prepaid expenses, and any other item that will or could be converted to cash in the normal course of business within one year.	Current Assets $_____	
Land, plant, equipment, leasehold improvements, and other items that have an expected useful business life measured in years. Depreciation is applied to those fixed assets that (unlike land) will wear out. The fixed asset value of a depreciable item is shown as the net of cost minus accumulated depreciation.	Fixed Assets $_____	
		Less Accumulated Depreciation $_____
	= Net Fixed Assets $_____	
Intangible assets such as patents, copyrights, exclusive use contracts, and notes receivable from officers and employees	Other Assets $_____	
	Total Assets: $_____	

	Assets	Liabilities
Accounts payable, notes payable, accrued expenses (wages, salaries, withholding tax, FICA), taxes payable, current portion of long-term debt, and other obligations coming due within one year.		Current Liabilities $_____
Mortgages, trust deeds, intermediate and long-term bank loans, and equipment loans (all of these net of the current portion of long-term debt, which appears as a current liability).		Long-Term Liabilities $_____
		Total Liabilities: $_____
Owner's equity, retained earnings, and other equity.	Total Assets minus Total Liabilities = Net Worth $_____	
	Total Liabilities and Net Worth $_____	
	Footnotes	
You should provide displays of any extraordinary item (for example, a schedule of payables). Contingent liabilities such as pending lawsuits should be included in the footnotes. Changes of accounting practices would also be mentioned here.		

The cash flow projection attempts to budget the cash needs of a business and shows how cash will flow in and out of the business over a stated period of time. Cash flows into the business from sales, collection of receivables, and capital injections, and flows out through cash payments for expenses of all kinds. Figure 10.9 outlines cash flow management.

Cash is generated primarily by sales. However, not all sales are cash sales. Perhaps your business is all cash, but if you offer any credit (charge accounts, term payments, trade credit) to your customers, you need to have a means of telling when those credit sales will turn into cash-in-hand. This is blurred in the income statement but made very clear by the cash flow. Your business may be subject to seasonal bills, and again, a cash flow makes the liquidity problems attending such large, occasional expenses clear.

A cash flow deals only with actual cash transactions. Depreciation, a non-cash expense, does not appear on a cash flow. Loan repayments (including interest), on the other hand, do, because they represent a cash disbursement.

Explanation of Cash Flow Projections

Let's go through the sample cash flow projections in Figures 10.10 through 10.12 line by line. The receipts shown on the sample cash flow projections for Wholesome Foods include both sales and other cash sources to emphasize their impact on Wholesome. The cash flow projections show how business operations affect cash flow, so some people prefer to isolate "other sources" of cash receipts in the cash reconciliation section (lines 40 to 43 in the year one cash flow projection).

Line 3, sales receivable. Sales are cash for retail, and cash or 10-day net for wholesale accounts. If Wholesome provided longer terms, their cash flow could be significantly altered. As it is, the cash flow assumes a conservative 10-day lag on all wholesale sales. Since wholesale sales in September were $6,400, $2,000 (10/30 of September wholesale sales) turns to cash in October. The same rationale applies to the rest of the year: One-third of wholesale receipts aren't collected until the following month.

The collection lag is not continued beyond the first quarter of year two. Experience will correct the cash flow, and new figures should be calculated for year two on a monthly basis for year-two business planning.

Line 4, wholesale. Note the total of $28,700 + 60,100 (total sales receivable and total wholesale) = $88,800, which is $1,200 less than the projected sales of $90,000 shown on the income statement. To reconcile the difference between these figures, note that $2,000 in cash receipts come from September of the preceding year, while $3,200 of cash receipts are postponed for September of year one. Sales figures are based on the income projections in Figures 10.3 through 10.6.

Line 5, retail. See income projections in Figures 10.3 through 10.6.

Line 6, other sources (year one).

October:	Inventory loan, using credit line
November:	Closing costs, using credit line
January:	Purchase building; $30,000 from Pendleton and Tellini as new equity investment, along with a $75,000 mortgage
April:	Equipment and building improvements, from term loan
June:	Inventory loan, credit line

Line 7, total. Cash receipts are the sum of line 3 through 6. Note that the total is distorted by loans and new investments.

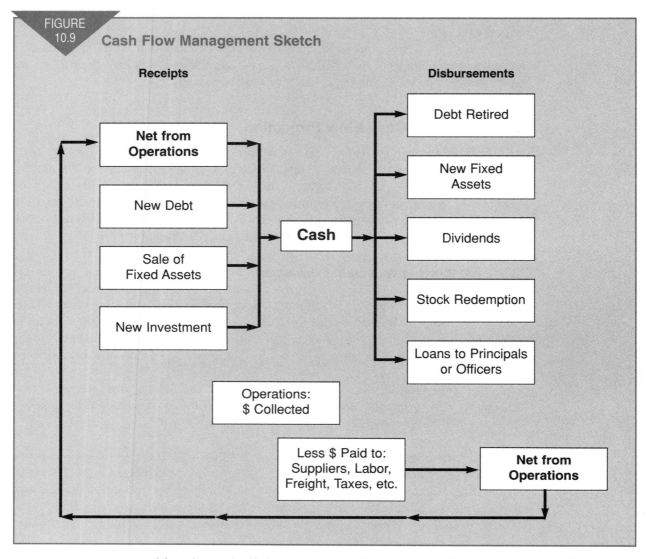

FIGURE 10.9 Cash Flow Management Sketch

Line 8, cash disbursements. These are the disbursements that will be made in cash (including checks) during the normal course of business plus any major anticipated cash outlays.

Line 9, cost of goods. Amount from income projection in Figure 10.4, line 10.

Line 10, variable labor. Amount from income projection in Figure 10.4, line 9.

Line 11, advertising. Budgeted at $400 per month for the first year, plus an extra $600 in October for a tourist-oriented ad campaign, and an extra $4,155 in April to an agency for the major wholesale marketing program, including implementation and execution.

Line 12, insurance. This disbursement payable quarterly.

FIGURE 10.10 Sample Cash Flow Projection: Year One by Month

Wholesome Foods, Inc.
Cash Flow Projection: Year One by Month

	A	B October	C November	D December	E January	F February	G March	H April	I May	J June	K July	L August	M September	N Total
1														
2	Cash Receipts:													
3	Sales Receivables	$2,000	$1,333	$1,333	$1,733	$1,867	$2,000	$2,333	$2,333	$2,800	$3,533	$3,767	$3,767	$28,800
4	Wholesale	$2,667	$2,667	$3,467	$3,733	$4,000	$4,667	$4,667	$5,600	$7,067	$7,533	$7,533	$6,400	$60,000
5	Retail	$9,730	$9,500	$9,500	$9,000	$8,400	$8,750	$10,300	$11,540	$12,165	$12,165	$12,475	$12,475	$126,000
6	Other Sources (see notes)	$7,500	$7,500	$0	$105,000	$0	$0	$30,000	$0	$15,000	$0	$0	$0	$165,000
7	**Total Cash Receipts**	**$21,897**	**$21,000**	**$14,300**	**$119,467**	**$14,267**	**$15,417**	**$47,300**	**$19,473**	**$37,032**	**$23,232**	**$23,775**	**$22,642**	**$379,800**
8	Cash Disbursements:													
9	Cost of Goods	$9,886	$9,720	$10,584	$10,512	$10,368	$11,340	$12,456	$14,357	$16,391	$16,895	$17,118	$15,894	$155,520
10	Variable Labor	$0	$0	$0	$0	$0	$0	$0	$0	$604	$796	$796	$604	$2,800
11	Advertising	$1,000	$400	$400	$400	$400	$400	$4,555	$400	$400	$400	$400	$400	$9,555
12	Insurance	$0	$300	$0	$0	$300	$0	$0	$300	$0	$0	$300	$0	$1,200
13	Legal and Accounting	$0	$0	$375	$0	$0	$375	$0	$0	$375	$0	$0	$375	$1,500
14	Delivery Expenses	$75	$75	$75	$100	$75	$100	$150	$200	$200	$250	$250	$250	$1,800
15	*Fixed Cash Disbursements	$2,535	$2,535	$2,535	$2,535	$2,535	$2,535	$2,535	$2,535	$2,535	$2,535	$2,535	$2,535	$30,425
16	Mortgage (rent)	$550	$550	$550	$876	$876	$876	$876	$876	$876	$876	$876	$876	$9,535
17	Term Loan	$0	$0	$0	$0	$0	$0	$534	$534	$534	$534	$534	$534	$3,202
18	Line of Credit	$0	$85	$15,085	$0	$0	$0	$0	$0	$165	$165	$15,000	$0	$30,500
19	Other Disbursements	$0	$0	$0	$105,000	$0	$30,000	$0	$0	$0	$0	$0	$0	$135,000
20	**Total Cash Disbursements**	**$14,046**	**$13,665**	**$29,604**	**$119,424**	**$14,555**	**$45,627**	**$21,106**	**$19,202**	**$22,080**	**$22,451**	**$37,809**	**$21,468**	**$381,037**
21														
22	**Net Cash Flow**	**$7,851**	**$7,335**	**($15,304)**	**$43**	**($288)**	**($30,210)**	**$26,194**	**$271**	**$14,952**	**$781**	**($14,034)**	**$1,174**	**($1,237)**
23														
24	**Cumulative Cash Flow**	**$7,851**	**$15,185**	**($119)**	**($76)**	**($364)**	**($30,574)**	**($4,380)**	**($4,109)**	**$10,843**	**$11,624**	**($2,410)**	**($1,237)**	
25														
26	*Fixed Cash Disbursements	(FCD)												
27	Utilities	$2,160												
28	Salaries	$22,800												
29	Payroll Taxes and Benefits	$2,850												
30	Office Supplies	$300												
31	Maintenance and Cleaning	$300												
32	Licenses	$115												
33	Boxes, Paper, etc.	$400												
34	Telephone	$1,020												
35	Miscellaneous	$480												
36	Total FCD	$30,425												
37	Avg FCD per month	$2,535												
38														
39	**Cash on Hand:**													
40	Opening Balance	$2,150	$10,001	$17,335	$2,031	$2,074	$1,786	($28,424)	($2,230)	($1,959)	$12,993	$13,774	($260)	
41	+Cash Receipts	$21,897	$21,000	$14,300	$119,467	$14,267	$15,417	$47,300	$19,473	$37,032	$23,232	$23,775	$22,642	$379,793
42	- Cash Disbursements	($14,046)	($13,665)	($29,604)	($119,424)	($14,555)	($45,627)	($21,106)	($19,202)	($22,080)	($22,451)	($37,809)	($21,468)	$381,037
43	Total = New Cash Balance	$10,001	$17,335	$2,031	$2,074	$1,786	($28,424)	($2,230)	($1,959)	$12,993	$13,774	($260)	$913	

FIGURE
10.10   **Sample Cash Flow Projection: Year One by Month, continued**

Cash Flow Sketch

1. Cash at Beginning of Period
   Add: Revenues, etc.:
2. Sales of products (cash)
3. Sales of products (receivables collected)
4. Cash received from assets sold
5. Cash received from equity investment
6. Cash received from loans
7. Cash received from bad debt recovery
8. Miscellaneous cash received
   Total: Cash Received

Subtract: Cash Disbursements

9. New inventory purchased for cash
10. Salaries/wages
11. FICA, federal and state withholding tax
12. Fringe benefits paid
13. New equipment to be purchased for cash
    14. Processing
    15. Office, sales equipment
    16. Transportation equipment
17. Insurance premiums
18. Fees
    19. Accounting
    20. Legal
21. Utilities
    22. Telephone
    23. Heat, light, power
24. Advertising
25. Principal and interest on debt

26. Transportation
    27. Oil, gas
    28. Vehicle maintenance
    29. Tires
30. Freight
31. Provision for bad debts (if funded with cash)
32. Taxes payable
    33. Income (state, federal, other if applicable)
    34. Property
    35. Excise
    36. Sales taxes (if applicable)
37. Dividends paid, cash withdrawal by partner, or contribution to profit-sharing plan
38. Provision for unforeseen circumstances (if funded)
39. Provision for replacement of depreciable assets (if funded)

Total Cash Received less Total Disbursements Equals Cash at End of Period

Note: Only cash disbursements are included. These are actual dollars that you pay out, not obligations that you incur now to be paid off at some future date. Those appear on the income projection and balance sheet.

Line 13, legal and accounting. This disbursement payable quarterly.

Line 14, delivery expenses. These expenses vary with volume of wholesale sales.

Line 15, fixed cash disbursements. These are relatively independent of sales, so they are allocated evenly throughout the year. See display on lines 26 through 37 for details. If salaries fluctuate widely, break them out as a separate item with the other disbursements. For example, if you meet your payroll every other week, two months of the year will have three paydays rather than two, which can make those months look alarmingly costly.

FIGURE 10.11

Sample Cash Flow Projection: Year Two by Quarter

Wholesome Foods, Inc.
Cash Flow Projection: Year Two by Quarter

	A	B	C	D	E	F
1		1st Qtr	2nd Qtr	3rd Qtr	4th Qtr	Total
2	Cash Receipts:					
3	Receivables	$3,200	$0	$0	$0	$3,200
4	Wholesale	$38,900	$54,800	$76,500	$94,800	$265,000
5	Retail	$41,000	$37,400	$48,600	$53,000	$180,000
6	Other Sources	$0	$0	$12,000	$15,000	$27,000
7	**Total Cash Receipts**	**$83,100**	**$92,200**	**$137,100**	**$162,800**	**$475,200**
8	Cash Disbursements:					
9	Cost of Goods	$57,528	$66,384	$90,072	$106,416	$320,400
10	Variable Labor	$0	$0	$604	$2,196	$2,800
11	Advertising	$1,998	$2,305	$3,128	$3,695	$11,125
12	Insurance	$950	$950	$950	$950	$3,800
13	Legal and Accounting	$500	$500	$500	$500	$2,000
14	Delivery Expenses	$1,598	$1,844	$2,502	$2,956	$8,900
15	* Fixed (FCD)	$12,638	$12,638	$12,638	$12,638	$50,550
16	Mortgage	$2,628	$2,628	$2,628	$2,628	$10,514
17	Term Loan	$1,601	$1,601	$1,601	$1,601	$6,403
18	Line of Credit	$0	$0	$12,140	$15,360	$27,500
19	Other Disbursements	$0	$0	$0	$0	$0
20	**Total Cash Disbursements**	**$79,440**	**$88,850**	**$126,762**	**$148,940**	**$443,992**
21						
22	**Net Cash Flow**	**$3,660**	**$3,350**	**$10,338**	**$13,860**	**$31,208**
23						
24	**Cumulative Cash Flow:**	**$3,662**	**$7,009**	**$17,348**	**$31,205**	
25						
26	***Fixed Cash Disbursements**					
27	Utilities	$2,640				
28	Salaries	$39,000				
29	Payroll Taxes/Benefits	$4,875				
30	Office Supplies	$360				
31	Maintenance/Cleaning	$360				
32	Licenses	$115				
33	Boxes, Paper, etc.	$800				
34	Telephone	$1,800				
35	Miscellaneous	$600				
36	Total: FCD/yr	$50,550				
37	Avg FCD per qtr	$12,638				

FIGURE
10.12
Sample Cash Flow Projection: Year Three by Quarter

Wholesome Foods, Inc.
Cash Flow Projection: Year Three by Quarter

	A	B	C	D	E	F
1		1st Qtr	2nd Qtr	3rd Qtr	4th Qtr	Total
2	Cash Receipts:					
3	Receivables	$0	$0	$0	$0	$0
4	Wholesale	$58,750	$55,000	$97,500	$113,750	$325,000
5	Retail	$47,400	$43,600	$56,000	$63,000	$210,000
6	Other Sources	$0	$0	$12,000	$15,000	$27,000
7	**Total Cash Receipts**	**$106,150**	**$98,600**	**$165,500**	**$191,750**	**$562,000**
8	Cash Disbursements					
9	Cost of Goods	$76,428	$70,992	$110,520	$127,260	$385,200
10	Variable Labor	$0	$0	$1,622	$5,898	$7,520
11	Advertising	$2,655	$2,465	$3,835	$4,420	$13,375
12	Insurance	$1,025	$1,025	$1,025	$1,025	$4,100
13	Legal and Accounting	$625	$625	$625	$625	$2,500
14	Delivery Expenses	$1,805	$1,675	$2,610	$3,010	$9,100
15	*Fixed Cash Disbursements	$15,216	$15,216	$15,216	$15,216	$60,865
16	Mortgage (rent)	$2,628	$2,628	$2,628	$2,628	$10,512
17	Term Loan	$1,602	$1,602	$1,602	$1,602	$6,408
18	Line of Credit	$0	$0	$12,140	$15,360	$27,500
19	Other Disbursements	$0	$0	$0	$0	$0
20	**Total Cash Disbursements**	**$101,984**	**$96,228**	**$151,823**	**$177,044**	**$527,080**
21						
22	**Net Cash Flow**	**$4,166**	**$2,372**	**$13,677**	**$14,706**	**$34,920**
23						
24	**Cumulative Cash Flow**	**$4,166**	**$6,538**	**$20,214**	**$34,920**	
25						
26	***Fixed Cash Disbursements:**					
27	Utilities	$2,880				
28	Salaries	$46,800				
29	Payroll Taxes/Benefits	$5,850				
30	Office Supplies	$480				
31	Maintenance/Cleaning	$420				
32	Licenses	$115				
33	Boxes, Paper, etc.	$1,200				
34	Telephone	$2,400				
35	Miscellaneous	$720				
36	Total FCD	$60,865				
37	Avg FCD per qtr	$15,216				

Line 16, mortgage (rent). Rent through December at $550 per month, mortgage payments (principal and interest) at $876 thereafter.

Line 17, term loan. $534 per month for seven years, which includes principal and interest.

Line 18, line of credit. This amount includes principal repayment and interest.

Line 19, other, (year one).

January: Purchase building.
March: Equipment purchase and building improvements to be paid in full.

Line 20, total cash disbursements. This is the sum of lines 9 through 19.

Line 22, net cash flow. This is the difference between total cash receipts and total cash disbursements.

Line 24, cumulative cash flow. For each month in year one this amount is the net cash flow plus the previous month's cumulative cash flow. This is useful on a periodic basis (monthly or quarterly). Over a longer time, it's of academic interest only.

Some experts advise pushing a cash flow until the cumulative cash flow is consistently positive.

Lines 39 through 43, cash balance reconciliation. The opening balance plus cash receipts less cash disbursements equals the new cash balance. This display (for year one only) may be used as a quick check on how well the budget is doing. For years two and three, it is not accurate enough to be useful.

Further explanation of these cash flow items appears in the notes supporting the income projections.

Samples of Notes and Explanations for a Cash Flow Projection

Further explanation of cash flow items appears on the notes supporting the income projections. The following are the notes that would support the projections for Wholesome Foods. You should notice that only the most important cash flow items are annotated. Such annotation helps you remember your thinking at some later time—and helps avoid repeating errors. It also makes your projections much more believable, since the numbers will be seen to have more foundation than guesswork.

Notes and Explanations for Wholesome Foods, Inc.
Cash Flow Projection: Year One by Month

Line 3, sales receivable. Our terms are cash retail, net 10 for wholesale accounts. Assumes 1/3 wholesale will turn to cash in the following month.

Line 4, wholesale. See income projections for derivation of these figures.

Line 5, retail. See income projections for derivation.

Line 6, other sources. October, November credit line, $7,500; January $75,000 mortgage and $30,000 new equity from owners; April term loan for improvements and equipment, $30,000; June inventory buildup, $15,000 from credit line.

Line 9, cost of goods. 72 percent of current month sales (line 6 of income projections).

Line 10, variable labor. Part-time help from May to September to handle extra weekend tourist trade and extra preparation requirements.

Line 11, advertising. $1,000 initial burst, $400 per month thereafter. Add $4,155 to April for wholesale marketing program.

Line 16, mortgage. $550 per month rent to December, mortgage payments from January on. Terms: $75,000, 15 year, 11.5 percent.

Line 17, term loan. $534 per month payments scheduled for term loan. Terms: $30,000, 7 year, 12.25 percent.

Cash Flow Projection: Years Two and Three by Quarter

Line 3, receivables turn from September, year one. Since this is a quarterly summary, no further allowance will be made for receivables turn.

Line 6, other sources. $12,000 for one month on line of credit third quarter, $15,000 for nine weeks on line of credit fourth quarter to meet inventory needs.

Line 15, fixed cash disbursements. Could have included mortgage and term loan payments, but to preserve parity with detail of year one, loan payments are displayed separately.

Line 24, cumulative cash flow. Subtract $1,238 from net cash flow, first quarter year two, to reflect the total cumulative cash flow of year one: ($1,238).

Line 26, fixed cash disbursements. From income projections.

PERSONAL WORKSHOP 23
Preparing Cash Flow Projections
▼ ▼ ▼ ▼ ▼

▼ You can develop your own cash flow projection by filling in the cash flow projection form in this workshop. If some of the lines don't apply to your business, or you don't have the facts at hand yet, leave them blank. You can fill them in later. You want to make sure that cash inflows and outflows are shown in the months in which they fall. Remember: The keys to cash flow are amounts and timing.

The level of detail you wish to provide is another judgment call. You may want to provide much more detail. For example, you might benefit from breaking down your cash flow into a series of cash flows, each representing one profit center or other business unit. This can be particularly handy if you have more than one source of revenue or if you are a manufacturer and need to prepare numerous bids. The accumulated information gained by several projections can be invaluable.

Preliminary Cash Flow Projection
By Month, Year One

	A	B	C	D	E	F	G	H	I
		Jan	Feb	Mar	1 QTR	Apr	May	Jun	2 QTR
1									
2	Cash Inflow								
3									
4									
5	Cash Sales								
6	Receivables								
7	Debts								
8	Investment								
9	Sale of Fixed Assets								
10	Other								
11									
12	Total Cash Inflow								
13									
14	Cash Disbursements								
15									
16	Owner Salary								
17	Other Salaries								
18	FICA, LAH, etc.								
19	Rent								
20	Utilities								
21	Phone								
22	Insurance								
23	Postage								
24	Advertising/Marketing								
25	Secretarial								
26	Travel								
27	Entertainment								
28	Equipment Rental								
29	Office Supplies								
30	Miscellaneous								
31	Start-up Costs (see notes)								
32	Term Loan Payments								
33									
34	Loan Payments (other)								
35	Taxes (see notes)								
36									
37	Total Cash Disbursement								
38									
39	Net Cash Flow								
40									
41	Cumulative Cash Flow								

Preliminary Cash Flow Projection
By Month, Year One

	A	J Jul	K Aug	L Sep	M 3 QTR	N Oct	O Nov	P Dec	Q 4 QTR	R Total: YR 1
1										
2	Cash Inflow									
3										
4	Cash Sales									
5	Receivables									
6	Debts									
7	Investment									
8	Sale of Fixed Assets									
9	Other									
10										
11	Total Cash Inflow									
12										
13	Cash Disbursements									
14										
15	Owner Salary									
16	Other Salaries									
17	FICA, LAH, etc.									
18	Rent									
19	Utilities									
20	Phone									
21	Insurance									
22	Postage									
23	Advertising/Marketing									
24	Secretarial									
25	Travel									
26	Entertainment									
27	Equipment Rental									
28	Office Supplies									
29	Miscellaneous									
30	Start-up Costs (see notes)									
31	Term Loan Payments									
32										
33	Loan Payments (other)									
34	Taxes (see notes)									
35										
36	Total Cash Disbursement									
37										
38	Net Cash Flow									
39										
40	Cumulative Cash Flow									

Step One: Start with the easy part. Fixed monthly payments can be accurately figured. These include rent, salaries and benefits, equipment rental payments, and any monthly term-loan payment.

Step Two: Payments that aren't necessarily made monthly, but whose size and timing can be scheduled, come next. Ongoing advertising and marketing disbursements, some loan payments, and equipment purchases are examples.

Step Three: Predictable payments are largely discretionary, though some are necessary but sporadic (licenses, for example). You have considerable choice over when to make most of these payments and will use these opportunities to juggle your cash flow.

Step Four: Now turn to the cash inflow section (lines 3 through 12). Try to spread out cash from sales and cash from receivables over the year. Each month will probably be different, depending on the seasonality of your business. Lines 7 through 10 (Debt, Investment, Sale of Fixed Assets, and Other) will be treated in steps seven and eight.

Seasonal patterns have such a dramatic effect on the shape of small business cash flows that you should seek out expert advice on the patterns your business will most likely face. SCORE and SBDC counselors may be able to provide this advice free. You may also want to check local business college Small Business Institute™ (SBI) programs.

Step Five: Variable payments depend on the level of sales. If sales are strong, you have to have inventories on hand to meet demand and may need extra help. Other variable costs will also increase. If sales are expected to be low, inventories can be low and other variable costs will shrink.

Step Six: For taxes, line 35, ask your accountant for help. Taxes are part of the cost of doing business, and if you make money, you have to pay taxes. Their timing and amount vary—not at your whim but at the behest of the IRS. (You always have Uncle Sam for a partner, whether you want to or not.)

Step Seven: At this point, you can make the first cut at your cash flow. (It will change after you add back capital investment and proceeds from loans as outlined in the next two steps.) Figure the cash flow for each month: net cash flow equals total cash inflows minus total cash outflows.

Step Eight: Figure cumulative cash flow for the entire first year. If it continues steadily downhill, keep projecting until the cumulative cash flow definitely begins to turn up toward a positive figure. (If it never turns up, don't start the business unless your advisers can show you where your numbers have gone wrong.) For the first month, cumulative cash flow equals net cash flow (that is, line 41 equals line 39). For the second month and beyond, add the new month's net cash flow to the previous month's cumulative cash flow to arrive at the new month's cumulative cash flow.

You can now calculate how much capital your business needs (invested capital plus bank debt).

In step four, certain cash inflows were deliberately left to be treated later. The reason is that in all start-ups there are negative cash flows from the beginning because revenues take a while to develop, while expenses start immediately. Inflows from new capital and loan proceeds cover these negative cash flows.

Cash flow projections lend themselves to computerization. Spreadsheet programs such as Lotus 1-2-3™ or Microsoft Excel™ are made even more valuable because you can tie in graphic displays to your hard numbers, link together several different financial statements, or play "what-if" with much greater speed and accuracy than is possible if you are limited to pencils, adding machines, 13-column accounting papers, and erasers.

THE NEXT STEP

The remainder of this chapter is devoted to a longer case study than usual. This one's also a little different from the others: rather that describing a problem and asking you to help resolve it, Hannah Kingman will simply walk you through her start-up process, with particular emphasis on the financial analysis aspects. Read it carefully, and consider how her experiences apply to your own situation.

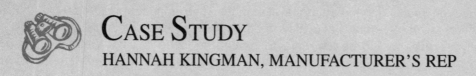

CASE STUDY
HANNAH KINGMAN, MANUFACTURER'S REP

*M*y name is Hannah Kingman. I'm 35 years old, and recently opened my own business as a manufacturer's rep in a medium-sized Southwestern city.

I planned my start-up over a period of several years. My initial steps involved researching businesses that appealed to me. Distribution businesses, manufacturer's reps, service businesses, and consulting had the closest fit with my interests, experience, and goals. I decided on starting a manufacturer's rep business for four basic reasons:

1. It offers compensation tied directly to my own efforts and abilities.
2. It allows me to manage my own time.
3. Its capital requirements are low, and well within my range.
4. I talked with some reps who heartily enjoyed their work.

I took time to gain experience before leaping into business for myself. That experience is difficult to overvalue. I learned how to work with principals (the manufacturers whose product lines I represent), how to identify prospects and decide which ones to approach, what the pitfalls of a rep business are, and (most importantly) how to make money in a notoriously competitive business. I also was paid for my efforts and was able to tuck away enough cash to make sure that when I did begin my business, I'd be able to survive until the business could support me.

I used "house money" to get started. Initially, I worked out of my house and car, to keep my overhead low. A home equity loan is one way to squeeze money out of a house like a sponge. Windfalls (inheritances, winning at the track, a bonus or profit share, and that sort of thing) can also be used if available, but successful small business owners don't rely on luck. They plan for their success. I planned for mine.

CONTINUED ▶

Although my undergraduate degree in English didn't teach me how to read financial statements and run a business, it did teach me research skills. I took the SCORE pre-business workshop and wrote a comprehensive business plan. I took a few sales courses, and since I want to expand my business eventually, I still take management courses and read trade publications.

I set goals and made sure I achieved them: positive, focused, directed efforts are much more productive than just sitting around thinking about how great things are going to be someday. I call that "somedaying," and I just don't do it. I knew that if I was going to be my own boss I had some hurdles: I needed new skills and experience; I needed capital; and I needed to meet people and form business relationships. You don't just walk into a manufacturer and say, "Hi, I'd like to rep your product lines."

I've included my financial model here for you to look at. It starts with a sales forecast and worksheet. This approach is more detailed than many start-ups, but because I gained access to more information I felt I could predict my start-up sales patterns and running expenses with considerable accuracy. I also use a P&L as an intermediate step in establishing my cash flow budget. You won't necessarily have to do this for your start-up, but I can personally recommend it.

I forecast sales and expenses for three years. I plan to add staff in the second year, which will dramatically change my business.

Let's walk through my financial plan.

I represent several storage unit, display case, and shelving manufacturers. I learned that there are three markets: institutional (schools, hospitals, and so forth), retail stores, and industrial firms. Sales split 20/80 between office and display uses, with over 40 percent of the sales coming from the retail sector. The remaining sales should split evenly between institutional and industrial markets. This detailed information can only come from careful research. A combination of data from trade associations and listening to individual sales reps' own experiences provided the basis for my conclusions. The business has seasonal fluctuations (lines 23 through 27) that can be anticipated and planned for.

The three forecasts are based on attaining market share the first year. The anticipated total sales in my industry, for my market area, will be $3.5 million. I think I can get a minimum of 10 percent and a maximum of 20 percent of the market the first year (line 4). Total sales can then be calculated, spread among the market segments, and with high and low ranges established, I chose a more probable 14 percent figure (Most Likely) as a base for my plans.

Trade commission rates in my field average 15 percent. Line 16 is figured by multiplying total sales (line 14) by 15 percent.

Expenses (line 18) are figured on the sales forecast worksheet to total $57,000 the first year. The profit or loss (line 20) is simply revenues (line 16) minus expenses (line 18).

Sales Forecast Worksheet

		Worst case	Most likely	Best case
1.	Sales forecasting			
2.		10% mkt share	14% mkt share	20% mkt share
3.				
4.	Office			
5.	Institutional	$20,000	$28,000	$40,000
6.	Retail	30,000	42,000	60,000
7.	Industrial	20,000	28,000	40,000
8.				
9.	Display			
10.	Institutional	$80,000	$112,000	$160,000
11.	Retail	120,000	168,000	240,000
12.	Industrial	80,000	112,000	160,000
13.				
14.	Total:	$350,000	$490,000	$700,000

CONTINUED ▶

		Worst case	Most likely	Best case
15.				
16.	Revenues (15% commission rate):			
17.		$52,500	$73,500	$105,000
18.	Expenses (from worksheet)			
19.		$57,000	$57,000	$57,000
20.	Profit (Loss):	($4,500)	$16,500	$48,000
21.				
22.				
23.	Sales Pattern (based on experience and trade information):			
24.	1st Qtr	15%	$11,025	
25.	2nd Qtr	30%	$22,050	
26.	3rd Qtr	20%	$14,700	
27.	4th Qtr	35%	$25,725	

Expense Forecast

This worksheet gives an overview of my expenses and determines the sales level needed to meet them. That's what's called my break-even point. The line items aren't exhaustive, but they cover pretty much all of the major expenses I'll be facing.

I want to make $24,000 the first year, $30,000 the second, $36,000 the third. FICA, life and health insurance, etc., are figured as 40 percent of salary total. In years two and three, this includes salaries and benefits for new employees.

My other expense figures are estimates, based on trade figures, experience, and conversations with other sales reps in similar lines.

Line 24, total monthly. Sum of lines 8 through 22.

Line 26, total full year. Line 24 times 12.

Line 28, break even. Line 26 divided by 15 percent (the commission rate). In order to cover expenses, sales have to be $392,000 or better for the year. Since my sales forecast showed $490,000 as the most likely first year sales figure, I have a comfortable margin. This is a very handy feasibility analysis. It shows that my business goals are within reach and gives a clear go-ahead sign.

Line 29, @ $600,000. What if sales hit $600,000 the first year?

I use a computer and a spreadsheet program to analyze possible outcomes under different sets of assumptions. This process is sometimes called "what-if" and is valuable in testing ideas. I also use an accountant. She doesn't fit into my desktop computer, but it's good to keep human experts around.

Years two and three: If I add another salesperson and a secretary to free my own time for more aggressive sales in the second year, I expect to achieve the results shown here. Sales would have to more than double in order for me to break even. Is this realistic? I believe it is, but I'm going to wait until I have more experience running my own business before committing to this sort of aggressive growth.

Expense Forecast Worksheet

		Year 1	Year 2	Year 3
1.				
2.	Costs	$4,900.00	$12,128.17	$13,386.86
3.	Monthly gross sales	32,666.67	80,854.44	89,245.71
4.	Gross sales	392,000.00	970,253.33	1,070,948.53
5.				
6.				
7.	Expenses			
8.	Salary (owner)	$2,000.00	$2,500.00	$3,000.00

CONTINUED ▶

		Year 1	Year 2	Year 3
9.	Salaries (other)	0.00	3,803.33	4,031.53
10.	FICA, LAH ins. etc.	800.00	2,521.33	2,812.61
11.	Rent	250.00	265.00	280.90
12.	Utilities	75.00	79.50	84.27
13.	Insurance	150.00	159.00	168.54
14.	Phone	250.00	397.50	421.35
15.	Mail etc.	100.00	159.00	168.54
16.	Adv/Mktg	150.00	318.00	337.08
17.	Secretarial	200.00	212.00	224.72
18.	Travel	600.00	1,272.00	1,348.32
19.	Entertainment	50.00	150.00	200.00
20.	Equipment rental	125.00	132.50	140.45
21.	Office supplies	50.00	53.00	56.18
22.	Miscellaneous	100.00	106.00	112.36
23.				
24.	Total monthly:	$4,900.00	$12,128.17	$13,386.86
25.				
26.	Total full year	$58,800.00	$145,538.00	$160,642.28
27.				
28.	Break even	$392,000.00	$970,253.33	$1,070,948.53
29.				
30.	@ $600K	$31,200.00		

Projected Profit and Loss

I asked my accountant what a P&L is, and she explained it this way: "A P&L," she said, "is based on anticipated revenues and expenses as they are incurred, unlike their treatment in a cash flow projection, where they are booked only when cash is exchanged. A P&L is used to determine whether your business is making money. It's optional until you are actually in business. The real key to survival is cash flow: You can go broke while making money if the cash isn't coming in as fast as it goes out."

My P&L projection for one year is used to support her cash flow projection. Some of the major differences between the cash flow and the income statement revolve around non-cash expenses (depreciation, amortization) that are reported on a P&L but not on the cash flow, while some cash disbursements (loan repayments including principal and interest) appear on the cash flow but not on the P&L.

Line 7, total income. Anticipated revenues of $484,000 (from the sales forecast) are spread over 12 months according to the anticipated pattern.

Lines 12 through 29, expenses. Anticipated expenses of $58,800 (from the worksheet) are distributed evenly over the 12 months.

Line 32, profit (loss) is shown monthly. A monthly P&L can be misleading, especially for a start-up business. Quarterly P&Ls are actually more useful, as they allow the surges and anomalies to even out. Studying three months at a time (current month plus the two immediately previous months) is even more handy. Profit is simply total income minus total expenses (line 7 minus line 30). Projected first year profit: $13,800.

Lines 35 through 39: Note the sales pattern provided at the bottom of the P & L. This is the same pattern as shown on the Sales Forecast.

CONTINUED ▶

Hannah's Profit and Loss Projection

		Jan	Feb	Mar	Apr	May	Jun
1.		Jan	Feb	Mar	Apr	May	Jun
2.							
3.							
4.	Income:						
5.	Office	$500.00	$1,000.00	$1,200.00	$1,600.00	$1,800.00	$2,000.00
6.	Display	$1,200.00	$2,000.00	$3,000.00	$3,600.00	$6,000.00	$7,000.00
7.	Total Income	$1,700.00	$3,000.00	$4,200.00	$5,200.00	$7,800.00	$9,000.00
8.							
9.	Quarters:			$8,900.00			$22,000.00
10.							
11.	Expenses:						
12.	Owner salary	$2,000.00	$2,000.00	$2,000.00	$2,000.00	$2,000.00	$2,000.00
13.	Salaries (other)	$0.00	$0.00	$0.00	$0.00	$0.00	$0.00
14.	FICA, LAH etc.	$800.00	$800.00	$800.00	$800.00	$800.00	$800.00
15.	Insurance	$150.00	$150.00	$150.00	$150.00	$150.00	$150.00
16.	Rent	$250.00	$250.00	$250.00	$250.00	$250.00	$250.00
17.	Utilities	$75.00	$75.00	$75.00	$75.00	$75.00	$75.00
18.	Phone	$250.00	$250.00	$250.00	$250.00	$250.00	$250.00
19.	Mail	$100.00	$100.00	$100.00	$100.00	$100.00	$100.00
20.	Advertising/marketing	$150.00	$150.00	$150.00	$150.00	$150.00	$150.00
21.	Secretarial	$200.00	$200.00	$200.00	$200.00	$200.00	$200.00
22.	Travel	$600.00	$600.00	$600.00	$600.00	$600.00	$600.00
23.	Entertainment	$50.00	$50.00	$50.00	$50.00	$50.00	$50.00
24.	Equipment lease	$125.00	$125.00	$125.00	$125.00	$125.00	$125.00
25.	Office supplies	$50.00	$50.00	$50.00	$50.00	$50.00	$50.00
26.	Miscellaneous	$100.00	$100.00	$100.00	$100.00	$100.00	$100.00
27.							
28.	Interest						
29.							
30.	Total Expenses:	$4,900.00	$4,900.00	$4,900.00	$4,900.00	$4,900.00	$4,900.00
31.							
32.	Profit (Loss):	($3,200.00)	($1,900.00)	($700.00)	$300.00	$2,900.00	$4,100.00
33.							
34.							
35.	Sales Pattern (based on experience and trade information:						
36.		1 Qtr.	15.00%		$11,025.00		
37.		2 Qtr.	30.00%		$22,050.00		
38.		3 Qtr.	20.00%		$14,700.00		
39.		4 Qtr.	35.00%		$25,725.00		

CONTINUED ▶

Hannah's Profit and Loss Projection

	Jul	Aug	Sep	Oct	Nov	Dec	Total
1.							
2.							
3.							
4.							
5.	$1,700.00	$500.00	$700.00	$1,200.00	$1,800.00	$3,000.00	$17,000.00
6.	$5,400.00	$2,400.00	$4,000.00	$6,500.00	$7,500.00	$7,000.00	$55,600.00
7.	$7,100.00	$2,900.00	$4,700.00	$7,700.00	$9,300.00	$10,000.00	$72,600.00
8.							
9.			$14,700.00			$27,000.00	
10.							
11.							
12.	$2,000.00	$2,000.00	$2,000.00	$2,000.00	$2,000.00	$2,000.00	$2,400.00
13.	$0.00	$0.00	$0.00	$0.00	$0.00	$0.00	$0.00
14.	$800.00	$800.00	$800.00	$800.00	$800.00	$800.00	$9,600.00
15.	$150.00	$150.00	$150.00	$150.00	$150.00	$150.00	$1,800.00
16.	$250.00	$250.00	$250.00	$250.00	$250.00	$250.00	$3,000.00
17.	$75.00	$75.00	$75.00	$75.00	$75.00	$75.00	$900.00
18.	$250.00	$250.00	$250.00	$250.00	$250.00	$250.00	$3,000.00
19.	$100.00	$100.00	$100.00	$100.00	$100.00	$100.00	$1,200.00
20.	$150.00	$150.00	$150.00	$150.00	$150.00	$150.00	$1,800.00
21.	$200.00	$200.00	$200.00	$200.00	$200.00	$200.00	$2,400.00
22.	$600.00	$600.00	$600.00	$600.00	$600.00	$600.00	$7,200.00
23.	$50.00	$50.00	$50.00	$50.00	$50.00	$50.00	$600.00
24.	$125.00	$125.00	$125.00	$125.00	$125.00	$125.00	$1,500.00
25.	$50.00	$50.00	$50.00	$50.00	$50.00	$50.00	$600.00
26.	$100.00	$100.00	$100.00	$100.00	$100.00	$100.00	$1,200.00
27.							
28.							$0.00
29.							
30.	$4,900.00	$4,900.00	$4,900.00	$4,900.00	$4,900.00	$4,900.00	$58,800.00
31.							
32.	$2,200.00	($2,000.00)	($200.00)	$2,800.00	$4,400.00	$5,100.00	$13,800.00
33.							
34.							
35.							
36.							
37.							
38.							
39.							

CONTINUED ▶

Asset List and Values

My asset list includes inventories for display (I have to maintain a sales room), necessary office equipment (some of which I own, some of which will be purchased during the first year and show up on the cash flow), and a variety of licenses that are part of the cost of doing business. This information will be used to support the cash flow projection and balance sheet.

Asset List and Values	
Inventories for display:	
Initial inventory	$2,000.00
New inventories	5,000.00
Total Inventories:	$7,000.00
Office equipment:	
Copier	$ 700.00
Computer and software	3,700.00
Printer	2,000.00
Typewriter	400.00
Filing cabinets	600.00
Telephones	1,200.00
Car phone (cellular)	600.00
Answering machine	300.00
Total Office Equipment:	$9,500.00
Permits, licenses etc.	$1,000.00
TOTAL:	$17,500.00

Cash Flow Projections

There are two projections presented here: an initial cash flow (to show where the holes are) and a revised cash flow (which reflects needed capital investment and new debt). This two-step approach is highly recommended, I understand, because it allows you to calculate with some accuracy how much you need to invest and/or borrow and when that cash will be needed in the business.

A cash flow projection is based on amounts of cash and the timing of that cash's movement. Balancing cash flow is a major survival skill for a small business, especially if access to additional capital or debt is in question.

Line 8. Cash sales are sales paid for at the time. Unlike the P&L, where sales are booked when made regardless of the payment schedule, cash flow projections demand that money (including checks) change hands.

Line 9. Receivables have been lagged according to a rather complex schedule. My schedule is based on two patterns: office sales are 50 percent cash, 50 percent in 30 days. Display sales are 50 percent cash, 50 percent in 90 days. Your pattern will depend on your business. For me, my research and experience suggested that I should take a conservative approach. (I really expect receivables to be significantly shorter, which would accelerate my cash flow, but like my dad always said, it's better to expect the worst and be surprised when something good happens, than to expect the best and be disappointed.)

Line 10, debt. No debt is shown on the preliminary cash flow, because I didn't know how much to borrow or when. That decision is made by looking at lines 42 and 44, cash flow and cumulative cash flow.

Line 11, investment. Similar considerations apply to new investment.

My combination of debt and investment is based on my analysis of the preliminary cash flow projection, equipment needs, and disbursement patterns. I had my bank and accountant help me make these decisions.

Line 19, salary. I plan to take $1,000 a month at first, then increase it as the business takes off.

Line 20: taxes and benefits. Currently figured at 40 percent of salary, these will increase as my salary goes up.

Line 22. Rent payments don't start until the third month.

Line 23. Utilities are a space cost, so they too are postponed.

Line 24. Phone costs are based on anticipated use: heavy at first, then following a well-known pattern.

Line 25. Insurance is paid quarterly. Compare with the P&L, as insurance is used evenly throughout the year. This kind of difference between the P&L and cash flow is important to understand.

Line 26, postage. Heavy, then light. Start-up mailing is expensive: see the notes that follow.

Line 28, advertising/marketing. An initial blitz, including direct mail, will get my firm off the ground. After that, advertising and marketing costs are governed by two factors: ongoing marketing expenses and special promotions.

Line 29, secretarial. Part-time help, as needed.

Line 30, travel. Seasonal adjustments.

Line 31, entertainment. Seasonal adjustments.

Line 32, equipment rental. Monthly payments.

Line 33, miscellaneous. January includes $200 of small items (paper, envelopes, etc.) as well as equipment to the tune of $9,500 (see asset list). In April, $5,000 of new inventory will be needed.

Line 34, start-up costs. In January, licenses and fees, plus starting inventory.

CONTINUED ▶

Hannah's Preliminary Cash Flow Projection

	A	B	C	D	E	F	G	H	I
1		Jan	Feb	Mar	1 QTR	Apr	May	Jun	2 QTR
2		($15,125.00)	($16,100.00)	($16,525.00)	($16,525.00)	($21,825.00)	($25,425.00)	($21,500.00)	($21,500.00)
3	Cash Inflow								
4									
5	Cash sales	$850.00	$1,500.00	$2,100.00	$4,450.00	$2,600.00	$3,900.00	$4,500.00	$11,000.00
6	Receivables		$850.00	$1,500.00	$2,350.00	$2,100.00	$2,600.00	$3,900.00	$8,600.00
7	Debt				$0.00				$0.00
8	Investment				$0.00				$0.00
9	Sale of fixed assets				$0.00				$0.00
10	Other				$0.00				$0.00
11									
12	Total Cash Inflow	$850.00	$2,350.00	$3,600.00	$6,800.00	$4,700.00	$6,500.00	$8,400.00	$19,600.00
13									
14	Cash Disbursements								
15									
16	Owner salary	$1,000.00	$1,000.00	$1,500.00	$3,500.00	$2,000.00	$2,000.00	$2,000.00	$6,000.00
17	Other salaries	$0.00	$0.00	$0.00	$0.00	$0.00	$0.00	$0.00	$0.00
18	FICA, LAH, etc.	$400.00	$400.00	$600.00	$1,400.00	$800.00	$800.00	$800.00	$2,400.00
19	Rent	$0.00	$0.00	$250.00	$250.00	$250.00	$250.00	$250.00	$750.00
20	Utilities	$0.00	$0.00	$125.00	$125.00	$100.00	$75.00	$50.00	$225.00
21	Phone	$350.00	$200.00	$300.00	$850.00	$350.00	$300.00	$250.00	$900.00
22	Insurance	$0.00	$800.00	$0.00	$800.00	$0.00	$0.00	$0.00	$0.00
23	Postage	$200.00	$100.00	$100.00	$400.00	$125.00	$100.00	$100.00	$325.00
24	Advertising/marketing	$600.00	$0.00	$50.00	$650.00	$150.00	$150.00	$100.00	$400.00
25	Secretarial	$100.00	$150.00	$200.00	$450.00	$200.00	$200.00	$200.00	$600.00
26	Travel	$300.00	$400.00	$600.00	$1,300.00	$750.00	$750.00	$600.00	$2,100.00
27	Entertainment	$50.00	$100.00	$100.00	$250.00	$100.00	$100.00	$0.00	$200.00
28	Equipment rental	$125.00	$125.00	$125.00	$375.00	$125.00	$125.00	$125.00	$375.00
29	Office supplies	$150.00	$0.00	$25.00	$175.00	$50.00	$50.00	$0.00	$100.00
30	Miscellaneous	$9,700.00	$50.00	$50.00	$9,800.00	$5,000.00	$200.00	$0.00	$5,200.00
31	Start-up costs (see notes)	$3,000.00			$3,000.00				
32	Term loan payments								
33									
34	Loan payments (other)				$0.00		$5,000.00		$5,000.00
35	Taxes (see notes)				$0.00	$0.00			$0.00
36									
37	Total Cash Disbursement	$15,975.00	$3,325.00	$4,025.00	$23,325.00	$10,000.00	$10,100.00	$4,475.00	$24,575.00
38									
39	Cash Flow	($15,125.00)	($975.00)	($425.00)	($16,525.00)	($5,300.00)	($3,600.00)	$3,925.00	($4,975.00)
40									
41	Cumulative Cash Flow	($15,125.00)	($16,100.00)	($16,525.00)	($16,525.00)	($21,825.00)	($25,425.00)	($21,500.00)	($21,500.00)

Hannah's Preliminary Cash Flow Projection

	J	K	L	M	N	O	P
		Jul	Aug	Sep	3 QTR	Oct	Nov
1							
2		($17,575.00)	($17,950.00)	($18,675.00)	($18,675.00)	($17,250.00)	($14,325.00)
3	Cash Inflow						
4							
5	Cash sales	$3,550.00	$1,450.00	$2,350.00	$7,350.00	$3,850.00	$4,650.00
6	Receivables	$4,500.00	$3,550.00	$1,450.00	$9,500.00	$2,350.00	$3,850.00
7	Debt				$0.00		
8	Investment				$0.00		
9	Sale of fixed assets				$0.00		
10	Other				$0.00		
11							
12	Total Cash Inflow	$8,050.00	$5,000.00	$3,800.00	$16,850.00	$6,200.00	$8,500.00
13							
14	Cash Disbursements						
15							
16	Owner salary	$2,000.00	$2,000.00	$2,000.00	$6,000.00	$2,000.00	$2,000.00
17	Other salaries	$0.00	$0.00	$0.00	$0.00	$0.00	$0.00
18	FICA, LAH, etc.	$800.00	$800.00	$800.00	$2,400.00	$800.00	$800.00
19	Rent	$250.00	$250.00	$250.00	$750.00	$250.00	$250.00
20	Utilities	$50.00	$50.00	$50.00	$150.00	$100.00	$175.00
21	Phone	$150.00	$150.00	$200.00	$500.00	$250.00	$300.00
22	Insurance	$0.00	$800.00	$0.00	$800.00	$300.00	$0.00
23	Postage	$50.00	$50.00	$150.00	$250.00	$100.00	$75.00
24	Advertising/marketing	$50.00	$350.00	$100.00	$500.00	$0.00	$300.00
25	Secretarial	$100.00	$200.00	$200.00	$500.00	$200.00	$350.00
26	Travel	$450.00	$500.00	$500.00	$1,450.00	$500.00	$750.00
27	Entertainment	$50.00	$50.00	$100.00	$200.00	$50.00	$100.00
28	Equipment rental	$125.00	$125.00	$125.00	$375.00	$125.00	$125.00
29	Office supplies	$0.00	$50.00	$0.00	$50.00	$0.00	$250.00
30	Miscellaneous	$50.00	$0.00	$50.00	$100.00	$100.00	$100.00
31	Start-up costs (see notes)						
32	Term loan payments				$0.00		
33							
34	Loan payments (other)				$0.00		
35	Taxes (see notes)				$0.00		
36							
37	Total Cash Disbursement	$4,125.00	$5,375.00	$4,525.00	$14,025.00	$4,775.00	$5,575.00
38							
39	Cash Flow	$3,925.00	($375.00)	($725.00)	$2,825.00	$1,425.00	$2,925.00
40							
41	Cumulative Cash Flow	($17,575.00)	($17,950.00)	($18,675.00)	($18,675.00)	($17,250.00)	($14,325.00)

Hannah's Revised Cash Flow Projection

	A	B Jan	C Feb	D Mar	E 1 QTR	F Apr	G May	H Jun	I 2 QTR
1		($125.00)	($1,100.00)	($1,525.00)	($1,525.00)	$5,675.00	$2,075.00	$11,000.00	$11,000.00
2									
3	Cash Inflow								
4									
5	Cash sales	$850.00	$1,500.00	$2,100.00	$4,450.00	$2,600.00	$3,900.00	$4,500.00	$11,000.00
6	Receivables		$850.00	$1,500.00	$2,350.00	$2,100.00	$2,600.00	$3,900.00	$8,600.00
7	Debt				$0.00	$12,500.00		$5,000.00	$17,500.00
8	Investment	$15,000.00			$15,000.00				$0.00
9	Sale of fixed assets				$0.00				$0.00
10	Other				$0.00				$0.00
11									
12	Total Cash Inflow	$15,850.00	$2,350.00	$3,600.00	$21,800.00	$17,200.00	$6,500.00	$13,400.00	$37,100.00
13									
14	Cash Disbursements								
15									
16	Owner salary	$1,000.00	$1,000.00	$1,500.00	$3,500.00	$2,000.00	$2,000.00	$2,000.00	$6,000.00
17	Other salaries	$0.00	$0.00	$0.00	$0.00	$0.00	$0.00	$0.00	$0.00
18	FICA, LAH, etc.	$400.00	$400.00	$600.00	$1,400.00	$800.00	$800.00	$800.00	$2,400.00
19	Rent	$0.00	$0.00	$250.00	$250.00	$250.00	$250.00	$250.00	$750.00
20	Utilities	$0.00	$0.00	$125.00	$125.00	$100.00	$75.00	$50.00	$225.00
21	Phone	$350.00	$200.00	$300.00	$850.00	$350.00	$300.00	$250.00	$900.00
22	Insurance	$0.00	$800.00	$0.00	$800.00	$0.00	$0.00	$0.00	$0.00
23	Postage	$200.00	$100.00	$100.00	$400.00	$125.00	$100.00	$100.00	$325.00
24	Advertising/marketing	$600.00	$0.00	$50.00	$650.00	$150.00	$150.00	$100.00	$400.00
25	Secretarial	$100.00	$150.00	$200.00	$450.00	$200.00	$200.00	$200.00	$600.00
26	Travel	$300.00	$400.00	$600.00	$1,300.00	$750.00	$750.00	$600.00	$2,100.00
27	Entertainment	$50.00	$100.00	$100.00	$250.00	$100.00	$100.00	$0.00	$200.00
28	Equipment rental	$125.00	$125.00	$125.00	$375.00	$125.00	$125.00	$125.00	$375.00
29	Office supplies	$150.00	$0.00	$25.00	$175.00	$50.00	$50.00	$0.00	$100.00
30	Miscellaneous (see notes)	$9,700.00	$50.00	$50.00	$9,800.00	$5,000.00	$200.00	$0.00	$5,200.00
31	Start-up costs	$3,000.00			$0.00				$0.00
32	Term loan payments								
33									
34	Loan payments (other)				$0.00		$5,000.00		$5,000.00
35	Taxes (see notes)				$0.00				$0.00
36									
37	Total Cash Disbursement	$15,975.00	$3,325.00	$4,025.00	$23,325.00	$10,000.00	$10,100.00	$4,475.00	$24,575.00
38									
39	Cash Flow	($125.00)	($975.00)	($425.00)	($1,525.00)	$7,200.00	($3,600.00)	$8,925.00	$12,525.00
40									
41	Cumulative Cash Flow	($125.00)	($1,100.00)	($1,525.00)	($1,525.00)	$5,675.00	$2,075.00	$11,000.00	$11,000.00

Hannah's Revised Cash Flow Projection

A	J Jul	K Aug	L Sep	M 3 QTR	N Oct	O Nov	P Dec	Q 4 QTR	R Total: Year 1
2	$8,355.00	$7,910.00	$7,115.00	$7,115.00	$6,970.00	$4,825.00	$9,375.00	$9,375.00	$9,375.00
3 Cash Inflow									
4									
5 Cash sales	$3,550.00	$1,450.00	$2,350.00	$7,350.00	$3,850.00	$4,650.00	$5,000.00	$13,500.00	$36,300.00
6 Receivables	$4,500.00	$3,550.00	$1,450.00	$9,500.00	$2,350.00	$3,850.00	$4,650.00	$10,850.00	$31,300.00
7 Debt				$0.00				$0.00	$17,500.00
8 Investment				$0.00				$0.00	$15,000.00
9 Sale of fixed assets				$0.00				$0.00	$0.00
10 Other								$0.00	$0.00
11									
12 Total Cash Inflow	$8,050.00	$5,000.00	$3,800.00	$16,850.00	$6,200.00	$8,500.00	$9,650.00	$24,350.00	$100,100.00
13									
14 Cash Disbursements									
15									
16 Owner salary	$2,000.00	$2,000.00	$2,000.00	$6,000.00	$2,000.00	$2,000.00	$2,000.00	$6,000.00	$21,500.00
17 Other salaries	$0.00	$0.00	$0.00	$0.00	$0.00	$0.00	$0.00	$0.00	$0.00
18 FICA, LAH, etc.	$800.00	$800.00	$800.00	$2,400.00	$800.00	$800.00	$800.00	$2,400.00	$8,600.00
19 Rent	$250.00	$250.00	$250.00	$750.00	$250.00	$250.00	$250.00	$750.00	$2,500.00
20 Utilities	$50.00	$50.00	$50.00	$150.00	$100.00	$175.00	$125.00	$400.00	$900.00
21 Phone	$150.00	$150.00	$200.00	$500.00	$250.00	$300.00	$250.00	$800.00	$3,050.00
22 Insurance	$0.00	$800.00	$0.00	$800.00	$300.00	$0.00	$0.00	$300.00	$1,900.00
23 Postage	$50.00	$50.00	$150.00	$250.00	$100.00	$75.00	$50.00	$225.00	$1,200.00
24 Advertising/marketing	$50.00	$350.00	$100.00	$500.00	$0.00	$300.00	$150.00	$450.00	$2,000.00
25 Secretarial	$100.00	$200.00	$200.00	$500.00	$200.00	$350.00	$300.00	$850.00	$2,400.00
26 Travel	$450.00	$500.00	$500.00	$1,450.00	$500.00	$750.00	$800.00	$2,050.00	$6,900.00
27 Entertainment	$50.00	$50.00	$100.00	$200.00	$50.00	$100.00	$100.00	$250.00	$900.00
28 Equipment rental	$125.00	$125.00	$125.00	$375.00	$125.00	$125.00	$125.00	$375.00	$1,500.00
29 Office supplies	$0.00	$50.00	$0.00	$50.00	$0.00	$250.00	$50.00	$300.00	$625.00
30 Miscellaneous (see notes)	$50.00	$0.00	$50.00	$100.00	$100.00	$100.00	$100.00	$300.00	$15,400.00
31 Start-up costs									
32 Term loan payments	$70.00	$70.00	$70.00	$210.00	$70.00	$70.00	$0.00	$140.00	$350.00
33									
34 Loan payments (other)	$6,500.00			$6,500.00	$1,500.00	$5,000.00		$6,500.00	$18,000.00
35 Taxes (see notes)				$0.00				$0.00	$0.00
36									
37 Total Cash Disbursement	$10,695.00	$5,445.00	$4,595.00	$20,735.00	$6,345.00	$10,645.00	$5,100.00	$22,090.00	$90,725.00
38									
39 Cash Flow	($2,645.00)	($445.00)	($795.00)	($3,885.00)	($145.00)	($2,145.00)	$4,550.00	$2,260.00	$9,375.00
40									
41 Cumulative Cash Flow	$8,355.00	$7,910.00	$7,115.00	$7,115.00	$6,970.00	$4,825.00	$9,375.00	$9,375.00	$9,375.00

Line 35, term loan payments.

Line 37, loan payments (other). A May payment of $5,000 will cover some pre-start-up costs I incurred, including my own car.

Line 38, taxes. None anticipated the first year.

Line 40, total cash disbursements. Sum of lines 19 through 39.

Line 42, cash flow. Line 15 (cash inflow) minus line 40. Monthly figures used to check progress.

Line 44, cumulative cash flow. Used as a guide to when new debt or capital is needed, when debt can be repaid, and similar major financial decisions.

Notes on the Cash Flow Projection

In my preliminary cash flow, negative cash flow peaks in the second quarter at –$25,425. I used this information to make an important decision: I will need to invest $15,000 in January to get my business off to a safe start.

Even with this investment, things will be tight in the second quarter, so I plan to borrow $12,500 after consulting with my bank and accountant. If I don't have to borrow this amount, though, I won't. But by planning for it before start-up, I know it will be available to me if I need it. If my projections don't hold true, I stand to lose some or all of my investment, and I don't want to compound that problem with a mountain of debt.

Cash flow should improve dramatically after this investment, so I plan to repay the loan: $6,500 in July, $1,500 in October, and $5,000 in November. This includes interest payments as well as principal.

These changes are reflected in the revised cash flow projection, which will also function as my cash flow budget. ▼

URLinks
http://www.smalloffice.com/miser/archive/mmsays44.htm
http://www1.bigyellow.com/ma/z_bz_971215.mat
http://sbinformation.miningco.com/MSUB18.HTM

CHAPTER BRIEFCASE

▼▼▼▼▼

- Policy and control are the key ingredients of any successful business. Policy establishes what your business will do, and control measures how you accomplish those goals. The heart of your control system is bookkeeping.

- At a minimum, you should be familiar with balance sheets, cash flow projections, P&L statements, and the break-even analysis. The balance sheet and the cash flow projection will help you answer the most pressing financial questions start-ups face. The profit and loss (P&L) statement (or income statement) is useful, but the cash flow projection is key. Profit is secondary to meeting your bills. The break-even analysis helps quantify the sales levels you must reach based on your projected expenses. You should consult experts, because the break-even analysis depends on some tricky judgments about expenses.

▲▲▲▲▲▲

See Also ...

▶ 2. The Economics
      of Small Business

▶ 4. Determining the
      Feasibility of Your
      Business

▶ 7. Positioning Your
      Business

▶ 10. Basic Financial
      Statements

▶ 12. Credit and
      Collections

▶ 25. Making
      Employment
      Decisions

▶ 26. Planning
      for Growth

Chapter 11

FINANCIAL HEALTH AND PRICING STRATEGIES

▼▼▼▼▼

Where large sums of money are concerned, it is advisable to trust nobody.

—Agatha Christie

MISSION STATEMENT

In this chapter, you will

*L*EARN how to use your financial statements to manage your business, and how to develop profitable pricing strategies.

*E*XPLORE a variety of strategies for setting price structures.

*A*PPLY your understanding of financial analysis to a case study.

*P*RODUCE a price structure for your business.

KEY TERMS

breakeven statement	deviation analysis	variance analysis
current ratio	quick test	working capital
debt-to-worth ratio		

INTRODUCTION TO FINANCIAL HEALTH AND PRICING STRATEGIES

Earlier, we learned about the basic financial statements and how to prepare them. This chapter is dedicated to how to use that information to make wise decisions for your business. Initially, people often dread time spent trying to understand this information. However, once you know what to look for, and understand how it can help you, it will (or should) become a regular habit.

Financial statements are not created to make your banker happy or to puff up your business plan. They aren't for your bookkeeper or accountant to analyze. They're for *you*. They are the most reliable source you have in

▼▼▼▼▼▼▼▼▼▼▼▼▼▼▼▼▼▼▼▼

making level-headed business decisions. As the owner, you need to understand what those numbers mean, and use them to manage your business.

By regularly analyzing your financial statements, you will be able to answer such questions as:

- How much cash do I need to keep my business running?
- Is this business a good investment?
- Can I make payroll this week?
- Am I making money?
- How much is my business worth?
- How does my business stack up against other businesses?
- How much do I have to sell to break even?
- Can I afford to buy this machine, hire that person, borrow more money, enter a new market?
- At what point will I be too deep in debt?

DEVIATION ANALYSIS

The **deviation analysis** (also referred to as a **variance analysis**) compares actual performance to projected or budgeted performance on a monthly basis. As a guard against runaway expenses or destroyed budgets, it's unbeatable. You should compare both income statement and cash flow projections to actual performance. Business experts agree that more businesses are destroyed by the cumulative effects of a lot of small, sloppy errors (which deviation analysis highlights and helps you correct) than by large, powerful, obvious mismanagement.

Together, the income statement, cash flow, breakeven, deviation analysis, and balance sheet afford a comprehensive model of the operations, liquidity, and the past and near future of your business. If you have a computer and spreadsheet software, the information can be easily manipulated to give you answers to many revealing what-if questions: What if we raised prices 5 percent? What if we lose 15 percent of our customer base? Would it make sense to add these fixed expenses to obtain 10 percent greater productivity? And so on.

The value of such an interactive model of your business is hard to overstate. If you are not familiar with computerized financial models, check with the nearest business school (or your accountant). Just being able to trace the short-term financial implications of a business decision can make a big difference in the quality of your judgments, to say nothing of your profits. Figures 11.1 through 11.4 are examples of budget deviation analysis formats.

BREAKEVEN STATEMENT

Let's review the breakeven. In Chapter 4, we talked about breakeven analysis, and how to compute your breakeven point for determining how much you would need to sell to meet start-up and operating obligations. It's obvious why this information is critical when starting a business. The breakeven is an important tool as your business continues to grow.

FIGURE 11.1 Budget Deviation Analysis by Month (from Income Statement)

From the Income Statement
For the Month of _____

	A Actual for Month	B Budget for Month	C Deviation (B – A)	D % Deviation (C/B x 100)
Sales				
Less Cost of Goods				
Gross Profit on Sales				
Operating Expenses:				
Variable Expenses				
Sales salaries (commissions)				
Advertising				
Miscellaneous variable				
Total Variable Expenses				
Fixed Expenses				
Utilities				
Salaries				
Payroll taxes and benefits				
Office supplies				
Insurance				
Maintenance and cleaning				
Legal and accounting				
Delivery				
Licenses				
Boxes, paper, etc.				
Telephone				
Miscellaneous				
Depreciation				
Interest				
Total Fixed Expenses				
Total Operating Expenses				
Net Profit (Gross Profit on Sales Less Total Operating Expenses)				
Tax Expense				
Net Profit after Taxes				

FIGURE 11.2 **Budget Deviation Analysis Year-to-Date (from Income Statement)**

From the Income Statement
Year-to-Date _____

	A Actual for Year-to-Date	B Budget for Year-to-Date	C Deviation (B – A)	D % Deviation (C/B x 100)
Sales				
Less Cost of Goods				
Gross Profit on Sales				
Operating Expenses:				
Variable Expenses				
Sales salaries (commissions)				
Advertising				
Miscellaneous variable				
Total Variable Expenses				
Fixed Expenses				
Utilities				
Salaries				
Payroll taxes and benefits				
Office supplies				
Insurance				
Maintenance and cleaning				
Legal and accounting				
Delivery				
Licenses				
Boxes, paper, etc.				
Telephone				
Miscellaneous				
Depreciation				
Interest				
Total Fixed Expenses				
Total Operating Expenses				
Net Profit (Gross Profit on Sales Less Total Operating Expenses)				
Tax Expense				
Net Profit after Taxes				

Calculations: A. Add current month actual to last month's year-to-date analysis.
B. Add current month budget to last month's year-to-date analysis.

FIGURE 11.3 Budget Deviation Analysis by Month (from Cash Flow Projection)

From the Cash Flow Statement
For the Month of _____

	A Actual for Month	B Budget for Month	C Deviation (B – A)	D % Deviation (C/B x 100)
Beginning Cash Balance				
Add:				
Cash sales				
Accounts receivable that have turned to cash				
Other cash inflows				
Total Available Cash				
Deduct Estimated Disbursements:				
Cost of materials Variable labor Advertising Insurance Legal and accounting Delivery Equipment* Loan payments Mortgage payment Property tax expense				
Deduct Fixed Cash Disbursements:				
Utilities Salaries Payroll taxes and benefits Office supplies Maintenance and cleaning Licenses Boxes, paper, etc. Telephone Miscellaneous				
Total Disbursements				
Ending Cash Balance				

Equipment expense represents actual expenditures made for purchase of equipment.

FIGURE
11.4

Budget Deviation Analysis Year-to-Date (from Cash Flow Projection)

From the Cash Flow Statement
Year-to-Date _____

	A Actual for Year-to-Date	B Budget for Year-to-Date	C Deviation (B – A)	D % Deviation (C/B x 100)
Beginning Cash Balance				
Add:				
Sales revenue				
Other revenue				
Total Available Cash				
Deduct Estimated Disbursements:				
Cost of materials				
Variable labor				
Advertising				
Insurance				
Legal and accounting				
Delivery				
Equipment*				
Loan payments				
Mortgage payment				
Property tax expense				
Deduct Fixed Cash Disbursements:				
Utilities				
Salaries				
Payroll taxes and benefits				
Office supplies				
Maintenance and cleaning				
Licenses				
Boxes, paper, etc.				
Telephone				
Miscellaneous				
Total Disbursements				
Ending Cash Balance				

Calculations: A. Add current month actual to last month's year-to-date analysis.
　　　　　　 B. Add current month budget to last month's year-to-date analysis.

*Equipment expense represents actual expenditures made for purchase of equipment.

The **breakeven statement** is based on the income and cash flow statements. Breakeven analysis is a technique that no business can afford to ignore. Basically, the breakeven shows the volume of revenue from sales you need to exactly balance the sum of your fixed and variable expenses. Once you know your breakeven point, you have an objective target that you can plan to reach by carefully reasoned steps. This document can be used to make decisions in such critically important areas as setting prices, whether to purchase or lease equipment, projecting profits or losses at different sales volumes, and even whether to hire a new employee.

It is essential to remember that increased sales do not necessarily mean increased profits. More than one company has gone broke by ignoring the need for breakeven analysis, especially in those cases where variable costs (those directly related to sales levels) get out of hand as sales volume grows.

Lori Snyder from FlapHappy discusses how she bootstrapped her start-up, works creatively, and carefully, to extend credit to customers and *always* keeps her eye on the bottom line.

REVIEW OF CALCULATING YOUR BREAKEVEN POINT

For a detailed walk-through of your breakeven point, go to Chapter 4.

Calculating the breakeven point can be simple (for a one-product business) or very complex (for a multi-line business). Whatever the complexity, the basic technique is the same. Some of the figures you will need to calculate will have to be estimates. It is a good idea to make your estimates conservative by using somewhat pessimistic sales and margin figures and by slightly overstating your expected costs.

The basic breakeven formula is:

$$S = FC + VC$$
where
S = Breakeven level of sales in dollars
FC = Fixed costs in dollars
VC = Variable costs in dollars

When you want to calculate a projected breakeven and you do not know what your total variable costs will be, you have to use a variation of the basic formula. If you know what gross margin (profit on sales) to expect as a percent of sales, use the following formula:

$$S = FC \div GM$$
where
GM = Gross margin expressed as a percentage of sales

If instead of calculating a dollar breakeven you want to determine how many units you need to sell to break even, simply divide the breakeven derived above in dollars by the unit price to get the number of units to be sold.

In Figure 11.5, because sales are projected at a total of $216,000 for the first year, Wholesome Foods doesn't expect to make a profit—but because they know what they are apt to face, they will be able to plan ahead to finance their business properly.

FIGURE
11.5

Sample Breakeven Analysis

**Projected Figures from Wholesome Foods
Three-Year Income Projection**

Fixed costs   FC = $62,220

Gross margin   GM = (57,680/216,000) = 26.7%

Thus, breakeven sales   = S = FC/GM

               =   ($62,220/.267)

               = $233,033/year

On a monthly basis,   S = $19,419/month

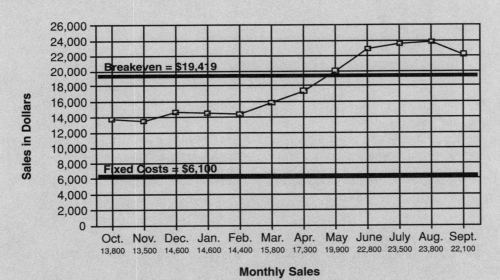

	Oct.	Nov.	Dec.	Jan.	Feb.	Mar.	Apr.	May	June	July	Aug.	Sept.
	13,800	13,500	14,600	14,600	14,400	15,800	17,300	19,900	22,800	23,500	23,800	22,100

Monthly Sales

This pictorial representation of breakeven points is a handy way to make objectives more tangible than the usual "$20,000 a month" kind of goal. It can be very illuminating (or daunting) to post your breakeven projections, then trace out—in some vivid color on a monthly basis—how near to the projection you have come.

You can also use breakeven charts to measure progress toward annual profit goals. Suppose Wholesome Foods had aimed at a $12,000 profit the first year. What sales would be needed?

S = (FC + Profit)/GM

where Profit = $12,000;

S = ($62,220 + 12,000)/.267 = ($74,220)/.267 = $277,977/year or $23,164/month.

FIGURE
11.5
Sample Breakeven Analysis, continued

Graphically,

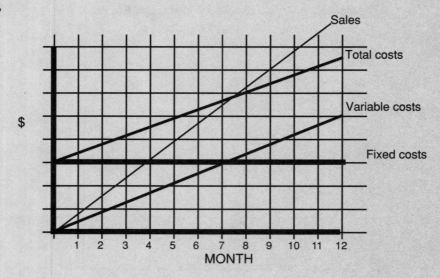

Any time you can help your employees visualize progress toward a goal, you benefit. Breakeven charts (again) are useful for more than financial planning purposes. Once you have calculated breakeven sales, you may find it very helpful to break the sales down in terms of customers needed— as a reality check, this can keep you from making overly optimistic projections.

Here is how Wholesome Foods determined the number of customers needed per month at breakeven:

Assumptions:

1. They assumed that the proportions of retail and wholesale will remain the same as in the income projections.

2. Breakeven in sales $=$ $233,033

   Retail = (126/216) x 233,033 $=$ $136,000/year

   Wholesale = (90/216) x 233,033 $=$ 97,000/year

Experience has shown that the average retail customer spends $16 per visit to Wholesome Foods and comes to the store (on average) twice a month.

Retail sales/month = $136,000/12 = around $11,000/month

$11,000/$16 (average sale) = approximately 700 transactions each month. Since Wholesome Foods' retail clientele consists of both steady local customers and tourist (one-time, drop-in) business, they plan in terms of gross sales.

| FIGURE 11.5 | Sample Breakeven Analysis, continued |

Wholesome Foods has projected retail sales of $126,000 for the first year, or $10,500/month. If they add $500/month to their retail sales, they will hit (retail) breakeven projections. Wholesome Foods currently has 17 wholesale customers who average 4 transactions per month at $60/transaction. To achieve breakeven as projected above,

Wholesale sales/month = $96,000/12 = around $8,000/month

$8,000/$60 (average sale) = approximately 130 transactions each month,

or 33 wholesale customers.

Wholesome Foods has projected wholesale sales of $90,000 for the first year, or $7,500/month. They currently average about $4,000/month wholesale but view the wholesale market as ripe for expansion. They think they can add the necessary 16 new customers and/or increase the average sale. In fact, their marketing plans depend on being able to achieve a market penetration of better than 12 percent over the next 12 months (12% of 300 = 36 customers).

Breakeven analysis may also be represented pictorially. The diagramming helps establish forecasts, budgets and projections. Using a chart lets you substitute different combinations of numbers to obtain a rough estimate of their effect on your business.

A helpful technique is to make worst case, best case, and most probable case assumptions, chart them to see how soon they cover fixed costs, and then derive more accurate figures by applying the various formulas and kinds of thinking displayed above. This is of particular value if you are thinking of making a capital investment and want a quick picture of the relative merits of buying or leasing.

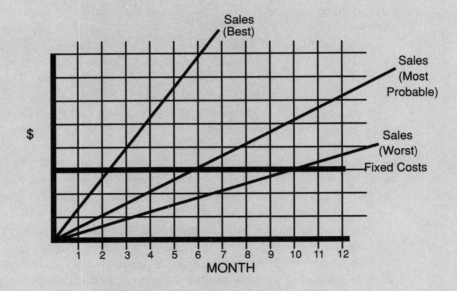

WHAT YOUR INCOME STATEMENT WILL TELL YOU

Income statements should be reviewed at least once a quarter to check their validity and, if necessary, to make adjustments or changes in your business' operations. As a budget tool, the actual progress of your business should be compared to the projections every month. You have to detect deviations as soon as possible to correct problems before they become major and to seize opportunities while they are still fresh.

There is nothing sacred about income projections. If they are wildly incorrect, correct them to make a more realistic guide. When to make corrections is a matter of judgment. A rule of thumb is if they are more than 20 percent off for a quarter (three months), redo them. If they are less than 20 percent off, wait another quarter. Do not change your projections more often. In a short period, certain trends will be magnified, and these distortions will usually even out over the long run. Of course, if you find you have omitted a major expense item or discovered a significant new source of revenue, you will want to make immediate corrections. Use your common sense.

The reasoning behind income projections is that most expenses are predictable and income doesn't fluctuate too drastically, so the future will be much like the past. For example, if your gross margin has historically been 30 percent of net sales, it will (barring strong evidence to the contrary) continue to be 30 percent of net sales. If you are in a start-up situation, look for financial statement information and income ratios for businesses similar to yours.

WHAT YOUR BALANCE SHEET WILL TELL YOU

The balance sheet records the past effect of such decisions. More to the point, it records what the cash position (liquidity) of the business is and what the owner's equity is at a given point in time. These are directly affected by the cash flow and income statement, which themselves are the records of how the business operates over time.

Comparing one business to another using balance sheets is always informative. For start-ups, comparisons are particularly valuable. You must have a good reason to depart from the average distribution of assets and liabilities. This doesn't mean you have to model your balance sheet on the norm. Start with how you want your business to be shaped, check to see how others have done it, then make changes that may be suggested by those other businesses. They represent experience, while you represent hope. Keep the two in some kind of tension, and you'll do better than going to the extremes of either slavishly copying the average or blundering heedlessly ahead on whim.

Once you have been in business for a while, looking for changes in the balance sheet can be instructive. A balance sheet is a picture of the business at a given time, so changes are inevitable. Look for changes in debt and current assets first, then compare other areas.

The difference between current assets and current liabilities is your working capital. The amount of working capital available is a good measure of your ability to meet current obligations and will be examined by your banker when you apply for a loan. Having adequate working capital is a necessity for long-term survival.

Three Essential Ratios

There are three ratios which can be quickly calculated from figures on your balance sheet that are particularly useful.

1. **Current Ratio:** Divide *current assets* by *current liabilities* to determine your business's liquidity (ability to meet current obligations).

$$\text{Current assets} \div \text{Current liabilities} = \text{Current ratio}$$

2. **Quick or Acid Test:** Divide *cash* plus *accounts receivable* by *current liabilities*. Since accounts receivable are close to cash, this is a better measure of liquidity (in some ways) than the current ratio.

$$(\text{Cash} + \text{Accounts receivable}) \div \text{Current liabilities} = \text{Quick test}$$

3. **Debt-to-Worth Ratio:** Divide *total liabilities* by *net worth*. Many bankers look at this to determine how much risk the owner should shoulder.

$$\text{Total liabilities} \div \text{Net worth} = \text{Debt-to-worth ratio}$$

The distinction between debt and equity is important to your banker because the more debt there is in relation to equity, the higher the risk. A high debt-to-worth ratio (worth being roughly equivalent to equity but may include some kinds of subordinated debt) indicates high risk—and high risk costs high interest if you can find new debt money at all. Why? Because debt money is rented money, and the rent must be paid no matter what the business is doing. If you can't meet your debt payments, you go out of business.

Not only that, but a highly leveraged business (higher than normal debt-to-worth ratio for that kind of business) must earn more money. Sometimes it's possible to find so much debt money that the business can never get ahead. Without capital (permanent non-repayable money invested in the business), you can spin your wheels forever, a problem called overtrading. Sales-to-worth ratios are guidelines that can help you pinpoint your capital needs relative to projected sales.

Once you have figured your three key ratios, compare them to other businesses in your industry. You can find industry standards from

- trade associations. These are apt to be very specific—a good example would be the Hardware Association's annual figures. Check with *Ayer's Directory of Associations* in your library and call the appropriate association for more information.
- annual statement studies. Your banker will usually have these available from Robert Morris and Associates.
- *Key Business Ratios, Cost of Doing Business: Partnerships & Proprietorships*, published by Dun & Bradstreet; also available for corporations.
- a friendly competitor, perhaps in a non-competing location.

- your banker and accountant.
- your local library, business school, or chamber of commerce.

WHAT YOUR CASH FLOW WILL TELL YOU

Your cash flow analysis will show you

- how much cash your business will need;
- when it will be needed;
- whether you should look for equity, debt, operating profits, or sale of fixed assets; and
- where the cash will come from.

This financial tool emphasizes the points in your calendar when money will be coming into and going out of your business. The advantage of knowing when cash outlays must be made is the ability to plan for those outlays and not be forced to resort to unexpected borrowing to meet cash needs. Illiquidity is a killer, even for profitable businesses. Lack of profits won't kill a business (non-cash expenses such as depreciation can make your profits look negative, while your cash flow is positive). Lack of cash to meet your trade and other payables will.

After it has been developed, use your cash flow projections as a budget. If the cash outlays for a given item increase over the amount allotted for a given month, you should find out why and take corrective action as soon as possible. If the figure is lower, you should also find out why. If the cash outlay is lower than expected, it is not necessarily a good sign. Maybe a bill wasn't paid. By reviewing the movement of your cash position you can better control your business.

On a more positive note, the savings may tip you off to a new way of economizing. Discrepancies between expected and actual cash flows are indicators of opportunities as well as problems. If the sales figures don't match the cash flow projections, look for the cause. Maybe the projections were too low. Maybe you've opened a new market or introduced a new product that can be pushed even harder.

PRICING STRATEGIES

Pricing is always frightening. Many small business owners feel that pricing is the only way to compete: they simply must have the lowest prices available anywhere in order to succeed, and being more expensive than anyone is certain commercial death. In fact, you have more choice in the matter of pricing at start-up than you will have once you've set a pricing strategy. That's because how you set prices determines (to some extent) how the market perceives your company. The wrong perception can be harmful. But remember, "wrong" can result from being too cheap as well as too expensive. A good pricing strategy starts with a base of measurables (for instance, costs and service expenses). Your price must be able to cover your cost per item or service element. Then, add in the more subjective elements of image or positioning, location, and market expectations. Finally, include a profit component. Don't be greedy, or you'll end up pricing yourself out of existence. On the other hand, don't be shy, or you won't be able to grow.

Research pays off here. Your aim is to make sure your price structure is such that you make a profit, sell enough product or service to stay in business, and find a way to avoid price competition. Pricing is a balancing act in many ways. You have to balance image, perceived value, price sensitivity in your markets, and your own cost structures. The safest route is to establish a price range based on your business's costs, compare the range to the competition, and constantly look for ways to keep out of price wars. In a price war, which is a state of intense downward ratcheting of prices among competitors, nobody wins— except the customers. That's very nice for them, but it creates expectations that will be difficult to deal with once the war's over, and doesn't do anything good for your bottom line.

Price and perceived value work together. Price is important. But it is not the main reason people buy things or pay for services. People weigh a wide range of other factors when making a purchasing decision: reputation, reliability, durability, and guarantee. Medical care, housing, cars, food, childcare, education—lots of things are purchased based on factors unrelated to their cost. Price is important, certainly, but price is not everything.

FIRST PERSON

David B., Dover, New Hampshire: Some years ago my company was trying to persuade Chase Manhattan Bank in New York to subscribe to our small business management newsletter. We offered what we thought was quite a bargain: reprint rights to 12 issues a year for $1,200. We got nowhere. Frustrated, I was complaining about this program to a friend who owned a leading business brokerage. "Go back and see them again," he said. "Tell them the price has gone up to $12,000 a year." I said no way would they go for that. "Lack of courage in pricing," he roared, now in full spate. "That's your problem. Raise your price. You'll see."

He was right. The VP we dealt with wasn't a bit shocked. Instead, as he reached for his pen, he told me, "You finally value your products."

Think about it. If you don't put a premium on your time and effort, why should the market buy at any price?

Pricing is a major marketing concern. Price, quality, service, and profitability are tied together in a complex web. While there are no mechanical formulas for cranking out price decisions, there are four basic strategies that will help you develop a price range you can work with—and profit from. Use one, two, three, or all four; mix and match elements from each to create your own strategy.

The Formula Strategy

Price equals product plus service plus image plus expenses plus profit. The prices you set on your goods and services should reflect not only the product or service itself but also an intangible image factor. In an ideal situation, you would know how your customers and prospects perceive the value of whatever you sell and price accordingly. You also have to cover costs and profits.

FIGURE 11.6 **Price-Quality Matrix**

Quality

High quality
Low price

High quality
High price

Price

Low quality
Low price

Low quality
High price

The Goal-Oriented Strategy

Determine your pricing objectives. Identify your objectives. Are you trying to buy market share with low prices? (It won't work but you can always try!) Maximize profits? Remain competitive? Build up a new product line? Your general marketing objectives apply here. Pricing is inherently strategic, so be clear on your objectives.

The Defensive Range Strategy

Establish price ranges. This is a defensive strategy. Make sure that you charge enough to cover your costs. You have to cover your fixed costs with enough margin to survive. At the high end, build in your desired profit levels and compare the prices you arrive at (on an item-by-item or product-line basis) to your sense of what the market will bear. Your customers won't pay more for your goods and services than they have to—and their perception of the value of your goods and services makes a very effective upper price limit.

The Flexible Pricing Strategy

Choose a flexible pricing approach. The four basic pricing approaches are (1) full-cost pricing (which reflects your costs), (2) flexible markups, (3) gross margin pricing (which takes operating costs and marketing factors into account), and (4) suggested or going rate. The last of these is the least desirable; it involves you in an endless game of follow-the-leader and ignores your cost structures. All of these approaches have their merits, however, and it makes sense for you to understand all of them.

PERSONAL WORKSHOP 24
Establishing a Price Structure
▼ ▼ ▼ ▼ ▼

▼ Use the worksheet below to get you started on setting your price structure. Then review the various strategies to determine the best price for your products or services.

Price Range Guidelines

Item _____

Price ranges $ _____ to $_____

1. Price floor

    Mark-on (gross margin) is _____% of retail price.

    Manufacturer's suggested price is $_____.

    Fixed costs are $_____.

    Variable costs are $_____.

    Breakeven point is $_____.

2. Special considerations for this product's or service's price are:

    ___ service

    ___ status

    ___ superior quality

    ___ demand/product life

    ___ overhead

    ___ downtime

    ___ competitive position

    ___ market penetration costs

3. Turnover rate is _____ times per year.

4. Industry average is _____.

5. Going rate is _____.

CONTINUED ▶

6. I estimate _____ units will be sold.

_____ (number of units) at $_____ will cover my fixed costs.

7. Top price possible is $_____. (Estimate customer's perception of value.)

Comments: _____

_____

_____

_____

Set Sensible Prices

Lack of courage in pricing is a common small business problem. Underpricing your goods or services (especially services) in order to gain market share is self-defeating. As we've pointed out, excessively low prices can actually deter prospects who take "you get what you pay for" literally. You must remember that:

- Lower prices don't necessarily mean higher sales—but they do mean that you have to make more sales to reach the same dollar totals. That may not be feasible.
- High quality and low prices don't fit well together. Low quality and high prices don't either.
- If you don't think your service is valuable, why should your markets?
- Raising prices is difficult, especially if you have established a reputation as a low-cost provider.
- Low-price strategies invite price competition in which everyone except the company with inordinately deep pockets loses.

Find Out What the Market Will Bear

A good starting point for your pricing strategies is to look around. What are other people charging? Compare their prices with what you plan to charge. If your prices are going to be much higher or lower than average, be prepared to explain why you differ. Most experienced business owners are pretty careful about how they set prices and base much of their reasoning on experience. Remember, though, that effective marketing can go a long way toward justifying significant price differences between you and your competitors. The market will likely accept higher prices for products that are a better quality, more economical, last longer, work better, or require fewer repairs than your competitors'. In many ways, pricing is a matter of image. At some point, of course, higher prices will eventually drive away your customers.

Avoid Competing on Price Alone

When you compete with other businesses, you don't necessarily have to limit yourself to competing on the basis of price. Some alternatives to price competition include:

- Personalization
- Specialization
- Emphasis on quality
- Emphasis on service
- Emphasis on value
- Emphasis on convenience
- Emphasis on safety
- Delivery
- Guarantees and warranties
- Attractive financing options
- Cleanliness

In short, don't make the mistake of underpricing in order to get customers. It just doesn't work.

URLinks

http://smallbizpartners.com/success/pricing.html
http://www.sba.gov/opc/pubs/co28.html

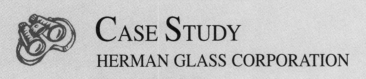

CASE STUDY
HERMAN GLASS CORPORATION

▼▼▼▼▼▼

*B*arbara Burke has been in the retail and wholesale glass business for nearly 20 years and is presently general manager of the Clark Glass Company. Her company specializes in auto glass, plate glass, windows, storefronts, glass tops, mirrors, and other glass products. Clark Glass caters to retail as well as industrial and commercial clients. A major part of Clark's business is with insurance companies and building contractors. Barbara has an excellent reputation in the glass business, and has been looking for an opportunity that would allow her to start her own business.

A few weeks ago, Barbara was contacted by her banker, who was aware of her interest. He told her that the Herman Glass Corporation was for sale. William Herman had passed away after a long illness, and Alice Herman, his wife, now wanted to sell the company and move to Hawaii. Barbara knew the company well; while it was not as big as Clark Glass Company,

CONTINUED ▶

it had a good reputation and sold essentially the same products. It is located in Riverdale, about 60 miles from Clark. The area had a good economic base and was considered a growth area. The competitors in the area were small and, in Barbara's opinion, did not present a threat to Herman Glass. Barbara felt that with a strong marketing campaign, Herman Glass could increase its sales dramatically.

Barbara met with Mrs. Herman and received the financial statements and tax returns for the past three years, as well as other information that she had requested (see Exhibits I and II). Mrs. Herman offered to either sell the stock of the corporation for $155,353 plus $100,000 goodwill, or permit the buyer to purchase assets (less cash and prepaid items) plus $100,000 goodwill. In either case, Mrs. Herman wanted cash and wanted to sell the business within 45 days. She offered to sign a noncompetitive clause and to stay with the business for 30 to 60 days to effect a smooth transition. She told Barbara that two other people also were interested in the company.

Exhibit I. Herman Glass Corporation, Balance Sheet, December 31, 1998.

Assets			Liabilities		
Current Assets			**Current Liabilities**		
Cash	$15,000		Accounts payable		$115,600
Accounts receivable	$140,000		Accrued state taxes payable		5,300
Less: allowance for doubtful accounts	$2,800	137,200	Accrued federal taxes payable		8,500
			Accrued interest payable		1,500
Notes receivable	5,400		Accrued sales taxes payable		$1,540
Prepaid items	5,900		Total Current Liabilities		$132,440
Inventory	$134,293				
Total current assets	$297,793		**Long-Term Liabilities**		
Fixed Assets			Note payable		$50,000
Equipment	$70,000		Total Long-Term Liabilities		$50,000
Less: allowance for depreciation	$38,500	$31,500	Total Liabilities		$182,440
Equipment, furniture and fixtures	$25,000		**Stockholders' Equity**		
			Common stock	$150,000	
Less: accumulated depreciation	$16,500	8,500	Retained earnings	$5,353	$155,353
Total Fixed Assets		$40,000	**Total Liabilities**		
Total Assets		**$337,793**	**and Stockholders' Equity**		**$337,793**

CONTINUED ▶

Exhibit II. Herman Glass Corporation, Comparative Income Statements, Years Ended December 31.

	1998	1997	1996
Sales	$550,950	$501,700	$476,548
Cost of sales	358,118	326,105	333,584
Gross profit	192,832	175,595	142,964
Operating Expenses			
Salary expense (owner)	40,000	30,000	25,000
Salaries (other)	70,050	69,150	47,000
Payroll taxes, 12%	13,206	11,898	8,640
Rent	24,000	24,000	18,000
Insurance	6,700	6,450	6,500
Advertising	145	275	190
Delivery, car, travel	3,260	4,105	3,750
Supplies	1,410	1,390	1,470
Accounting and legal	4,000	4,000	4,500
Telephone	3,967	3,892	3,600
Utilities	6,840	6,715	6,200
Repairs and maintenance	950	1,140	980
Depreciation—equipment	3,500	3,500	3,500
Depreciation—furniture/fixtures	1,500	1,500	I,500
Interest expense	6,000	6,000	6,000
Miscellaneous	750	871	650
Total expenses	186,278	174,886	137,480
Net before Taxes	6,554	709	5,484
Income Tax	983	106	823
Net after Taxes	5,571	603	4,661

Mrs. Herman, who owned the building under her own name, offered to rent it to Barbara for the first two years at an annual rate of $24,000. She would give Barbara an option for five more years, but the rental per annum would be tied to the preceding year's Consumer Price Index. Barbara asked if she would consider an option to purchase the building, and Mrs. Herman agreed to sell the building any time during a five-year period for $360,000 cash (the current market value of the building was $260,000).

A few days after the first meeting, Mrs. Herman sent the additional material Barbara had requested, including copies of the proposed lease, aging of accounts payable and accounts receivable, payroll breakdown, and a list of all equipment, furniture, and fixtures. After several conferences with her attorney and accountant, Barbara decided to make a cash offer of $148,880. She also decided to take her lawyer's advice and purchase only the assets of the business and assume the accounts payable. Her attorney believed that because the Herman Corporation had been around for nearly 25 years, there was the possibility some unknown contingent liability might arise, spelling disaster. Barbara also felt it was important to assume the accounts payable; if for some reason they were not paid as expected, it could impact negatively upon the company.

Barbara computed the purchase price as follows:

CONTINUED ▶

Accounts receivable (gross)	$140,000	$47,775	$92,225
Notes receivable	5,400		5,400
Inventory	134,293	40,288	94,005
Equipment (book value)	31,500		31,500
Furniture and fixtures (book value)	8,500		8,500
Total asset value for each party	319,693		231,630
Less: accounts payable	115,600		115,600
Balance	204,093		116,030
Plus goodwill	100,000		32,770
Price desired by each party	304,093		148,800

Notes:
- Barbara's accountant felt the accounts receivables over 90 days should be excluded.
- Barbara estimated that 30 percent of the inventory was obsolete.
- Barbara based goodwill on five times 1998 earnings before taxes ($6,554 x 5 years = $32,770).

She met with Mrs. Herman and offered her $231,630 for the assets plus $32,770 for goodwill, less $115,600 for the accounts payable, or a total amount of $148,800. Barbara said that she wanted the name of the business plus a lease for two years at $24,000 per annum and the option to renew for an additional five years at the same price adjusted by the Consumer Price Index. In addition, Barbara wanted an option to purchase the building for $260,000 any time during a five-year period. Further, Barbara wanted the non-competitive agreement plus assistance for 30 days.

The following day, Mrs. Herman presented her final offer to Barbara. Mrs. Herman acknowledged that the accounts receivable and inventory were overvalued, but she felt strongly that the goodwill figure of $32,770 was grossly inadequate. Since Mr. Herman had been ill for several years, he could not devote full attention to the business; however, if he had been active, the profits would have been substantial. She also pointed out that the area was growing, the personnel were experienced, and the company had an excellent reputation. Mrs. Herman said that she would sell only the assets of the business and, because Mr. Herman contracted those obligations with the suppliers, she would pay them off herself and provide whatever proof Barbara needed to substantiate that fact. She agreed to sell the assets to Barbara for $231,630, but the goodwill figure could not be less than $64,370, thus making the selling price $296,000. Further, Mrs. Herman said she would sell the name for one year only, but she would give a rental lease for two years at $24,000 per annum and the additional five-year rental option would be tied to the Consumer Price Index. In addition, she would grant an option to purchase the

building for $300,000, but the option at that price would only be valid for two years. If Barbara did not purchase the building in two years, the purchase option price in three years would be $350,000; a fourth year option price would be $400,000; and the fifth-year final option price could be negotiated, but it could be no less than $450,000. Mrs. Herman also agreed to the noncompetitive clause and said she would remain 30 days to assist as directed. She added that her offer was final, and that she expected Barbara's answer the following day.

Barbara thought about the terms; while they weren't all she had hoped for, she felt this was an opportunity she couldn't pass up. After having her lawyer prepare the agreement, she met with Mrs. Herman and gave her a $25,000 deposit.

Barbara discussed the finances with her accountant and he informed her that, in addition to the $296,000, she would need $38,600 for initial working capital. Barbara analyzed her personal resources and determined that she could raise all but $100,000. She talked to bank officers, who were willing to extend a ten-year loan at 12 percent providing the SBA was willing to guarantee the loan. If she borrowed the money from the bank, the monthly payments would be $1,435. (For our purposes, we will assume that $602 was for interest expense and $833 for principal.)

A second option was to sell $100,000 of stock to her sister Lilyann. Lilyann was close to Barbara and more than willing to invest in her new business. The problem was that Lilyann would be investing every cent of her resources. While Barbara was quite confident about the business, its failure could have a tremendous impact on her sister.

CONTINUED ▶

Lilyann offered to forgo dividends the first year, but wanted to earn at least 10 percent on her investment starting with the second year. She was flexible with respect to the rate, but thought it should be comparable to bank money market funds. When her children start college in a few years, Lilyann wants also to come into the business in some capacity, either full time or part time.

If Barbara does sell stock to her sister instead of borrowing from the bank, she would not have to give her personal guarantees. The latter option could be an advantage if she needed to borrow additional funds from the bank. ▼

CASE STUDY ROUNDTABLE

▼ ▼ ▼ ▼ ▼ ▼

Barbara: I understand that ratio analysis is important when looking at financial statements. Could you please walk me through some ratios? Here are the industry averages to help you understand the big picture.

Industry Averages

Current ratio	2.7
Quick ratio	1.1
Debt ratio	60.0
Total debt to net worth	1.1
Average inventory turnover	3.5 times/year
Receivables turnover	5.61
Average collection period	65 days
Net sales to total assets	3.0
Net profit on sales	5.6%
Net profit/Net worth	10.7%

(See Exhibits I and II in the case study for financial data.)

Discussion Points

- When calculating the average inventory turnover, the inventory at the beginning of 1998 was $127,500. When calculating the receivables turnover, you will use 70 percent of 1998's total sales ($550,950) as credit sales for the numerator and gross accounts receivable plus notes receivable for the denominator.

- To calculate the average collection period ratio, use 365 days as the numerator and the receivables turnover as your denominator.

- Prepare a monthly cash budget for this year (1999) and the next. Assume that you are going to borrow the money from the bank. (See Cash Budget Financial Assumptions Barbara has provided following this roundtable.)

- Prepare a monthly income statement for this year and the next. (See Monthly Income Financial Assumptions following the Cash Budget Financial Assumptions.)

Barbara: Should I borrow the money or sell stock to my sister? Do you have any other suggestions? Will I have sufficient funds in the business to buy the building by June of next year and be able to put up the $60,000 which includes closing costs? The bank is willing to finance $250,000 at 12 percent for 15 years. Monthly payments would be $3,000. If there aren't going to be sufficient funds in the business at that time, where could I get the $60,000? Should I defer the decision to purchase the building? Help!

Discussion Points

- Calculate the breakeven point for this year and next year. Consider $227,034 as your fixed expense this year and $291,000 as your fixed expense for next year. What conclusions can you draw from your results?

    Cash Budget Financial Assumptions
    - Initial cash balance: $38,600.
    - Sales are 30% cash and 70% credit.

    Credit sales are collected in the following manner:
    - 25% of credit sales collected in 30 days
    - 50% of credit sales collected in 60 days
    - 25% of credit sales collected in 90 days

    Note: The accounts receivable and notes receivable purchased by Barbara were $145,400. This amount will be collected as follows and must be included in the cash budget forecast for the present year:

January	$33,425
February	25,900
March	14,150 (includes $8,750 + $5,400 note receivable)
Total	73,475

    The attorney received a check for $50 in May of 1999 and forwarded it to Barbara. The balance of the accounts receivable is in dispute at this time and has been turned over to her lawyer for collection. All of the accounts making up this list are contractors, but there is a good possibility that about 50 percent might be collected at some time in the future.

- Sales forecasts are as follows:

	Sales Forecast 1999	Sales Forecast 2000
January	$ 60,000	$ 80,000
February	63,000	84,000
March	66,000	88,000
April	63,000	84,000
May	60,000	80,000
June	57,000	76,000
July	60,000	80,000
August	63,000	84,000

	Sales Forecast 1999	**Sales Forecast 2000**
September	66,000	88,000
October	72,000	96,000
November	75,000	100,000
December	80,000	106,664
Total	$785,000	$1,046,664

Note: The sales forecast for January 1997 is $106,664. This amount is needed to calculate purchases in December of 2000. Barbara feels those forecasts are very likely because of her experience, her clients, the business she will be personally bringing to the firm, and her marketing plan.

- Purchase (Cost of Sales)
  Cost of sales is 65 percent of each month's sales. Barbara will have to pay 65 percent of each month's sales in the preceding month. For example, in February, sales are forecasted at $63,000. Barbara will have to pay out 65 percent of $63,000, or $40,950, during the month of January. The same procedure will apply to each succeeding month.

- Loan payment
  If Barbara borrows $100,000 through the bank, her monthly payments will be $1,435. In the cash budget, deduct $1,435 as a cash disbursement under loan prepayment. Note: When you prepare your monthly income statement, consider $602 as interest expense for purposes of this problem.

- Estimated federal taxes payable
  In your cash budget, consider $2,500 as tax prepayments in the months of April, June, September, and December of the current year. Next year you will budget the same amounts.

- Other cash disbursements
  In the first month of this year, other disbursements will be heavier because of start-up costs. In the succeeding 11 months they will remain constant.

	January this year	**Each remaining month**
Deposits (utilities, phone, etc.)	$ 2,800	0
Equipment purchase	6,600	0
Insurance (lump-sum payment)	7,200	0
Salary and wage group	9,000	9,000
Payroll taxes (12%)	1,080	1,080
Supplies	150	150
Repairs and maintenance	100	100
Advertising	5,000	2,000
Car, delivery, and travel	1,000	1,000
Accounting and legal	2,000	350
Rent	2,000	2,000
Telephone	350	350
Utilities	600	600
Miscellaneous	100	100
Total other disbursements	37,980	16,730

In the following year, the other cash disbursements will be as follows:

- In January the disbursements will amount to $29,200 exclusive of the loan prepayment of $1,435, which also will have to be considered.
- In the remaining 11 months the cash disbursements will amount to $22,000 exclusive of $1,435, which also will have to be considered.
- New capital purchases

The company will have to pay for new equipment purchases of $15,000 in December of this year. Bank officers have agreed that if an overdraft does occur they will lend the company additional funds on a short-term basis up to 120 days at 14 percent interest.

Monthly Income Statement Assumptions

- Sales: Use sales forecast figures presented in cash budget.
- Cost of sales: Use 65 percent monthly sales.
- Gross profit is 35 percent of sales.
- Expenses for 1999 are as follows:

January: $23,182, taking into account some initial expenses such as additional legal and accounting to set up the business, advertising, promotion, and some other items.
Balance of year: $18,532 for each of the remaining 11 months.
January through April of 2000: $24,425 (to reflect $175 interest expense on a $15,000 loan). The remaining months will be $24,250.

BACK TO THE TABLE
Angelo Bandelo

In Chapter 8, you met Angelo Bandelo, and learned about his efforts to start a service station. Based on what you now know, how would you advise Angelo to:

- increase his sales and profits?
- be more competitive with the highway stations? Should he lower his prices?

 # CHAPTER BRIEFCASE

- The best way to keep a pulse on your business is to regularly analyze your financial statements.
- Deviation analysis is an excellent comparison tool. It is unbeatable in guarding against runaway expenses and destroyed budgets.
- Breakeven shows the volume of revenue from sales you need to balance the sum of your expenses.

- Review your income statements at least once every three months to check their validity.

- Your balance sheet is another fine comparison tool. Use it to compute ratios and match them against your industry standards.

- Your cash flow statement is your most important financial analysis tool. It shows how cash flows in and out of your business over a period of time.

- Price is determined by what the market will bear and what you need to break even. There are several strategies for developing a price structure that works. Lack of courage in pricing is a common small business problem.

- Even if you have altruistic motives for starting your business, you still must make a profit.

- To avoid setting unrealistic sales objectives, you should become as familiar as you can with your industry and question people experienced in your field.

- Price and perceived value work together. Price is important, but it is not the main reason people buy things or pay for services. People weigh a wide range of other factors in making a purchasing decision. Many small businesses make the error of thinking they have to have the lowest price in order to compete. That assumption can be dangerous—or fatal.

- A good starting point for your pricing strategies is to look around. What are other people charging? Compare their prices with what you plan to charge. If your prices are going to be much higher or lower than average, be prepared to explain why you differ.

- The cash flow projection is the most important financial planning tool available to you. If you were limited to one financial statement (which fortunately isn't the case), use the cash flow.

▲▲▲▲▲▲

Chapter 12

CREDIT AND COLLECTIONS

▼▼▼▼▼

Neither a borrower nor a lender be
For loan oft loses both itself and friend

—*William Shakespeare,* Hamlet I, iii

MISSION STATEMENT

In this chapter, you will

*L*EARN about the issues involved in extending credit to your suppliers and customers.

*E*XPLORE the legal issues involving consumer bankruptcy as they affect your business.

*A*PPLY your understanding to a case study.

*P*RODUCE an evaluation of a commercial customer's financial viability, as well as a sample retail credit policy.

KEY TERMS

bankruptcy	COD	Net 30
CBD	creditor	2/10/Net 30
CCOD	debtor	

INTRODUCTION TO CREDIT ISSUES

Undoubtedly, your business, like most businesses, extends credit. To compete for customers, encourage sales, and maintain good relations with existing customers, you often must extend credit. Credit is also an effective marketing tool: it provides potential customers with the attraction of enhanced purchasing power (that is, getting the goods today and paying for them later). By extending credit, we mean any time you receive payment other than cash in advance at the time of sale, whether to a consumer or to a commercial customer.

Shakespeare's advice certainly simplifies life in a household, business, or castle in Denmark, but it does not reflect today's economy, where credit has become a fixture in the operations of nearly all businesses. A basic knowledge of collection measures will help you

- evaluate your current credit policies,
- gather useful collection information from customers at the time of sale, and
- work with your lawyer to collect from insolvent or recalcitrant debtors.

As a small business owner, you have many roles. An important first step in understanding your collection rights is to determine the point when, in addition to being an entrepreneur, marketer, accountant, comptroller, inventory control specialist, manufacturer, service provider, manager, adviser, and occasional gofer, you also suddenly, one day, become a lender.

REVIEWING YOUR BAD DEBT EXPOSURE

Any business, even one as modest as a 10-year-old's lemonade stand or a teenager's babysitting enterprise, is exposed to customers who promise to pay later. And then don't. Companies view potential bad debts in different ways. Some accept collection losses as simply a necessary cost of doing business. Other companies, for financial or moral reasons, cannot tolerate collection losses and do not enjoy or cannot afford the legal pursuit to collect debts.

Your company can become a lender and be exposed to the risk of collection by

- accepting a check that is ultimately returned for insufficient funds (that is, that bounces like a rubber ball);
- providing goods or services based on a customer's promise to pay later;
- offering goods on a tryout basis with payment deferred;
- selling goods and taking a security interest in the goods;
- prepaying wages or salaries; or
- prepaying orders of goods or services to be provided in the future by another business.

You should begin the analysis of your company's lender status by identifying the various ways in which you extend credit. The term *credit* can have a formal, statutory meaning involving the execution of many documents. It can also refer to the informal ways in which money is advanced or goods or services are provided without your business receiving cash or services in exchange. In reviewing your operations, consider the relationships you have with your employees, customers, and the business vendors that provide your company with services, supplies, and inventory. When does the potential for a debt (and thus the potential for a bad debt) exist?

Some businesses have the good fortune of rarely having collection problems. Their type of business, the local economy within which they operate, or the goodwill the business has with its customers and employers are among the reasons for such good fortune. Most businesses, however, must develop and administer an active and alert credit program.

Review Your Credit Guidelines

The next step in developing a thoughtful and knowledgeable credit and collection program is to review your credit policies. Shakespeare's adage about never lending aside, you should have in place policies to govern those times when you do extend credit.

Just as preventive health measures reduce medical costs, smart credit terms and policies can save you the irritation, disappointment, financial losses, and collection costs that come with late paying accounts and bad debts.

You must develop policies responsive to your customers' needs, and your competitive environment, but also to your own tolerance (financially and mentally) for slow- or non-paying customers.

FIRST PERSON

Shawna P., Charlotte, North Carolina: I'm sorry, but I have been burned more times than I want to talk about by customers who abused my credit policy. When I started out, I wanted to attract people by making credit really easy and low pressure. That might work for some people, but it didn't for me. I found out my customers took advantage of a lenient credit policy to find every loophole and stretch everything as far as they could. I just about lost my shirt. I tightened up my policy so much, I'm practically cash-only now. Sure, I lost some customers, but just the worst offenders. I gained peace of mind—and my profit line!

Terms

The following is a list of alternative methods of payment that can be used by manufacturers and wholesalers, and, to a limited extent, retailers. Retailers, however, need to be aware of state and federal laws governing the extension of credit to customers.

- **COD (Cash on Delivery).** The carrier is required to release the shipment only after the customer pays the C.O.D. amount in cash.
- **CCOD (Certified Check on Delivery).** The carrier is required to release the shipment only after the customer pays the COD amount in the form of a certified check.
- **CBD (Cash Before Delivery).** The customer is contacted on the shipping date and agrees to mail payment that day.
- **Pro Forma.** The customer is contacted that the order is ready to be shipped and is instructed to mail payment. When payment is received, and the check clears, the order is shipped.
- **Net 30.** The customer is shipped goods and is given 30 days (calculated either from shipment or invoicing) to pay. Other common terms are 10 days, 15 days, or 45 days.
- **2/10/Net 30.** Customers are given a 2 percent discount if they pay within 10 days but are still allowed 30 days to pay, if they elect not to take advantage of

the discount. Variations of this technique include giving a 1 percent discount (1/10/Net 30) or extending the term (2/10/Net 60).

Collecting Useful Information

A key part of any credit policy is the collection of information about the customer at a time when getting this information is the easiest. This is usually before or at the time the customer orders your goods or services and requests credit. Having a standard application for the customer to complete will allow you to gather information that will

- help you decide whether you want to extend the credit and/or
- allow you or your lawyer to begin legal action against the customer if the debt goes bad.

Credit Application

A credit application form is the most obvious place to collect information about a customer. A credit application may take many forms, but should ask for the following useful information:

Business Credit Applicants	**Individual Credit Applicants**
A third party to contact	A third party to contact (references)
Longevity of the business	Place and length of employment
Legal status of the customer, corporate agent and officers	Source(s) of income
Important tax numbers	Car and home ownership status
Trade references	Credit references
Bank references	Bank references

The standard form also provides you with the customer's authorization for you to receive his or her information. It will generally contain an explanation of your credit terms as well.

Credit Information

Credit information gathered directly from the customer can be supplemented by you with information from local or national credit reporting agencies. You can find the telephone numbers of these agencies in the yellow pages of your phone directory. It would be worthwhile for you to speak with representatives from several agencies to learn what information they can provide to help you in credit determinations or collecting a bad debt.

This information-gathering process should continue throughout your relationship with each customer. You should record changes of address and ownership. You should also periodically make copies of checks sent in as payments. The checks can provide the new address of the borrower and reveal the financial institution at which the borrower maintains his or her checking account.

FIGURE
12.1

**Common Danger Signs of a
Commercial Customer's Financial Difficulties**

Event	Yes	No
Staff turnover (insiders at a business may be aware of problems long before it is apparent to outsiders)		
Nonpayment of local, state, or federal taxes		
Published judgments against the customer (check the business section of your local newspaper)		
Conversion of collateral by the borrower		
Expansion of the business		
Unusually large or small orders		
Delinquencies on payments due you		

Danger Signs to Help You Avoid or Reduce Losses

As part of your effort to maintain up-to-date information on each business borrower, you should be aware of danger signals that can alert you to a worsening financial condition for the borrower. Although a financial collapse of one of your customers can occur without warning, there are often warning signs of deteriorating financial well-being from which collection problems may arise. Review your bad debt history (as painful as this might be) and recall if there were signs that the problem customers were heading for financial difficulties. Figure 12.1 provides a checklist of some common danger signs.

LEGAL TOOLS TO PROTECT AGAINST BAD DEBTS

Even the most vigilant business can experience a bad debt. However, the law provides several protections for your business in the event a borrower does not turn out to be the honest, financially stable, and prompt-paying person he or she seemed to be. Fortunately, the credit reporting industry generally provides timely and accurate information on businesses and customers. Often, though, good accounts go bad, a contractual dispute results in a default, or you send goods to a disreputable account.

It is good for you to be aware of the full lineup of legal tools available to reduce your risk of loss or to collect from an account that has defaulted on a financial obligation to you. Lawyers refer to this as your "quiver of arrows." Any businessperson (at least any businessperson with a healthy business) knows that a lawsuit is one of the arrows in the quiver. But it's usually the last one you'll want to use, because a lawsuit can be costly, time-consuming, and ineffective if you cannot find the debtor or if the debtor has insufficient funds.

Getting a Guaranty

Consumer transactions. If you suspect the customer does not have an established credit record or, conversely, may not have a sufficient financial base for the size of the debt, then you can suggest or require that another person formally agree to provide a guaranty that the loan or debt will be repaid. This is commonly called **cosigning**. This guaranty should be in writing and the laws in most states require that you have the *cosigner* provide the guaranty each time you extend credit to the borrower.

Business debts. Obtaining a personal guaranty for a business debt is also common. Here again, the business borrower may not have established a sufficiently good credit history and a personal guaranty will provide additional support. But with business debt, a personal guaranty is also advisable because of the limited liability corporate officers and shareholders enjoy for the debts of their corporation. If you lend to a corporate borrower, you will generally be limited to collecting your debt from the assets of the business and not the personal wealth of the individuals who own or operate the business, unless you obtain a guaranty from an individual that he or she will personally provide payment in the event of nonpayment.

Securing Your Interest

The laws in all states allow you to take a **security interest** in the goods you sell on credit. The **Uniform Commercial Code (UCC)**, which has been adopted in full or in large part by all 50 states, gives a seller of goods the right to take a secured interest in the property sold to a customer, or even in other property owned by the customer. The security interest gives you the legal right to take back and sell the property to offset your loss if the customer defaults and does not pay his or her debt.

You create this security interest by filing a UCC financing statement with the secretary of state or county clerk of courts, depending on your state. You and the debtor must sign a security agreement and the financing statement.

As a *secured creditor*, you also will have priority over unsecured creditors if the customer files a bankruptcy petition.

COLLECTIONS AND LEGAL REMEDIES

Two legal terms, *creditor* and *debtor*, are used throughout this section. **Creditor** means the business that is owed money: that is, you. **Debtor** means the customer or business that owes money to your company. The discussion in this section assumes that informal methods of collection such as calling your customer and writing friendly (or not so friendly) reminders to the customer have not been successful and that you have decided to apply one or more of the legal measures available to you.

Commence a Lawsuit

When you or your attorney have exhausted all nonjudicial means to collect a bad debt, you must decide whether to file a lawsuit to collect the debt. Before you do, you need to keep two hard facts in mind:

1. Lawyers are expensive and legal fees can grow to be greater than the debt.
2. Even if your lawyer (or you in a small claims action) wins, the judgment you get against the debtor-defendant may be meaningless if the debtor cannot be found, has no valuable assets, or does not have a sufficiently well-paying job.

If you decide that the potential legal expenses are reasonable and the chance of enforcing the judgment is sufficiently high, you might want to begin a lawsuit. The ultimate goal of the lawsuit is to have the trial court enter a monetary **judgment** in your favor against the debtor. Entry of a judgment against the debtor in court records is an important step because it permits you or your lawyer to pursue postjudgment collection alternatives.

Small Claims

Most states have established procedures to handle smaller contract disputes. Although the specifics may vary, the procedures typically create a small claims court with simplified procedures and shorter waiting periods to settle disputes for more modest amounts of money. The maximum amount permitted in a small claims action varies from state to state.

The procedures for a small claims action are more relaxed than in regular court. The parties don't need to be represented by lawyers, for instance. The simplified procedures allow you to represent yourself against your debtor. The exact procedures and court rules can vary from county to county, even within a state. It is important, therefore, to contact the clerk of court in your county or in the counties where you do business to learn the specific procedures to be followed in that county.

Large Claims

In all cases in which the creditor seeks payment of a sum in excess of the legal small claims limit, a regular civil action must be filed with the clerk of circuit court in the county where the trial will be held.

While the rules of procedure will vary from place to place across the country, a general outline of a collection action might be helpful. The following steps must be taken:

1. The creditor, through his or her attorney, drafts and files a summons and complaint with the clerk of court.
2. The summons tells the debtor the time within which to file a written answer with the court. The summons also advises the debtor where to send the answer and, further, that failure to answer may result in the entry of a default judgment.

3. If no answer is filed, the creditor may, after filing a default motion and typically after a short hearing, have a default judgment entered against the defendant/debtor.

4. If the defendant/debtor files an answer within the time limits, the case proceeds to trial subject to whatever scheduling, terms, and conditions the trial judge established.

5. Once a decision or judgment by the trial judge is made, it must be entered by the clerk of court in court records to be enforceable against the debtor. To be enforceable as a lien against the debtor's real estate so that collection efforts can be taken against that real estate, the judgment must be "docketed" in the county where the real estate is located. That means it must be formally entered into the legal records of the county.

Uniform Enforcement of Foreign Judgments Act

The Uniform Enforcement of Foreign Judgments Act is a law that allows creditors to collect from debtors who leave the state where a judgment has been obtained. "Foreign" refers only to judgments entered in other states; it does not refer to other countries. This act allows creditors to docket judgment obtained against debtors in any other state the debtor moves to, and to pursue all postjudgment collection remedies normally available to a creditor in the debtor's new state.

Collecting Money

Just because a creditor obtains a judgment against a customer or business it does not mean the creditor will receive that money. Many people unfamiliar with the court system assume that the losing party is required to pay the winning payment immediately after the trial judge makes his or her decision. This is a substantial mistake. A debtor may still balk at paying or may not have sufficient funds to pay the judgment. Fortunately, the laws of most states establish mechanisms to assist you to collect a judgment involuntarily from a recalcitrant debtor. Of course, if the debtor failed to pay because he or she has no assets, the creditor's judgment is worth the paper it's printed on—and no more.

Typically, the first step following the entry of a judgment is a supplementary proceeding. Supplementary orders (and orders for financial disclosure) are court orders which, if not adhered to, place the debtor in "contempt of court." If a debtor fails to appear at a contempt motion hearing to explain why the debtor failed to appear for the supplementary examination (or return the order for financial disclosure form), the court may authorize the sheriff to take the debtor into custody to compel the debtor's appearance or response.

Garnishment

A garnishment action is a court procedure in which the court orders a third party (for example, an individual, employer, or bank) that is holding some property of a debtor to transfer all or a part of the property to a creditor who has received a judgment against the debtor. Generally, the property is the debtor's wages or checking account.

The debtor is liable for the cost of garnishment actions. The creditor recovers the cost of the garnishment from the amounts recovered or adds the cost to the balance owed. Assets subject to garnishment include:

- Wages
- Accounts receivable
- Bank accounts
- Promissory notes

Wage Assignment

Under certain circumstances, and to avoid the cost of garnishment actions, the debtor may also authorize the debtor's employer to withhold a certain portion of the debtor's paycheck and send that portion to you. Wage assignments must be voluntary and revocable by the debtor. If the debtor revokes the assignment, you can still resort to garnishments or other collection avenues.

Execution

"Execution" is a legal term that (unfortunately, in some cases) has nothing to do with lining the debtor up against a wall. Rather, it refers to an action taken by the creditor to recover money or property in the debtor's possession to satisfy a judgment.

An execution may proceed against both personal or real property. It is a direction to the sheriff to recover the judgment amount from the real or personal property of the judgment debtor which may be located in the sheriff's county.

Attachments

The law also allows you to have the sheriff seize property belonging to the debtor and hold it as security for the payment and satisfaction of a judgment upon the conclusion of a collection action. This remedy is of limited availability. It is useful in those situations in which you can convince a judge that the debtor will try to fraudulently sell the property to avoid payment, conceal assets in the debtor's control, or run off with the property that would be the subject of post-judgment collection remedies.

Reclaiming the Goods (Repossession)

When faced with a bad debt by a commercial customer, a business owner in a show of initiative, anger, or unwise bravado will occasionally attempt to repossess the goods which the customer obtained but has not paid for.

LAWS AFFECTING COLLECTIONS

Congress and state legislatures have enacted laws that regulate or impact a creditor's collection practices. You need to be alert to changes in these laws because, as the use of credit by business and customer becomes even more pervasive, there will undoubtedly be more legislative initiatives which target either creditor rights or consumer and debtor protections. Here, we will look at several major laws with which you should be familiar.

Federal Laws

Fair Debt Collection Practices Act (FDCPA). This federal act became law in 1968 to protect consumers from abusive debt collection practices and create consistent debt collection practices. The act only applies to "debt collectors" who attempt to collect consumer debts. A debt collector is defined by this law as a person who regularly attempts to collect the debts of another. Thus, if you are solely collecting consumer debts for your own business, you would not be a debt collector under this law. If you turn your bad debts over to a collection agency, then the collectors for that agency must conform their collection practices to the requirements of this law. If your business begins to pursue collections on behalf of other businesses then you should consult with your attorney to understand what you are permitted to do when communicating with the debtor. Penalties for noncompliance are substantial.

Federal Truth-in-Lending Act. This act created by Congress, and the administrative rules adopted to implement it, require that certain disclosures of credit terms be given when you extend credit to a consumer. The credit terms you must disclose include:

- Total sales price (which is the price of the good or service plus any other charges you add)
- Monthly finance charge
- Annual interest rate
- Explanation of when payments are due
- Late payment charges and an explanation of when they will be added

Fair Credit Billing Act. This federal law imposes requirements on you if a consumer alleges that you have mistakenly billed him or her. If the consumer notifies you of the mistake within 60 days after you mailed the allegedly erroneous bill, you have 30 days to respond unless the dispute is resolved. You are given 90 days to investigate and determine if the bill is correct or to correct an error. Here is an example of why you must be attentive to the federal and state regulations on your billing and collection practices. The penalties for noncompliance can be harsh and substantial; if you do not comply with the law's time limits you are required to give the customer a $50 credit even if you ultimately determine your billing was accurate.

State Laws

State consumer protection laws. Some states have consumer protection laws which restrict the contacts a lender can have with a consumer to collect a bad debt. Some of these state laws are even more restrictive than the federal Fair Debt Collection

Practices Act. First, some states do not exempt those collecting their own debts from the definition of debt collector. Second, states can adopt limits on collection practices that are more restrictive than the federal law.

Exempt assets. Not all property belonging to a debtor is available to recover money that is owed you. It has been long recognized in law that everyone (including a debtor) is entitled to retain some minimal amount of assets with which to carry on life. As a result, the laws of each state typically protect or exempt certain assets from creditor collection efforts.

BANKRUPTCY

The stated purpose of the Bankruptcy Code is to grant honest debtors a fresh start through a discharge of their debts. To help with this fresh start, debtors are permitted to elect certain assets exempt from the claims of creditors. The concept of exemptions grew out of the early 19th century English practice of permitting tradesmen to except the tools of their trade from the claims of their general creditors in order that they not become a burden on the public welfare. That concept has been expanded greatly under the Bankruptcy Code and state law. Most states exempt some property from the claims of general creditors.

Bankruptcy petitions can be filed under different chapters of the United States Bankruptcy Code. Each chapter has its own advantages and requirements depending on the type of the debt and the debtor's financial condition.

Chapter 7

This form of bankruptcy is frequently referred to as a "liquidation proceeding" or "straight bankruptcy." A Chapter 7 case involves the appointment of a trustee to gather together the debtor's nonexempt assets, liquidate those assets, and pay a dividend to the debtor's creditors.

The objective of a Chapter 7 debtor is to discharge the debtor's obligations to his or her creditors. Creditors may object to discharge on certain grounds. A creditor may file a "Proof of Claim" but this is not always required. In addition, a debtor may reaffirm certain debts.

Chapter 11

A Chapter 11 proceeding allows a debtor to reorganize or to achieve an orderly liquidation of its assets. Normally, the debtor retains control of his or her assets and is referred to as a debtor-in-possession (DIP). A Chapter 11 debtor stays in control of the business and operates it as opposed to a trustee being appointed by the court to do so. A creditor's committee is formed to represent the interests of unsecured creditors. To encourage creditors to work with the bankrupt entity to reorganize, "postpetition" debts are afforded priority over "prepetition" unsecured debts.

Chapter 12

Chapter 12 is designed to allow farmers to continue running their farming operations while reorganizing their financial affairs. The debtor has "debt limitations" that affect eligibility for Chapter 12.

Chapter 12 contains a "codebtor stay," which means that creditors cannot take collection action without court permission against any codebtor or guarantor once the petition is filed.

Chapter 13

Chapter 13 is referred to as the "wage earner's" bankruptcy. It allows the debtor with a regular income to propose a plan by which a portion of the debtor's indebtedness will be repaid normally over a three-year period of time. A trustee is appointed by the court to receive payment from the debtor (generally an assignment of wages) and make distributions to creditors.

Involuntary Bankruptcy

Although most bankruptcy proceedings are voluntary acts by the debtor, creditors may also begin involuntary bankruptcy proceedings against certain debtors. Involuntary petitions can be commenced under Chapter 7 or 11. Creditors must show either that the debtor is not paying debts as they come due, or that a receiver has been appointed over the debtor's assets.

The beginning of the process after the debtor has filed a petition for bankruptcy protection is the *automatic stay*. Provisions covering the stay are effective immediately upon the filing of the petition. Generally, unsecured trade creditors of a debtor who is the subject of a bankruptcy proceeding are barred from any further attempts to collect the debt.

A creditor who violates the automatic stay may be held in contempt of court. A creditor, however, may take certain actions to protect lien rights. There are also provisions that allow a creditor to petition the court for relief from the automatic stay to take possession of collateral. However, any time a creditor receives a notice of bankruptcy or knows that a petition has been filed, he or she needs to preserve their rights while proceeding carefully in any further attempts at collection. It is especially helpful to consult with an attorney to determine what steps should be taken to preserve your rights in the bankruptcy.

 URLinks
http://www.toolkit.cch.com/Text/P06_4244.stm
http://www.equifax.com/
http://www.experian.com/

PERSONAL WORKSHOP 25
Credit Inquiry Considerations
▼ ▼ ▼ ▼ ▼ ▼

▼ If your business extends credit, consider how this sample credit inquiry form worksheet might be useful. Does it address the specific realities of your marketplace? If not, what elements would you add (or remove) to make it relevant to your business?

Credit Inquiry

Name _____ Date of birth _____

Address _____

Telephone number _____ Years there _____

Former Address _____

_____ Years there _____

Marital Status _____ Name of Spouse _____ No. dependents (inc. spouse) ____

Employer _____ Years there _____

Address _____

Phone _____ Kind of business _____

Position _____ Net income $/ _____

Former employer and address _____ Years there _____

Spouse's employer and address _____

Net income $/ _____ Other income sources: $/month _____

Account	Bank	Acct. No.	Balance
Checking			
Savings			

Auto owned (year and make) _____ Purchased from _____ $ _____

Financed by _____ Balance owed $ _____ Monthly _____

Rent or mortgage payment/mo. $ _____ Paid to _____

Real estate owned in name of _____ Purchase price _____ Mtge. bal. _____

Credit references and all debts owing—other than above
(Bank, loan or finance companies, credit unions, budget)

Name	Address	Orig. amt.	Bal.	Mo. payment

Life insurance amount _____ Company _____

If co-maker for others, state where and for whom _____

Nearest relative or friend not living with you/relationship _____

Address _____

CASE STUDY
KORZINSKI'S DEPARTMENT STORE
▾▾▼▼▼▼▼

Stephen Korzinski owns and operates Korzinski's Department Store in Providence, Rhode Island. Korzinski's has been in business for more than 40 years. Stephen's father, Karl, started the business in the mid-1950s as a small general store that sold about 100 products. Gradually, though, the store began to change in response to economic changes and the demands of customers for greater variety. Today, Korzinski's sells more than $10 million of merchandise a year, and is a city fixture with an even wider reputation for excellent products at reasonable prices. Many of Korzinski's longtime customers (or their children), however, have moved to outlying suburban areas. Stephen expects that if Korzinski's expands into the suburbs he can double or triple his sales within a matter of a year or two.

The one thing that worries Stephen is credit sales. Korzinski's policy through the years was always to sell for cash. His father had designed a sign that was all over the store, and that appeared as a kind of logo in Korzinski's newspaper ads: a dollar bill with a picture of Korzinski's building in place of George Washington, and in money-style type, "In God We Trust: All Others Pay Cash." Because of the store's prices and the quality of the goods, the cash-only policy worked. Several years ago, Stephen talked his father into installing a local bank's ATM machine in the store, as a service to customers. It was a unique situation, and many of his competitors felt that Korzinski's was a "miracle store," for they were burdened with a variety of costly and often frustrating credit plans.

Stephen finally realized that he would have to change the store's famous policy, and the opening of a suburban Korzinski's seemed like a convenient time to do it. While it went against the entire commercial value system he'd been taught by his father, he knew that to survive and grow, Korzinski's would have to offer credit to customers. Yet, he was determined that there would be strict requirements for eligibility. Stephen examined all the credit card companies, but didn't like the idea of having to pay a percentage to them. So he decided to set up his own credit department. He was quite aware that according to industry surveys, department stores with industry assets over $1 million were averaging only 1.3 percent net profit after taxes. Since Stephen was making about 2.5 percent, it was all the more reason not to give away a percentage of his sales to credit card companies. He could depend on commercial databases such as Experian or Equifax for credit reports of individuals to reduce bad-debt losses.

Stephen hired Rhonda Alvarado, a thorough financial whiz he'd met in business school, as manager of the new department. He outlined the requirements of a new system for her:

- A credit application form that is complete and nondiscriminatory, but one that goes beyond the usual three credit references. Stephen was especially interested in applicants' credit histories, occupations, and addresses where they could be found in case of nonpayment.
- A grading system in which each customer would be assigned an appropriate credit limit, along with specified conditions that would have to be met to increase the limit.
- A subsystem that would weed out marginal accounts.
- A revolving credit program for approved accounts that would charge the maximum interest rate allowed by the state.
- An installment credit program for big-ticket items, which would be financed over a period of not more than three years. Stephen wanted all installment contracts discounted with the bank on a nonrecourse basis. (That is, if the client didn't pay, then the bank lost the money and couldn't come back to Korzinski's.) Included in the installment program would be requirements for down payment and criteria for establishing the length of a contract.
- A rapid evaluation procedure that was effective and would not cost the company sales. (Customers often lose interest while waiting for credit departments to approve them.) Stephen would rather lose an account, how-

CONTINUED ▶

ever, than approve someone not up to his standards.

- A system in which all accounts receivable were aged, and Stephen could obtain a perfect view at a glance of how much credit was out on the street. He suggested that Rhonda get a computer in the department that would provide all the information he needed, when he needed it.
- A procedure whereby active accounts who paid their bills on time would receive advertising brochures, inserts, and other promotional items in their billing envelopes.
- A procedure for collection of all accounts over 45 days past due without resorting to collection agencies or use of the company's attorneys unless Stephen so directed.

- A means to identify that the person using the card was authorized to do so.

Rhonda pointed out that it was important for the accounts receivable subsidiary ledger to be kept up to date on a daily basis. If a client had a credit limit of $700 and the accounting department was 10 days behind in posting invoices, then a client could exceed the limit before they would catch it. She also pointed out that billing should take place promptly. If the bills didn't go out on time, then payments wouldn't come in on time.

This was a major challenge for Rhonda. It was clear that Stephen was holding her responsible for credit sales. She sat down to design a system that would meet his requirements. ▼

Case Study Roundtable

▼ ▼ ▼ ▼ ▼

Rhonda: Stephen has very specific ideas about what he wants for Korzinski's credit program. I'm sure I can come up with something suitable, but I'd still like your input.

Discussion Points

- Design a credit application that meets Stephen's expectations. Remember that it cannot violate any existing credit laws and cannot be discriminatory.
- Design a grading system in order to assign clients a credit limit. How would you handle a client who wanted a higher limit than you had determined should be granted? Would you extend credit to students or young people who were just out of school and working, or would you consider them marginal or undesirable accounts? What additional conditions would make them acceptable?
- Provide clear definitions of what would constitute an undesirable client, and the characteristics of an acceptable client.

BACK TO THE TABLE
Latonya Ellis and Kate Petrakis

In Chapter 1, you met Latonya and Kate, owners of Grandmother's Attic Heirloom Dresses, a small shop specializing in custom replicas of women's dresses and children's clothing from the late 1800s and early 1900s. Based on what you now know, how would you advise them to handle the problem of when to order the fabric and lace for the heirloom dresses and at what quantity, given the business's current lack of a credit line?

▲▲▲▲▲▲

CHAPTER BRIEFCASE

▼▼▼▼▼▼

- To compete for customers, encourage sales, and maintain good relations with existing customers, you often must extend credit. Credit is also an effective marketing tool: it provides potential customers with the attraction of enhanced purchasing power.

- A key part of any credit policy is the collection of information about the customer at a time when getting this information is the easiest.

- It is good for you to be aware of the full lineup of legal tools available to reduce your risk of loss or to collect from an account that has defaulted on a financial obligation to you. Lawyers refer to this as your "quiver of arrows." A lawsuit is usually the last one you'll want to use, because a lawsuit can be costly, time-consuming, and ineffective if you cannot find the debtor or if the debtor has insufficient funds.

- The laws in all states allow you to take a security interest in the goods you sell on credit. The Uniform Commercial Code (UCC), which has been adopted in full or in large part by all 50 states, gives a seller of goods the right to take a secured interest in the property sold to a customer, or even in other property owned by the customer.

- Congress and state legislatures have enacted laws that regulate or impact a creditor's collection practices. You need to be alert to changes in these laws because, as the use of credit by business and customer becomes even more pervasive, there will undoubtedly be more legislative initiatives that target either creditor rights or consumer and debtor protections.

▲▲▲▲▲▲

BUSINESS BUILDING

Paul and Vickie Scharfman
(Lowell, Wisconsin)
Specialty Cheese Company

Adapted with permission from
Small Business 2000, the
series on public television.

"*V*ickie: There are many people who go out and say, 'I have God's gift to the product world. I have this fabulous invention. Everyone's gonna love it. I'm gonna make a mint. I'm gonna sell a gazillion of them.' They go out and they make this wonderful product, and it sits there and nothing happens. And they can't understand why people aren't buying this, all right? That is completely the backwards approach to marketing. Marketing says, 'Find out what your consumer wants, what your consumer needs, and what they're not getting from the current offerings in the marketplace, and go out and tailor your dream to what they want.' And that's gonna be the right fit that sells product, okay? So that's the start of it.

Paul: The gist of it is simple: ask. People love talking. Ask them about something they care about, and they will tell you more than you want to know. You want to go and become a manufacturer of golf balls. Have you started by asking people who use golf balls about the product? Have you asked people who play golf a lot, heavy users, about it? You want to go and make stuffing mix. When was the last time you made stuffing? Probably not recently. Who makes a lot of stuffing? Have you talked to them? What are the problems? What do they like? What don't they like? It's free. You can do it. "

Chapter 13

CREATING AN IDENTITY AND CHOOSING A NAME

▼▼▼▼▼

Thou art thyself, though not a Montague.
What's Montague? It is nor hand nor foot,
Nor arm nor face, nor any other part
Belonging to a man. O, be some other name!
What's in a name? That which we call a rose
By any other word would smell as sweet

—*William Shakespeare*, Romeo and Juliet, II, ii

MISSION STATEMENT

In this chapter, you will

*L*EARN about the importance of choosing an effective name that communicates the image you want for your business.

*E*XPLORE the legal issues involved in selecting and protecting your business's name and image.

*A*PPLY your understanding to a real world case study.

*P*RODUCE a name for your business based on a systematic creative process.

KEY TERMS

brochure	graphic identity	logo
DBA	letterhead	logotype
fictitious name		

INTRODUCTION: WHAT'S IN A NAME?

Naming your business is a pleasant task. It makes it easier to visualize the business, and somehow makes the entire start-up process feel more real. Some people know exactly what they want to name their business; others have to list all the possibilities and think about it long and hard.

Not only is choosing a name one of the more "fun" parts of starting a business, it's also one of the most important decisions you'll make. The name you choose will position your business in people's minds, affect the image you project, and have a major impact on your success. Some guidelines may help you think through the naming process and decide what image you want to project with your name, letterhead, logo, and business cards.

This analysis is not intended to prevent you from being creative or whimsical (any book from a company called Upstart Publishing has to be careful about being more-serious-than-thou about names). It is, however, intended to help you avoid the unintended consequences of a hastily chosen (and unprotected) name.

HOW TO NAME YOUR BUSINESS

Naming your business is an important marketing decision. Keep in mind that one major marketing rule is to minimize customer (and prospect) discontent. Here are some basic business-naming tips:

- Keep the name straightforward and descriptive. The name you pick should tell your markets what your business is about, not baffle them. "Jack's Joke Shop" is straightforward. But what's an "EXXON"? A "Primerica"? To answer these questions, these companies spend millions of dollars every year.
- Make the name distinctive, if possible. You still want to stand out from the crowd. A veterinarian who specializes in feline medicine decided to call her office "The Cat Practice." The name is clear and direct, yet distinctive: you'd be unlikely to stop in with your sick Labrador.
- Avoid humor. What you think is funny your markets may not. Humor is a dangerous marketing tool at best. On the other hand, if you know that your market has a high tolerance for the whimsical, humor can work to your advantage (a hair styling salon called "Curl Up & Dye," for example, or a high-end used clothing store called "Rags from Riches").
- Shun grandiose descriptors. "Supreme," "Universal," "Federal," and so forth have been overworked to the point where they are meaningless.
- Don't necessarily pick the first name that comes to you. Make a list. Ask your friends. Check the yellow pages and local business directories, not just in your area but in other places. Don't use a famous name, or one similar to a famous name. In these litigious days, calling your shop "McDonuts" will probably get you nothing but angry cease-and-desist letters from corporate lawyers. If your own name is like another famous company's, you even need to be careful naming your business for yourself. A few years ago, a woman named Sony found herself on the losing end of a major lawsuit when the electronics company felt that her use of her own name on her newly opened restaurant threatened their trademark. Similarly, the Not-A-Stetson hat store in Texas had to pick another name when the actual Stetson company was not amused. More recently, a little boy nicknamed Pokey set up a noncommercial Web site called "Pokey's Web" and found himself threatened with a lawsuit by Prema Toy Company, the owner of the Gumby® and Pokey® trademarks. If in doubt, consult your own attorney. Run an Internet search on some of your ideas to see if they're already being used (at least on the Web).
- Try your business name out on some people who don't know you and your business idea. They may give you positive feedback, or constructive criticism. If they stare at you blankly, or make faces, rethink the idea. Run it by an ad agency

or marketing advisers. It's easy to change the name now. It won't be once you develop a logo, stationery, business cards, signs, and put your phone number in the yellow pages and business directories.

- Finally, be flexible. Avoid locking on to a name that your company is likely to outgrow. And don't become so fond of your company's original name that you're unwilling to change it if your business (or the times) change.

PERSONAL WORKSHOP 26
Naming Your Business

▾ As we've discussed in this chapter, naming your business is an important process. This three-step workshop is designed to help you work through the process in an organized and efficient way.

Step One: Keep the name straightforward and descriptive.

Use this form to do some "organized brainstorming" about your business name. First, fill in all the categories, and then spend some time playing with the resulting words and phrases to make a list of possible names. Don't judge their quality yet: just make the list!

My name	What do I do or make?	What do people value in my product or service?	Appropriate descriptive words
Your own name can be an important part of your business name, especially if it's a personal service or special skill.	Your company's name might include a reference to exactly what your business does.	List some adjectives that describe what your customers want.	List colorful and specific words that describe what you do and how well you do it.

CONTINUED ▶

Step Two: Do research.

Use this form to list all your competitors' names, and judge what you like and don't like about each one (the name, that is, not the competitor!).

Competitor name	Does it clearly say what they do?		Does it grab my attention?		Is it distinctive and recognizable?		Other reactions
	YES	NO	YES	NO	YES	NO	

Step Three: Get reactions.

Once you've brainstormed a bunch of names, and compared them with your competitors' names, choose your top three or four possible names and present them to five other people for their reactions. Keep a tally of your results here.

Potential name	Excellent name	Neutral about it	Didn't like it	Really hated it	Comments

FIRST PERSON

Daria M., San Francisco, California: My mom started Fannie's Fancy Hats about twenty years ago. It's always been a small operation—just a few women who like to make creative, custom hats—that seems to be pretty consistently popular with a small clientele, mostly artists and some tourists who happen to walk by. Fannie's Fancy Hats has been in the same tiny storefront for twenty years, and is a real fixture in what's become quite a trendy neighborhood. Well, mom turned the business over to me five years ago and then went to Peru to find herself. What she ended up finding was a women's weaving cooperative that made blankets, shawls, bags, and all sorts of things in wonderful traditional colors and patterns, and she shipped a bunch back to the shop. I put them out, and they were gone in a week. Then she went to Tibet and found some other artisans, and the same thing happened. Suddenly, she was our international buyer, and I was running what was turning into a store that sold a lot more than just hats. In fact, our hat sales have been declining fast since the locals got a look at the stuff from Peru, Mexico, Nigeria, and Tibet. So I did it: I changed the venerable, time-honored name of Fannie's Fancy Hats to just Fannie's—I figured that left room for a wider inventory without just dumping all the name recognition we'd earned over the decades. I took out an ad in the local paper announcing the change and listing all the new items, sent letters to our regular customers (with coupons), and a couple of months ago we had the big switchover. Mom was terrified (and a little sad) but you know what? Nothing bad happened, no one complained, and sales are as strong as ever. In fact, I think they'll grow now that people don't see our store and say "I don't need a hat." Now they say, "Fannie's? Look at those wonderful things in the window!" and come on in to check us out.

URLinks
http://www.new-direction.com/NAME.HTM
http://www.namestormers.com/nameg.htm
http://www.entrepreneurmag.com/page.hts?N=923&Ad=D

FICTITIOUS NAMES

A fictitious name is commonly referred to as a DBA, which stands for "Doing Business As." A fictitious name is any business name that does not contain your own name. In some states, that means your legal name (frequently first and last).

If you are not a corporation and you plan to conduct business under a fictitious name, you must file a DBA. If you are a corporation, ownership of your name is ensured when you incorporate. Also, if your legal name is considered very common, you may be required to file a DBA.

These examples may more clearly illustrate DBA registration:

Name	DBA Registration Required	DBA Registration NOT Required
Ocean Adventures	x (no name)	
Glenn's Ocean Adventures	x (common name)	
Sullivan's Ocean Adventures	x (common name)	
Glenn Sullivan's Ocean Adventures		x (full name)

Name	DBA Registration Required	DBA Registration NOT Required
John Smith's Ocean Adventures	x (common name)	
Ocean Adventures, Inc.		x (corporation)

Filing your DBA is one of the first tasks you must undertake because every other piece of paperwork requires the business name. Your bank will also require a copy of your DBA before they will open a business account under that name. This is the only authorization they have for depositing or cashing checks made out to that business name or written against its account.

Your business name should be free of conflict with names already registered in your area. Find out if a corporation has staked a claim to your name by calling your state's office of name availability. You may also wish to check the DBA books at the county clerk's office. Finding out at a later date that your name is already legally registered to another business will result in having to redo all of your paperwork.

Failing to File

Registering a business name is very important for your own protection as well as for compliance with the law. Registration of that name gives you exclusive rights to it. It also keeps others from filing the same or a similar name and capitalizing on the hard work and investments you have made in your business.

Unfortunately, there are individuals who lurk in the shadows waiting for just such an opportunity. About eight years ago, we had a business owner in one of our classes who had built a very successful electronics firm. However, he failed to file a DBA. Someone else discovered his error, filed under his business name and offered him the option of either paying to buy the name back or ceasing to do business under that name. The business owner refused to pay the blackmail and chose to reestablish under a new name. However, the continuity of his business was set back and he lost a large amount of business trying to reestablish under the new name.

The time and money spent to file a DBA is very small compared to the benefits you will derive from becoming the legal owner of your business name. (In Chapter 20, we discuss the Internet version of DBA filing: domain name registration.)

GRAPHIC IDENTITY

First impressions are lasting. The first impression often made by a business is through *graphic identity*. **Graphic identity** refers to the visual representation of your company. It includes the design of your logo and the style of your promotional materials.

You may be a small company competing with larger companies or a new company entering an existing market. You need to look competent and established. A carefully planned and implemented graphic identity can give you the edge you need and should last for many years.

A company's graphic or visual identity usually includes a logo, a logotype (type style), and company colors. The combinations you choose will create your identity and will make your promotional and packaging materials recognizable. In today's highly competitive world, it is important to be recognized, to be remembered, and to be viewed as an established business.

Logo

A **logo** is a symbol that represents the company. It may be a monogram of the company's initials or a design. A logo is a quick way of getting people to notice and remember your business. When designing your logo, you want to be sure that it is appropriate to your business and that the art work is timely. You can design your own, select from standard logos available from a printer, hire a professional artist, or work with a high school or college art student.

Be sure to register your logo with the Copyright Office or the Patent and Trademark Office in Washington, D.C. Refer to Chapter 8 regarding these protections. Some famous logos are illustrated in Figure 13.1 (note IBM's extra protections).

Logotype

Logotype refers to the type style used in the writing of your business name. The type size, placement, and style can communicate a great deal about your company. There are hundreds of fonts available and, within each type family, there are plain, italic, and bold versions (see Figure 13.2).

 URLinks

http://thelogofactory.com/case/gallery1.html
http://windows.microsoft.com/typography/links/link6.htm

Colors

Often a company will wish to adopt company colors. For example, IBM is closely associated with blue (and is commonly referred to as "Big Blue"). Century 21's real estate agents are known by their gold jackets. Most often two colors are used. As with type style, the colors you choose can set the tone for your marketing materials. Make sure the colors fit your company and the identity you wish to project. Use colors consistently: select particular shades, and use them all the time, without variation.

Business Cards

Business cards are one of the most universally used marketing tools. Not only do they give your business credibility, they serve as a visual reminder of you and your business. Be sure to have business cards printed as soon as possible. Whenever you attempt to deal with another business or individual, you should give them your card.

Begin to gather cards as you network in the business community, deal with suppliers, and evaluate competitors. When you have collected 30 to 40 of them, arrange them on a tabletop. Now scan the cards and see which ones catch your eye. Then evaluate the cards that caught your attention in terms of the following questions:

FIGURE
13.1 **Well-Known Logos**

IBM and the IBM logotype are registered trademarks of International Business Machines Corporation.

> FIGURE
> 13.2   Logotype
>
> When Daria decided to change the name of her store from Fannie's Fancy Hats to just Fannie's, she wanted to change the look of the store's logotype, too. Below are the final five choices she narrowed it down to. Which one would you suggest she choose? Why? (You may want to reread Daria's First Person story on page 303.)
>
> *Fannie's Fancy Hats*
>
> **Fannie's**
>
> Fannie's
>
> FANNIE'S
>
> *Fannie's*
>
> *Fannie's*

- What is it about this card that first draws your attention?
- Is the logo appropriate and descriptive?
- Is the company name legible?
- Is the contact person's name and phone number included?
- Does the card tell what product is offered?
- Does the card tell the service provided?
- Does the card tell the location of the business?
- Is the overall appearance pleasing?
- Is the card one you will remember?

Ask these same questions of your card as you plan the design. Keep in mind the following items:

- The logo must be appropriate and descriptive.
- The company name must be legible and in the correct type size.
- A contact person's name and phone number must appear.
- Include a statement about the product or service offered.
- The overall appearance of the card must be pleasing.
- The card should be one the customer will remember.

A business card is like a mini-billboard. It should tell the what, why, who, how, when, and where of your business.

Be patient. Do not buy your first cards in large quantity. Even though the purchase of a large quantity of business cards will save you money on a per unit basis, one thousand cards will do you no good if the information on your cards is no longer valid. They will just have to be discarded and the money you saved will be lost. In a very short time you may want to change your card for any number of reasons: change of address, addition of a logo, inclusion of a fax number or e-mail address, or addition of new products or services. All businesses change as they grow. By purchasing your cards in reasonable amounts, you can avoid having to discard ones which no longer apply to your situation.

FIRST PERSON

Linda P., Tustin, California: I've kept all our old business cards over the years. Today, it's interesting for newer employees to see how far this little company's come, and the business cards reflect that. Figure 13.3 displays four examples that show how our business cards were changed to add a logo and a fax number, to change addresses and phone numbers, and to reflect changes in the nature of a business. *Out of Your Mind...And Into the Marketplace* started as a small, home-based consulting service located in Fullerton, California. Later, we added a logo, expanded our service to include seminars and textbooks, and relocated the main office to Tustin. At the same time, we opened another office in Camarillo. My partner and I became pretty well recognized as business consultants, and wrote a few books. Then along came the computer revolution, and we had to respond quickly, adding educational programs and business planning software. Today, we offer business plan and publishing consulting. I think the lesson we learned just from these four cards is that in order to grow, your business has to be dynamic. In order to keep your market informed, the changes you make have to be reflected on that "mini-billboard" you hand out like candy.

Letterhead

Your letterhead is your business stationery. It should be used for all business correspondence. It also lends credibility to your business. The color, type, and quality of the paper you use will reflect on your company. Expand the information formatted for your business card and develop a "look" that appears on all your promotional materials and carries over to your package design. Duplicate the format, type style, and colors used on your business card for continuity. When you have your letterhead printed, purchase a smaller quantity of second sheets. When writing a business letter, the letterhead is used only for the first page.

Brochures

Brochures are essential for any business for which the prospective customer needs detailed information about the qualifications and expertise of the owner and the services and products offered. More information can be supplied in a brochure than would be practical for a classified ad. Brochures can be mailed, distributed door to door, or given out at community events and trade shows.

FIGURE
13.3
Business Card Development

OUT OF YOUR MIND . . . .
AND INTO THE MARKETPLACE
SMALL & HOME-BASED BUSINESS CONSULTING

JERRY JINNETT
&
LINDA PINSON

3031 Colt Way #223
Fullerton, CA 92633
Tel. No. (714) 523-1849

Small Business Consulting
Textbooks
Seminars

OUT OF YOUR MIND...
AND INTO THE MARKETPLACE™

LINDA PINSON
13381 WHITE SAND DRIVE
TUSTIN, CA 92680
Tel. No. (714) 544-0248

JERRY JINNETT
1734 SHORELINE STREET
CAMARILLO, CA 93010
Tel. No. (805) 484-2135

OUT OF YOUR MIND...
AND INTO THE MARKETPLACE™

PUBLISHER OF BUSINESS BOOKS & BUSINESS PLAN SOFTWARE

LINDA PINSON
President

13381 White Sand Drive
Tustin, CA 92680

Tel: (714) 544-0248
FAX: (714) 730-1414
EMail: LPinson@AOL.com

International Business Consulting
Business Plan Consulting
Business Education Programs

OUT OF YOUR MIND...
AND INTO THE MARKETPLACE™

AUTHORS OF BUSINESS BOOKS & BUSINESS PLAN SOFTWARE

JERRY JINNETT
2824 Bedford Street
Johnstown, PA 15904

(814) 266-9187
CA Office: (714) 544-0248

Business Education Programs
Business Plan Consulting
Publishing Consulting

The following guidelines should help you with your design and content issues. A brochure is a general term for a promotional piece that contains the following information about your business. It should contain certain specific elements, in a clearly readable and attractive format that is appropriate for your type of business and your market's expectations (that is, a computer dealer's brochure would not be likely to resemble a florist's). You should include the following information:

- Company name
- Company address (be sure to include the full address and zip code)
- Telephone and fax number (be sure to include the area code; also your e-mail address)
- Key people (Clients and customers want to know the background and expertise of the people with whom they will be doing business and feel more comfortable if they can ask for a contact person by name. You may wish to include short biographies or photos of key people within your business.)
- Features (characteristics or attributes of your product or service that "tell" about your business)
- Benefits (advantages of purchasing and using your product or service that "sell" your business)

- Statement of purpose (the mission statement of your business can convey your business philosophy and goals to the customer)
- Testimonials from satisfied customers

Other Promotional Materials

A business card, letterhead, and a brochure are the primary promotional materials of all businesses. As your business grows, you may want to develop these other materials:

- Invoices
- Building sign
- Business cards
- Business reply envelopes
- Checks
- Contracts/agreements
- Display signs
- Envelopes
- Flyers
- Letterhead
- Mailing labels
- Name badges
- Presentation folders
- Promotional giveaways
- Purchase orders
- Uniforms
- Vehicle signs

If you are a retailer, you may decide to have a catalog printed and mailed to your customers. You may even want to go into color processing. Eventually you may need signs for a display, your building, or your vehicle. To create a "total look" for your business, you can expand your graphic identity to include business checks, mailing labels, purchase order forms, and invoices. For the small business just starting up, business cards, letterhead, and a basic brochure or order form are enough to get the business off to a good start.

Choosing a Printer

Two of the major considerations in choosing a printer are quality of work and price. Sometimes the lowest bid is not the most cost-effective. If the workmanship on the project and the quality of materials are poor, your business image will suffer. After all, the presentation materials you use often determine how your customers, suppliers, and competitors will perceive your business.

Quality and price vary among printers. You will want to visit three or four printers in your area. Get a price list and view samples of their work. You may have your cards and letterhead done at one shop and your brochures printed at another shop that specializes in that type of printed matter.

In order to save money, much of your printing can be done from camera-ready copy. This means that you take the printer a finished product ready to be reproduced. Note that camera-ready copy should only be used if you can make your layout look professional and businesslike. Desktop publishing companies can help you with this work. With the right software and equipment, of course, you can desktop-publish your own business cards and other promotional materials. Just be sure you have the professional design and application skills necessary to achieve a high-quality appearance.

FIRST PERSON

Greg N., Hancock, Michigan: Here's an important thing: before you have *any* printing done, be sure to get an estimate *in writing*. I was given a quote over the phone for printing booklets and boxes for the juggling balls my company makes. One of my employees dropped off the designs at the printer. They printed up the booklets and boxes and I paid the bill in full when they were delivered. A month later, I received another bill, this one for something called "setup charges." The printer said that the setup charges covering setting up and inking the printing press were separate. I called my attorney, but it turned out I was legally responsible for the additional charges. Since there was no written agreement, I couldn't prove that the printer hadn't told me about the extra charges. So remember: *get it in writing*!

CASE STUDY
AUTUMN LEAVES PET CEMETERY

*B*everly Pickford and Donnel Jenkins were sisters who were widowed and living together. They had not inherited much money from their husbands, and it would be nearly 10 years before they would be eligible to receive Social Security. They decided to open a business that would be both satisfying and meaningful to them. Of course, they also wanted to make enough money to live comfortably.

After much research, Beverly and Donnel decided to establish a pet cemetery. The nearest one was approximately 75 miles away. If they established one nearby, just outside Lincoln, Nebraska, it would have great appeal. Beverly already owned a 100-acre piece of property with an abundance of beautiful trees that would make an ideal cemetery.

The sisters hired an architect to create a design and layout for the cemetery. The environment had to be serene, so that pet lovers would want to bury their pets there. In a month, the architect came up with a design with a distinctive brick wall surrounding the facility. The wall facing the main highway was low enough for people to see how beautiful the cemetery was. The landscaping included separate areas ringed by shrubs and trees, small waterfalls, and statues of all types of animals. The cemetery exuded peace and harmony.

The architect designed a building to house the inventory of stones, tools, and other equipment. The building also had a display room for caskets and other products for sale, and a small chapel. He also designed a crematorium to accommodate animals up to 200 pounds. The proposed layout was simply magnificent. The architect estimated the entire project would cost $150,000 to construct. The sisters approved the design and construction began.

Next, the sisters had to decide how to advertise the cemetery. Since neither of them had any marketing experience, they thought that maybe an advertisement in the papers or on television would be sufficient.

The big question, however, was the name. Throughout the early stages of start-up, the sisters had discussed a wide array of possible names for the cemetery. Beverly liked Fond Farewells, Peaceful Pets, The Final Walk, and Dreamland. Donnel preferred Pearly Gates, Best Friend's Rest, Fur, Feather 'n' Halo, and Always In My Heart. After weeks of sometimes heated argument, they finally settled on a name—Autumn Leaves—that neither one hated. Even though neither sister liked the name much, they needed to have a sign made and advertisements laid out. ▼

CASE STUDY ROUNDTABLE

▼ ▼ ▼ ▼ ▼ ▼

Beverly: I still think Fond Farewells is a vastly better name than Autumn Leaves. I mean, what does Autumn Leaves have to do with anything anyway? Am I right?

Donnel: No. It's too gloomy. That's why I like Pearly Gates or Fur, Feather 'n' Halo— people don't need to be reminded how miserable they feel.

Beverly: See what we're doing? We just go round and round on this. What do you think?

Discussion Points

- Is the name issue really the central problem? If not, what is? In any case, do you think the resolution of the dispute (picking a name that no one hated) was the best way to do it? What are the possible problems with such a solution?
- What are the strengths and weaknesses of the sisters' preferred choices?
- Sketch a logo concept for the sisters that you think will be effective in establishing name and product identification. Also, which of these logotypes would you recommend for their signs, cards, and letterhead? Why?

Autumn Leaves	**Autumn Leaves**	Autumn Leaves	AUTUMN LEAVES	**Autuan Leaves**	Autumn Leaves	**Autumn Leaves**
1	2	3	4	5	6	7

▲ ▲ ▲ ▲ ▲ ▲

CHAPTER BRIEFCASE

▼ ▼ ▼ ▼ ▼

- Choosing a name for your business is one of the most important decisions you will make during the start-up process. Keep it simple and descriptive yet distinctive; avoid inappropriate humor and superlatives.
- If you are not a corporation and you plan to conduct business under a fictitious name, you must make a Doing Business As (DBA) filing in accordance with the laws of your state.
- First impressions are lasting, and often the first impression made by a business is through its graphic identity: the visual representation of the company through a logo or logotype. You may want your company to be associated with certain colors. Once you've selected a "graphic identity" you must use it often

and consistently in order to embed it in the public consciousness. Business cards, letterhead, brochures, and other promotional materials are ways to ensure that your name and graphic identity are given maximum exposure.

▲▲▲▲▲▲

Chapter 14

MARKET RESEARCH TECHNIQUES

▼▼▼▼▼▼

Scorn also to depress thy competitor by any dishonest or unworthy method; strive to raise thyself above him only by excelling him; so shall thy contest for superiority be crowned with honor...

—*Pharoah Akhenaton (c. 1350 BC)*

MISSION STATEMENT

In this chapter, you will

*L*EARN about the importance of defining your market and your competitors, and establishing effective communication with your prospective customers.

*E*XPLORE the steps and strategies behind creating questionnaires.

*A*PPLY your understanding to a case study.

*P*RODUCE an evaluation of your competitors and draft a questionnaire for your business.

KEY TERMS

demographics	market research	target markets
fad	psychographics	trend
markets	questionnaire	

INTRODUCTION TO MARKET RESEARCH AND ANALYSIS

Markets are those persons or organizations who *will* be your customers, while **target markets** are those persons or organizations *most likely* to become your customers. Target markets are small and tightly defined. A common start-up error is to assume that everyone is a prospective customer. Everyone is not. Your markets are limited by a wide variety of factors, including:

▼▼▼▼▼▼▼▼▼▼▼▼▼▼▼▼▼▼▼▼▼▼▼

314

- Geography
- Age
- Education
- Income
- Competition
- Your skill at promoting and advertising your business

Even your target markets will have different subgroups of greater or lesser value to you. Think of a bull's eye (most valuable prospects) versus outer rings (less valuable prospects) on an archery target. You want to focus on the bull's eye and not squander your efforts and resources trying to reach less likely prospects. In this chapter, we will examine the strategies and techniques you can use to measure, evaluate, and effectively target a market for your business.

HOW TO SURVEY YOUR MARKET

In order to be successful, a business must know its market. **Market research** is an organized and objective way of learning about your customers. It involves finding out what a customer wants and needs and determining how your company can meet those wants and needs.

Evaluate Current Buying Trends

One method of learning about customers, products, and services is to look at what is being purchased and who is doing the purchasing. In marketing, this is known as evaluating trends.

A **trend** is a behavior or buying pattern that lasts between five and ten years and is generally widespread. Current trends include environmentalism, alternative medicines, relationships, exotic and organically grown spices and foods, and concern for health and aging. For instance, foods, cosmetics, and packaging materials are removing color additives and promoting themselves as "clear" or "crystal" as a response to health and environmental issues. The use of recycled paper has increased. Evidence of current trends surrounds us.

Be careful not to confuse trends with fads. **Fads** are short-term surges of popularity (and usually sales) for a particular type of product or service. After the initial wave, in which it seems that everyone absolutely must have a pet rock, home gym, or gourmet jelly bean, there is a dramatic and relatively quick dropoff in sales (and profits). Garage sales and resale shops are filled with items that people had to have, and then somehow learned they didn't really need. Fads seem to occur among smaller groups and last for only a year or two at most. Although large sums of money can often be made by being the first to present a fad, business longevity is tied to trends. The smart businessperson looks at the current trends, as well as those being predicted for the future, and finds ways of tailoring products or services to meet the needs of consumers in terms of those trends. It's great to be the person whose product enjoys six months of dizzying sales as a popular fad; it's better to be the one who's out in front of a long-term trend.

Don't underestimate personal observation as a means of tracking trends. A great deal can be learned about the buying habits in your area by watching the purchases made in the supermarket checkout line and the stores in the mall. What specialty shops are opening? What colors seem to be popular? What books are on the bestseller lists and what subjects do they cover? What foods are being featured in restaurants? When are most purchases made? Who is making these purchases? Your eyes can be one (or two) of your most important market-analysis tools.

MARKETING STEP ONE: KNOW YOUR COMPETITORS

You have two main types of competitors: direct and indirect. Direct competition is a business that offers the same product or service to the same market. Indirect competition is a company with the same product or service but a *different* market. That is, you may both provide the same product or service, but one of you is exclusive based on walk-ins, and the other is strictly a catalog. Evaluate both direct and indirect competition, because they both have one thing in common: you want their business, and they want your profits. Look for the strengths and weaknesses of your competitors. You need to identify your competitor's image. To what part of the market does the company appeal? Can you appeal to the same market in a better way? Or can you discover an untapped market?

In a retail business, the toughest competition generally comes from established stores and wholesalers that can offer lower prices because of higher sales volume. In the service industry, strong competition comes from established businesses that have a loyal clientele. Examine the extent and nature of the competition in terms of location, product or service, pricing, methods of distribution, packaging, and source of supply.

Look for the strengths and weaknesses of your competitors. You need to identify your competitor's image. To what part of the market does he or she appeal? Can you appeal to the same market in a better way? Or can you discover an untapped market?

Finding the Competition

If your marketing questionnaire contains questions regarding current service businesses and products used by your market, you will have a head start. The business listings in your telephone directory can provide a wide variety of useful information. The total listing in your business category will give you an idea of the range of your competition. You will be able to pinpoint their locations within your geographical area. Analyze the type and style of each ad. What image do you have of the business based solely on your reaction to the ad? When you make an inspection trip to the places of business, do you retain that same image?

The chamber of commerce can give you a wealth of information on business in general and your business area in particular for the region that you wish to investigate. National trade and professional associations publish newsletters and magazines that not only predict trends, but also tell about current business. Directories that list these associations are available in the library. Identify those in your field, write to them on your letterhead, and request sample copies of their publications and membership information.

PERSONAL WORKSHOP 27
Competition Evaluation Form
▼ ▼ ▼ ▼ ▼

▼ Use this form to help you pinpoint your competitors' competitive vulnerabilities. First, do an objective analysis of each competitor's business, from the point of view of the customer or client. Then use the right-hand column to check off areas where your business could immediately compete. The Shortstop's Sporting Goods example in Figure 14.1 shows how one business owner used this form.

Competitor		
Location		
Products or services offered		
Methods of distribution		
Image		
Packaging		
Promotional materials		
Methods of advertising		
Quality of product or service		
Pricing structure		
History and performance		
Market share		
Strengths		
Weaknesses		
Date of site visit/service use		
Observations/experience		

When you have compiled a list of competitors, plan to visit each one. Make copies of the Competition Evaluation Form in Personal Workshop 27. Use them to help you gather the data you need.

Evaluating a Competitive Service

The most effective way to evaluate a competitive service is to pose as a customer. Call and ask for job rates, delivery schedules, terms of payment, discount policies, and warranties or guarantees. What was your overall reaction after your phone call to the competition? Do you have confidence in the company? Were you treated in a courteous manner? Were you put on hold and forced to listen to inane music or a series of ads? Your reactions will reflect those of the buying public.

Visit your competitor's place of business. Rate the personnel. Is service prompt and efficient?

Now make use of the competitor's service. Was it acceptable? What could be improved? Your analysis of this information about the competition will help you plan your own market entry.

FIRST PERSON

Jim M., Oak Park, Illinois: Three years ago, I first got the entrepreneurial bug. I was interested in opening a dry cleaning service that would cater to the commuters who live in town. I even found a prime spot near the train station. The only trouble was a dry cleaner already operated within a couple of blocks of where I wanted to locate. So I decided to do a little investigation. I parked outside the competitor's shop at 6:30 on a Tuesday morning. The shop was due to open at 7:00. During the half hour before he opened, I counted eight customers in business suits who drove into the lot, parked, walked up to the door with bundles of clothes and then left again because the cleaner was closed. So I thought, here's an opening for me. I went ahead with the deal and opened up my business with a big ad push that emphasized that we were right next to the train station parking lot and that we opened for business at 6:00 in the morning. At the moment, Early To Rise Dry Cleaning is the only cleaner in town: the other guy tried changing his hours, but we'd gotten out ahead and he couldn't catch up.

Evaluating a Competitive Product

Visit shops where products similar to yours are displayed. Are the personnel knowledgeable? Ask a sales clerk to explain the product's advantages. Is the explanation enough to encourage you to buy the merchandise? How well is the competing product packaged and displayed? Packaging sells your product, not the sales clerk, so you can help by making your product's advantages clear on the package. You might even consider a training session for retailers of your products, or at least a flyer outlining the sales benefits.

Visit the shop at different times on different days of the week. You will begin to get an idea of traffic flow patterns. Watch the displays of similar products. Do the products seem to be moving? How soon are they marked down or moved to the sale table? Most stores keystone, or double the wholesale cost, so you can get an estimate of what your competitors' wholesale prices may be.

FIGURE 14.1 Sample Competition Evaluation Form: Shortstop's Sporting Goods

Competitor	Smith Sporting Goods	
Location	724 King Drive, Blair, WI in Tall Creek Shopping Center	
Products or services offered	Full line of sports equipment with emphasis on golf	X
Methods of distribution	Retail sales, catalog	
Image	Blue and white colors used in decor and uniforms	
Packaging	Plastic sales bags with logo	
Promotional materials	Baseball caps and T-shirts with name and logo	
Methods of advertising	KLXY radio ads, flyers-mail, Sunday supplement-newspaper	
Quality of product or service	Major brands, excellent sales staff	
Pricing structure	100% markup on golf items, 75% markup on other merchandise	X
History and performance	In current location for five years	
Market share	One of two sporting goods stores in town, has high school and university trade pretty much locked	
Strengths	Knowledgeable, friendly sales staff. Established contacts with local golf courses and associations.	
Weaknesses	Does not offer classes or sports clinics	X
	Closed Sundays	X
	Does not stock fishing gear	X
	Does not sponsor a youth team	X
Date of site visit/service use	Visited on 3/6 and 4/8; called for product info on 3/20 and 3/21	
Observations/experience	Staff was courteous, service was efficient and unrushed. Checkout was quick. Phone help was slow: on hold for 10 minutes waiting to find out if they carry Dolfer clubs (they don't).	X

Your competition is just as smart and motivated as you are: maybe even more so, because they've had more time to learn from their early mistakes. Some are better established, some are better financed, some have more experience, and some have solid reputations that may give them considerable flexibility in pricing and service. What can you do to fight back?

Keep track of everything your nearest competitors do. Keep records of their ads, their promotions, their financial dealings. If they add a branch office or close a satellite operation, take note. If they merge with another business, you need to know.

Keep these files up to date and periodically review them, and you will know more about your competitors than they know about themselves. When do they run sales? What benefits do they stress? Are they going after new target markets, trying to buy market share, or competing on quality? Are they consistent or scatterbrained? Do they drive the market, or follow it? Your analysis of the competition will help you plan your own market entry.

As you evaluate your competition, strengths and weaknesses will appear. You will bring the strengths of the competition to your business and you will learn from their weaknesses. The weaknesses are your inroads to success. They point the way toward what will be unique about your business. They will help you target what will benefit your customer.

CUSTOMER DEMOGRAPHICS: RESEARCHING YOUR MARKET

Niche marketers Paul and Vickie Scharfman applied their expertise to a sluggish cheese manufacturing business they purchased—and grew it into a profitable enterprise.

Market research involves finding out if there is a need for your product or service before committing a great deal of time and money to the project. Your product or service may be in demand and your pricing competitive. You may have found the lowest prices for your raw materials and may have secured adequate financing for your business. All of this will be of no use if you have not taken the time to identify your customers and find the means to get your product or service to them. The key word here is time. It takes time to research and develop a marketing plan, but it is time well spent.

So far, your focus has been on starting your business and developing your product or service. A person concerned with marketing must be consumer-oriented. You must now change your focus. Try to be objective and think like a customer. Will the customer have an interest in what you have to offer? Market research involves finding out what a customer wants and needs and determining how your business can satisfy those wants and needs. It also involves examining your competition's abilities and successes in the marketplace.

Markets are described in terms of **demographics**, such as age, sex, ethnic background, education, occupation, income, family status, and geographic location. Based upon your observations while analyzing the competition and your results from questionnaire evaluations, you will develop a profile of your customers. You then want to find customers who will fit this profile.

The information you need is available in census reports published by the Department of Commerce, in directories available in the reference section of the library, and in data available through the chamber of commerce. You should look for information about:

- *Population size.* This is one of several factors you can use to help you determine the size of the market. A study of population tables in the Statistical Abstract of the United States (reference material published by the Department of Commerce) will show population shifts. When studied, trends begin to emerge.
- *Population distribution tables.* These show trends such as a shift of the more affluent city dwellers to suburban communities. This change requires an adjustment on the part of business. Where does your market live? Where do they work? Do they shop where they live or where they work? If your potential customers shop where they work and work in another city, it will do no good to offer your product or service to them during normal working hours in the city of their residence.
- *Age distribution.* These figures also dictate trends. In the mid-1980s, the number of people age 65 or over surpassed the number of teenagers. This gap continues to widen as we move toward the year 2000.
- *Sex.* An obvious basis for consumer market analysis shows that many of the traditional buying patterns are changing. Men are frequent food shoppers, women are buying gas and arranging for car repair, and both are now concerned with home maintenance and repair. The number of working women has risen considerably in all age groups. In the late 1980s, well over one half of all American women were working outside the home, and this trend will continue to grow into the next century.
- *Ethnic origin.* Because it can affect the population base, it is also useful in the analysis of demographics for some products and services. Product preferences, age distribution, population shifts, and language will vary. You should be aware of the ethnic breakdown of the geographical area that you are targeting. This data is found in the Census Bureau information dealing with general population characteristics. A business reference librarian can direct you to resources such as the City and County Data Book, which contains statistical information on population distribution.
- *Family status.* During the past decade, two distinct and new groups have emerged: single people living alone and unmarried people living together. Census reports break down family status by number of children and their age ranges, and indicate a rise in the number of single parents.
- *Education level, occupation and income.* These are other demographics to be considered. Education level often points to changes in product preference. People with higher levels of education may have more specialized tastes and higher incomes. Occupation must also be considered as a meaningful criterion for analyzing the market.

URLinks
http://www.bea.doc.gov/
http://www.census.gov/
http://www.ita.doc.gov/
http://www.state.ia.us/sbro/tools.htm

Psychographics

Markets are also defined in terms of psychographics. These are the psychological characteristics of your market and are as important as demographics. The traditional demographic studies gave no insight into why people bought certain products over those of the competition. Marketers began to see the need for analyzing lifestyle, personal behavior, self-concept, and buying style. The study of psychographics and its relationship to marketing is relatively new. It had its beginnings in the early 1950s. At the present time, it is a widely used tool for analyzing the market.

- *Lifestyle* refers to a person's manner of living. It is a broad category and involves personality characteristics. Lifestyle relates to a customer's activities, interests, and opinions. It reflects how leisure time is spent.
- *Personal behavior* is tied to personal values. The degree of community involvement, political activity, and neighborhood participation reflects the psychological makeup of a person. The degree of cautiousness, skepticism, and ambition reflects on buying patterns.
- *Self-concept* refers to how we see ourselves and hope to be seen by others. The demographics of family size, location, occupation, and income level may indicate that an individual would purchase a station wagon, but the psychographics of self-image show that the individual would buy a sports car.
- *Buying style* of your market is critical. How often do they make a purchase? Was there a specific reason for the purchase or was it an impulse buy? New products are first purchased by individuals who perceive themselves as adventuresome and open-minded.

Market Surveys

Unless you know who your customers, prospects, and competition are you can't even begin to ask the kinds of questions that will get you the answers you need. You can get help with marketing surveys from Small Business Development Centers, Small Business Institutes, marketing courses at local business schools, or your trade association. Surveys can be tricky. Customers don't always give straight answers to direct questions, and interpreting the data can be a challenge. Often, the way a question is worded can dramatically influence the kind of answers you receive.

You will be surprised at what information surveys reveal. Maybe customers buy from you because your location is convenient, or your sales force is polite and well informed, or they think your competitors are arrogant, rude, brusque, and disdainful. You may learn that your services are not perceived as superior, or your goods price-competitive. You may learn the reasons why you get customers' trade and your competitors do not. And when you lose customers to the competition, you can find out what you are doing wrong—or what your competitors are doing better than you.

Questionnaires

The key to market research is gathering useful information: information that is timely and reliable. It is an orderly, objective way of learning about the people who will buy your product or use your service. Remember that marketing is a dynamic process. Customers move, lifestyles change, income levels vary. To work effectively, market research must occur continuously throughout the lifetime of your business. Always be alert for new competition, new products and services, population shifts, and new trends.

A cost-effective method for gaining a response from the market regarding your product or service is through the use of a **questionnaire**. Surveys are an excellent means of determining the response to what you have to offer, and a questionnaire is the most common means of collecting data. A questionnaire begins with an introduction. Explain the nature of your business. Describe your product or your service, tell what is unique about it and how it will benefit the customer. Your initial contact with the reader is established in the opening statement.

A well-designed questionnaire can gather data covering four main areas:

1. *Interest in your product or service.* For example, include questions aimed at determining a need for your product or service: Would you be interested in home delivery of gourmet meals? Would you be interested in a gift-buying service? Are you looking for housekeeping services?
2. *Demographics.* Questions can be structured to show the kind of people your prospects are. These questions gather the demographic and psychographic information on your market: Do you work away from your home city? Do you shop where you work? Do you shop where you live? What price would you expect to pay for this product? What would you expect to pay for this service? What is your age? What is your household income? Do you own or rent your home?
3. *The means for reaching your market.* Questions can be included that will show you how to reach your customers: What newspapers do you read? What radio stations do you listen to? What TV programs do you watch? Do you use discount coupons? Do you order through catalogs? Where would you expect to buy this product?
4. *The competition.* Questions about the competition can show you ways in which your company can be unique and can benefit the customer: What company do you currently use? What do you like about their product or service? How can the product or service be improved?

CREATING EFFECTIVE QUESTIONNAIRES

The Use of Questionnaires

Because marketing is a dynamic process, you must find a cost-effective method of keeping up with the changes occurring within the marketplace. You want to get a response from the public regarding the product or service you are interested in providing. Before you invest time and money in developing your idea, determine whether a need or desire for it exists in the buying community. Surveys are an excellent means of determining the response to what you have to offer. A questionnaire is the most common means of collecting data.

Format

In formulating a questionnaire, care must be given to the structure, word choice, and sequence of the questions. Determine what you need to know, then choose your questions. Wording is important; be simple, unbiased, and direct. Be aware of the sequence of your questions. The first question should generate interest.

A questionnaire begins with an introduction. Establish your initial contact with the reader in the opening statement. Tell just enough about the nature of your survey to arouse interest. Point out that you value the reader's response. We all like to feel that our opinions are important.

Next, begin work on the body of the questionnaire by making a list of the information you need. Don't worry about phrasing or order at this point. Get everything down on paper, then go back and develop your wording and sequence. There are three types of questions and they vary according to structure and response.

1. Open-ended questions. This type of question requires the respondent to provide the reply. Choices are not given; the respondent must fill in the blanks. These are considered qualitative questions because they allow the person being surveyed to express an opinion in words. These questions often gather the most subjective information.

2. Multiple-choice questions. With these questions, you provide the respondent with a selection of answers. One example would be a question requiring a yes or no answer. Because there are only two responses, there is little chance of a biased answer. Some questions will warrant more choices. When using multiple-choice questions, run different copies of the questionnaire and vary the order in which the choices appear following the question. People tend to select an answer from the front of the list and your results may be biased. If the question requires the respondent to choose an answer from a numerical list, there is a tendency to select an answer from the middle of the list. People wish to appear "average" or "normal" and assume that choices at either end of the range reflect extremes.

3. Rating questions. These are sometimes called value-judgment questions. The respondent is asked to reflect an opinion on a ranking scale; for example, a scale of one to ten. If a ranking scale is used, be sure to indicate the value of the number range (i.e., one is equal to the least and ten is equal to the most).

Try to phrase your questions so they are clear and easily understood. Choose language that is appropriate to the group who will be responding. Use terms that are familiar to the consumer, and avoid words or phrases that are unique to your industry and not in common usage.

Ask questions in a logical sequence. Questions in a subject area should be grouped together. The first question creates interest. Begin with general questions and build to the more specific. Ask the most difficult or involved questions at the end. They will turn off the respondent if they appear early in the questionnaire. Since respondents will have completed most of the work by the time they get to the more involved questions, they will be less apt to abandon the project.

The questionnaire should end with the basic data: the name, address, and phone number of the respondent. Often, a more honest and subjective response will result if providing this information is optional. Many questionnaire respondents prefer to remain anonymous.

Types of Information

A well-designed questionnaire can gather data covering four main areas: (1) interest in your product or service, (2) data on demographics, (3) methods for reaching the market, and (4) information on the competition. Figure 14.2 suggests some question types for each of these areas.

To illustrate how specific data can be gathered, sample questionnaires are provided in Figures 14.3 (for a product-based business) and 14.4 (for a service-related business).

Distributing Questionnaires

Reach your market by giving the questionnaire to valid, potential customers—don't just circulate it among your family and friends, and don't just pick a random spot and hand them out. Mass-mailings are considered successful if they yield a 7 percent return: that is, if 7 percent of recipients respond. Target your mailings and questionnaires carefully, to achieve the greatest response rate possible. For instance, if your business will serve a specific neighborhood (like a dry cleaner or video store), you should probably not waste your time by sending out questionnaires to the entire metropolitan area. Renting a mailing list is often the most effective procedure in preparing a mass mailing. The company that provides the list will already have subdivided a master list into core interest groups, geographic regions, income, and lifestyle categories. This will allow you to "cherry pick" your target market.

In addition to mailings, your market can be contacted by telephone or through personal or group interviews. You may use a geographical phone directory or conduct interviews through clubs and organizations. Display tables at community events are also a good way to make contact with the buying public and gather information.

Your questionnaire results can form a basis for zeroing in on your customers. They can give you feedback regarding the demographics and psychographics of your study group. Include questions that will generate the information that you need.

FIRST PERSON

Lonnie W., Lincoln, Nebraska: I started Shortstop's Sporting Goods ten years ago. Today, our business is thriving, in no small part because we keep in touch with our customers. We send out follow-up cards and questionnaires, and have hired a telemarketing company to contact our regular customers and prospective markets and find out what they want in the way of the athletic supplies and services we can offer. Two years ago, I started thinking that maybe we could branch out. We did a questionnaire to research if there was a market for fishing lessons and guided fishing trips that Shortstop's could fill. (OK, I admit it, I love to fish, and I thought this would be a good way to combine business and pleasure!) I guess you could say it was a good step, because things certainly have worked out very well. We've expanded our business and

FIGURE
14.2

Market Research Question Types by Category

Product/Service	Demographics	Market Research	Competitors
Do you like to _____?	Where do you work?	What newspapers do you read? What section do you read first?	What company do you currently use?
Do you own a _____?	Do you shop where you work?	What radio stations do you listen to?	Are you satisfied with its product or service?
In the past two months, how often have you _____?	Do you shop where you live?	What television programs do you regularly watch?	How could that product or service be improved to meet your needs?
Would you be likely to purchase/use _____?	Into which of these age groups do you fall?	What magazines do you read?	What do you currently pay for this product or service?
Are you interested in _____?	What is your occupation?	Do you use discount coupons?	
	Do you own or rent your home?	Do you shop on the Internet?	
	What is your household income?	Do you prefer catalog shopping?	
	How much would you expect to pay for this product or service?	In the last six months, how many times did you order a product from a catalog?	
		Where would you expect to buy this product?	

FIGURE
14.3 **Sample Questionnaire: Product**

I am developing a new product and am contacting a few people in your neighborhood for an important and quick survey. I hope you will take a moment to tell me how you feel about **board games**.

1. Do you play any board games? ☐ Yes ☐ No (If NO, please go to #7)

2. What is your favorite board game?
   ☐ Backgammon ☐ Checkers ☐ Pictionary ☐ Life
   ☐ Clue ☐ Monopoly ☐ Sorry ☐ Other _____

3. On the average, how often do you play board games?
   ☐ Less than once per month ☐ Once per month
   ☐ Twice per month ☐ Once per week ☐ More than once per week

4. Would you consider playing a new board game about the stock market?
   ☐ Yes ☐ No ☐ Maybe ☐ I don't know

5. How much would you pay for a board game about the stock market?
   ☐ $6.00 to $10.00 ☐ $10.01 to $15.00
   ☐ $15.01 to $20.00 ☐ Over $20.00

6. What is the first word that comes to mind when you think of the stock market?
   _____

7. On the average, how many hours of television do you watch per week?
   ☐ Less than one hour ☐ 1 to 3 hours ☐ 3 to 6 hours
   ☐ 6 to 9 hours ☐ 9 hours or more

8. Do you clip coupons from the newspaper? ☐ Yes ☐ No

9. What radio station do you listen to most often? _____

10. What is your age group?
    ☐ 18 to 24 years ☐ 25 to 34 years ☐ 35 to 44 years
    ☐ 45 to 54 years ☐ Over 55 years

11. What is your average household income?
    ☐ Under $25,000 ☐ $25,000 to $45,000
    ☐ $45,000 to $60,000 ☐ Over $60,000

Thank you for your response. The following information is helpful to my study but is optional.

Name_____

Address_____

City_____ State_____ Zip _____

Phone (____)_____

> **FIGURE 14.4** Sample Questionnaire: Service

I am developing a new service and am contacting a few people in your neighborhood for an important and quick survey. I hope you will take a moment to tell me how you feel about **take-out food**.

1. Do you order take-out food? ❑ Yes ❑ No

2. What is your favorite take-out food?
   ❑ Chinese ❑ Mexican ❑ Pizza
   ❑ Deli ❑ Burgers ❑ Other _____

3. On the average, how often do you order take-out food?
   ❑ Less than once a month ❑ Once a month
   ❑ Twice a month ❑ Once a week ❑ More than once a week

4. Would you consider full-course take-out food? ❑ Yes ❑ No

5. Would you consider home-delivered meals? ❑ Yes ❑ No

6. How much would you be willing to pay for a full-course, home-delivered meal?
   ❑ $10.00 ❑ $15.00 ❑ $17.50 ❑ $20.00

7. What is the first word that comes into your mind when you think of full-course, home-delivered meals?

   _____

8. On a scale of 1 to 5, with 5 signifying very important and 1 signifying unimportant, please rank the following items as they relate to your feelings about take-out food: (Please circle)

Containers	1	2	3	4	5
Variety of foods offered	1	2	3	4	5
Temperature when delivered	1	2	3	4	5
Taste	1	2	3	4	5
Delivery time	1	2	3	4	5
Type of food	1	2	3	4	5
Price	1	2	3	4	5

9. Do you clip coupons from the newspaper? ❑ Yes ❑ No

10. What newspaper do you read? _____

11. What is your age group?
    ❑ 18 to 24 years ❑ 25 to 34 years ❑ 35 to 44 years
    ❑ 45 to 54 years ❑ Over 55 years

12. What is your average household income?
    ❑ Under $25,000 ❑ $25,000 to $45,000
    ❑ $45,000 to $60,000 ❑ Over $60,000

Thank you for your response.

the lessons and trips are looking very profitable. I set up a table at the shopping mall where we're located, and gave out free lures to everyone who filled out a form. I also did a mailing to people who subscribe to a couple of fishing magazines, and, on my daughter's advice, to students at a local community college. The mailing to the students got a good response, and I think this group will likely form a good part of the target market. Through the mailings and the table in the mall, I developed my own mailing list of 349 individuals interested in fishing trips and classes.

Here's the questionnaire I wrote. You can feel free to tweak it to make it suit whatever kind of business you're in, or you can even use it just as it is if you're starting a fishing trip business—unless you're planning to open up in my area! I've also included my analysis of the results, if you're interested—and not a competitor.

Questionnaire for Shortstop's Sporting Goods
Your One-Stop Sporting Supply Source at WestParc Mall!

Date _____   Location _____

Please circle your answers:

Sex: Male   Female

Marital Status: Single   Married   Divorced   Other

Age: 18 to 25   26 to 35   36 to 45   46 and over

Your Occupation/Profession _____

1. Do you enjoy outdoor activities?   Yes   No

2. Do you enjoy fishing?   Yes   No

3. Have you ever been fly fishing?   Yes   No

   If yes:

   a) What did you think of the experience? _____

   b) Where did you go? _____

   c) Were instructors/guides present?   Yes   No

   d) Would you be interested in classes on fly fishing?   Yes   No

   e) Would you be interested in professionally guided
      fishing trips?   Yes   No

   f) How much would you expect to pay for a 10-hour
      guided fishing trip? _____

   g) Do you own a boat?   Yes   No

      If yes, what kind? _____

Questionnaire for Shortstop's Sporting Goods

If no:

a) Would you be interested in fishing lessons? Yes No

b) Would you be interested in rental equipment? Yes No

c) Would you be interested in a 10-hour guided
   wilderness fishing trip? Yes No

4. Do you use discount coupons? Yes No

5. What newspapers do you read? *Advertiser* *Herald*
   Sun *Fisherman Times*

6. What radio station do you listen to? T-98 WTXU
   WBGF ZZ101 Other _____

7. Have you heard of Shortstop's Sporting Goods? Yes No

8. Have you ever shopped at Shortstop's Sporting Goods? Yes No

   If yes:

   What was your most recent purchase, and approximately when did you buy it?

   _____

   If no:

   Why not?

   _____

Thank you for your response. The following information is helpful, but optional.
Your personal information will not be resold, rented, or distributed to anyone
else!

Name _____

Address _____

City/State/Zip _____

Phone (____)_____

May we call you with more information? Yes No

Here's how the results worked out:

Shortstop's Sporting Goods: Analysis of Questionnaire Results

Sex: Male = 57%   Female = 43%

Marital Status: Single 45%   Married 32%   Divorced 19%   Other 4%

Age: Average age = 32

Your Occupation/Profession   25% services   38% students
                        29% professionals   10% industrial   8% retired

1. Do you enjoy outdoor activities?   Yes 84%   No 26%

2. Do you enjoy fishing?   Yes 63%   No 25%   No response: 22%

3. Have you ever been fly fishing?   Yes 23%   No 77%
   If yes:
   a) What did you think of the experience?   Enjoyed it: 85%   Disliked: 7%
   b) Where did you go?   WI: 80%   IL 15%   MN 68%   MI 44%
   c) Were instructors/guides present?   Yes 12% No 89%
   d) Would you be interested in classes on fly fishing?   Yes 58% No 42%
   e) Would you be interested in professionally guided
      fishing trips?   Yes 49% No 51%
   f) How much would you expect to pay for a 10-hour
      guided fishing trip?   Average $80
   g) Do you own a boat?   Yes 11% No 89%
   If no:
   a) Would you be interested in fishing lessons?   Yes 63% No 37%
   b) Would you be interested in rental equipment?   Yes 72% No 38%
   c) Would you be interested in a 10-hour guided fishing trip? Yes 68% No 32%

4. Do you use discount coupons?   Yes 34% No 66%

5. What newspapers do you read?   *Advertiser* 15%   *Herald* 46%
                                        Sun 33%   *Fisherman Times* 11%

6. What radio station do you listen to?   T-98 22%   WTXU 64%
                                            WBGF 2%   ZZ101 36%

7. Have you heard of Shortstop's Sporting Goods?   Yes 83% No 17%

8. Have you ever shopped at Shortstop's Sporting Goods?   Yes 75% No 25%
   If yes:
   What was your most recent purchase, and approximately when did you buy it?
   Responses inconclusive: no product pattern or purchase cycle beyond holidays
   and major sale initiative.
   If no:
   "Not into sports" 8%   "Too expensive" 12%   "New in town" 3%
   "Poor product quality" 2%   "Incompetent staff" 3%   No response 50%
   "Better prices at Wal-Mart/Kmart/Doley's" 22%

Applying the Questionnaire: Shortstop's Sporting Goods

Target Market:

Target group represents 20% of total population within city limits.

Total population = 52,000; 20% = 10,400.

Projections indicate that I can serve 10% of the targeted group for a customer base of 1040.

And here's the analysis form I filled in. For me, it really helped a lot.

What Are the Customers' Needs?	How Can I Meet Those Needs?	What Is the Benefit to Customers?
Sports instruction. Opportunity to "try" equipment prior to purchase.	Offer rental equipment. Offer free sports clinics and inexpensive youth and adult classes. Offer "how-to" sports videos for in-store viewing. If demand is present, will sell copies of videos.	Only store in region to provide free sports clinics: emphasize family fishing. Only store in region to provide an area for viewing sport instructional videos.
Have interest in fishing, especially fly fishing. Currently no store stocks a full product line of fishing gear.	Stock full line of fishing gear. Provide in-store demos.	Only sporting goods store in the county to stock and specialize in fishing equipment.
Due to commute time and number of two-income families, store should be open at times convenient to the consumer.	Will open on Sunday. Will stay open until 10 p.m. on Thursday and Friday.	Only sporting goods store open on Sunday. Longest hours on Thurs/Fri.
Business commitment to the community.	Sponsor youth or adult amateur sports team.	Competition does not demonstrate "community values."
Knowledgeable staff.	Training program for employees: sales techniques, customer service, sports knowledge.	Efficient, effective assistance makes shopping more pleasant.
Reliability of merchandise.	Offer in-store guarantee on all merchandise.	In-store guarantee on all equipment.

Finally, I came up with my Action Plan:

> 349 people indicated an interest in guided fishing trips. Realistically, 5 percent (or 17 people) will actually register for the trip. The results indicate that $80 is the average amount registrants would expect to pay for a ten-hour guided fishing trip. This involves the following expenses:

> - Salaries for two guides
> - Rental of a 12-person van
> - Insurance
> - Fishing permits
> - Equipment

> The trip would have to include ten people at a charge of $87.50 per person in order to meet our expenses, with zero profit. If we want to make a profit, more people could be included and costs may be cut. We could consider accepting the breakeven in the hope of generating future equipment sales. One trip could be scheduled to test the response.

PERSONAL WORKSHOP 28
Creating a Market Survey Questionnaire

▼ Use this template to construct a questionnaire for your own business. We've helped you get started by including some basic demographic questions. You can, of course, change these or add more to customize the questionnaire to your own needs. Then compose appropriate questions for each of the fields 2 through 8, following the general directions in each. For instance, for "lifestyle," you might want to ask about jobs or recreational activities.

1. Sex	M		F					
Marital Status	Single		Married		Divorced		Other	
Age	18 to 25		26 to 35		36 to 45		over 45	
Occupation								
2. lifestyle								
3. use of your type of product or service in general	Always		Sometimes		Never			

CONTINUED ▶

4.	use of your competitor's product or service	Always	Sometimes	Never	
5.	rating of competitors' overall product or service	Good	No Opinion	Poor	Comment
6.	rank of generic product or service features (list)	Necessary	Important	No Opinion	Not Important
7.	interest in your business's special feature(s) (list)	Necessary	Important	No Opinion	Not Important
8.	interest in trying your product or service	Interested	More Info	Uninterested	Comments

9. If you'd like more information about _____[your business name]_____ or to be notified about special offers, please provide your name and address below:

CASE STUDY
FRANKLIN PUBLISHING COMPANY

▼▼▼▼▼

Jack Belcher and Elmar Huntly sat back and looked at one another, each trying to figure out what had gone wrong. They had entered the printing business ten years ago with great enthusiasm and energy, and even had dreams of building their own empire. Today the business was not breaking even. Both were taking about $100 a week out of the business, and even this made them feel guilty. How different it was now than when they started the business. Then, they faced no competition and could afford to drive luxury cars, pay their mortgages, and have everything their families could ever want. Today it seemed that everyone was selling business cards and stationery. Even as they bemoaned their troubles, they still retained their sense of humor. Jack suggested they burn the business down and collect the insurance money. Elmar retorted that they were both worth more dead than alive and both should let their wives collect on the insurance. Finally, Jack said, "You know Elmar, we could write a book about this business and it would be a best seller." Elmar replied, "Jack, if you printed that book the churches would ban it."

Suddenly Jack jumped out of his chair. "Elmar," he said, "you just gave me an idea. I think we'll publish books." Elmar thought he was kidding. However, he listened as Jack went on, "Look, Elmar, everyone wants to write a book. They all want to write the great American novel and be famous. Let's help them accomplish that dream by putting their novels or whatever they want published in print." Elmar replied, "We don't have the capability and where are we going to get the money?" But Jack just told him to forget that point for a moment and think about the concept. All they had to do was advertise in the right papers and magazines and then help the people publish their books. He pointed out to Elmar that because most people couldn't write well, they would offer help, if requested; or they could just print whatever was submitted without change. They would print as many copies as the client wanted. They could even help clients market their books. Elmar thought it sounded great, and might be a way out of their difficulties. However, he wondered how they were going to get the start-up money and how they were going to market the books.

Elmar had another idea that could work. He felt they were spending too much time selling forms, and competing with many cutthroat firms. What they needed was a marketing differentiation that would set them apart and give them a new niche in the field. If they could sell accounting systems for small firms, both profit and nonprofit, as well as other business systems, they could make a great deal of money. They would approach a prospective client and request to be permitted to conduct a business systems audit free of charge. They could then look at all their forms and make recommendations for an entire systems package. This would increase their printing business. The only problems Elmar could foresee would be finding a designer for the systems and actually conducting the audits.

Jack listened intently while Elmar was talking. There were some concepts here that could revolutionize their business. Both of them liked the concepts and they decided to think about them and talk again the next day. Jack called Elmar at about 3 A.M. and asked if he was awake. Elmar said, "Of course, I am. What do you think I've been working on half the night?"

The next day they met, and Jack calculated the amount of money they would need to enter the book publishing business. He could get good used equipment from a friend whom he had already contacted, and he could have six months to pay for it. Jack estimated they would need $85,000 to purchase the equipment and make the concept a reality. However, he still did not know how to market a book once it was published.

Elmar reported that he had contacted a friend who was a certified public accountant. He had agreed to design accounting systems for small business firms as well as nonprofit organizations. He could also set up a procedure for the salespeople to follow when they made their audits. After they completed the audit, he would offer his services to evaluate the results. He promised to charge a reasonable fee. However, Elmar was faced with the problem of finding salespeople. They would have to be trained in the new field of selling business systems. Because it was a new approach, there would be no restrictions on territory.

CONTINUED ▶

They would not be restricted to only Nevada, but could cover Utah, Arizona, Idaho, and other nearby states. The training would have to be intensive and the salespeople would have to be compensated while they were learning; it would take some time before they would be really productive. Elmar estimated that they would need at least four salespeople.

Jack and Elmar went to the bank and were told they could get a total of $100,000 through second mortgages on their homes. Jack and Elmar were not able to raise the balance of the money locally, but they knew of a loan broker in Reno with whom they discussed their situation. The broker examined their package and in a few days came back with a proposal to pay off the first mortgages on their homes; take a first position on all of the properties, including the building where the business was now located; and lend them the money they wanted plus $25,000 for working capital. Jack and Elmar would have to pay a fee of 4 percent of the money they borrowed in addition to the lender fee and closing costs. The loan company would also factor all their receivables and establish a credit line on sales made on credit, thus helping the company grow. The rate for the factoring was 6 percent over New York prime. While Jack and Elmar felt this was somewhat high, it was the best deal available, and the loan broker promised to work fast. Within three weeks they were ready for the closing.

With the money they had obtained, Jack purchased the equipment for book publishing and was ready for business. He advertised in the local papers and was surprised to receive more than ten calls from people who wanted to have their manuscripts published. He made separate deals with each of them. They were willing to pay anywhere from $2,500 to $20,000 to have a hundred copies of their books published. The only problem was how to promote the books, but Jack put that problem on hold.

After the books were published, the authors were pleased. However, they wondered what to do to make themselves famous. Jack told them to give the books to their relatives and friends, and soon word of mouth would sell them. He also suggested that they donate the books to libraries and send copies to newspaper editors for review. However, none of the authors made a single sale, and they all felt cheated. ▼

CASE STUDY ROUNDTABLE

▼ ▼ ▼ ▼ ▼ ▼

Jack: I understand now the importance of doing some basic market research. What do you think we should have done in this case?

Discussion Points

- How might the techniques of market research discussed in this chapter have been used effectively by Jack and Elmar? What might they have learned?

Elmar: Do you think it was a good idea for Jack and me to go into the book publishing business?

Discussion Points

- Do you really think a lot of people want to publish their own books, even though they are not likely to sell? Consider the fact that the average client would be spending a minimum of $10,000 for 100 books.

Jack: I think a big reason why the publishing company might fail is our inability to promote the books. What methods would you recommend to promote newly published books?

Discussion Points

- Do you think a professional marketing firm could assist the company?
- Do you think Jack and Elmar misled their clients who hoped their books would bring them fame?

▲▲▲▲▲▲▲

CHAPTER BRIEFCASE

▼▼▼▼▼▼▼

- **Markets** are those persons or organizations who *will* be your customers, while **target markets** are those persons or organizations *most likely* to become your customers. Target markets are small and tightly defined.

- **Market research** is an organized and objective way of learning about your customers. It involves finding out what a customer wants and needs and determining how your company can meet those wants and needs.

- A **trend** is a behavior or buying pattern that lasts between five and ten years and is generally widespread. **Fads** are short-term surges of popularity (and usually sales) for a particular type of product or service.

- Markets are described in terms of **demographics**, such as age, sex, ethnic background, education, occupation, income, family status, and geographic location. Markets are also defined in terms of psychographics. These are the psychological characteristics of your market and are as important as demographics.

- Before you invest time and money in developing your idea, determine whether a need or desire for it exists in the buying community. A cost-effective method of gaining a response from the market regarding your product or service is through the use of a **questionnaire**.

▲▲▲▲▲▲▲

Chapter 15

PROMOTIONS AND ADVERTISING

▼▼▼▼▼▼

A good reputation is more valuable than money.

—*Publius Syrus, 42 BC*

MISSION STATEMENT

In this chapter, you will

*L*EARN about the role of advertising and promotional strategies in building a strong reputation for your business, product, or service.

*E*XPLORE the essential elements of advertising as part of your overall public relations approach.

*A*PPLY your understanding to a case study.

*P*RODUCE an analysis of your business's market-driven qualities to design effective advertising copy for a print campaign.

KEY TERMS

advertising

campaign

copy

demographics

media

networking

promotion

INTRODUCTION TO PROMOTING YOUR BUSINESS

As good as your product may be, as excellent a service you may offer, the buying public is not psychic (except for some particular niche markets). People will not just become aware of your business simply because you exist. "Hanging out your shingle" is a terrific accomplishment, a sign of the fearless risktaking entrepreneurial spirit that built America. But it's not enough just to hang out your shingle and wait for the world to beat a path to your door. You must announce your existence to the world, over and over again, and convince the buying public that what you have to offer is worth a look. That sounds a lot easier than it is: the commercial marketplace is highly competitive, and there are often more choices than customers. You have to convince the public that what you have serves their needs better than what anyone else has to offer.

But it's important to know that it costs you much more to *attract* a new customer through advertising than to *keep* a current customer through good customer service. According to the American Productivity and Quality Center, nearly 70 percent of customers say they have stopped doing business with a company because they received poor service. Customers are five times more likely to stop doing business with a company due to poor service than poor product quality or high cost. Clearly, poor customer service does not pay.

Taken together, advertising and customer service are the way you present your business to the world, the way you sell yourself and your business. One brings customers to your door; the other determines what they think about you once they're there.

ADVERTISING

Advertising is the means for getting information about your product or service to your market. The first step in developing an advertising plan is to define potential customers in the geographic area or industry served by your business. Conduct some preliminary surveys and interviews to determine which means of advertising will reach them. What newspapers or trade journals do they read? What radio stations do they listen to? Do they use discount coupons? Do they respond to direct mail? Do they have e-mail? Tailor your advertising efforts to your market.

By now you will have identified what is unique about your business and how that uniqueness will benefit the customer. This theme or image for your product or service should carry through all of your advertising. It is what sets you apart from the competition and it is what will attract the customer.

Through the design of your advertising, the image and identity of your business can be established. After you have determined which forms of media you will use in your advertising campaign, decide on the format you want to use and the theme you wish to project. There are professionals in each type of media to help you. Typically, effective advertisements rely on the three "I"s:

1. *Involve* the audience by inviting them to participate, arousing their curiosity, or convincing them that they need your product or service.
2. *Inform* the customer about the benefits and uniqueness of your product or service in terms that they can understand. The ad must also let the customer know how, where, and when the item or service can be purchased.
3. *Illustrate* the benefits through words, images, or sounds that get the audience's attention and convey your information.

A good ad arouses curiosity, illustrates the benefits of using the product or service, invites the viewer to participate, and tells the customer how, where, and when the item may be purchased and used. With this in mind, we will now examine different types of advertising.

MEDIA ADVERTISING

Media advertising and publicity can be obtained through interviews, articles, and paid advertisements in newspapers and magazines, and on radio and television.

Newspapers

Newspaper advertising usually reaches a large audience, has a short life span, is relatively inexpensive, and is quickly and easily changed. Tailor your ad to the editorial content of the paper: an ad in the *Wall Street Journal* will not look like an ad in the *National Enquirer*. The two papers serve two different markets, and have distinctly different editorial looks. Determine what special feature sections are being planned by calling the newspaper's editorial staff. If the paper is planning to do a special feature relevant to your business, you may want to advertise in that feature. In any case, you should select a part of the paper that is most likely to be read by your target market. Look at any city paper. The sports section is dominated by advertisements for products and services that appeal to sports fans. The arts and entertainment section includes more ads for restaurants than for hair replacement products. (Interestingly, however, the sports sections often include many ads for hair replacement products.)

The cost of the ad will vary according to frequency of publication and area of circulation. Ads are available in various sizes and in several formats such as *display* or *classified* ads. Analyze the advertising of your competition regarding size, placement, and frequency. Your questionnaires and market research will have indicated the newspapers read by your target market. Those are the papers in which you will place your advertising.

Consumer and Trade Magazines

Magazine advertising is often overlooked by small business owners because ads are thought to be too costly to prepare and run. In fact, you don't have to run your ad in the entire edition of a magazine—admittedly a costly undertaking. Rather, you can reach specific geographic and demographic markets by placing your ad in regional editions. Even big national companies take advantage of regional editions by running slightly different ads to appeal to the interests or characteristics of different regions.

You may also cut down your cost by making use of "remnant space." Often a magazine will not have sold all of its advertising space prior to press time. These remnant spaces are often sold at a deep discount in order to fill the page. Contact the publication and determine their policies. Some magazines will also provide extra services such as reader response cards which enable you to develop a mailing list of individuals interested in what you have to offer. Magazine ads carry a large degree of credibility and prestige and are worth considering as an advertising option.

Of course, no advertising medium is without its disadvantages. One of the downsides of magazine advertising is that your ad must be placed well in advance of the issue's publication: this does not allow for last-minute changes. Also, you will have very little control over where your ad will appear in the magazine.

Radio

Radio advertising has many advantages:

- It is usually local.
- It reaches an identifiable (and loyal) audience who generally tune in at specific times.
- Ads can be changed frequently.
- Advertising time is relatively inexpensive and can be repeated frequently.

Radio advertising is linked to listenership: the more people who are tuned in to the station at a specific time of day (according to ratings services such as Arbitron), the more expensive the advertising time. Figure 15.1 is an example of the correlation between radio advertising costs and listenership throughout the day. An advertiser would pay more for an ad during Bill and Bob's morning show than during the two-hour afternoon music show. The rate even varies during Bill and Bob's show.

Radio advertising also is priced according to length of the message (more minutes equals more money) and frequency of broadcast (an ad run several times during the day may cost more than an ad run only once, although volume discounts may be arranged in some cases).

The ads are either read live by broadcasters or taped in advance. Taped ads can include music and special audio effects, and are generally more expensive than simple voice-only announcements. And don't forget public radio. Public radio listeners tend to be more affluent, educated, and intensely loyal to their station and its sponsors. Surveys have consistently shown that sponsorship of local public radio stations yields the highest consumer response, as well as the greatest loyalty among customers who are brought in from the radio sponsorship announcement.

There are two types of radio programming: background and foreground. Background programs feature mostly music. Foreground programs follow news and talk formats. Foreground programs involve more active listeners who will probably pay more attention to your commercials. Another approach to radio coverage of your business would be to offer your service as an expert in your field on a radio talk show. You can answer questions from listeners and talk about your business.

Radio advertising tips:

- You must catch the listener's attention in the first three seconds.
- Your ad will be read live or taped in advance. Taped ads offer more opportunity for special effects and are less prone to error. Live ads can be more interesting and timely (for instance, if your product or service is linked to current events), but run the risk of irreversible mistakes or technical glitches.

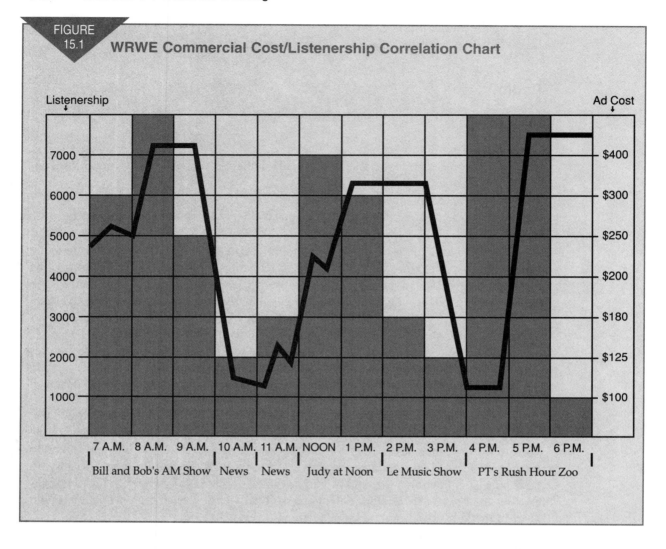

FIGURE 15.1 WRWE Commercial Cost/Listenership Correlation Chart

- The three biggest complaints about radio commercials: (1) they are noisy, (2) they have inane humor, and (3) they lack sincerity. Be direct, be straightforward, and be yourself.

Television

Television advertising reaches large marketing areas, but it is relatively expensive, and limited to brief copy. This form of advertising is usually highly professional and is priced according to length of message, time of broadcast, frequency of broadcast, time of year, and whether the station is an independent or a member of a network. For small start-ups, it may be beyond their advertising budget. However, federal communications law requires cable television companies to provide local access programming, and this is often an option for smaller businesses. Keep in mind, though, that while local access cable time may be affordable, it also has generally low ratings, even in the community it serves.

The cost of television advertising is based on gross rating points (GRP). One point equals 1 percent of the television sets in the TV marketing area. The GRP unit cost is determined by the competitive situation, size of area, and time of year. Advertising costs may be higher during the holiday season, which is considered to be October through December. Prime time covers the period from 8:00 to 11:00 PM, Eastern time, and is more costly because more people are tuned in. The "fringe time" before and after prime time may be more cost-effective for you.

SELECTING MEDIA

You need to know which media are most likely to influence your target audience. The public library has media source books available that list newspapers, magazines, and radio and television stations. Find out what shows your customers watch. Television stations will have demographic and psychographic breakdowns of their viewing audiences. Most commercial media use market studies to effectively help position advertising where it will be seen by those interested in the products or services offered. Newspaper, magazine, radio, and television advertising departments will be pleased to share this information with you, and help you determine the most effective placement for your advertising.

FIRST PERSON

Lydia W., St. Louis, Missouri: Advertising takes planning, time, persistence—and especially money. And the frustrating thing, at least for me, is that the effectiveness of your advertising is measured over time: you rarely get that big bang for your buck the next day, unless you're advertising a special sale or something. Your market just has to be reminded and reminded and reminded about why it's so great to do business with you! It's like a circle: the more you advertise, the more people come to think of you as an established, reliable business, because you advertise so much. And I don't care if it's in the newspaper, on the radio, during the TV weather report (or the Super Bowl!), being pulled behind a plane, or dropped in people's mailboxes, the whole point of advertising is to get your name out there in front of people, and get them used to you.

PERSONAL WORKSHOP 29
Three Steps to Do-It-Yourself Advertising

▼ Follow these simple steps to developing and analyzing your promotional copy. Keep in mind that copy produced for print media will be limited by space and production considerations, while copy produced for broadcast media will have time and technology challenges. Also remember that there are professional advertising agencies (many of them small businesses themselves!) that specialize in promoting small businesses. Your advertising is the face you present to the marketplace: you want to be sure you look your best. If you have any question about your ability to produce your own promotional campaigns, take the best advice we can give: turn it over to the pros!

CONTINUED ▶

Step One: Building a Campaign from Concepts

Use these common advertising copy words and phrases to help you get started drafting an ad for your product or service. Choose the three or four words that are most relevant to your business.

act	how to	now you can	secrets
advantage	hurry	offer expires	send no money
benefit	imagine	only	now
boost	invite	opportunity	thanks
build	just arrived	profit	today
convenient	know	protect	unique
delight	last chance	proven	valuable
discover	learn	results	value
easy	limited time offer	reward	win
exciting	new	save	worth
free	never before	save time	
fast	no obligation	satisfaction	
guaranteed	not sold in stores	guaranteed	

Step Two: Brainstorming Promotional Copy

Using the words you picked in step one as your focus, write several sentences to describe or promote your product, service, or business. Your advertising copy should answer five basic questions for customers:

1. Who are you (and why should I believe you)?

2. What is the product (or service)?

3. How can I use it?

4. What do you want me to do?

5. Why should I do it?

CONTINUED ▶

Now analyze your promotional copy using the following checklist:

	Yes	No
Is the promotional copy written like you would say it yourself? (It should be! A conversational tone is most effective.)		
Does the copy address a specific market?		
Does the copy tell the reader about the benefits, advantages, and features of my product or service?		
Does the copy use specific terms, not generalities?		
Could a competitor put his or her name on this copy and have it be just as effective?		
Are there excessive words that could be eliminated or long sentences that could be shorter?		

If you answered "yes" to the first four questions, and "no" to the last two, then your copy is probably very effective.

Step Three: Headlines

The headline is where you grab your potential customer's attention. An effective headline should:

- Offer a benefit. (Finally! A product that will help you more effectively target your customers!)

- Make a promise. (You won't have to pay for repairs, belts, hoses, or oil for three years!)

- Provide news. (Introducing the new SandTrap XC50 custom-designed golf bag!)

- Identify a problem. (Washing the outside of your home's windows can be dangerous and frustrating!)

- Propose an offer. (Let us help you find your ideal match!)

- Set a scenario. ("They laughed when I brought out my ukelele...")

CONTINUED ▶

Write some headlines that support the promotional copy you've written.

Now evaluate your headlines using the following checklist

	Yes	No
Is the headline's meaning clear?		
Does the headline communicate the benefit of my product or service?		
Does the headline appeal to my most likely market?		
Is the headline interesting and attention-getting?		
Could it be more specific?		
Could it be more closely related to the promotional copy it supports?		
Does it work well with any visual elements in the ad?		

Revise your headlines as necessary according to your analysis.

PUBLICITY

In addition to paid advertising, don't overlook publicity. Publicity is also known as "free advertising." Call programmers for the radio and television talk programs and editors of the newspapers and magazines in your area. Ask if they will be doing any features on your area of expertise. If they are, offer your services as an expert working in that field. You may be interviewed and profiled, you may be able to submit an article for publication, or you may wish to place some targeted advertising to coincide with the feature. If no features are being planned, explain why this would be a timely topic and would be of interest to their audiences. Offer your services as an expert in your type of business who can provide background information for any future reports. You can also send out press releases offering your services as a resource for news stories and talk shows.

It is not enough to just tell about your business. You must be prepared to present a unique angle. You must convince the editor or programmer that what you have to say will appeal and will be of interest to their readers, listeners, or viewers. The information you submit and the ideas with which you approach the media must be timely, important, and interesting to a large segment of their audience. While commercial media are driven by advertising sales (a cynical television executive once referred to programming as "the stuff in between the commercials"), they are not interested in providing a free forum for you to advertise your product. You must be newsworthy enough, or of sufficient interest, that large numbers of people will tune in and stay tuned to listen to what you have to say. The more people the program attracts, the more the medium can charge advertisers (such as yourself) to reach them.

What Makes Great PR?

When developing news angles, consider the kinds of stories reporters are looking for. Figure 15.2 lists some of the specific news areas that are most likely to generate media interest. As always, consider these and seek PR input as early in the development of your product or service as possible.

FIGURE 15.2 News Angles

Controversy	Creating/bucking a trend
Timeliness	Local hook
Celebrity/personalities	Usefulness
Shock value	Tie-in to current news

Source: Courtesy Communications Dept., Kaplan Educational Centers.

Press Releases

You may wish to distribute a press release in order to let people know who you are and what you have to offer. When preparing a press release, there are two primary concerns:

1. Content
2. Structure

News releases should be as short as possible while containing all of the important facts. Make every effort to write it in good journalistic style: the idea is to do the reporters' work for them. Prepare a release that could be printed in the paper with little or no revision. That means you need to think like a journalist.

Read news releases in your target news outlets and study their format and content. News writing follows the *inverted pyramid* style in which every paragraph is considered more important than the ones following it. That is, the story is written in descending order of importance: the main idea is up front. A busy reader whose interest is not caught in the first paragraph will not read the second one. A news release format sheet and a sample news release are included in Figures 15.3 and 15.4.

How to Prepare a Press Release

While some media outlets will have their own preferred formats for press releases, some basic rules can generally be applied.

Identification. The business sending the release should be plainly identified. Use your letterhead or printed news release forms. The name and telephone number of a contact person for additional information must appear at the top of the page.

Release date. Most releases should be "immediate" or "for use upon receipt." Designate a release time only if there is a specific reason, such as a scheduled speech, meeting, news announcement, or planned event.

Appearance. Leave wide margins and space at the top so the editor can edit and include notations. Double-space your text. News releases should be cleanly printed on standard letter-size white paper.

Headline. The headline you submit should be to summarize your writing. The media will generally create their own headline. Nonetheless, your headlines should conform to the general style of the media to which you submit the release.

Length. Most press releases are one page in length. If you have a longer release, write the highlights into an attached news memo and include the news release as background material. If you must use more than one page, do not split a paragraph from the first to second page. Center the word "more" at the bottom of the first page.

Classic journalism style. Use a **summary lead** and the **five Ws** (*who, what, when, where, why*—and sometimes *how*.) A summary lead is a brief, one-sentence statement that tells the reader exactly what the article is about: everything else is just detail in support of the summary lead. (The summary lead was called a "thesis statement" in your high school and college writing classes.) Use *short sentences* with *active verbs*. Make sure it is accurate and timely, and try to use an objective (not self-serving) writing style.

Proofread. Proofread names, spelling, numbers, and grammar carefully: nothing destroys the credibility of a press release like a glaring typographical error.

Logistics. Your news release should be in the hands of editors well in advance of deadlines. Contact the city desk, assignment editor, or feature editor with whom you are working to clarify deadlines and publication schedules. Make sure your release is on time and properly hand-delivered or mailed first class to the designated media contact.

FIGURE 15.3 **News Release Format**

[Company Letterhead]

FOR IMMEDIATE RELEASE

TO: Designated editor or reporter

FROM: Your name, address, and phone number

RE: A one or two sentence statement regarding the story you are suggesting, the event to which you are inviting reporters, the meeting, class or seminar you have scheduled, or other purpose of the news release.

Text:

❏ Time and Date: Specific time, date, and year of event.

❏ Location: Specific location, including directions if the location is not well known or easily found.

❏ Why: You must have a reason for the news release or the event.

❏ Contact: The name and phone number of someone the news editor or reporters can contact with questions about the news release.

FIGURE
15.4
Sample News Release

blair **Sporting Goods**

!! F O R   I M M E D I A T E   R E L E A S E !!

September 6

Contact: David Blair

(555) 613-7965

Fly Fishing Demonstration and Contest to Feature Professional Fisherman

John Bacon, well-known professional fly fisherman, will demonstrate techniques for dry and wet fly casting and will judge a contest in the parking lot of **Blair Sporting Goods** on Saturday, September 26 from 10 AM to 4 PM.

Blair Sporting Goods' owner, **David Blair**, stated that the popularity of the book and movie, *A River Runs Through It*, has led to an increased interest in the sport of fly fishing. Participants will pay a $5 participation fee, with all proceeds going to the **Memorial Hospital Children's Wing Fund**. All contestants will receive a **10 percent discount** coupon from **Blair Sporting Goods**.

After receiving instruction from Mr. Bacon, contestants will be judged on form, distance, and accuracy. **Prizes** include theater passes, dinner coupons, and sporting event tickets. The contest is **open to everyone regardless of skill**. Information and pre-registration are available at Blair Sporting Goods, 271 Adams St., Laketown, New York or by phoning (555) 613-7965.

OTHER METHODS

In addition to advertising and publicity, there are other means of getting the message about your business to your customers.

Displays

Displays may be set up at community-oriented functions such as city fairs, community events, and civic meetings. This is a good way to present your product or service to the buying public. You can also get an immediate positive (or negative) response—that can be very valuable feedback.

Networking

Community involvement is also an effective means of advertising. Membership in civic organizations can pave the way to being a guest speaker. Active membership affords you the opportunity for **networking**. Networking is the exchange of ideas and information that takes place every day in your life. What changes a simple social conversation into a networking opportunity is the conscious directing of that exchange to your benefit and to the benefit of those around you. The more you meet with people, the more you will be able to promote your business, learn more about the business community around you, and become more self-confident. Membership in civic and business organizations, such as the chamber of commerce, is an excellent means of accomplishing this.

Trade Shows

Trade show and exhibit participation allow you to take advantage of promotional campaigns that would be too expensive for a small business to undertake alone. You can request listings of trade events from malls and convention centers. Participation in trade shows and membership in trade organizations give you visibility in your business field. These shows are usually attended only by those interested in your particular field. This is an excellent way to reach your target market.

Direct Mail

Direct mail can be an effective way to deliver specific information in a personal way to large numbers of people. Direct mail can take the form of inexpensive fact sheets, letters, promotional giveaways, contests, discount coupons, and brochures. It can be used to solicit mail-order or phone-order business, to announce new products or services, to notify customers of price changes, to welcome new customers, to thank current customers, and to announce special events such as sales. To be cost-effective, you must target your market. Rent a good list from a list broker.

PROMOTION AND PUBLIC RELATIONS STRATEGIES

As in every other aspect of your business, be strategic, analytical, methodical, and selective in choosing advertising, promotional, and public relations assistance. Shop to find the right marketing help for your business. Ideally, the expert becomes part of your management team, helps you save money by sparing you the expense of learning to do it yourself, and most importantly, helps ensure that your promotional efforts are targeted to the right people through the right media for your business.

This assumes that you have already done a lot of groundwork. You should know:

- The market you want to reach
- What that market wants
- What benefits you can offer your target market
- How much you can afford to spend to support your marketing efforts

A general word of caution: Make sure to budget enough money for *two* kinds of promotional activity. The first is the ongoing campaign to keep your name in front of your markets. This is usually going to be general media (newspaper, yellow pages, and perhaps radio or cable TV). The second is for special events, opportunities, or challenges such as sudden intense competition.

Promotional campaigns in the form of T-shirts, pens, key rings, plastic shopping bags, calendars, balloons, contests, and bumper stickers can also get your name in front of the public. The most effective promotional materials are useful items that are appropriate to (and directly associated with) the business that they represent. For example, a logo or business name on a T-shirt is an effective way of advertising a business dealing with the outdoors, such as a bicycle shop or a kite maker. Pens would be a good item for a manufacturer of note cards and stationery. Balloons could represent a company specializing in children's items. Be creative in your use of this advertising form. There are many companies that specialize in printing and manufacturing promotional materials.

Use Outside Experts

The dangers of do-it-yourself marketing strategies, or using inexperienced or amateur advertising designers, is that you risk putting out the wrong message to the wrong people at the wrong time through the wrong media. If any one of these—message, market, timing, or media—is bungled, you are simply throwing your money away. Advertising that fails to achieve any positive goal is expensive no matter how little cash you spend on it. Talk to ad agencies and other experts. Use your advisers to corroborate your instincts or back up your decisions, but be prepared to pay for marketing and promotional skills. Once you know what you are doing—once you've learned from the experts—you may be able to do some of this work yourself, in-house. A business that's just starting up, however, shouldn't even think of cutting corners here. It just won't work.

Promotions Response Record

It is vital that you keep track of the performance of each type of promotions vehicle you use, and compare the return generated by each medium and campaign. Personal Workshop 31 features a blank promotions response record, and shows how it can be used to track a month of advertising and promotions. Remember, though, that

PERSONAL WORKSHOP 30
Promotions Worksheet

▼ Use this worksheet to help you focus and design your promotions strategy. As an example, look at the sample worksheet from Shortstop's Sporting Goods. Then, after you've designed your strategy, use the response record in Personal Workshop 31 to measure the effectiveness of your campaign.

Name of business:	
What are the features and benefits of my product or service?	
Who is my audience?	
Who is my competition and how do they promote their businesses?	
What are the goals of my promotions campaign?	
How much do I plan to invest for promotions?	
What promotion methods will I use?	__ Newspapers __ Magazines __ Yellow pages __ Radio __ Television __ Direct mail __ Telemarketing __ Flyers __ Brochures __ Coupons __ Press release __ Promotional items Other _____
When will I use them and what will they cost?	
How will I measure the effectiveness of the promotion?	

CONTINUED ▶

Sample Completed Promotions Worksheet

Name of business:	Shortstop's Sporting Goods
What are the features and benefits of my product or service?	Knowledgeable trained staff; open until 9 PM weekdays, 1-5 PM Sunday; full sports product line, specializing in fishing gear; offer fly tying and fly fishing classes; in-house guarantee of sports equipment
Who is my audience?	Youth, high school, university students Active, middle-income sports enthusiasts Live within 10-mile radius
Who is my competition and how do they promote their businesses?	Smith Sporting Goods—radio ads KLXY Mailings, newspaper ad—Sunday supplement Promotions—caps, T-shirts
What are the goals of my promotions campaign?	Reach high school and university market Reach youth market Reach fishing enthusiasts
How much do I plan to invest for promotions?	$1,300 per month
What promotions methods will I use?	_x_ Newspapers __ Magazines _x_ Yellow Pages __ Radio __ Television _x_ Direct mail __ Telemarketing __ Flyers __ Brochures __ Coupons __ Press release _x_ Promotional items Other ___ sponsor youth team ___
When will I use them and what will they cost?	Newspaper: start 1/3/99 weekly ad x 5 = $500/mo. Direct mail flyers: 1/7/99 and 1/14/99 = $550 total Youth team: 1/26/99 = $150/mo. Promo items: 1/16/99 = $100/mo. Yellow pages ad: (Spring directory) = $200/mo.

How will I measure the effectiveness of the advertising plan?	A. Ask customers how they heard about the store.
	B. Compare cost/income on Advertising Response Record
	  1. Change or delete methods that cost more than income generated.
	  2. Adjust or increase budget to include radio ad, brochure, larger yellow pages and newspaper ads.

PERSONAL WORKSHOP 31
Promotions Response Record

▶ Record the response to your promotions on this worksheet. A completed sample is provided for you to follow.

Promotions Response Record for Month of: _____

Medium	Description	Period of Appearance	Cost	Total Exposure	Responses Generated	Sales Generated	Per Unit Return/Cost per Exposure*

* (Sales generated − Cost) ÷ Circulation or exposure = Per unit return (PUR)
Cost ÷ Total exposure = Cost per exposure (CPE)

CONTINUED ▶

Sample Completed Promotions Response Record

Shortstop's Sporting Goods Promotions Response Record for Month of: January

Medium	Description	Period of Appearance	Cost	Total Exposure	Responses Generated	Sales Generated	Per Unit Return/Cost per Exposure*
Register	2" x 4" in sports section	Weekly	$300	15,000	26 phone orders	$6,600	0.42 / 0.02
Flyers — high school, university	10% discount coupon	Mailed 1/3, 1/10, 1/17, 1/24, 1/31	$350	750	264 coupons returned	$520	0.23 / 0.47
Flyers	10% discount for fishermen	Mailed 1/7, 1/14, 1/26	$200	500	96 coupons returned	$260	0.12 / 0.40
caps/shirts (20% team discount)	Youth team sponsorship	Distributed 1/12	$150	12	6 team members	$135	-1.25 /12.5

* (Sales generated − Cost) ÷ Circulation or exposure = Per unit return (PUR)
Cost ÷ Total exposure = Cost per exposure (CPE)

the promotions response record is just a snapshot of the response. You need to analyze the effectiveness of your efforts throughout the lifetime of the business.

In the sample record in Personal Workshop 31, notice that the newspaper ad, which included the 10 percent off coupon, generated income of $6,600 with an expense of $300. The discount flyers mailed to the high school and university students were not cost-effective. The flyers mailed to a targeted mailing list of fishermen were more effective: at a cost of $200, 96 new customers responded and spent $1,152. The sponsorship of a youth sports team may appear to lose money, but the good will and visibility generated is worth the small loss.

The far right column of the response record helps make the effectiveness of each type of promotion more obvious. By applying two simple formulas, you can compare the average rate of return on each unit of advertising—that is, the amount you spend versus the average amount you make on each coupon, ad, or promotional item. These formulas help you understand how much you are spending to bring in customers, and whether your money is being spent in the most effective way.

Per unit return (PUR). The financial return on each unit of advertising is determined by using this formula:

$$(\text{Sales generated} - \text{Cost}) \div \text{Circulation or exposure} = \text{PUR}$$

This formula tells you how much money each advertising vehicle or promotional item generated for you.

Cost per exposure (CPE). A different formula demonstrates how much you spend on each item of advertising:

$$\text{Cost} \div \text{Total exposure} = \text{CPE}$$

By comparing the CPE with the PUR, you can see how much you spend and how much you get back on each individual promotional item.

Figure 15.5 compares the advantages and disadvantages of various advertising media. Some of them may not apply to your business.

URLinks
http://www.sbaer.uca.edu/docs/Publications/pub00028.txt
http://www.whcsb.com/

FIGURE 15.5	The Advantages and Disadvantages of Various Advertising Media

Medium	Advantages	Disadvantages
Newspapers	short lead time	low readership under 18
	limits distribution to your geographic market	read in a hurry
	size and shape flexibility	overfilled with ads on some days
	broad consumer acceptance	low selectivity
	in-house layout help for advertisers	price-oriented: most ads are for sales
Magazines	high selectivity of market niche	circulation beyond niche market
	audience tends to be receptive, self-selected	long lead time required to place ad
	repeat exposures, as magazines circulate informally	space and creative costs are high; design restrictions may apply
	high production values	
	small page sizes permit even small ads to stand out	
Television	multimedia—combination of visual and sound	enormous market: nonselective
	mass audience	subject to selective consumer non-viewing via remotes and VCRs
	approximates face-to-face contact	fleeting impression
	low cost per exposure (i.e., high production cost offset by number of viewers)	high cost for creation and production
	mere fact of presence in medium builds credibility	limited amount of information can be communicated
Radio	wide accessibility to medium	fleeting impression
	low cost	enormous, nonselective market
	target demographics	spoken word limitation

FIGURE
15.5 **The Advantages and Disadvantages of Various Advertising Media, continued**

Medium	Advantages	Disadvantages
Web page Banner ads	massive exposure to literally millions of potential customers graphically creative can be selectively placed on relevant Web sites of interest to your customers direct click-through to your Web page	unfocused market: no sure control over exposure banner message limited to slogan and graphics may rotate with competitors or be displayed with competing products
Direct mail	personal and selective specifically target market flexible copy content, message length message hidden from competition	long lead time for creation, printing, database generation and mailing high cost-per-prospect reached poor public perception ("junk mail" image) limits actual access high quality mailing lists can be expensive, hard to find and difficult to maintain
Outdoor	flexible location choices low cost per contact good for "reminder" type ads	no lengthy copy unfocused: wasted circulation
Yellow pages	self-selective: prospects reach for your ad when they need your product/service relatively inexpensive long life	competitors are listed in close proximity difficult to be creative difficult to update or change

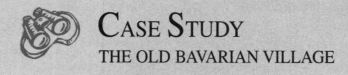

CASE STUDY
THE OLD BAVARIAN VILLAGE

Frances Wright inherited 100 acres of prime land just outside Houston, Texas. She decided to convert the land into a unique shopping center, called The Old Bavarian Village. It would have shops with authentic German features and products. She asked her uncle, a construction contractor, if he would help her build her shopping center. He suggested she hire a well-known Houston architect to design the shops, which she did. Together Frances and the architect traveled to Germany to get that "special feel" needed to carry out the village concept.

The architect designed a center containing 100 stores. Frances felt there should be more, but the architect felt ample space was left for expansion, if necessary. He also pointed out that she might want to include another concept, such as a Far Eastern group of stores, which could be set apart from the Old Bavarian Village; however, Frances decided to stick with the Bavarian theme.

In the meantime, at the suggestion of her uncle, Frances contacted a marketing expert to prepare a marketing plan for the village. About four months before the project was to open, he started teaser advertising and announcements written in German in the papers and on billboards. He had actors appear on television dressed in typical Bavarian costume. They talked about the center using the High German dialect of Bavaria. Of course, only a few people knew what the actors were saying. However, the mysterious ads created quite a stir in Houston. The local papers ran feature stories about the ads, and explained what they were about. Then, on television, about two weeks before the center was to open, an actor began talking in German, and then switched to English. The actor turned out to be a "good old Texas country boy" whose parents were from the old country. When he switched to English with his Texan accent, he talked about the Old Bavarian Village and suggested that people go on opening day because everyone would receive prizes and get to see some of the most unusual merchandise ever offered for sale in Texas.

When the shops opened, the parking lots were jammed. The decor was so authentic that those people who had visited Germany were stunned to find that such a place existed just outside Houston. There were stores selling antiques, clocks, toys, jewelry, furniture, and countless other products not likely to be found in the local department stores. The prices were high, but the people didn't mind, and business was brisk. Frances had brought some musicians over from Germany who played Bavarian music and danced on a stage and, of course, Bavarian beer was being served in all the restaurants. There seemed to be something for everyone. All in all, the opening was a fantastic success and Frances, her uncle, the architect, and the promoter were happy. However, they wondered how to sustain this interest.

After a few months, the novelty started to wear off and sales were down. Frances went to the promoter and asked him to get things moving. He replied that they would always get business, but they could never expect it to equal opening-day sales. Frances could not understand this and informed him that it was his job to find a way to keep things in high gear.

Several of the store owners decided to pull out, citing lack of sales. Although sales had been great in the beginning, they were now sagging, and the owners could not go on paying the high rent Frances demanded. Frances lowered the rent in these stores and the other store owners found out about it. They also demanded rental adjustments. Finally, the clock maker and the antique dealer left the center. Frances tried to find some other tenants to fill the space, but she was not successful.

She then had an offer from a supermarket chain to move into the location and give her the rent she demanded on a long-term lease. She also received similar offers from a pizza parlor and a Chinese restaurant. The space was available, and expenses were creeping up to the point where she was now losing money on the entire operation. She went to her uncle, and he told her that the concept for the Bavarian Village was great, but she had to face reality. He felt she should accept the three tenants who wanted to come in on a long-term lease and pay the rent she needed. He thought that as long as she had some stores related to the Bavarian concept, she

CONTINUED ▶

shouldn't be concerned. Frances signed the leases, and business started picking up again.

However, a few more tenants left, including the German furniture store, the art gallery, the toy store, and the German variety store. They felt that Frances had betrayed the original concept and that they were now no longer in the type of environment they had expected. They each indicated they would find their own location in Houston and create a lasting Bavarian image that would attract clients. In their place Frances signed up a pharmacy, a dry cleaner, a bookstore, and a shoe store. Not many of the original businesses remained except the German restaurants, which were booming.

The marketing promoter tried to get the stores to advertise as a group, but they declined. After a year, Frances saw that her basic concept had been destroyed. The tenants that remained were not balanced. The drug store sold some of the same products as the supermarket, and there were other stores that competed with one another. The Chinese restaurant, which had served great food, went out of business and its space was vacant. As soon as she signed up one tenant, another would close or go bankrupt, and the store would have court notices plastered on the doors. Finally, the supermarket announced it was closing its doors because business was not as good as expected. Frances reminded the store owners that the lease had ten years remaining at $10,000 a month. They stated that they would continue to pay it, but would use the location as a storage center for their Houston stores. When they boarded up the store, the entire complexion of the center changed. People thought that the center was closing. The owners of the German restaurant told her that she had to do something or they, too, were going to close. The village had lost its image, and people were not calling for dinner reservations so their sales were down.

With the supermarket closed and 24 other stores vacant, Frances was losing money and did not know what to do. She was not afraid of going bankrupt because she had inherited a fortune from her father's estate. However, she wanted to be a success. She went back to the architect to talk to him about the entire matter. He suggested that maybe it was time to renovate the entire center with a new concept. He recommended a large movie theater and, in general, a switch to more traditional architecture, still maintaining as much of the Bavarian concept as possible. He also suggested adding a day-care center to attract parents who found it difficult to shop with their children.

At this point, Frances was confused, especially when she received an offer from a donut shop eager to open in the center on a one-year lease. In addition, a flower shop, a computer store, a video rental, an adult bookstore, a small loan company, a firm selling used clothing, and a surplus store selling army and navy goods also indicated interest. Frances knew she needed to find an expert in business to help her solve her problems. ▼

Case Study Roundtable

▼▼▼▼▼

Frances: Was I too hasty in my decision to build a shopping center based on the Bavarian concept? I thought it was a good idea.

Discussion Points

- How would a business or marketing plan have helped Frances?
- Was Frances prepared to enter a business venture of this scale? Why or why not?
- Do you think that the types of stores Frances selected for the center had anything to do with its failure? What types of stores should she have looked for?

Frances: I think the high point was that first couple of weeks, when everyone was all excited because of the ad campaign. What did you think of it?

Discussion Points

- Did the ad campaign generate too much interest? How could it have been handled differently, and perhaps have avoided the sudden drop in sales?

BACK TO THE TABLE
Latonya Ellis and Kate Petrakis

In Chapter 1, you met Latonya and Kate, owners of Grandmother's Attic Heirloom Dresses, a small shop specializing in custom replicas of women's dresses and children's clothing from the late 1800s and early 1900s. Based on what you now know, how would you advise Latonya and Kate to more effectively promote their business?

▲▲▲▲▲▲

Chapter Briefcase
▼▼▼▼▼▼

- Advertising is the means for getting information about your product or service to your market. Tailor your advertising efforts to your market. A good ad arouses curiosity, illustrates the benefits of using the product or service, invites the viewer to participate, and tells the customer how, where, and when the item may be purchased and used.

- Typically, effective advertisements rely on the "three I"s:
    1. *Involve* the audience by inviting them to participate, by arousing their curiosity, by convincing them that they need your product or service.
    2. *Inform* the customer about the benefits and uniqueness of your product or service in terms that they can understand. The ad must also let the customer know how, where, and when the item or service can be purchased.
    3. *Illustrate* the benefits through words, images, or sounds that get the audience's attention and convey your information.

- Media advertising and publicity can be obtained through interviews, articles, and paid advertisements in newspapers and magazines, or on radio and on television. Other resources include phone directories, Web site banner ads, and outdoor advertising. Each medium has its own distinct advantages and disadvantages.

- It is vital that you keep track of the performance of each type of advertising you use, and compare the return generated by each medium and campaign.

- In addition to paid advertising, don't overlook publicity. Publicity is also known as "free advertising."

- The financial return on each unit of advertising is determined by using this formula:

$$(\text{Sales generated} - \text{Cost}) \div \text{Circulation or exposure} = \text{PUR}$$

This formula tells you how much money each advertising vehicle or promotional item generated for you.

- Cost per exposure. A different formula demonstrates how much you spend on each item of advertising:

$$\text{Cost} \div \text{Total exposure} = \text{CPE}$$

By comparing the CPE with the PUR, you can see how much you spend and how much you get back on each individual promotional item.

Chapter 16

CUSTOMER SERVICE AND SALES

▼▼▼▼▼

Give the lady what she wants. The customer is always right.

—Marshall Field, department store owner
(1834–1906)

MISSION STATEMENT

In this chapter, you will

*L*EARN about the role of customer service strategies in building a strong reputation for your business, product, or service.

*E*XPLORE the essential elements of customer service as part of your overall public relations approach.

*A*PPLY your understanding to a case study.

*P*RODUCE an analysis of your business's market-driven qualities and your awareness of customer service needs.

KEY TERMS

communications   feedback   questionnaire
complaints   guarantee   warranty
Federal Trade
 Commission

INTRODUCTION TO CUSTOMER SERVICE

So now your advertising and promotional campaign has done its work, and your customers have arrived at your door. (This can be a real door, of course, or a virtual one: the "door" of your telephone, or your Web site—it's all the same to the customer.) What happens next is the final step in your public relations strategy: customer service. If the advertising has attracted the customer, it's the customer service strategy that seals the deal. If your customer feels abused, neglected, unsafe, or cheated, the very best advertising campaign put together by Madison Avenue's finest minds will not bring them back.

▼▼▼▼▼▼▼▼▼▼▼▼▼▼▼▼▼▼▼▼▼

CUSTOMER SATISFACTION

Listen to your customers. You are not really selling products or services as much as you are selling customer satisfaction. Satisfied customers return to spend more money and are likely to refer new customers to you. Dissatisfied customers terminate their spending and discourage potential customers. It has been estimated that when customers are displeased, they tell from 7 to 11 people about their dissatisfaction. But only one in 26 dissatisfied customers complains to the company offering the poor service. Providing an atmosphere and the means for allowing a customer to voice a complaint is a matter of maintaining open communication. Warranties and guarantees are the most powerful marketing statements a company can make. They are especially effective for a new company. They create a relationship that says "we stand behind what we sell."

There is one simple difference between a warranty and a guarantee: a warranty is provided by a *manufacturer*. A guarantee is provided by the *seller* of a product or the performer of a service. Of course, to the consumer they're often one and the same.

Warranties

A **warranty** explains what the seller promises about the product being sold. It is a written statement of the manufacturer's commitment if a product is defective or performs poorly. Common law says that producers must stand behind their products. The federal Magnuson-Moss Act of 1975 states that producers must provide a "clearly written" warranty. This means stating the limits of any warranty including its length, specific areas of performance, and whether it includes labor and routine maintenance. The act also requires full warranties to meet certain minimum standards, which include reasonable repairs and replacement.

The **Federal Trade Commission (FTC)** has established guidelines to ensure that warranties are clear and definite and not deceptive or unfair. Some companies used to say their products were "fully warranted" or "absolutely guaranteed." However, they didn't state the time period or spell out the meaning of the warranty. Now a company is required by law to make clear whether it is offering a "full" or "limited" warranty (the law defines what "full" means). The warranty must also be available for inspection before the purchase.

A company that produces a product must make specific decisions about what the warranty will cover, and then the warranty should be communicated clearly to the customer.

LIABILITY ALERT!

In general, the FTC requires that if an ad for a consumer product that costs more than $15 mentions a warranty, the ad must inform consumers that a copy of the warranty is available for them to read prior to sale. If the ad promises a warranty on products available through the mail, the ad must tell consumers how to get a copy.

For advertisements of products costing $15 or less, the FTC does not require disclosures. Instead, the FTC's legal decisions and policy statements are the sole sources of guidance on how to avoid unfairness or deception in advertising warranties.

Obviously, you should consult your attorney for help in applying the FTC's decisions and policy statements to your company's warranty policy.

Regardless of the price of the product, however, advertising phrases such as "satisfaction guaranteed" or "money back guarantee" may be used only if the advertiser is willing to fulfill the promise to customers who return the merchandise for any reason.

An ad that mentions a satisfaction guarantee should tell consumers of any conditions or limitations on the offer. For example, a restriction based on a specific time period, such as 30 days, is a material condition that must be disclosed.

"Lifetime" warranties or guarantees can be confusing for consumers, because it is difficult to know just whose life is involved. For example, one person may intend the warranty to last for the expected useful life of the product, while another may intend it to last for the life of the purchaser. Others may assume that the lifetime warranty they offer is for the time the original purchaser owns the product. To avoid confusing consumers about the duration of a "lifetime" warranty or guarantee, the FTC requires that ads should define for consumers precisely which "life" measures the warranty.

Guarantees

A **guarantee** implies making oneself or one's business liable or responsible for the performance of something. It is a pledge or promise. Ideally the best guarantee is unconditional, easy to understand, meaningful, easy to invoke, and quick to pay off.

Stand by your guarantees, no matter what. Let your customers know that your commitment to customer satisfaction is of the utmost importance to you. Adopt a liberal return policy. Of course, some customers may abuse this policy, but your good customers will appreciate the policy and spread the word. Word-of-mouth endorsements are the best and least expensive advertising you can get.

Making good on customer returns shouldn't be viewed solely as an expense. It is a learning opportunity: a chance to engage in some market analysis and head off disasters before they get out of control. Why was the item returned? How could the return have been avoided? Did the customer feel that the matter was resolved in a timely and cordial way? Is the problem with the product limited to just that one item, or could it be a sign that an entire shipment is flawed?

Accept responsibility for all mistakes. When an error is made on a customer's order, respond by saying, "I'm sorry for the mistake. What can I do to correct the problem to your satisfaction?" No matter how angry the customer may be, this response will usually defuse the situation. Answer all customer inquiries and complaints as promptly as possible. Meet all time commitments. Quality begins with the owner and is an ongoing process. Never stop asking how you can do better. Find out what your customer expects from your product or service. Then deliver it and guarantee it.

COMMUNICATION

If you want your business to be successful, you must listen to and talk with customers in order to learn how you can better serve them. The most successful business owners identify with and stay close to their customers. They give their customers the level of service they themselves would expect to receive. These business owners also maintain a two-way communication channel with their employees. They educate employees about the company and its products and services. They listen to employees' concerns. Employees often know your customers best. Their input should be encouraged. This chapter will look at the importance of establishing ways to generate customer feedback and encourage employee communication.

Mailing Lists

Mailing lists can be developed from your own customer files. You can capture names and addresses from checks, credit cards, business cards, and questionnaires. Encourage customers to drop their business cards into a basket or bowl by providing a monthly prize drawing. For customers without cards, provide forms to fill out.

Stay in touch. Educate your customers about new products, alert customers about sales, introduce a new staff member, or take a survey to determine customer satisfaction. If you see something that might interest them, even if it is not related to your business, write them a note or give them a call. Follow up a purchase with a phone call or a response card to make sure they are satisfied. Remember birthdays and special events by sending cards or other appropriate acknowledgments. A birthday wish is personal and has relatively little competition from other cards. Most businesses send holiday greeting cards that arrive in bunches during the holidays and the individual thought is lost in the volume of cards.

To cut the cost of mailing, consider using postcards to announce an address change, to introduce new personnel, to invite customers to a sale, to announce the arrival of new merchandise, or to tell about the addition of an 800 number, fax line, or Internet Web site. Postcards can also be sent to advertise single items, mention a special discount, or offer a free item.

Customer Feedback

Communication, of course, is a two-way street. Let customers know that you value their opinions whether good or bad. Provide ways for them to communicate with you. Most unhappy customers who do not complain will simply not buy from you again. The reason they do not complain to the business owner is that they think the complaint will do no good or they aren't sure how to voice their complaint. Your job is to show the customer that complaints and comments do make a difference. Some methods for encouraging customer communication include:

- *Face-to-face communication.* Listen to what customers say about you, your company, and your competition. Talk and meet with your customers to learn about their attitudes, and what they like and dislike. Ask questions. Share knowledge of your industry and educate them with seminars or talks about your product or service.
- *The telephone.* Phone calls can be an effective method of communication for a small business. Personal phone contact is a good way to get information and to give explanations. Make sure that you and your employees use good telephone techniques. Always introduce yourself by giving your name as well as the name of the company that you represent. Use tact and a friendly tone. Use the words "thank you" and "appreciate" often. Successful salespeople follow

up with customers, usually by phone, to see that the purchases made or services received were satisfactory. On incoming calls, use "hold" sparingly and keep the caller informed. Some businesses with clients nationwide may find an 800 phone number a good tool for getting a prompt response.

- *The Internet.* You can communicate with customers and potential customers anywhere in the world with the Internet. E-mail service can be built in to your Web site, so you can inform your customers while simultaneously soliciting their feedback. Many people seem to feel more comfortable communicating electronically, which is seen as "safer" and more anonymous than phone conversations or face-to-face meetings.
- *Formal suggestion and complaint system.* A simple, accessible, and visible complaint and suggestion system should be established to show customers that your company will listen. Post signs explaining your policy, use a suggestion box, print a customer service name and number on cards or bills. Designate someone to handle the comments and to respond when appropriate. Comment cards are often used for restaurants and other businesses with many customers whose identities are not known. Customers should be asked about problems and impressions and their comments must be noted.
- *Questionnaires.* In Chapter 14, we discussed how questionnaires can be used for strategic marketing. Questionnaires can form the basis for face-to-face, mail, and phone surveys. Make the survey short, clear, and specific in order to gather meaningful information. Offer premiums related to your business to boost the response rate. (A sample customer service questionnaire for a retail store has been included in Figure 16.1.)

Community Involvement

Community involvement is another form of communication. It shows that you are committed to your business for the long haul. It demonstrates to your customers, your suppliers, your competitors, other businesses, and the community, in general, that you have a vested interest in the welfare of your home and business community.

Active participation in community organizations and events can help project the identity or image you have chosen for your company. Membership in civic groups and business organizations such as the chamber of commerce can give you opportunities for public speaking, conference exhibiting, and networking. Offer to share your expertise by guest lecturing at high schools or offering evening adult seminars. Sponsorship of youth athletic teams can also get visibility for your business and show your commitment.

Consider donating your product or service to a charitable cause. This often results in positive exposure to community leaders and civic groups. While consumer products are usually desired the most, many organizations also look for donations of professional service time. If you have a restaurant, consider hosting an event for a charitable organization. Of course, this works best if volunteers for that charity are potential customers.

Project an image as an integral part of your community. It is the friendly feelings people have that draw them to you and your business. It has been said that the best form of advertising is "word of mouth." The most successful businesses are based upon customer and community loyalty.

FIGURE
16.1

Customer Service Questionnaire for a Retail Business

In an effort to meet the needs of our customers, we have developed the following questionnaire. We hope you will take a few moments to tell us how you feel about our store, how we rate next to our competition and what we can do to improve our product line and our service.

1. Is this your first visit to our store? ☐ Yes ☐ No

2. Which of the following stores do you consider our closest competition?
   ☐ Dolber's ☐ Things-n-Such
   ☐ Lafky & Sutherton ☐ Brenberger's

3. What do you value most about our store?
   ☐ Selection ☐ Service ☐ Pricing
   ☐ Convenience ☐ Other _____

4. How could our store be improved?
   _____

5. What other products or services would you like us to offer?
   _____

6. How did you first hear about our product/service?
   _____

7. What newspapers and magazines do you read regularly?
   _____

8. What radio and television stations do you tune in to regularly?
   _____

9. Do you respond to direct mailings? ☐ Yes ☐ No

10. Do you use discount coupons? ☐ Yes ☐ No

11. Please indicate your sex and age:
    ☐ Male ☐ 18–34 ☐ 35–49
    ☐ Female ☐ 50–65 ☐ 66+

12. Please indicate your annual household income:
    ☐ Under $15,000 ☐ $15,000–$25,000 ☐ $25,000–$49,000
    ☐ $50,000–$74,000 ☐ Over $75,000

Thank you for your responses. If you would like to be included in our mailings for in-store promotions and sales, please complete the following:

Name _____ Birthdate: _____

Address _____

City/State/Zip _____

Phone (_____)_____

Addressing Customer Complaints

The most common customer complaints can be broken down into three areas, shown in Figure 16.2. As you can see, customers can express dissatisfaction regarding your employees, your location, and/or your product or service.

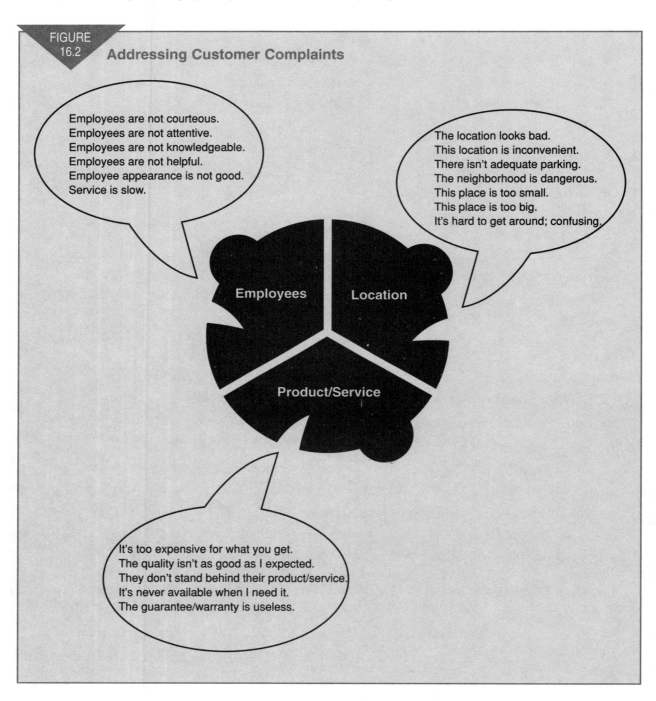

FIGURE 16.2 **Addressing Customer Complaints**

Employee-oriented complaints. The two most frequently cited customer complaints are:

1. Being ignored by salespeople
2. Being treated in a rude manner

The average American company will lose 10 to 30 percent of its customers per year due to poor service. When customers have a choice, they will go to the competition almost one-third of the time. In a highly competitive marketplace, these are customers you cannot afford to lose.

Successful companies realize that their strongest selling point can be high-quality service. Small businesses that put their emphasis on customer service are more likely to survive and succeed than companies that emphasize the advantages of lower price, convenience, speed of delivery, or product performance. While these are important to the consumer, the personal dealings with staff can be what brings that customer back for repeat business. (Of course, if your company can promise—and deliver—low prices *and* high quality customer service, your business will thrive!)

There are some specific steps you can take to address employee-oriented customer complaints.

- *Provide training.* Let your employees know what you expect of them, so they'll know exactly what to do in every situation. Lack of knowledge on the part of the employees reflects on the business owner. Also, when you are not around your employees are your company's contact with the public: it's in your own best interest to train and educate them so they know your product, service, and industry inside and out. Make sure that they understand your company's purpose, philosophy, products, and services. They must be able to locate items, explain features, and understand warranty and guarantee policies. Involve your employees as part of your team.
- *Encourage initiative.* As an entrepreneur, you know the value of being able to take charge of a situation and think independently on your feet. Encourage that trait in your employees, and reward them when they demonstrate initiative. They must be able to help customers make informed decisions, even if it means no immediate sale or referring them to the competition. Customers will remember that help. (Remember the movie, *Miracle on 34th Street*? When the Macy's Santa Claus started sending customers to Gimbel's, Macy's business skyrocketed because their customers felt valued.) As your points of contact with the world, your employees need to be able to respond to customer suggestions and complaints, too.
- *Demand civility.* Customers must be greeted promptly and courteously. Stress to your employees the importance of maintaining eye contact. Make sure that personal appearance and grooming are appropriate to the business type and setting. You may want to institute a dress code or provide uniforms. This also reinforces the identity and image you have designed for your company. Of course, this applies to the business owner as well as the employee!

Location-oriented complaints. The appearance of your business location or work area reflects the image or identity you have adopted for your company, your products, and your services. The importance of choosing a location takes into account the needs and expectations of your market, as well as traffic patterns for customers, availability of parking, and safety issues. (This will be discussed further in Chapter 21.)

Make sure that your customers know how to reach your business. Include a small map or directions for reaching your business on your brochure or flyer. Make sure that employees who may be answering the phone can give good directions to your business location. Designate the nearest parking area on your map. If you are a service business and your clients must use public parking, validate their parking tickets. The amount of money you will spend reimbursing parking fees will seem small in comparison to the goodwill you'll generate.

PERSONAL WORKSHOP 32
Customer Security Checklist

▼ The following checklist might help as you survey your facilities periodically.

	Yes	No
Are all interior lights functioning?		
Are all exterior building lights functioning?		
Is the parking lot properly lit?		
Are the exterior premises free of vandalism or graffiti?		
Are the exterior premises free of litter?		
Is the interior floor clean?		
Are shelves, racks, or display surfaces orderly?		
Is the sidewalk in good repair?		
Is the parking lot surface in good repair?		
Are public restrooms clean?		

Be aware of a customer's personal needs. Can you assign an employee to carry merchandise to vehicles? Look out for your customers' safety. Are your establishment and the surrounding area properly lighted? What is the condition of the pavement and sidewalk? Would your customers feel safer with a security person on the premises? Evaluating your location and its appearance in terms of your customers' needs is an ongoing process throughout the life of your business.

If you don't have a physical location, you should analyze your virtual one. If you are a phone-based business, is the voice mail system user-friendly and easy to navigate through? Are customers abandoned on hold, or unclear whether they're in the right place? When they're on hold, do they receive repeated assurances that they haven't been forgotten? Such "location" issues are just as important to your customers as they would be in a brick-and-mortar context.

Product/service-oriented complaints. Customers want to feel that they are getting value for their money. Give customers the quality of product or service you would want. Put yourself in the "buyer's seat" when dealing with your customers.

If you want to retain your customer base (which you probably do), you must always anticipate the competition. Make sure that your pricing structure is in line with your competitors'. Keep up with trends in order to be aware of new products and services you can provide.

No business can provide all things to all people, however. Know your customer base. Understand what they are interested in purchasing and what you are comfortable providing. Plan your business start-up and growth with the goal of establishing a niche for yourself in the marketplace. Build a reputation for depth and expertise in a selected area. By focusing on that niche, you will be able to avoid many product or service complaints. You will be aware of the needs and wants of your target market, you will be dealing with merchandise you understand, can explain, and will stand behind, and you will know when to refer customers to a competitor.

 URLinks
http://www.toolkit.cch.com/Text/P03_7020.stm
http://www.cba.neu.edu/alumni/molloy/art-32.html
http://www.toolkit.cch.com/text/P01_2240.stm
http://sbinformation.miningco.com/msub19.htm

 CASE STUDY ROUNDTABLE
▾ ▾ ▾ ▾ ▾ ▾

Case Study: Grandmother's Attic

In Chapter 1, you met Latonya and Kate, owners of Grandmother's Attic Heirloom Dresses, a small shop specializing in custom replicas of women's dresses and children's clothing from the late 1800s and early 1900s. Here we will revisit the entire case study (beginning on page 16), because it raises a number of issues that are particularly relevant to what you've just read.

Kate: I can't help feeling sometimes like we're running this business by the seat of our pants—or the backs of our bustles, if you want. Projects just seem to last forever, but we believe we have to get every detail just the way the customer wants it. Is that wrong?

Discussion Points

- Grandmother's Attic has no formal customer service policy. Currently, Latonya and Kate will alter the heirloom dresses until the customer is satisfied. What are the implications of this, assuming they are doing the alterations at no additional cost?
- If you were asked to draft a reasonable customer service policy for Grandmother's Attic, what would be its main points?

▲▲▲▲▲▲

Chapter Briefcase

▼▼▼▼▼▼

- You are not really selling products or services as much as you are selling customer satisfaction. Satisfied customers return to spend more money and are likely to refer new customers to you. Dissatisfied customers terminate their spending and discourage potential customers.
- A warranty explains what the seller promises about the product being sold. It is a written statement of the manufacturer's commitment if a product is defective or performs poorly. The Federal Trade Commission has established guidelines to ensure that warranties are clear and definite and not deceptive or unfair.
- An ad that mentions a satisfaction guarantee should tell consumers of any conditions or limitations on the offer. For example, a restriction based on a specific time period, such as 30 days, is a material condition that must be disclosed.
- A guarantee is a pledge or promise. Ideally, the best guarantee is unconditional, easy to understand, meaningful, easy to invoke, and quick to pay off.
- If you want your business to be successful, you must listen to and talk with customers in order to learn how you can better serve them. The most successful business owners identify with and stay close to their customers.
- Some methods for encouraging customer communication include *face-to-face communication, telephone, the Internet, a formal suggestion and complaint system, and questionnaires.*
- Community involvement is another form of communication. It shows that you are committed to your business for the long haul.
- The most common customer complaints can be broken down into three areas:
  1. Employee-oriented complaints
  2. Location-oriented complaints
  3. Product/service-oriented complaints

▲▲▲▲▲▲

Chapter 17

DEVELOPING A WEB PRESENCE

Five years ago, the World Wide Web barely existed; I think there were about 50 sites. Today, there are 1.5 million new Web pages created every day, 65,000 every hour. This phenomenon has absolutely staggering possibilities to democratize, to empower people all over the world... The next big step in our economic transformation, it seems to me, is the full development of this remarkable device and the electronic commerce it makes possible.

—President Bill Clinton to the Technology '98 Conference, February 26, 1998

MISSION STATEMENT

In this chapter, you will

*L*EARN about the concepts underlying Internet-based commercial activity (e-commerce).

*E*XPLORE whether an Internet presence is a good idea for your company.

*A*PPLY principles of effective e-commerce to a case study.

*P*RODUCE an effective analysis of Internet service vendors to select the ones best suited to your business's needs.

KEY TERMS

e-commerce	Internet	URL
homepage	navigation	Web site
hyperlink	page-clicker	World Wide Web
interactive		

INTRODUCTION TO E-COMMERCE

The Internet can be defined as a *network* of networks; a *community* of people who use and develop those networks; and a *collection* of resources that can be reached through those networks. That is, it's not just another computer thing: it's a vibrant, interconnected community of resources and information. There are, at latest estimate, more than 320 million different Web pages available to tireless surfers. That makes it quite a promising tool for small businesses. Imagine the marketing and sales potential of a medium to which 30 million adults in the United States alone have access. Read this chapter's opening quote again: "1.5 million new Web pages created every day, 65,000 every hour." Do the math. That's the Internet.

Nearly 12 million people use the World Wide Web regularly, and a little over 1.5 million people have purchased something through it. That statistic alone is worthy of further discussion: with all those potential customers out there, why are so relatively few people actual customers? An interesting question for Web entrepreneurs. Of course, the number is growing daily, as people become used to the idea of buying things electronically, and as fears about security and privacy are increasingly resolved. In 1998, consumer Internet sales were nearly $2.5 billion, and conservative estimates suggest that by the turn of the century Web-based commerce will account for more than $17.3 billion. Try to think of another sector of the economy in which sales activity grew so dramatically in so little time.

E-commerce (the shorthand, high-tech way of saying commercial transactions handled over the Internet) is one of the hottest growing areas of Internet use, and one of the hottest growing markets of any kind, anywhere.

One of the significant downsides of the proliferation of Web sites and the growing popularity of the Internet as a commercial tool is that far too many entrepreneurs, caught up in the thrilling discovery of a new, attractive, and effective tool for reaching potential customers and conveying information, fail to make the intuitive leap from paper to screen.

Worse, companies post Web sites and leave them languishing on the Web, failing to update them or keep people coming back.

Word processors haven't helped much, because what you key in on the keyboard gets displayed on the monitor as if it were a piece of paper: typing with a stream of electrons rather than messy ribbons. The Internet, however, is much more than a lavishly high-tech copyholder: it's literally a whole new world of marketing opportunity. But like any other whole new world, it has its own rules, its own expectations, and its own demands—many of which its discoverers have yet to notice, much less understand. Here, we'll examine some of those, and consider the challenge of taking the printed marketing material you've been using, and uploading it onto the Web in the most commercially effective way possible.

While we're at it, we'll also answer these questions:

- Why do I need an Internet presence at all?
- Is the Internet right for my business?
- How can I most effectively use the Internet?

A word about what this chapter won't do: We aren't going to discuss the nuts-and-bolts of authoring systems, upload procedures, or HTML. We will not address the comparative virtues of the various browsers, or how many megs can dance on the head of a pin. While it is certainly vital for a Web-based entrepreneur to understand the technology behind the design, here we will deal with the design itself, and the theory underlying it. There are many sound training systems out there (many of them on the Web itself) that can give you the kinds of technical skills you need. And there are so many consumer-oriented comparisons of Internet services and Internet-related products that no one can claim to be uninformed about their cyber-decisions any more. Whole books are written explaining the qualities and mechanics of one or two Internet products or services; a single chapter here can't hope to do as much.

THE INTERNET

Let's take a low-tech comparison approach first. The Internet is similar in concept to the yellow pages: it's a place people go when they want to find out who supplies what products or services. (Of course, people go onto the World Wide Web for other reasons, too: entertainment, research, education, and communication, for instance.) The World Wide Web, though, is *infinitely* more interactive, *infinitely* larger, and *infinitely* more flexible to the individual needs of both business and customers than any printed media could ever hope to be. Instead of a two-inch-by-three-inch advertisement on a printed page, every business on the Net has a full-page display ad called a homepage or Web site. A visible presence on the World Wide Web isn't expensive: it can cost less than a hundred dollars to post a perfectly attractive and effective home page. Of course, the amount you can spend on your virtual storefront is virtually limitless. If you start small, though, you can grow into the demand.

Remember that your homepage—whether simple or complex—will be accessible by anyone in the world, at any time. If you decide to sell your products, you may find yourself getting orders from Scotland or Brazil mixed in with ones from what you might usually consider your "region." You may need to be prepared to deal with international shipments, exchange rates, and other exciting aspects of the growing worldwide economy.

Remember: the Internet is just another site for your store. It's more than an advertisement in a high-tech yellow pages: it's the opportunity to create a virtual branch outlet for your company. On the other hand, a lot of companies waste a lot of time (and money) on Web sites that no one visits and that fail to create revenue. You wouldn't think of renting office or shop space if you had no idea how customers would find you, and you certainly wouldn't go out of your way to locate in a place far from your customer base. For the same reason, you shouldn't locate in cyberspace, if cyberspace is not where your customers are. Personal Workshop 33 will help you decide.

URLinks
http://www.net101.com/reasons.html

GOING ONLINE THE RIGHT WAY

A successful business Web site incorporates four basic characteristics:

1. A sound, carefully considered **business strategy**. That is, you should have a good business reason for going online. A good business reason doesn't necessarily mean your site will generate direct income: it may even lose money, at least at first, costing more to set up and maintain than it generates in sales. But if a Web presence generates interest (and income) for the rest of your business,

PERSONAL WORKSHOP 33
Should You Be on the Web?
▾▾▾▾▾

▾ Before you even start thinking about the design and content issues of entering into the world of online commerce, you need to ask whether the Internet is the place for you. Why do you want to be on the Web? Check off the three statements that apply most to you:

I want to set up a Web site because:

❑ 1. Everyone else is.

❑ 2. It's fashionable.

❑ 3. If I have a Web site, my company will look like it's on the cutting edge.

❑ 4. My old company had a Web site.

❑ 5. My competition has a Web site.

❑ 6. I want to show my products and services to potential customers.

❑ 7. I want to sell my products and services electronically to customers.

❑ 8. I want to provide customers with information about my product, service, and company.

❑ 9. I want to provide customers with useful information related to my product or service.

❑ 10. My customers are Web surfers.

❑ 11. My customers are geographically scattered.

❑ 12. My customers are accustomed to Internet commerce.

Scoring: Give yourself 2 points for each checkmark for statements 5 through 9, and 3 points for checking 10, 11, or 12. Deduct 1 point for each checkmark for the first four statements. Now total your score.

–3 to +2	You should probably not bother with a Web site right now.
3 to 6	Give it some more thought: what do you want your Web site to do, exactly, and why do you want to do it that way?
7 to 9	It looks like you have a pretty clear idea what you want from the Web, why you want it, and how you're going to get it done.

a Web presence can still be a wise move. Your Web presence may be pure PR, but good PR is good marketing, and good marketing is how businesses are built. The point is, have a sound, cold-hearted, capitalist reason for going on the Web—not just because you think it would be a good idea.

2. A clear **market analysis**. Do your customers go online? Are your clients Web surfers, or does your market consider an electric typewriter the height of high-tech equipment? If your customers (or your potential customers) aren't on the Web, why should you be? Think of it this way: it might be "cool" to advertise in *Esquire*, or *The New Yorker*, or *Vanity Fair*, but if your customers read *Ladies Home Journal*, *Fish 'n' Tackle*, and *Reader's Digest*, then you wouldn't do it, right? You would spend the money where it would be most likely to reach your customers. The same thing with the Internet. If your customers don't have computers, or don't like computers, or will never go onto the Internet, then you should allocate your resources elsewhere. Know your market, and act accordingly. On the other hand, if you're interested in building a new market, and your potential customers are Web surfers, then obviously you should have a place for them to surf to.

3. An **appealing, effective page design**. You wouldn't put up an ugly sign on your store, or take out a nasty-looking advertisement in the paper, right? So be careful when designing your Web presence. We'll discuss this issue more below.

4. A **secure method for conducting commercial transactions**. That means, if you're going to take orders online, you'll need to establish a **secure server**—a technology that will encrypt your customers' personal and credit card information so it is as safe as possible as it zips through the phone lines at 186,000 miles per second. Keep that in mind, if your customers balk: you're offering greater security than when they order from a catalog over the same phone lines, because anyone can listen in on their conversation. Decrypting electronic information, however, is a daunting task for all but the most dedicated cyber criminals. Also remember this: Amazon.com handles thousands of orders electronically every day, and has experienced no incidents of credit card fraud or theft from online bad guys. That doesn't mean the Internet is 100 percent secure—nothing is. But it does mean that a lot of your customers' concerns can be addressed.

Doing business on the Internet, Bill Tobin of PC Flowers and Gifts earned the *Inc.* Small Business Person of the Year award by doing what people said couldn't be done. Here he shares his insight into doing business on the Internet.

THINKING ABOUT WEB-BASED COMMERCE

It might help to step outside the realm of high technology for a moment, to not think about the lightning-fast stream of "0"s and "1"s whipping through your modem and hurling themselves into the global network of interconnected computers that is the Internet. Instead, think for a moment of a languid pond, shimmering in the shade of the pine trees, the warble of birds, and the rustling of squirrels. Think of that pond as a piece of newspaper, lying flat on the ground. Traditionally, the potential customer gets information from a printed document like a bird that swoops down and skims the pond, barely breaking through the placid surface. A document on the Internet, on the other hand, is approached by a different kind of hunter, who dives in and finds food underwater. Web-based consumers are diving hunters: they can reenter the pond at different points, going to different depths, until their hunger (whether for creepy-crawlies or widgets) has been completely satisfied.

This is not the usual way companies deliver information.

Obviously, the entrepreneur is giving up a good deal of control when offering marketing material on the Internet. In a newspaper, magazine, or catalog setting, the business calls the shots: when specific material should be read, when pictures should be included, in what order, and at what level the description of the goods or services should be written. If you want to just suggest an image for your product, you design that type of ad. If you want to provide specs and mechanical details, that's what you write. The business can control how much "nice to know" information is included, and lead customers through the material point by point in an order carefully designed to build toward the point of purchase.

No such luck on the Internet. A well-designed Internet marketing site will have a number of special characteristics, all of which run exactly counter to the expectations of traditional marketing. Let's consider some of them.

Multiple Points of Entry

Customers on the Web expect to be able to start and stop their experience of your site at virtually any point. Of course, in many circumstances it is essential that one concept be understood in order to understand the next, and the site can be designed to do that. However, insofar as it is possible to do so, a commercial Web site must permit the visitor to essentially structure his or her own visit.

One way to do that is by breaking your content into separate, self-supporting modules that can be accessed by the customer in any order. Another way is by providing hyperlinks.

In print advertising, the marketer is bound by constraints of time and logistics. There may be fascinating historical, theoretical, or otherwise interesting but nonessential information that the business would love to share with the customer—information that could build loyalty, create a positive product image, or encourage greater understanding of need—but the demands of the medium force the business to stick to the essentials.

On the Internet, however, all that information can be made available through hyperlinks. A hyperlink is a URL, a Web address, like *http://www.dearborn.com*, where a specific file resides. URL stands for *uniform resource locator*. The "http" part of the URL is the *hypertext transfer protocol* that tells the browser you're looking for a specific Web page. By including hyperlinks, the Web-based entrepreneur can provide front-door access to additional depths of information about his or her product or service. Figure 17.1 describes the components of a URL.

A simple HTML tag does the trick:

> <italic>For more about small business issues, click <A HREF="http://www.companyline.com/internet/webpage.html">here</A>!</italic>

On a Web page, a hyperlink might look like this:

*For more about small business issues, click **here**!*

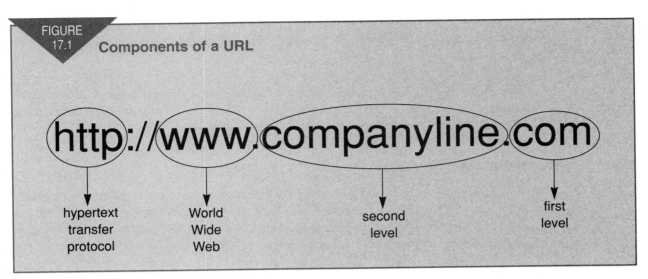

FIGURE 17.1 Components of a URL

The user is clued to the hyperlink because the underlined word or words are a different color or otherwise stand out on the page. When the user positions the cursor over the word and clicks on his or her mouse, the file is accessed and the information retrieved. He or she is transferred to the new Web page. The new file may contain additional hyperlinks, permitting the user to construct a custom-tailored chain of topical data that directly addresses his or her information needs. The hyperlink may be represented on the screen by underlined words that are a different color from the surrounding text, or by buttons or icons.

FIRST PERSON

Joan K., Mahomet, Illinois: I thought a Web site would be just the thing for my business, which grew out of my experience as a florist. Essentially, I—that is, my two employees and I—create baskets of dried flowers and prairie grasses, and then sell them through local gift "shoppes." We do a pretty brisk business. I like surfing the Web, so my husband (a computer guy over at the university) put together a beautiful site, with photos of different kinds of baskets, and an online order form. Well, I found out you can have too much of a good thing! All of a sudden I was getting orders from Chicago and Milwaukee and St. Louis—and those were the close ones! I had a shop in Bozeman, Montana that wanted a dozen of them, and a lady in Ottawa that wanted one delivered in three days. Well, I had my husband turn off that Web site right away, and I went ahead and filled the orders that had come in. I found out that the local merchants in the towns and suburbs around Champaign-Urbana (where the university is) had a cooperative Web site, kind of like an online services directory, or yellow pages, I guess. I joined up with them, and now we get orders pretty much only from local customers: people who've gone to the Internet looking for a local business to deal with. I love the Internet, but it can get out of control if you're not careful.

But here's the really good news: My sales are up 25 percent since I went online, and after that first false start, I think it's great. The biggest hurdle was getting people to feel OK about using their credit cards online. We have a secure server, which means their personal information is coded and scrambled—"encrypted" is the word the tech guys use—so it's at least as safe as giving your credit card number over the phone. We haven't had any problems at all. So that's my "Internet experience"—a mixed bag, but overall really good.

After looking at the basic information about your business, product, or service, a customer who wants to order, or needs to know more, can go to your hyperlinked files. Other customers can proceed to other parts of your Web site.

Navigability

Research has shown that Web users still want a sense of place, even in a hypertext environment. The "look and feel" of the Web site should be consistent throughout all levels of interactivity, and the user should always have a clear path back to where they started (i.e., recurring directional and "home" buttons).

Thus, there are two fundamental (and somewhat contradictory) characteristics shared by most consumers in an electronic environment: (1) the desire for self-direction, and (2) the desire for a clear sense of structure. Users need to be "in control" of the site to the greatest possible extent, while at the same time having access to support and information from credible, reliable sources, and continuous positive reinforcement that they are going in the right direction and that what they want to see is there.

At the same time, Web site developers must not create too many options for users, or relinquish so much control over content that the site becomes little more than a Web browser or search engine. While potential customers may appear to be empowered by high levels of user-directed content delivery, the basic objectives of the site—be it sales or marketing—may be lost if there are no clearly specified directions.

All of these navigability goals can be achieved by consistent screen design, clear content and positional mapping, and multiple user choices. Screens should be designed to achieve the "ACE" standard: Attractiveness, Clarity, and Efficiency.

Attractiveness. Certainly beauty is subjective, but in the world of computer screens, there are some basic, standard measures. On the Internet, a screen is attractive if it downloads quickly, and doesn't make the viewer squint or pass out. The most brilliant content is going to go unread if it's embedded in a screen full of garish, flashing colors and a confusing array of frames. An attractive site can be accomplished by following three simple rules. (See Figure 17.2.)

1. *Keep it simple.* The screen should be pleasant to look at: use large, uncluttered typefaces, and add color to highlight rather than dazzle. Design the elements of your screen to work on the "sideways" layout of a screen (11 by 8½ inches), rather than the standard catalog page (8½ by 11). *Content always dictates appearance.* Make it simple. Don't include elements just because you can; include elements because you have to in order to get your information across to your customers. And remember: the fancier your site, the longer it's going to take for a customer to see it. Downloading time is a significant concern to Web-based consumers.
2. *Don't overload the screen.* One of the most important things to remember when designing a commercial Web site is *don't overload the screen.* In print-based

marketing, costs are often tied to the amount and quality of paper used, or the number of newspaper columns your ad takes up. In e-commerce, you are liberated from printer's costs. Remember that computer-based consumers don't want to spend more than 15 seconds lingering over a single screen, and a typical screen should contain no more than thirty lines of legible text. Use pictures if you can.

3. *Don't create a page-clicker.* The corollary to the "don't overload" rule is *don't create a page-clicker.* That is, you don't want to put your Web visitors in the position of click-click-clicking their way through an endless parade of nearly identical screens. The scholarly term for that is "reactive pacing." Reactive pacing is the electronic equivalent of page-turning. It runs precisely counter to the interactive character of Web-based education: it's a waste of the capability of the resource, and will definitely affect the attractiveness of your product and its profitability.

Clarity. Don't confuse your customers with banners or obscure icons. Functionality on a Web-based instructional screen should be clear and consistent: if your icons are at the bottom of the screen on the first page, they should stay there. Viewers should know where to look for a particular element. The icons themselves should be obvious, not require too much in the way of interpretation or guesswork, and should not overwhelm the page.

Audio. Studies have indicated that the use of audio may "contaminate" effective design if it fails to provide valuable content, is purely decorative or distracting, or slows file access times. Relying on audio to deliver content unsupported by screen text or graphics is dangerous, too, because your customers' computers or speakers may not be capable of handling the material. (Or, from a diversity standpoint, if you rely on audio delivery of important information you will exclude hearing-impaired customers.)

Think, too, about where people use the Internet. If they're accessing your Web site from their workplace, they may be sitting in an open sea of cubicles (the sort of place you decided not to be in when you set out on your own). If they come to your site for information about your product or service and are greeted by a loud eagle's cry or the blare of trumpets, you can bet they'll be out of there as fast as possible. Far from attracting new business, the use of sound can scare customers away.

Perhaps most important from a cost-benefits standpoint, audio files take up a lot of memory. Also, like other special features, audio will slow down the delivery of content. If content delivery is slowed noticeably, your customers will lose interest.

Animations. Sadly, the same principle is true of graphics, particularly animations. It is relatively easy to add animated graphics to your Web site, and pretty tempting to put in a spinning, three-dimensional view of your brand-new patented widget for all to see. The question is, however, does the animation contribute to the experience, or detract from the content?

An animation that illustrates, for instance, different views of your product, or the ease with which it can be used, has more commercial value than gaily colored little fuzzy bears dancing across the bottom of the screen. While less charming, the

FIGURE
17.2 **The Three Fundamentals of Web Page Design**

1.  Keep *it* Simple

2. Don't Over-load The Screen

3.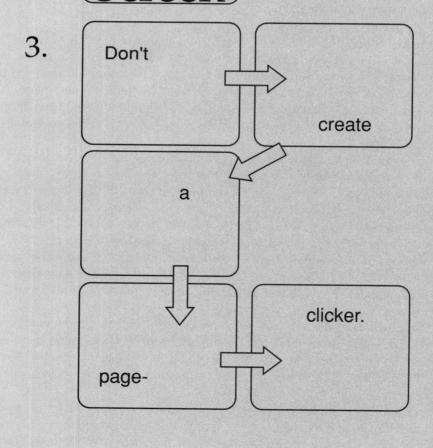

Don't create a page- clicker.

product-views graphic takes up memory space for a reason. The bears, while cuter than concrete, do not serve an objectively useful function for consumers. Sometimes, the bears just have to go.

Efficiency. Remember that sometimes (particularly in Web-based marketing) enough is enough. Despite the high-tech whizzbang of the delivery system, you are still engaged in delivering information. Make the delivery as efficient as if you were doing it in a newspaper, magazine, or catalog. The fact that customers are empowered to access that content in a more-or-less free manner is immaterial. Think of your Web site as a dictionary. Even though a user rarely reads a dictionary from front to back, it would be much more difficult to use efficiently if the publisher decided to order it in a way other than alphabetically; say, in the order in which some editor most frequently looks for words. Don't overanticipate how customers will want to access the information.

Interactivity

This is a popular word, and much bigger than its six syllables suggest. It also gets thrown around a lot these days, applied to topics from books and software to voicemail systems, so we ought to pause for a moment and consider what it means in a Web-based context. Webster's tells us that *interactive* means "mutually or reciprocally active," or "of, relating to, or being a two-way electronic communication system that involves a user's orders or responses." Nice, but limited. Let's look a little further in the same source. The prefix *inter* means "between or among." The adjective *active* means, among other things, "productive of action." Put them together this way, and you have a new definition of *interactive* for our Web-based context:

> **in•ter•ac•tive** *adj* (1998): that which is productive of action between or among users

Note that this new definition is broad enough to encompass the Webster's definition, which is limited to two-way interaction between user and machine, as well as more complex levels of communication. The point is, interactive is an active word, one that requires both an actor and a thing acted upon. More importantly, the "thing acted upon" must be an actor, too.

That is, *interactive* does not mean typing in an order for a bestselling novel and sending it to Amazon.com with a mouse click. Interactive means submitting your order and getting back a confirmation message, or a request for more information that demonstrates that the information you've sent has been received, analyzed, and questioned.

Remember how the Internet experience can be compared to the hunting habits of various birds? Here's a more urban metaphor: Interactivity is *not* a two-way street: it's a narrow one-way street with two big cars headed directly toward each other at high speeds from opposite ends. The point is, interactivity requires contact: cause and effect, action and result, decision and consequence. Anything less than interactive is called a page-clicker, and simply means that the user is scrolling down through your on-screen text just like they would a book. That's a tremendous waste of a resource's potential.

Something for Nothing

For businesses engaged in e-commerce, the hard truth is that surfing consumers want value, and they want something for nothing. If you want to keep customers coming back to your site, you're going to have to keep it vibrant, active, and changing. Promise monthly product updates, downloadable coupons (if you don't do online ordering; periodic electronic discounts if you do), online newsletters with useful information, and updated links to other sites of interest (but not competitors!)—anything that your customers perceive as having value and being free will get them to "bookmark" your site on their computers and come back regularly. When you set up an Internet presence, you're almost going into the entertainment business along with whatever business you're really in. Entertain your customers with information, and they'll keep coming back.

 URLinks
http://www.homeofficemag.com/page.hts?N=6475&Ad=S
http://microsoft.com/magazine/guides/internet/history.htm
http://www.icat.com/mall

A FINAL WORD

Just as the Web-based customer should be able to enter your information flow at any point, depending on his or her needs, the user should be able to select the level of information. Your online marketing or sales effort must have depth. That is, users should be able to pick up just the essentials necessary for making a quick buying decision, delve deeper into a specific subject area, or totally immerse themselves in the minute details of your product or service. For the business, this means that Web-based sales and marketing will contain much more information than a catalog or other printed medium. Up-front development work on a Web site is intense, and the greater content depth required creates more work.

But remember, just because your product or service is offered on the Internet, its fundamental character doesn't change. This is a product or service like any other; only the medium of exchange is different. Like so many other technological wonders that promised the elimination of the marketplace as we know it, the Information Superhighway is just another road for entrepreneurs to drive on: that is, to market, promote, and sell their products and services.

CASE STUDY
THE OLDE-FASHIONED SWEET SHOPPE

▾▾▾▾▾▾

For some time, Janet and several of her closest friends had talked about going into a small business that would produce additional income with the possibility of growing into a chain of stores. However, they were not sure what type of business they should enter, nor where to get the capital to start it. They figured that between the four of them they could split the working hours so they would not have to hire outside employees.

Finally, Janet called her friends together and said, "I have a terrific idea that I think will make money." Her friends were fascinated when Janet told them she had surveyed the entire area, and that there was not one candy store in the entire town. She felt that if they started a sweet shop like those of years ago that sold homemade cookies and candy they could make money. A quality product and nostalgia would combine into a profitable venture.

The idea sounded ideal to her friends. To begin with, Beth made delicious candy, a skill she learned from her mother. Beth felt she could teach everyone how to make candy within a few weeks so they all could eventually pitch in with the candy making. Janet was famous in the neighborhood for her amazing cookies, delicacies that were both beautiful and delicious.

Sherry and Tracy said they would look for an appropriate location in the area. Tracy was a real estate agent and felt she could be very helpful in that direction. Sherry worked for a plastics firm in the purchasing department, so she offered to contact all the vendors who sold the basic materials needed to make candy and the other items they expected to produce. Sherry also offered to contact all the ice cream companies, including some of the bigger ones in the state, to see if they would sell to them wholesale. Janet offered to calculate all the finances and work on the marketing package since she had some experience in that field.

Beth and Janet had given Sherry a list of all the ingredients needed for making cookies and candy, and Sherry reported that she had numerous vendors eagerly lined up to do business. She could not get any of them to buy the machinery to make the candy, but Sherry had found some used equipment with a six-month guarantee that they could purchase for $3,500. The price included all the other pieces of equipment and utensils needed to make the candy. They could also get a discount on ovens and other bakery equipment. Sherry brought up the point that two of the major costs would be shopping bags with the shop's name printed on them and containers for the candy and cookies.

Janet estimated that $35,000 was needed to get started in the business. This would cover start-up fees, equipment, furniture and fixtures, signs, uniforms, deposits for utilities, and telephones. Janet also included money for materials and supplies to get the business started. In addition, Janet set aside $5,000 for a one-month advertising campaign to start the business with a bang. The campaign would include some local television spots she had obtained through her friends who were willing to give her special rates on time slots that were not already sold. While these might be 10- or 20-second spots for as little as $30 per spot, they almost certainly would not be prime-time slots. However, Janet felt it was a terrific idea because it would give them exposure. She intended to make up her own television commercials in the TV studio featuring each one of the owners doing something that would get everyone's attention. They decided to call the candy "Beth's Olde-Fashioned Candy" and Janet agreed to design a box that would really be a stand-out. ▾

CASE STUDY ROUNDTABLE

▼▼▼▼▼▼

Janet: Last night I was up to my knees in paperwork, and my daughter (who works at one of those new high-tech companies) calls me on the phone and says, "Mom, you should have a Web site!" She's all excited about it—how it could look like an old-fashioned needlepoint sampler, and have audio files of old player piano music. I think that's great, but I can't help wondering: *why*?

Discussion Points

- The big question is, what would The Olde-Fashioned Sweet Shoppe gain from a Web site?
- Are there potential dangers to this business in going online? What are they, and can they be dealt with?
- Using the Web design template that follows, design a prototype Web site for The Olde-Fashioned Sweet Shoppe. What would it look like? What features would it include? What would be its function?
- As an alternative, select any of the other case studies covered in this book and design a Web site for them. Answer the other questions for this case study with regard to the one you choose.

PERSONAL WORKSHOP 34
Assessing Web Site Design Vendor Services and Web Design
▼▼▼▼▼▼

▼ Use this worksheet to evaluate the services offered by competing Web site designers. The results should help you make a sound, objective decision based on standard criteria of service type, quality, and price. You can access thousands of Web site designers and other Internet service providers by using the World Wide Web itself.

Vendor:_____

	Service	Yes	No	Price	Details
B	Home page design				
	Image scanning 1 2 3 4 No limit				
A	Cost per additional images				
	Site registration				
S	Link to search engine				

CONTINUED ▶

	Service	Yes	No	Price	Details
	Metatagging				
I	Icon design				
	Logo design				
C	Domain name registration (InterNIC)				
	Additional Web pages ($ per page)				
	Site hosting				
	Look-and-feel design				
	Hit counter				
F	Scrolling marquee				
E	Guest book				
A	Separate company profile page				
T	Separate contacts/clients page				
U	Separate links page				
R	Address book				
E	Online help				
S	❏ e-mail ❏ memo ❏ fax				
	Updates				
C					
O	Catalog				
M	Interactive customer demographics form				
M	Clickable product/service images				
E	Online ordering				
R	Secure transactions				
C	Customer history database				
E					

CONTINUED ▶

Web Design Template

▼ Use these forms to help you organize your Web site plan. If you intend to build your site yourself, this will be a good start toward a blueprint. If you plan to have your site professionally designed and managed, these templates will help your vendor serve you more efficiently.

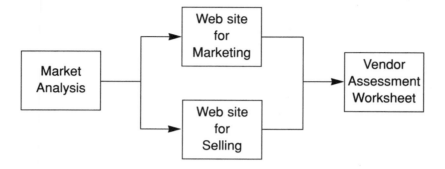

Web Site for Marketing

1.	What are the *3 **most important things*** people need to know about my business? (SCREEN ONE)
	①
	②
	③
2.	Of ***those three items***, what is the ***single most important thing?*** Why?

3.	Do I want to use ***images***? ❏ Yes ❏ No	
	Describe each image:	***Why*** do I want to use it?
	Image 1	
	Image 2	
	Image 3	
	Image 4	
4.	What is my ***something-for-nothing*** value-adding lure?	

CONTINUED ▶

Web Site for Marketing

5.	Do I want to provide *links* to other sites? ☐ Yes ☐ No To which sites?

6.	Map the *structure* of your site. Identify page topics and show links among pages.

Home				

7.	What is the overall *look and feel* of my Web site? (*Check all descriptive words that apply*) ☐ Formal ☐ Playful ☐ Businesslike ☐ Friendly ☐ Authoritative ☐ Casual ☐ Enthusiastic ☐ Objective ☐ Funny

8.	List the *search terms* that potential customers might use when searching for your product or service.

9.	Can customers *e-mail* me? ☐ Yes ☐ No

10.	Other *special features* or content:

CONTINUED ▶

Web Site for Selling

(Use the *Marketing* form, and then complete the following additional items:)							
		Yes	No			Yes	No
11.	Catalog?			12.	Online ordering?		
13.	Illustrations?			14.	Mail-in order form printout?		
15.	Text descriptions?			16.	Confirmation e-mail?		
17.	Price list?			18.	Secure credit card transaction?		
19.	Phone help?			20.	Calculate ❑ Sales tax ❑ Discount ❑ Exchange rate?		
21.	Other						

CHAPTER BRIEFCASE

- The Internet can be defined as a *network* of networks; a *community* of people who use and develop those networks; and a *collection* of resources that can be reached through those networks.

- There are, at latest estimate, more than 320 million different Web pages available to tireless surfers. Today, there are 1.5 million new Web pages created every day, 65,000 every hour.

- **E-commerce** (the shorthand, high-tech way of saying commercial transactions handled over the Internet) is one of the hottest growing areas of Internet use, and one of the hottest growing markets of any kind, anywhere.

- A successful business Web site incorporates four basic characteristics: (1) a business strategy, (2) market analysis, (3) an appealing page design, and (4) a secure method for conducting transactions.

- Interactivity is key to effective Web-based marketing. Commercial Web sites also have to be updated, revised, and kept current and provide customers with valuable information and tips—essentially, to give them something for nothing.

- Three keys to effective Web site design: (1) keep it simple, (2) don't overload the screen, and (3) don't create a page-clicker. Keep your customers' needs in mind, and work within the capabilities and limitations of the medium.

Adapted with permission from *Small Business 2000*, the series on public television.

SMALL BUSINESS LEGAL ISSUES

Albert Black (Dallas, Texas)
On Target Supplies and Logistics

"*I* think my purpose is to build a business and to do those things... hire people, improve infrastructure, pay taxes, provide leadership, and get rich along the way.

I think my mother is a driver. She expected nothing but the best. She is an elitist in her own right. And she didn't think that she should expect anything but the best from her children, and that drives the way we run On Target Supplies and Logistics now.

I think we had to speak correctly. We had to walk correctly. We had to have good posture. We had to be clean. We had to make the best grades in school. We had to look at ourselves as champions of whatever cause we're part of. We lived in the ghetto, but my mother wouldn't permit us to think that way. She used to say, 'You may live in the ghetto, but you're not ghetto material. And I don't—I won't—stand for you acting that way.'

My character, whatever character that I may be able to have, was formed by my grandmother. To treat people with passion...to always look out, as she would say, for the other fella; to do what you say you're gonna do; to take care of others before you take care of yourself; to tell the truth; to love and expect to be loved; to put God first, your family second, and everything else somewhere after that. "

Chapter 18

FORMS OF ORGANIZATION

▼▼▼▼▼▼

Corporations cannot commit treason, nor be outlawed nor excommunicated, for they have no souls.

—*Sir Edward Coke (1549-1634) Case of Sutton's Hospital*

MISSION STATEMENT

In this chapter, you will

*L*EARN about the various forms of legal organization available to your business, and their requirements, structures, and relevant tax issues.

*E*XPLORE the differences, advantages, and disadvantages of each form.

*A*PPLY your understanding to a case study.

*P*RODUCE personal evaluations that will help you decide how to organize your business.

KEY TERMS

articles of incorporation	liability	partnership
corporation	limited partnership	S corporation
dual taxation	limited liability	sole
general partnership	company (LLC)	proprietorship

INTRODUCTION TO CHOOSING A BUSINESS STRUCTURE

One of the most important decisions you will make is how to structure your business. There are advantages and disadvantages of each form of organization. The type of legal format you choose will depend on the following factors:

- *The size of risk.* Look at the owner's liability for debts and taxes under each structure. How much liability are you willing to assume? How would you want your earnings to be taxed?
- *The continuity of the business.* If something should unexpectedly happen to you, what would happen to your business?
- *Your access to capital.* How much money will you need to develop and run your business? Where will you get this money?
- *Your skills.* What is your business experience? What are the skills and abilities you bring to the company?
- *Your purpose for starting a business.* What is your ultimate goal? What are the possibilities for business growth?
- *Your state's law.* What kinds of business organizations are legal in your state? Some states do not recognize limited liability companies; others impose very strict requirements on new incorporations.

There are basically four different ways to organize your business: (1) sole proprietorship, (2) partnership, (3) corporation, and (4) limited liability company. In this chapter, we'll examine each of them in some detail. The legal structure you choose will be a major factor in determining how much paperwork you will have to do, how much personal liability you will incur, how you will be able to raise money, and how your business will be taxed.

DOING BUSINESS AS A SOLE PROPRIETORSHIP

This is the easiest, least expensive, and least regulated business legal structure available to start-up entrepreneurs. A sole proprietorship is owned and operated by one person, although it may have employees. The sole proprietorship is the most common form of business and comprises 70 percent of all American business entities. Many who are just starting a business choose this form until it becomes practical to enter into a partnership or to incorporate. Let's consider some of the advantages and disadvantages of doing business as a sole proprietorship (see Figure 18.1).

Advantages

Easy to establish. There are fewer legal restrictions associated with forming a sole proprietorship than any other business structure. While regulations vary by state, a sole proprietorship can generally be established by registering the company's name (filing a DBA) and by obtaining a business license.

Inexpensive to set up. Just as there are fewer legal restrictions on setting up a sole proprietorship, it's also the least expensive to establish. Costs vary according to the city in which the business is formed, but usually include a license fee and possibly a business tax.

Simple tax treatment. Businesses that are sole proprietorships are taxed as individuals. (The significance of this treatment will become more obvious as we explore the tax ramifications of other structures.) As the sole owner, your business profit and loss is recorded on your Form 1040, Schedule C. The bottom line amount is transferred to your personal tax form. (You will also file Schedule SE, which is your contribution to Social Security.)

Control. The sole proprietor has total control, and is not answerable to any board or group of stockholders. The business is owned and operated by one person. All decision-making is vested in the owner, who has complete responsibility.

Disadvantages

Unlimited personal liability. The owner is responsible for the full amount of business debt, which may exceed his or her initial investment. This liability extends to all assets, including the owner's home and vehicles.

Less available capital. Funding for the venture must come from the proprietor, who may find obtaining long-term financing difficult.

Limited growth potential. The future of the company is dependent upon the owner's capabilities, knowledge, drive, and financial potential. With only one person involved in the creative decision-making, opportunities for growth may be missed.

Heavy responsibility. The owner is the person ultimately responsible for the success or failure of the business. There are no requisitions to central supply when he or she runs out of envelopes. The owner alone is responsible for the purchase of supplies, equipment, advertising, and insurance, as well as handling employee issues, marketing, bill paying, and customer relations.

Death, illness, or injury can endanger the business. The business ceases to exist as a legal entity upon the death of the owner. Of course, that's not a problem for the owner, but it may be awkward for employees and customers. More difficult for the owner (in a day-to-day operations sense) is his or her own illness or injury. With no partners to pick up the slack, a sole proprietor's long-term illness can permanently disable even a thriving business.

FIRST PERSON

Lily B., San Francisco, California: What's the biggest advantage of being a sole proprietor? I don't care what anyone says, the biggest advantage is that *I keep all the profits*! It's great: I take all the risk, I do all the work, and I get all the money. No partners, no shareholders, no investors, no sharing. It's only fair. Of course, there's the flip side of that, which is I also get to deal with all the losses and the liabilities, too. That just means I'm really motivated to minimize those.

&TAXES
Sole Proprietorship

If you are a sole proprietor, there is no tax effect if you take money to or from your business, or transfer money to or from your business. You should, however, set up a drawing account to keep track of amounts that are for personal use and not for business expenses.

PERSONAL WORKSHOP 35
Should You Be a Sole Proprietor?
▼ ▼ ▼ ▼ ▼ ▼

	Agree	Disagree
Limiting tax liability is NOT a central focus of my business life.		
Product liability and personal injury issues are NOT a factor for my business.		
I have adequate financial resources to fund my new business.		
I don't want to spend much of my start-up money on lawyers.		
I don't want to deal with a lot of legal paperwork.		
I'm most happy when I'm in control of every detail of a project.		
I'm a detail-oriented person.		
I'm equally comfortable with day-to-day operations and big picture issues.		
I'm NOT interested in setting up a business that will go on after I die.		

If you agreed with all of these statements, you should definitely consider the sole proprietorship business structure. If you disagreed with more than three of them, you might be more comfortable with some other form of doing business.

FIGURE 18.1   Advantages and Disadvantages of a Sole Proprietorship

Advantages	Disadvantages
Easy to form	Unlimited personal liability
Sole owner	Less available capital
Least expensive	Limited growth potential
Taxed as an individual	Heavy responsibility
Have total control	Death, illness, or injury can end the business

Filing: Sole proprietors file their taxes using **Schedule C (Form 1040),** "Profit or (Loss) from Business or Profession."

File Schedule C with your Form 1040 and report the amount of net profit or (loss) from Schedule C on your 1040. If you operate more than one business as a sole proprietor, you prepare a separate Schedule C for each business.

If you are a sole proprietor, you may have to make **estimated tax** payments if the total of your estimated income tax and self-employment tax for the year exceeds your total withholding and credits by specified amounts. Form **1040-ES** is used to estimate your tax. It includes four vouchers, filed on April 15th, June 15th, September 15th, and January 15th. (Notice that there are only two months between the second and third payments and four months between the third and fourth payments.) Your estimated tax payments include both federal income tax and self-employment tax liabilities.

Sole proprietors file **self-employment tax** on **Schedule SE (Form 1040),** "Computation of Social Security Self-Employment Tax." The self-employment tax is a Social Security and Medicare tax for individuals who work for themselves. Social Security benefits are available to the self-employed individual just as they are to wage earners. Your payments of self-employment tax contribute to your coverage under the Social Security system. This is one of the downsides, or "anti-benefits" of entrepreneurship: when you work for someone else, a portion of your Social Security taxes are paid by your employer. The same is true for the self-employed; the only difference is, you are your own employer.

You do not have to carry on regular full-time business activities to be self-employed. Part-time work, including work you do on the side in addition to your regular job, may also be self-employment. Complete Personal Workshop 35 to determine if sole proprietorship is a good decision for your business.

Your Government at Work:

Publication 334, Tax Guide for Small Business.

Taxpayer Education Coordinator: 800-829-1040

http://www.irs.ustreas.gov/prod/bus_info/index.html

http://www.irs.ustreas.gov/prod/cover.html

http://www.irs.ustreas.gov/prod/tax_edu/teletax/tc408.html

http://www.irs.ustreas.gov/prod/tax_edu/teletax/tc306.html

http://www.irs.ustreas.gov/prod/tax_edu/teletax/tc554.html

FIRST PERSON

Carla S., Salt Lake City, Utah: I used to work for the IRS, and I can tell you that one of the main things that most small businesses mess up on most are the quarterly filing requirements. Even if you are a sole proprietorship filing on a Schedule C as part of your personal 1040, you will probably be subject to quarterly filing requirements, and to get behind on your quarterly payments can cost you big money in state and federal penalties.

DOING BUSINESS AS A PARTNERSHIP

A partnership is an association of two or more people who carry on a business for profit as co-owners. That is, a partnership is a legal business relationship in which ownership and management of a business is shared between or among the partners.

Often, people choose to go into partnership to compensate for each individual's inadequate expertise in a particular area of a business, or because two experts are often better than one. Sometimes, sharing ownership of a business may also be a way to gain more start-up money by sharing responsibility in exchange for a bigger infusion of working capital. Figure 18.2 lists the advantages and disadvantages of a partnership.

FIRST PERSON

"Bud" Q., Albuquerque, New Mexico: I think a business partnership is more than just an arm's length legal relationship: it's a lot like a marriage in many ways—I find that I spend more time with my partners than with my wife sometimes! Anyway, just like a marriage, you have people with different personalities, different interests, and different personal values and you tie them together in a legal thing. It can lead to real growth and opportunity and, I admit it, fun. Or it can result in these incredible conflicts that tear the business apart. So I'd say, before you go into business with someone else, you should both carefully think through the advantages and disadvantages involved. Don't go into it all fuzzy-headed with big romantic dreams about making a million. Go in with your eyes open and your head screwed on straight. Those are the partnerships that last. Marriages, too, I think.

Advantages

Ease of formation. The legal requirements and expenses are fewer than those involved with forming a corporation. While regulations vary by state, a partnership can generally be established by registering the company's name (filing a DBA) and by obtaining a business license.

Shared responsibility. Two or more heads are better than one! By sharing in the profits, partners are motivated to succeed. This form of legal structure allows for distribution of the work load and sharing of ideas, skills, and responsibilities.

Increased growth potential. A partnership makes it possible to obtain more capital and tap into more skills.

Ease of operation. The partnership has more freedom from government control and special taxation than the corporation.

Disadvantages

Unlimited personal liability. Owners are *personally responsible* for the business debt. A partnership is not a separate legal entity, even though its income is reported on a separate informational tax return. Profits must be included on each partner's individual tax return according to their percentage of interest in the business.

Lack of continuity. Like the sole proprietorship, the partnership terminates upon the death or the withdrawal of a general partner, unless the partnership agreement provides otherwise. Death, withdrawal, or bankruptcy of one partner endangers the entire business.

Relative difficulty in obtaining large sums of capital. While the opportunity for getting long-term financing is greater in a partnership (a lender might be more comfortable with two people taking responsibility for the debt), it is still dependent upon review of each individual partner's assets.

Difficulty in disposing of the partnership interest. The terms and procedures for buying out of a partnership or sale to another party must be spelled out in the partnership agreement.

Distribution of responsibility in bankruptcy. In case of bankruptcy, the partner with more personal assets will lose more.

Partner's responsibility. Each general partner can act on behalf of the company in conducting business. Each partner represents the company and can individually hire employees, borrow money, and operate the business. Choose someone you trust; you will be bound by each other's decisions.

Profits. Profits are shared among the partners according to the terms set out in the partnership agreement.

Taxation. Profits and losses are passed directly through the partnership to each partner, each of whose individual tax situation determines his or her tax consequences.

FIGURE 18.2 Advantages and Disadvantages of a Partnership	
Advantages	**Disadvantages**
Easy to form	Unlimited personal liability
Shared responsibility	Death, illness, or injury can endanger the business
Increased growth potential	Somewhat difficult to obtain large sums of capital
Ease of operation	Difficulty in changing the partnership interest
Hands-on control possible	Distribution of assets in bankruptcy
	Both partners can take action
	No tax benefits
	Profits are shared

PERSONAL WORKSHOP 36
Should You Be in a Partnership?
▼▼▼▼▼▼

	Agree	Disagree
Limiting tax liability is NOT a central focus of my business life.		
Product liability and personal injury issues are NOT a factor for my business.		
My potential partner has strengths and competencies I lack.		
I have always worked well in a team or cooperative environment.		
I am able to share authority and control with others.		
I am NOT especially concerned about the business going on after my death.		
My partner and I will have adequate financial resources to fund operations.		
I am comfortable sharing details of my finances with a partner.		
I'm comfortable with sharing profits—and losses—with a partner.		

If you agreed with all of these statements, you should consider the partnership form of business organization. If you disagreed with three or more of them, another structure may be better for you.

Limited Partnerships

Partnerships are defined by how active a role the partners play in the business. In a general partnership, all the partners participate in the operation and management of the business and share full liability for business losses and obligations. General partnerships are dissolved and must be reorganized if one partner dies, withdraws, or goes bankrupt.

A limited partnership, on the other hand, consists of one or more general partners as well as limited partners. The business is run by the general partner or partners. The limited partners are not legally permitted to participate, and each can be held liable for business losses only to the extent of his or her investment. The limited partnership is a popular method of organizing investors, because it permits investors with small amounts of capital to participate in large or elaborate projects with minimal personal risk. In a limited partnership, the partnership agreement may provide for the continuation of the organization following the death or withdrawal of one of the partners.

Limited partnerships are often used as a way of raising capital. A general partner can take on limited partners as a means of raising cash without involving outside investors in the management of the business. A limited partnership is more expensive to create, involves extensive paperwork, and is used mainly for companies that invest in real estate or speculative ventures.

Partnership Agreements

A partnership agreement is a contract that states how you want your business relationship to work. The Uniform Partnership Act (UPA) is a body of law that establishes the basic legal rules applicable to partnerships. It has been adopted in all states (except Louisiana). But the UPA does not dictate the content of your agreement: its rules can be changed by provisions of your partnership agreement. Unless the agreement itself specifies a different date, a written agreement is effective when it is signed.

Do not underestimate the need for a partnership agreement. Many friendships and good working relationships have ended over business disagreements. When financial considerations enter the picture, friendships are often put aside. Carefully prepare your partnership agreement (have an attorney help you) and have it properly notarized. It will serve as the guideline for your working relationship with your partners. It will outline the financial, managerial, and material contributions of the partners into the business and delineate the roles of the partners in the business relationship.

The following subjects should be covered in a partnership agreement:

- The *purpose* of the partnership business
- The *terms* of the partnership
- The *goals* of the partners and the partnership
- The *financial contributions* made by each partner for start-up and throughout the lifetime of the business
- The *distribution* of profits and losses
- The *withdrawal* of contributed assets or capital by a partner
- The *management* powers and work responsibilities of each partner
- Procedures for admitting *new partners*
- Procedures for *expelling* a partner
- Provisions for *continuing* the business in the event of a partner's death, illness, disability, or resignation
- Provision for determining the *value* of a departing partner's interest and how that interest will be compensated
- The methods of *settling disputes* through mediation or arbitration
- The *duration* of the agreement
- The terms of *dissolution* of the business

&TAXES
Partnership

A *partnership* is the relationship between two or more persons who join together to carry on a trade or business with each person contributing money, property, labor, or skill, and each expecting to share in the profits and losses of the business.

Filing: Every partnership doing business in or having income from sources within the United States is required to file **Form 1065** for its tax year. This is mainly an information return. *Partnership profits are not taxed to the partnership.* Each partner must take into account his or her distributive share of partnership items and report it on his or her own income tax return (whether distributed or not).

Tax is not withheld on partnership distributions and partners may have to make estimated tax payments. A partner's distributive share of income is usually included in figuring net earnings from self-employment. **IRS Form 1040-ES** is used to estimate your tax. It includes four vouchers, filed on April 15th, June 15th, September 15th, and January 15th.

Schedules K and K-1 (Form 1065) are used to show partners' distributive shares of reportable partnership items. Form 1065 and its Schedules K or K-1 are filed separately and not attached to your income tax return.

Schedule E (Form 1040), "Supplemental Income Schedule, Part II," is used to report partnership items on your individual tax return. Failure to treat your individual and partnership returns consistently will allow the IRS to assess and take action to collect deficiencies and penalties.

Partners in a partnership file self-employment tax on **Schedule SE (Form 1040)**, "Computation of Social Security Self-Employment Tax." The self-employment tax is a Social Security and Medicare tax for individuals who work for themselves. Social Security benefits are available to the self-employed individual just as they are to wage earners. Your payments of self-employment tax contribute to your coverage under the Social Security system. This is one of the "anti-benefits" of being an entrepreneur: when you work for someone else, a portion of your Social Security taxes are paid by your employer. The same is true for the self-employed: the only difference is, you are your own employer.

You do not have to carry on regular full-time business activities to be considered self-employed for tax purposes. Part-time work, including work you do on the side in addition to your regular job, may also be self-employment.

Your Government at Work:

Publication 334, Tax Guide for Small Business.
Taxpayer Education Coordinator: 800-829-1040
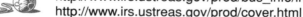
http://www.irs.ustreas.gov/prod/bus_info/index.html
http://www.irs.ustreas.gov/prod/cover.html
http://www.irs.ustreas.gov/prod/forms_pubs/pubs/p54114.htm
http://www.irs.ustreas.gov/prod/tax_edu/teletax/tc554.html

DOING BUSINESS AS A CORPORATION

The corporate form of business organization is the most complex and highly regulated of all the various business structures. A corporation is a distinct legal entity, separate from the individuals who own it. In legal terms, it is an "artificial person," created under the laws of the state from which it received its charter. A corporation is managed and operated by its board of directors. The charter establishes the corporation's powers, including the limits of its permissible operations and its ability to buy and sell property. Individuals participate, or invest, in a corporation by purchasing stock. Each shareholder's liability for the corporation's losses is usually limited to the amount of his or her investment. As a legal entity, a corporation continues to exist independently of the presence or absence of any individual director. A corporation exists until it is formally dissolved in accordance with the terms of its charter.

There are many advantages to the corporate form of business, which is probably why there are so many corporations. One of the main disadvantages, however, is that profits are subject to double taxation: as a person (in the eyes of the law), a corporation must file an income tax return and pay tax on its profits (even artificial people can't escape taxes!). The remaining profits are passed on to the shareholders as dividends.

The investors in turn pay tax on the dividends as individual income. Figure 18.3 lists the advantages and disadvantages of a corporation.

Advantages

There are several distinct advantages to incorporation, including:

- Ownership is readily transferable. The corporation does not cease to exist with the death of an individual director.
- Increased options for growth and fundraising. A corporation has access to numerous investors and can raise substantial capital through the sale of stock.
- The corporation is a separate legal entity. It is responsible and liable for all debts. The shareholders are liable only for the amount they have invested. A corporation has an existence apart from the people who own it.
- Authority can be delegated. The corporation has the ability to draw on the expertise and skills of more than one individual.

Disadvantages

However, there are certain disadvantages to the corporate form. These include:

- Extensive government regulations. Corporations are complex to manage and are highly regulated.
- Burdensome local, state, and federal reports must be filed and regular stockholder meetings must be held.
- Expensive to form and maintain. The fees for setting up a corporate structure, the costs of stockholders' meetings, and the expense for legal fees and paperwork are some of the costs unique to the corporation.
- Increased tax load. Income tax is paid on the corporate net income (profit) and on individual salaries and dividends. This is referred to as **dual taxation**.

Because of the complexity of the corporation, you may wish to consult an attorney regarding its formation. Whether you choose to form the corporation on your own or with legal help, you will have to consider the following items in order to be knowledgeable and prepared.

Articles of Incorporation

The preparation of articles of incorporation (also referred to as a certificate of incorporation in some states) is generally the first step to incorporating. Many states have a standard certificate of incorporation form that may be used by small businesses. Copies may be obtained from the state official who grants charters or from larger stationers or office suppliers. The following information is usually required:

- **Corporate name:** The name chosen must not be *similar* to any other corporation authorized to do business in the state. The name must not be *deceptive* so as to mislead the public. To be certain that the name you select is suitable, check the name availability through the designated state official in each state in which you intend to do business before drawing up the certificate of incorporation.

- **Purpose** for which the corporation is formed. Purposes should be broad enough to allow for expansion and specific enough to give a clear idea of the business to be performed.
- **Length of time** for which the corporation will exist. The term may cover a number of years or be *perpetual*, again, depending on state law.
- Names and addresses of **incorporators**. In some areas, at least one or more of the incorporators is required to be a resident of the state in which the corporation is being organized.
- Location of the **registered office** of the corporation in the state of incorporation. If you decide to obtain your charter from another state, you will be required to have an office there. You may appoint an agent in that state to act for you.
- Proposed **capital structure**. The maximum amount and type of capital stock your corporation wishes authorization to issue. State the amount of capital required at the time of incorporation.
- **Management**. Provisions for the regulation of the corporation's internal affairs.
- **Director**. The name and address of the person who will serve as the director until the first meeting of the stockholders.

The charter will be issued when and if the designated state official determines that the corporate name is available, the certificate has been completely and properly executed, and there has been no violation of state law.

In order to complete the incorporation process, the stockholders must meet. They must elect a board of directors and adopt bylaws. The board of directors will in turn elect the officers who will actually have charge of operating the corporation. Usually, the officers include a president, a secretary, and a treasurer. In small corporations, the members of the board of directors are frequently elected as officers of the corporation.

Bylaws

The bylaws of the corporation may repeat some of the provisions of the charter and usually cover such items as:

- The location of the principal office and other offices
- The time, location, and notice of shareholder meetings
- Number of directors, their compensation, terms of office, method of election, and the filling of vacancies
- The time and location of director's meetings
- Quorum and voting methods
- Issuance and form of stock certificates
- Methods of selecting officers and designating their titles, duties, terms of office, and salaries
- Method of paying dividends
- Decisions regarding the fiscal year
- Procedure for amending the bylaws

> FIGURE
> 18.3   **Advantages and Disadvantages of a Corporation**
>
> | **Advantages** | **Disadvantages** |
> |---|---|
> | Ownership readily transferable | Extensive government regulations |
> | Corporation exists after the death of an individual director | Burdensome local, state, and federal reports |
> | Better options for growth and raising capital | Increased tax load |
> | A separate legal entity, liable for all debts | Expensive to form and maintain |
> | Authority can be delegated | |

In general, the cost and complexity of the corporate legal structure make it an unrealistic option for many small businesses.

&TAXES
Corporation

Forming a ***corporation*** involves a transfer of either money, property, or both, by the prospective shareholders in exchange for capital stock in the corporation. Every corporation, unless it is specifically exempt or has dissolved, must file a tax return even if it has no taxable income for the year and regardless of the amount of its gross income. Corporate profits normally are taxed to the corporation. When the profits are distributed as dividends, the dividends are then taxed to the shareholders.

Filing: The income tax return for ordinary corporations (that is, corporations formed under Subchapter C of the Internal Revenue Code, or C Corporations) is **Form 1120**. Form **1120-A** is for companies having gross receipts, total income, and total assets that total less than $500,000. In addition there are other requirements that must be met. Corporation returns are due on March 15th. A corporation using a fiscal year not beginning January 1st and ending December 31st will have to file the return on or before the 15th day of the third month following the close of its fiscal year.

Every corporation whose tax is expected to be $500 or more must make estimated tax payments. If a corporation's estimated tax is $500 or more, its estimated tax payments are deposited with an authorized financial institution or Federal Reserve bank. Each deposit must be accompanied by **Form 8109**. (Some deposits may now be made through electronic funds transfer technology.) A corporation's estimated tax is the amount of its expected tax liability (including alternative minimum tax and environmental tax) less its allowable tax credits. Amounts of estimated tax should be refigured each quarter and amended to reflect changes.

A corporation that fails to pay in full a correct installment of estimated tax by the due date is generally subject to a penalty. The penalty is figured at a rate of interest published quarterly by the IRS in the *Internal Revenue Bulletin*.

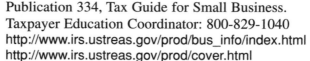

Your Government at Work:
Publication 334, Tax Guide for Small Business.
Taxpayer Education Coordinator: 800-829-1040
http://www.irs.ustreas.gov/prod/bus_info/index.html
http://www.irs.ustreas.gov/prod/cover.html

S CORPORATION

An alternative form of business ownership that provides the benefits of a corporation as a legal entity but avoids double taxation is known as an **S corporation** (in reference to *Subchapter S* of the Internal Revenue Code). An S corporation is really a special *type* of corporation recognized by the IRS: it is a creation of the tax code. To set up an S corporation, it is necessary to first create a standard corporation (a C corporation, discussed previously). Then file an election with the IRS, claiming tax treatment as a corporation. If your corporation meets the requirements of Subchapter S, it is transformed into an S corporation.

In an S corporation, only that portion of the corporation's profits that are passed to the shareholders are taxed. The S corporation's own profits are not taxed. However, S corporations are subject to strict requirements regulating their structure, membership, and operation (see Figure 18.4). If the IRS determines that an S corporation has failed to comply with these detailed rules, the entity will be redefined as some other form of business organization, and its favorable tax treatment will be lost. S corporation status allows the small business corporation to have its income taxed to the shareholders as if the corporation were a partnership. It must, however, meet the following requirements:

- It must have 75 or fewer shareholders, all of whom are individuals or estates (corporations or partnerships cannot be shareholders in a valid S corporation).
- There can be no nonresident alien shareholders.
- There can be only one class of outstanding stock.
- All shareholders must consent to the election to claim S corporation status.
- A specific portion of the corporation's receipts must be derived from active business rather than passive investments.
- No limit can be placed on the size of the corporation's income and assets.

Talk to your attorney or accountant to determine if this form of legal structure is right for your business.

&TAXES
S Corporation

Definition: Some corporations may elect not to be subject to income tax. If a corporation qualifies and chooses to become an S corporation, its income usually will be taxed only to the shareholders.

The formation of an S corporation is only allowable under certain circumstances. The formation of an S corporation can be an advantageous form of legal structure, but if entered into without careful planning, it can result in more taxes instead of less.

FIGURE 18.4 **Advantages and Disadvantages of a S Corporation**

Advantages	Disadvantages
Avoids double taxation: only that portion of the profits that are passed to shareholders are taxed.	Subject to strict requirements regulating structure, membership, and operation

---

Filing: File **Form 1120S**, U.S. Income Tax Return for an S Corporation. This form is used to file an income tax return for an S corporation. **Schedule K and K-1** are extremely important parts of Form 1120S. Schedule K summarizes the corporation's income, deductions, and credits, reportable by the shareholders. Schedule K-1 shows each shareholder's separate share. The individual shareholders report their income taxes on **Form 1040**. Form 1120S is due on the 15th day of the third month after the end of the tax year.

Shareholders in an S Corporation file self-employment tax on **Schedule SE (Form 1040)**, Computation of Social Security Self-Employment Tax. The self-employment tax is a Social Security and Medicare tax for individuals who work for themselves. Social Security benefits are available to the self-employed individual just as they are to wage earners. Your payments of self-employment tax contribute to your coverage under the Social Security system. This is one of the major downsides of entrepreneurship: when you work for someone else, a portion of your Social Security taxes are paid by your employer. The same is true for the self-employed: the only difference is, you are your own employer. You do not have to carry on regular full-time business activities to be self-employed. Part-time work, including work you do on the side in addition to your regular job, may also be self-employment.

Your Government at Work:

Publication 334, Tax Guide for Small Business.

 Taxpayer Education Coordinator: 800-829-1040

http://www.irs.ustreas.gov/prod/bus_info/index.html

http://www.irs.ustreas.gov/prod/cover.html

http://www.irs.ustreas.gov/prod/tax_edu/teletax/tc554.html

DOING BUSINESS AS A LIMITED LIABILITY COMPANY (LLC)

The **limited liability company (LLC)** is a relatively recent form of business organization. An LLC combines the most attractive features of limited partnerships and corporations. The members of an LLC enjoy the limited liability offered by a corporate form of ownership and the tax advantages of a partnership. In addition, the LLC offers flexible management structures without the complicated requirements of an S corporation election or the restrictions of a limited partnership. This means that all debts, obligations, and liabilities of an LLC will remain the debts, obligations, and liabilities of the LLC and not its members. The structure and methods of establishing a new LLC, or of converting an existing entity to the LLC form, vary from state to state. All United States

states and the District of Columbia recognize limited liability companies as legitimate business organizations.

Although LLCs are created in accordance with state laws, some uniform characteristics apply and generalizations can be made. However, as with forming any type of business entity, you should consult with competent legal counsel to ensure that you form your company in accordance with your state's law.

A limited liability company must consist of two or more members. A member can be an individual, as well as a general partnership, a limited partnership, a domestic or foreign limited liability company, a trust, an estate, an association, a corporation, or any other legal commercial entity.

Another corporate characteristic of an LLC is the ability to centralize management. That is, a core group of people can control the business, either by electing a board of managers or a single manager. Each member has an interest in the LLC equal to each member's contribution to the LLC. The interest represents a member's rights in the LLC, including a share of profits and losses, distributions upon liquidation, and the right to participate in management. Generally, agreement of more than half of the LLC members is required to approve or authorize LLC actions.

There are two types of management forms for an LLC; (1) the member-managed form, and (2) the manager-managed form. In a manager-managed LLC each manager has an equal vote. Generally, in a member-managed LLC, members vote in proportion to their respective interests in the LLC. In a manager-managed LLC, managers oversee the day-to-day operations within the scope of their delegated authority and are agents with the authority to contract on behalf of the LLC in the ordinary course of business. In a member-managed LLC, agency and partnership principles apply, so each member may contract on behalf of the LLC.

Under either management form, a unanimous member vote is usually required in connection with certain extraordinary events, such as the admission of new members and the acceptance of additional contributions by any member. Figure 18.5 lists the advantages and disadvantages of an LLC. Figure 18.6 compares an S corporation to an LLC.

&TAXES

If an LLC is structured correctly, it is taxed as a partnership. This pass-through treatment resembles an S corporation's tax treatment. An S corporation limits the number of shareholders to 75. Unlike an S corporation, an LLC has no limit on the number of members that can hold an interest in the LLC, and owners can include not only individuals but also partnerships, corporations, trusts, or other legal or commercial entities.

Advantages

More liberal loss deductions. The owners of an LLC do not assume liability for the business's debt and any losses can be used as tax deductions against active income. Loss deductions are more limited under an S Corporation than under an LLC.

More stock options. LLCs can offer several different classes of stock with different rights.

FIGURE
18.5

Advantages and Disadvantages of a Limited Liability Company

Advantages	Disadvantages
More liberal loss deductions	Difficulty in business expansion out of state
More stock options	Restrictions on transferring ownership
No restrictions on the number of owners	Different requirements from state to state
	Restriction on type of business

FIGURE
18.6

S Corporation Versus LLC

	Pass-Through Tax Treatment	Limited Liability (Interstate)	Limitation on Number of Shareholders	Limitation on Nature of Shareholders	Limitation on Stock Classes	Taxation of Property Distributions on Liquidation
S Corporation	guaranteed	guaranteed	75	individuals, specified trusts	one class	taxable
LLC	only if correctly structured, otherwise LLC taxed as a corporation	recognized in all 50 states	no limit	no restrictions	may create multiple classes	not taxable

Fewer restrictions on participation. There are no restrictions on the number or type of owners. An unlimited number of individuals, corporations, and/or partnerships may participate in an LLC.

Disadvantages

Transferability restriction test. Ownership interests cannot be transferred to other parties without some restrictions.

Lack of uniform code. In some states, the business is dissolved upon the death, retirement, resignation, or expulsion of an owner. Some states impose a corporate tax on LLCs.

Restriction on type of business. An LLC cannot be used for professional services such as an accountant, attorney, or insurance agent.

Establishing an LLC

To set up an LLC, its management follows a path similar to the formation of a corporation. First, an article of organization and the appropriate filing fees must be submitted to the Secretary of State in the state in which the business is organized. Because states differ in the information required, it is wise to consult an attorney or accountant when the Limited Liability Company form of legal structure is being considered.

CONCLUSION

Keep in mind that your initial choice of a business form doesn't have to be permanent. You can start out as a *sole proprietor*. As your business develops, you may wish to take on *partners*. As the risks of personal liability increase, you may decide to form a *corporation*. If you are unsure about which type of business structure is best for your business, you may wish to consult an attorney who is knowledgeable about the various types of business organization. In any case, it's always a good idea to have an attorney draft your articles, declarations, and other documents, and ensure proper registration of your chosen form of business with the appropriate state agencies.

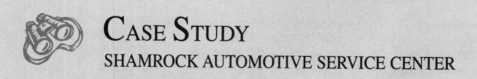

CASE STUDY
SHAMROCK AUTOMOTIVE SERVICE CENTER

*F*or many years, Tom thought about going into business with his friends Matt, Jim, and John. They had grown up together, and each had gone into a different area of the automotive field with a different company. They often talked about pooling their resources and starting an automotive center that would be economical, efficient, and consumer-friendly. Their skills were diverse, and put together, Tom and his friends felt they had what it takes to run an honest operation. Tom was a good administrator as well as an excellent mechanic; Matt was an excellent painter; Jim was an outstanding body and fender man; and John knew exactly where to get parts for any type or model car.

Finally, they agreed to start an operation together. They estimated that they needed about $50,000 to get started, and they each agreed to put up an equal share of the money. They also agreed that they would limit their paychecks to $400 each per week until the business started making money. Their wives agreed to help out part-time without compensation.

The group then searched and found a good location, signing a one-year lease with a renewal

CONTINUED ▶

option for three years, plus another renewal option for five more years. They also obtained a purchase option to buy the building for $100,000 if bought within two years. (The present market value of the building was $60,000.)

Because the partners all knew one another, and because money was tight, they decided that they didn't need a lawyer. Tom's wife, Cathy, had taken a bookkeeping course in high school, so she agreed to handle all the accounting records. After much discussion at their favorite bar, they decided to draw up their own partnership agreement:

We, Thomas Dooley, Matt Boyle, James Reynolds, and John O'Toole, hereby agree to call the new undertaking Shamrock Automotive Service Center. It is all agreed between each of us that as friends and partners we will all take $400 a week out of the business and not one penny more until the enterprise is out of the woods. As soon as the business makes a lot of money, then and only then will all partners of the first part be able to take money out of the business. Further, it is agreed as friends that all decisions will be made as we have done since we grew up, and that is we will discuss what has to be discussed and then agree. If someone does not agree, then the others will try and convince the disagreeing friend and partner, and it is understood that there will be no fighting to make the disagreeable partner agree to whatever is being discussed. Further, it is understood that there will be no drinking on the premises to be rented in the city of Chicago and especially Matt will not bring beer or whiskey to work and will not drink on the job. Each partner will put up $12,500 in cash in the business tomorrow after we sign this paper tonight and the money will be kept in a bank account. Since we are all friends and partners, each of the partners will be able to sign checks because of the mutual trust we have for one another. However, we all agree to tell Cathy, who is going to handle the books, how much we made out the check for so she can keep the books straight. Each friend and partner will tell Cathy how much to charge for the work on the cars and trucks and Tom, who knows about how to manage a business, will prepare bills for the customers and see they are paid.

At the end of each month Cathy will tell us how much money the enterprise has made, and at the end of the year or sooner, we will all take out our share of the profits from the pot that will be building up with profits from the endeavors of the four partners. If the friends and partners think that the money should stay in the company or enterprise because it needs it, then everyone will have to wait until we can get the money out.

Each wife of the partners and friends will try to do her share of work in the business and offer her services without charging a dime for what she does. Cathy will handle the books. Debbie will answer the phone since she used to answer the phone for a big company when she used to work before she married Matt. Eileen will meet people who come in to pay their bills and help in the cleaning because she is good at meeting people and likes to talk. And finally Jane will help everybody any way she can and bring lunch and dinner since she is the best cook of all the wives. When the business can afford to employ people, each wife will be allowed to stop working.

Everybody agrees to get to work early in the morning and stay as long as they can at night. The enterprise will remain open every day of the week except on Sundays when it will not open until after church services. Finally, no vacations will be allowed until we all make money and it is now agreed that the party of the first part will now affix their valid legal and binding personal signatures to the line at the bottom of the page and we all agree to be friends and partners in the new enterprise which shall hereinafter forever forward be called Shamrock Automotive Service Center. One last thing is that we will charge prices that will be pleasing to the public and we all will turn out good work. After we affix our names we will all be partners.

Tom Dooley   Matt Boyle

Jim Reynolds   John O'Toole

CONTINUED ▶

Each of the partners put $12,500 in the local bank under the name of Shamrock Automotive Service Center, and they all signed the signature cards giving them the right to sign checks. After doing this, they each quit their jobs and started getting the location ready for business. Tom purchased a sign and told the others that it would be ready in about two weeks. According to Tom, it was a big, beautiful sign that would clearly advertise their name to consumers, and anyone driving down the street on either side could not miss it. All the partners seemed to be quite pleased.

Each of the partners stuck to their specialties and purchased whatever they needed for their respective departments. In about two weeks they had the business stocked with parts, tools, and all the necessary equipment. They also had business cards and stationery made for use in the business. Just before opening day, Tom went to the local newspaper, and the staff prepared a full-page ad announcing the opening of Shamrock Automotive Service Center. The ad stated that the new business offered full services to the public at reduced prices. The ad promised guaranteed efficient service.

After the ad was placed, the traffic was tremendous and the business brisk. Customers flocked in and all four men were constantly busy. At the end of the first month, Cathy presented a statement that showed sales of $25,000 and a cash balance of $900.

Needless to say, the partners were disappointed and could not understand how they could be so busy and end the month with such a small profit. To make matters worse, they received a letter from a lawyer stating that because they had not answered his correspondence asking them to desist from using his client's name in the Chicago area, he was filing suit against them within 20 days. He stated that this was the final opportunity to discuss a possible settlement with his client regarding the name. Further, the City of Chicago informed them that the sign violated zoning laws and must come down.

As it turned out, Tom had not thought it was important that another company already was using the name Shamrock Automotive Service Center and had thrown all the notices away without bringing them to anyone's attention. This other company was a small parts store on the other side of town, and would be willing to sell the name for $10,000.

During the month, Cathy called everyone into her office and insisted on knowing who was writing checks because some were missing from the checkbook. Jim and Matt could not remember all of the checks or the exact amounts of the checks they had written. Cathy also could not reconcile the accounts payable because each of the partners made purchases for cash or on account, and purchase invoices were lost or misplaced. However, they thought they owed $37,900 to various vendors. ▼

 ## CASE STUDY ROUNDTABLE

Tom: I've got to say, at this point, we're all a little depressed about how things are going.

Matt: But we want to keep going, right?

Jim: Sure, but we thought that all we needed was a little cash, a lot of determination and skill, and honesty and we'd make a fortune.

John: We know we have some problems and don't know where to turn. What do you think? What did we do wrong when we decided to go into business?

Discussion Points

- What specific problems can you identify in the partnership agreement? Outline all mistakes and indicate what you feel should have been included in the agreement.
- What kind of expert advice might have helped avoid the problems the partners now face?

Tom: We used to all get along real well, the wives and us guys did everything together; no fights, no arguments. Now it's different. I wonder if it was a bad idea to go into business with each other.

Discussion Points

- What are the special challenges that face partners who aren't friends?
- Do you think it's a good idea for friends to go into business together? Identify both the positive aspects and the possible challenges friends face.

Cathy: Do you think the guys should pay the other Shamrock company $10,000? I think they should just change the name, and get a new sign made that the city won't gripe about.

Discussion Points

- Based on the material covered in Chapter 13, what issues are involved with the name question, and what do you think the partners should do?

BACK TO THE TABLE
Ludwig and Greta

In Chapter 3, you met Ludwig and Greta, and learned about their plans to base a small business on their hobbies. Based on what you know now, do you think they should remain as sole proprietorships, or should they form a partnership or a corporation? If so, how should control, ownership, and profits be divided?

BACK TO THE TABLE

In Chapter 11, you met Barbara Burke, who was dealing with some fairly complicated problems involving Herman Glass Corporation. Based on what you've learned in this chapter, how would you answer her new question:

Barbara: I've been thinking that the way to go might be as a Subchapter S corporation, but I'm not sure that'll solve all my issues here. What do you think?

CHAPTER BRIEFCASE

▼▼▼▼▼▼

- One of the most important decisions you will make is how to structure your business. There are advantages and disadvantages to each form of organization. The type of legal format you choose will depend on: the size of the risk, the continuity of the business, your access to capital, your skills, and your purpose for starting a business. What is your ultimate goal? What are the possibilities for business growth? What are your state's laws?

- The easiest, least expensive, and least regulated business legal structure available to startup entrepreneurs is the sole proprietorship. A sole proprietorship, which is owned and operated by one person, is the most common form of business in the United States today.

- A partnership is an association of two or more people who carry on a business for profit as co-owners. Partnerships are defined by how active a role each partner plays in the business. In a general partnership, all partners participate in the running of the operation; in a limited partnership, the general partner (or partners) makes day-to-day decisions and the limited partners participate only by virtue of having invested.

- The corporate form of business organization is the most complex and highly regulated of all business structures. A corporation is a distinct legal entity, an "artificial person" created under the laws of the state in which it is chartered. A corporation assumes liability on behalf of its officers and shareholders, but must also pay tax on its income before it is distributed to investors.

- An S corporation combines the benefit of a corporation as a legal entity but avoids double taxation. Only those profits distributed to shareholders are subject to tax. S corporations are subject to strict organizational regulations.

- A limited liability company (LLC) combines the most attractive features of partnerships and corporations. Members of an LLC enjoy a corporation's limited liability while avoiding double taxation. In addition, the requirements for LLCs are more flexible than those governing S corporations.

▲▲▲▲▲▲

Chapter 19

CONTRACTS, FORMS, AND AGREEMENTS

▼▼▼▼▼

*He's a businessman. I'll make him an
offer he can't refuse.*

—Mario Puzo, The Godfather

MISSION STATEMENT

In this chapter, you will

*L*EARN what a contract is, what its basic elements are, and some of
the underlying legal principles that make a contractual agreement
valid.

*E*XPLORE various types of contracts.

*A*PPLY your understanding to a case study.

*P*RODUCE an organized analysis of your past agreements as learning experiences.

KEY TERMS

acceptance	discharge	offer
addendum	executed contract	offeree
amendment	executory contract	offeror
assignment	express contract	option
bilateral contract	implied contract	unenforceable
breach	legal capacity	unilateral contract
consideration	meeting of the minds	valid
contract	mutual assent	void
damages	novation	voidable

INTRODUCTION

As you run your business, you will enter into countless agreements with other people: agreements with vendors to supply you with products and services; agreements with customers to deliver your product or service to them; lease agreements; telephone service agreements—the list is a long one. In this chapter, we will consider the legal basis that supports these agreements, and that makes the market economy run productively and profitably on what amounts to nothing more than promises. This chapter is not an introduction to legal theory, of course. Rather, it is designed to help you understand the basics of what your lawyer spent years studying, so that you can more clearly appreciate the whys and wherefores of each contract you sign.

Of course, in highly complex circumstances, or if you have any doubts, it is important that you never sign a binding contractual agreement without consulting with legal counsel.

CONTRACTS

A lawyer will tell you that a **contract** is a voluntary agreement or promise between legally competent parties, supported by legal consideration, to perform (or refrain from performing) some legal act. That definition may be easier to understand if we take it apart and consider its various parts separately.

A contract must be

- *voluntary*—no one may be forced into a contract.
- an *agreement or a promise*—a contract is essentially a legally enforceable promise.
- made by *legally competent parties*—the parties must be viewed by the law as capable of making a legally binding promise.
- supported by *legal consideration*—a contract must be supported by some valuable thing that induces a party to enter into the contract. That "thing" must be legally sufficient to support a contract.
- about a *legal act*—no one may make a legal contract to do something illegal.

Essentially, a contract is an enforceable promise—a promise that someone may be compelled by a court to keep. The general body of law that governs such agreements is known as contract law.

FIRST PERSON

Terry K., Northwood, California: I used to think that another businessperson's word was good enough. I mean, you can call me naive if you want, but if you can't look another person in the eye and say "I'll do that" or "I'll pay such-and-such a price for 'x' of your product," then what's the point of being in business? Well, I found out the hard way that you can't always think that way. I had a guy put in a big order of our product a few months after we opened, and I just said, sure, we'll have them ready. So the delivery day came—no guy. Next day I called, he said he'd changed his mind, he couldn't remember the order, maybe next week—every excuse in the book! I was stuck. I mean, 98 percent of the people you deal with follow through on what they promise, but that other 2 percent can really do you in! Now, even though I'm a Democrat, I do like what Reagan said: trust, but verify. I get it in writing, I make sure it's all done the legal way, and everyone's better off. Just because you sign a paper doesn't mean you don't trust each other. It's just insurance.

Express and Implied Contracts

A contract may be express or implied, depending on how it is created. An **express contract** exists when the parties state the terms and show their intentions in words. An express contract may be either oral or written. Under each state's statute of frauds, certain types of contracts—particularly those involving real property—must be in writing to be enforceable in a court of law. (Enforceable means that the parties may be forced to comply with the contract's terms and conditions.)

For example, suppose you go to your neighbor and say, "I will paint your house today for $50." Your neighbor is pleased with the offer, and replies, "If you paint my house today, I will pay you $50." The two of you have entered into an oral express contract.

In an **implied contract**, the agreement of the parties is demonstrated by their acts and conduct. When you go into a restaurant and order a meal, you have entered into an implied contract with the restaurant to pay for the meal, even though payment was not mentioned before the meal was ordered.

Bilateral and Unilateral Contracts

Contracts may be classified as either bilateral or unilateral. In a **bilateral contract**, both parties promise to do something: one promise is given in exchange for another. A real estate sales contract, for example, is a bilateral contract because the seller promises to sell a house to the buyer, who promises to pay the seller a certain sum of money.

A **unilateral contract**, on the other hand, is a one-sided agreement. One party makes a promise in order to induce a second party to do something. The second party is not legally obligated to act. However, if the second party does comply, the first party is obligated to keep the promise. For instance, a law enforcement agency might offer a monetary payment to anyone who can aid in the capture of a criminal. Only if someone does aid in the capture is the reward paid. An option contract, which will be discussed later, is another example of a unilateral contract.

Assume your neighbor puts up a sign that says, "If you paint my house today, I will pay you $50." If you paint the house, your neighbor will be legally obligated to pay you. You and your neighbor have a unilateral contract.

Executed and Executory Contracts

A contract may be classified as either executed or executory, depending on whether the agreement is performed. An **executed contract** is one in which all parties have fulfilled their promises: the contract has been performed. This should not be confused with the word *execute*, which refers to the signing of a contract. An **executory contract** exists when one or both parties still have an act to perform. A contract is an executory contract from the time it is signed until the parties have performed what they promised to do. Once performed, the contract is executed.

Essential Elements of a Valid Contract

A contract must meet certain minimum requirements to be considered legally valid. The following are the basic essential elements of a contract.

Offer and acceptance. There must be an offer by one party that is accepted by the other. The person who makes the offer is the **offeror**. The person who accepts the offer is the **offeree**. This requirement is also called **mutual assent**. It means that there must be, in legal terms, a *meeting of the minds*. That means complete agreement about the purpose and terms of the contract. Courts look to the objective intent of the parties to determine whether they intended to enter into a binding agreement. The wording of the contract must express all the agreed-upon terms and must be clearly understood by the parties.

An **offer** is a promise made by one party, requesting something in exchange for that promise. The offer is made with the intention that the offeror will be bound to the terms if the offer is accepted. The terms of the offer must be definite and specific and must be communicated to the offeree.

An **acceptance** is a promise by the offeree to be bound by the exact terms proposed by the offeror. The acceptance must be communicated to the offeror. Proposing *any* deviation from the terms of the offer constitutes a rejection of the original offer and becomes a new offer. This is known as a **counteroffer**, and it must be communicated to the original offering party. The counteroffer must be accepted for a contract to exist.

Besides being terminated by a counteroffer, an offer may be terminated by the offeree's outright rejection of it. Alternatively, an offeree may fail to accept the offer before it expires. The offeror may revoke the offer at any time before receiving the acceptance. This revocation must be communicated to the offeree by the offeror, either directly or through the parties' agents. The offer is also revoked if the offeree learns of the revocation and observes the offeror acting in a manner that indicates that the offer no longer exists.

Consideration. The contract must be based on consideration. **Consideration** is something of legal value offered by one party and accepted by another as an inducement to perform or to refrain from some act. There must be a definite statement of consideration in a contract to show that something of value was given in exchange for the promise.

Consideration must be "good and valuable" between the parties. The courts do not inquire into the adequacy of consideration. Adequate consideration ranges from as little as a promise of "love and affection" to a substantial sum of money. Anything that has been bargained for and exchanged is legally sufficient to satisfy the requirement for consideration. The only requirements are that the parties agree and that no undue influence or fraud has occurred.

Legally competent parties. All parties to the contract must have **legal capacity**. That is, they must be of legal age and have enough mental capacity to understand the nature or consequences of their actions in the contract. In most states, 18 is the age of contractual capacity. Under state law, an imprisoned felon or certain mentally ill persons may be legally incompetent to enter into a contract.

Validity of Contracts

A contract can be described as valid, void, voidable, or unenforceable, depending on the circumstances. A contract is **valid** when it meets all the essential elements that make it legally sufficient, or enforceable. A contract is **void** when it has no legal force or effect because it lacks some or all of the essential elements of a contract. A contract that is **voidable** appears on the surface to be valid, but may be rescinded or disaffirmed by one or both parties based on some legal principle. A voidable contract is considered by the courts to be valid if the party who has the option to disaffirm the agreement does not do so within a period of time prescribed by state law.

A contract with a minor, for instance, is usually voidable. This is because minors are generally permitted to disaffirm certain contracts at any time while under age and for a certain period of time after reaching majority age. A contract entered into by a mentally ill person is usually voidable during the mental illness and for a reasonable period after the person is cured. On the other hand, a contract made by a person who has been adjudicated insane (that is, found to be insane by a court) is void on the theory that the judgment is a matter of public record.

Mental capacity to enter into a contract is not the same as medical sanity. The test is whether the individual in question is *capable of understanding what he or she is doing*. A party may suffer from a mental illness, but have a clear understanding of the significance of his or her actions. This is a thorny legal and psychological question that requires consultation with experts.

A contract that is **unenforceable** also seems on the surface to be valid; however, neither party can sue the other to force performance. For example, an oral agreement to sell a warehouse would be unenforceable. Because the statute of frauds requires real estate sales contracts to be in writing, the defaulting party could not be taken to court and forced to perform. There is, however, a distinction between a suit to *force performance* and a suit for *damages*. A party who is harmed by another's default of an oral contract may seek **damages**: a financial penalty paid by the offending party in an amount sufficient to compensate for the injury suffered. An unenforceable contract is said to be "valid as between the parties." This means that once the agreement is fully executed and both parties are satisfied, neither has reason to initiate a lawsuit to force performance.

Reality of consent. A contract that complies with all of the basic requirements may still be either void or voidable. This is because of the doctrine of **reality of consent**. A contract must be entered into as the *free and voluntary act of each party*. Each party must be able to make a prudent and knowledgeable decision without undue influence. A mistake, misrepresentation, fraud, undue influence, or duress would deprive a person of that ability. If any of these circumstances is present, the contract is voidable by the injured party. If the other party were to sue for breach, the injured party could use lack of voluntary assent as a defense.

Discharge of Contracts

A contract is **discharged** when the agreement is terminated. Obviously, the most desirable case is when a contract terminates because it has been completely performed, with all its terms carried out. However, a contract may be terminated for other reasons, such as a party's breach or default.

Performance of a Contract

Each party has certain rights and duties to fulfill. The question of when a contract must be performed is an important factor. Many contracts call for a specific time by which the agreed-upon acts must be completely performed. In addition, many contracts provide that "time is of the essence." This means that the contract must be performed strictly within the time limit specified. A party who fails to perform on time is liable for breach of contract.

When a contract does not specify a date for performance, the acts it requires should be performed within a reasonable time. The interpretation of what constitutes a *reasonable time* depends on the situation. Generally, unless the parties agree otherwise, if the act can be done immediately, it should be performed immediately. Courts have sometimes declared contracts to be invalid because they did not contain a time or date for performance.

Assignment

Assignment is a transfer of rights or duties under a contract. Rights may be assigned to a third party (called the **assignee**) unless the contract forbids it. Obligations may also be assigned (or delegated), but the original party remains primarily liable unless specifically released. Many contracts include a clause that either permits or forbids assignment.

For instance, assume you and your neighbor enter into a contract to paint your toolshed. Under the terms of the contract, your neighbor will be paid $1,000 when she finishes the job. Your neighbor owes $1,000 to her uncle, and so she assigns to her uncle the right to receive the payment. When the job is done, you will pay $1,000 to your neighbor's uncle. On the other hand, suppose that the day after your neighbor signs the contract to paint your toolshed for $1,000, she receives an offer from someone else who will pay her $3,000 to paint a gazebo. Your neighbor wants to take the better-paying job, but doesn't want to breach the contract with you (because, knowing you, you'll probably sue). If your contract permits it, your neighbor may assign both the right to be paid and the duty to paint the toolshed to her friend, another painter. If your neighbor's friend fails to paint the toolshed, however, your neighbor will still be liable to you for breach of contract.

Novation

A contract may be performed by **novation**—that is, the substitution of a new contract in place of the original. The new agreement may be between the same parties, or a new party may be substituted for either (this is novation of the parties). The parties' intent must be to discharge the old obligation. For instance, when a real estate purchaser assumes the seller's existing mortgage loan, the lender may choose to release the seller and substitute the buyer as the party primarily liable for the mortgage debt.

Breach of Contract

A contract may be terminated if it is breached by one of the parties. A **breach of contract** is a violation of any of the terms or conditions of a contract without legal excuse. For instance, a seller who fails to deliver promised goods to a buyer breaches a sales contract. The breaching or *defaulting* party assumes certain burdens, and the non-defaulting party has certain remedies.

The contract may limit the remedies available to the parties, however. A liquidated damages clause permits the seller to keep any deposit and any other payments received from the buyer as the seller's sole remedy. The clause may limit the buyer's remedy to a return of the deposit and other payments should the seller default.

Statute of Limitations

The law of every state limits the time within which parties to a contract may bring legal suit to enforce their rights. The **statute of limitations** varies for different legal actions, and any rights not enforced within the applicable time period are lost.

Discharged or Terminated Contracts

Contracts may also be discharged or terminated when any of the following occurs:

- *Partial performance* of the terms, along with a written acceptance by the other party
- *Substantial performance*, in which one party has substantially performed on the contract, but does not complete all the details exactly as the contract requires. (Such performance may be enough to force payment, with certain adjustments for any damages suffered by the other party.) For instance, where a newly constructed restaurant is finished except for polishing the brass railings, the contractor is entitled to the final payment.
- *Impossibility of performance*, in which an act required by the contract cannot be legally accomplished
- *Mutual agreement* of the parties to cancel
- *Operation of law*, such as in the voiding of a contract by a minor, as a result of fraud, due to the expiration of the statute of limitations, or because a contract was altered without the written consent of all parties involved

Contract Forms

Because so many commercial transactions are very similar in nature, preprinted forms are available for most kinds of contracts. The use of preprinted forms raises three problems: (1) what to write in the blanks, (2) what words and phrases should be ruled out by drawing lines through them because they don't apply, and (3) what additional clauses or agreements (called riders or addenda) should be added. All changes and additions are usually initialed in the margin or on the rider by both parties when a contract is signed.

It is essential that both parties to a contract understand exactly what they are agreeing to. Poorly drafted documents, especially those containing extensive legal language, may be subject to various interpretations and lead to litigation. The parties to a transaction should be advised to have contracts and other legal documents examined by their lawyers before they sign to ensure that the agreements accurately reflect their intentions. When preprinted forms do not sufficiently cover special provisions in a transaction, the parties should have an attorney draft an appropriate contract.

Amendments and Addendums

An **amendment** is a change to the existing content of a contract. Any time words or provisions are added to or deleted from the body of the contract, the contract has been amended. For instance, a form contract's provision requiring delivery in 90 days might be crossed out and replaced with a 60-day period. *Amendments must be initialed by all parties.*

On the other hand, an **addendum** is any provision added to an existing contract without altering the content of the original. An addendum is essentially a new contract between the parties that includes the original contract's provisions "by reference"; that is, the addendum mentions the original contract. *An addendum must be signed by the parties.*

OPTIONS

An **option** is a contract by which an **optionor** (generally a seller) gives an **optionee** (a prospective purchaser) the right to buy or lease the owner's goods, services, or property at a fixed price within a certain period of time. The optionee pays a fee (the agreed-upon consideration) for this option right. The optionee has no other obligation until he or she decides to either exercise the option right or allow the option to expire. An option is enforceable by only one party—the optionee. In an option contract, the optionee is essentially freezing the price of the goods, services, or property for a specific period of time. During that time, the optionee can think about the purchase, look for better bargains, arrange for financing, or even do nothing at all.

An option contract is not a sales contract. At the time the option is signed by the parties, the seller does not sell, and the optionee does not buy. The parties merely agree that the optionee has the right to buy and the owner is obligated to sell if the optionee decides to exercise his or her right of option. Options must contain all the terms and provisions required for a valid contract.

The option agreement (which is a unilateral contract) requires the optionor to act only after the optionee gives notice that he or she elects to execute the option. If the option is not exercised within the time specified in the contract, both the optionor's obligation and the optionee's right expire. An option contract may provide for renewal, which often requires additional consideration. The optionee cannot recover the consideration paid for the option right. The contract may state whether the money paid for the option is to be applied to the price of the goods, service, or property if the option is exercised.

A common application of an option is a lease that includes an option for the tenant to purchase the property. Options on commercial real estate frequently depend on some specific conditions being fulfilled, such as obtaining a zoning change or a building permit. The optionee may be obligated to exercise the option if the conditions are met. Similar terms could also be included in a sales contract.

URLinks
http://www.toolkit.cch.com/text/p06_4488.stm

PERSONAL WORKSHOP 37
Learning from Experience

▾ For this workshop, reflect on agreements you've entered into in the past: who were you agreeing with, what was the agreement about, and what were its terms? Did you have a written contract? If you did, reflect on why it was necessary. If you didn't, would the transaction have worked out better with a written contract, or did it work out fine without one? Use a variety of transactions for this analysis: buying a car, accepting a job, ordering a hamburger (we've done that one for you as an example)—all of these are business transactions, and all of them involve some sort of contract, whether written or oral. Be creative in this workshop, and have fun with the "legal" issues.

Type of Transaction	Parties (You + ____)	Terms (item, limits, time)	Writing? Y	Writing? N	Reflection
Buying a hamburger	counter clerk	1 cheeseburger, no onions, now		X	This was a basic goods-for-money oral contract. No writing was required: a writing would have been silly.

CASE STUDY

SNERT ELECTRICAL MACHINERY CORPORATION

▼▼▼▼▼▼

*T*hree years ago, Rupert Schuler purchased an electrical machinery equipment manufacturing firm with the intention of eventually entering the international field. Although Schuler had worked for a year in the international department of his former employer, he did not think he knew enough about the international scene. He thought there should be a good international market for his equipment because his products were well built, he used high-tech equipment to manufacture his products, and his quality control was excellent. The high-profile interest in international trading activity generated by NAFTA seemed to be the final door opening. So, he appointed Henri Villard to investigate the possibilities. Henri spoke French, Spanish, and German fluently and had traveled extensively through Latin America, Africa, and Asia. Although Villard was not familiar with the entire product line, Schuler felt he could quickly learn about it.

Schuler's venture into the international field had the backing of the Department of Commerce and other international agencies, and Henri had been working with them to gather information. He decided to make a trip to Central and South America to assess the market. Henri's first stop was in Venezuela. He checked in with the correspondent bank in Caracas and was immediately welcomed with open arms. The bank representative gave Henri a complete analysis of the Venezuelan market and offered his assistance. Henri then asked to meet with some interested and reliable firms. The banker contacted several companies and made appointments with four firms. Henri was elated and made plans to visit each of them.

After two days of conferences and meetings, Henri found that there was genuine interest in many of the products Schuler manufactured, partly to cover the domestic market, but mainly to compete for government bids. Each applicant wanted an exclusive agreement with Schuler in Venezuela, and each expressed interest in a long-term contract. Henri agreed to get back to them soon regarding the contract and conditions. Henri went back to the banker and asked for credit checks on all the firms. One company, Productos Electricos, turned out to be especially attractive. The company had substantial assets, and the management team was good and aggressive. Henri began negotiations with the company agent, Don Ulloa, for a representation agreement. Ulloa stated clearly what he wanted:

- Exclusive representation for five years.
- Credit conditions including 30 days' sight draft against documents and longer terms, if necessary, for sales to large companies or the government.
- Engineering assistance when necessary, for special projects and installations.
- Catalogs, price lists, brochures, and bulletins, all in Spanish.

Henri was willing to do the following:

- Grant a one-year exclusive representation agreement for Ulloa in Venezuela. If the arrangement proved to be satisfactory after one year, he would be glad to entertain a five-year exclusive contract. The agreement would be granted, however, only if the distributor stocked at least $350,000 worth of equipment. The first order had to be opened by a letter of credit.
- Give credit terms for 30 days. Extensions would be on a case-by-case basis.

Ulloa agreed to the one-year contract and accepted the credit terms, but he did not immediately want to invest $350,000 in stock. He first wanted to assume the line and then select particular inventory based on perceived needs. After much discussion, Henri went along with this. Ulloa agreed to purchase the beginning inventory within six months. He signed a contract prepared by Henri in Spanish, which made Ulloa the exclusive distributor in Venezuela.

All in all, Henri had a good trip, considering that it was the first he had made for the company. On his return, he immediately met with Schuler, who

CONTINUED ▶

was pleased with the sales and made arrangements for the products to be shipped. He did not quite understand the 30-day sight draft, so Henri explained that the goods would be shipped and 30 days after document presentation by the bank to the client and acceptance of the draft, the total amount would be paid by the distributor. All shipments would have to be invoiced with the price broken down to indicate the factory shipping cost, insurance, freight, and handling costs to the destination.

Henri hired an engineer from Spain to translate catalogs, brochures, price lists, bulletins, and service manuals into Spanish. He also contacted the Department of Commerce and discussed handling transactions with foreign countries.

Soon after the trip, orders started flowing into the company, and Schuler was very pleased. However, many difficulties began to emerge. One problem developed soon after the first shipment was sent abroad. Customs would not accept the goods because they were not packed and marked as required. Henri called the distributor, who was getting the matter resolved through his political connections, but all shipments would have to be forwarded correctly in the future. Shipping overseas involved a tremendous amount of paperwork: commercial invoices, packing lists, the shipper's export declaration, export licenses, insurance certificates, consular invoices, and certificates of origin. The paperwork, as well as the packing, was too much for Henri and he wondered if some firm could handle this function for him. Another problem was that transportation costs were quite high, but Henri learned that if he used nonconference freighters instead of conference lines, he could save a great deal of money on the freight costs and make himself more competitive.

One incident illustrated a third area for concern. The distributor did not pay a $15,000 sight draft when it was presented to him at the end of the 30-day period. Bank officials cabled that they were filing a protest within 24 hours and would have a local attorney handle the collection, but it was not guaranteed. When Henri called, the distributor reported that the client who ordered the goods would not pay as agreed, and he needed more time, specifically 90 days. Henri could see no other alternative and agreed to the terms. He cabled the bank officials and told them he had made other arrangements. However, Henri felt that there had to be some other way of protecting the company against bad debt losses overseas.

Finally, Henri faced the problem of the brochures and catalogs being seized at the Venezuelan border because some of the wording was "obscene." It seems that the Spanish words used had connotations in many parts of Latin America considered highly inappropriate. These written materials would have to be changed.

In the face of all these difficulties, Schuler decided to reexamine his involvement with international business. Sales had reached $10 million, but more than $1 million in receivables was outstanding. Collection was likely, but the timing of receipt was uncertain. It was difficult for him to carry the accounts, and he wondered if he should continue in this business. ▾

CASE STUDY ROUNDTABLE

▾ ▾ ▾ ▾ ▾ ▾

Rupert: I don't know if it was such a good idea to get started in this. And I'm really getting uncomfortable with the terms of the agreement. I think Henri did a great job, but he doesn't really know our industry. Can you people help me out?

Discussion Points

- Do you think it was a good idea for Schuler to enter the international market?
- Would you have made contractual arrangements with a distributor who refused to carry your suggested stock of products? What other conditions would you

want included in the agreement? Try drafting an agreement that you think would have worked better.

- What can Henri do about the nonpayment of invoices? How is he going to handle shipments to foreign countries that demand terms of up to one year or more? Is there any way Henri can protect the company from bad debt losses?

- How would you handle the problem of vocabulary for brochures and other publications that must be translated from English to Spanish?

▲▲▲▲▲▲

 CHAPTER BRIEFCASE

▼▼▼▼▼▼

- A contract is a voluntary agreement or promise between legally competent parties, supported by legal consideration, to perform some legal act.

- Contracts may be implied (demonstrated by the parties' actions) or express (written or oral agreement). Contracts may be bilateral (an exchange of promises, such as "I'll do" or "I'll pay") or unilateral (such as a promise of a reward).

- Rights or obligations under a contract may be assigned to other parties.

- A breach of contract is a violation of any of the agreement's terms and conditions. The contract may include an agreement on damages in case of breach.

▲▲▲▲▲▲

Chapter 20

INTELLECTUAL PROPERTY ISSUES

▼▼▼▼▼

*The Congress shall have power to...
promote the progress of science and
useful arts, by securing for limited
times to authors and inventors the
exclusive right to their respective
writings and discoveries...*

—*U.S. Constitution, Article I, Section 8*

MISSION STATEMENT

In this chapter, you will

*L*EARN about the various ways in which you can protect your business ideas, your words, and your Web site.

*E*XPLORE the ways that legal changes in response to new technologies enhance your ability to protect your intellectual property.

*A*PPLY your understanding to a real-life case study.

*P*RODUCE an analysis form that will help you think of products and intellectual property as protected goods, and help you evaluate the types of protections you should seek for your products.

KEY TERMS

copyright	fair use	patent
disclosure letter	NET Act	provisional patent application
domain name	passing off	trademark

INTRODUCTION TO PROTECTING YOUR IDEA

When you are developing your product or service, you want to make certain that you are not infringing on the rights of others. You also want to get protection for your own work. Don't let the fear of having your idea stolen keep you from the marketplace. In order to develop and sell ideas, you have to disclose them to somebody: no one can buy your product (or produce

▼▼▼▼▼▼▼▼▼▼▼▼▼▼▼▼▼▼▼▼▼

one based on your idea) if you keep it a secret. On the other hand, it's also important not to share your ideas with others without first protecting them. That's kind of like putting your family heirloom jewelry on your front porch and relying on the goodness of human nature to keep it safe. Of course, you can't copyright an idea, but you can protect it. The development and market research stage is a good time to review the safeguards and protections available to entrepreneurs under the federal law of copyright, trademark, and patent.

As with our discussion of other legal issues (forms of organization, taxes, contracts, etc.) you should be sure to consult a competent attorney about these issues before you do anything. In the world of patent and copyright, failure to cross all the "t"s and dot all the "i"s can leave you unprotected.

DISCLOSURE LETTER

One simple way of protecting your idea is through the use of a **disclosure letter**. This is a letter outlining your idea for your new product or service, detailing the research and work you have done to date and citing the people you have contacted while doing your research. Date the letter and have it notarized. The purpose of the disclosure letter is to verify the date on which the idea was yours. Place the letter in a sealed envelope and file it in a safe place.

Establishing a date by means of a disclosure letter alone is not enough, however. You must be able to demonstrate that you are involved in an active business as opposed to a passive business activity. An active business is able to show continuous work and progress in developing the idea into a viable product or service. You can demonstrate the active nature of your business by keeping a log or journal. This is a diary that will show daily entries verifying ongoing work.

To be considered a legal document, the log must

- be a bound book (not loose-leaf).
- have consecutively numbered pages.
- be written in ink and contain no erasures (if you make an error, line through it, initial it and make the correction—do not use correction fluid).

Include information regarding the people to whom you have spoken about your idea and the dates and locations of the meetings. The journal and the disclosure letter give you the security you need to begin your market research.

COPYRIGHT

United States copyright law gives copyright owners five exclusive rights:

1. The right to *reproduce* the work
2. The right to *create derivative works* based on an original copyrighted work
3. The right to *distribute copies* of the work to the public
4. The right to *perform* the work publicly (including via electronic media)
5. The right to *display* the work publicly

According to the Copyright Office, "Copyright protection subsists from the time a work is created in a fixed form; that is, it is an incident of the process of authorship. The copyright in the work of authorship *immediately* (sic) becomes the property of the author who created it. Only the author or those deriving their rights through the author can rightfully claim copyright."

Copyright protection for works created after January 1, 1978, lasts for the author's life plus 50 years, beginning at the moment of creation. In the case of joint works, the term is 50 years after the death of the last surviving author. For works made for hire, or for anonymous or pseudonymous works, the duration is 75 years from publication or 100 years from creation, whichever term is shorter.

It is important to note, however, that it is not necessary to publish or register anything with the Copyright Office to secure copyright protection. Benefits of registration, however, include:

- Establishment of a public record of the copyright claim
- The right to file an infringement suit in court
- Absolute (prima facie) evidence of the copyright's validity
- Statutory damages and attorney's fees to be available to the copyright owner, who is otherwise limited to actual damages and lost profits

Use of the **copyright notice** is optional, but recommended by the Copyright Office. Among other things, use of the notice alerts the public that the work is protected by United States copyright laws. Use of the notice also deprives defendants of the right to claim "innocent infringement" in a lawsuit.

For "visually perceptible copies," the copyright notice should contain three elements:

1. The © symbol or the word "Copyright" or the abbreviation "copr."
2. The year in which the work was first published
3. The name of the copyright owner, or an abbreviation by which the name can be recognized

The notice should be obvious enough to "give reasonable notice of the claim of a copyright."

TRADEMARK

A **trademark** is a word, symbol, unique name, design, logo, slogan, or some combination of these elements used by a company to identify its products. A **service mark** identifies and distinguishes a service rather than a product. A **trade name** is used to designate a company rather than a product or service.

In general, the federal trademark statute covers trademarks, service marks, and words, names, or symbols that identify or are capable of distinguishing goods or services. *Copyright registration cannot be made for names, titles, or other short phrases or expressions.*

U.S. trademark law allows a company or individual to file a trademark application for the purpose of "reserving" that trademark for future licensing and to protect the

PERSONAL WORKSHOP 38
Trademark Recognition

▾ For this workshop, you should look around your home for examples of each of the various types of copyright and trademark notification on books, magazines, Web sites, and products. Where does it appear? What types of items bear which marks? This should help you learn about the kinds of protections you should seek for your business, intellectual property, and products. On this worksheet, note the type of item and the placing of the symbol.

Protection	Type of Item	Placement
®		
SM		
TM		
©		
pat. pend.		

▾ These marks serve to identify and distinguish an owner's products, goods, or services from those of the competition. They can serve as good marketing tools, provided the quality and reputation of goods and services is maintained.

trademark for up to three years before it is actually used in commerce. These are known as "intent-to-use" applications.

Trademark renewals take place every ten years. There is a fee for renewal and a penalty for late renewal applications.

Notice of Trademark

There is a standard format for the use of the trademark symbol. The letters "TM" must be placed after every use of the trademark or symbol, like this: ™. The letters "SM" are used for a service mark, like this: ℠. Once the trademark registration has been completed and confirmed, the symbol ® will be placed after every use of the trademarked word or symbol.

PATENT

A patent protects your invention against being copied by others for 20 years. What a patent offers inventors is really a negative right: the right to keep others from producing, selling, or copying your invention.

What Can Be Patented?

You are entitled by law to obtain a patent if you invent or discover any new and useful process, machine, manufacture, composition of matter, or any new and useful *improvement* of an existing process, machine, manufacture, or composition. That is, just because the mousetrap has been invented doesn't mean you can't get a patent on your better one.

For purposes of the patent law, a *process* mostly refers to industrial or technical processes or systems. The term *machine* refers to machines (of course), and *manufacture* means both making things and the things that are made. The phrase *composition of matter* has to do with chemical compositions, mixtures of ingredients, and new compounds.

Note that, under the patent law, the thing or process to be patented has to be useful. That is, it has to do what it's intended to do. A machine designed to make shoes that did not, in fact, make shoes would not be patentable because it would not be very useful. You should also be aware that the laws of nature, physical phenomena, and ideas or suggestions are not patentable. You can patent your better mousetrap, but you can't patent your idea for a better mousetrap.

Finally, be aware that *you cannot obtain a patent if your invention was known or used by others in this country, or was described in a printed publication in this country or any other prior to your application for a patent!* And if your invention was in public use or on sale in the United States for more than one year prior to the application for a patent, you will not be able to obtain one. In short, get the patent before you let the cat out of the bag. Once you've published an article about your wonderful new machine in *Popular Mechanics, Scientific American,* or *National Enquirer,* you are out of luck for getting a patent. In other words, get the patent first, then tell everybody about your invention.

Obtaining a Patent

When you have an idea for a new invention or process, it is important to analyze that idea for *originality* and *patentability*. A patented item is assigned a file number, which should be displayed. Patentable products that are marketed prior to final assignment of a patent may display the phrase, "pat. pend." or "patent pending." This puts others on notice that you have initiated the patent process, and that your product will be protected against infringement. Note that the patent law imposes strict penalties on people who falsely claim to have applied for a patent. If you're going to display the "pat. pend." you must have actually initiated the process.

Novelty

One of the most difficult and crucial steps to securing a patent is to determine **novelty**. Establishing novelty involves two steps:

1. Analysis according to specific standards set down by the Patent Office
2. Determining if anyone has patented it first

The only sure way to do this is to conduct a search of Patent Office files. To help make these files available to the public, the federal government established the Depository Library Program. These libraries offer the publications of the U.S. Patent Classification System, contain current issues of U.S. Patents, maintain collections of earlier issued patents, and provide technical staff assistance in their use. A listing of Depository Libraries is available through the Government Printing Office.

A search of patents can be informative. Besides indicating if your device is patentable, it may disclose patents better than yours, but not in production. You may be able to contact the inventor and arrange to have his or her idea manufactured and sold by your company. In any event, you may be forewarned of potential competition.

The preparation of an application for a patent and the proceedings in the Patent and Trademark Office to obtain that patent are undertakings that require a thorough knowledge of the scientific or technical matters involved in the particular invention, as well as knowledge of the legal aspects of the patent process. Although inventors may prepare and file their own applications and may conduct their own proceedings, they may find it difficult. The patent process can be tedious, complicated, and lengthy. Most inventors employ the services of registered patent attorneys or patent agents. However, it is to your advantage to be as knowledgeable as possible about the patent process.

Provisional Patent Application

The **Provisional Patent Application (PPA)** is designed to allow individual inventors to show their inventions to potential manufacturers and investors without fear of having their ideas stolen. Along with a filing fee, inventors submit a one-page cover sheet, a declaration statement, informal drawings, and a detailed description of the invention to the Patent Office. The PPA information is retained in confidence and is automatically abandoned 12 months after filing. *It does not replace the need for applying for a regular patent.* Before the PPA expires, the applicant must file a nonprovisional application to obtain a patent.

URLinks
http://www.uspto.gov/
http://www.jonesaskew.com/patent.html

COPYRIGHT ON THE WEB: THE NO ELECTRONIC THEFT (NET) ACT

This law, signed by President Clinton in December, 1997, amends the existing Copyright Act to eliminate the profit requirement for prosecution. Under the old law, copyright violators were subject to federal criminal penalties (one to ten years' imprisonment or fines between $100,000 and $500,000, depending on the nature and specific facts of the infringement) *only if they realized some profit from the infringement.*

Under NET, any person who "willfully" infringes copyrighted material worth $1,000 or more is subject to criminal prosecution *whether he or she realized or intended to realize any profit from the infringement.*

NET originated, like so many federal laws, in a lawsuit: *United States v. LaMacchia* (871 F Supp 535 (D. Mass. 1994)). In brief, LaMacchia was a graduate student at MIT who set up two electronic bulletin boards on the Internet. He then encouraged people who had purchased computer games and other software to upload the products onto the first bulletin board. LaMacchia then transferred the electronic files to the second bulletin board, where others were encouraged to download the software to their own computers. LaMacchia did not charge any fee for this system, and did not ever benefit financially from the transactions.

Because federal criminal copyright laws did not envision prosecutions for acts that did not involve a profit by the defendant, the Massachusetts District Court dismissed the case. Congress was horrified, and enacted HR 2265, which President Clinton signed.

> "HR 2265 . . . criminalizes computer theft of copyrighted works whether or not the defendant derives a direct financial benefit from the act(s) of misappropriation, thereby preventing such willful conduct from destroying businesses, especially small businesses, that depend on licensing agreements and royalties for survival."

URLinks
http://lcweb.loc.gob/copyright/circs/circ01.html
http://nt.excite.com/webcrawler/reuters/971217/15.TECH-COPYRIGHT.html

INTERNET COPYRIGHT ISSUES

As more business is conducted over the Internet, businesses need to be aware of how to protect their proprietary information. There are four major areas in which copyright law impacts individual and corporate Web sites:

1. Appropriation of text
2. Copying of images
3. Linking
4. Domain names

Appropriation of Text

Remember: only the holder of the copyright has the right to make any reproductions or copies of the protected work.

In the absence of a fair use exception, the unauthorized appropriation of text (by, for instance, cut-and-paste functions) from another's Web site to your own is an illegal copyright infringement.

The "fair use exception" is a copyright law doctrine that, essentially, recognizes that not all unauthorized copying is illegal. The Copyright Act applies a four-pronged test to determine whether an infringement falls under the "fair use" doctrine. The four conditions in question are:

1. What is the purpose and character of the use in question? Is it commercial or academic?

2. What is the nature of the copyrighted work?
3. How much of the copyrighted work was copied in relation to the work as a whole? (The Act uses a "substantial and material" test.)
4. What is the effect of the infringement on the work's value or market potential?

So, for instance, if a few sentences from a commercial Web site's copyrighted text are reproduced in a review of the site, and if the review appears at a nonprofit, scholarly Web site dedicated to providing in-depth evaluations of the quality of a class of Web sites, a court would likely find that the copying fell under the "fair use" exception. This is true even if the review was scathing, and would likely diminish the number of customers who accessed the reviewed site. Courts do not tend to look at the nature of the review, only at the material copied, in determining market effect. For example, if the material copied constituted the "meat" of the product being marketed, the use in a review might be found to have had an adverse effect on the work's value.

FIRST PERSON

Carla R., Dallas, Texas: That's an interesting experience they had at CompanyLine *(see the case study at the end of this chapter).* As a lawyer, though, I can't help but want to consider an alternative reality for a moment. What if CompanyLine's text was part of an online corporate communications project, sold to the public and delivered over the Internet? If CommuniLine had done in these circumstances exactly what it did in reality, the copyright issues would be slightly different. For one thing, the protected text would have demonstrable value. Assuming that value was more than $1,000, the copyright law's criminal penalties are effective. For another thing, any claim of "fair use" would certainly fail, because all four prongs are satisfied: the unauthorized use of the protected material results in a direct decrease in the value of the hypothetical online product, based on the famous old legal argument that they won't buy the cow if they can get the milk for free.

In 1998, Congress passed the Digital Millenium Copyright Act. This act defines a new crime—circumvention—as the willful removal of copy protection technologies from software and other digital media. Once the protective programs are removed, of course, the unprotected content can be copied freely. The act imposes a $500,000 fine and up to five years in prison for violators.

Copying of Images

Any unauthorized copying of site images (gifs, jpegs, etc.) infringes on the creator's copyright. This rule is simple: clip art images, for instance, may be used by the purchaser under the license purchased along with the software. Anyone else who copies the images is committing a copyright infringement.

This is a particular issue on the Internet, where images (like text) may be easily copied, transferred, downloaded, or manipulated.

Linking

One of the primary features of the Internet, the thing in fact that gives it its "net-ness," is the ability to link from one Web site to another with a simple click of a mouse button. That's very wonderful, and full of opportunities, but linking can raise copyright issues. This is particularly true if it's not absolutely crystal clear that the site being linked to is not authored by the originating site, a practice referred to as "passing off." For instance, in our case study example, if CommuniLine had simply created a link to CompanyLine's "Pursuit of Clarity" page with the text, "To find out about creating effective corporate communications materials, click ***here***," it would be passing off CompanyLine's material as its own—essentially the same thing it did by cutting-and-pasting text from one site to another.

Domain Name Issues

A **domain name** is an individual's or company's Web address. Domain names have two levels. Current top-level domain names are .com, .org, .net, .gov, and .edu (more top-level names are being developed for the Internet). Second-level names are the address *before* the "dot"—*real-estate-ed*, for instance, or *amazon*. Second-level domain names are registered with InterNIC/Network Solutions, Inc. on a "first come, first served" basis. Network Solutions serves only as a registry. It does not evaluate the legality of the domain name or determine whether the name infringes upon the rights of a third party. It determines only if the name is available for registration (that is, has not been previously claimed).

URLinks
http://rs.internic.net/domain-info/nic-rev03.html

To legally protect a domain name, the owner should secure trademark registration of the name. For domain names, Tunisia is currently the favored country in which to register the trademark, due to the speed and relative inexpensiveness of the process there.

Because of the first come, first served basis of domain name registration, a company entering cyberspace for the first time may find that its name has already been taken. For instance, Real Estate Education Company, the publisher known nationwide as REEC, might have preferred the domain name *reec.com* to its current domain name, *real-estate-ed.com*, but Real Estate Education Company, a Chicago-based proprietary school known locally as REEC, registered first.

Other companies have found that enterprising entrepreneurs have registered whole bundles of valuable domain names with an eye toward reselling them to desperate buyers. For example, a savvy Web-trepreneur, seeing which way the electronic wind was blowing a few years ago, might have rushed to register *lawyer.com, software.com*, or *computer.com,* knowing that those names, being easy to remember, would be desired by individuals and companies, who would be willing to pay for them.

InterNIC has a procedure in place for handling disputes over domain names, and for suspending domain names during litigation.

What, finally, can Web site owners do to protect the integrity of their intangible text from the scoundrels who prowl the Net? According to the House Judiciary Committee, copyright piracy on the Internet cost the affected holders more than $11 billion in 1996. By the year 2000, the Internet is expected to have over 200 million users, vastly increasing the potential for copyright infringement and theft of intellectual property.

The following are some tips for protecting your own site and avoiding infringement of others' sites:

- Be sure that a complete copyright notice appears on every page of your site.
- Include tags in your text that identify it as yours when printed or copied.
- Consider registering your copyright.
- Consider trademarking your domain name.
- Be sure that all links are clearly identified as "foreign sites."
- Monitor any bulletin boards or e-mail facilities on your site for copyrighted material imported by users.
- Conduct periodic "policing" Web searches for your domain name or key identifiable words and phrases from your site, to identify possible infringement.
- Act immediately when infringements are located. Know your legal rights and let the infringer know that you are prepared to vigorously defend the integrity of your intellectual property. Don't be bashful: your property has been stolen as much as if the infringer came into your house and took your VCR. Let cyber-thieves know they've committed a crime. And once you've dealt with an infringer, periodically check his or her site to ensure that they haven't backslid. Let them know you're "watching."
- Don't take anything off the Internet that doesn't belong to you. That is, don't copy text, images, sound files, or anything else onto your Web site without authorization. Respect others' rights just as you expect them to respect yours.

In the best of all possible worlds, the Internet would be a vast, interlinked repository of thought, opinion, art, entertainment, facts, and commerce with no need for rules and regulations about its use and access to its resources. But while the Internet itself may have the potential to be such an idyllic cyber-network of all the world's knowledge and products, it is a virtual web accessed and operated by humans, who have human weaknesses. There is no reason to assume that the same rascals and scoundrels who populate the real world won't work their wickedness in the virtual one. That's why copyright laws exist both here, and there.

CASE STUDY
COMPANYLINE

▼▼▼▼▼▼

*F*ive years ago, Matt Evans and his partner David Nikko started CompanyLine, a professional communications service that focuses on writing in-house communications materials for large companies, like newsletters and benefits memos for accounting houses and law firms. Two years ago they made the decision to go online, with a Web site that provides illustrations of their services, a list of their former clients, a price list for their services, and humorous biographies of the owners. They also have a section called "The Pursuit of Clarity," where they offer free tips and guidelines for clear corporate communication. They use real-life horror stories as examples, as well as fictional accounts used for illustration.

Periodically, Matt surfs the Web to research their competitors across the country. Even though they're local, they think it's a good idea to know what other similar companies are doing. One day, Matt was doing his competitor research and discovered a company called CommuniLine. CommuniLine's Web site had a headline that said "California's Single Source for Cutting-Edge, High-Quality Professional Communications Services."

That was almost exactly the same as CompanyLine's headline, "Chicagoland's Single Source for Cutting-Edge, High-Quality Professional Communications Services." Intrigued, Matt went into the site, and there it was: the complete text of his site's "Pursuit of Clarity" feature from a couple of months ago, which he had written himself. It was reproduced word for word. While imitation may be the sincerest form of flattery, this was just too much for Matt.

After Matt finished yelling and throwing things around the office, he took a deep breath and calmed down. He called CommuniLine, and was automatically connected to the Web site manager's voicemail. Putting on his best "lawyer-sounding" voice, Matt left an ominous and unfriendly message about the legal consequences of plagiarism and his company's policy of "vigilantly and vigorously defending its proprietary content on the Internet"—a policy he'd just made up at that moment. As if by a miracle, however, the threat worked: CommuniLine's site was "under construction" the next day. When it reappeared a week later, all the CompanyLine content was gone. ▼

CASE STUDY ROUNDTABLE

▼▼▼▼▼▼

Matt: So I took care of the CommuniLine problem, but it got me thinking about what we'd gotten ourselves into, putting our product—our words—out on the Web for everyone to see. What else could we do?

Discussion Points

- What actual legal options would have been available to CompanyLine under the facts as you understand them?
- How do you think this incident would be treated under NET?

Matt: CompanyLine hadn't registered our Web site text with the Copyright Office prior to the infringement. Would that have been a problem? What kind of luck do you think we'd have if we sued?

Discussion Points

- How could CompanyLine establish actual damages? Was there any actual financial injury to the company?
- If you were a judge, what would you have done with the case?

Matt: Any of the pages on CompanyLine's site can be accessed independently via a search engine (Yahoo!, Lycos, Excite, etc.). One of the first things we did after the incident was to have copyright notices placed on every page.

Discussion Points

- Does that matter?
- Is there anything else CompanyLine can or should do to protect its content?

▲▲▲▲▲▲

CHAPTER BRIEFCASE

▼▼▼▼▼▼

- While you can't copyright an idea, you can provide certain legal protections, such as through a disclosure letter supported by a journal
- U.S. copyright law gives owners the right to reproduce their work, to create derivative works based on an original copyrighted work, to distribute copies to the public, to perform the work publicly (including through a digital transmission), and to display the work publicly.
- A trademark is a word, symbol, unique name, design, logo, slogan, or combination of elements used by a company to identify its products.
- The only sure way to establish the novelty of a product, invention, or process (and its patentability) is to conduct a search of the Patent Office files. A Provisional Patent Application (PPA) lets inventors show their product, invention, or process to others without fear of having their idea stolen.
- Intellectual property on the Internet is particularly susceptible to infringement, and the No Electronic Theft (NET) Act seeks to address these risks by providing special protections and penalties. Common Web-based infringements include appropriation of text and images (through simple cut-and-paste) and passing off linked Web sites as one's own.

▲▲▲▲▲▲

SMALL BUSINESS CHOICES

Sue Kaufman (Dallas, Texas)
Words Worth

Adapted with permission from
Small Business 2000, the
series on public television.

" ***S***ue: I realized I had this opportunity—to begin my own business full-time doing something I really know how to do—and I was going to be extremely valuable. And the interesting thing is that I'm much more valuable in the business community than I am in academia.

With 30 years of experience and a Ph.D. I was a dime a dozen. But in the business community, I'm one in a million.

The very month that I began my own business full-time, in 1992, I decided it was important to join at least one organization for networking purposes, and I joined the National Association of Women Business Owners, which has been a godsend to me in many ways. I have met many people. I have learned a lot about how to market my services because, of course, most people who are in business for themselves or for other people—but particularly for themselves—are marketing and selling, and that's not their expertise. My expertise is language but I had to learn how to sell my services, and I learned a great deal from that organization. And that has helped me to get new clients, to learn how to work better with the clients that I have. We function, really, as a chairman, as a board together.

Hattie: Board of advisers to one another.

Sue: That's right. And we come in with our problems, with our ideas, our goals, and then we bounce them off the other folks and they have been very helpful. We all have been helpful to each other. "

URLink
http://www.nawbo.org

441

Chapter 21

CHOOSING A LOCATION

▼▼▼▼▼

"Would you tell me, please, which way I ought to go from here?"
"That depends a good deal on where you want to get to," said the Cat.
"I don't much care where—" said Alice.
"Then it doesn't matter which way you go," said the Cat.
"—so long as I get SOMEWHERE," Alice added as an explanation.
"Oh, you're sure to do that," said the Cat, "If you only walk long
enough."

—*Lewis Carroll*, Alice's Adventures in Wonderland

MISSION STATEMENT

In this chapter, you will

*L*EARN about the various considerations involved in selecting a
location for your business, and understand the essential elements
of a standard lease.

*E*XPLORE your business's location needs with organizing tools.

*A*PPLY your understanding of business locations to a case study
scenario.

*P*RODUCE location analyses to help you select possible real world
locations for your business.

KEY TERMS

Americans with Disabilities Act (ADA)	ground lease	net lease
business incubator	percentage lease	shopping center
enterprise zone	image	statute of frauds
gross lease	lease	variable lease
	location	

INTRODUCTION TO CHOOSING A LOCATION

So you know what you want to do, and why you want to do it. You've
decided how to implement your idea, and how to present yourself to the
world. The next step is to decide *where* your business will be. Whether it's
in your basement or a shopping mall, office, industrial incubator, storefront,

or Web site, your choice of location is one of the most significant decisions you'll make at this early stage.

Choosing a location is not a simple matter of how much space you need and how much you can afford to pay (although those are certainly key considerations). The dynamics of a location choice can exert a significant impact on the success or failure of your business. In fact, *poor location is generally listed as one of the primary reasons for small business failure*.

Rating the relative strength of a location involves examining some rather obvious issues. Location may be a source of considerable strength if it provides visibility to the target market or customers. On the other hand, a superb product or service may never be accepted if the business is in a bad location. The old saying, "Build a better mouse-trap and the world will beat a path to your door" is only partly true. If your door is too hard to get to, the world will make do with the mousetraps it has.

Key location factors include:

- Amenities
- Availability of parking
- Competitors
- Cost
- Demographics
- Ease of access

- Neighborhood reputation and image
- Neighboring businesses
- Resources and supplies
- Traffic patterns
- Visibility

In this chapter, we'll look at each of these elements, as well as other considerations in selecting the best location for your business.

THE BEST LOCATION FOR YOUR TYPE OF BUSINESS

Your business location should be chosen with great care. Investing time to choose a good location well ahead of start-up pays off handsomely.

For some kinds of businesses, location is all-important. For other businesses, location is less vital. Manufacturers and wholesalers value low space costs and good access to transit routes over exposure to and accessibility by the public. For retail operations, access and exposure are very important. A storefront is vital to a retail business in part because it is the most direct channel of distribution between store and customer. If you provide a service, you must also think in terms of distribution channels. How will you keep your prospects alert to your business existence? Where will you deliver the service—your place or theirs? If you are a manufacturer (including crafts), how will you get the products from your site to the stores or intermediaries who take your products to the consumer? Line up your distribution channels early, and include distribution considerations in your search for the right location for your business. Traffic studies may be available for the area you are interested in and can give you information to make the right location decision for your business. If you're going to rely on walk-in traffic, make sure you're in an area where people walk around to shop, rather than just engage in point-to-point driving trips. Will your customers drive to your site? If so, parking is an important consideration. Making a decision on cost concerns alone is risky. Location and image are so tightly intertwined that the wrong location can undermine an otherwise sound business.

Talk with Real Estate Brokers, Bankers, and Your Chamber of Commerce

Before settling on a location, consult the people who can help you make a wise choice. Real estate brokers are knowledgeable about markets for commercial property, but talk to more than one, and don't rely on them alone.

Talk to your banker and other advisers. Bankers provide another viewpoint for evaluating commercial locations and often are aware of trends earlier than other people. Your choice of location may also affect your qualification for a loan.

Information about specific areas is also available from chambers of commerce, industrial development commissions (they may also have information about tax breaks and financing incentives for businesses that will employ substantial numbers of people in towns under their commission), trade sources such as magazines and associations, planning commissions, and lawyers. Try these first. And don't forget to talk to owners of existing businesses.

Once you have a feel for how much space you need and the location cost requirements, interview some commercial real estate agents to find out what is available that meets your specifications. Don't jump at the first good site. Choose from a variety of locations, and take your time. If you decide to rent, remember that leases are negotiable. They are also hard to get out of, so be sure to get legal advice before you sign.

Flexibility

As always, the successful entrepreneur is alert to change. Once you get started, or if you are already in a good location, keep a constant eye on changes in your location—new roads get built, populations change, people move, zoning ordinances change, and your business needs may change too. Prepare to anticipate these changes. Compare census reports over a period of time to find long-term shifts. Keep in touch with real estate people who have to know what's happening.

IMAGE

One important set of questions involved in choosing a location revolves around the image you wish your business to project. Since money spent on space is a fixed cost, one that you have to pay every month no matter how sales are, this is no trivial matter. Some questions you should ask include:

- How do you want your target markets to perceive your business?
- Is there a "gasoline alley" or "fast food row" or professional office park where your business should be located?
- Will you depend on walk-in business?
- Is the location consistent with the image you want to project? A discount store in a luxury location or a luxury store in a downscale area is discordant.
- Where do your competitors set up shop? Why did they choose their location?
- What sort of help does your trade association offer for site selection?
- Check with your advisers (SCORE, SBDC, and student consulting projects, for instance). What do they recommend?

- What is the rent versus advertising cost trade-off? Low rent and high advertising costs tend to go together.

If location is not very important to your business, you still have to ask how your customers will find you, what the impact of the location on your image will be, and how you will justify your choice. As an example, consultants often use a fancy accommodation address to impress prospective clients, even if the actual client meetings take place at the client's place of business. Mail order companies prefer to use a street address rather than a post office box number, which has implications of here today, gone tomorrow.

Location is a major choice. Take your time. For now, just look around and ask questions. You can make your choice later.

FIRST PERSON

Nancy G., Minneapolis, Minnesota: This is a real sore spot for me! I opened my first Nancy's Nails salon in a little strip center that was near my home. It was easy to get to, the rent was low and the other shops were pleasant: a dry cleaner, a convenience store, and a video rental place. After six months, I had about sixteen customers—way too low for this kind of business. By the time the one-year lease was up, Nancy's Nails was closed. But I like doing nail art, and I'm good at it, and so after I took a few months off to recuperate I decided to give it another try. This time I was a little more careful: I talked to some real estate people I knew from the parents' association at the elementary school, and I drove around town scoping out possibilities. Then I was complaining about all this to the woman who does my hair, and I'll never forget what she said: "People don't get their nails done when they go pick up a loaf of bread or drop off their laundry." She was so right. I started looking for good spots near hair and tanning salons, day spas, even health clubs. I found a perfect location at a good price in a shopping center right next to a hair salon and three stores down from a place that sells party dresses. I've been there ever since, and business is booming: I've hired three assistants and I'm thinking about expanding next year!

CHOOSING THE BEST BUSINESS LOCATION

Your choice of location should be made early. Base your decision on the type of products or services you provide and your target market rather than on your personal convenience. Your most important consideration when choosing a location is your ability to satisfy your target market. Your customers must be able to reach your business easily, safely, and pleasantly. Other considerations are location of the competition, sources of supply, availability of a labor force, and square footage costs.

Location Choice Mapping System

One of the most effective ways to evaluate a location is to do a map analysis. Draw a map of the area in which you wish to locate. Have a copy shop run off some

PERSONAL WORKSHOP 39
Location Selection Organizer

▼ Use this worksheet to record information about prospective locations.

What is the business ADDRESS?	
What are the building's PHYSICAL FEATURES?	
Would you LEASE or OWN your space?	
LEASE: Rent per square foot or month	
OWN: Sales price and interest costs	
What RENOVATIONS are needed?	
How much will they COST?	
Do ZONING LAWS permit your business?	
What OTHER BUSINESSES are in the area?	
Are there any COMPETITORS in the area?	
Why is this the RIGHT LOCATION for you?	
Why is this the WRONG LOCATION for you?	

duplicates and one transparency. On the transparency, indicate the location sites available within your target area and mark them with a colored pen or assign each of them a number. Because you will be coding information onto the duplicate maps, you will be able to place the transparency over the coded map to get a feeling for each site.

Crime. Take one of the duplicate maps to the police department. Ask about crime rates. Shade the high crime area on your map. When you place the transparency over the shaded duplicate, you will be able to see if any of your potential locations fall within high crime areas.

Market. On a duplicate map, shade in the areas in which your target market lives, shops, or works. Again use the transparency overlay to see if your customers will be able to reach you easily. Retail stores and restaurants have to be located near their customers. Is there freeway access, good traffic flow, and adequate parking? Customers are concerned about safety. Can they reach your place of business with a feeling of security? Your crime rate map will show if they have to pass through any high crime areas on the way to your establishment. Customers' trips to your business should be pleasant. Drive and walk the routes your customers will have to take and get a feeling for the neighborhood.

Competition. Find out where your competition is located and try to determine their sales volume. Most businesses try to distance themselves from the competition. However, some types of businesses, such as restaurants and auto dealerships, seem to have great success when clustered together. Professional services tend to locate within an area around a main support facility, such as doctor's offices near a hospital and attorney's offices near the court house. The consumer expects to locate such services in these areas. Sometimes, businesses will take special note of where a particularly successful competitor chooses to locate. They assume, often correctly, that the competitor has undertaken a thorough demographic and market analysis, and that, in short, what's good for the competitor is good for them, too. For instance, notice how often several fast-food restaurants will suddenly appear once one national franchise has located in a particular spot.

Sources of supply. Manufacturing companies may need to locate close to suppliers and will have to consider transportation, labor, and power costs; the tax base; and the zoning regulations of a site. If certain raw materials are crucial to the manufacture of your products, you may need to locate close to your suppliers in order to reduce freight costs and delivery times.

Labor force. Another location consideration is the availability of employees. As your business grows, it becomes increasingly important to have a pool of qualified potential employees. Some areas do not have an adequate group of people to form a labor pool. The prevailing wage rate in the area may be out of line with competitors' rates in other areas. The local chamber of commerce will be able to give you wage and labor statistics for the neighborhoods and other areas around the location you are considering.

COST

Do not go into business in a particular spot just because the price is low. Rent and purchase prices are fixed by market forces, and a low price usually reflects low desirability. While for some operations this doesn't matter, for others (merchandising and restaurant businesses in particular) the three most important success factors are said to be *location, location,* and *location.*

Office space for minimal rent is not always the best reason for choosing a site. Remember: if the rent seems too good to be true, it probably is—there's usually a reason why a property's rent is below the prevailing market rate. Find out why the space is available, how long it has been vacant, and the history of the previous tenants. If there has been a frequent turnover in occupancy, it may be considered a "bad location." The chamber of commerce can give you information on average square footage costs for your area. Check with the local zoning commission regarding any rezoning being planned for the surrounding area. Take a walk around the area. Does the location project the image that you have for your business?

Plan, Plan, Plan

Before beginning a search for the perfect location, outline your present requirements and project your future needs. If you plan to grow your business, will the location allow for expansion? It is often difficult to relocate a successful business without losing some of your customer base.

Proper site location can help your business make money. If you are going into business, first try to locate the ideal site, then figure out how close you can come to it. Remember:

$$\text{Rent} = \text{The costs of space} + \text{Advertising}$$

TYPES OF BUSINESS LOCATIONS

Shopping Centers

You may consider locating your business in a minimall or shopping center. These sites are preplanned as merchandising units. On-site parking is available, which makes it easy for your customers to drive in, park, and shop. You can take advantage of the foot traffic that is drawn to the area by other stores, as well as taking advantage of cooperative marketing efforts or publicity by the center's developers.

There may be some disadvantages, however. You will be a part of a merchant team. You will be expected to pay your share of the site budget, which may include items such as building, landscaping, and parking lot maintenance, and cooperative advertising and promotional activities. You may have to keep regular store hours in concert with other businesses, maintain your windows and premises in a prescribed manner, and conform to established display guidelines. In larger shopping centers, you may be required to pay a percentage of your gross sales to the developers or mall owners in addition to the rent or lease payments.

Business Incubators

A relatively new type of location particularly well suited to light manufacturing and service businesses that do not require large facilities is called a business incubator. While some incubators are new structures, many are converted factories and warehouses, mostly in urban locations, which have been subdivided into smaller space appropriate for several tenants. Incubators are also found at colleges or universities. Because converted incubators were originally industrial-type structures, they offer tenants large, open floor spaces, reinforced structures, and the type of equipment and infrastructure needed by manufacturers.

To reduce overhead costs for new businesses, the incubator programs often provide services to tenants through a centralized resource station, and additional incentives and resources are often available through local and federal urban renewal programs. Usually included in the tenant package are reception and telephone answering, maintenance of the building and grounds, conference room facilities, and shipping and receiving services. Other incubator services may include complete clerical services at a nominal charge. Incubator facilities are targeted toward small start-ups and new firms. Square footage costs are low. The new businesses are expected to remain for two to three years. At that point it is hoped they will be successful enough to relocate.

Incubators typically have a manager who is skilled at the business start-up processes. That person is available for one-on-one or group technical assistance to the incubator tenants. The goal of a business incubator is to strengthen the local economy: the success of each participating business is vital to the incubator's success. Incubator start-ups that recognize and exploit this relationship are the ones with the best chance of moving out of "incubation" and on to independence.

Enterprise Zones

There are many advantages to locating in enterprise zones as communities work toward redeveloping depressed areas. Companies located in these zones can take advantage of significant tax incentives, technical assistance, and marketing programs. Enterprise zone communities are committed to attracting new business investment and offer such incentives as reduction or elimination of local permit and construction-related fees and faster processing of plans and permits. Information on enterprise zones in your area can be obtained through the Department of Commerce, the Small Business Administration, and the local chamber of commerce.

LEASES

A lease is a contract between an owner of real estate (usually called the *lessor*) and a tenant (the *lessee*). It is a contract that transfers the lessor's rights to the exclusive possession and use of the property to the tenant for a specific period of time. The lease states the length of time the contract is to run and the amount the lessee is required to pay for the use of the property.

Before you sign a lease on any location, have your lawyer and insurance agent review it. There are several basic facts you'll want to know:

- How much is the rent and how is it determined?
- How does the rent compare to other property in the area?
- Who will pay for alterations and remodeling?
- What is the amount of insurance held by the landlord?
- How much insurance coverage is required by the tenant?
- What are the lease renewal provisions?
- Does the tenant have the right to sublet?
- Are there any zoning restrictions on the property?

A lease is a binding legal agreement and it spells out the rights and obligations of the landlord and the tenant. Be sure you understand all of the provisions of the lease and that they fit with your plans for the site and your business.

Statute of Frauds

The statute of frauds in most states requires lease agreements for more than one year to be in writing in order to be enforceable in court. If the lease cannot be performed within one year of being entered into, the statute of frauds also requires a written document.

Requirements of a Valid Lease

A lease is a form of contract. To be valid, a lease must meet the same requirements as any other contract. We discussed contracts in more detail in Chapter 19, but here is a review of the basic requirements of a valid contract:

- *Offer and acceptance.* The parties must reach a mutual agreement on all the terms and conditions of the contract.
- *Consideration.* The term "consideration" refers to something of value that is given by one party to a contract in exchange for the other party's promise to do something. Because it is a contract, a lease must be supported by valid consideration. Rent is the normal consideration given for the right to occupy the leased premises: the tenant pays rent to the lessor in exchange for the lessor's promise to give up his or her rights to the property for a period of time.
- *Capacity.* The parties must be of legal age and understand that they are entering into a contract.
- *Legal objective.* The purpose of the lease must be legal, or the contract will not be valid. A valid contract cannot be for an illegal purpose.

The leased premises should be clearly described. The legal description of the real estate should be used if the lease involves land, such as a ground lease, on which you're going to build a new building. If the lease is for a part of a building, such as an apartment or office, the space itself or the apartment designation should be described specifically. The lease should describe any other space included, such as storage space or common areas.

Use of Premises

The lessor may restrict the lessee's use of the premises through provisions included in the lease. For instance, the lessor may limit the types of business activities that may be conducted in a building or shopping center.

Use restrictions, in fact, are particularly common in leases for stores or commercial space. For example, a lease may provide that the leased premises are to be used "only as a gourmet coffee shop and for no other purpose." In the absence of such a clear limitation, a lessee may use the premises for a coffee shop, a used bookstore, or a fingernail painting salon—any lawful purpose.

Term of Lease

The term of a lease is the period for which it will run. It should be stated precisely, including the beginning and ending dates, together with a statement of the total period of the lease. For instance, a lease might run "for a term of 30 years beginning June 1, 1999, and ending May 31, 2029." A perpetual lease for an inordinate amount of time or an indefinite term will usually be ruled invalid by a court. However, if the language of the lease and the surrounding circumstances clearly indicate that the parties intended such a term, the lease will be binding on the parties. Some states prohibit leases that run for more than 100 years.

Security Deposit

Most leases require the tenant to provide some sort of security deposit, to be held by the landlord during the lease term. If the tenant fails to pay the rent, or damages the premises, the lessor may keep all or part of the deposit as compensation for the loss.

The lease should specify whether a payment is a security deposit or an advance rental. If it is a security deposit, the tenant is usually not entitled to apply it to the final month's rent.

Improvements

Neither the landlord nor the tenant is required to make any improvements to leased property. The lease may, however, give a commercial tenant the right to install trade fixtures. A fixture is a substantial piece of personal property that is "affixed" to the real estate in such a way that, by law, it is transformed into a part of the real estate. In a house, for instance, a built-in bookcase is a fixture. In a commercial context, trade fixtures are a special category of property. While they are "affixed" to the property, they may be removed when the lease expires. Examples of trade fixtures include shelving, booths, and bakery ovens. Just because you bolt it to the landlord's wall doesn't mean it belongs to the landlord when you leave.

Build-Outs and Americans with Disabilities Act (ADA)

The **Americans with Disabilities Act (ADA)** requires that commercial, nonresidential property in which public goods or services are provided be free of all architectural barriers. That is, all publicly accessible property must provide reasonable accommodation for people with disabilities. When dealing with existing properties, it is advisable for a lease to require the lessor to ensure that the property is in compliance with the ADA.

Frequently, lessors will be willing to remodel existing premises to suit the needs of a new tenant. For instance, an open floor plan may be modified to include several offices, or a maze of office space may be opened up into spacious suites. This is called a "build-out provision." The lessor may perform the build-out before the tenant moves in, or may simply provide an allowance for the tenant to undertake the work himself or herself.

Destruction of the Premises

In leases involving agricultural land, the tenant is obligated to pay rent to the end of the term, even if all the buildings on the land are destroyed. The tenant's liability does not depend on whether the destruction was his or her fault. In many states, this principle has been extended to include ground leases for land on which the tenant has constructed a building.

A tenant who leases only part of a building, such as office or commercial space, however, is not required to continue to pay rent after the leased premises are destroyed.

In some states, if the property was destroyed as a result of the landlord's negligence, the tenant can even recover damages.

Note: All of these general statements about lease provisions are controlled by the terms of the agreement and applicable state law. Great care must be taken to read the *entire lease* before signing it. Every clause in the lease has an economic and legal impact on either the landlord or the tenant. While preprinted lease forms are available, there is no such thing as a "standard" lease. *When complicated leasing situations arise, particularly in commercial lease contexts, competent legal counsel should be sought.*

TYPES OF LEASES

The manner in which rent is determined is often a key indicator of the type of lease.

Gross Lease

In a gross lease, the tenant pays a fixed rental, and the landlord pays all taxes, insurance, repairs, utilities, and other costs connected with the property. Usually, these are called property charges or operating expenses. This is the type of lease structure typically found in residential leases.

Net Lease

In a net lease, the tenant pays all or some of the property charges in addition to rent. Leases for entire commercial or industrial buildings and the land on which they are located, ground leases, and long-term leases are usually net leases.

In a triple-net lease, the tenant pays all operating and other expenses in addition to a periodic rent. These expenses include taxes, insurance, assessments, maintenance, utilities, and other charges.

Percentage Lease

Either a gross lease or a net lease may be a percentage lease. The rent is based on a minimum fixed rental fee plus a percentage of the gross income received by the tenant doing business on the leased property. This type of lease is usually used for retail businesses. The percentage charged is negotiable and varies depending on the nature of the business, the location of the property, and general economic conditions.

Variable Lease

Several types of variable leases allow for increases in rental charges during the lease period. One of the more common is the graduated lease. A graduated lease provides for specified rent increases at set future dates. Another is the index lease, which allows rent to be increased or decreased periodically based on changes in the Consumer Price Index or some other indicator.

Ground Lease

As discussed earlier, a ground lease involves the lease of unimproved land to a tenant who agrees to erect a building on the land. Ground leases usually involve separate ownership of the land and buildings. These leases must be for a long enough term to make the transaction desirable for the tenant; they often run for terms of 50 up to 99 years. Ground leases are generally net leases—the lessee must pay rent on the ground, as well as real estate taxes, insurance, upkeep, and repairs.

CALCULATING RENT

Regardless of the type of lease involved, it's good to know how much rent you're paying. Let's look at the different methods of calculating rent based on a percentage lease and square footage method.

Percentage leases usually call for a minimum monthly rent plus a percentage of gross sales income exceeding a stated annual amount. For example, a lease might require minimum rent of $1,300 per month plus 5 percent of the business's sales exceeding $160,000. On an annual sales volume of $250,000, the annual rent would be calculated as follows:

First find the total annual rent:

$$\$1,300 \text{ per month x } 12 \text{ months} = \$15,600$$

Then determine the sales amount above the stated level:

$$\$250,000 - \$160,000 = \$90,000$$

Next, multiply that sales amount by the stated percentage to determine the percentage rent:

$$\$90,000 \text{ x } 5\% = \$4,500$$

Finally, add the base rent and the percentage rent to determine total annual rent:

$$\$15,600 \text{ base rent} + \$4,500 \text{ percentage rent} = \$20,100 \text{ total annual rent}$$

To calculate monthly rent per square foot, first determine the total square footage of the rental premises. Generally, this includes only floor space, not total enclosed space. For example, here's how to calculate the monthly rent per square foot of a property that is 50 feet by 30 feet, and rents for $1,850 a month.

First, find the total annual rent:

$$\$1,850 \text{ per month x } 12 \text{ months} = \$22,200 \text{ per year}$$

Then determine the total number of square feet:

$$50 \text{ feet x } 30 \text{ feet} = 1,500 \text{ square feet}$$

Next, divide the total annual rent by the total square feet to determine the annual rate per square foot:

$$\$22,200 \div 1,500 \text{ square feet} = \$14.80 \text{ per square foot per year}$$

Finally, convert the annual rate to a monthly rate:

$$\$14.80 \div 12 \text{ months} = \$1.23 \text{ per square foot}$$

PERSONAL WORKSHOP 40
Location Factor Checklists

▾ The following checklists are designed to help you evaluate and compare potential business locations. We've included two sets of factors: those for a retail business and those for a manufacturer.

Property Address:	Excellent	Good	Poor	Bad	
Factor	**4**	**3**	**2**	**1**	**Notes**
General location					
Proximity to customers					
Proximity to competitors					
Demographics of target market					
Size of building					
Size of parking lot					
Number of cars passing location					
Speed of cars passing location					
Distance from traffic signal					
Distance from corner					
Entrance/exit					
Visibility distance					
Setback from street					
Placement of utilities, drainage, etc.					
Distance to nearest commercial neighbor					
Compatibility of commercial neighbors					
SUBTOTAL:					
TOTAL PROPERTY SCORE:					

CONTINUED ▶

Location Factor Checklist for Manufacturing Business

Property Address:	Excellent	Good	Poor	Bad	
Factor	4	3	2	1	Notes
General region					
Proximity to raw materials					
Proximity to transportation					
Types of available transportation					
Condition of available structures					
Zoning restrictions					
Tax rates					
Inducements from city					
Availability of utilities					
Availability of labor					
SUBTOTAL:					
TOTAL PROPERTY SCORE:					

VIRTUAL LOCATION

In Chapter 17, we discussed the small business ramifications of the Internet, World Wide Web, and e-commerce. It's important for small business developers to understand that a *non-physical* location may be a possibility to consider in addition to, or even instead of, an actual physical location.

 URLinks
http://www.onlinewbc.org/docs/starting/location.html
http://www.entrepreneurmag.com/radio/tip155.hts

PERSONAL WORKSHOP 41
Location Analysis Worksheet
▼ ▼ ▼ ▼ ▼

▼ Earlier in this chapter in Personal Workshop 39 (page 447), you were given a tool with which to evaluate a single potential location. Use the following worksheet to prepare the kind of detailed analysis you need before making a final rent or purchase decision.

Location Analysis Worksheet

1. ADDRESS:

2. NAME, ADDRESS, PHONE NUMBER OF REALTOR/CONTACT PERSON:
   Agent Name:
   Brokerage:
   Broker's Name:
   Address:

3. SQUARE FOOTAGE/COST:
   _____ square feet @ $_____/sq. ft.
   _____ feet of window display area fronting on _____.
   Other specialized areas:
   ❑ Break room
   ❑ Classroom
   ❑ Changing room
   ❑ Office (number = _____)
   ❑ Meeting room
   ❑ Restroom
   ❑ Storage room
   ❑ Supply room
   ❑ Workroom
   ❑ Other:

4. HISTORY OF LOCATION:
   Previous occupant type: _____
   Occupied site for _____ years.
   Reason for leaving: _____
   Vacant _____ months.

CONTINUED ▶

5. LOCATION IN RELATION TO TARGET MARKET:

    Draws customers from _____ mile radius.

    Other factors:

6. TRAFFIC PATTERNS FOR CUSTOMERS:

    Mass transit stop _____ block.

    Access from street: ❑ easy ❑ difficult ❑ other: _____

    Traffic lights at crosswalks ❑ yes ❑ no

    Stop signs at crosswalks ❑ yes ❑ no

7. TRAFFIC PATTERNS FOR SUPPLIERS:

    Access for deliveries ❑ easy ❑ difficult ❑ other:

    Loading dock ❑ yes ❑ no

8. AVAILABILITY OF PARKING (include diagram):

    _____ spaces in front of location

    Parking type: ❑ head-in diagonal ❑ head-in straight ❑ parallel

    Metered parking ❑ yes ❑ no

    Metered parking rate ___ ¢/hour

    Parking lot on site ❑ yes ❑ no

    Public lot _____ block(s) from site

    Private lot _____ block(s) from site

    Parking lot rate ❑ free $_____/hour

9. CRIME RATE FOR THE AREA:

    ❑ Electronic security system

    ❑ 24-hour private security additional cost: $_____

    ❑ active neighborhood watch in surrounding residential area

    ❑ police foot patrols

    ❑ police drive-by patrols

    Reported crime rate for area:_____

10. QUALITY OF PUBLIC SERVICES (e.g., police, fire protection):

    Police station _____ blocks

    Fire station _____ miles

    ❑ fire alarm

    ❑ sprinkler system

    ❑ smoke alarms

CONTINUED ▶

11. NOTES OF WALKING TOUR OF IMMEDIATE AREA:

Quality of single-family home maintenance ❑ high ❑ good ❑ mixed ❑ poor

Quality of rental residences ❑ high ❑ good ❑ mixed ❑ poor

Quality of commercial properties ❑ high ❑ good ❑ mixed ❑ poor

Red Flags: ❑ abandoned cars ❑ litter ❑ graffiti ❑ vandalism

❑ vagrancy ❑ abandoned buildings ❑ burned-out buildings

❑ poor sidewalk maintenance ❑ vacant lots ❑ debris in vacant lots

12. NEIGHBORING SHOPS AND LOCAL BUSINESS CLIMATE:

13. ZONING REGULATIONS:

❑ Residential ❑ Mixed Use ❑ Commercial ❑ Industrial

14. ADEQUACY OF UTILITIES

_____ phone lines

_____ bathrooms

_____ water faucets

_____ electrical outlets

_____ wiring in place

❑ water service

❑ sewer

❑ gas available

15. AVAILABILITY OF RAW MATERIALS/SUPPLIES:

16. AVAILABILITY OF LABOR FORCE:

❑ Employment service:

❑ Public ❑ Private

❑ Temp agency

❑ University

❑ Community college

❑ Technical school

❑ High school

CONTINUED ▶

17. LABOR RATE OF PAY FOR THE AREA:

   $_____/hour average for part-time _____ employees

   $_____/hour average for full-time _____ employees

   $_____/hour, managerial

18. HOUSING AVAILABILITY FOR EMPLOYEES:

   Affordable rental apartments in 10 mile radius _____

   Average rental for 2 bedroom = $_____

CASE STUDY
MAINLINE GIFT SHOP

▼▼▼▼▼▼

*L*ucinda Alvarado owns and operates the Mainline Gift Shop in suburban Houston. Lucinda purchased the business seven years ago, and its annual sales have gradually grown to over $900,000. The business has an excellent reputation. The shop is beautifully decorated, and is stocked with gifts from all parts of the world. Lucinda is pleased with her success and attributes her prosperity to total dedication, close contact with her clients, appropriate merchandise, and a good marketing plan. However, Lucinda admits to having serious problems and has talked about them to several of her friends, including her accountant, lawyer, and banker. One of the biggest problems concerns location.

When Lucinda purchased the business seven years ago, the landlord would not give her more than a one-year lease. Because the previous owner had no difficulty renewing the lease each year, Lucinda felt she would not encounter problems either. Plus, she had doubts about her ability to run the business successfully, and was happy not to commit to a longer term. However, the business succeeded, and for the past seven years the $1,000-a-month lease has been renewed each year.

Three months ago, though, the landlord died and his widow turned over all property management to her son, Andrew. Naturally, Lucinda expected the lease arrangement to remain the same as it had in the past. Indeed, Andrew assured her that when her present lease expired she would receive a new one. At the end of the year, Lucinda received a new five-year lease, which was fine with Lucinda, but the new lease was a "net lease" that raised her rent to $3,000 or 5 percent of total annual gross receipts, whichever was higher. Needless to say, Lucinda was furious and immediately called Andrew. He told her that if she didn't like the new terms, she could move. Andrew insisted that based on comparable rental values throughout the community, the rent was more than fair. Andrew did offer to give her a six-month extension on her present lease at the new rate. Lucinda told him she would give him an answer in a few weeks.

Lucinda is reluctant to move. She spent a lot of time building her business at that location and she doesn't want to risk $900,000 in sales and profits. On the other hand, she can't afford either 5 percent or $45,000 a year in rent. Since her business is growing

CONTINUED ▶

at the rate of 20 percent a year, she knows moving would set her back. She decided to contact several real estate brokers and finally located a vacant lot ten blocks from her present location. The new location would have room for parking and future expansion and still be close enough to keep most of her present customers. The total cost of the building would be $375,000. She could get a mortgage for $300,000, which would require payments of $3,600 monthly for 15 years. She would not be able to move into the new building for six to eight months. The builder said he could make the location reasonably presentable and functional sooner, but it would not be totally complete for about eight months.

In the meantime, Lucinda has heard that Andrew is thinking about opening his own gift shop in her present location. When Lucinda confronted Andrew about this, he confirmed that his wife, Sally May, was going to open up a shop as soon as Lucinda left. Sally May had worked part time for Lucinda for several years. She was very capable, and, in fact, knew the suppliers, customers, and price structure necessary to operate the business.

Lucinda asked Andrew if he would be willing to sell the building. Andrew immediately told her that he would be willing to sell it for $400,000. He would take $100,000 down and hold the mortgage himself at 11.5 percent fixed for 20 years. The monthly payments would be $3,200. Lucinda knew that the building was not worth that much, and that there was little room for expansion. She wasn't sure whether Andrew was bluffing in order to sell the building, or if he really intended to open a gift shop. Since the old lease clearly indicated that all improvements she had made became part of the property of the landlord, Sally May would be opening with the same decor Lucinda had used for years. Lucinda worried about whether all her customers would shop at her new location. She was also concerned that the local market couldn't support two gift shops on the same street. If sales dropped, she might not be able to afford the mortgage payment on the new building. Lucinda asked for an extension of eight months on her lease, but Andrew insisted that she would have to sign a five-year lease.

Lucinda is considering another alternative. For some time she had been contemplating opening a second shop. She had finally settled on a new growth area in another section of Houston. A new building was available there that Lucinda could either lease or purchase. The property was strategically located among a cluster of stores that would complement her business. There was plenty of parking space and room for future expansion. The owner was willing to lease the facility for $2,000 per month on a three-, five-, or ten-year basis, or sell the property for $250,000. The owner would accept $50,000 down and could arrange financing at 12 percent over a 20-year period. The monthly payments, including principal and interest, would be $2,202. Lucinda is tempted to call it quits at the old location and start from the beginning in this new growth area. When she thinks about the time and effort she put into the original location, however, she is reluctant to start over again. ▼

CASE STUDY ROUNDTABLE

▼ ▼ ▼ ▼ ▼ ▼

Lucinda: There's really only one question here: What should I do?

Discussion Points

- Lucinda seems to have only four options, none of which is clearly perfect for her:
  1. Pay an exorbitant rent under a five-year lease at the present location
  2. Purchase her present location, which would probably be too small within five years and is overvalued at $400,000
  3. Build a new building 10 blocks away and take on a mortgage of $3,600 per month, with the threat of having Sally May open the same type of business and perhaps cut into her sales

4. Open a new location in the growth area and start over again, with uncertain sales and income

- Discuss the positive and negative aspects of each element, and decide which one Lucinda should choose.

- What could Lucinda have done earlier to help her decision-making process?

▲▲▲▲▲▲

CHAPTER BRIEFCASE

▼▼▼▼▼▼

- Before you settle on a location, consult the people who can help you make a wise choice: real estate brokers, bankers, your local chamber of commerce, and existing business owners.

- The most important consideration when choosing a location is your ability to satisfy your target market. Customers must be able to reach your business easily, safely, and pleasantly. It's up to you to ensure that you locate in a place that provides those essential things.

- Don't go into business in a particular spot just because the rent is low. Rent and purchase prices are fixed by market forces, and a low price usually reflects low desirability.

- Before you sign any lease, have your lawyer and insurance agent review it. A lease is a binding legal document—be sure you understand what you're signing. In particular, be able to answer these questions:
  - How much is the rent and how is it determined?
  - How does the rent compare to other property in the area?
  - Who will pay for alterations and remodeling?
  - What is the amount of insurance held by the landlord?
  - How much insurance coverage is required by the tenant?
  - What are the lease renewal provisions?
  - Does the tenant have the right to sublet?
  - Are there any zoning restrictions on the property?

▲▲▲▲▲▲

Chapter 22

HOME-BASED BUSINESS ISSUES

▼▼▼▼▼▼

There's no place like home...
there's no place like home...
there's no place like home...

—*Dorothy,* The Wizard of Oz

MISSION STATEMENT

In this chapter, you will

*L*EARN about the challenges (as well as the pleasures) of running a business from your home.

*E*XPLORE the basic requirements of the IRS's home office deduction as guidelines for building an efficient home business environment.

*A*PPLY your understanding to evaluate your suitability for running a home-based business.

*P*RODUCE a cost/efficiency analysis for your own business.

KEY TERMS

credibility	principal place of business
home office deduction	Publication 587
organization	self-discipline

INTRODUCTION TO THE FASTEST-GROWING MARKET

One of the fastest-growing markets in the United States is the home-based business. It's interesting to note that one in five businesses located in an office or industrial area started in somebody's home, including such well-known companies as Ford and Apple Computers.

▼▼▼▼▼▼▼▼▼▼▼▼▼▼▼▼

463

The top five home-based occupations are:

1. Marketing/sales
2. Contracting
3. Mechanical/transportation
4. Services
5. Professional/technical

According to the American Association of Home-Based Businesses, there are more than 24 million people running companies out of their homes. They are accountants, artists, business consultants, caterers, contractors, craftspersons, desktop publishers, financial planners, insurance brokers, lawyers, writers—virtually any occupation short of heavy-equipment operation. Women are going into business at a rate five times that of men, and (according to the U.S. Census Bureau) some 300,000 of them start their businesses from their homes.

Some home business owners have assistants, support staffs, and employees. All of them have freedom and flexibility, and the successful ones are highly organized, self-disciplined, and focused on their vision.

HOME-BASED BUSINESS

The trend toward home-based business has occurred for several reasons. From the beginning, the electronic revolution, with its computers, fax machines, copiers, and generally faster, better, smaller and cheaper office technology has made it possible for almost every family to start a business from home. Job insecurities and lay-offs have forced white-collar workers out of corporations. Many of these displaced middle managers have translated their skills into viable businesses run from their home offices. The trend toward home-based business has also been fueled by economic considerations such as eliminating rent and utilizing other home-office deductions. As an additional bonus, having a home-based business has allowed parents to stay home with their families and address elder care and parental leave without added costs.

Home-based businesses are popular because they can be very successful. They can also turn into disasters or, at the very least, become unproductive or halfhearted efforts. To help you get off to a good start, we have devoted this chapter to some of the most important considerations that will contribute to the success of your home-based business.

 URLinks
http://www.aahbb.org/
http://207.240.161.90/index2.html
http://www.homeofficemag.com/
http://www.home-bus.com/
http://www.homebusinessmag.com/
http://www.bizoffice.com/

CREDIBILITY PROBLEM

Home-based business has come to represent a large segment of today's workforce and a powerful force in the economy. Almost every kind of business imaginable is being run out of a home office somewhere. Unfortunately, those same home businesses are often regarded as "little hobbies." The home-based entrepreneur has to get used to looks from neighbors, delivery people, retailers, and messengers that say, "Why aren't you at work?" It may be that a trip out to the discount store for paper and ink cartridges is the equivalent of a walk down the hall to the supply cabinet, but home-based entrepreneurs are constantly asked how they're enjoying their vacations, and if this is their day off.

The truth is that a home-based business owner has to expend extra effort to prove his or her credibility and attract customers. Many professional business organizations, including chambers of commerce, are forming networking groups to help people overcome this stigma. Further, the advent of electronic commerce via the Internet makes the physical location of a business increasingly meaningless: if a customer is ordering widgets or baskets or anything else from the comfort of his or her living room by using a PC with a modem, it doesn't matter one bit whether the company he or she is ordering from is filling the orders out of a vast suburban warehouse center, a midtown highrise, or a corner of the laundry room. However, until the day comes when all business is conducted online and no one commutes to work ever again, professionalism is the only weapon that can be effectively used to overcome misconceptions about the seriousness of this major economic force. It may seem contradictory, but home-based entrepreneurs are in many ways as tied to their "offices" as their white-collar counterparts languishing in cubicles downtown.

The key to success in running a home-based business is to act like you're not at home. That is, set business hours (and stick to them as if you were punching a time clock at the door). Tempting as it may be, don't do your work in your bathrobe: get dressed and be professional about what you do, even when no one but the cat is looking.

Home-based business issues: Two entrepreneurs give compelling reasons for working out of their homes. And two other entrepreneurs tell why they decided *not* to operate a home-based business.

The Importance of Business Hours

It is very important for the home-based entrepreneur to establish regular business hours. Credibility is hard to come by, especially if you work out of your home. Your customers will take you more seriously if they see that you are operating on a schedule. If you are not available when they call, you will soon find that they will be looking elsewhere for the same service or product.

When you are required to be away from your business during normal working hours, be sure that you have provided for a way to take a message and return your customer's call. If you can't afford a "live" answering service, invest in a good answering machine and leave a new message stating when you will be back in your office and assuring the customer that you will return the call. E-mail and voicemail are excellent for fielding calls and taking messages while you're out or unavailable, and for prioritizing your responses, too. There's a wide range of affordable technology and services available to make sure you don't miss an opportunity: use them to your advantage.

FIRST PERSON

Haley B., Amherst, Massachusetts: I knew this one home-business owner who really hated to change messages on his answering machine. So he put on a generic message that said, "I am away from my office right now and will return in two hours." The problem was that the callers never knew what time the message was left or when the two hours would be up. Of course, people stopped calling eventually when he was so hard to get a hold of and didn't reliably return calls. He still works at home, only now he just works on mailing out his resumes!

Protect Your Work Hours

In Chapter 3, we talked about how important it is to the long-term success of your new business to have supportive emotional buy-in from your family and friends. This is particularly vital for home-based businesses. In addition to all the strains that a start-up places on any family, business functions added to the chaotic mix of home activities cause more stress than ever. While it is important that you understand what you're doing to your family, it's equally important that they understand that this isn't a hobby or an early retirement. Just because you work at home, it doesn't make you the convenient new errand-runner, babysitter, and housekeeper.

Politely, but firmly, inform your family and friends that you are serious about your business and will need to work without interruption. For some reason, a home-based business is usually perceived as a place where visitors are welcome to show up and stay for a friendly visit. They would never think of popping into a corporate office for a cup of coffee, but freely assume that you would welcome a break in your working hours at home! Many tender-hearted home-based entrepreneurs have had to work late into the night because well-meaning friends decided that they needed some company during the day!

Unfortunately, this is one of the most serious problems encountered in home-based businesses and one that is difficult to solve. It not only applies to family and friends, but to some of your customers who are anxious to establish a friendly relationship. We have used every trick in the book to get rid of unwanted visitors without offending them. We have resorted to proclaiming nonexistent appointments, calling each other from a telephone in the other room, walking the visitor slowly out the door, and any other means within our imaginations. When all else fails, tell the truth—it might just work.

Protect Your Free Hours

In addition to protecting your business hours, you will also have to decide what days and hours you wish to be closed and promise yourself that you will use them for non-business pursuits. In fact, guard that free time with your life. Just as family and friends may forget that your home-based business is a business, it's equally easy for the home-based entrepreneur to forget that he or she can leave work "at the office." It's hard: that work is sitting there on your desk or work table all the time—during your official working hours and during the time you should be spending with yourself, your friends, and your family. Too many home-based entrepreneurs burn out quickly, simply because they are always "at work."

Be sure to inform your customers about your working hours. If they want to come during your off hours, tell them nicely but firmly that you are closed. Most will respect you and return during your regular business hours.

At the end of your working day, turn on your answering machine and shut the door to your business. Plan activities with your family or friends and try not to overwhelm them with your business problems. The idea is to have fun and give yourself a break. You will soon feel overwhelmed and tired of your business if you never have the opportunity to get away from it.

It would be naive to pretend that a business owner will never have to work extra hours to make the business prosper. Do what you need to do to run your business, but don't let it run you. And don't let it cause you to burn out your enthusiasm and create problems with the people you care about. Remember, owning your own business is supposed to be a *positive* part of your life!

Be Self-Disciplined

Owning your own business requires a great deal of time and effort. Some potential business owners exclaim that they are going to quit working eight hours a day for a company and be free to set their own hours. It is true that you can decide on your hours. However, working for yourself will probably be equivalent to holding down two jobs, at least for the first three or four years until the business is functioning smoothly. For this reason, it will be necessary to develop a high degree of self-discipline.

Be willing to work long hours when necessary. If an extra effort is needed to get a job done, you will have to do it. Decide what hours you are willing to work and stick to your schedule. Don't fall into the trap of thinking that you are free. You are your own boss and you will have to treat yourself as you would an employee.

Dress for Success

Just because you are working at home, don't use it as an excuse to be a slob. Every trade has an acceptable mode of dress that should be adhered to. A home business is the perfect target for a 24-hour-a-day onslaught by customers. They will call on the telephone and ring the doorbell seven days a week from dawn to dark—and that includes holidays. No one can see what you look like on the other end of the phone, but if you are going to answer the door, look like a businessperson. Obviously, that doesn't mean you should wear a suit around the house: just dress like you take yourself seriously. When you run your own business, there's no reason why you can't have a "business casual" dress code.

FIRST PERSON

Becky L., Nashville, Tennessee: I was thrilled to be working at home. It was an exciting time for me after I quit working for someone else and became my own boss. Mostly, it's worked out great, but it took some getting used to at first. For instance, I started working one morning at 8 AM, but since I wasn't expecting anyone, I was still in my bathrobe at 10. Of course, that's when a customer rang the doorbell! I hid behind the door and lost the customer—something no one who's starting a new business at home or otherwise can afford to do. After that, I learned that I had to get dressed in the morning, almost like I was going downtown. And I didn't just get dressed in my weekend clothes. I wore my "business clothes" anytime I was "at work." I'm sure that everyone's been turned off to one business or another because the owners didn't act and look like they could get the job done. You need to dress the part, wherever you are. If your customer is going to have confidence in your products or services, they have to have confidence in you.

Organize Your Work Space

Setting aside your work space is not only an IRS requirement, but a necessary element of any business. It is important to understand that a home-based business is the same as a business in a commercial location with the exception of some special tax considerations. That's exactly the way you should treat it.

Organize your work space in an efficient manner and eliminate non-work items so that you will not be tempted to mix the two during working hours. If you are operating a lawn mower repair shop out of your garage, don't use it to house your cars, bicycles, freezer, and old clothes. If you have an office in your family room, get rid of the TV, pool table, exercise machine, and ironing board. When a customer steps through the door into your office, it should feel like a business.

Compare the three different approaches in Figures 22.1, 22.2, and 22.3 from a home-based business spread all over the house to a fully functional separate office space. Obviously, your ability to set aside separate space for your home-based business will depend on your home. It may be difficult to convince a landlord to let you wall off part of the living room in an apartment, for instance. Renters can use bookcases or folding screens to create separate office areas. Homeowners may prefer to change an extra bedroom into an office, or equip a basement or garage for the business.

Time is Money

This is not an issue just for people who run businesses out of their homes: everyone who's self-employed should think carefully about how they spend their time, and what it's costing them. For home workers, however, the cost/efficiency analysis is particularly important. With so many distractions lying around the house, or calling you on the phone, or ringing your doorbell (not to mention the domestic responsibilities you'd have no matter where you worked, and the ever-present temptation of a cup of coffee and mindless daytime television!), you need to be aware of just what you're doing every minute, and how much you're spending to do it.

Many people forget that they're spending money even when they aren't writing a check or handing someone a credit card, but they are. Every minute you're not being paid by someone else, you're spending your own money.

Think of it this way: The house has to be cleaned by someone, and since you work at home you're the obvious candidate: after all, you're there all day anyway, right? Try looking at four basic figures; they'll tell you a lot!

1. How much do I charge for my time, on an hourly basis? $_____
2. How much does a good housekeeper charge, per hour? $_____

FIGURE
22.1   **Poor Home Office Approach**

▼ This home business is spread all over the house. The computer and printer are on a card table in the living room, the answering machine is on the household phone line in the kitchen, the fax machine is in the bedroom, and the business records, documents, notes, and files are piled in the dining area.

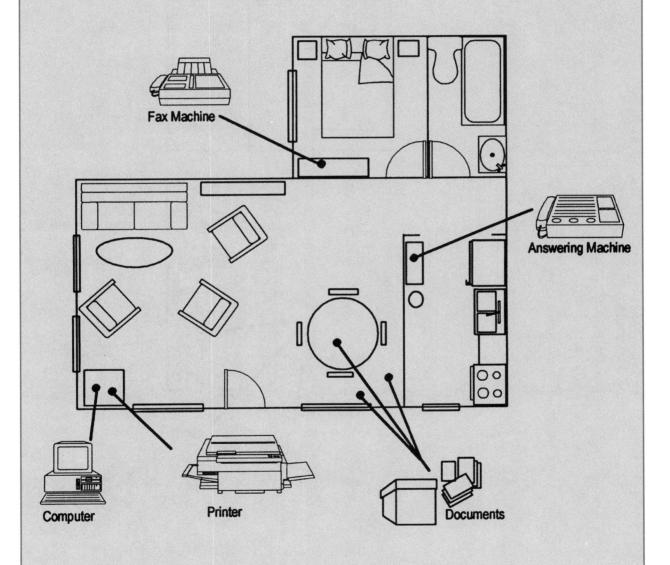

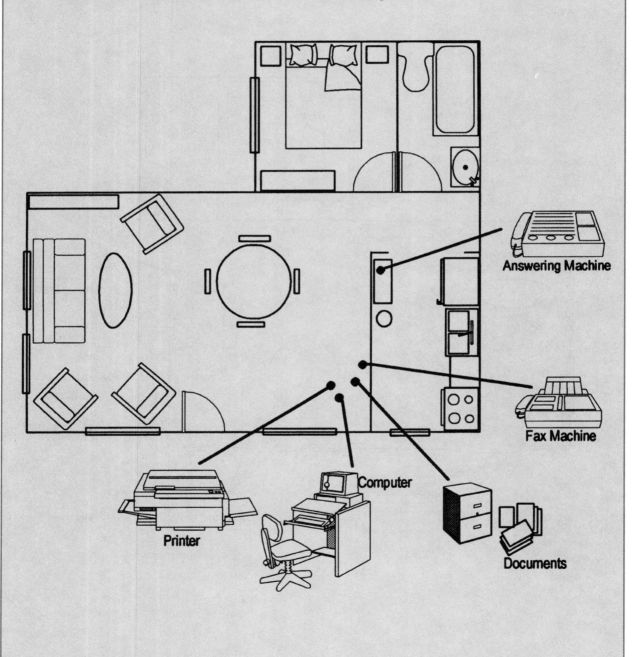

FIGURE
22.2
Better Home Office Approach

▾ The home business owner has made a modest investment in a workstation and file cabinet and has consolidated the business operations in one part of the living room. Although the answering machine is still in the kitchen, this is a much better arrangement.

Answering Machine

Fax Machine

Printer

Computer

Documents

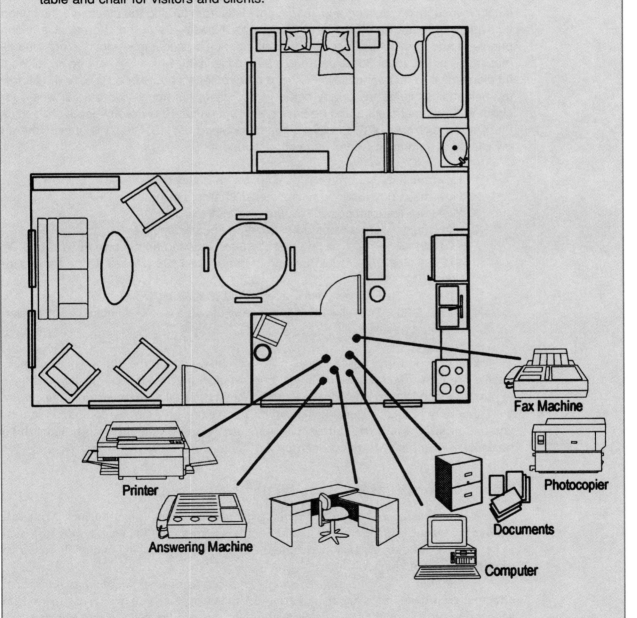

FIGURE 22.3 Best Home Office Approach

▼ The home business owner was able to add a partition wall in the living room, creating a small but completely separate private workspace. The office is on its own phone line and even has an extra table and chair for visitors and clients.

Printer

Answering Machine

Computer

Fax Machine

Photocopier

Documents

3. What are the total possible hours a week I could bill? _____
4. How many hours a week do I spend on housekeeping? _____

FIRST PERSON

Frank N., Rochester, New York: OK, I'll play along with your little system here. Let's see, I guess I spend about six hours a week on household chores like the laundry, vacuuming, dusting and keeping my kids from turning the place into the condo equivalent of a landfill. That'd be Step 4, right? Now, figure in the chores, plus taking people to and from school, soccer, cello, and dance practice, the grocery store, and all that stuff. I put in about 35 hours a week as a consultant, which is what I do for a living. If I didn't have to do the housework, that'd be another six hours or so. That's 41. I know my neighbor upstairs has a lady come in and clean his house two days a week, for about four hours at a shot, and he pays her $10 an hour. She's pretty good, and I think that's about average for this neighborhood. So Step 2 is $10. Step 1 is easy: I charge my clients $18 an hour. So how does that work out?

1. How much do I charge for my time, on an hourly basis? $18
2. How much does a good housekeeper charge, per hour? $10
3. What are the total possible hours a week I could bill?   41
4. How many hours a week do I spend on housekeeping?   6

$18 - $10 = $8—I'm paying myself $8 too much to do my own housework!

$18 x 6 = $108—I could be earning an extra $108 a week if I had a house-keeper?

$10 x 6 = $60—The housekeeper would cost $60 a week.

$108 - $ 60 = $48—I would have a profit of $48 a week—almost $2,500 a year! This is a no-brainer!

You can perform this analysis with virtually any of the tasks your business involves, not just the household chores. For instance, figure out how much you'd have to pay someone to stuff envelopes, do photocopying, or take on other time-consuming work that only indirectly generates income. If you can earn more by doing the big jobs you had in mind when you started, pay someone else to do the little stuff, and still be financially ahead, it's worth considering.

Take Care of Legal Responsibilities

A home business has the same legal requirements as any other business. You will still need a business license, a DBA, and a seller's permit—all the legal hoops still need to be jumped through. You also need to go through all the focusing and analysis we've discussed in other chapters.

You should never mix your business finances with your personal finances. An effective recordkeeping system will have to be set up and you will need to find an accounting professional who can help you maximize your tax benefits and prepare your final tax return. You will need a separate bank account and a business telephone. You will need business insurance tailored to your products and services.

In other words, pretend that you have just opened business in a commercial location and do the same things that you would have to do to get your business underway.

 **URLinks**
http://www.aahbb.org

HOME OFFICE TAX CONSIDERATIONS

There are many financial advantages available to you if you operate out of your home. You don't have to pay rent, you don't have to worry (as much) about childcare. If the business use of your home meets specific tests, you may be able to deduct a percentage of your regular expenses, such as rent, interest, taxes, insurance, repair, and maintenance. This is one of the principal attractions of basing a start-up business in the home for many entrepreneurs. However, to do so, your home office must meet specific tests and your deduction is limited.

Of course, this is not a tax book, it's a book about developing a small business. But in the real world of small business, home-based businesses face the same developmental issues as any other business; that's what this book is about. Where the difference lies, as we've been saying over and over again in this chapter, is in people's perception of the home-based entrepreneur: the customer's view, the family's view, and the entrepreneur's own view of himself or herself as a home-based worker. That is, business is business: the only difference is the location.

The rest of this chapter will focus on the home business deduction that may be available to home-based entrepreneurs. We will focus on it, though, not so much because we're giving out tax advice (please read the warning that follows to understand that we absolutely are *not* giving tax advice), but to help you be more aware of your home-based business and its true physical reality as a workplace. That is, if the Internal Revenue Service takes your home-based business seriously, so should you. As you read this material, think of how it applies to your own perceptions of what you do at home and how you do it. Remember, too, that tax laws change. However, the guidelines here are good ones for you to keep in mind whether you're thinking about taxes or just about your business.

WARNING! CONSULT A COMPETENT TAX ATTORNEY BEFORE YOU DECIDE TO CLAIM A HOME OFFICE DEDUCTION! **The home office deduction is one of the most difficult to defend against an IRS audit, and the IRS seems to be particularly suspicious of people who claim home office deductions! The information provided here, based on IRS Publication 587, is for informational purposes only, and should not be relied on as legal advice!**

 **URLinks**
http://www.irs.ustreas.gov/

Under the Internal Revenue Code, the part of your home for which you are claiming the home office deduction must be used exclusively and regularly

PERSONAL WORKSHOP 42
Advantages and Disadvantages of a Home-Based Business
▼ ▼ ▼ ▼ ▼ ▼

▼ Check all that apply to you to see if the advantages of basing your new business in your home outweigh the disadvantages.

Advantages	Disadvantages
❑ **Address domestic responsibilities:** I would be free to care for children, parents, and household duties.	❑ **Demands on family members to cooperate:** I'm not sure my spouse/parents/ children will like the disruption of a business being run out of their home.
❑ **Control over work hours:** If I don't feel that I have time in my life for another client, I can say no. I can cut back during the summers, and work longer hours during the school year.	❑ **Difficult to set aside long blocks of time:** Soccer games, doctors' appointments, car repairs, plumbers—the list of things I have to fit in work around is a long one.
❑ **Convenience:** I would have all the aspects of my life—work, family, social— consolidated in one place.	❑ **Domestic interruptions:** If I'm at home, it's going to be hard for family and friends to realize I'm working.
❑ **Decreased commuting time:** I'd be able to really use the time I spend now traveling from home to work and back.	❑ **Household chores:** I really won't have any excuse for not keeping up with the house.
❑ **Flexible hours and pace:** If I wanted to put in my hours late at night or early in the morning, I'd be able to do it.	❑ **Informal, cramped, insufficient work-space:** I don't have very good "private" space for working.
❑ **Independence:** I'd not only be my own boss, I'd be my own landlord.	❑ **Lack of respect:** People will think I'm unemployed, or they'll think of my business as a hobby.
❑ **Lack of workplace distractions:** It seems like I spend half my days chatting with other workers—I could take back that time for working, and earning money.	❑ **Lack of workplace camaraderie:** It can get quiet and lonely around the house all day.
❑ **Low overhead expenses:** I'm already paying for the space I live in and the utilities I use; why not make the most of it?	❑ **Total responsibility for workflow and efficiency:** It's a lot to be responsible for, and I won't have anyone to blame but myself.
❑ **Tax advantages:** The IRS offers tax breaks for business use of the home: I could use a tax break.	❑ **Zoning issues:** I'm not sure my town permits businesses like mine to be operated out of residential neighborhoods.

- as the *principal place of business* for any trade or business in which you engage;
- as a place to meet or deal with your *patients, clients, or customers* in the normal course of business; or
- in *connection with your trade or business* if you are using a separate structure that is not attached to your home or residence.

Beginning in 1999, however, the definition is significantly simplified and broadened. Under the new rule, your home office generally will qualify as a principal place of business if

- you use it *exclusively and regularly* for the administrative or management activities of your trade or business, and
- you *have no other fixed location* where you conduct substantial administrative or management activities of your trade or business.

That is, if you work from home, and don't work from anywhere else, then your home office will likely qualify in 1999 and after.

Qualifying for the Deduction

To qualify for a home office deduction for the business use of your home, you must meet the following tests:
Your use must be

- exclusive,
- regular, and
- for your trade or business.

The business part of your home must be

- for your trade or business, or
- the place where you meet or deal with patients, clients, or customers in the normal course of your trade or business, or
- a separate structure (not attached to your home) that you use in connection with your trade or business.

Let's consider each part of the requirement individually.

Exclusive use. To qualify as exclusive use, you must use a *specific area* of your *home only for your trade or business*. The area you use can be a room or any other identifiably separate space. The space does not need to be separated from the rest of the house by a permanent partition; it must only be clearly separate.

However, you will not satisfy the exclusive use test if you use the area for both business and personal purposes. For example, an attorney uses a den in his home to write legal briefs and prepare client tax returns. His family also uses the den for playing video games, doing homework, entertaining friends, and watching a big-screen television. Because the den is not used exclusively by the attorney for his professional activities, he cannot claim a business deduction for its use.

There are some exceptions to the exclusive use requirement, however. The IRS does not require you to meet the exclusive use test if you use part of your home for storing inventory or product samples, or if you use part of your home as a day care facility.

When you use part of your home for storing inventory or product samples, you don't have to meet the exclusive use test. However, you must meet *all* of the following requirements:

- You keep the inventory or product samples for use in your trade or business.
- Your trade or business is the wholesale or retail selling of products.
- Your home is the only fixed location of your trade or business.
- You use the storage space on a regular basis.
- The space you use is identifiably separate space suitable for storage.

For instance, assume your home is the sole fixed location of your business selling mechanics' tools at retail. You regularly use half of your basement for storage of inventory and product samples. Sometimes, you use the area for personal purposes. The expenses for the storage space are deductible even though you do not use this part of your basement exclusively for business.

Regular use. To qualify under the regular use test, you must use a specific area of your home for business on a continuing basis. You do not meet the test if the business use is only occasional, even if you don't use the area for any other purpose.

Trade or business use. To qualify under the trade or business use test, part of your home must be used in connection with a trade or business. If you use your home for a profit-seeking activity that is not a trade or business, you cannot take a deduction for its business use.

For example, if you use your study exclusively to read financial periodicals and reports, clip bond coupons, call your broker, and generally manage your investments, you cannot take a deduction for the business use of your study. Because you do not make investments professionally as a broker or dealer, your activities are not considered part of a trade or business.

Principal place of business. To qualify for a home business deduction, your home must be your principal place of business for that trade or business. You can, of course, have more than one business location, including your home, for a single trade or business. If your home is the main place where you conduct your business, you can likely deduct its use.

There is no hard and fast rule for identifying what constitutes a "principal" place of business: the IRS will consider all the facts and circumstances of each individual case. There are two primary factors in this consideration.

1. The relative *importance* of the activities performed at each location. To determine whether your home is the principal place of business, consider the relative importance of the activities carried out at each business location. The relative importance of the activities performed at each business location is

determined by the basic characteristics of the business. That is, if your business requires that you meet with clients or patients, or that you deliver goods or services to a customer, then the place where you make contact must be given great weight in determining where the most important activities are performed, and the activities that occur in your home office (such as planning for services or the delivery of goods, or the accounting or billing for those activities or goods) is not as important.

2. The *time* spent at each location. Compare the time you spend on business at your home office with the time you spend at other locations.

The following First Person account gives examples of the principal place of business.

FIRST PERSON

Mary R., Little Rock, Arkansas: Joe and I are both in sales. But I was interested to see how the IRS treats us differently, at least as far as the home office deduction is concerned. Joe's only office is a room in his house used every day, exclusively to set up appointments, store product samples, and write up orders and other reports for the companies whose products he sells.

Joe sells to customers all over the metro area. He goes from site to site, visiting customers to explain the products and (hopefully!) take orders. He only makes a few sales from his home office. I'd say he spends about 30 hours a week visiting customers and maybe 12 working at home.

This is what the IRS said about Joe, when he wanted to claim a deduction for his home office:

> The essence of the taxpayer's business as a salesperson requires him to meet with customers primarily at the customer's place of business. The home office activities, although essential, are less important to the taxpayer's business and take less time than the sales activities he performs when visiting customers. Therefore, his home office is not his principal place of business and he cannot deduct expenses for the business use of his home.

Now, I'm in sales, too, and I do pretty much the same thing Joe does (of course, I think I do it a little better!). I do the same things in my home office as Joe, except I make most of my sales to customers by telephone or mail from my home office. I'm just the opposite of Joe: I spend an average of probably 30 hours a week working at home, and 12 to 14 hours a week out visiting prospects, delivering products, and sometimes taking orders.

The IRS said this about my home office deduction:

> The essence of the taxpayer's business as a salesperson requires her to make telephone or mail contact with customers primarily from her office, which is in her home. Actually visiting customers is less important to her business and

takes less time than the sales activities she performs from her home office. Therefore, the taxpayer can deduct expenses for the business use of her home.

More than one trade or business. Whether your home office is the principal place of business must be determined separately for each trade or business activity. While one home office may be the principal place of business for more than one activity, each activity has to satisfy all the tests for the business use of the home deduction.

Place to meet patients, clients, or customers. If you meet or deal with patients, clients, or customers in your home as part of the normal operation of your business, you can probably deduct your expenses for the "business" part of your home if

- you *physically* meet with patients, clients, or customers on the premises, *and*
- their use of your home is *vital* to your business.

Occasional meetings and telephone calls with customers or clients will not qualify for the home business deduction.

Separate structures. You can deduct expenses for a separate free-standing structure, such as a garage or barn, if you use it only for your business. The structure does not have to meet the other tests: it doesn't have to be your principal place of business or the place where you meet patients, clients, or customers.

Figuring the Deduction

Once you've determined that your home business qualifies, you still have to figure out how much you can deduct. Your deduction is limited by the percentage of your home used for business, and the deduction limit.

Business percentage. Although you can use any reasonable method to figure what percentage of your home qualifies for the home business deduction, there are two basic methods.

1. The area (length multiplied by the width) used for business divided by the total area of your home.
2. If the rooms in your house are about the same size, you can simply divide the number of rooms used for business by the total number of rooms in your home.

For example, assume Mary's home office is 12 feet x 20 feet (240 square feet), and her home is 1,200 square feet. Her office is 20 percent of the total area of her home (240 ÷ 1,200). Her business percentage is 20 percent.

Or, using the second method, Mark uses only one room in his home for business. His home has four rooms, all of which are about the same size. Mark's office is 25 percent of the total area of his home (1 room ÷ 4 rooms). Mark's business percentage is 25 percent.

You can try using the worksheet in Figure 22.4 to figure your business percentage.

FIGURE
22.4

Worksheet to Figure the Deduction for Business Use of Your Home

PART 1—Part of Your Home Used for Business:

1) Area of home used for business . . . . 1) _____

2) Total area of home . . . . 2) _____

3) Percentage of home used for business (divide line 1 by line 2 and show result as percentage) . . . . 3) _____ %

PART 2—Figure Your Allowable Deduction

4) Gross income from business (see instructions) . . . . 4) _____

	(a) Direct Expenses	(b) Indirect Expenses
5) Casualty losses	5) _____	_____
6) Deductible mortgage interest	6) _____	_____
7) Real estate taxes	7) _____	_____
8) Total of lines 5 through 7	8) _____	

9) Multiply line 8, column (b), by line 3 . . . . 9) _____

10) Add line 8, column (a), and line 9 . . . . 10) _____

11) Business expenses not from business use of home (see instructions) . . . . . 11) _____

12) Add lines 10 and 11 . . . . 12) _____

13) Gross income limit. Subtract line 12 from line 4 . . . . 13) _____

14) Excess mortgage interest	14) _____	_____
15) Insurance	15) _____	_____
16) Repairs and maintenance	16) _____	_____
17) Utilities	17) _____	_____
18) Other Expenses	18) _____	_____
19) Add lines 14 through 18	19) _____	_____

20) Multiply line 19, column (b) by line 3 . . . . 20) _____

21) Carryover of operating expenses from prior year (see Instructions) . . . . . . 21) _____

22) Add line 19, column (a), line 20, and line 21 . . . . 22) _____

23) Allowable operating expenses. Enter the **smaller** of line 13 or line 22 . . . . 23) _____

24) Limit on excess casualty losses and depreciation. Subtract line 23 from line 13 . . . . . . 24) _____

25) Excess casualty losses (see instructions) . . . . 25) _____

26) Depreciation of your home from line 38 below . . . . 26) _____

27) Carryover of excess casualty losses and depreciation from prior year (see instructions) 27) _____

28) Add lines 25 through 27 . . . . 28) _____

29) Allowable excess casualty losses and depreciation. Enter the **smaller** of line 24 or line 28 . . . . . . 29) _____

30) Add lines 10, 23, and 29 . . . . 30) _____

31) Casualty losses included on lines 10 and 29 (see instructions) . . . . 31) _____

32) Allowable expenses for business use of your home. (Subtract line 31 from line 30.) See instructions for where to enter on your return . . . . 32) _____

PART 3—Depreciation of Your Home

33) Smaller of adjusted basis or fair market value of home (see instructions) . . . . 33) _____

34) Basis of land . . . . 34) _____

35) Basis of building (subtract line 34 from line 33) . . . . 35) _____

36) Business basis of building (multiply line 35 by line 3) . . . . 36) _____

37) Depreciation percentage (from applicable table or method) . . . . 37) _____

38) Depreciation allowable (multiply line 36 by line 37) . . . . 38) _____

PART 4—Carryover of Unallowed Expenses to Next Year

39) Operating expenses. Subtract line 23 from line 22. If less than zero, enter -0- . . . . 39) _____

40) Excess casualty losses and depreciation. Subtract line 29 from line 28. If less than zero, enter -0- . . . 40) _____

Deduction Limit

If your gross income from the business use of your home is the same as or more than your total business expenses, good for you! Also, the IRS will permit you to deduct *all* your business expenses. On the other hand, if your gross income from the use of your home is *less* than your total business expenses, your deduction is limited. Check with IRS publications and your accountant or tax lawyer for information on these calculations.

Business Furniture and Equipment

There are complicated rules that govern the calculation of deductions for business furniture and equipment purchased for your home business. Furniture and equipment deductions may be available even if you do not qualify for the home business deduction. The calculation of these deductions, however, involves technical rules for figuring depreciation.

Depreciation. Most business property used in a home office is considered by the IRS to be either five-year or seven-year property for purposes of depreciation deductions. That is, the total cost of the business property can be depreciated over five or seven years, depending on the type of property.

Five-year property, for instance, includes computers and peripheral equipment, typewriters, calculators, adding machines, and copiers. Office furniture, on the other hand, is considered seven-year property. IRS Publication 946 provides more detailed information and tables for figuring depreciation.

PERSONAL WORKSHOP 43
Home Office Tax Deduction Eligibility

▼ Use this worksheet to determine whether or not your home office may be eligible for the home office deduction. Remember, however, to consult a competent tax attorney or accountant before you make any home office claims on your income tax form!

Qualification	Yes	No
Is part of your home used in connection with a trade or business?		
Are you an employee?		
Do you work at home for the convenience of your employer?		
Is the use regular and exclusive?		
Is it your principal place of business?		
Do you meet patients, clients, or customers in your home?		
Is it a separate structure?		

Note: Day care and inventory storage are exceptions to the exclusive use test.

SPECIAL CASE STUDY
THE REAL WORLD PAPER CHASE (A HOME BUSINESS DEDUCTION EXAMPLE FROM IRS PUBLICATION 587)

▼▼▼▼▼▼

*T*he filled-in forms for John Stephens that follow (the first page of John's Schedule C, and completed Forms 8829 and 4562) show how to report deductions for the business use of your home if you file Schedule C (Form 1040). Only the expenses and information that relate to the business use of the home are discussed here. You can follow along with the description of John's tax preparations.

Schedule C
Line 13. John enters his section 179 expense deduction for assets used in his home office on Form 4562.

When John began using part of his home for business in 1992, his office furniture was five-year property under ACRS. Tax year 1997 was the last year of the recovery period for that property. He has recovered his total depreciable basis in that property. He cannot deduct any depreciation for that property in 1998.

In March 1998 he bought a file cabinet for $600 and a copier for $2,500 to use in his business. He elects to take a section 179 deduction for both items.

Form 4562
Part I. John enters the cost of both items, $3,100, on line 2 and completes lines 4 and 5. On line 6, he enters a description of each item, its cost, and the cost he is electing to expense. He completes the remaining lines in Part I. He then enters $3,100, the total section 179 deduction, on line 13 of Schedule C.

Line 16b. This amount is the interest on installment payments for the business assets John uses in his home office.

Line 25. Because he had a separate telephone line in his home office that he used only for business, he can deduct the expense for it of $347.

Lines 28-30. On line 28, he totals all his expenses other than those for the business use of his home, and then he subtracts that total from his gross income. He uses the result, on line 29, to figure the deduction limit on his expenses for the business use of his home. He enters that amount on line 8 of Form 8829 and then completes the form. He enters the amount of his home office deduction from line 34, Form 8829, on line 30 of Schedule C.

Form 8829, Part I
John began to use one room of his home exclusively and regularly to meet clients in August 1998. In Part I of Form 8829 he shows that, based on the square footage, the room is 10 percent of his home.

Form 8829, Part II
He uses Part II of Form 8829 to figure his allowable home office deduction.

Step 1. First, he figures the business part of expenses that would be deductible even if he did not use part of his home for business. Because these expenses ($4,500 deductible mortgage interest and $1,000 real estate taxes) relate to his entire home, he enters them in column (b) of lines 10 and 11. He then subtracts the $550 business part of these expenses (line 14) from his tentative business profit (line 8). The result, $25,781 on line 15, is the most he can deduct for his other home office expenses.

Step 2. Next, he figures his deduction for operating expenses. He paid $300 to have his office repainted. He enters this amount on line 18, column (a) because it is a direct expense. All of his other expenses ($400 homeowner's insurance, $1,400 roof repairs, and $1,800 heating and lighting) relate to his entire home. Therefore, he enters them in column (b) on the appropriate lines. He adds the $300 direct expenses (line 21) to the $360 total for indirect expenses (line 22) and enters the total, $660, on line 24. Because this amount is less than his deduction limit, he can deduct it in full. The $25,121 balance of his deduction limit (line 26) is the most he can deduct for depreciation.

Form 8829, Part III
Step 3. Next, he figures his allowable depreciation deduction for the business use of his home. In Part III of Form 8829, he determines that the basis of his home office (line 38) is $6,000. Because he began using the office in August 1986, it is 19-year real property under ACRS. 1999 is the 13th year of the recovery

CONTINUED ▶

SCHEDULE C
(Form 1040)

Department of the Treasury
Internal Revenue Service

Profit or Loss From Business
(Sole Proprietorship)

▶ Partnerships, joint ventures, etc., must file Form 1065.

▶ Attach to Form 1040 or Form 1041. ▶ See Instructions for Schedule C (Form 1040).

OMB No. 1545-0074

1997

Attachment
Sequence No. 09

Name of proprietor	Social security number (SSN)
John Stephens	465 00 0001

A Principal business or profession, including product or service (see page C-1)
Tax Preparation

B Enter principal business code
(see page C-6) ▶ 7 6 3 3

C Business name. If no separate business name, leave blank.
Stephens Tax Service

D Employer ID number (EIN), if any

E Business address (including suite or room no.) ▶ 821 Union Street
City, town or post office, state, and ZIP code   Hometown, IA 52761

F Accounting method: (1) ☒ Cash (2) ☐ Accrual (3) ☐ Other (specify) ▶ ....

G Did you "materially participate" in the operation of this business during 1997? If "No," see page C-2 for limit on losses. ☒ Yes ☐ No

H If you started or acquired this business during 1997, check here . . . . ▶ ☐

Part I   Income

1	Gross receipts or sales. **Caution:** *If this income was reported to you on Form W-2 and the "Statutory employee" box on that form was checked, see page C-2 and check here* . . . . ▶ ☐	1	34,280
2	Returns and allowances	2	– 0 –
3	Subtract line 2 from line 1	3	34,280
4	Cost of goods sold (from line 42 on page 2)	4	– 0 –
5	**Gross profit.** Subtract line 4 from line 3	5	34,280
6	Other income, including Federal and state gasoline or fuel tax credit or refund (see page C-2) . . .	6	– 0 –
7	**Gross income.** Add lines 5 and 6 . . . . ▶	7	34,280

Part II   Expenses. Enter expenses for business use of your home **only** on line 30.

8	Advertising	8	250	19	Pension and profit-sharing plans	19	
9	Bad debts from sales or services (see page C-3) . .	9		20	Rent or lease (see page C-4):		
10	Car and truck expenses (see page C-3)	10	1,266		a Vehicles, machinery, and equipment .	20a	
					b Other business property . .	20b	
11	Commissions and fees . .	11		21	Repairs and maintenance . .	21	
12	Depletion	12		22	Supplies (not included in Part III) .	22	253
13	Depreciation and section 179 expense deduction (not included in Part III) (see page C-3) . .	13	3,100	23	Taxes and licenses	23	
				24	Travel, meals, and entertainment		
14	Employee benefit programs (other than on line 19) . . .	14			a Travel	24a	310
					b Meals and entertainment .		512
15	Insurance (other than health) .	15	750		c Enter 50% of line 24b subject to limitations (see page C-4) .		256
16	Interest				d Subtract line 24c from line 24b .	24d	256
	a Mortgage (paid to banks, etc.) .	16a		25	Utilities	25	347
	b Other	16b	200	26	Wages (less employment credits) .	26	
17	Legal and professional services	17	350	27	Other expenses (from line 48 on page 2)	27	267
18	Office expense	18	600				

28	**Total expenses** before expenses for business use of home. Add lines 8 through 27 in columns . ▶	28	7,949
29	Tentative profit (loss). Subtract line 28 from line 7	29	26,331
30	Expenses for business use of your home. Attach **Form 8829**	30	1,462
31	**Net profit or (loss).** Subtract line 30 from line 29.		
	• If a profit, enter on **Form 1040, line 12,** and ALSO on **Schedule SE, line 2** (statutory employees, see page C-5). Estates and trusts, enter on Form 1041, line 3.	31	24,869
	• If a loss, you MUST go on to line 32.		
32	If you have a loss, check the box that describes your investment in this activity (see page C-6).		
	• If you checked 32a, enter the loss on **Form 1040, line 12,** and ALSO on **Schedule SE, line 2** (statutory employees, see page C-5). Estates and trusts, enter on Form 1041, line 3.	32a ☐	All investment is at risk.
	• If you checked 32b, you MUST attach **Form 6198.**	32b ☐	Some investment is not at risk.

For Paperwork Reduction Act Notice, see Form 1040 instructions.   Cat. No. 11334P   **Schedule C (Form 1040) 1997**

CONTINUED ▶

Form **4562**	**Depreciation and Amortization** (Including Information on Listed Property)	OMB No. 1545-0172 **1997**
Department of the Treasury Internal Revenue Service	▶ See separate instructions. ▶ Attach this form to your return.	Attachment Sequence No. **67**

Name(s) shown on return: John Stephens	Business or activity to which this form relates: Tax Preparations	Identifying number: 465-00-0001

Part I Election To Expense Certain Tangible Property (Section 179) (Note: *If you have any "listed property," complete Part V before you complete Part I.*)

1	Maximum dollar limitation. If an enterprise zone business, see page 2 of the instructions . .	**1**	$18,000
2	Total cost of section 179 property placed in service. See page 2 of the instructions	**2**	3,100
3	Threshold cost of section 179 property before reduction in limitation	**3**	$200,000
4	Reduction in limitation. Subtract line 3 from line 2. If zero or less, enter -0-	**4**	– 0 –
5	Dollar limitation for tax year. Subtract line 4 from line 1. If zero or less, enter -0-. If married filing separately, see page 2 of the instructions	**5**	18,000

(a) Description of property	(b) Cost (business use only)	(c) Elected cost
6 File Cabinet	600	600
Copier	2,500	2,500

7	Listed property. Enter amount from line 27 . . . . **7**		
8	Total elected cost of section 179 property. Add amounts in column (c), lines 6 and 7 . . .	**8**	3,100
9	Tentative deduction. Enter the smaller of line 5 or line 8	**9**	3,100
10	Carryover of disallowed deduction from 1996. See page 3 of the instructions	**10**	– 0 –
11	Business income limitation. Enter the smaller of business income (not less than zero) or line 5 (see instructions)	**11**	18,000
12	Section 179 expense deduction. Add lines 9 and 10, but do not enter more than line 11 . .	**12**	3,100
13	Carryover of disallowed deduction to 1998. Add lines 9 and 10, less line 12 ▶ **13**		

Note: *Do not use Part II or Part III below for listed property (automobiles, certain other vehicles, cellular telephones, certain computers, or property used for entertainment, recreation, or amusement). Instead, use Part V for listed property.*

Part II MACRS Depreciation For Assets Placed in Service ONLY During Your 1997 Tax Year (Do Not Include Listed Property.)

Section A—General Asset Account Election

14 If you are making the election under section 168(i)(4) to group any assets placed in service during the tax year into one or more general asset accounts, check this box. See page 3 of the instructions . . . . ▶ ☐

Section B—General Depreciation System (GDS) (See page 3 of the instructions.)

(a) Classification of property	(b) Month and year placed in service	(c) Basis for depreciation (business/investment use only—see instructions)	(d) Recovery period	(e) Convention	(f) Method	(g) Depreciation deduction
15a 3-year property						
b 5-year property						
c 7-year property						
d 10-year property						
e 15-year property						
f 20-year property						
g 25-year property			25 yrs.		S/L	
h Residential rental property			27.5 yrs.	MM	S/L	
			27.5 yrs.	MM	S/L	
i Nonresidential real property			39 yrs.	MM	S/L	
				MM	S/L	

Section C—Alternative Depreciation System (ADS) (See page 6 of the instructions.)

16a Class life					S/L	
b 12-year			12 yrs.		S/L	
c 40-year			40 yrs.	MM	S/L	

Part III Other Depreciation (Do Not Include Listed Property.) (See page 6 of the instructions.)

17	GDS and ADS deductions for assets placed in service in tax years beginning before 1997	**17**	
18	Property subject to section 168(f)(1) election	**18**	
19	ACRS and other depreciation	**19**	252

Part IV Summary (See page 7 of the instructions.)

20	Listed property. Enter amount from line 26	**20**	
21	**Total.** Add deductions on line 12, lines 15 and 16 in column (g), and lines 17 through 20. Enter here and on the appropriate lines of your return. Partnerships and S corporations—see instructions . .	**21**	3,352
22	For assets shown above and placed in service during the current year, enter the portion of the basis attributable to section 263A costs **22**		

For Paperwork Reduction Act Notice, see the separate instructions.   Cat. No. 12906N   Form **4562** (1997)

CONTINUED ▶

Form **8829**	**Expenses for Business Use of Your Home**	OMB No. 1545-1266
Department of the Treasury Internal Revenue Service	▶ File only with Schedule C (Form 1040). Use a separate Form 8829 for each home you used for business during the year. ▶ See separate instructions.	**1997** Attachment Sequence No. **66**

Name(s) of proprietor(s)   John Stephens

Your social security number   465 ¦ 00 ¦ 0001

Part I Part of Your Home Used for Business

1	Area used regularly and exclusively for business, regularly for day care, or for storage of inventory or product samples. See instructions	**1**	200
2	Total area of home	**2**	2,000
3	Divide line 1 by line 2. Enter the result as a percentage	**3**	10 %

• For day-care facilities not used exclusively for business, also complete lines 4–6.
• All others, skip lines 4–6 and enter the amount from line 3 on line 7.

4	Multiply days used for day care during year by hours used per day .	**4**		hr.
5	Total hours available for use during the year (365 days × 24 hours). See instructions	**5**	8,760 hr.	
6	Divide line 4 by line 5. Enter the result as a decimal amount . . .	**6**	.	
7	Business percentage. For day-care facilities not used exclusively for business, multiply line 6 by line 3 (enter the result as a percentage). All others, enter the amount from line 3 . . . . ▶	**7**	10 %	

Part II Figure Your Allowable Deduction

8	Enter the amount from Schedule C, line 29, **plus** any net gain or (loss) derived from the business use of your home and shown on Schedule D or Form 4797. If more than one place of business, see instructions			**8**	26,331

See instructions for columns (a) and (b) before completing lines 9–20.

			(a) Direct expenses	(b) Indirect expenses	
9	Casualty losses. See instructions	**9**			
10	Deductible mortgage interest. See instructions .	**10**		4,500	
11	Real estate taxes. See instructions	**11**		1,000	
12	Add lines 9, 10, and 11	**12**		5,500	
13	Multiply line 12, column (b) by line 7		**13**	550	
14	Add line 12, column (a) and line 13				**14**	550
15	Subtract line 14 from line 8. If zero or less, enter -0- .				**15**	25,781
16	Excess mortgage interest. See instructions . .	**16**			
17	Insurance	**17**		400	
18	Repairs and maintenance	**18**	300	1,400	
19	Utilities	**19**		1,800	
20	Other expenses. See instructions	**20**			
21	Add lines 16 through 20	**21**	300	3,600	
22	Multiply line 21, column (b) by line 7		**22**	360	
23	Carryover of operating expenses from 1996 Form 8829, line 41 . .		**23**	– 0 –	
24	Add line 21 in column (a), line 22, and line 23				**24**	660
25	Allowable operating expenses. Enter the **smaller** of line 15 or line 24				**25**	660
26	Limit on excess casualty losses and depreciation. Subtract line 25 from line 15				**26**	25,121
27	Excess casualty losses. See instructions		**27**		
28	Depreciation of your home from Part III below		**28**	252	
29	Carryover of excess casualty losses and depreciation from 1996 Form 8829, line 42		**29**		
30	Add lines 27 through 29				**30**	252
31	Allowable excess casualty losses and depreciation. Enter the **smaller** of line 26 or line 30 . .				**31**	252
32	Add lines 14, 25, and 31				**32**	1,462
33	Casualty loss portion, if any, from lines 14 and 31. Carry amount to **Form 4684**, Section B . .				**33**	
34	Allowable expenses for business use of your home. Subtract line 33 from line 32. Enter here and on Schedule C, line 30. If your home was used for more than one business, see instructions ▶				**34**	1,462

Part III Depreciation of Your Home

35	Enter the **smaller** of your home's adjusted basis or its fair market value. See instructions . .	**35**	75,000
36	Value of land included on line 35	**36**	15,000
37	Basis of building. Subtract line 36 from line 35	**37**	60,000
38	Business basis of building. Multiply line 37 by line 7	**38**	6,000
39	Depreciation percentage. See instructions	**39**	4.2 %
40	Depreciation allowable. Multiply line 38 by line 39. Enter here and on line 28 above. See instructions	**40**	252

Part IV Carryover of Unallowed Expenses to 1998

41	Operating expenses. Subtract line 25 from line 24. If less than zero, enter -0-	**41**	
42	Excess casualty losses and depreciation. Subtract line 31 from line 30. If less than zero, enter -0- . .	**42**	

For Paperwork Reduction Act Notice, see page 3 of separate instructions.   Ⓐ *Printed on recycled paper*   Cat. No. 13232M   Form **8829** (1997)

CONTINUED ▶

period and, because he files his return based on the calendar year, August is the eighth month of his tax year. Using Table 6 in the Appendix of Publication 534, he finds that the depreciation percentage for the 12th year of the recovery period, for assets placed in service in the 8th month, is 4.2 percent. Therefore, his depreciation for 1997 (line 40) is $252. He enters that amount in Part II on lines 28 and 30. Because it is less than the available balance of his deduction limit (line 26), he can deduct the full depreciation.

Step 4. Finally, he figures his total deduction for his home office by adding together his otherwise deductible expenses (line 14), his operating expenses (line 25), and depreciation (line 31).

He enters the result, $1,462, on lines 32 and 34, and on Schedule C, line 30. ▼

CHAPTER BRIEFCASE

▼▼▼▼▼▼

- One of the fastest-growing markets in the United States is the home-based business. One in five businesses currently located in an established office or industrial area began in somebody's home.

- There are advantages and disadvantages to operating a home-based business. The advantages include flexibility, independence, and convenience. The disadvantages include a lack of credibility, isolation, and inadequate workspace.

- The key characteristics of a successful home-based businessperson include self-discipline, organization, flexibility, and attention to detail.

- The Internal Revenue Service offers tax advantages to operators of home-based businesses who qualify for the home-based business deduction. Tax regulations are subject to change, but the IRS requirements provide valuable guidelines for setting up a successful home-based business.

▲▲▲▲▲▲

Chapter 23

PURCHASING A FRANCHISE

▼▼▼▼▼

I believe in God, family, and McDonald's—and in the office, that order is reversed.

—*Ray Kroc, founder of McDonald's*

MISSION STATEMENT

In this chapter, you will

*L*EARN about the distinct advantages and disadvantages of franchise operations.

*E*XPLORE the different interests and responsibilities of franchisors and franchisees.

*A*PPLY your understanding of the rights, duties, and expectations of franchisors and franchisees to a case study.

*P*RODUCE an organized analysis of potential franchise opportunities.

KEY TERMS

Federal Trade Commission	franchisee	franchisor
franchise fee	franchising	royalty

INTRODUCTION TO FRANCHISES

In the real world, not all small businesses get started when someone has a new idea. Frequently, small business start-ups happen because of someone else's idea, and the new entrepreneur brings his or her own special brand of expertise, skill, and experience to enrich an existing operation. There is an almost bewildering variety of opportunities out there to join a community of franchisees.

In this chapter, we'll look at franchising, and in Chapter 24, we'll focus on buying existing independent businesses. We'll discuss some of the opportunities and challenges posed by franchising, and what to watch out for when taking over an ongoing operation.

FRANCHISING OPPORTUNITIES

Many small business owners have minimized their risks by investing in a franchise. **Franchising** is a plan of distribution under which an individually owned business is operated as a part of a large chain. The products and services offered are standardized. There are two key terms to remember: franchisor and franchisee.

The company is the **franchisor**. It gives the individual dealer, the **franchisee**, the right to market the franchisor's product or service and to use the franchisor's trade name, trademarks, reputation, and way of doing business. The franchise agreement usually gives the franchisee the exclusive right to sell in a specified area. In return, the franchisee agrees to pay to the franchisor a fee, and usually a percentage of gross sales as well.

Advantages of Franchising

There are several distinct advantages to choosing the franchising route.

- **Name identification.** You will be able to start your business under a name and trademark that is already accepted by the public. The immediate identification many franchise operations enjoy can bring pre-sold customers to your door.
- **Training and assistance.** You may be able to receive training and management assistance from people who are experienced in your type of business. Some franchisors will guide you in day-to-day operations until you are proficient. Often, the franchisor provides management consulting on a continuing basis. This usually includes help with recordkeeping.
- **Financing.** Many franchisors provide financial assistance to qualified franchisees.
- **Quantity savings.** You may be able to enjoy significant savings through the franchisor's quantity purchasing of products, equipment, supplies, and advertising materials. Often, equipment and supplies must be purchased from the franchisor.
- **Marketing.** National and regional promotions by the franchisor will help your business.

Disadvantages of Franchising

For all its advantages, there are also some disadvantages to becoming a franchisee.

- **Less freedom.** Because of the required standardized operations, you cannot make all of the rules. You often lose the freedom to be your own boss and to make most of the decisions. The franchisor will probably exercise a pre-approval option of sites for outlets. While this is advantageous in some ways (the franchisor probably has a pretty good idea about what sort of site works best), it may be frustrating if the franchisor refuses to approve the site you want.

Franchisors commonly impose (and strictly enforce) design and appearance standards. While such standards ensure a uniform quality of goods and services in all the outlets, complying with the standards may be expensive.

- **Expenses.** Your initial franchise fee may cost several thousand or several hundred thousand dollars. It is frequently nonrefundable. You also may be required to pay a marketing or advertising fee to the franchisor to promote your new outlet. The franchisor usually charges a royalty on a percentage of gross sales (that is, you pay the royalty for the use of the franchisor's name and trademarks whether or not you make a profit). On the other hand, the franchisor does not usually share your losses. You may have to pay into a pooled advertising fund which underwrites national or regional advertising, but not necessarily targeting your particular operation.

- **Business restrictions.** You may be restricted in establishing selling prices, in introducing new products or services, and in dropping unprofitable ones, thus limiting your ability to be competitive. Even if you are certain that a product or service would do well in your market, you may not be able to offer it. The franchisor may set your hours, limit your territory, dictate dress codes, design advertising campaigns, or demand adherence to certain bookkeeping methods. All of this control helps achieve a uniform quality among franchises, but you may feel that such restrictions prevent you from operating your outlet the way you want to.

- **Paperwork and accountability.** Franchisors take a keen interest in the details of each franchise operation's day-to-day profitability. As a result, they usually require specific, regular reports and you may consider the time and effort spent in preparing them to be burdensome.

URLinks

http://entrepreneurmag.com/homebiz/home200.hts
http://www.bbbmbc.com/bbbtips/tip65.htm
http://www.entrepreneurmag.com/resource/buying_tips.hts

Making the Decision

Making the decision to franchise is not a matter to take lightly. Before entering into a franchise contract, you should follow these steps:

- *Examine your interests and abilities.* What do you like to do? What do you do well?
- *Consult a directory of franchise opportunities.* A number of organizations publish information that includes descriptions of franchisor companies and the qualifications and capital that a franchisee needs.
- *Narrow your options.* Write to the companies that interest you and ask them to give you the names of franchisees that you could contact.
- *Talk to franchisees.* Other franchisees have firsthand experience at operating the type of business that interests you.
- *Contact the Federal Trade Commission.* The FTC can provide free information on the FTC Franchise Rule, which requires franchisors to disclose certain information before a potential franchisee invests any money in the opportunity. For an information packet, write to the Division of Marketing Practices, FTC, Washington, DC 20580. You can call the FTC at 202-326-2502.

- *Consult a lawyer and an accountant before signing a franchise contract.* Make sure that you understand all of the details and ramifications of the contract.

FTC Disclosure Requirements

Most of the franchising opportunities available today are legitimate ones, although any business undertaking includes a significant degree of risk. There are unscrupulous franchisors, however, who lure unsuspecting franchisees with promises of quick wealth or easy loans, and then disappear with their victim's cash in hand.

To help potential franchisees avoid franchisor fraud, and to ensure that franchisors provide potential franchisees with all the information they need to make a clear and sensible business decision, the FTC has established disclosure rules. These rules, which have the force and effect of federal law, require franchisors to disclose the required information to potential franchisees, at the first face-to-face meeting or ten business days before any money is paid or a contract is signed.

If the franchisor has made any claims about actual or potential sales, profits, or earnings, the franchisor is required by federal law (and the law of about half of the states) to provide detailed disclosures. There must be a documentable, reasonable basis for any earnings claim, and projected or historical earnings data must be relevant to the potential franchisee's geographic market area. Earnings claims based on operating results are required to be prepared in accordance with generally accepted accounting principles.

The earnings claim document must follow a specific format. It must include a statement of the assumptions used in making the claim along with required cautionary language. The document must tell you the number (and percentage) of franchise outlets that have achieved the claimed results. Various other additional information is required, although franchisors are not required to disclose actual or projected earnings information.

URLinks
http://www.ftc.gov/
http://www.ftc.gov/bcp/conline/pubs/invest/buyfran.htm

FIRST PERSON

Peter N., Omaha, Nebraska: I am a Mama's Pizza franchisee in Nebraska. I signed my first franchise agreement with Mama's Pizza in 1989, my second in 1992 and my third in 1996. I will have to sign a new agreement in 2002. Each of the agreements I signed was more restrictive than the last one, and I'm sure the next agreement I sign will be more restrictive than the one I am currently operating under. The agreements offered by my franchisor are strictly non-negotiable: either I sign their agreement or sell the business.

Selling is not an option because Mama's Pizza controls the market. They regulate the value of the business, and they control the list of potential buyers.

Recently, Mama's Pizza made an offer to purchase my store at the contract purchase price. After deducting for all the various obligations required in the franchise agreement, paying my debt, and paying my capital gains taxes, I would have had to pay Mama's to buy my store! Last month I had the business independently appraised. It was valued for sale at nearly $2 million. Mama's offered me $600,000—which they are entitled to do under our agreement. And of course, I can't sell to anyone but a Mama's Pizza employee who is approved by Mama's Pizza. It's all there in the franchise agreement.

You might ask, why I don't I just get out—refuse to renew? Unfortunately, when you've invested even a couple of years, and in my case now hundreds of thousands of dollars, and have your family's livelihood in the business, it's a little bit difficult to take your cheese and go home.

PERSONAL WORKSHOP 44
Buying a Franchise
▼ ▼ ▼ ▼ ▼ ▼

▼ Use this worksheet to organize your research and opinions about various franchising opportunities.

Name of franchise	
Type of business	
Address	
Contact person	
What is the franchisor's reputation?	
Current franchisees' opinions	
Is franchisor involved in litigation?	
Training and start-up assistance?	
Continuing assistance?	
What is the management structure of the organization?	
Franchisor have site approval?	
Is the location and territory protected?	
What are the operating practices of the franchise?	
What are the operating control policies?	
What are the franchise costs?	
Initial license fee	
Continuing royalty fees	
Other fees	
How will the sale be financed?	
Do I have the right to sell the franchise?	
What are the terms of renewal and termination?	
Notes	

CONTINUED ▶

Sample Completed Franchise Worksheet

Name of franchise	American Sports and Trophies
Type of business	Retail store featuring full line of baseball, football, tennis equipment, footwear, clothing, and trophy and engraving sales.
Address	762 Industrial Parkway, Atlanta, GA 30601
Contact person	Al Casey (401) 555-6250
What is the franchisor's reputation?	Well-established (1984). Name recognition and public awareness are good.
Current franchisees' opinions	positive
Is franchisor involved in litigation?	None
Training and start-up assistance?	Six weeks management training in Atlanta (cost included in franchise fee)
Continuing assistance?	Location assistance, inventory control system, bookkeeping system, promotion and advertising assistance.
What is the management structure of the organization?	Regional manager — Tom Anderson District manager — Ann Johnstone
Franchisor have site approval?	Yes
Is the location and territory protected?	No other AST franchise w/in 6 mile radius
What are the operating practices of the franchise?	Product line and pricing selected by franchisor.
What are the operating control policies?	Quarterly financial reports.
What are the franchise costs?	$280,000
Initial license fee	$100,000
Continuing royalty fees	Continuing royalty fees: 2% of gross sales annually
Other fees	Equipment - $60,000 Opening inventory - $120,000 (from company)
How will the sale be financed?	Through franchisor
Do I have the right to sell the franchise?	Must be sold through franchisor.
What are the terms of renewal and termination?	Contract written from year to year.
Notes	"Escape clause" favors franchisor. Non-renewal by franchisor if sales do not reach projections in agreement. Franchisor can repurchase franchise at will.

CASE STUDY

SILVER SCREEN VIDEOPLEX

*L*arry Hanson graduated from college with a degree in retail marketing, and went to work as a distribution manager for a major auto parts chain in Atlanta. There, Larry gained experience in purchasing, inventory management and control, human resource management, and financial budgeting and analysis. Larry enjoyed the challenges of his position, but never really felt comfortable with the large metropolitan lifestyle. One summer, Larry returned to his hometown in the Blue Ridge area of central Virginia for a vacation. While walking around the small downtown, he noticed there was no business specializing in movie rentals, in spite of the popularity of these businesses in communities across America.

Larry's hometown is a community of 14,000 people. An additional 9,000 live in the surrounding villages. The town has a small liberal arts college with an enrollment of about 1,000 students. Lynchburg, with its population of about 70,000, is the closest city, less than an hour's drive away. Larry did some research and discovered that the only places in town where residents could rent videos were all retailers of other types of goods, who rented movies only as a supplement to their primary business activities. For example, the local drugstore offered a selection of video rentals. These stores, Larry learned, received their movies from video rental stores in Lynchburg and, in effect, were satellite operations of the video businesses in the larger market.

Larry also noticed that all the stores in town that rented movies had only a limited variety of selections of both older classics and current new release rentals. He also observed that customers were clearly annoyed at the lack of choices. As he was leaving one location, a customer turned to him and said, "What this town needs is a good movie rental store. It would make a fortune!"

Larry had always wanted to resettle in his hometown and go into business for himself. The problem with this dream was that he never could think of a viable opportunity that was within both his area of expertise and his somewhat limited financial capabilities. However, a movie rental establishment might just be the opportunity he was seeking. It seemed to Larry that there were two ways to go: franchise and independent.

As a video customer in Atlanta, Larry had become familiar with the major movie rental franchises. He decided to contact a few of these organizations to determine their basic franchise requirements. After careful review, he identified one franchise, SilverScreen Videoplex, that had features and benefits he thought would work in his hometown's market environment.

The general franchise agreement of SilverScreen Videoplex is as follows:

- The initial **franchise fee** is $25,000, which does not include any inventory, store racks and fixtures, or other operating equipment.
- There is a 4 percent **royalty** on all monthly sales, paid by the fifteenth of each month for the previous month's activity.
- In return for these fees, SilverScreen Videoplex provides the franchisee with a two-week **training program** at the corporate office. The training covers the basic methods of operating a retail movie rental business, including store layout and design, checkout, inventory control, pricing and promotion, and store site selection. Additional training and consulting is available as needed throughout the life of the franchise at no extra cost.
- SilverScreen Videoplex also provides its franchisees with the latest and most current rentals at a 10 percent **discount** compared to the prices independent movie distributors have to pay. SilverScreen Videoplex has a vast inventory of movie classics and previous "hot" rentals. These can be purchased at one half of their original offering price, which represents a 20 percent savings over prices offered by most independent vendors.
- SilverScreen Videoplex provides **marketing assistance**: promotional posters and other point-of-purchase displays for current hits, preprinted advertising materials, and marketing support and guidance. To promote the

CONTINUED ▶

services of their franchisees, SilverScreen Videoplex advertises in the Southeastern United States through regional television feeds and regional editions of national magazines.

• SilverScreen Videoplex requires that each location be open seven days a week, except for Christmas, Easter, and Thanksgiving, and stay open a minimum of twelve hours a day. In addition, they require a location that has either a high pedestrian or vehicular traffic count. SilverScreen Videoplex reserves the right to rescind the franchise agreement with a 30-day notice if these conditions are not met.

While researching the possibility of entering into the franchise agreement, Larry visited an independent movie rental operation in a neighboring county. This store had been operating successfully for more than ten years, from the time the video rental market first opened up. The owner suggested that Larry explore the possibility of opening a movie rental business as an independent. He told Larry he would supply him with several vendor sources of movies and would give him advice on specific operations as needed. (The owner did not view Larry as a direct competitor since they were located over 30 miles apart, and was pleased to be in the position of mentor to an industry newcomer.) In addition, the owner even raised the possibility of cooperative buying.

Larry is sure that his experience in the automotive warehouse would be transferable to a rental business. However, he feels he knows very little about the specifics and details of the movie rental business. Still, he is convinced that owning his own business in his hometown would be a satisfying career move.

He estimates that his business would require an opening inventory of approximately $60,000 (1,500 tapes, representing approximately 1,000 titles). This would include both current "hot" rentals and classics purchased from an independent vendor, and would represent an inventory three times larger than any of the "sideline" movie rental establishments in town. He estimates that it would take an additional $40,000 to lease a building, remodel it, and purchase fixtures appropriate for movie rentals. This would also allow for about $5,000 in working capital for initial payrolls, opening promotions, and other miscellaneous expenses. SilverScreen Videoplex had projected that a store of the size that Larry was envisioning (1,000 titles), operating in a community with the demographics of Larry's hometown, should do about $20,000 a month in rentals.

When Larry contacted SilverScreen Videoplex for franchise information, they let it be clearly known that they had been interested in establishing a franchise in his county for some time and may actively seek one even if he elected not to do business with their company. ▼

CASE STUDY ROUNDTABLE

▼ ▼ ▼ ▼ ▼ ▼

Larry: So, I'm going to go ahead with this move; the only question is, which way to go? If you were in my position, what would you do: establish the movie rental business as an independent or as a franchise?

Discussion Points

• What advantages are there for Larry in franchising?

• What advantages are there in establishing an independent operation?

• What are the disadvantages in both cases?

• Do the advantages normally enjoyed by franchises relate to the movie rental business?

Larry: Do you think I should be influenced by the comment made by SilverScreen that they might establish a franchise operation in my county if I don't?

Discussion Points

- Was it ethical for SilverScreen Videoplex to make this comment?
- What are the implications?

Larry: I don't think that the current movie rental places in my town pose a significant competitive threat. Do you agree?

Discussion Points

- What are the possible competitive issues Larry might have to face from the existing vendors?
- Is loyalty a factor to be considered? To what extent might tradition or simple habit be a consideration?
- Are there any other possible sources of competition Larry should be worried about?

▲▲▲▲▲▲

CHAPTER BRIEFCASE

▼ ▼ ▼ ▼ ▼ ▼

- Franchising is a plan of distribution under which an individually owned business is operated as a part of a large chain. The products and services offered are standardized. The company is the franchisor, and the individual dealer is the franchisee.
- The advantages of franchising include name identification, training and assistance, financing, quantity savings, and marketing help. The disadvantages include less freedom for the individual owner, initial expenses, restrictions on operations, and considerable paperwork and accountability.
- The Federal Trade Commission monitors and regulates franchisors, and can assist franchisees and help protect them against fraud and abusive practices.

▲▲▲▲▲▲

Chapter 24

PURCHASING AN EXISTING BUSINESS

▼▼▼▼▼

Eat before shopping. If you go to the store hungry, you are likely to make unnecessary purchases.

—American Heart Association Cookbook

MISSION STATEMENT

In this chapter, you will

*L*EARN how to make informed decisions about buying an ongoing business, and how to analyze an existing business to determine its value.

*E*XPLORE the risks and potentials involved in buying an existing business.

*A*PPLY your understanding to a real world case study.

*P*RODUCE detailed analyses of potential existing business opportunities.

KEY TERMS

assets   purchase price   risk

INTRODUCTION TO ONGOING BUSINESSES

According to the President's Report on the State of Small Business, about 20 percent of all businesses in the United States are for sale at any given time. That's about 1,200,000 businesses with "For Sale" signs hung on their doors. There are some advantages to buying an existing business. It may be the only way to get a good location in the area in which you want to do business. You can save some of the time, work, and money that go into the start-up phase of business development. Often you are able to make use of the seller's invested capital. Many sellers will finance a large part of the sale for a lower interest rate than a lending institution would offer. An existing business already has an organizational plan and operating system in place. The customer base is already established. Often the seller will also consult with the buyer on the management of the company.

For all the advantages and possibilities involved, however, the entrepreneur interested in taking over a business that was started by someone else needs to keep two words in mind: *caveat emptor*—buyer beware. Know what you're looking for, and find out whether the business meets your needs. Know what you're buying, and be aware of the values and the risks of the business. The fundamental question you should keep in mind is, "If this business is such a great deal, then why is it being sold?" Suspicious? Not really, just cautious.

For most people using this book, buying an existing business isn't really high on the list of goals. Most entrepreneurs are interested in creating—from the vision to the window dressing—not in taking over what someone else has already started. For that reason, our coverage of the topic is more of a "heads up" to this opportunity, than a "how to." But keep this in mind: just because someone already did the groundwork doesn't necessarily mean you can't take over and make the business your own.

BUYING AN EXISTING BUSINESS

There are a number of ways to find businesses for sale. Trade associations and neighborhood business groups are usually the first to know about a business that is for sale and about the business's performance and reputation. Business brokers are a good professional resource for information on available properties, locations, markets and financing. They can represent sellers or buyers and are paid a percentage of the sale price. The "Business Opportunity" advertising section of a newspaper will have local listings. Bankers, the chamber of commerce and other professional people within the community often know people who are selling or are about to sell a business.

Why Is the Business for Sale?

When you find a business in which you are interested, first determine why it is for sale. There may be serious business problems such as new competition, relocation of the primary customer base, obsolescence of a product line, or cash flow problems that have prompted the sale. Study the business and research its market carefully. Study the trends of the specific business. Learn about the competition, the surrounding neighborhood, the local business community, and the current customer base. If a business is being sold, there's always a reason. It may be a perfectly good reason (the owner is retiring or moving) or it may be a big warning sign. If you aren't satisfied with the seller's reason for selling the business, don't buy.

An experienced and independent accountant can help you analyze the seller's financial statements and tax records to determine profitability and purchase price. *Do not take the word of the seller's accountant.* Even if you know the seller's accountant—even if the seller's accountant is your mother—have the books independently audited.

Evaluate the seller's projections for future growth and performance. In an eagerness to sell, the owner might make claims that are in conflict with reality. By the same token the seller's view of past performance may be based on a set of expectations and market assumptions that are far different from your own. If you have difficulty getting the financial information you need, it might be wise to move on to another opportunity.

Know What You're Buying

When you buy a business, you purchase a number of tangible and intangible assets. You want to know what you will be purchasing and its current value before you set a price and close a sale. You want to know if any of the company's assets have been pledged as collateral for outstanding debt. It is wise to hire an appraiser to determine the value of the assets being purchased. These items may include items such as those listed in Personal Workshop 45.

PERSONAL WORKSHOP 45
Valuing Assets

▼ This form lists some of the most common commercial assets typically included when a business is sold. Use it when working with your professional appraiser to help you evaluate what you're buying.

❑ Accounts payable and other liabilities

❑ Accounts receivable

❑ Building

❑ Business name

❑ Business clientele and customer list

❑ Consulting agreement with seller

❑ Covenant not to compete

❑ Credit relationships

❑ Equipment

❑ Furniture and fixtures

❑ Inventory

❑ Lease agreements

❑ Liabilities and liens

❑ Personnel

❑ Trademark, copyright, patent

❑ Unpaid taxes

Determining the Best Price

Pricing a business—especially a small or closely held company that is not publicly traded—is a delicate and demanding process. It calls for both expertise and ethics. Paying for a professional appraisal may turn out to be an excellent investment as it not only establishes a fair price for the business, but also provides justification for the price should outside financing be needed.

The simplest way to establish a justifiable and understandable price for a business is to reconstruct its financial statements. Every business accumulates unnecessary expenses over time. Some of them are compensation to the owner (company car, insurance and retirement plans, travel and entertainment expenses). Some are just poor habits, such as awarding contracts on the basis of personal relationships, without soliciting comparison bids. Inventories and property have to be evaluated; real estate may be understated, while inventories may be stale and lose value.

Include a copy of the appraisal as a document supporting the price you offer. The price should reflect the value of the assets of the business, the rate of expected return on your investment (including new investment in the business during the first few years), and some "going concern" or goodwill figure.

Making It Work

Certainly there's less risk in buying a thriving, well-run business than there is in buying one that's failing. On the other hand, poor past performance will reduce the business's value, and your profits will be all the greater if you can turn it around. Just make

---

PERSONAL WORKSHOP 46
Buying a Business

▾ Use this worksheet to answer the six fundamental questions you need to ask before you can seriously consider buying a business.

1.	When was the business founded? Who founded it? What is its history?	
2.	Why is the current owner selling?	
3.	What is the current financial health of the business?	
4.	What is the trend of sales?	
5.	What post-sale expenses will be incurred?	
6.	How will your management make the business more profitable?	

sure that you have the skills, capital, and patience required to reinvigorate a faltering business before you commit yourself.

 URLinks
http://www.smartbiz.com/sbs/cats/buysell.htm
http://www.bizbooksoftware.com/links.htm
http://www.moneyminded.com/worklife/uboss/c7stbu11.htm
http://www.toolkit.cch.com/columns/starting/buybiz.stm

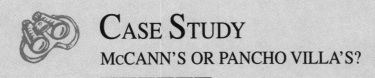

CASE STUDY
MCCANN'S OR PANCHO VILLA'S?
▼▼▼▼▼▼

*F*or several years Ernie York had been looking for a restaurant to buy in the Portland area. He contacted real estate brokers, answered advertisements in newspapers, and talked to bankers about his interest. Ernie felt well qualified to operate his own restaurant, because he had been a successful chef for more than 20 years. He worked for one of the best restaurants in the Portland area, and people constantly commended him on his excellent cooking. He always managed to come up with cuisine and other personal creative touches that made the business very lucrative for his employer. Ernie realized he was weak at administration, yet felt that his wife Belinda, and perhaps his grown children, could help out. Ernie and his wife had managed to accumulate more than $400,000 over the years as a result of investing in stocks and real estate. Ernie did not want to invest all the savings, but felt that he had enough to start out in a business. Ernie made $55,000 as a chef, and Belinda made $25,000 as office manager for a local accounting firm.

Two months ago, Ernie identified two strong possibilities: McCann's Restaurant and Pancho Villa's Hideaway.

McCann's Restaurant

McCann's was a locally well-known steak and lobster house. The owner, Harry McCann, wanted to sell the restaurant so he could retire. McCann's included a bar, but no catering facilities. Because his religion forbids drinking, Ernie had tried to avoid purchasing a restaurant with a bar. On the other hand, Belinda, whose religious views don't include a prohibition of alcohol, felt that a restaurant without a bar would

almost certainly fail. Their son George agreed, but their daughter Melissa took her father's side.

Ernie decided to look at the business. Harry McCann told him that their dealings would have to be confidential, because he didn't want his employees to become aware of the possible sale. He also said that if Ernie wanted to examine the books, he would have to put up a $50,000 deposit, which would be refundable if the deal didn't go through.

Sheila Dixon, the real estate agent, told Ernie that a deposit was standard when looking at a business of this type, and that his lawyer could prepare an agreement that would give him the protection he needed.

Harry said the restaurant was doing approximately $2 million in business annually and was making a profit. The selling price was $650,000, which included the property. Belinda knew of the restaurant and was quite excited. She even had a solution to the alcohol issue: if they did purchase McCann's, she would handle the bar and Ernie could handle the food. Ernie didn't especially like this idea, but decided to explore the business anyway. McCann took the $50,000 deposit and gave Ernie and his accountant all the books of the business.

When Ernie's accountant examined the books and the tax statements, he found some large discrepancies in what McCann had said. The tax statements indicated that the business was doing only a little over $1 million a year and was losing about $125,000 annually. The business was a corporation and was solely owned by McCann. McCann was taking $75,000 plus expenses out of the business each year. The business had been operating for nearly 15 years and, from what

CONTINUED ▶

the accountant could learn, had never shown much of a profit. It was clear that McCann was not reporting all the income, or was constantly investing more money to take care of losses. The accountant informed Ernie that the building was probably worth more than the $150,000 net book value, but that based on the statements he could not see where any goodwill was evident. The accountant pointed out that in his experience when he came across books that were not kept as they should be, it was best to avoid the situation. McCann also wanted to sell the entire corporation intact; however, he did state he would give his personal guarantee for six months to take care of any unforeseen problems that might arise.

Ernie met several times with McCann and they became good friends. When Ernie mentioned the discrepancies in the books, McCann insisted that the sales and profits were there. McCann stated that he never could have lasted 15 years if he was losing money. But he finally admitted that he had been skimming cash sales off the top. He told Ernie that he never reported all his sales to his accountant because the IRS would take all the money in taxes. He said that all cash businesses do this, and since his restaurant was a cash business, he had to take advantage of profit any way he possibly could. McCann offered to show Ernie a few things that might impress him and help him understand McCann's position.

McCann took Ernie on a tour. First they went through the restaurant, and then he showed Ernie other properties, including his house, which was magnificent. He even showed Ernie pictures of a home he had in Acapulco, where he intended to retire, and a beautiful estate in Lake Tahoe. He showed Ernie lists of stocks and bonds that he had outside the country and, in general, impressed Ernie with his wealth. "Ernie," he said, "I owe everything to my restaurant and you can have the same thing if you want it." He also informed Ernie that nothing could be traced because he had been careful over the years. Ernie never thought that he could make so much money, but he resolved that if he took over McCann's business he would not operate in the same manner.

When Ernie discussed the price, McCann stated that the corporation had a book value of $250,000 (after deducting all the liabilities from the assets) and that he felt the goodwill was worth $400,000. McCann said that the business was still growing and Ernie could recoup the goodwill within a few years. Ernie pointed out that while McCann insisted that profits were being made, his accountant found absolutely nothing but losses indicated on the books. McCann

invited Ernie to come into his business at the end of each business day for a few weeks and together they would add up the cash and the sales tickets. He even proposed that Ernie take two weeks of vacation and work in his place as a chef because he had several chefs who needed vacations. Ernie liked that idea and felt it would give him better insight into the business.

Finally, McCann suggested that if Ernie would come up with cash for the purchase he would sell him the business on paper for $350,000 and take $200,000 "under the table" to save Ernie $100,000. Ernie thanked McCann for the information and assured him that everything would remain confidential.

Ernie went home and talked to his wife about what had happened. While they both felt that McCann was a thief in many respects, they felt his business could be viable, and did not want to dismiss it without thought. Over the next week they found that McCann was highly respected in the community. He was associated with several charities and was involved in community affairs. They visited the restaurant quite a few times and each time found it busy. Ernie went to work as a substitute chef for two weeks. At the end of each day, Ernie and McCann went over sales and cash receipts and Ernie went away at the end of two weeks convinced that the business was profitable.

Ernie's accountant was still afraid of the business, and the lawyer felt that since McCann admitted being unethical, Ernie could get hurt. Ernie and his wife agreed with all their comments, but still liked the facts that the business was established, the personnel were experienced, the facilities appeared to be adequate, and a catering business could be developed. Ernie also felt that he could add a few items to the menu to make it more attractive.

Pancho Villa's Hideaway

The second restaurant that Dixon showed Ernie and Belinda was called Pancho Villa's Hideaway. It was a three-year-old Mexican restaurant that was becoming very popular in the area. The cuisine was excellent and the atmosphere and decor were charming and authentic. Ernie knew a little about Mexican food and at times prepared some of the more popular dishes. The restaurant did not have a bar. Carlos Rivera, the owner, told them that he had been thinking about getting a liquor license, but because he was returning to Mexico he did not follow through on it. Carlos's father was ill, and Carlos wanted to look after the family. During the three years that Carlos had the business he had become quite a local celebrity, and personally greeted people as they came into the

CONTINUED ▶

restaurant. He had run a series of commercials on local television urging people to come and try his authentic Mexican food.

Carlos was very receptive to Ernie's interest in the business. He told Ernie that the business did about $1 million a year in sales and that it was making money. He wanted $300,000 in cash for the business and would not consider financing any part of the sales price. The business did not have any property other than the name, the business itself, and the equipment and fixtures. He had a lease with five years left on it, but the annual rental payments were to be increased each year by 5 percent or the rate of inflation, whichever was higher. He felt that the owner would transfer the new lease and even give Ernie a longer one if he wished. Carlos said that he was personally taking $60,000 out of the business plus other household expenses. Ernie sent his accountant to examine the books, for which Carlos did not require a deposit.

The accountant found the books to be completely in order. Carlos could account for every penny, and the sales from the previous year, according to the tax statement, were $976,000. The net profit after taxes was $20,000 and Carlos did take $60,000 in compensation out of the business. The business was mainly cash, which amounted to about 50 percent of sales, and the balance was credit cards. In addition, some local clients kept open accounts. At present time there was about $24,000 in accounts receivable that were between 60 and 90 days old. Carlos stated that the money was entirely collectible because the clients involved were established firms. The facilities were adequate and parking was sufficient for the current amount of business.

When Ernie discussed the business with Belinda, she felt that it looked like a good opportunity, but that it did not have the potential of McCann's. She pointed out that unless the Mexican restaurant obtained a liquor license, profits did not seem promising. She also pointed out that neither of them spoke Spanish and some of the staff were Hispanic. Finally, Belinda pointed out that one of the main attractions of the business was Carlos himself. When he left, the business might go with him since he was so well known.

Finally, Ernie and Belinda sat down with their family to thrash out which business to purchase. Both agreed that the prices were a little high, but hoped that they could negotiate down the price on the one they decided to buy. The entire family agreed that they would abide by the majority decision. After much discussion and argument the family decided to buy McCann's, but only if the price was reduced to $575,000 and if the down payment was reduced to $300,000.

Dixon discussed the matter with McCann, and he agreed to a final price of $600,000, but would accept $300,000 down. Ernie and his wife agreed to McCann's terms. They contacted their attorney to make up the agreement, but found that he was on a 30-day vacation. Dixon recommended another lawyer, but McCann offered to have the agreement prepared by his attorney at no cost to Ernie and his wife. Dixon prepared an offer and used the $50,000 as a deposit, with the balance of $250,000 due in 20 days. ▼

 Case Study Roundtable

▼▼▼▼▼

Ernie: So what do you think? Did we make the right decision?

Discussion Points

- What are the issues in this decision-making process?
- Assess the positive and negative aspects of both possible purchases.
- Would you have purchased the corporation? Why or why not?

Belinda: I still think that Ernie was emotional about the bar. I even talked to his pastor, and he said that there was no church "rule" about serving alcohol in a restaurant, and that it was up to us. I really believe that you have to set that sort of thing aside when it comes to business decisions. Am I right?

Discussion Points

- Do you feel Ernie's religious values should have played a role in this decision? Why or why not?
- What other so-called moral issues can you identify in this transaction? How were they dealt with by the parties?
- Would you enter into an agreement with a business person who had consistently defrauded the IRS?
- Do you think that Ernie and his wife will have any personal problems with the business as a result of their differences about the bar?

Ernie: My attorney was pretty mad when he got back from vacation and found out I'd let McCann prepare the sales agreement. Was that wrong?

Discussion Points

- What is the risk in having McCann draft the agreement? Does there seem to be any problem?
- What terms and conditions would you have insisted on before you signed the agreement?

▲▲▲▲▲▲

CHAPTER BRIEFCASE

▼▼▼▼▼▼

- There are certain distinct advantages to buying an existing business: location, efficiency, organization, financing, and reputation are among the most significant.
- When considering buying an existing business, ask yourself: Why is this business for sale? and What am I buying?
- Pricing a business is a delicate and demanding process. A professional appraisal not only establishes a fair price, but also provides justification for the price should you need to obtain outside financing.

▲▲▲▲▲▲

CREATING AND MANAGING GROWTH

Albert Black (Dallas, Texas)
On Target Supplies and Logistics

"*I* think we should approach the future with a degree of optimism that says that we have to find the next growth curve in whatever industry we want to be a part of. We have to make sure that we put those factors of production together. We have to make sure that we train labor to take a look at the future and embrace it, as you would say. We have to make sure that we are prepared by making sure that we've saved, we've invested properly in order to finance the future. I think that we also have to make sure that we've got our proper place and understand where it is in the communities that we're a part of; that we have some sort of equity with our customers in the communities that we're a part of so that they will do fluent thinking with us and help create that future.

The future is developed by suppliers like myself or service providers going out there thinking with the customers, defining what we think the future should be, and building that future. I'm looking forward to building a better supply future with my customers. "

Chapter 25

MAKING EMPLOYMENT DECISIONS

▼▼▼▼▼

The man who knows how *will always have a job. The man who also knows* why *will always be his boss.*

—*Ralph Waldo Emerson*

MISSION STATEMENT

In this chapter, you will

*L*EARN about the employment options available when you decide that your business needs more workers.

*E*XPLORE the best ways to recruit the best new employees.

*A*PPLY your understanding of the process to a case study.

*P*RODUCE an analysis of your employees' status and a form to help you create an effective job description and want ad.

KEY TERMS

discrimination

employee

independent contractor

interview

job analysis

job specifications

recruiting

INTRODUCTION TO ASSESSING YOUR HIRING NEEDS

All small business owners have a vision of what they want their business to be. If that vision includes growth, then hiring decisions will become an important part of the equation sooner or later. After all, you can't do it yourself forever: at some point, you're going to need some help. Good hiring decisions are critical to the success of any business, large or small. Hiring the right people can mean higher productivity and profit for your business. Hiring the wrong people, however, can threaten your business's survival.

Although finding and hiring the right employees can take time and cost money, finding the right employees may be one of your most valuable investments.

Most small business employers have no formal training in how to make hiring decisions. Most have no real sense of the time it takes nor the costs involved. All they know is that they need help in the form of a "good" sales manager, a "good" secretary, a "good" welder, or whatever. And they know they need someone they can work with, who's willing to put in the time to learn the business and do the job enthusiastically, or at least competently. It sounds simple, but it isn't. Before you begin your search for a "good" anything, you need to do your homework.

This isn't a book about employing people, human resource issues, or managing multiple employees. What we *can* give you here are some guidelines to get you started once you decide you can't do everything by yourself. In spite of what many people think, hiring employees is not a blind gamble. You can develop the skills needed for finding and hiring the right employees. That's what this chapter is all about.

Managing employees: Awarded Small Business Person of the Year by the U.S. Small Business Administration, Lorraine Miller from Cactus and Tropicals shows how her "fun is fundamental" philosophy empowers employees and creates a productive work environment for the people she hires.

DO YOU REALLY NEED A NEW EMPLOYEE?

Sometimes the need for a new employee is planned: you knew you would need someone to supervise your salespeople when sales reached a certain level, and now you are there. Sometimes you have to hire a new employee because of the resignation or retirement of an old trusted one who was there with you from the start. Maybe you want to get more involved in some special high-tech process, so you must hire an individual with the necessary technical skills. But sometimes the need isn't so obvious or planned. Maybe this is the first time you have felt the need for some additional help, and you aren't sure if hiring an employee is really justified. How do you know if you really need a new employee?

Whether replacing a current employee or hiring for a new position, whether this is your first employee or your fiftieth, any personnel change should be considered an opportunity for rethinking your organizational structure. Do not get caught in the trap of hiring based only on your immediate needs. Instead, think about your business plan and your vision for the company, and ask yourself the following questions:

- Do I currently have the right number of employees with the right skills to get the work done?
- Am I properly utilizing my employees? Are there new or different things my current employees could learn or do to enhance the business without having to hire new ones?
- Do I have the people and talent needed to satisfy future needs?

If you answered "no" to any of these questions, you probably need to make some different decisions. This doesn't necessarily mean you should hire someone. Actually, there are several alternative options. You could:

- Reorganize the work load that currently exists to better take advantage of employees' talents and skills.
- Delegate, and provide training, if needed, to develop the people you have.

- Refocus the efforts of your employees on the immediate needs of the company and drop low-priority activities.
- Contract out excess work, hire temporary workers through an agency, or allow current employees to work overtime (especially if the need is seasonal or short term).

If, after careful consideration, none of these solutions seems reasonable, you should consider hiring a new employee. But, again, ask yourself these questions:

- Can the business support a new employee?
- Will the business's growth be limited without a new employee?
- What kind of employee do I need? Full-time or part-time? Permanent or for some limited term? Would two part-time employees be preferable to one full-time employee?
- What level of increased production is needed to cover the costs of a new employee?

You should hire only when the business's growth can support a new employee or the business cannot grow without additional help. If that is your situation, then it is time to decide exactly what job the new employee will do.

THE NON-EMPLOYEE EMPLOYMENT DECISION: INDEPENDENT CONTRACTORS

If you are still undecided about the need to hire employees, or if the financial obligations of an employed workforce are not yet quite within your business's grasp, you should consider the independent contractor option. **Independent contractors** are, as their name suggests, independent business people who are hired to perform specific tasks. They are just like any other vendor, except they perform services rather than provide tangible goods. Independent contractors are in business for themselves. They are not employees. They are not eligible for unemployment, disability, or workers' compensation benefits. The hiring firm does not have to pay employee-employer taxes or provide workers' compensation insurance, and usually is not liable for the contractor's actions. Independent contractors include consultants and temporary employees (temps) hired from agencies for short-term, limited tasks. Figure 25.1 lists the benefits and risks of hiring independent contractors.

The Basic Rules

Government rules determine if a worker is an independent contractor, not written agreements. That is, this is one area in which you can write "independent contractor" all over an agreement, but the federal (or state) government may disagree. There are significant legal and tax implications of the independent contractor label, and you should be careful to adhere precisely to the necessary formalities.

As a general rule, all workers are assumed to be employees. The burden is on the employer to demonstrate otherwise. According to IRS Code Section 3121(d) the following workers are automatically employees:

FIGURE
25.1

The Benefits and Risks of Hiring Independent Contractors

Benefit	Risk
Save money: Hiring firms don't have to pay Social Security taxes, workers' compensation premiums, health insurance, and retirement benefits or unemployment insurance	**Government fines:** The government looks negatively at the misclassification of bona fide employees as independent contractors for two reasons: 1) independent contractors can contribute to the underground economy by not paying taxes; 2) the Social Security, disability and unemployment insurance programs were all designed to protect average workers. The government does not want businesses to circumvent these programs (and their costs) simply by calling their workers "independent contractors."
Avoid a long-term employee commitment: Particularly in seasonal businesses, it can be uneconomical for an employer to hold on to a fully staffed full-time workforce. On the other hand, layoffs are painful for all parties and result in increased retraining and restaffing costs later on.	**Lawsuits from independent contractors:** When an employee is injured, he or she can usually only receive workers' compensation benefits. However, independent contractors may sue their hiring firm.
Avoid liability for the worker's actions: Under the concept of "respondeat superior," an employer may be held liable for the unlawful acts, injuries, or damage caused by his or her employees. The owner of a company is not liable for the acts of an independent contractor.	**No control over the work:** A hiring firm cannot control an independent contractor's work. If it does, the worker's legal status will automatically convert to an employer-employee relationship and the hiring firm will be liable for employment taxes and benefits. Because hiring firms can't control their contracts, deadlines may be missed, customers may become angry, or other situations may arise that are detrimental to the hiring firm.
Avoid dealing with labor unions: With independent contractors, the relationship between management and worker is a direct, contractual one. It lacks the sometimes adversarial relationship that results from unionization. (On the other hand, the relationship can be less consistent over time than dealing with a union representative.)	**Limited right to fire independent contractors:** Hiring firms can fire independent contractors only if they breach their contract or if the completed work is unacceptable. If a hiring firm keeps the right to fire the worker at will, the worker's legal status usually converts to an employer-employee relationship.

- Officers of corporations who provide services to that corporation
- Food and laundry drivers
- Full-time traveling or city salespeople who sell goods to people (or firms) for resale
- Full-time life insurance agents, working mainly for one company (IRS only)
- At-home workers who are supplied with materials or goods and are given specifications for the work to be done

In 1982, the Tax Equity and Fiscal Responsibility Act (TEFRA) created two categories of workers who are, by law, *not* to be treated as employees for tax purposes:

1. Direct sellers who sell a product to the final user (such as door-to-door and home demonstration salespeople)
2. Licensed real estate agents

Common Law Factors

In the case of all other workers who don't fall into a special category, there are twenty common law factors that can be applied to distinguish an employee from an independent contractor. Independent contractors do not have to satisfy all twenty factors. The courts have given different weights for each factor according to the industry and job and the courts have not always been consistent in weighing these factors. Figure 25.2 lists and explains the twenty factors.

FIGURE 25.2	Twenty Common Law Factors for Determining Independent Contractor Status (Rev Rul 87–41)
1. No instructions	Contractors are not required to follow, nor are they furnished with instructions to accomplish a job. They can be provided with job specifications by the hiring firm.
2. No training	Contractors typically do not receive training by the hiring firm. They use their own methods to accomplish the work.
3. Services don't have to be rendered personally	Contractors are hired to provide a result and usually have the right to hire others to do the actual work.
4. The work being performed is not essential to the hiring firm	A company's success or continuation should not depend on the service of outside contractors. An example violating this would be a law firm which called their lawyers independent contractors.
5. Own work hours	Contractors set their own work hours.

FIGURE
25.2
Twenty Common Law Factors, continued

6. Not a continuing relationship	Usually contractors don't have a continuing relationship with a hiring company. The relationship can be frequent, but it must be at irregular intervals, on call, or whenever work is available. Warning: Part-time, seasonal, or short duration relationships have nothing to do with independent contractor status.
7. Control their own assistants	Contractors shouldn't hire, supervise, or pay assistants at the direction of the hiring company. If assistants are hired, it should be at the contractor's sole discretion.
8. Time to pursue other work	Contractors should have enough time available to pursue other gainful work.
9. Job location	Contractors control where they work. If they work on the premises of the hiring company, it is not under that company's direction or supervision.
10. Order of work set	Contractors determine the order and sequence that they will perform their work.
11. No interim reports	Contractors are hired for the final result, and so should not be asked for progress or interim reports.
12. Payment timing	Contractors are paid by the job, not by time. Payment by the job can include periodic payments based on a percentage of job completed. Payment can be based on the number of hours needed to do the job times a fixed hourly rate. However, this should be determined before the job commences.
13. Working for multiple firms	Contractors often work for more than one firm at a time.
14. Business expenses	Contractors are generally responsible for their incidental expenses.
15. Own tools	Usually contractors furnish their own tools. Some hiring firms have leased equipment to their independent contractors, so they could show that the contractor had his or her "own" tools and an investment in their business (see 16). This strategy won't work if the lease is for a nominal amount or can be voided by the hiring firm at will. *In short, the lease must be equivalent to what an independent business-person could have obtained in the open market.*

FIGURE
25.2 **Twenty Common Law Factors, continued**

16. Significant investment	Contractors should be able to perform their services without the hiring company's facilities (equipment, office furniture, machinery, etc.). The contractor's investment in his or her trade must be real, essential, and adequate.
17. Services available to general public	Contractors make their services available to the general public by one or more of the following: • having an office and assistants • having business signs • having a business license • listing their services in a business directory • advertising their services
18. Limited right to discharge	Contractors can't be fired as long as they produce a result that meets the contract specifications.
19. No compensation for non-completion	Contractors are responsible for the satisfactory completion of a job or they may be legally obligated to compensate the hiring firm for failure to complete.
20. Possible profit or loss	Contractors should be able to make a profit or a loss. Employees can't suffer a loss. Five circumstances show that a profit or loss is possible: 1. The contractor hires, directs, and pays assistants. 2. The contractor has his own office, equipment, materials, or facilities. 3. The contractor has continuing and recurring liabilities. 4. The contractor has agreed to perform specific jobs for certain agreed prices. 5. If the contractor's services affect his or her own business reputation.

& TAXES

Employers are required by law to deduct and withhold income tax from the salaries and wages of employees. On the other hand, no such requirement exists for business owners who enter into valid agreements with legitimate independent contractors. That's why it is especially important to accurately determine whether a worker is an employee or an independent contractor. In the event that the hiring firm mistakenly misidentifies the worker as an independent contractor, the penalty for the innocent error is

- 1.5 percent of the worker's gross wages,
- 20 percent of the amount that would have been the employee's share of FICA taxes,
- the appropriate employer's share of FICA.

On the other hand, if an employer's misidentification of the worker is intentional, and the employer fails to file information returns or fails to provide W-2s to employees, the penalty is doubled:

- 3 percent of the gross wages (federal withholding), plus
- 40 percent of the amount that would have been the employee's share of FICA taxes, and
- the appropriate employer's share of FICA.

PERSONAL WORKSHOP 47
Employees or Independent Contractors?

▼ Use the following checklist to help you identify whether your workers are employees or independent contractors. For each statement, mark the statement true or false. True statements refer to employees. False statements are independent contractors. If you have more true than false responses, your workers are most likely classified as employees. If you have more false than true responses, then your workers are more likely to be considered independent contractors.

Factor The worker...	True (Employee)	False (Independent Contractor)
Is required to comply with employer instructions about when, where, and how work is to be performed.		
Is required to undergo job-related training.		
Does not hire, supervise, or pay others to perform work for which he or she is responsible.		
Must perform his or her job during certain set hours.		

CONTINUED ▶

Factor The worker...	True (Employee)	False (Independent Contractor)
Must devote to the job full time.		
Must perform his or her job on the employer's property.		
Must perform job-related tasks in a certain order set by the employer.		
Is required to submit regular written or oral reports to the employer.		
Is paid on an hourly, weekly, or monthly basis.		
Is furnished with the tools and materials required for his or her job.		
Is entitled to have his or her business and travel expenses paid by the employer.		
Does not rent his or her office or working space from the employer.		
Will not realize a profit or loss as a direct result of his or her services.		
Does not work for more than one company at a time.		
Does not make his or her services available to the general public.		
May be fired by the employer.		
Has the right to quit the job at any time, regardless of whether the required tasks are completed.		

Note: these factors are only possible indicators of a worker's status. Each case must be determined on its own facts, based on all the information.

FIRST PERSON

Carla S., Nashville, Tennessee: Here's a clue from someone who used to work for the IRS: if there's any question—any question at all about a worker's status—the IRS is going to characterize them as an employee. If you absolutely clearly and scrupulously comply with the Revenue Ruling's guidelines, you'll probably be OK; but if there's any question, like I said, they're employees. The IRS takes this one very seriously, because there's a lot of employment fraud and abuse out there.

THE HIRING DECISION: DEFINE THE JOB AND THE TYPE OF EMPLOYEE YOU NEED

So now you've analyzed your options and have made the decision to hire employees. Before you can hire the right employee with the right skills, you need to understand exactly what the job will be. After all, how can you decide what qualifications are required until you understand what you want the person to do? You accomplish this by doing a job analysis. With the information you gather, you can write a job description and specifications for the skills, knowledge, and abilities needed to perform the job. These tools will help you locate and attract the best qualified applicants to your business. The information gained through job analysis will also help you determine the appropriate job title or classification, pay, and benefits.

Job Analysis

Job analysis is the first step in understanding what any job involves. The information you gather will be used to write both a job description and job specifications for the individual to be hired.

By completing this process, you will have a better understanding of the job you are analyzing. You can use this information to develop a clear description of the job and the qualifications needed to successfully do the job. Your job analysis can also help you determine the appropriate classification or job title, pay level, and other factors.

Job analysis involves studying the job to understand exactly what needs to be done. At this point in the process, do not be concerned with what characteristics the right employee should have. If you are analyzing an existing job, try to forget the characteristics of the person currently in the job. On the other hand, it is important to involve other employees in the job analysis process, because they may have the best understanding about how much time certain tasks take and how the position relates to other positions in the company. The goal of job analysis is to identify what duties any person in the job will have, what tasks will need to be done, and clarify the conditions of the job, such as reporting relationships and travel requirements.

If the position you are analyzing is a new one, you can essentially design the job from scratch through this process. If it is an existing job, you should observe and talk to the current employee. Or, you may find that other employees can be helpful in analyzing a job. If they have similar tasks, they can help you determine the time and skills needed to do the job, whether your expectations are realistic, and how the position fits in with the total operation.

A job description typically includes:

- A job title
- A paragraph-long overview of the job
- A list of primary duties and responsibilities
- Reporting relationships
- Working conditions

A good job description, however, goes a step further to describe the results you expect from the person in the job. By including performance expectations for the duties and key activities of the position, you minimize the chances that the person hired misunderstands what the job is all about and what you expect the results to be. Defining your expectations also will help you write clear and valid specifications for the job, which is the next step in the process. The clearer your expectations are up front, the better the odds that the right person will be selected for the job.

Building a Results-Oriented Job Description

Use the information gathered on your job analysis worksheet to write a job description. Add statements regarding your performance expectations for each of the major duties or responsibilities listed. Remember that you want the employee to know exactly what the job is and the results you expect by reading this document. Be as specific as possible in your description. For each duty, write at least one measurable result you expect. If it is a new position and you are not sure how realistic your expectations are, that's okay. Most jobs evolve over time, and most job descriptions need to be changed frequently, as the needs of the company change. Think of this job description as a starting point, and, if you would feel better, note on the job description that it is a draft or that it is subject to change.

Check the job description you have written. Does it clearly describe the job and your performance expectations for any employee in that job? To be sure it is clear, ask a few employees who are close to the job to read it over and give you feedback. Does the description accurately describe what the job entails? Are your performance expectations reasonable and workable? When you are confident that you have clearly described the job, you are ready to think about the type of person needed to fill the job.

Most job specifications include two very different aspects: required (or absolute) qualifications and desired (or preferred) qualifications. The required qualifications should include the minimum levels of education, work experience, skills, and personal characteristics needed to do the job. During the selection process, applicants who are missing a required qualification will usually be eliminated from the pool.

The Role of Experience

It is often said that the best predictor of what a person will accomplish in the future is what he or she has accomplished in the past. This suggests that work experience should be an important consideration when selecting employees. Many advertisements will specify the need for a certain number of years of experience. But is it *quantity* or the *quality* of the work experience that really counts? In developing job specifications, clearly state the work accomplishments you consider important for success in this position, and don't get hung up on the number of years someone might have warmed a seat or carried a business card with an impressive-sounding title. Later, when you review the work histories of applicants, look for evidence of track records or progressive experience which suggests an applicant has actually made some significant accomplishments.

Desired Qualifications

Desired qualifications are like topping on ice cream—nice but not necessary. Desired qualifications should be so noted and might give a particular applicant an edge over the others in the selection process. In fact, you might want to think about the relative value of different desired qualifications to your business—is it more important to have chocolate sauce or sprinkles on your ice cream?—considering your immediate and future needs. Desired qualifications are not minimum requirements, and it would be unusual for an applicant to have all the desired qualifications listed.

WRITING JOB SPECIFICATIONS

Job specifications describe what type of person is qualified for the job. It is important that both required and desired skills and qualifications are clearly noted. This will help assure that only qualified applicants apply for the job, and it will help you when making selection decisions later. All skills and qualifications need to be valid indicators of job success. In other words, you cannot require that an applicant have a certain qualification or personal characteristic if there is no relationship between that characteristic and the ability to do the job.

When writing a job specification, ask these three questions:

1. Is the description clear? Does it give you a basic understanding of what the job entails?
2. Do the duties and tasks required sound reasonable? Are the performance expectations realistic? Is there anything that should be added or deleted?
3. Are the required and desired skills and characteristics reasonable? Is there anything that should be added or deleted?

THE SEARCH

To find the right employee, you need to recruit a pool of qualified applicants. The goal of recruitment is to attract a number of applicants who possess *all* the required qualifications for the job and *some* of the desired qualifications.

If your applicant pool is too small, you might be forced to compromise what you consider to be a necessary skill or characteristic. That might result in a poor selection or, at least, an employee who will require a good deal of additional training and/or time from you. Do not be concerned about attracting too large an applicant pool. If you've done a good job of creating clear, specific job specifications, your pool of candidates will essentially be self-screening, allowing you to have a manageable number of qualified applicants to interview.

Advertising

Start by writing a position announcement for the job, using the job description and specifications you have created. Most position announcements are relatively brief (no more than one or two paragraphs), and include instructions for getting more information or how to apply for the position.

PERSONAL WORKSHOP 48
Building a Job Specification

▼ Use this form to help you focus your job analysis (and also to construct an effective advertisement).

In the **Goal** column, list the goals you have: what is the reason for hiring this person? What will the new employee help your company do? Be specific.

In the **Task** column, list the various jobs that the new person will have to do to achieve the goal.

In the **Skill** column, list the kinds of skills required to perform each task.

In the **Qualification** column, list any special training, education, or characteristics necessary to perform each task.

In the **Experience** column, put a checkmark if experience alone is a sufficient qualification.

Goal	Task	Skill	Qualification	Experience

How Should You Recruit Applicants?

To develop a pool of qualified applicants, you should consider using several different methods to announce your job opening. The effectiveness of different sources depends primarily on the type of job. The costs of recruiting also vary with the method and scope of your search. Typically, the higher the level of the position, or the more specialized the skills required, the greater the need to recruit beyond your local area, and the higher the costs. Possible sources of qualified applicants include those that follow.

Referrals. Ask your current employees to tell any qualified people they know about the job vacancy. In some cases, employers offer finder rewards to an employee who refers the individual hired—although such rewards should not be paid until the new employee has been with the company for a reasonable period of time. Employee referral should never be the exclusive method of recruiting, however, because it could limit workplace diversity.

Networking. Take every opportunity to tell others about your job opening. Call friends and professional associates. Announce it at social meetings or service organizations you belong to. Send a copy of the position announcement to your professional or technical association and ask that it be posted in the next newsletter. Or take the announcement to a professional conference and post it on the message board. Don't be afraid to call people you think might be qualified to tell them about the position. Even if they aren't personally interested, they may know someone with similar skills who is. Most of these recruitment strategies are free, and they could result in some excellent, highly qualified applicants.

Employment agencies. Employment agencies can be either public or private. Some provide general services to employers and job applicants for all types of employment, while others specialize in specific businesses or skills. Through computerized databases, agencies can target your search to particular categories, experience groupings, or geographic areas. They can also can provide you with local labor statistics, information about fair employment practices and affirmative action, and recruitment assistance.

There are two types of private employment agencies: **retainer search firms** and **contingency recruiting firms**. Employers generally hire retainer search firms to locate highly specialized people or top-level managers. These agencies require an up-front fee and typically handle only positions that pay higher salaries. You can expect to pay approximately one-third of the position's annual salary for this service.

Contingency search firms, on the other hand, make their money in volume, collecting fees from employers only when they place a candidate. While hiring is a good thing, be careful: you can expect a contingency search firm to want to fill the position as quickly as possible, even if it means compromising your job specifications. Some temporary employment agencies also serve as contingency search firms. If you find that you need to hire temporary help until a permanent employee is found, check with the agency to find out the terms and conditions of hiring someone permanently that they may have placed with you as a temp. The advantage of this approach is that you get to try out the employee without obligation, perhaps even while you are conducting your search.

Advertising in the newspaper. Placing a classified ad in a newspaper can be costly, but can be a good source for finding qualified applicants, depending upon the type of job. Before placing an ad, look at the kinds of ads the paper currently runs. Larger newspapers tend to list classified ads by job category. Also look at the ads for style tips: note which ones grab your attention and which get lost on the page. It might be worthwhile to pay a little more and run a well-designed display ad one time than to run a smaller, nondescript classified ad several times. Contact your newspaper to find out the best days to advertise, the costs, and what services they offer to help you design an attractive ad. The cost of a newspaper ad depends on the size of the ad and the circulation of the paper.

Keep in mind, though, that any advertisement placed in the newspaper will be read by thousands of unqualified applicants. To avoid receiving thousands of unwanted applications, be as specific as possible about the required qualifications in the ad. If you definitely don't want telephone calls or applicants dropping by your business without an appointment, you might consider asking job applicants to send a letter and resume to a post office box and not even list your company's name in the advertisement.

Advertising in professional trade journals. If the skills required for the job are highly specialized or technical, or if you need to do a regional or national search, you might consider placing an advertisement in a professional association or trade journal, or an association newsletter. For example, if you need to hire a veterinarian, you may have greater success advertising your position in the various trade journals that veterinarians read, rather than the local newspaper. There are thousands of professional and trade associations, some statewide, some regional, some national and international; and most of them at least have a newsletter. To find out the names of appropriate trade and professional associations, talk to people in the field, or go to the reference section of your local library. Costs for advertising in professional trade journals and newsletters range from free to very expensive, depending upon the association and the circulation of the publication.

School placement services. Most colleges, trade schools, and vocational schools have placement offices for their students and graduates. Just call the school or send them your job announcement, and they will include it in their job bank or place it on a job bulletin board. Needless to say, the educational requirements and skills needed for the job will help you decide which schools to contact. If the position can be filled by a high school student, also contact your area high schools. This service is typically free.

"Help wanted" signs in your window. This is an inexpensive way to get the word out and is especially effective for retail and food service businesses. If the main qualification for the job is a warm body and willingness to work, this technique may be the most effective. Your pool of potential applicants will, of course, be limited to passers-by, so this strategy only works if your business is located in a heavy traffic area. Your sign should be large, easy to read, and specify times when applicants should stop in, if appropriate.

LIABILITY ALERT!
The Application Form

You may use your own employment application form, but make sure the questions are reasonably related to the job you are trying to fill. Use caution if you use a preprinted form: it may ask questions that are not reasonably related to the job or violate your state's employment laws. It is also important that the questions are not aimed at eliciting information as to whether the applicant is a member of a protected class.

You must also make *reasonable accommodations* to enable a disabled person to apply for the job. The **Americans with Disabilities Act** requires employers to provide equal opportunity to applicants with disabilities.

Make sure you use an up-to-date application form that contains questions strictly related to the applicant's ability to perform the job.

SELECTION: HOW TO SCREEN
AND EVALUATE JOB APPLICANTS

Now that you have a pool of applicants to consider for your job opening, your next task is to screen the applications. Never assume that everyone who applies is qualified for the job. In fact, as you read through the application materials, you are likely to be amazed at the breadth of backgrounds and experiences represented, no matter how precise your job specifications were! Many applicants seem to think that a "willingness to learn" makes up for a complete lack of the required qualifications.

If you have any questions about an application, jot them down so you will remember to ask the candidate about them later. As you screen the applicants, you should make four piles of applications:

1. Applicants who are not qualified
2. Applicants who have all the required qualifications, but lack the desired ones
3. Applicants who are qualified, but for whom you have unanswered questions regarding their application
4. Applicants who are clearly qualified and could be hired immediately

Conducting the Personal Interview

Never assume that everyone who applies is qualified for the job. The purpose of a job interview is for both parties to assess how well the candidate matches the job. Both parties need to come out of the interview with more information, so everyone needs to be able to get answers. Be sure to allow time for the applicant to ask questions about the company and the job. Set the interview format and develop an interview agenda accordingly.

PERSONAL WORKSHOP 49
Screening Worksheet

▼ Before you begin your review of the applications, you might find it helpful to develop a screening worksheet such as the one we've provided here. Use the worksheet as a tool to help you determine if an applicant has the required and/or desired qualifications for the job, and make a few notes about the applicant. A screening worksheet will be particularly useful if you have several applicants for the vacant position. It can also serve as a record of your decision-making process, which could be especially useful should anyone ever make a discrimination charge against you.

Design a screening worksheet to fit your needs. Use the job specifications you established to customize the worksheet to the position. Be sure that your worksheet includes all the required and desired qualifications and skills you noted in the job description.

CONTINUED ▶

Applicant Name or Identifier:

Required Qualifications for Job as Advertised	Applicant Has? Yes	No	If Yes, Describe Applicant's Qualifications	*Desired* Qualifications for Job as Advertised	Applicant Has? Yes	No	If Yes, Describe Applicant's Qualifications
Educational							
1.							
2.							
3.							
Experience							
1.							
2.							
3.							
Expertise							
1.							
2.							
3.							
Other							
1.							
2.							
3.							

Positive Comments about This Applicant:

Negative Comments about This Applicant:

LIABILITY ALERT!
The Interview

Many employers are not aware that some traditional interviewing questions might be illegal or interpreted by the courts as discriminatory under state or federal employment laws. In addition to federal antidiscrimination laws, each state has civil rights statutes and provisions in their constitutions that protect against discrimination. State civil rights laws and constitutional provisions may prohibit discrimination based on the following:

- Color
- Race
- Religious creed
- Sex
- National origin
- Marital status
- Change in marital status
- Sexual orientation
- Parenthood
- Pregnancy
- Personal appearance
- Status with regard to public assistance
- Workers' compensation claims
- Political party
- Physical disability

- Handicap
- Medical condition
- Smoking habit
- Atypical hereditary cell or blood type
- Matriculation
- Arrest record
- Unfavorable military discharge
- Expunged arrest record of juvenile
- Conviction record
- Participation in lawful activities during off-hours
- Family responsibilities
- Mental disorder
- Age

The interview questions. Using the job description and specifications as a guide, develop a set of interview questions to ask each candidate. These questions should cover the important aspects of the candidate's work experiences and accomplishments, education and training, and career goals or aspirations, as they relate to the position.

Questions unrelated to the job should be avoided. Questions should primarily be open-ended, requiring more than a "yes" or "no" answer. Open-ended questions force candidates to think, organize, and express their thoughts. They also allow candidates to say as little or as much as they want about a topic. But as each candidate talks, look for openings to ask clarifying and probing questions that will help you learn a little more about that person. For example, if a candidate mentions having accomplished a certain goal, ask how he or she went about achieving that goal, overcoming obstacles, or what was learned from the accomplishment. The answers to such questions can give you insight into the candidate's work style, organizational skills, conflict management skills, determination, motivation, and values. This information will be useful in deciding whether this person is a good fit for your company, as well as whether he or she has the appropriate skills and abilities to do the job.

LIABILITY ALERT!
Questioning a Job Applicant

The key to lawful employment inquiries is to ask only about those areas which will provide information about the person's ability to do the job with reasonable accommodation.

Review the following types of questions and be aware of them as you prepare to interview applicants for employment.

Age or Date of Birth	The Federal Age Discrimination in Employment Act prohibits discrimination on the basis of age. This applies particularly to anyone age 40 or over. State laws also prohibit questions of this type.
Arrest Records or Criminal Charges	State law may prohibit you from asking about criminal arrest records or convictions. If an applicant has a pending criminal charge that is related to the job to be performed, an employer should either suspend judgment until the court decision on the charge, if possible, or advise the applicant to reapply when the pending charge has been resolved. An employer should never reject an applicant outright, or discharge an employee, because of a pending criminal charge.
Availability for Saturday or Sunday Work	Questions about working on Saturday or Sunday may discourage applications from persons of certain religions which prohibit their adherents from working on Saturday or Sunday. On the other hand, employers may need to know whether an applicant can work on these days. Title VII of the Civil Rights Act of 1964 prohibits discrimination on the basis of religious beliefs and practices. Employers are exempt from compliance if they can demonstrate that they are unable to reasonably accommodate an employee's (or prospective employee's) religious observance or practice without undue hardship on the conduct of the business. If you do need to ask about Saturday and Sunday work, you should state that a reasonable effort is made to accommodate the religious needs of all employees.
Children, Age of Children, Child Care Arrangements	The purpose of questions about parental status and child care arrangements is usually to explore what the employer believes to be a common source of absenteeism and tardiness. There are a number of common causes of absenteeism and tardiness that affect both men and women which would be worthy of exploration if this is a matter of concern to the employer. In the absence of proof of business necessity, employers are prohibited from having one hiring policy for women with preschool children and another for men with preschool children.

Checking References

Don't skip this step! Check the applicant's references, both those offered directly by the candidate and those developed in the interview. Ask the applicant's permission before calling anyone. Sometimes, a candidate will ask that you not contact the current employer. While that's understandable, you should be wary if a candidate declines to authorize *any* reference checks, or if the candidate still won't allow you to call the current employer when you are ready to make an offer. These situations suggest the candidate may be trying to hide something negative.

Past supervisors and coworkers are usually the best sources for objective job-related information about the candidate. Call the candidate's former supervisors, identify yourself and the purpose of your call, verify the candidate's length of employment and position(s) held, and then ask a few key questions about the candidate's work performance and job-related characteristics. Take notes during each call. As in the candidate interview, do not ask questions which might be illegal or interpreted as discriminatory. Personal references are rarely helpful: you already know that applicants' aunts, childhood friends, or spiritual advisors are likely to say nice things about them.

FIRST PERSON

Rathna C., Somerville, Massachusetts: Here are two things I do: First, I always narrow my first interviews down to at least three candidates. Then, in the second interview, I try to learn as much about the personality of each one as I can. Do they handle stress? Are they good at juggling more than one project at a time? Will they treat my clients and the other employees with respect and professional courtesy? Usually I take them to lunch, which helps them relax and gives us time for real conversation. That way I get an idea of the whole person, and that helps me make the right decision.

YOUR FINAL DECISION

You should now have all the information needed to select the best candidate for the position. It might be helpful to put this information into some standard format. For each of your final job candidates, review the screening worksheet, your notes from the interview and reference checks, and all other application materials that you have gathered. Compare each candidate's strengths and weaknesses to the written job specifications.

The important thing is to be as fair and objective as possible as you determine which candidate will be the best fit for the job. Document your decision-making along the way, noting your evaluation of applicants' job-related criteria only.

The Offer

Sometimes an offer is pretty straightforward; other times it involves negotiations. Before contacting your top choice for the job, determine what you believe to be a fair and reasonable offer for this person in this job. Have some salary and benefit limits in mind, if you are interested in negotiating. Never make an offer during the employment interview: you both need some time to think about whether the situation is right. Invite your top candidate to come in, or make a verbal offer by phone. Follow any verbal offer with a letter stating the general terms of the offer, but do not imply that the letter is an employment contract. Give the candidate a reasonable period of time to make a decision, and invite him or her to call you if any questions come to mind. If you and the candidate cannot come to terms, then make an offer to your next choice on the list of acceptable candidates.

ARE YOU FINALLY FINISHED?

At this point you should feel terrific about finding a well-qualified new employee, but your work isn't done. While you have no obligation to tell any applicant why they did not get the job (in fact, you should absolutely *avoid* doing so), you should notify anyone you interviewed that you have selected the candidate whose qualifications best met your needs. You should not tell any other applicant anything about the individual who was selected. Simply thank other applicants for their interest in the job, and enjoy the challenge, opportunity, and excitement of welcoming a new employee aboard.

LIABILITY ALERT!
Be Aware of Federal and State Employment Laws

Employers need to be aware of federal and state employment laws, particularly those affecting child labor and the hiring of immigrants.

&TAXES

If you have one or more employees, you will be required to withhold federal income tax from their wages. You also must collect the employee's part and pay your matching share of Social Security (FICA) and Medicare taxes. FICA provides for a federal system of old-age, survivors, disability, and hospital insurance. The old-age, survivors, and disability part is financed through Social Security taxes, and the hospital part is financed by the Medicare tax. Each of these taxes is reported separately. Social Security taxes are levied on both you and your employees. You as an employer must collect and pay the employee's part of the tax by withholding it from the employee's wages. As employer, you are also liable for a matching share of Social Security taxes.

You are required by law to deduct and withhold income tax from the salaries and wages of your employees. You are liable for payment of that tax to the federal government whether or not you collect it from your employees.

Generally, you must withhold income from wages you pay employees if their wages for any payroll period are more than the dollar amount of their withholding allowances claimed for that period. The amount to be withheld is figured separately for each payroll period. You should figure withholding on gross wages before any deductions for Social Security tax, pension, union dues, insurance, or other expenses are made. The IRS publishes Circular E, Employer's Tax Guide, which contains the applicable tables and detailed instructions for using withholding methods.

Filing: Social Security (FICA) and Medicare taxes and withheld income tax are reported together on Form 941, Employee's Quarterly Federal Tax Return. Forms 942, 943, and 945 are used for other than the usual type of employee. (See Publication

334.) Form 943 (for Agricultural Employees) is an annual return due one month after the end of the calendar year. The other forms are quarterly returns and are due one month after the end of each calendar quarter. Due dates are April 30, July 31, October 31, and January 31. An extra 10 days are given if taxes are deposited on time and in full.

You will probably have to make deposits of Social Security and Medicare taxes and withheld income taxes before the return is due. Deposits are not required for taxes reported on Form 942. You must deposit both your part and your employee's part of Social Security taxes in an authorized financial institution or a Federal Reserve Bank. Forms 8109, Federal Tax Deposit Coupons, are used to make deposits (some deposits may be permitted through electronic funds transfer technologies).

You must furnish copies of Form W-2 to each employee from whom income tax or Social Security tax has been withheld. Form W-2 shows the total wages and other compensations paid, total wages subject to Social Security and Medicare taxes, amounts deducted for income, Social Security and Medicare taxes, and any other information required on the statement. Furnish copies of Form W-2 to employees as soon as possible after December 31, so they may file their income tax returns early. It must be sent to the employee no later than January 31st. W-2s must also be transmitted annually to the Social Security Administration.

Employers must file Form W-3 annually to transmit Forms W-2 and W-2P to the Social Security Administration. These forms will be processed by the Social Security Administration, which will then furnish the Internal Revenue Service with the income tax data that it needs from the forms.

In general, an employee can claim withholding allowances equal to the number of exemptions he or she is entitled to claim on an income tax return. Each new employee should give you a Form W-4, Employee's Withholding Allowance Certificate, on or before the first day of work. The certificate must include the employee's Social Security number.

Your Government at Work:

Publication 334, Tax Guide for Small Business.

Taxpayer Education Coordinator: 800-829 1040

http://www.irs.ustreas.gov/prod/tax_edu/teletax/tc751.html
http://www.irs.ustreas.gov/prod/tax_edu/teletax/tc752.html
http://www.irs.ustreas.gov/prod/tax_edu/teletax/tc753.html
http://www.irs.ustreas.gov/prod/tax_edu/teletax/tc755.html
http://www.irs.ustreas.gov/prod/tax_edu/teletax/tc757.html
http://www.irs.ustreas.gov/prod/tax_edu/teletax/tc762.html
http://www.irs.ustreas.gov/prod/tax_edu/teletax/tc750.html
http://www.lawcrawler.com/bookstore/ixbusiness.html
http://www.toolkit.cch.com/text/P01_5450.STM
http://www.toolkit.cch.com/text/P05_0005.stm

FIRST PERSON

Nick B., Houston, Texas: I used to work for the IRS national office, and I can tell you that one thing that really messes people up all the time is the requirement to withhold payroll taxes and pay them to the state and federal authorities on a quarterly basis. When small businesses find themselves in a cash crunch, they sometimes are tempted to use the money set aside from payroll tax withholding rather than paying it on a timely basis. At the time, it probably doesn't seem like a big deal. But this can run into big money in penalties. And the really important thing to remember is that the penalties are assessed against anyone who had the power to make the payment, and they are assessed personally, not against the company. That means they can come and take your house. It's not a joke.

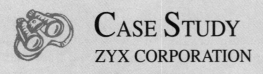

CASE STUDY
ZYX CORPORATION

▾▾▾▾▾▾

*M*onique Fein owns ZYX Corporation, a small manufacturer of electronic components. When she took over the company from her father in 1989, it had seven full-time employees, all of whom were kept regularly busy throughout the year. ZYX has a core of regular customers it supplies with various components, although lately it has tended to concentrate on circuit boards. Monique's father founded the company in 1962, and worked hard over the years to build up the core customers, all of whom have become both loyal and, to a large degree, dependent on ZYX for their components. The company has exclusive supplier contracts with many of them.

For the past two years, Monique has devoted much of her time to winning a contract from VerTek, a large Silicon Valley company, to supply it with circuit boards. She traveled to California regularly, met with VerTek's officers, and even flew them out to visit ZYX's recently modernized facility. Finally, a few months ago, her efforts paid off: VerTek awarded ZYX an order for 10,000 circuit boards. If ZYX could meet the delivery and quality specifications set by VerTek, they were promised additional orders which would virtually double their annual production. Clearly, this was an important account, and some strategic thinking was in order. This one account could change the whole direction, focus, and market power of ZYX.

There was one problem: ZYX did not have enough employees to meet the deadline without sacrificing quality, not just on the VerTek order, but on standing orders from longtime customers. To

Monique, this was an unacceptable option. Trouble was, she didn't know what the company's long-term future needs would be, because keeping the new account depended upon her success with this first order. She knew what she wanted for the company: growth, expansion, and an emphasis on the profitable high-tech end of their business. On the other hand, ZYX's future growth could definitely be jeopardized if it failed to meet VerTek's order on time. And falling behind on existing orders from old customers was not even an option. Monique was aware that because of the goodwill and strong relationships her father had built with the base customers over the years, she could probably go to them and ask for extensions on delivery dates. But Monique also knew that while they'd probably be very understanding about the situation, they all had their own businesses to run, and ZYX's failure to deliver on time would put them all in an awkward position. They might be willing to let ZYX slide this once, but years of customer relations work would be undermined. They might also get nervous about ZYX's new direction, and take their orders elsewhere. There was certainly no shortage of suppliers, as Monique well knew.

Monique sat down to consider the alternative. Hiring and training an entire second shift didn't seem reasonable, since an increased future level of production was not yet guaranteed. But contracting out the extra work or hiring temporary employees weren't reasonable options, either, since the work of an assembler requires special skills, technical training,

CONTINUED ▶

and training in the special quality control process ZYX was famous for. Hiring a bunch of temps could be disastrous for ZYX's reputation if they didn't get everything exactly right. The other employees had spent years learning the system; it wouldn't be possible to master it in a few weeks. But that left Monique right back where she'd been in the first place: staring at the VerTek orders at her desk, late into the night. ▼

CASE STUDY ROUNDTABLE

▼▼▼▼▼▼

Monique: You people have a lot of experience...do you have any suggestions for how we can handle this? How many people should I hire? Where should I get them from? Help!

Discussion Points

- Did Monique make any mistakes in this case? How could they have been avoided?
- What is the basic problem she has? Is it long-term or short-term?
- Is hiring new employees the answer for Monique? Can you think of alternative solutions?

▲▲▲▲▲▲

CHAPTER BRIEFCASE

▼▼▼▼▼▼

- Whether replacing a current employee or hiring for a new position, whether this is your first employee or your fiftieth, any personnel change should be considered an opportunity for rethinking your organizational structure.
- Do not get caught in the trap of hiring based only on your immediate needs. Instead, think about your business plan and your vision for the company.
- Independent contractors are independent business people who are hired to perform specific tasks. They are just like any other vendor, except they perform services rather than provide tangible goods. Independent contractors are in business for themselves. They are not employees. They are not eligible for unemployment, disability, or workers' compensation benefits. The hiring firm does not have to pay employee-employer taxes or provide workers' compensation insurance, and usually is not liable for the contractor's actions. The IRS has strict guidelines for independent contractor status.
- Before you can hire the right employee with the right skills, you need to understand exactly what the job will be. Job analysis involves studying the job

to understand exactly what needs to be done. Remember to think in terms of what the job should be, and not necessarily in terms of how someone might currently be doing it.

- To develop a pool of qualified applicants, you should consider using several different methods to announce your job opening. Once you have a pool of applicants to consider for your job opening, your next task is to screen the applications. Never assume that everyone who applies is qualified for the job. The purpose of a job interview is for both parties to assess how well the candidate and job match. Both parties need to come out of the interview with enough information to make that determination.

▲▲▲▲▲▲

Chapter 26

PLANNING FOR GROWTH

▼▼▼▼▼▼

Time is a sort of river of passing events, and strong is its current; no sooner is a thing brought to sight than it is swept by and another takes its place, and this too will be swept away.
—*Emperor Marcus Aurelius, 121–180 AD*

The strongest principle of growth lies in human choice.
—*George Eliot*

MISSION STATEMENT

In this chapter, you will

*L*EARN about the importance of environmental and internal analysis as you move your business forward.

*E*XPLORE the strengths and weaknesses of your business idea and identify distinctive competencies.

*A*PPLY your understanding to a case study of an ongoing business.

*P*RODUCE competitive objectives for growing your business.

KEY TERMS

competitive weakness

distinctive competence

environmental analysis

internal analysis

sustainable competency

INTRODUCTION TO PLANNING FOR GROWTH

People often say there are only two certainties in life: death and taxes. In the real world of small business development, however, there is another one—change. No new business stays the same forever. It grows, or it dies; it changes, or it fails to thrive; it meets new challenges, or it falls behind. Sure, death and taxes are always with us, but for small business owners, so is change. As your business moves forward and it finds its way in the marketplace, you need to be prepared to deal effectively with its growth and evolution, and with the new challenges you will face both internally and from your competitors.

▼▼▼▼▼▼▼▼▼▼▼▼▼▼▼▼▼▼

As your business moves ahead, there are two principal challenges that need to be planned for: (1) change itself, and (2) the effect of your business's change and growth on your competitors. You'll be surprised how quickly a friendly rivalry can become alarmingly intense when one of you grows and changes, posing a new and unexpected threat to the other. The opposite is true, too: a "professional" relationship between competitors can become ugly when one of them exposes a weakness. That's the thing about change: it always has two sides, a good and a not-so-good effect. That's why you need to plan and be prepared.

BE PREPARED FOR CHANGE

In the first few months your business is in operation, you will be busier than you ever have been or will be again. The key to getting through these months successfully: Maintain your focus. You spent months deciding what your business is, who your markets are, and what (and why) they will buy from you. You decided what promotions made sense, what kind of image to project, and what to do if things didn't go exactly as planned. In the early phases, you'll experience a lot of change, and have to make a lot of adjustments. But remember, don't change your basic strategic plan without strong reasons.

Under the pressure of daily business, with experience correcting your forecasts (often in a negative way), it becomes very tempting to try to do a little more, add a product or service, go after a different market, buy market share, or any of thousands of possible responses to outside forces. Be stalwart. Stick to your plan for three months. That gives you enough time (in most cases) to get over the initial excitement of running your own business, meet the payroll and other fixed expenses several times, and have a better grip on what your business patterns actually will be.

Sales may be higher than anticipated initially, followed by a substantially lower sales pattern than hoped for. This is a common pattern and doesn't mean that your plans were off the mark. Initial sales often come from the newness factor, and after the novelty for your customers wears off, sales will slowly build in a more normal pattern. Assuming that you did your homework in the pre-start-up period, these swings will even out.

Some ways to keep your enthusiasm high include scheduling your time effectively (that is, doing the right things at the right times), updating your product/benefit list from your customers' viewpoint and paying extra attention to communications with your markets. Expect to make mistakes—you're human. But plan to learn from your mistakes (and from your successes). You will learn more about your business in the first three to six months than you will in the next five years. That's exhilarating.

Throughout the life of your business, you'll want to keep these three fundamentals in mind:

1. Update your product or service.
2. Adapt your plans.
3. Budget your time.

Continuously Update Your Product or Service

This is where your interests and those of your customers intersect. If you remain attuned to their wants and preferences and shape your product or service to their needs,

Managing for growth: Minority entrepreneur Albert Black, from On Target Supplies and Logistics, delivers a compelling message on ownership and growth issues, and how he created a board of advisers to help grow his business strategically.

you win. If you try to force what you have to sell on a public that doesn't want to buy, you're in deep trouble.

Update Your Plans as Needed

Don't become so fond of looking down to admire your plans that you forget to watch the road ahead. The sudden, unanticipated head-on crash into reality is the biggest danger small business owners run into, on or off the highway.

Budget Your Time

Continually review your work habits and patterns: You go to work, open the door, and then what? How do you spend your time? Time is a finite and precious resource, and your best investment is budgeting your own time to make sure you don't leave any major aspect of your business undernourished. In successful businesses every important management area is given adequate attention. Lopsided businesses are unsuccessful ones. We all prefer to spend time doing things we enjoy doing, and avoiding (if possible) those tasks we dislike. This poses a simple choice: either budget your time to avoid those gaps, or don't manage your time and wake up in a sweat at 3:00 AM wondering if you remembered to fill in that tax form or make that loan payment.

When budgeting your time, keep these points in mind:

- The tasks of management are: to plan, coordinate, direct, control, monitor, evaluate, correct, review, and innovate. These areas require attention on a regular basis.
- Set aside time for your family and for yourself to avoid burnout. The temptation to spend all your time at work is beguiling, but the costs in personal terms are excessive. Build in some downtime for yourself as well. Getting away from the hurly burly of business pays off in having better judgment and making better decisions.
- Set aside time for learning more about your business. Information pays. You can never know too much about your business, the industry, and general management and economic issues.
- Set aside time to get to know your customers better. Talk with them. Ask them questions; listen to their answers. There's a good reason you have two ears and one tongue. Listen twice as much as you talk, and you'll become wise. Make sure to get as many of their names, addresses, interests, and preferences as you can for marketing purposes.
- Set aside time to research your competition. The more you know about your competition, both direct and indirect, the better. Religiously maintain those competitor files. Shop your competition. Speak with their customers and suppliers. They act as a mirror for your own business's improvement.

Listen—
- To customers
- To your family and friends
- To your employees
- To vendors
- To competitors
- To advisers

Don't forget to listen to yourself. People like to give advice. Your role as business owner is to listen, evaluate what you hear, and act accordingly based upon your judgment and experience. This is not a recommendation that you weigh every bit of input equally. You learn from others, selectively, by applying the intelligence and experience that urged you to go into business on your own in the first place.

IDENTIFYING AND DEVELOPING AREAS OF DISTINCTIVE COMPETENCE

In Chapter 4, we discussed the nine basic competencies likely to be found in a successful small business.

1. Filling a special niche
2. Flexibility and adaptability
3. Location
4. Personnel
5. Price
6. Quality
7. Reputation and image
8. Service
9. Strong consumer orientation

A business that has one or more of these competencies is able to distinguish itself from its competitors, and create a special place for itself in the market.

As a child gets older, it not only improves its basic skills and abilities (walking, eating, talking), but adds new ones (algebra, driving, and, eventually, small business development). It's the same with your business: as it ages and grows, it will not only improve its existing competencies, but will develop new ones, too.

Evolving Competency

Distinctive competencies may appear in either of two ways. First, the competency may be present as part of the firm's operations. As the business exists over time, it operates in such a manner that clear and important areas of competence are stressed. These competencies may have initially developed out of the firm's mission or management style. Over time, they become an integral part of the business.

In some situations, though, distinctive competencies may need to be developed or nurtured. Here, you analyze the competitive environment, scrutinize internal resources, and carefully decide which areas are most fruitful for development. In this approach, you actually build areas of competence, rather than simply recognizing them.

Such a building process can be a challenge. Investigate areas where you can create a meaningful competence, realizing that competencies are dictated by your competitive environment, your company's internal capacities, and how you react to your competitors.

Making the Connection: Relating Distinctive Competencies to Specific Business Opportunities

As noted earlier, not all opportunities are good ones for your business to pursue. How do you know which ones are right? In general, you should select those opportunities in areas that offer you some unique or special advantage over your competitors. In other words, you should focus on those opportunities for which your business has distinctive competencies.

PERSONAL WORKSHOP 50
Product Comparison Form

▾ Fill out this form for each product or service you offer. For simplicity's sake, and to keep your focus, make comparisons only to your leading competitor's products or services. (Note that this is similar to the *competitor* comparison in Personal Workshop 10.)

Product/Service _____

	Mine	**Theirs**
Target markets		
Benefits offered:		
1.		
2.		
3.		
Quality		
Price		
Improved versions		
Delivery		
Follow-up service		
Availability		
Convenience		
Reliability		
Service		
Guarantees		
Other (specify):		
1.		
2.		
3.		

The significance of this point is often overlooked or misunderstood. Often, owners believe that if they see a business opportunity, they should capitalize on it even though it may be a poor use of their resources. For example, a number of competitors may respond to the same opportunity, and some of these competitors may be better able to do so. To commit to something because everyone else is doing it, even though you are at a competitive disadvantage, is poor business sense. Areas where the business possesses a meaningful competitive edge over its competitors are the areas that should be emphasized. Of course, doing what you do well is easier said than done.

Sustainable Competencies

It's one thing to have or develop a distinctive competency. It's quite another to maintain it. The more successful a company is because of a competency, the more competitors will attempt to copy or improve on it. Anything you can do to sustain a competency and prevent competitors from encroaching on your territory will go far in ensuring the success of your business. You might patent a product or process, keep formulas for products secret, advertise the product heavily to develop brand loyalty, or develop unique packaging and catchy slogans or product names that encourage customers to identify the product with your company.

Few competencies are sustainable forever. Even IBM, once the epitome of success in the computer industry, has fallen on hard times in recent years. This happens all the time with real estate companies in medium-size cities. For a few years, one company dominates the community's sale of real estate. A few years later, another firm leads the pack. Still later, another will take over as number one. A real estate agency can ward off competitors for a few years because of its size or because its key executives are well known in the city. The success of that firm, however, eventually fades when a competitor tries some other approach that customers find appealing. The tenuous nature of distinctive competencies should prompt you to constantly search for ways to sustain your competencies.

DISTINCTIVE COMPETENCIES AND PLANNING FOR GROWTH

The recognition of your distinctive competencies is one of the critical, culminating events of planning for growth. Distinctive competencies become the focus or driving force behind selecting relevant business opportunities, preparing mission and goal statements, and planning strategic actions. Eventually, this will bring you back to reconsider your mission statement (discussed in Chapter 7).

It may be useful to refine the steps that make up the planning model (see Figure 26.1). First, **environmental analysis** yields a series of opportunities in the real world in which the business will operate. These are then subjected to the scrutiny of **internal analysis** to determine if they are in fact relevant business opportunities. Additional analysis focusing on competitors and key internal strengths helps you clearly recognize your company's distinctive competencies (or pinpoint those areas most fruitful for development). Then, the relevant business opportunities are evaluated in terms of the recognized distinctive competency. Those opportunities most consistent with your

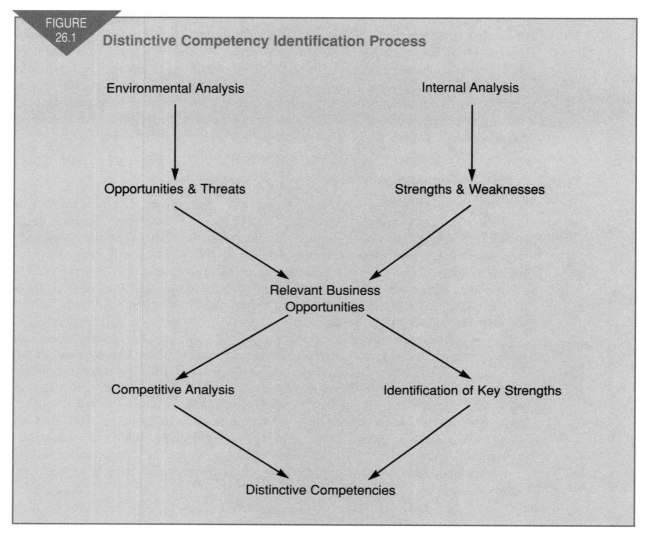

FIGURE 26.1

Distinctive Competency Identification Process

competencies are the ones you should pursue, and they should become the focus for your planning efforts.

Competitive Weaknesses

While careful environmental and internal analyses lets you identify areas of distinctive competence, they also suggest areas of competitive weakness. A **competitive weakness** is an area of vulnerability, an area in which your competitors have a meaningful edge. In a highly competitive situation, one company's distinctive competency is often another company's competitive weakness. Just as distinctive competencies are developed over time, competitive weaknesses also evolve over time.

Throughout its business life, the things your company has done and failed to do can accrue into competitive weaknesses. Once you've recognized them, however, your competitive weaknesses can spur the planning process.

However, small business owners are a proud group. To be successful, you have to be enthusiastic believers in your products and services. As a result, it is often difficult to recognize, much less act on, your competitive weaknesses. Generally, this is the result of a combination of factors: an unrealistic analysis of the competitive environment, and an inadequate internal analysis. That's why it's so important to undertake a clear-headed analysis, and why you must be open and ready to accept *and respond* to the results of your analysis. Indeed, one or two key areas of competitive weakness can, if ignored, destroy all the strength you get from your distinctive competencies. Since few businesses are the best at everything, identifying competitive weaknesses is not a sign of failure. Instead, it lets you know that there are challenges you must deal with as you develop a strategy for competitive action.

Determining the Planning Horizon

A three-year period is often the target for medium-term plans. Short-term plans are generally for one year or less. Accountants, on the other hand, often refer to any-

---

PERSONAL WORKSHOP 51
Competitive Objectives
▾ ▾ ▾ ▾ ▾

▾ Use this worksheet to help you focus on your strengths, weaknesses, and areas for improvements as you plan to develop your business's competitive objectives.

Prepared by: _____   Date: _____

Reviewed by: _____   Date: _____

We need to improve our competitive position in these areas:

1._____

2._____

3._____

We can build on our competitive strengths in these areas:

1._____

2._____

3._____

We can attack our competition in their weak areas:

1._____

2._____

3._____

thing over one year as long range. In high-technology industry, six months is virtually forever. Time, as Einstein showed us, is a relative thing: it depends on who's watching the clock.

Determining long- versus short-range goals depends on your industry and the type of product or service you provide. A utility company has to look 15 to 20 years ahead because of the time it takes to build a power plant. A small janitorial service may have no reason to look beyond one year. A small manufacturer is somewhere in between.

These examples introduce a key factor in planning: the *planning horizon*. The **planning horizon** is the time required to implement a major strategic change. Beyond that time period, a manager need only do some casual monitoring, because the business can react to any change that might develop.

Just don't get carried away with planning and analysis. The details can be attractive and interesting, but it's like trying to run in a swamp: you can get (literally) "bogged down" in the data, and never get anywhere. You have to constantly watch the marketplace so you can spot developing trends. But you can't react to every fad or market blip. Trying to do that will only paralyze you, leaving your business unable to respond over the long run.

FIRST PERSON

Sergio O., Chicago, Illinois: I opened my Italian restaurant several years ago, in a space and neighborhood I could afford at the time. The restaurant did pretty well and developed a reputation for good, moderately priced food. But its out-of-the-way location and small size eliminated a big part of the city's population as potential customers. So I decided to open a new location in a pretty trendy part of town, close to a new shopping mall. The move went well, and profits went up because there were few similar restaurants in the area: lots of fast food and coffee shops, but no lasagna. Four years later, two big, well-known Italian restaurant chains opened sites within two blocks on either side of my place.

People said to me, "Boy, that was really a classic case of bad planning!" Should I have been able to predict three to five years in advance? The answer is no. Even though my restaurant is now in what you could call a highly competitive market, there was no way that the competition could have been predicted. My planning horizon was not that far down the road: how could it have been? The move was the right move at the time. If I'd worried about what might happen five years later, I'd still be back in my little hole in the wall. Even though I don't dominate the market here anymore, we're still doing fine.

Realistic Planning

If you extend the horizon too far, you may lock yourself into a strategy that's outdated before you've fully set it in motion. Imagine, for instance, how those companies felt that pinned their hopes on the punchcard input devices that were the leading edge of computer technology in the 1970s. On the other hand, if the horizon is too short, you may miss opportunities. Like Goldilocks, you have to find the horizon that's "just right."

THE ACTION PHASE

After you have evaluated your company's competencies and identified any competitive weaknesses, you're ready to move on to the **action phase** of planning for your company's growth. It's time to create a working plan to guide your company's activities.

The first step requires determining (or even rethinking) the **mission** of your business and its strategic posture. (Mission statements are discussed in detail in Chapter 7.)

Once you have a clear understanding of your company's mission and overall strategic posture in mind (and written down), you can focus on your specific business goals. Setting achievable and measurable goals for the company as a whole as well as each of its separate functions is an important process.

Strategies breathe life into goals. Essentially, a goal statement says, "This is what we want to do or what we want to be," while strategies say, "This is how we are going to do it." Decisions to segment the market, change pricing, alter sales policies, acquire additional funds, and change production methods are examples of **unit strategies** undertaken to move the company toward the realization of its goals. The best strategies in the world are of limited value, though, if they are not written down.

URLinks
http://www.toolkit.cch.com/text/P02_3201.STM
http://www.vandoren.net/default2.htm
http://www.hp.com/sbso/tips/tips.html

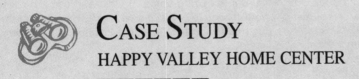

CASE STUDY
HAPPY VALLEY HOME CENTER

▼▼▼▼▼▼

*F*ive years ago, Bob Adams purchased the Happy Valley Home Center for $375,000. It was located in a small town near Richmond, Indiana. The price included the building, equipment, fixtures, inventory, and some goodwill. At the time of the purchase, the business was selling about $2,500,000 annually and earning about 5 percent before taxes. Although the parking facilities were inadequate, people still bought more from Happy Valley than from any other appliance store in town, because of the Happy Valley reputation for service and the brands it carried. In order to attract new customers, Adams took the initiative to launch a major advertising campaign. This proved to be a wise decision. After several months of intense advertising in newspapers and radio, sales and profits were higher than ever.

Just when everything seemed to be going so well, Murdock's Appliance Discount Center opened directly across the street. Murdock carried the same brands as Adams, but he was not an appointed appliance dealer. He purchased his stock from out-of-state dealers who were carrying excess inventory and were all too glad to dump the excess stock for less than cost. Murdock's strategy was to let Adams advertise to attract customers. The customers would notice the signs in Murdock's windows advertising discounts far below what Adams could offer. Thus, Murdock was attracting clients without cost. He also cut overhead by offering no services or part replacements. Murdock did not deliver appliances, but instead used a local trucker who charged the customer a small delivery fee.

As a result of the competition from Murdock's, Adams's sales and profits suffered. He was at a loss as to what to do. The manufacturers would not give

CONTINUED ▶

him better prices because it would be a violation of the Robinson-Patman Act. They did promise to find out which dealers were selling to Murdock from out of state and try to make those dealers desist. But Adams knew that this action was useless because the dealers would claim that they thought they were selling to builders or contractors, and that they didn't know the products were going to be used as inventory for an illegitimate appliance dealer.

Adams tried to teach his sales force how to overcome the competition from Murdock, but many already had a mental block about price and had difficulty telling potential clients that Murdock was not a legitimate dealer. Adams tried advertising, warning customers to beware of dealers who were not authorized to sell the brands he was selling. He also emphasized his large inventory of spare parts and emergency service. He even reduced his prices somewhat to promote sales. However, people would still come to his store, talk to his salespeople, notice the signs at Murdock's, and leave without buying. They would cross the street and purchase the appliance at Murdock's. Murdock would also follow Adams's advertising lead. If Adams offered a particular brand at a special price, Murdock would offer the same brand at a lower price.

After doing all he could in marketing, Adams decided to find out about Murdock's background and financial status. Adams discovered that Murdock was operating on a one-year lease at $2,500 per month. The building Murdock occupied had been vacant for nearly 18 months before Murdock came along. The owner had been trying to sell the building for $175,000, but resorted to leasing it on an annual basis. Adams found out that the building had an appraised value of $150,000, and that he could get a mortgage on the building for $100,000 if he purchased it at that price. Thus, one avenue open to Adams was to buy the building and throw out Murdock at the end of the lease.

However, if Adams decided to buy the building he would have to come up with $50,000 in cash plus closing costs. And once he had it, what would he do with it? He was not yet at a stage where he could use it himself, and leasing it would be difficult. Another alternative was to try to pick up the lease when Murdock's expired, even if he had to pay more than the $2,500 a month. But if he offered to pay $3,000 per month and Murdock offered the same amount, they could get into a battle, leaving the owner of the building the winner.

A third alternative was to match Murdock's prices. He could also find out-of-state dealers who were interested in dumping excess stock and then advertise dramatic discounts to drive Murdock out of business. Adams made a short trip to various cities in Ohio. He talked to some of the dealers he had met at a convention last year, and some of them were willing to sell him excess stock. Adams thought this was a great idea until one of the manufacturer's representatives informed him that if he purchased from other sources it would be a clear violation of his franchise agreement. He would risk losing some of his lines that were the backbone of his business. Adams understood the manufacturers' position, yet he needed their assistance. He called each manufacturer and asked for a period of 90 days in which to make purchases in Ohio. He was making this urgent request so he could drive Murdock out of business and get back the profitable position he once enjoyed. The manufacturers finally agreed to the proposition; they felt that Adams would deplete their Ohio dealers' stock and they would be able to make further sales in those areas. They also didn't want to lose a good dealer like Adams.

The manufacturers made it clear that Adams could not use their floor plan, and he would have to make arrangements with a local bank to handle the financing. After the arrangements were made, Adams went on a buying spree in Ohio and came back with more than $250,000 of new stock. He then put a full page advertisement in all the local papers as follows:

GREATEST APPLIANCE SALE IN
NEWFIELD HISTORY
NONE, AND WE MEAN NONE,
CAN MATCH
HAPPY VALLEY'S APPLIANCE PRICES
ALL APPLIANCES WILL BE SOLD
AT DEALER COST PLUS 5%
AND YOU STILL GET THE FAMOUS
HAPPY VALLEY SERVICE AND
PARTS WARRANTY
PLUS 24-HOUR EMERGENCY SERVICE
IF YOU CAN GET A LOWER PRICE
WE WILL MEET IT
EVEN IF WE LOSE
MONEY ON THE SALE
HAPPY VALLEY HOME CENTER
52 MAIN STREET
277-5555

CONTINUED ▶

People started coming back to Happy Valley Home Center and sales were brisk. Murdock's sales appeared to halt, yet he still remained in business after 65 days. Adams's sales were higher than ever, but his profits were next to zero. He was just giving too much away and expenses were cutting into the profits. At this point, Adams was quite worried because his 90 days were running out.

One day Mr. Murdock called Adams and asked him out to lunch. Adams agreed and they met (for the first time) at the local country club. Murdock was very direct; he said he knew he was a thorn in Adams's side. He knew Adams was buying from Ohio dealers just as he was, but he also knew that Adams could not survive in the long run because his expenses would consume him and he would eventually go out of business. Adams protested, but Murdock held his ground. Finally, Adams said, "Tell me what you want, Murdock. I'm a very busy man." Murdock said that he would leave if Adams gave him $50,000 in cash. In addition, he wanted Adams to pay off the balance of the lease (which had five months to go), amounting to another $12,500. Adams was shocked at the proposal and said he would never consider it under any circumstances. Murdock responded, "Look, Adams, think about it for a few days and then get back to me.

But remember one thing—if you don't take my offer, I'll stick around a little longer and drive you out of business."

Adams was upset and confused. He was still the largest dealer in town, but he had destroyed his price structure by offering large discounts to compete with Murdock. If he did get rid of Murdock, it would take months before he would be able to get his pricing back in line. Adams also knew that the manufacturers were not going to stand for his purchasing from other dealers again when he was the appointed dealer for his area. After the 90 days were up, they would expect Adams to resume his purchasing as before.

So Adams was in a difficult position. All his money was tied up in this business. It was a good business until Murdock entered the picture. Should he hang in there for the balance of the 90 days and then make an offer to Murdock? Or should he call Murdock and make him an outright offer? If he did get rid of Murdock, the building would be vacant and someone else like Murdock might do the same thing. Adams wondered if he should purchase the building and use the $50,000 as the down payment and mortgage the rest. Should he attempt to lease the building when Murdock's lease expired? At this point, Adams felt totally confused. ▼

CASE STUDY ROUNDTABLE

▼ ▼ ▼ ▼ ▼ ▼

Bob: Did I handle Murdock properly? Do you think I pushed the panic button too soon?

Discussion Points

- What competitive strategy would you have used to overcome Murdock? Explain.
- How could Adams have benefited from a more careful strategic analysis?
- Do you think Murdock would have been able to "stick around?" Was he bluffing?
- Did the manufacturers give Adams all the assistance they could? What else might they have done?
- What other advice would you give to Adams to get his company back into its former position?

BACK TO THE TABLE
Ludwig and Greta

In Chapter 3, you met Ludwig and Greta, and learned about their plan to start a craft shop. Based on what you now know, how would you advise Ludwig and Greta about how a strategic plan could help them resolve many of their issues?

▲▲▲▲▲▲▲

 C<small>HAPTER</small> B<small>RIEFCASE</small>

▼▼▼▼▼▼

- A **distinctive competency** is any area in which the firm possesses a meaningful edge over its competitors. Similarly, **competitive weaknesses** represent areas in which the competitors' relative strengths are significant or overwhelming.

- Distinctive competencies may appear in either of two ways. The competency may be present as part of the firm's operations, and as the business exists over time, clear and important areas of competence are stressed, or distinctive competencies may need to be developed or nurtured by analyzing the competitive environment, scrutinizing internal resources, and deciding which areas to develop.

- Distinctive competencies include quality, strong consumer orientation, service, reputation and image, location, personnel, filling a special niche, price, flexibility, and adaptability.

- To be successful, small business owners must be enthusiastic believers in their products and services. As a result, they may find it difficult to recognize competitive weaknesses.

- During the **analysis phase**, the owner develops a clear recognition of the key threats and opportunities in the firm's external environment. Owners must not only identify and track changes in key factors outside their business, they must carefully assess the impact these forces and changes will have on the firm and its operations. External (or *environmental* analysis) is future-oriented, seeking to recognize the problems and potential created for the firm by changes in its environment.

▲▲▲▲▲▲

SAMPLE BUSINESS PLANS

MARINE ART OF CALIFORNIA
P.O. Box 10059-251
Newport Beach, CA 92658
(714) 997-9100

BUSINESS PLAN

Robert A. Garcia, President
P.O. Box 10059-251
Newport Beach, CA 92658
(714) 997-9100

Plan prepared

by

Robert A. Garcia

(Private and Confidential)

* Financial history updated through December 31, 1999 by the developers of Automate Your Business Plan. Historical financial statements in this plan show what could have happened in 1999. The 1999 year-end financial statements and financial statement analysis were prepared by *Automate Your Business Plan* developers and are intended to be used for educational purposes only. They were not meant to and <u>do not</u> reflect the actual financial history of Marine Art of California. *See Explanatory notes at beginning of Appendix II.*

Table of Contents

MARINE ART OF CALIFORNIA

Statement of Purpose

Marine Art of California is a Limited Partnership to be established in 1998. The direct mail order and show-room company will be located in Newport Beach, CA. The company is seeking working capital in the amount of $130,000 for the purpose of start-up operations and to cover estimated operating expenses for a six-month period.

Twenty limited partnerships (2.25% each) are being offered in return investments of $6,500 to be treated as loan funds to be repaid over a 15-year period at the rate of 11%. Limited partnerships will have a dura-tion of four years, at which time the partners' shares will be bought back at the rate of $3,250 for each 2.25% share. At the end of the 15-year loan period, it is projected that the Return on Investment (ROI) for each $6,500 share will amount to $34,084.

The $130,000 in loan funds will enable the company to effectively market its products and services while maintaining proper cash flow. Funding is needed in time for the first catalog issue to be distributed in November 1998 and for a showroom to be operational in the same month for the Christmas buying season. There is a two- to three-week period between order placement and delivery date.

It is projected that the company will reach its breakeven point in the latter part of the second year of operation.

Repayment of the loan and interest can begin promptly within 30 days of receipt and can be secured by the percentage of the business to be held as collateral.

I. ORGANIZATIONAL PLAN
Marine Art of California

<u>Description of Business</u>

Marine Art of California is a start-up company in Newport Beach, marketing the works of California artists through a direct mail-order catalog. The product line is a unique combination of art, gift items and jewelry, all tied together by a marine or nautical theme. This marketing concept is a first! There is no known retailer or catalog company exclusively featuring the works of California artists in either a retail store or by mail-order catalog. I'm targeting a specific genre of the art market that, in terms of marketability, is on the cutting edge.

Having managed Sea Fantasies Art Gallery at Fashion Island Mall in Newport Beach from November 1996 to November 1997, I was able to discuss my idea personally and collect more than 700 names and addresses of highly interested customers who were marine art lovers. Of these, 90% lived in the surrounding communities and the rest came from across the U.S. and other nations.

Currently, I have begun mailings, taking orders, and making sales. I have a large number of artists and vendors throughout California with marketing agreements already in place.

I have assets of about $10,000 of miscellaneous items. These include framed and unframed originals, lithographs, posters, bronzes, acrylic boats, jewelry, videos, cassettes, CDs, T-shirts, glass figurines, greeting cards, shells, and coral.

Sales will be processed by a 4-step marketing plan. First is a direct mail-order catalog published bimonthly (six times a year). This allows for complete marketing freedom targeting high-income households, interior designers, and other businesses located in coastal areas. The second is to generate sales through a retail showroom where merchandise can be purchased on-site and large high-end pieces (exhibited on consignment) can be ordered by catalog and drop shipped from artist/vendor directly to the customer. Third, a comprehensive advertising campaign targeting the surrounding high-income communities shall be conducted, e.g., yellow pages, high-profile magazines, monthly guest artist shows, Grand Opening mailings, and flyers with discount coupons. Fourth is to conduct an ongoing telemarketing program aimed at customers on our mail lists in our local area at minimal cost.

Industry trends have stabilized with the bottoming of the current recession. My plan to counter this situation is to obtain exclusive marketing rights on unique designs and the widest selection in the market of quality items priced affordably under $100.00.

My plan is to secure my ranking as the #2 marine art dealer in Southern California, second only to the Wyland Galleries, by the end of 2000 and by 2001, through steadily increasing catalog distribution to more than 150,000 copies per mailing, to rank as the #1 dealer in California in gross sales! From 2001 through 2003, projected catalog distribution will increase at a rate of at least 100,000 catalogs per year.

Legal Structure

The structure of the company will consist of one (1) General Partner and up to twenty (20) Limited Partners. The amount of funds needed from the Limited Partners is $130,000, which will equal 45% ownership of the business. Each Limited Partner's investment of $6,500 shall equal 2.25% of the business.

The investment will be treated as a loan and will be paid back over 15 years at 11% interest. The loan repayment amount for each 2.25% share will be $79.03 per month.

No Limited Partner shall have any right to be active in the conduct of the Partnership's business or have the power to bind the Partnership with any contract, agreement, promise, or undertaking.

Provisions for Exit and Dissolution of the Company

The duration of the Partnership is 4 years. The General Partner will have the option of buying out the Limited Partners at the end of 4 years for $3,250 for each 2.25% interest. The buyout will not affect the outstanding loan, but the General Partner will provide collateral equal to the loan balance. The value of the business will be used as that collateral.

The distribution of profits shall be made within 75 days of the end of the year. Each Limited Partner will receive 2.25% per share of investment on any profits over and above the following two months' operating expenses (January and February). This amount will be required to maintain operations and generate revenues necessary to keep the company solvent.

In the event of a loss, each Limited Partner will assume a 2.25% liability for tax purposes and no profits will be paid. The General Partner will assume 55% of the loss for tax purposes.

A Key Man Insurance Policy in the amount of $250,000 shall be taken out on the General Partner to be paid to the Limited Partners in the event of the General Partner's death. The policy will be divided among the Limited Partners according to their percentage of interest in the company.

* See Copy of Contract in Supporting Documents for remainder of details.

Products and Service

The product line of **Marine Art of California** consists of hand-signed limited editions of bronzes, acrylics, lithographs, and posters with certificates. Included are exclusive designs (covered by signed contracts) of (1) originals and prints, (2) glass figurines, and (3) fine jewelry. Rounding out the line are ceramic figures, videos, cassettes, CDs, marine life books, nautical clocks, marine jewelry (14k gold, sterling silver, genuine gemstones) and many more gift items, as well as a specific line for children. The marketing areas covered are both Northern California and Southern California.

The suppliers are artists and vendors from throughout California. They number over 260! I chose them because they best express, artistically, the growing interest in the marine environment. However, due to catalog space, only 30 to 50 artists/vendors can be represented. The retail showroom will be able to accommodate more.

My framing source for art images is a wholesale operation in Fullerton that services many large accounts, including Disney Studios.

With an extremely large artist/vendor pool to draw from, I virtually eliminate any supply shortage that cannot be replaced quickly. Also, my shipping policy specifies a maximum of 3 weeks delivery time for custom-made pieces such as limited edition bronzes that need to be poured at foundries. Almost all of my suppliers have been in business for years and understand the yearly marketing trends.

Management

At present, I, Robert A. Garcia, am sole proprietor. I possess a wealth of business environment experience as indicated on my resume. My first long-term job was in the grocery industry with Stater Bros. Markets. I worked from high school through college, rising to the position of second assistant manager. The most valuable experience I came away with was the ability to work cohesively with a variety of personalities in demanding customer situations. It was at this point that I learned the importance and value of the customer in American business. The customers' needs are placed first! They are the most important link in the chain.

With the opportunity for better pay and regular weekday hours, I left Stater Bros. for employment with General Dynamics Pomona Division. For the next eleven years I was employed in Production Control and earned the title of Manufacturing Coordinator, supervising a small number of key individuals. I was responsible for all printed circuit board assemblies fabricated in off-site facilities located in Arizona and Arkansas. My duties included traveling between these facilities as needed. On a daily basis, I interfaced with supporting departments of Engineering, Quality Assurance, Procurement, Shipping and Receiving, Inspection, Stockroom and Inventory Control, Data Control Center, Electronic Fabrication, Machine Shop, and Final Assembly areas.

The programs involved were the Standard Missile (Surface to Air Weapon System), Phalanx Close I Weapons System, Stinger System, and Sparrow Missile. My group was responsible for all analysis reports for upper management, Naval personnel, and corporate headquarters in St. Louis, Missouri. Duties

Management (cont.)

included: solving material shortages, scheduling work to be released to maintain starts and completions, and to drive all support departments to meet Final Assembly needs for contract delivery. Problem solving was the name of the game. The importance of follow-up was critical. Three key concepts that we used as business guidelines were (1) production of a **QUALITY PRODUCT** (2) at a **COMPETITIVE PRICE** (3) delivered **ON SCHEDULE**.

I'm currently in contact on a regular basis with 8 advisors varying in backgrounds of marketing, advertising, corporate law, small business start-up, finance, direct mail-order business, and catalog production. Two individuals are college professors with active businesses, one a publisher of my business plan reference book, and two are retired executives with backgrounds in marketing and corporate law involved in the SCORE program through the Small Business Administration (SBA). I meet with these two executives every week.

Pertinent Courses and Seminars Completed

College Course	Supervisory Training	Mt. San Antonio College
College Course	Successful Business Writing	Mt. San Antonio College
Seminar	Producing a Direct Mail Catalog	Coastline Community College
Seminar	Business Taxes & Recordkeeping	SCORE Workshop
Seminar	Business Plan Road Map	SCORE Workshop

Note: See resume in Supporting Documents

Manager Salary Plan: Upon the signing of limited partnership agreements, I will maintain the status as managing partner and decision maker. For the duration of the partnership (planned for four years), as the manager, I will draw a monthly salary of $2,000, as per the agreement. In addition, I will retain 55% ownership of the company.

Personnel

The total number of employees to be hired initially will be four. Interviews have been conducted for each position, and all are tentatively filled. I will be on the premises during all business hours for both retail and catalog ordering operations during the first month of business. It will be the owner's duty to hire the following employees:

1. **Store Manager** - part time - $11.00 per hour

2. **1st Asst. Manager** - part time - $9.00 per hour

3. **2nd Asst. Manager** - part time - $8.00 per hour

4. **Sales Consultant** - part time - $5.50 per hour

5. **Administrative Asst.** - part time - $10.00 per hour

Personnel (cont.)

TRAINING:

1. **All employees** will be cross-trained in the following areas:
    a. Knowledge of product line
    b. Daily Sales Reconciliation Report (DSR)
    c. Catalog order processing
    d. Familiarity with key suppliers
    e. Company policy regarding customer relations
    f. Charges: VISA/MasterCard

PERSONNEL DUTIES:

1. **Manager:** Reports directly to Owner
    a. Open store (Key) - dust and vacuum
    b. Write work schedule
    c. Verify previous day's sales figures
    d. Follow up on any problems of previous day
    e. Head biweekly wall-to-wall inventory
    f. Reconcile any business discrepancies
    g. Responsible for store and catalog operations
    h. Order inventory
    i. Have access to safe
    j. Process catalog orders
    k. Conduct telemarketing in spare time
    l. Authorize employee purchase program (EPP)

2. **Administrative Assistant:** Reports to Manager
    a. Open store (Key)
    b. Write work schedule
    c. Perform office functions
        (1) Daily Sales Reconciliation Report   (DSR)
        (2) Accounts Receivable   (A/R)
        (3) Accounts Payable   (A/P)
        (4) Payroll   (P/R)
        (5) General Ledger   (G/L)
        (6) Typing - 60 wpm
        (7) Computer - WP/Lotus/D-Base
        (8) 10-Key Adding Machine
    d. Have access to safe
    e. Process catalog orders
    f. Authorize employee purchase program (EPP)

6

Personnel (cont.)

3. **1st Assistant Manager:** Reports to Manager
    a. Close store (Key)
    b. Order inventory
    c. Complete Daily Sales Reconciliation Report (DSR)
    d. Follow up on day's problems not yet solved
    e. Have access to safe
    f. Process catalog orders
    g. Conduct telemarketing in spare time

4. **2nd Assistant Manager:** Reports to 1st Assistant Manager
    a. Is familiar with all 1st Assistant Manager tasks
    b. Process catalog orders
    c. Assist in Customer Relations follow-up
    d. Dust and vacuum showroom
    e. Conduct telemarketing in spare time

5. **Sales Consultant:** Reports to 2nd Assistant Manager
    a. Cover showroom floor
    b. Process catalog orders
    c. Assist in Customer Relations follow-up
    d. Dust and vacuum showroom
    e. Conduct telemarketing in spare time

EMPLOYEE PROFILE

1. Personable, outgoing, reliable, in good health
2. College background
3. High integrity and dedication
4. Neat in appearance
5. Able to take on responsibilities
6. Able to follow directives
7. Demonstrates leadership qualities
8. Previous retail experience
9. Basic office skills
10. Sincere interest in marine art and environment
11. Likes water sports
12. Team worker

7

Methods of Recordkeeping

All bookkeeping activities shall be done by the Administrative Assistant. Financial Reports will be filed by John Horist, CPA. John brings more than 40 years of experience in his field. His hourly fee is very reasonable.

I would like to point out the key areas of recordkeeping required in the business and explain the software to be used and why. The areas are as follows:

Mail Lists: List & Mail Plus Software from Avery. It stores, sorts, and prints up to 64,000 addresses with no programming required. It contains predefined label formats, or I can create my own. Searching and extracting subsets of the mailing list is possible. It also checks for duplicate entries.

Labels: MacLabel Pro Software from Avery. The features include preset layouts for Avery laser labels and dot matrix labels, drawing tools and graphic sizing, built-in clip art, and easy mail merge.

Accounting: Sybiz Windows Accounting Software. This program automatically updates all accounts, customers, payroll, suppliers, inventory, and ledgers in one step. Windows graphics, fonts, and integration make it easy to use.

The simplicity and power of these reasonably priced programs makes them very attractive.

Insurance

Prospective Carrier:	State Farm Insurance 2610 Avon, Suite C Newport Beach, CA 92660 (714) 645-6000	
Agent:	Kim Hiller	
Type of Insurance:	Business/Personal:	$ 150,000.00
	Deductible:	$ 1,000.00
	Liability:	$1,000,000.00
Premium:	Annual Premium:	$ 3,100.00
	Monthly Premium:	$ 258.00
	Workers' Comp: 1.43 per/1K of Gross Payroll	

<u>Security</u>

**PROBLEM SITUATIONS TO BE CONSIDERED
AND PROTECTIVE MEASURES TO BE USED:**

1. **Internal Theft:** Employee Dishonesty

    a. Shoplifting of store merchandise: 2 closed circuit monitoring cameras recording showroom activity each business day.

    b. Cash theft: $400 limit of cash on hand. Timely safe drops and daily maintenance of Daily Sales Reconciliation Report will balance cash with receipts.

    c. Falsifying receipts: DSR will detect discrepancies.

    d. Employee Purchase Plan: will reduce inclination to steal. Employee discount is 35% off retail price. Can purchase layaway (20% down—balance over 60 days) or by payroll deduction (deducted from each check over 4 pay periods). Processed by authorized personnel other than oneself (2 signatures required).

    e. Employee Orientation Program: will stress security procedures and employee integrity.

    f. Biweekly wall-to-wall inventory: will reveal any losses.

2. **External Theft:** Customer shoplifting or Robbery

    a. Walk-in theft: 2 closed circuit monitoring cameras recording showroom activity each business day.

    b. Break-in theft: robbery—alarm system plus closed circuit monitoring cameras. All fine jewelry is displayed in locked cases, removed and stored in safe each night.

    c. Wall-to-wall biweekly inventory will reveal any merchandise loss.

9

II.   MARKETING PLAN
Marine Art of California

<u>Target Marketing</u>

Who are my customers?

1. Profile:

Economic level: middle to upper class.

Psychological makeup: art lover, jewelry lover, fashion conscious, ocean lover, eclectic taste, college educated, discriminating buyer, upwardly mobile life-style.

Age: 35 to 55.

Sex: Male/Female.

Income level: $75,000 and above.

Habits: high-expense entertainment, travel, marine-oriented hobbies (shell/dolphin collectors, scuba diver, boat/yacht owner, etc.), patrons of performing arts, concerts and museums.

Work: professional, business owners, business executives, middle management, interior designers.

Shop: middle to high-profile retail establishments.

2. Location:

Orange County: coastal areas - home value of $500,000 and above.

San Francisco County, San Diego County, San Bernardino County

3. Market size:

Mail list purchased through wholesale mail list companies. The consumer base will range from 20,000 to 100,000 in the first year of operations.

4. Competition:

Minimal due to unique 2-pronged marketing concept of marketing exclusively California marine art, custom-designed jewelry and giftware by way of (1) direct mail-order catalog and (2) retail show-room. No known operation in either category.

5. Other factors:

As acting distributor for several artists I am able to retain exclusive marketing rights and, in most cases, have contracted to purchase at **10 - 15% below published wholesale price lists.**

10

Competition

The two areas of competition to consider will be (1) competitors to the retail showroom and (2) competitors to the direct mail-order operation.

(1) Competition to Retail Showroom

Following this page are attached Competition Evaluation Worksheets for each competitor within a radius of 3 miles of proposed store site.[1] Retail Stores to be evaluated will have at least 1 of the 4 categories of my product line:

> A. MARINE ART: Framed (custom) and framed
>
> B. MARINE SCULPTING: Cast in bronze and acrylic
>
> C. MARINE AND NAUTICAL GIFT ITEMS
>
> D. MARINE AND CONTEMPORARY JEWELRY DESIGNS: Fine and fashion

(2) Competition to Direct Mail-Order Catalog

After investigating scores of catalog companies across the nation for the past year and speaking to artists and vendors across the state of California, we are aware of only one mail-order company with a similar theme but with a very different line and profile than Marine Art of California.

Methods of Distribution

Two-Way Distribution Program

A. Direct Mail-Order Catalog

> 1. Catalog mailings are distributed through target marketing.
>
> 2. Orders are processed via telephone (1-800 #) or by return mail-order forms, accepting checks, VISA/MC, or American Express.
>
> 3. Shipping in most cases is done by the artist or vendor directly to the customer per my instructions. All other shipping is done by Marine Art of California.
>
> 4. Shipping costs are indicated in the catalog for each item. The customer is charged for shipping costs to reimburse the vendor.
>
> 5. UPS shipping is available throughout the United States.

---

[1] Supporting documents are not included in this sample.

Methods of Distribution (cont.)

B. Retail Showroom

    1. All items shown in the catalog will be available for purchase in the retail store.

    2. High-ticket items will be carried on consignment with previous agreements already made with individual artists.

    3. General Catalogs will be displayed on an order counter for all products not stocked in the store and that can be shipped on request.

    4. All large items will be delivered anywhere in Orange County at no charge.

Since I am dealing with more than 260 artists and vendors across the state there should be no problem with the availability of merchandise. I am only able to carry about 55 artists and vendors in the catalog. Most items can be ordered for the store and be in stock within a 2 to 3 day turnaround.

For more detailed information on shipping arrangements, please see copy of Terms and Conditions for Participants in Supporting Documents section.[2]

Advertising

Pacific Bell:	Yellow/white pages: 1 line	No charge
	Bold: $5.00 extra each	
Pac Bell/Sammy:	Sales order # N74717625 (8/21)	
740-5211	Business line installation	$70.45
	Monthly rate	$11.85
	DEADLINE: August 19 Cannot change without $18.00 per month rate increase	
	Display: 1/4 column listing (per month) (Yearly cost $588.00)	$49.00
	Disconnect w/message (new #) 1 year	No charge
Donnelly:	White pages - 1 line	No charge
1-800-834-8425	Yellow pages - 2 lines	No charge
	3 or more	$10.00
	1/2 add (per month)	$27.00
	DEADLINE - August 21 (30 days to cancel)	
	Change deadline - September 10	
	Deposit due September 11	$183.00
	Monthly rate	$91.50
	(Yearly cost $1098.00)	

---

[2] Supporting documents are not included in this sample.

Advertising (cont.)

Metropolitan Magazine: 757-1404	Circulation 40,000 Monthly rate	129.00

Kim Moore
4940 Campus Drive
Newport Beach, CA 92660

California Riveria:	1/6 page (per month)	$300.00
494-2659	Art charge - one time	$50.00
Leslie	40% discount - new subscriber	
Box 536	Can hold rate for 6 months (Reg. $575.00)	
Laguna Beach,	Color (per month)	$600.00
CA 92652	Articles	No charge
	Print month end	
	Circulation: 50,000:29K High Traffic	
	21K Direct Mail (92660 - 92625)	

Grand Opening:	4 x 6 Postcard - color	$400.00
	Catering	$200.00
	Artist show	
	Discount coupons	
	Flyers	
	Newspaper ads (OC Register: one time cost - $100)	

Orange County News: (714) 565-3881	Will get advertising estimates after 6 months in business	

Orange County Register:	Monthly rate	$100.00

Advertising (cont.)

DONNELLY LISTINGS:

5 Categories:

     1. Art Dealer, Galleries

     2. Interior Designers and Decorators

     3. Framers

     4. Jewelers

     5. Gift Shops

1.   ART DEALERS:

    Original Art, Lithos, Posters, Custom Framing, Bronze & Acrylic Sculptings, Int. Designer Prices, Ask for Catalog.

2.   INTERIOR DECORATORS AND DESIGNERS:

    Original Art, Lithos, Posters, Custom Framing, Bronze & Acrylic Sculptings, Dealer Prices, Ask for Catalog.

3.   FRAMERS:

    Large Selection of California Marine Art, Coastal Scenes, Custom Framing, Matting, Ask for Mail-Order Catalog

4.   JEWELERS:

    Specialty, Marine/Nautical Custom Designs by California Artists, 14K Gold, Sterling, Gemstones, Ask for Catalog

5.   GIFT SHOPS:

    Unique Line of Marine/Nautical Gifts, Glass Figurines, Acrylic Boats, Clocks, Art, Jewelry, Bronzes, Ask for Catalog

Pricing

A. **Purchasing:** As stipulated in my Terms and Conditions, I request a 10 - 15% discount off published wholesale prices from artists and vendors in lieu of a participation fee. In about 95% of all agreements made, I am receiving this important discount!

B. **Catalog Pricing**

    1. Non-Jewelry Items: To recover publication costs, I have "keystoned" (100% markup) all items plus an additional 10-50%. Keystoning is typical in the retail industry. The added margin will cover any additional shipping charges that may not be covered by the indicated shipping fee paid by the customer.

    2. Jewelry Items: Typical pricing in the industry is "Key" plus 50% (150% markup) to triple "Key" (200% markup). My markup is "Key" plus 10-30% to stay competitive.

C. **Store Pricing:** All items will be "Keystone" plus 10 - 20% to allow a good margin for sales on selected items.

D. **Wholesale:** Mailings and advertising will target Interior Decorators and Designers. To purchase wholesale, one must present a copy of their ASID or ISID license number and order a minimum purchase of $500.00 or more. The discount will be 20% off retail price.

Below is a sample of the computer database with 17 fields of information on each item in inventory and how the retail price is computed.

File: Price List
Record 1 of 49

Item:	Fisherman's Wharf
Make:	Poster
Vendor	A Chrasta
Exclusive:	So California
Size:	21.5 26 Sq.
Vendor #:	NAC102WM
Image Pr:	$5.00
Type:	Poster
Frame:	PT4XW
Frame Price:	$31.50
Whsl. Price:	$36.50
Disc:	50% IM
Adj. Whsl:	$36.50
Key+:	10%
Retail Price:	$79.50
Group:	1

Gallery Design

After managing Sea Fantasies Gallery at Fashion Island Mall in Newport Beach, I have decided to recreate its basic layout. My goal is to create the most stunning and unique showroom design in Orange County with a product line that appeals to the high-profile customer's taste.

The design theme is to give the customer a feeling of being underwater when they enter. This would be accomplished by the use of glass display stands, and live potted tropical plants to simulate lush, green underwater vegetation. Overhead curtains 18 inches wide would cleverly hide the track lighting while reflecting the light on the curtain sides, creating the illusion of an underwater scene with sunlight reflecting on the ocean surface.

A large-screen TV would continuously play videos of colorful underwater scenes with mood music playing on the store's sound system. A loveseat for shoppers to relax in would face the screen. Along with creating a soothing and relaxing atmosphere, the videos, CDs, and cassettes would be available for sale. All fine art pieces (bronzes and framed art) would be accented with overhead track lighting, creating a strong visual effect.

Large coral pieces would be used for display purposes, such as for jewelry. Others would be strewn around the showroom floor area for a natural ocean floor effect.

Certain end displays would be constructed of glass with ocean floor scenes set inside consisting of an arrangement of coral, shells, and brightly painted wooden tropical fish on a two-inch bed of sand! All display stands would be available for sale.

This design concept was generally considered to be the most outstanding original store plan in Fashion Island as expressed by Mall customers and the Management Office. By incorporating these tried and proven concepts with my own creative designs, this gallery will have the most outstanding and unique appearance of any gallery from Long Beach to San Clemente.

The showroom area will be approximately 800 square feet. The rear and stock area is about 200 sq. ft.

Timing of Market Entry

Considering the fact that most of my product line could be viewed as gift items, the upcoming Holiday Season is of **CRITICAL IMPORTANCE**! This is typically the peak sales period in the retail industry. Catalogs from large retailers and mail-order houses are already appearing in the mail for the holidays. These are the dates to consider:

1. **OCTOBER 8:**   Camera-ready artwork goes to film separator.

             Turnaround time: 3 days!

2. **OCTOBER 11:**   All slides and artwork must be ready to be delivered to the printer, Bertco Graphics, in Los Angeles.

             Turnaround time: 11 working days!

3. **OCTOBER 22:**   Printed catalogs must be delivered to Towne House Marketing in Santa Ana.

             Turnaround time: 3 days!

4. **OCTOBER 29:**   Catalogs shipped to Santa Ana Main Post Office.

             Turnaround time: 2 working days!

5. **NOVEMBER 1:**   **CUSTOMER RECEIVES CATALOG** - Ordering begins.

6. **DECEMBER 4:**   Last ordering date to ensure Christmas delivery! Can send via Federal Express all stocked items and all stocked items at vendors.

             Problem Items:

                  a) High-end cast bronzes

                  b) Hand-made glass figurines

                  c) Original paintings

             Turnaround time: 3 weeks!

17

Location

The prime business location targeted for **Marine Art of California** retail showroom is 1000 square feet at 106 Bayview Circle, Newport Beach, CA 92660. This site was chosen because of large front display windows, excellent visibility and access for the showroom, as well as adequate floor space to house inventory for catalog shipping. Both operations require certain square footage to operate successfully. Demographics and surrounding stores are extremely favorable.

Proposed site: Newport Beach, California

Features: * Retail Shop space of 1000 sq. ft.

* Located in the primary retail and business sector of Newport Beach, Orange County's most affluent and growing community

* Excellent visibility and access

* Median household income in 1 mile radius is $90,000.00

Demographics[3]	1 Mile	3 Miles	5 Miles
Population:	1,043	111,983	308,906
Income:	$90,000	$61,990	$59,600

Private Sector Employment (Daytime pop.)

	1 Mile	3 Miles	5 miles
	43,921	113,061	306,313

Socio-Economic Status Indicator (SESI)

	1 Mile	3 Miles	5 Miles
	73	79	79

Population by Age

	1 Mile		3 Miles	5 Miles
25 - 29			9.2%	8.4%
30 - 34			9.4%	9.9%
35 - 44			16.1%	18.6%
45 - 54			12.3%	12.1%
25 - 54		**TOTAL**	**47.0%**	**49.0%**

Leasing Agent: Chuck Sullivan
CB Commercial
4040 MacArthur Blvd.
Newport Beach CA 92660
(714) 955-6431

---

[3] Donnelly Marketing Information Service

Industry Trends

Information extracted from: ABI/INFORM DATABASE at UCI Library for Business Research.

Title: **Sharper Image Revamps Product Line. Sells Items Consumers Can Actually Buy.**

Journal: **Marketing News** Vol.: 26 Issue: 10 Pg.: 2

Summary: Although shoppers will still find upscale items at Sharper Image, the company has doubled the amount of goods that are more affordable. The addition of low-priced items is part of a continuing shift that will last, even if the economy improves.

Title: **What's Selling, and Why**

Journal: **Catalog Age** Vol.: 9 Issue: 5 Pg.: 5

Summary: Market researcher Judith Langer believes today's mailers must create a value package that combines quality and price. Merchandise is reflecting consumer sentiment about the economy and the desire to buy U.S. goods and services.

Title: **Tripping the Gift Market Fantastic**

Journal: **Catalog Age** Vol.: 9 Issue: 6 Pg.: 30

Summary: Christmas Fantastic and Celebration Fantastic catalogs feature gifts and decorative accessories and target upscale females age 25 and over. Response has been strong. Average orders of $95.00 for Christmas Fantastic and $85.00 for Celebration Fantastic have surpassed company expectations.

Title: **Spring Sales Blossom**

Journal: **Catalog Age** Vol.: 9 Issue: 6 Pg.: 36

Summary: Spring sales appear to be much stronger than in the previous year. Many mailers believe the latest upturn in sales will be long-lasting.

Title: **Your Catalog's List Is Its Greatest Asset**

Journal: **Target Marketing** Vol.: 15 Issue: 2 Pg.: 44-45

Summary: There are a number of reasons why greater attention should be paid to the customer mail list rather than prospecting for new customers: 1. It is the primary source of profit for the company. 2. It is the cataloger's most valuable asset. 3. It will outperform a rented list by as much as 10 times in response rate and average order.

Note: The above articles have been condensed for brevity.

Publications and Services Utilized

Art Business News (Monthly)

Monthly trade magazine for art dealers and framers. Foremost business journal in the art industry. It provided readers with a wide range of art industry news, features, sales and marketing trends, and new product information. Reports on trade shows nationally and internationally.

National Jeweler (Monthly)

Dealer magazine. Provides jewelry industry news, features, sales and marketing trends, fashions, and styles. Lists major manufacturers and wholesalers.

Catalog Age (Monthly)

Monthly journal featuring articles on mail-order companies. Provides inside information on statistics for mail-order business. Highly informative.

Target Marketing (Monthly): Monthly trade journal.

Orange County Business Journal (Weekly)

Small Business Administration

Free Publications: **Selling by Mail Order**
Tax & Regulatory Requirements in Orange County
Partnership Agreements - Planning Checklist
Understanding Cash Flow
Developing A Strategic Business Plan
Insurance Checklist for Small Business

Anatomy of a Business Plan: Pinson & Jinnett (Dearborn Financial Publishing)

Automate Your Business Plan 6.0: Pinson (Out of Your Mind...and Into the Marketplace)

Direct Marketing Handbook: Edward L. Nash (McGraw-Hill)

The Catalog Handbook: James Holland

Direct Marketing Association: Membership organization for catalogers.

Orange County Demographic Overview: Demographic reports, charts and maps provided by the market research department of the Orange County Register.

ABI/INFORM Data Base: University of California, Irvine (see Industry Trends section)

On-line database located in the library. Contained in this database are abstracts and indexes to business articles published in more than 800 different journals. ABI/INFORM is an excellent source of information on:

Companies	Trends	Marketing & Advertising
Products	Corporate Strategies	
Business Conditions	Management Strategies	

Orange County Demographic Overview - Demographic reports, charts, and maps provided by the market research department of the *Orange County Register*.

20

III. FINANCIAL DOCUMENTS
Marine Art of California

<u>Summary of Financial Needs</u>

I. **Marine Art of California**, a limited partnership, is seeking equity capital for start-up purposes.

    A. Direct Mail-Order Catalog

    B. Retail/Wholesale Showroom

II. **Funds needed to accomplish above goal** will be $130,000.00. See "Loan Fund Dispersal Statement" for distribution of funds and backup statement.

<u>Loan Fund Dispersal Statement</u>

I. DISPERSAL OF LOAN FUNDS

    Marine Art of California will utilize funds in the amount of $130,000.00 for start-up of two retail functions: (1) A direct mail-order catalog and (2) a retail showroom to conduct related functions.

II. BACKUP STATEMENT

Direct mail-order catalog:	a) 24 pages		
	b) 2 editions		
	c) Quantities:	20K:	**$ 20,000.00**
		30K:	**23,200.00**

Start-up expense of warehouse — One Time Cost: **25,275.00**

3 Months Operating Expense:	**58,364.00**
3 Month Total Loan Repayment Cost:	**3,161.00**
(@ $1,560.00 per month)	
TOTAL:	**$130,000.00**

Catalog revenues will result in a net profit sufficient to pay all expenses and loan payments beginning in 30 days and continuing.

PRO FORMA CASH FLOW STATEMENT

Page 1 (Pre-Start-Up & January thru May)

Marine Art of California

For the Year 1999	Start-Up Nov-Dec	Jan	Feb	Mar	Apr	May
BEGINNING CASH BALANCE	0	75,575	65,312	50,837	49,397	37,807
CASH RECEIPTS						
A. Sales/Revenues	41,620	22,065	16,040	42,350	30,300	67,744
B. Receivables (Credit Accts.)	0	0	0	0	0	0
C. Interest Income	0	0	0	0	0	0
D. Sale of Long-Term Assets	0	0	0	0	0	0
TOTAL CASH AVAILABLE	41,620	97,640	81,352	93,187	79,697	105,551
CASH PAYMENTS						
A. Cost of goods to be sold						
Inventory Purchases	29,900	12,213	9,200	22,375	16,375	35,122
B. Variable Expenses						
1. Advertising/Marketing	1,042	221	221	221	521	521
2. Car Delivery/Travel	200	100	100	100	100	100
3. Catalog Expense	27,600	9,600	10,800	10,800	14,600	14,600
4. Gross Wages	5,120	2,560	2,560	2,560	2,560	3,520
5. Payroll Expense	384	192	192	192	192	269
6. Shipping	800	400	400	400	400	400
7. Misc. Var. Exp.	3,000	500	500	500	500	500
Total Variable Expenses	38,146	13,573	14,773	14,773	18,873	19,910
C. Fixed Expenses						
1. Accounting & Legal	820	160	160	160	160	160
2. Insurance + Workers' Comp	904	302	302	302	302	320
3. Rent	3,900	1,300	1,300	1,300	1,300	1,300
4. Repairs & Maintenance	60	30	30	30	30	30
5. Guaranteed Pay't (Mgr. Partner)	4,000	2,000	2,000	2,000	2,000	2,000
6. Supplies	600	300	300	300	300	300
7. Telephone	1,050	600	600	700	700	1,000
8. Utilities	630	290	290	290	290	290
9. Misc. (inc. Licenses/Permits)	175	0	0	0	0	0
Total Fixed Expenses	12,139	4,982	4,982	5,082	5,082	5,400
D. Interest Expense	1,192	1,192	1,192	1,192	1,192	1,192
E. Federal/State Income Tax	0	0	0	0	0	0
F. Capital Purchases (Office)	9,000	0	0	0	0	0
G. Capital Purchases (Showroom)	5,300	0	0	0	0	0
H. Loan payments	368	368	368	368	368	368
I. Equity Withdrawals	0	0	0	0	0	0
TOTAL CASH PAID OUT	96,045	32,328	30,515	43,790	41,890	61,992
CASH BALANCE/DEFICIENCY	(54,425)	65,312	50,837	49,397	37,807	43,559
LOANS TO BE RECEIVED	130,000	0	0	0	0	0
EQUITY DEPOSITS	0	0	0	0	0	0
ENDING CASH BALANCE	75,575	65,312	50,837	49,397	37,807	43,559

1. $130,000 15-year loan. 20 limited partners @ $6,500 in exchange for 2.5% equity (each) in company (see proposal in Supporting Documents)
2. Cash business: Prepaid orders and paid on-site purchases only; no open accounts or receivables.

22

PRO FORMA CASH FLOW STATEMENT
Page 2 (May thru December + 6 & 12-month Totals)
Marine Art of California

Jun	6-MONTH TOTALS	Jul	Aug	Sep	Oct	Nov	Dec	12-MONTH TOTALS
43,559	75,575	37,462	48,996	46,287	47,992	37,772	80,527	75,575
47,696	226,195	83,508	58,672	67,950	47,700	154,200	105,700	743,925
0	0	0	0	0	0	0	0	0
0	0	0	0	0	0	0	0	0
0	0	0	0	0	0	0	0	0
91,255	301,770	120,970	107,668	114,237	95,692	191,972	186,227	819,500
25,123	120,408	43,054	30,661	35,275	25,150	78,375	54,125	387,048
521	2,226	521	521	521	521	521	521	5,352
100	600	100	100	100	100	100	100	1,200
16,400	76,800	16,400	18,200	18,200	20,000	20,000	20,000	189,600
3,520	17,280	3,520	3,520	3,520	3,520	3,520	3,520	38,400
269	1,306	269	269	269	269	269	269	2,920
400	2,400	400	400	400	400	400	400	4,800
500	3,000	500	500	500	500	500	500	6,000
21,710	103,612	21,710	23,510	23,510	25,310	25,310	25,310	248,272
160	960	160	160	160	160	160	160	1,920
320	1,848	320	320	320	320	320	320	3,768
1,300	7,800	1,300	1,300	1,300	1,300	1,300	1,300	15,600
30	180	30	30	30	30	30	30	360
2,000	12,000	2,000	2,000	2,000	2,000	2,000	2,000	24,000
300	1,800	300	300	300	300	300	300	3,600
1,000	4,600	1,250	1,250	1,500	1,500	1,800	1,800	13,700
290	1,740	290	290	290	290	290	290	3,480
0	0	0	0	0	0	0	0	0
5,400	30,928	5,650	5,650	5,900	5,900	6,200	6,200	66,428
1,192	7,152	1,192	1,192	1,192	1,192	1,190	1,190	14,300
0	0	0	0	0	0	0	0	0
0	0	0	0	0	0	0	0	0
0	0	0	0	0	0	0	0	0
368	2,208	368	368	368	368	370	370	4,420
0	0	0	0	0	0	0	0	0
53,793	264,308	71,974	61,381	66,245	57,920	111,445	87,195	720,468
37,462	37,462	48,996	46,287	47,992	37,772	80,527	99,032	99,032
0	0	0	0	0	0	0	0	0
0	0	0	0	0	0	0	0	0
37,462	37,462	48,996	46,287	47,992	37,772	80,527	99,032	99,032

23

QUARTERLY BUDGET ANALYSIS
Marine Art of California

For the Quarter Ending: December 31, 1999

BUDGET ITEM	THIS QUARTER			YEAR-TO-DATE		
	Budget	Actual	Var.	Budget	Actual	Var.
SALES/REVENUES	307,600	300,196	(7,404)	743,925	730,379	(13,546)
a. Catalog Sales	285,500	275,238	(10,262)	672,920	647,380	(25,540)
b. Showroom Sales	15,300	16,382	1,082	46,325	53,805	7,480
c. Wholesale Sales	6,800	8,576	1,776	24,680	29,194	4,514
Less Cost of Goods	159,650	146,315	13,335	375,048	369,502	5,546
a. Purchases	167,650	154,172	13,478	387,048	380,914	6,134
Catalog Products	152,750	137,619	15,131	336,460	323,690	12,770
Showroom Products	10,650	11,191	(541)	35,163	38,903	(3,740)
Wholesale Products	4,250	5,362	(1,112)	15,425	18,321	(2,896)
b. Less Change in Ending Inventory	8,000	7,857	143	12,000	11,412	588
GROSS PROFITS	147,950	153,881	5,931	368,877	360,877	(8,000)
VARIABLE EXPENSES						
1. Advertising/Marketing	1,563	4,641	(3,078)	5,352	16,431	(11,079)
2. Car Delivery/Travel	300	268	32	1,200	1,193	7
3. Catalog Expense	60,000	54,852	5,148	189,600	172,263	17,337
4. Gross Wages	10,560	10,560	0	38,400	38,400	0
5. Payroll Expense	807	807	0	2,920	2,920	0
6. Shipping	1,200	1,732	(532)	4,800	5,591	(791)
7. Miscellaneious Selling Expense	1,500	1,328	172	6,000	4,460	1,540
8. Depreciation (Showroom assets)	265	265	0	1,060	1,060	0
FIXED EXPENSES						
1. Accounting & Legal	480	450	30	1,920	2,035	(115)
2. Insurance + Workers' Comp	960	960	0	3,768	3,768	0
3. Rent	3,900	3,900	0	15,600	15,600	0
4. Repairs & Maintenance	90	46	44	360	299	61
5. Guaranteed Pay't (Mgr. Partner)	6,000	6,000	0	24,000	24,000	0
6. Supplies	900	500	400	3,600	2,770	830
7. Telephone	5,100	5,134	(34)	13,700	13,024	676
8. Utilities	870	673	197	3,480	2,447	1,033
9. Miscellaneous Admin. Expense	0	197	(197)	0	372	(372)
10. Depreciation (Office equip)	450	450	0	1,800	1,800	0
NET INCOME FROM OPERATIONS	53,005	61,118	8,113	51,317	52,444	1,127
INTEREST INCOME	0	0	0	0	0	0
INTEREST EXPENSE	3,858	3,858	0	14,300	14,300	0
NET PROFIT (LOSS) BEFORE TAXES	49,147	57,260	8,113	37,017	38,144	1,127
TAXES (Partnership*)	0	0	0	0	0	0
(Partners taxed individually according to distributive shares of profit/loss)						
PARTNERSHIP: NET PROFIT (LOSS)	49,147	57,260	8,113	37,017	38,144	1,127

NON-INCOME STATEMENT ITEMS

1. Long-term Asset Repayments	0	0	0	0	0	0
2. Loan Repayments	1,104	1,104	0	4,420	4,420	0
3. Equity Withdrawals	0	0	0	0	0	0
4. Inventory Assets	8,000	7,857	143	12,000	11,412	588

BUDGET DEVIATIONS

	This Quarter	Year-To-Date
1. Income Statement Items:	$ 8,113	$ 1,127
2. Non-Income Statement Items:	$ 143	$ 588
3. Total Deviation	$ 8,256	$ 1,715
Cash Position Year-To-Date:	Projected = $99,032	Actual = $100,747

24

THREE-YEAR INCOME PROJECTION
Marine Art of California

Updated: September 26, 1998	Nov-Dec 1998 Pre-Start-Up	YEAR 1 1999	YEAR 2 2000	YEAR 3 2001	TOTAL 3 YEARS
INCOME					
1. SALES/REVENUES	41,620	743,930	2,651,856	4,515,406	7,952,812
Catalog Sales	33,820	672,925	2,570,200	4,421,500	7,698,445
Showroom Sales	4,600	46,325	53,274	61,266	165,465
Wholesale Sales	3,200	24,680	28,382	32,640	88,902
2. Cost of Goods Sold (c-d)	23,900	375,048	1,329,476	2,261,783	3,990,207
a. Beginning Inventory	6,000	6,000	18,000	25,000	6,000
b. Purchases	23,900	387,048	1,336,476	2,268,783	4,016,207
Catalog	19,600	336,460	1,285,100	2,210,750	3,851,910
Showroom (Walk-in)	2,300	35,163	33,637	37,633	108,733
Wholesale	2,000	15,425	17,739	20,400	55,564
c. C.O.G. Avail. Sale (a+b)	29,900	393,048	1,354,476	2,293,783	4,022,207
d. Less Ending Iventory (12/31)	6,000	18,000	25,000	32,000	32,000
3. GROSS PROFIT ON SALES (1-2)	17,720	368,882	1,322,380	2,253,623	3,962,605
EXPENSES					
1. VARIABLE (Selling) (a thru h)	38,146	249,332	734,263	1,316,291	2,338,032
a. Advertising/Marketing	1,042	5,352	5,727	6,127	18,248
b. Car Delivery/Travel	200	1,200	1,284	1,374	4,058
c. Catalog Expense	27,600	189,600	670,400	1,248,000	2,135,600
d. Gross Wages	5,120	38,400	41,088	43,964	128,572
e. Payroll Expenses	384	2,920	3,124	3,343	9,771
f. Shipping	800	4,800	5,280	5,808	16,688
g. Miscellaneous Selling Expenses	3,000	6,000	6,300	6,615	21,915
h. Depreciation (Showroom Assets)	0	1,060	1,060	1,060	3,180
2. FIXED (Administrative) (a thru h)	12,139	68,228	71,609	75,268	227,244
a. Accounting & Legal	820	1,920	2,054	2,198	6,992
b. Insurance + Workers' Comp	904	3,768	4,032	4,314	13,018
c. Rent	3,900	15,600	16,692	17,860	54,052
d. Repairs & Maintenance	60	360	385	412	1,217
e. Guaranteed Pay't (Mgr. Partner)	4,000	24,000	24,000	24,000	76,000
f. Supplies	600	3,600	3,852	4,123	12,175
g. Telephone	1,050	13,700	15,070	16,577	46,397
h. Utilities	630	3,480	3,724	3,984	11,818
i. Miscellaneous Fixed Expense	175	0	0	0	175
j. Depreciation (Office Assets)	0	1,800	1,800	1,800	5,400
TOTAL OPERATING EXPENSES (1+2)	50,285	317,560	805,872	1,391,559	2,565,276
NET INCOME OPERATIONS (GPr - Exp)	(32,565)	51,322	516,508	862,064	1,397,329
OTHER INCOME (Interest Income)	0	0	0	0	0
OTHER EXPENSE (Interest Expense)	1,192	14,300	13,814	13,274	42,580
NET PROFIT (LOSS) FOR PARTNERSHIP	(33,757)	37,022	502,694	848,790	1,354,749
TAXES: (Partnership)*	0	0	0	0	0
(partners taxed individually according to	0	0	0	0	0
distributive shares of profit or loss)	0	0	0	0	0
PARTNERSHIP: NET PROFIT (LOSS)	(33,757)	37,022	502,694	848,790	1,354,749

PROJECTED BALANCE SHEET

Business Name:
Marine Art of California

Date of Projection: September 30, 1998
Date Projected for: December 31, 1999

ASSETS			% of Assets
Current Assets			
Cash	$	98,032	73.96%
Petty Cash	$	1,000	0.75%
Sales Tax Holding Account	$	4,067	3.07%
Accounts Receivable	$	0	0.00%
Inventory	$	18,000	13.58%
Short-Term Investments	$	0	0.00%
L-Term Investments	$	0	0.00%
Fixed Assets			
Land (valued at cost)	$	0	0.00%
Buildings	$	0	0.00%
1. Cost	0		
2. Less Acc. Depr.	0		
Showroom Improvements	$	4,240	3.20%
1. Cost	5,300		
2. Less Acc. Depr.	1,060		
Office Improvements	$	4,160	3.14%
1. Cost	5,200		
2. Less Acc. Depr.	1,040		
Office Equipment	$	3,040	2.29%
1. Cost	3,800		
2. Less Acc. Depr.	760		
Autos/Vehicles	$	0	0.00%
1. Cost	0		
2. Less Acc. Depr.	0		
Other Assets			
1.	$	0	0.00%
2.	$	0	0.00%

LIABILITIES			% of Liabilities
Current Liabilities			
Accounts Payable	$	0	0.00%
Notes Payable	$	4,906	3.79%
Interest Payable	$	0	0.00%
Taxes Payable (Partnership)			
Federal Income Tax	$	0	0.00%
Self-Employment Tax	$	0	0.00%
State Income Tax	$	0	0.00%
Sales Tax Accrual	$	4,067	3.15%
Property Tax	$	0	0.00%
Payroll Accrual	$	0	0.00%
Long-Term Liabilities			
Notes Payable to Investors	$	120,306	93.06%
Notes Payable Others	$	0	0.00%
TOTAL LIABILITIES	$	129,279	100.00%

NET WORTH (EQUITY)			% of Net Worth
Proprietorship	$	0	0.00%
or			
Partnership			
1. Bob Garcia, 55% Equity	$	1,793	55.00%
2. Ltd. Prtnrs., 45% Equity	$	1,467	45.00%
or			
Corporation			
Capital Stock	$	0	0.00%
Surplus Paid In	$	0	0.00%
Retained Earnings	$	0	0.00%
TOTAL NET WORTH	$	3,260	100.00%

TOTAL ASSETS $ 132,539 100.00%

Assets - Liabilities = Net Worth
and
Liabilities + Equity = Total Assets

1. See Financial Statement Analysis for ratios and notations.

BREAKEVEN ANALYSIS

Marine Art of California

Date of Analysis: September 29, 1998

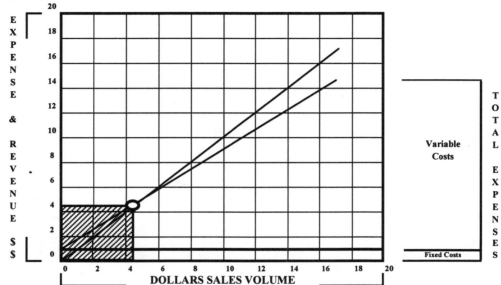

NOTE: Figures shown in 2 hundreds of thousands of dollars (Ex: 2 = $ 400,000)

Marine Art of California
BREAK-EVEN POINT CALCULATION

B-E POINT (SALES) = Fixed costs + [(Variable Costs/Est. Revenues) X Sales]

B-E Point (Sales) = $ 181,282.00 + [($ 2,750,165.00 / $ 3,437,406.00) X Sales]

B-E Point (Sales) = $ 181,282.00 + [.8001 X Sales]

S - .8001S = $181,282.00   S - .8001S = $181,282.00   .19992S = $181,282.00

S = $181,282.00/.1999

Break-Even Point
S = $906,800*
*rounded figure

FC (Fixed Costs) =	(Administrative Expenses + Interest)		$	181,282
VC (Variable Costs) =	(Cost of Goods + Selling Expenses)		$	2,750,165
R (Est. Revenues) =	(Income from sale of products and services)		$	3,437,406
BREAK-EVEN POINT =			$	906,727

27

The financial figures below in no way represent an actual Profit & Loss Statement for Mr. Garcia's business.
This statement is for illustrative purposes only and is an example of what "might have happened" during Marine Art of California's first year of business.

PROFIT & LOSS (INCOME) STATEMENT
Marine Art of California

Page 1 (January thru June + 6-Month Totals)

For the Year: 1999	Jan	Feb	Mar	Apr	May	Jun	6-MONTH TOTALS AMOUNT	% of Total Revenues PERCENT
INCOME								
1. Sales/Revenues	21,073	17,916	40,640	31,408	66,858	50,034	227,929	100.00%
a. Catalog Sales (60%-40%)	16,700	13,700	34,786	24,600	61,540	42,846	194,172	85.19%
b. Showroom Sales (Walk-in)	1,825	2,356	3,900	4,670	3,170	4,648	20,569	9.02%
c. Wholesale Sales	2,548	1,860	1,954	2,138	2,148	2,540	13,188	5.79%
2. Cost of Goods Sold	10,622	9,960	22,799	16,417	35,137	25,580	120,515	52.87%
a. Beginning Inventory	6,000	7,234	7,465	6,230	6,784	6,345	6,000	2.63%
b. Purchases	11,856	10,191	21,564	16,971	34,698	26,335	121,615	53.36%
(1) Catalog Goods (50%)	8,350	6,850	17,393	12,300	30,770	21,423	97,086	42.59%
(2) Showroom (50%+$1Kp/m)	1,913	2,178	2,950	3,335	2,585	3,324	16,285	7.14%
(3) Wholesales (x.625)	1,593	1,163	1,221	1,336	1,343	1,588	8,244	3.62%
c. C.O.G. Available for Sale	17,856	17,425	29,029	23,201	41,482	32,680	127,615	55.99%
d. Less Ending Inventory	7,234	7,465	6,230	6,784	6,345	7,100	7,100	3.12%
3. GROSS PROFIT	10,451	7,956	17,841	14,991	31,721	24,454	107,414	47.13%
EXPENSES								
1. Variable (Selling) Expenses								
a. Advertising/Marketing	836	836	836	1,547	1,547	1,547	7,149	3.14%
b. Car Delivery/Travel	94	126	78	83	112	97	590	0.26%
c. Catalog Expense	9,600	10,770	10,770	11,960	11,960	11,960	67,020	29.40%
d. Gross Wages	2,560	2,560	2,560	2,560	3,520	3,520	17,280	7.58%
e. Payroll Expense	192	192	192	192	269	269	1,306	0.57%
f. Shipping	385	432	391	406	389	391	2,394	1.05%
g. Miscell. Variable Expenses	538	147	268	621	382	211	2,167	0.95%
h. Deprec. (Showroom)	88	88	89	88	88	89	530	0.23%
Total Variable Expenses	14,293	15,151	15,184	17,457	18,267	18,084	98,436	43.19%
1. Fixed (Admin) Expenses								
a. Accounting & Legal	150	150	150	385	150	150	1,135	0.50%
b. Insurance + Workers' Comp	302	302	302	302	320	320	1,848	0.81%
c. Rent	1,300	1,300	1,300	1,300	1,300	1,300	7,800	3.42%
d. Repairs & Maintenance	0	12	56	0	0	72	140	0.06%
e. Guar. Pay't (Mgr. Partner)	2,000	2,000	2,000	2,000	2,000	2,000	12,000	5.26%
f. Supplies	287	246	301	223	259	172	1,488	0.65%
g. Telephone	542	634	556	621	836	872	4,061	1.78%
h. Utilities	287	263	246	164	168	172	1,300	0.57%
i. Miscell Fixed Expenses	23	17	0	46	39	0	125	0.05%
j. Deprec. (Office equip)	150	150	150	150	150	150	900	0.39%
Total Fixed Expenses	5,041	5,074	5,061	5,191	5,222	5,208	30,797	13.51%
Total Operating Expense	19,334	20,225	20,245	22,648	23,489	23,292	129,233	56.70%
Net Income From Operations	(8,883)	(12,269)	(2,404)	(7,657)	8,232	1,162	(21,819)	-9.57%
Other Income (Interest)	0	0	0	0	0	0	0	0.00%
Other Expense (Interest)	1,192	1,192	1,192	1,192	1,192	1,192	7,152	3.14%
Net Profit (Loss) Before Taxes	(10,075)	(13,461)	(3,596)	(8,849)	7,040	(30)	(28,971)	-12.71%
Taxes: Partnership*	0	0	0	0	0	0	0	0.00%
*(partners taxed individually on	0	0	0	0	0	0	0	0.00%
distributive shares of profits)	0	0	0	0	0	0	0	0.00%
PARTNERSHIP: NET PROFIT (LOSS)	(10,075)	(13,461)	(3,596)	(8,849)	7,040	(30)	(28,971)	-12.71%

28

The financial figures below in no way represent an actual Profit & Loss Statement for Mr. Garcia's business.
This statement is for illustrative purposes only and is an example of what "might have happened" during Marine Art of California's first year of business.

PROFIT & LOSS (INCOME) STATEMENT
Marine Art of California

Page 2 (July thru December + 12-Month Totals)

For the Year: 1999	Jul	Aug	Sep	Oct	Nov	Dec	12-MONTH TOTALS AMOUNT	of Total Revenues PERCENT
INCOME								
1. Sales/Revenues	81,092	57,014	64,148	67,684	127,390	105,122	730,379	100.00%
a. Catalog Sales (60%-40%)	72,740	47,890	57,340	57,468	120,550	97,220	647,380	88.64%
b. Showroom Sales (Walk-in)	5,490	6,734	4,630	6,340	4,280	5,762	53,805	7.37%
c. Wholesale Sales	2,862	2,390	2,178	3,876	2,560	2,140	29,194	4.00%
2. Cost of Goods Sold	41,819	28,641	32,212	33,942	63,689	48,684	369,502	50.59%
a. Beginning Inventory	7,100	7,256	8,421	9,555	10,940	12,267	6,000	0.82%
b. Purchases	41,975	29,806	33,346	35,327	65,016	53,829	380,914	52.15%
(1) Catalog Goods (50%)	36,370	23,945	28,670	28,734	60,275	48,610	323,690	44.32%
(2) Showroom (50%+$1Kp/m)	3,745	4,367	3,315	4,170	3,140	3,881	38,903	5.33%
(3) Wholesales (x.625)	1,860	1,494	1,361	2,423	1,601	1,338	18,321	2.51%
c. C.O.G. Available for Sale	49,075	37,062	41,767	44,882	75,956	66,096	386,914	52.97%
d. Less Ending Inventory	7,256	8,421	9,555	10,940	12,267	17,412	17,412	2.38%
3. GROSS PROFIT	39,273	28,373	31,936	33,742	63,701	56,438	360,877	49.41%
EXPENSES								
1. Variable (Selling) Expenses								
a. Advertising/Marketing	1,547	1,547	1,547	1,547	1,547	1,547	16,431	2.25%
b. Car Delivery/Travel	136	107	92	96	84	88	1,193	0.16%
c. Catalog Expense	15,125	17,633	17,633	18,284	18,284	18,284	172,263	23.59%
d. Gross Wages	3,520	3,520	3,520	3,520	3,520	3,520	38,400	5.26%
e. Payroll Expense	269	269	269	269	269	269	2,920	0.40%
f. Shipping	516	467	482	534	617	581	5,591	0.77%
g. Miscell. Variable Expenses	459	184	322	721	265	342	4,460	0.61%
h. Deprec. (Showroom)	88	88	89	88	88	89	1,060	0.15%
Total Variable Expenses	21,660	23,815	23,954	25,059	24,674	24,720	242,318	33.18%
1. Fixed (Admin) Expenses								
a. Accounting & Legal	150	150	150	150	150	150	2,035	0.28%
b. Insurance + Workers' Comp	320	320	320	320	320	320	3,768	0.52%
c. Rent	1,300	1,300	1,300	1,300	1,300	1,300	15,600	2.14%
d. Repairs & Maintenance	0	0	113	46	0	0	299	0.04%
e. Guar. Pay't (Mgr. Partner)	2,000	2,000	2,000	2,000	2,000	2,000	24,000	3.29%
f. Supplies	164	231	387	143	164	193	2,770	0.38%
g. Telephone	1,164	1,287	1,378	1,422	1,943	1,769	13,024	1.78%
h. Utilities	159	148	167	193	217	263	2,447	0.34%
i. Miscell Fixed Expenses	41	9	0	22	0	175	372	0.05%
j. Depreciation	150	150	150	150	150	150	1,800	0.25%
Total Fixed Expenses	5,448	5,595	5,965	5,746	6,244	6,320	66,115	9.05%
Total Operating Expense	27,108	29,410	29,919	30,805	30,918	31,040	308,433	42.23%
Net Income From Operations	12,165	(1,037)	2,017	2,937	32,783	25,398	52,444	7.18%
Other Income (Interest)	0	0	0	0	0	0	0	0.00%
Other Expense (Interest)	1,192	1,192	1,192	1,192	1,190	1,190	14,300	1.96%
Net Profit (Loss) Before Taxes	10,973	(2,229)	825	1,745	31,593	24,208	38,144	5.22%
Taxes: Partnership*	0	0	0	0	0	0	0	0.00%
*(partners taxed individually on	0	0	0	0	0	0	0	0.00%
distributive shares of profits)	0	0	0	0	0	0	0	0.00%
PARTNERSHIP: NET PROFIT (LOSS)	10,973	(2,229)	825	1,745	31,593	24,208	38,144	5.22%

29

The financial figures below in no way represent an actual Profit & Loss Statement for Mr. Garcia's business.

This statement is for illustrative purposes only and is an example of what "might have happened" during Marine Art of California's first year of business.

PROFIT & LOSS (INCOME) STATEMENT
Marine Art of California

Beginning: January 1, 1999 **Ending: December 31, 1999**

			% Total Revenues
INCOME			
1. Sales Revenues		$ 730,379	100.00%
a. Catalog Sales (60%-40%)	647,380		88.64%
b. Showroom Sales (Walk-in)	53,805		7.37%
c. Wholesale Sales	29,194		4.00%
2. Cost of Goods Sold (c-d)		369,502	50.59%
a. Beginning Inventory	6,000		0.82%
b. Purchases	380,914		52.15%
(1) Catalog Goods (50%)	323,690		44.32%
(2) Showroom (50%+$1K p/m)	38,903		5.33%
(3) Wholesale (x .625)	18,321		2.51%
c. C.O.G. Avail. Sale (a+b)	386,914		52.97%
d. Less Ending Inventory (12/31)	17,412		2.38%
3. Gross Profit on Sales (1-2)		$ 360,877	49.41%
EXPENSES			
1. Variable (Selling) (a thru I)		242,318	33.18%
a. Advertising/Marketing	16,431		2.25%
b. Car Delivery/Travel	1,193		0.16%
c. Catalog Expense	172,263		23.59%
d. Gross Wages	38,400		5.26%
e. Payroll Expense	2,920		0.40%
f. Shipping	5,591		0.77%
g. Miscell. Variable Selling Expense	4,460		0.61%
h. Depreciation (Showroom)	1,060		0.15%
2. Fixed (Administrative) (a thru I)		66,115	9.05%
a. Accounting & Legal	2,035		0.28%
b. Insurance & Workers' Comp	3,768		0.52%
c. Rent	15,600		2.14%
d. Repairs & Maintenance	299		0.04%
e. Guaranteed Payment (Mgr. Partner)	24,000		3.29%
f. Supplies	2,770		0.38%
g. Telephone	13,024		1.78%
h. Utilities	2,447		0.34%
i. Miscell. Fixed (Admin) Expenses	372		0.05%
j. Depreciation (Administrative Assets)	1,800		0.25%
Total Operating Expenses (1+2)		308,433	42.23%
Net Income from Operations (GP-Exp)		$ 52,444	7.18%
Other Income (Interest Income)	0		0.00%
Other Expense (Interest Expense)	14,300		1.96%
Net Profit (Loss) Before Taxes		$ 38,144	5.22%
Taxes: Partnership*	0		0.00%
* (partners taxed individually on distributive	0	0	0.00%
shares of profits or losses)	0		0.00%
PARTNERSHIP: NET PROFIT (LOSS)		$ 38,144	5.22%

30

BALANCE SHEET

Business Name:
Marine Art of California

Date: December 31, 1999

ASSETS			% of Assets
Current Assets			
Cash	$	100,102	75.43%
Petty Cash	$	645	0.49%
Sales Tax Holding Account	$	3,107	2.34%
Accounts Receivable	$	0	0.00%
Inventory	$	17,412	13.12%
Short-Term Investments	$	0	0.00%
L-Term Investments	$	0	0.00%
Fixed Assets			
Land (valued at cost)	$	0	0.00%
Buildings	$	0	0.00%
1. Cost	0		
2. Less Acc. Depr.	0		
Showroom Improvements	$	4,240	3.20%
1. Cost	5,300		
2. Less Acc. Depr.	1,060		
Office Improvements	$	4,160	3.13%
1. Cost	5,200		
2. Less Acc. Depr.	1,040		
Office Equipment	$	3,040	2.29%
1. Cost	3,800		
2. Less Acc. Depr.	760		
Autos/Vehicles	$	0	0.00%
1. Cost	0		
2. Less Acc. Depr.	0		
Other Assets			
1.	$	0	0.00%
2.	$	0	0.00%
TOTAL ASSETS	$	132,706	100.00%

LIABILITIES			% of Liabilities
Current Liabilities			
Accounts Payable	$	0	0.00%
Notes Payable	$	4,906	3.82%
Interest Payable	$	0	0.00%
Taxes Payable			
Federal Income Tax	$	0	0.00%
Self-Employment Tax	$	0	0.00%
State Income Tax	$	0	0.00%
Sales Tax Accrual	$	3,107	2.42%
Property Tax	$	0	0.00%
Payroll Accrual	$	0	0.00%
Long-Term Liabilities			
Notes Payable to Investors	$	120,306	93.76%
Notes Payable Others	$	0	0.00%
TOTAL LIABILITIES	$	128,319	100.00%

NET WORTH (EQUITY)			% of Net Worth
Proprietorship	$	0	0.00%
or			
Partnership			
1. Bob Garcia, 55% Equity	$	2,413	55.00%
2. Ltd. Prtnrs., 45% Equity	$	1,974	45.00%
or			
Corporation			
Capital Stock	$	0	0.00%
Surplus Paid In	$	0	0.00%
Retained Earnings	$	0	0.00%
TOTAL NET WORTH	$	4,387	100.00%

Assets - Liabilities = Net Worth
and
Liabilities + Equity = Total Assets

FINANCIAL STATEMENT ANALYSIS SUMMARY

The following is a summary of the 1999 financial statement analysis information developed on the next five pages of spreadsheets (pages 33-37):

*Writer must research industry for standards.

1999	PROJECTED	ACTUAL	INDUSTRY* STANDARD
1. Net Working Capital	$112,126	$113,253	$100,000 +
2. Current Ratio	13.5	15.1	2.0 +
3. Quick Ratio	11.5	13.0	1.0 +
4. Gross Profit Margin	49.60%	49.4%	45.0%
5. Operating Profit Margin	6.9%	7.2%	6.8%
6. Net Profit Margin	5.0%	5.2%	12.4%
7. Debt to Assets	97.5%	96.7%	33.0%
8. Debt to Equity	39.7:1	29.3:1	1.0:1 +
9. ROI (Return on Investment	28.0%	28.7%	11% +
10. Vertical Income Statement Analysis **			
Sales/Revenues	100.0%	100.0%	
Cost of Goods	50.4%	50.6%	50.0% -
Gross Profit	49.6%	49.4%	40.0% +
Operating Expense	42.7%	42.2%	35.0% +
Net Income Operations	6.9%	7.2%	15.0% +
Interest Income	0/0%	0.0%	N/A
Interest Expense	1.9%	2.0%	Variable
Net Profit (Pre-Tax)	5.0%	5.2%	10.0% +
** All items stated as % of total revenues			
11. Vertical Balance Sheet Analysis ***			
Current Assets	91.2%	91.4%	85.0%
Inventory	13.6%	13.1%	28.0%
Total Assets	3.7%	96.7%	
Current Liabilities	3.7%	3.7%	20.0% -
Total Liabilities	97.5%	96.7%	
Net Worth	2.5%	3.3%	50.0% +
Total Liabilities + Net Worth	100.0%	100.0%	

*** *All Asset items stated as % of Total Assets;*

Liability & Net Worth items stated as % of Total Liabilities + Net Worth

Notes:

Marine Art of California has an excessively high debt ratio (96.7%). However, the company has survived the first year of business, maintained its cash flow ($100,000+), and returned a higher amount than origin-ally promised to its investors. Sales for the first year were less than projected (-2%), but the net profit was still in excess of projections by 0.2%. Good management of the company by Mr. Garcia + a timely product with a solid niche would seem to be a good indicator that this company's profits will continue to increase rapidly and that the company will be more than able to fulfill its obligations to its limited partners/investors.

FINANCIAL STATEMENT ANALYSIS
Marine Art of California

For the Year: 1999

Type of Analysis	Formula	Projected: Year 1		Historical: Year 1	
1. Liquidity Analysis a. Net Working Capital	Balance Sheet Current Assets — Current Liabilities	Current Assets Current Liabilities **Net Working Capital**	121,099 8,973 **$112,126**	Current Assets Current Liabilities **Net Working Capital**	121,266 8,013 **$113,253**
b. Current Ratio	Balance Sheet Current Assets Current Liabilities	Current Assets Current Liabilities **Current Ratio**	121,099 8,973 **13.50**	Current Assets Current Liabilities **Current Ratio**	121,266 8,013 **15.13**
c. Quick Ratio	Balance Sheet Current Assets minus Inventory Current Liabilities	Current Assets Inventory Current Liabilities **Quick Ratio**	121,099 18,000 8,973 **11.49**	Current Assets Inventory Current Liabilities **Quick Ratio**	121,266 17,412 8,013 **12.96**
2. Profitability Analysis a. Gross Profit Margin	Income Statement Gross Profits Sales	Gross Profits Sales **Gross Profit Margin**	368,882 743,930 **49.59%**	Gross Profits Sales **Gross Profit Margin**	360,877 730,379 **49.41%**
b. Operating Profit Margin	Income From Operations Sales	Income From Ops. Sales **Op. Profit Margin**	51,322 743,930 **6.90%**	Income From Ops. Sales **Op. Profit argin**	52,444 730,379 **7.18%**
c. Net Profit Margin	Net Profits Sales	Net Profits Sales **Net Profit Margin**	37,022 743,930 **4.98%**	Net Profits Sales **Net Profit Margin**	38,144 730,379 **5.22%**
4. Debt Ratios a. Debt to Assets	Balance Sheet Total Liabilities Total Assets	Total Liabilities Total Assets **Debt to Assets Ratio**	129,279 132,539 **97.54%**	Total Liabilities Total Assets **Debt to Assets Ratio**	128,319 132,706 **96.69%**
b. Debt to Equity	Total Liabilities Total Owners' Equity	Total Liabilities Total Owners' Equity **Debt to Equity Ratio**	129,279 3,260 **3965.61%**	Total Liabilities Total Owners' Equity **Debt to Equity Ratio**	128,319 4,387 **2924.98%**
4. Measures of a. ROI *(Return on Investment)*	Balance Sheet Net Profits Total Assets	Net Profits Total Assets **ROI (Ret. on Invest.)**	37,022 132,539 **27.93%**	Net Profits Total Assets **ROI (Ret. on Invest.)**	38,144 132,706 **28.74%**
5. Vertical Financial Statement Analysis	Balance Sheet 1. Each asset % of Total Assets 2. Liability & Equity % of Total L&E Income Statement 3. All items % of Total Revenues	**NOTE:** *See Attached* Balance Sheet and Income Statement		**NOTE:** *See Attached* Balance Sheet and Income Statement	
6. Horizontal Financial Statement Analysis	Balance Sheet 1. Assets, Liab & Equity measured against 2nd year. Increases and decreases stated as amount & % Income Statement 2. Revenues & Expenses measured against 2nd year. Increases and decreases stated as amount & %	**NOTE:** **Horizontal Analysis** **Not Applicable** Only one year in business		**NOTE:** **Horizontal Analysis** **Not Applicable** Only one year in business	

33

The financial figures below in no way represent an actual Profit & Loss (Income) Statement for Mr. Garcia's business.
This statement is for illustrative purposes only and is an example of what "might have happened" during Marine Art of California's first year of business.

VERTICAL INCOME STATEMENT ANALYSIS
Marine Art of California

Historical For the Year: 1999	Begin: January 1, 1999 End: December 31, 1999		% Total Revenues
INCOME	AMOUNT		
1. **Sales/Revenues**		$ 730,379	**100.00%**
a. Catalog Sales	647,380		88.64%
b. Showroom Sales	53,805		7.37%
c. Wholesale Sales	29,194		4.00%
2. **Cost of Goods Sold (c-d)**		369,502	50.59%
a. Beginning Inventory	6,000		0.82%
b. Purchases	380,914		52.15%
(1) Catalog Products	323,690		44.32%
(2) Showroom (Walk-In) Products	38,903		5.33%
(3) Wholesale Products	18,321		2.51%
c. C.O.G. Avail. Sale (a+b)	386,914		52.97%
d. Less Ending Inventory (12/31)	17,412		2.38%
3. **Gross Profit on Sales (1-2)**		$ 360,877	**49.41%**
EXPENSES			
1. **Variable (Selling) (a thru l)**		242,318	**33.18%**
a. Advertising/Marketing	16,431		2.25%
b. Car Delivery/Travel	1,193		0.16%
c. Catalog Expense	172,263		23.59%
d. Gross Wages	38,400		5.26%
e. Payroll Expense	2,920		0.40%
f. Shipping	5,591		0.77%
g. Miscell. Variable Selling Expense	4,460		0.61%
h. Depreciation (Prod/Serv Assets)	1,060		0.15%
2. **Fixed (Administrative) (a thru l)**		66,115	**9.05%**
a. Accounting & Legal	2,035		0.28%
b. Insurance & Workers' Comp	3,768		0.52%
c. Rent	15,600		2.14%
d. Repairs & Maintenance	299		0.04%
e. Guaranteed Payment (Mgr. Partner)	24,000		3.29%
f. Supplies	2,770		0.38%
g. Telephone	13,024		1.78%
h. Utilities	2,447		0.34%
i. Miscell. Fixed (Admin) Expenses	372		0.05%
j. Depreciation (Administrative Assets)	1,800		0.25%
Total Operating Expenses (1+2)		308,433	**42.23%**
Net Income from Operations (GP-Exp)		$ 52,444	**7.18%**
Other Income (Interest Income)	0		0.00%
Other Expense (Interest Expense)	14,300		1.96%
Net Profit (Loss) Before Taxes		$ 38,144	**5.22%**
TAXES: (Partnership)			
	0		0.00%
* *(partners taxed individually according to*	0	0	0.00%
distributive shares of profit or loss)	0		0.00%
PARTNERSHIP: NET PROFIT (LOSS)		$ 38,144	**5.22%**

This financial statement is for illustrative purposes only and the figures in no way represent an actual Balance Sheet for Mr. Garcia's business.
The example below represents a "possible scenario" for the asset, liability, and net worth positions of Marine Art of California after one year of business.

VERTICAL BALANCE SHEET ANALYSIS

(All Asset %'s represent % of Total Assets; All Liability or Equity %'s represent % of Total Liabilities + Total Equity)

Analysis of Historical Balance Sheet			Date of Balance Sheet: December 31, 1999		
		Marine Art of California			

ASSETS			% of Total Assets	LIABILITIES			% of Total L + NW
Current Assets				**Current Liabilities**			
Cash	$	100,102	75.43%	Accounts Payable	$	0	0.00%
Petty Cash	$	645	0.49%	Notes Payable	$	4,906	3.70%
Sales Tax Holding Account	$	3,107	2.34%	Interest Payable	$	0	0.00%
Accounts Receivable	$	0	0.00%				
Inventory	$	17,412	13.12%	Taxes Payable			
Short-Term Investments	$	0	0.00%	Federal Income Tax	$	0	0.00%
				Self-Employment Tax	$	0	0.00%
L-Term Investments	$	0	0.00%	State Income Tax	$	0	0.00%
				Sales Tax Accrual	$	3,107	2.34%
Fixed Assets				Property Tax	$	0	0.00%
Land (valued at cost)	$	0	0.00%				
				Payroll Accrual	$	0	0.00%
Buildings	$	0	0.00%				
1. Cost	0			**Long-Term Liabilities**			
2. Less Acc. Depr.	0			Notes Payable to Investors	$	120,306	90.66%
				Notes Payable Others	$	0	0.00%
Showroom Improvements	$	4,240	3.20%				
1. Cost	5,300						
2. Less Acc. Depr.	1,060			**TOTAL LIABILITIES**	$	128,319	96.69%
Office Improvements	$	4,160	3.13%				
1. Cost	5,200						
2. Less Acc. Depr.	1,040			**NET WORTH (EQUITY)**			
Office Equipment	$	3,040	2.29%	**Proprietorship**	$	0	0.00%
1. Cost	3,800			or			
2. Less Acc. Depr.	760			**Partnership**			
				1. Bob Garcia, 55% Equity	$	2,413	1.82%
Autos/Vehicles	$	0	0.00%	2. Ltd. Prtnrs., 45% Equity	$	1,974	1.49%
1. Cost	0			or			
2. Less Acc. Depr.	0			**Corporation**			
				Capital Stock	$	0	0.00%
Other Assets				Surplus Paid In	$	0	0.00%
1.	$	0	0.00%	Retained Earnings	$	0	0.00%
2.	$	0	0.00%				
				TOTAL NET WORTH	$	4,387	3.31%
TOTAL ASSETS	$	132,706	100.00%	**LIABILITIES + N. WORTH**	$	132,706	100.00%

Assets - Liabilities = Net Worth -or- Liabilities + Equity = Assets

PROJECTED
VERTICAL INCOME STATEMENT ANALYSIS
(Percentages for all categories are in terms of % of Total Sales/Revenues)

Marine Art of California

Projections For Years Ended: 12/31/98   12/31/99   12/31/00 +   1992-2000 Combined Analysis

	Pre-Start-Up: 1998		Year 2: 1999		Year 3: 2000		Total: 2 Yrs. + Pre-Start-Up	
	AMOUNT	%	AMOUNT	%	AMOUNT	%	AMOUNT	%
INCOME								
1. SALES/REVENUES	41,620	100.00%	743,930	100.00%	2,651,856	100.00%	3,437,406	100.00%
a. Catalog Sales	33,820	81.26%	672,925	90.46%	2,570,200	96.92%	3,276,945	95.33%
b. Showroom Sales	4,600	11.05%	46,325	6.23%	53,274	2.01%	104,199	3.03%
c. Wholesale Sales	3,200	7.69%	24,680	3.32%	28,382	1.07%	56,262	1.64%
2. Cost of Goods Sold (c-d)	23,900	57.42%	375,048	50.41%	1,329,476	50.13%	1,728,424	50.28%
a. Beginning Inventory	6,000	14.42%	6,000	0.81%	18,000	0.68%	6,000	0.17%
b. Purchases	23,900	57.42%	387,048	52.03%	1,336,476	50.40%	1,747,424	50.84%
(1) Catalog Products	19,600	47.09%	336,460	45.23%	1,285,100	48.46%	1,641,160	47.74%
(2) Showroom (Walk-In)	2,300	5.53%	35,163	4.73%	33,637	1.27%	71,100	2.07%
(3) Wholesale Products	2,000	4.81%	15,425	2.07%	17,739	0.67%	35,164	1.02%
c. C.O.G. Avail. Sale (a+b)	29,900	71.84%	393,048	52.83%	1,354,476	51.08%	1,753,424	51.01%
d. Less Ending Iventory (12/31)	6,000	14.42%	18,000	2.42%	25,000	0.94%	25,000	0.73%
3. GROSS PROFIT ON SALES (1-2)	17,720	42.58%	368,882	49.59%	1,322,380	49.87%	1,708,982	49.72%
EXPENSES								
1. VARIABLE (Selling) (a thru h)	38,146	91.65%	249,332	33.52%	734,263	27.69%	1,021,741	29.72%
a. Advertising/Marketing	1,042	2.50%	5,352	0.72%	5,727	0.22%	12,121	0.35%
b. Car Delivery/Travel	200	0.48%	1,200	0.16%	1,284	0.05%	2,684	0.08%
c. Catalog Expense	27,600	66.31%	189,600	25.49%	670,400	25.28%	887,600	25.82%
d. Gross Wages	5,120	12.30%	38,400	5.16%	41,088	1.55%	84,608	2.46%
e. Payroll Expense	384	0.92%	2,920	0.39%	3,124	0.12%	6,428	0.19%
f. Shipping	800	1.92%	4,800	0.65%	5,280	0.20%	10,880	0.32%
g. Miscellaneous Selling Expense	3,000	7.21%	6,000	0.81%	6,300	0.24%	15,300	0.45%
h. Depreciation (Showroom Assets)	0	0.00%	1,060	0.14%	1,060	0.04%	2,120	0.06%
2. FIXED (Administrative) (a thru h)	12,139	29.17%	68,228	9.17%	71,609	2.70%	151,976	4.42%
a. Accounting & Legal	820	1.97%	1,920	0.26%	2,054	0.08%	4,794	0.14%
b. Insurance + Workers' Comp	904	2.17%	3,768	0.51%	4,032	0.15%	8,704	0.25%
c. Rent	3,900	9.37%	15,600	2.10%	16,692	0.63%	36,192	1.05%
d. Repairs & Maintenance	60	0.14%	360	0.05%	385	0.01%	805	0.02%
e. Guar. Payment (Mgr. Partner)	4,000	9.61%	24,000	3.23%	24,000	0.91%	52,000	1.51%
f. Supplies	600	1.44%	3,600	0.48%	3,852	0.15%	8,052	0.23%
g. Telephone	1,050	2.52%	13,700	1.84%	15,070	0.57%	29,820	0.87%
h. Utilities	630	1.51%	3,480	0.47%	3,724	0.14%	7,834	0.23%
i. Miscell. Fixed Expenses	175	0.42%	0	0.00%	0	0.00%	175	0.01%
j. Depreciation (Office Assets)	0	0.00%	1,800	0.24%	1,800	0.07%	3,600	0.10%
TOTAL OPERATING EXPENSES (1+2)	50,285	120.82%	317,560	42.69%	805,872	30.39%	1,173,717	34.15%
NET INCOME OPERATIONS (GPr - Exp)	(32,565)	-78.24%	51,322	6.90%	516,508	19.48%	535,265	15.57%
OTHER INCOME (Interest Income)	0	0.00%	0	0.00%	0	0.00%	0	0.00%
OTHER EXPENSE (Interest Expense)	1,192	2.86%	14,300	1.92%	13,814	0.52%	29,306	0.85%
NET PROFIT (LOSS) BEFORE TAXES	(33,757)	-81.11%	37,022	4.98%	502,694	18.96%	505,959	14.72%
TAXES: (Partnership)	0	0.00%	0	0.00%	0	0.00%	0	0.00%
* *(partners taxed individually according to*	0	0.00%	0	0.00%	0	0.00%	0	0.00%
distributive shares of profit or loss)	0	0.00%	0	0.00%	0	0.00%	0	0.00%
PARTNERSHIP: NET PROFIT (LOSS)	(33,757)	-81.11%	37,022	4.98%	502,694	18.96%	505,959	14.72%

PROJECTED
VERTICAL BALANCE SHEET ANALYSIS

(All Asset %'s represent % of Total Assets; All Liability or Equity %'s represent % of Total Liabilities + Total Equity)

Date Projected for: December 31, 1999	Date of Projection: September 30, 1998

Marine Art of California

ASSETS			% of Total Assets	LIABILITIES			% of Total L + NW
Current Assets				**Current Liabilities**			
Cash	$	98,032	73.96%	Accounts Payable	$	0	0.00%
Petty Cash	$	1,000	0.75%	Notes Payable	$	4,906	3.70%
Sales Tax Holding Account	$	4,067	3.07%	Interest Payable	$	0	0.00%
Accounts Receivable	$	0	0.00%				
Inventory	$	18,000	13.58%	Taxes Payable			
Short-Term Investments	$	0	0.00%	Federal Income Tax	$	0	0.00%
				Self-Employment Tax	$	0	0.00%
L-Term Investments	$	0	0.00%	State Income Tax	$	0	0.00%
				Sales Tax Accrual	$	4,067	3.07%
Fixed Assets				Property Tax	$	0	0.00%
Land (valued at cost)	$	0	0.00%				
				Payroll Accrual	$	0	0.00%
Buildings	$	0	0.00%				
1. Cost	0			**Long-Term Liabilities**			
2. Less Acc. Depr.	0			Notes Payable to Investors	$	120,306	90.77%
				Notes Payable Others	$	0	0.00%
Showroom Improvements	$	4,240	3.20%				
1. Cost	5,300			**TOTAL LIABILITIES**	$	129,279	97.54%
2. Less Acc. Depr.	1,060						
Office Improvements	$	4,160	3.14%				
1. Cost	5,200						
2. Less Acc. Depr.	1,040			**NET WORTH (EQUITY)**			
Office Equipment	$	3,040	2.29%	**Proprietorship**	$	0	0.00%
1. Cost	3,800			or			
2. Less Acc. Depr.	760			**Partnership**			
				1. Bob Garcia, 55% Equity	$	1,793	1.35%
Autos/Vehicles	$	0	0.00%	2. Ltd. Prtnrs., 45% Equity	$	1,467	1.11%
1. Cost	0			or			
2. Less Acc. Depr.	0			**Corporation**			
				Capital Stock	$	0	0.00%
Other Assets				Surplus Paid In	$	0	0.00%
1.	$	0	0.00%	Retained Earnings	$	0	0.00%
2.	$	0	0.00%				
				TOTAL NET WORTH	$	3,260	2.46%
TOTAL ASSETS	$	132,539	100.00%	**LIABILITIES + N. WORTH**	$	132,539	100.00%

Assets - Liabilities = Net Worth -or- Liabilities + Equity = Assets

37

IV. SUPPORTING DOCUMENTS
Marine Art of California

Personal Resume

Letter of Reference

Proposal for Limited Partnership

Catalog Cost Analysis

Competition Comparison Analysis

Terms & Conditions for Participants

Robert A. Garcia

P.O. Box 10059-251
Newport Beach, CA 92658

(714) 722-6478

Manufacturing Management

Record of accomplishments in 12+ years in manufacturing and distribution. Experience in start-up and turnaround operations. In-depth understanding of multi-facility high-tech production systems/methods. Strengths in project management, problem solving and coordinating/managing critical manufacturing functions: purchasing, engineering, inventory control, tracking, scheduling, and quality assurance developed with General Dynamics.

PROFILE

Hands-on management style: coordinated five support groups in Arizona, Arkansas, and California facilities in production of 57 complex assemblies, each having up to 100 components per circuit board.

Experience in product development for target markets; multi-product experience.

Set priorities, provided clear direction, energized others, got positive results.

Enthusiastic rapport builder, analytical self-starter, persistent, persuasive.

ACHIEVEMENT OVERVIEW

Turnaround Operations

Production of systems seven months behind schedule, inventory control unreliable, purchasing not aggressively seeking critical components from vendors.

* Procured materials for electronic circuit card assemblies in support of off-site and final assembly of missile systems.
* Created, along with other members of special task team, procedures and internal tracking system to show how specific part shortages would impact production schedules up to six months ahead.
* Chaired weekly inventory status meetings with Purchasing and Quality Assurance representatives.
* Supervised five analysts.
* Coordinated sub-assembly activities between offsite facilities in Arizona and Arkansas and final assembly in California in order to deliver product to customers against tight time constraints.
* Trained new hires.
* Provided data analysis to upper management for review.

Results Achieved: Corrected inventory accuracy from 70% to 97% within nine months.

cont. next page

39

Robert A. Garcia Page 2

Start-up Production/Distribution—Part Time Operation (secondary income)

* Researched market, found great potential for product, Bonsai trees.
* Studied plant propagation methods, built large greenhouse, implemented methods learned, marketed product.
* Participated in various home and garden shows, county fairs, three major shows/year.
* Employed staff of 8, wholesaled products to nurseries in LA and Orange Counties.

Results Achieved: Grew and operated business successfully for eight years, increased net profit from $4500 to $12,000 within four years.

CAREER HISTORY

Freelance Photography/Marine Art of California *Owner/President*	1992 - Current
Sea Fantasies Gallery *Store Manager*	1991 - 1992
General Dynamics Corporation *Manufacturing Coordinator*	1980 - 1989
Casa Vallarta Restaurant *Controller (part-time)*	1986 - 1987
B & D Nursery (secondary income) *Operations Manager*	1973 - 1981
Stater Bros. Markets *Journeyman Clerk*	1969 - 1980

EDUCATION

Completed course work in History, California State Polytechnic University. Independent studies in Psychology of Supervision, Written Communication.

AFFILIATIONS/INTERESTS

Coordinator on Service Board for Orange County
Alanon and Alateen Family Groups, 1988–1990

Regularly cast in musical productions.
Have appeared at Orange County Performing Arts Center and Fullerton Civic Light Opera.

40

Powell and Associates
Marketing Consultants

1215 West Imperial Highway - Suite 103 - Brea, CA 92621 Keith Powell - President Tel: (714) 680-8306

Dear Prospective Investor:

It is indeed a pleasure to write a reference letter for Bob A. Garcia.

I have known Bob over the past five years and have found him to be an extremely creative and enthusiastic individual. I have been associated with Bob through several community and civic organizations for which he is an active participant. He has also held office in several of these organizations and has always fulfilled his duties with aplomb.

Bob approached me well over a year ago to meet with him on a regular basis to become a "mentor" of a then-dream, now a reality, his company, MARINE ART OF CALIFORNIA. Along with several other mentors that he has been seeking advice from, I have had the privilege of reviewing, commenting, and assisting in the development of his plan. He has evidenced great discipline, follow through, creativity, and a willingness to do his homework on this business venture.

I would most highly recommend he be given the consideration he seeks. Bob has evidenced the qualities needed to succeed in any business venture, that of commitment, dedication, optimism, and follow through.

If you have any further questions, please do not hesitate to contact me. My direct line is 714-680-8306.

Cordially,

Keith P. Powell
President

41

PROPOSAL FOR LIMITED PARTNERSHIP

Borrow $130,000.00 from private investors as limited partners as outlined:

$130,000.00 = 45% of Marine Art of California

$130,000.00 = 20 shares @ $6,500.00 each

1 share = 2.25% of Marine Art of California

Limited Partners will own 2.25% of the business for each $6,500.00 invested. The investment will be treated as a loan and paid back at 11% interest over 15 years at $78.00 per month per shareholder.

1 share = $78.00 per month for 15 years

20 shares = $1560.00 per month

The General Partner, Robert A. Garcia, will own 55% of the business. The Limited Partners will own 45% of the business for the duration of the partnership.

The duration of the partnership is 4 years. The General Partner will have the option of buying out the Limited Partners at the end of four years for $3,250.00 for each 2.25% interest. The buyout will not affect the outstanding loan, but the General Partner will provide collateral equal to the loan balance. The value of inventory will be used as that collateral.

Return On Investment (ROI) for each $6,500.00 share:

A.

Principal (15 years)		Interest (15 years)		Buy-out (4 years)		Total (15 years)
$6,500.00	+	$7,540.00	+	$3,250.00	=	$17,290.00

B. PROJECTED Annual Profits (Loss) for 1 share (2.25%):

1998	1999	2000	2001		4 Year Total
($759.53)	$833.00	$11,310.62	$19,097.78	=	$30,481.87

- Principal & Interest (6 years) $17,290.00
- Buy-Out (4 years) $ 3,250.00
- Projected Profits/loss (4 years) $30,481.87
- **Total Projected Return on Investment**   **$34,083.56**

Contract Highlights:

1. **1st Right of Refusal:** Limited Partners agree to extend the 1st Right of Refusal to the General Partner, Robert A. Garcia, in the event the Limited Partner desires to sell, grant, or trade his share of the business.

2. **Key Man Insurance:** A Life Insurance Policy valued at $250,000.00 shall be taken out on General Partner, Robert A. Garcia, which is approximately double the amount of the $130,000.00 loan needed. In the event of the death of Robert A Garcia, the payments of the full policy amount will be divided among the Limited Partners equal to the amount invested (e.g., 2.25% investment would equal a 1/20th layout of $12,500.00)

3. **Limited Partner Purchase Program:** General Partner, Robert A. Garcia, agrees to grant **at cost buying privileges** on all product line items for the purchase of 3 or more shares. For 1-2 shares, a 45% discount shall be extended. These shall be in effect for the life of the Limited Partnership Contract (minimum 4 years before exercising buyout option). For remainder of the loan contract, (2 years) a discount of 35% off retail price will be extended. At the completion of the loan repayment, a **Lifetime Discount of 20%** off retail will be extended to Limited Partners. These privileges are non-transferable.

42

CATALOG COST ANALYSIS

PRINTING QUANTITY	20,000	30,000	40,000	50,000	60,000
CATALOG ITEMS					
24-Page: Price per 1000	521.37	413.92	360.07	336.11	306.49
WEIGHT - 2.208 OZ.					
Extended Cost	10,427.40	12,417.60	14,402.80	16,305.50	18,389.40
Prep & Delivery	756.00	970.00	1,235.00	1,500.00	1,765.00
Mail List Costs - $50.00 per/1000	1,000.00	1,500.00	2,000.00	2,500.00	3,000.00
Postage - $170 per/1000	3,200.00	4,800.00	6,400.00	8,000.00	9,600.00
Film Separations - $64 per/page	3,600.00	2,500.00	2,500.00	2,500.00	2,500.00
Art Work	1,000.00	1,000.00	1,000.00	1,000.00	1,000.00
TOTAL COSTS	**19,983.40**	**23,187.60**	**27,537.80**	**31,805.50**	**36,254.40**
Rounded Numbers	20,000.00	23,200.00	27,600.00	32,000.00	36,500.00
UNIT COSTS	1.00	0.77	0.69	0.64	0.61
COSTS PER PAGE	0.04	0.03	0.03	0.03	0.03
COSTS PER/1000	999.17	772.92	688.44	636.11	604.24
PRINTING QUANTITY	70,000	80,000	90,000	100,000	
CATALOG ITEMS					
24-Page: Price per 1000	291.72	280.29	268.85	261.00	
WEIGHT - 2.208 OZ.					
Extended Cost	20,420.40	22,423.20	24,196.50	26,100.00	
Prep & Delivery	2,030.00	2,295.00	2,560.00	2,825.00	
Mail List Costs - $50.00 per/1000	3,500.00	4,000.00	4,500.00	5,000.00	
Postage - $170 per/1000	11,900.00	13,600.00	15,300.00	17,000.00	
Film Separations - $64 per/page	2,500.00	2,500.00	2,500.00	2,500.00	
Art Work	1,000.00	1,000.00	1,000.00	1,000.00	
TOTAL COSTS	**41,350.40**	**45,818.20**	**50,056.50**	**54,425.00**	
Rounded Numbers	41,500.00	46,000.00	50,500.00	55,000.00	
UNIT COSTS	0.59	0.57	0.56	0.54	
COSTS PER PAGE	0.02	0.02	0.02	0.02	
COSTS PER/1000	590.72	572.73	556.18	544.25	
FOREIGN PRINTING QUANTITY	40,000.00	50,000.00	60,000.00	70,000.00	
NOTE: 20% will be deducted for foreign printing. Prices are reflected in Profit Analysis	27,600.00	32,000.00	36,500.00	41,500.00	
	0.80	0.80	0.80	0.80	
FOREIGN PRINTING COSTS	**22,080.00**	**25,600.00**	**29,200.00**	**33,200.00**	
FOREIGN PRINTING QUANTITY	80,000.00	90,000.00	100,000.00		
	46,000.00	50,500.00	55,000.00		
	0.80	0.80	0.80		
FOREIGN PRINTING COSTS	**36,800.00**	**40,400.00**	**44,000.00**		

COMPETITION COMPARISON ANALYSIS

	Price Range	Total Retail Prices	% of Total Prices	# of Items	Item Range %		
COMPANY NAME							
Wild Wings	-50.00	2,092.35	3%	68	19%		
Spring 1992	-100.00	5,269.50	7%	68	19%	-100.00	38%
32 Pages	-200.00	11,302.00	15%	78	22%		
	-500.00	39,905.00	54%	124	34%		
	-999.00	11,045.00	15%	19	5%		
	$1,000.00	4,745.00	6%	2	1%		
		$74,358.85	100%	359	100%		
						Avg Item Price	$207.13
			(Based on keystone pricing)			Avg Item Profit	$103.56
Sharper Image	-50.00	1,580.65	9%	47	39%		
Jul/Aug	-100.00	2,418.45	14%	31	26%	-100.00	64%
24 of 60 Pages	-200.00	3,898.75	23%	25	21%		
	-500.00	4,879.45	29%	13	10%		
	-999.00	2,797.85	17%	4	3%		
	$1,000.00	1,195.00	7%	1	1%		
		$16,770.15	100%	121	100%		
						Avg Item Price	$138.60
			(Based on keystone pricing)			Avg Item Profit	$69.30
Sharper Image	-50.00	2,223.60	10%	73	42%		
Jul/Aug	-100.00	3,227.95	15%	41	24%	-100.00	66%
32 of 60 Pages	-200.00	5,088.35	23%	33	19%		
	-500.00	7,129.10	33%	20	12%		
	-999.00	4,047.75	19%	6	3%		
	$1,000.00	0.00	0%	0	0%		
		$21,716.75	100%	173	100%		
						Avg Item Price	$125.53
			(Based on keystone pricing)			Avg Item Profit	$62.77
Marine Art of California	-50.00	2,826.95	13%	108	54%		
Nov/Dec	-100.00	3,587.65	17%	46	23%	-100.00	77%
40 Pages	-200.00	3,461.85	16%	23	12%		
	-500.00	4,528.25	21%	15	7%		
	-999.00	4,281.00	20%	6	3%		
	$1,000.00	2,600.00	12%	1	1%		
		$21,285.70	100%	199	100%		
						Avg Item Price	$106.96
			(Based on keystone pricing)			Avg Item Profit	$53.48

MARINE ART OF CALIFORNIA
Robert A. Garcia
P.O. Box 10059-251
Newport Beach, CA 92658
(714) 722-6478

TERMS AND CONDITIONS FOR PARTICIPANTS

1. **Artist/Vendor** agrees to drop ship stocked items within 48 hours of notification to indicated customer with Instructions for Shipping provided by **Marine Art of California**. A time schedule is needed for custom made pieces such as bronzes acrylics, or original art works requiring longer delivery. Customer will pay shipping.

2. **Artist/Vendor** agrees to provide 48 hour Federal Express Delivery with added shipping charges for all stocked items.

3. **Artist/Vendor** agrees to use only shipping labels provided by **Marine Art of California**.

4. **Artist/Vendor** guarantees that all items shipped will be free of any business names, logos, addresses, phone numbers or any other printed material referencing said **Artist/Vendor** (engravings or signatures of **Artist** on pieces not included).

5. Each **Artist** shall include a pre-approved autobiographical sheet with each shipment.

6. **Artist/Vendor** shall include required Certificates of Authenticity on all Limited Edition pieces shipped.

7. Exclusive marketing rights for a selected art item made for **Marine Art of California** shall be covered in a separate contract.

8. **Artist/Vendor** agrees to fax a copy of the shipping manifest or phone in shipping information and date of pickup on same day of transaction.

9. **Artist/Vendor** guarantees insurance coverage for the full retail value.

10. **Artist/Vendor** shall agree to 10 day full refund period beginning from the date customer receives shipped merchandise.

11. **Artist/Vendor** agrees to extend 30 days net payment plan to **Marine Art of California**.

12. **Artist/Vendor** shall not record names nor addresses of buyers for purposes of any sales or marketing contact within 24 months of shipment of the order.

45

Terms and Conditions, page 2

13. In lieu of any participation fee, **Artist/Vendor** agrees to extend a 15% discount on published whole-sale prices to **Marine Art of California**. This is justifiable due to advertising, printing, mailing, and target marketing costs and project volume sales.

14. Each **Artist/Vendor** shall be notified 2 weeks prior to the mailing of the first catalog issue.

15. **Artist/Vendor** agrees to provide goods and services as stated above for a minimum duration of 60 days after publication date.

I hereby acknowledge and accept these terms and conditions set forth by **Marine Art of California**.

_____
(Company)

_____
(Print Name and Title)

_____
(Signature and Title of Authorized Representative)

Date:_____

World Beat Tours
Dance the world with us!

871 Islington Street, Suite 9
Portsmouth, NH 03801
603-430-6868

Business Plan by Christine Johnson

SECTION ONE: THE BUSINESS

Statement of Purpose

World Beat Music Tour seeks investments totaling $20,000 to purchase equipment; fund the initial marketing campaign; provide deposit monies for hotel and airline reservations; and maintain sufficient cash reserves to provide adequate working capital to successfully expand into a national tour operator. This sum will finance development through the expansion phase so that the company can operate at a high level of profitability. Initial investment plus a guaranteed 20 percent return will be repaid in full within 18 months of disbursement.

Table of Contents

Description of the Business

World Beat Tours is an exciting new company that provides clients with a travel experience that engages body, mind, and spirit and enhances awareness of different cultures through music. Both international and domestic full-service music tours will be offered to individuals and groups from specialty markets across the United States. Products will include travel packages from major U.S. cities to events such as the following:

- Reggae Sunsplash—Montego Bay, Jamaica—February

- New Orleans Jazz Festival—New Orleans, Louisiana—May

- Telluride Bluegrass Festival—Telluride, Colorado—June

- Montreux Jazz Festival—Montreux, Switzerland—July

- Beatles Tour—London, England—August

- Bumbershoot—Seattle, Washington—Labor Day Weekend

World Beat Tours may also sell concert ticket/bus ride packages via radio promotions to clients locally who don't have access to major concert events in nearby cities (such as the recent Rolling Stones concert tour). This could provide a more immediate source of cash flow because the above tours have deposit schedules that span longer periods of time.

World Beat Tours began in September 1997 as a sole proprietorship (with plans to incorporate within two years). The office is located at 871 Islington Street, Portsmouth, New Hampshire. Hours are Monday through Friday, 10 AM to 6 PM. Because this is not a venture that anticipates walk-in clients (our customers will access us through a toll-free phone number), we currently share office space rent-free with a related business, Big World Productions. Big World is a concert production company whose owner, Joe Fletcher, is on our advisory board. Our office rental agreement is secure for one year, at which time we will negotiate a lease or choose another Portsmouth location. At that time, we may also consider the feasibility of opening a satellite office on the West Coast.

World Beat Tours has a high probability of success due to current favorable trends in adventure travel (see Attachment A) and to projected demographic trends (see Attachment B). Success will be realized through well-executed niche marketing. Our heaviest travel season will be from May to September annually, with the remainder of the year spent on marketing and preparation for upcoming seasons.

The Market

Our company is designed to cater to the needs of music lovers who are interested in incorporating their passion for music into a travel itinerary and have the means to do so. Through researching mailing lists companies, we have determined the potential client and market size to be as follows:

Customer Profile: Jazz music enthusiast, frequent traveler, income over $50,000 annually.

Metropolitan Area	# of Potential Clients
Boston	3,150
New York City	6,150
Seattle	1,950
Los Angeles	6,050
Total Sample Market	**17,300**

This is only a sample market size determined by selecting one musical genre preference and four major metropolitan areas. Market size can potentially be increased by thousands merely by adding other music preferences or cities. To keep growth manageable, only the above four cities will be initially targeted.

Marketing Plan

Our goal is to become the best music tour operator in the United States by providing a fully escorted adventure that will satiate all the senses and leave our clients feeling fulfilled, uplifted, and grateful for our services. We will offer this quality experience at an excellent value to our customers. The average price of a trip is $1,000. The customer benefits include adventure, relaxation, musical education, and peace of mind—a wonderful respite from the stresses of daily existence.

We will market to targeted individuals in choice metropolitan areas (Boston, New York, Los Angeles, Seattle) who have the desire and the means to travel to these events. Our main marketing vehicle will be our compelling brochure, which will drive a direct mail/telemarketing campaign. We will supplement the mailings with print advertising in high-profile music publications such as *Rolling Stone,* special radio promotions (offer stations a trip to give away), and an Internet presence. We will also market to the general public through an existing national sales force of travel agents who sell our packages on commission and are educated about our company through familiarization trips. We will focus special advertising efforts on group travelers such as student or college music groups, fan clubs of festival featured artists, and groups of music industry professionals (i.e., record label executives). Of course, we will also use publicity tools as a way to raise awareness and incur sales of our tours.

Competition

Currently, the biggest source of competition comes from two sources:

1. **Festival Organizers.** Individuals call the promoter's office directly and are given information on where to secure lodging, purchase festival tickets, and so forth. The disadvantage to clients is that they still have to go to a travel agency to purchase their airline ticket. Also, they have to spend time and money on long distance phone calls and must work with more than one person. Unless they have personal experience with the area and the festival, they are relying on a promoter (not a travel professional) to make recommendations on lodging and transportation.

2. **Travel Agencies.** Individuals compelled to attend a world music festival who are not familiar with the promoter would likely visit their travel agent for more information. Their travel agent (trained only in general leisure travel) would then call festival organizers and put the trip together, adding the air service for the client. Again, the disadvantage to clients is not having an expert assisting them with their very specialized tour package.

Currently, we are not aware of existing tour operators that specialize in this category of travel.

Business Risks

Risk	Minimizing Strategy
Cancellation from client	Nonrefundable deposits required; cancellation insurance offered
Limited hotel space	Reserve space early; hold with deposits
Fluctuating foreign currency	Build extra percentage into cost of sales on all international trips; put currency clause into literature
General liability issues	Purchase professional liability insurance; require all participating vendors to provide certificates of insurance; require clients to sign liability waivers

Management

Christine Johnson is a 1989 Babson College graduate with a dual degree in entrepreneurial studies and marketing. Her passion for and industry experience in the areas of both music and travel make her uniquely qualified for this venture. She possesses excellent management and organizational skills as outlined in her résumé (see Attachment D). Of course, Christine has personal experience with all of the products she offers.

Professional Relationships

World Beat Tours is advised by the following professionals:

Cindy Vandewater, CPA
Foy Insurance Group
Lizabeth MacDonald, J.D.

5

Professional partnerships will be formed with a travel agency (to assist with airline ticketing) and a production/promotion company (to assist with ticket acquisition from festival promoters). These are:

Glen Fouers, Word Wide Travel
Joe Fletcher, Big World Productions

Summary

World Beat Tours is a specialty tour operator servicing the needs of travelers attending music festivals worldwide. Christine Johnson, the owner, is seeking $20,000 in outside investments to fund the startup phase. The majority of the funds will be used for marketing expenses and for deposits required by the hotels and airlines. This investment will provide ample working capital to carry World Beat Tours through the first four months of operation until positive cash flows begin.

Careful analysis of the market has revealed that the travel industry is undergoing significant changes that favor this type of venture. More and more tour operators and agencies are being forced to specialize within specific markets. Travel consumers are significantly more sophisticated and expect an expert to assist them with their plans. Statistics show that over 6 million Americans now book their travel direct with suppliers via the Internet (see Attachment C). World Beat Tours will capitalize on these trends with a well-executed niche marketing plan that focuses strictly on the music enthusiast who is in the $50,000+ annual income bracket and has a history of traveling more than three times a year.

Christine Johnson's knowledge and operational experience, combined with professional partnerships in both the music promotions and travel industries, will greatly increase the likelihood of success in this venture. The funds sought will result in a healthy financial beginning. An immediate client base will emerge as a direct result of initial expenditures on marketing. The remaining funds will be carried forward as reserve cash flow. Based on very conservative projections, the initial investment can be repaid during the 18th month of operations.

SECTION TWO: FINANCIAL DATA

Application and Expected Effect of Investment

The $20,000 investment will be used primarily to meet working capital needs until the first profits are realized. Each hotel property (one per tour) will require a minimum deposit of $2,000 to hold the necessary lodging space. These payments will be due early in 1998. We also require the following to kick off our marketing campaign:

Brochure design	$1,000
Mailing lists	600
Printing (brochures, business cards, letterhead)	2,340
Postage	625
Internet fees	150
Total Phase I marketing	**$4,715**

Equipment needs of $400 include a scanner (for Web site design) and a two-line telephone.

We also anticipate $2,000 in initial accounting and legal fees for basic accounting setup and trademark research.

Capital Equipment List

Item	Date of Purchase	Approximate Value
NEC 9733 166mhz 32 meg RAM computer with MMX technology with peripherals:	8/97	
NEC CS500 monitor		
Keyboard		
HP Desk Jet 820Cse color printer		$2,500
Smith Corona x11800 typewriter	8/97	150
BellSouth 232x telephone	8/97	100
Sharp UX-106 fax machine	8/97	300
Canon NP2020 copier	used	500
Total		**$3,550**

World Beat Tours
November 20,1997
Balance Sheet

Assets		Liabilities and Equity	
CURRENT ASSETS		**CURRENT LIABILITIES**	
Cash	$ 300	Accounts Payable	$ 0
Accounts Receivable	0	Payroll Taxes Payable	0
Prepaid Expenses	0	Line of Credit	0
		Current Portion of Debt	0
Total Current Assets	**$ 300**	**Total Current Liabilities**	**$ 0**
FIXED ASSETS		**LONG-TERM LIABILITIES**	
Equipment	$3,550	Note Payable	$1,339
Vehicles	0	Equity Loan Payable	0
Real Estate	0		
Total Fixed Assets	**$3,550**	**Total Long-Term Liabilities**	**$1,339**
OTHER ASSETS		**Total Liabilities**	**$1,339**
Rental Deposit	$ 0		
Utility Deposit	0		
Other	0		
Total Other Assets	**$ 0**	**Owner's Equity**	**$2,511**
Total Assets	**$3,850**	**Total Liabilities and Owner's Equity**	**$3,850**

8

Breakeven Analysis

Year One

Total fixed costs of $24,300 ÷ $250 (per traveler gross profit margin) = 98 travelers.

Breakeven for the first year of operations will occur after the 98th client has paid for their travel with us. This should occur by July 1998.

Explanation for Income Statement and Cash Flow Projections

Year One Sales Assumptions

- A 7,500-piece direct mailer should yield a 2 percent buy response; this equals 150 travelers.

- 150 travelers spread out over 6 trips = 25 travelers per trip.

- Marketing in only 4 cities would require sales of only 6 people per trip from each city.

- This does not include sales derived from other advertising/marketing campaigns.

- This is a highly conservative estimate for first-year sales.

- Average sale = $1,000. Gross profit margin = 25 percent per sale = $250 gross profit margin per traveler.

Year Two Sales Assumptions

- A 15,000-piece direct mailer should yield a 2 percent buy response; this equals 300 travelers.

- This does not include sales derived from other advertising/marketing campaigns.

- Average gross profit margin per sales still equals $250.

Year Three Sales Assumptions

- A 25,000-piece direct mailer should yield a 2 percent buy response; this equals 500 travelers.

- This does not include sales derived from other advertising/marketing campaigns.

- Average gross profit margin per sales still estimated at $250.

9

WORLD BEAT TOURS

Income Projection: Three-Year Summary

	A	B	C	D
		1998	**1999**	**2000**
1				
2	Projected Sales	$150,000	$300,000	$500,000
3	Cost of Sales (75%)	$112,500	$225,000	$375,000
4	**Gross Profit**	**$37,500**	**$75,000**	**$125,000**
5				
6	Operating Expenses			
7	Bad Debts	$0	$0	$0
8	Bank Charges	$120	$240	$360
9	Commissions	$0	$0	$0
10	Consumable Supplies	$0	$0	$0
11	Donations	$0	$0	$0
12	Employee Benefits	$0	$0	$0
13	Equipment Leases	$0	$0	$0
14	Equipment Maintenance	$0	$0	$0
15	Insurance	$1,500	$1,500	$2,000
16	Interest	$0	$0	$0
17	Legal and Accounting	$2,000	$2,000	$3,500
18	Marketing			
19	Advertising	$2,500	$3,500	$8,500
20	Brochure Design	$1,000	$1,250	$1,500
21	Internet Fees	$700	$600	$600
22	Mailing Lists	$600	$600	$600
23	Promotional Items	$1,500	$3,000	$5,000
24	Trade Shows	$0	$1,500	$2,000
25				
26	Memberships and Subscriptions	$195	$610	$610
27	Office Supplies	$300	$600	$900
28	Payroll Salaries	$0	$6,000	$12,000
29	Payroll Taxes	$0	$600	$1,200
30	Postage	$2,975	$4,850	$7,950
31	Printing	$2,340	$4,500	$7,000
32	Rent	$0	$6,000	$9,000
33	Repairs and Maintenance	$0	$0	$0
34	Taxes and Licenses	$0	$0	$0
35	Telephone			
36	Business Line	$535	$900	$1,200
37	Toll-Free 800 Number	$630	$1,500	$2,100
38				
39	Travel (contract negotiations)	$6,863	$6,000	$6,000
40	Uniforms	$500	$1,000	$1,000
41	Utilities	$0	$0	$0
42	**Total Operating Expenses**	**$24,258**	**$46,750**	**$73,020**
43				
44	Other Expenses			
45	Equipment Purchases	$400	$2,400	$1,000
46	Miscellaneous	$0	$1,000	$2,000
47	Total Other Expenses	$400	$3,400	$3,000
48				
49	**Total Expenses**	**$24,658**	**$50,150**	**$76,020**
50				
51	**Net Profit before Taxes**	**$12,842**	**$24,850**	**$48,980**

WORLD BEAT TOURS
Income Projection: Three-Year Summary
(Investment Added)

	A	B	C	D
		1998	1999	2000
1		**1998**	**1999**	**2000**
2	Projected Sales	$150,000	$300,000	$500,000
3	Cost of Sales (75%)	$112,500	$225,000	$375,000
4	**Gross Profit**	**$37,500**	**$75,000**	**$125,000**
5				
6	Operating Expenses			
7	Bad Debts	$0	$0	$0
8	Bank Charges	$120	$240	$360
9	Commissions	$0	$0	$0
10	Consumable Supplies	$0	$0	$0
11	Donations	$0	$0	$0
12	Employee Benefits	$0	$0	$0
13	Equipment Leases	$0	$0	$0
14	Equipment Maintenance	$0	$0	$0
15	Insurance	$1,500	$1,500	$2,000
16	Interest	$0	$4,000	$0
17	Legal and Accounting	$2,000	$2,000	$3,500
18	Marketing			
19	Advertising	$2,500	$3,500	$8,500
20	Brochure Design	$1,000	$1,250	$1,500
21	Internet Fees	$700	$600	$600
22	Mailing Lists	$600	$600	$600
23	Promotional Items	$1,500	$3,000	$5,000
24	Trade Shows	$0	$1,500	$2,000
25				
26	Memberships and Subscriptions	$195	$610	$610
27	Office Supplies	$300	$600	$900
28	Payroll Salaries	$0	$6,000	$12,000
29	Payroll Taxes	$0	$600	$1,200
30	Postage	$2,975	$4,850	$7,950
31	Printing	$2,340	$4,500	$7,000
32	Rent	$0	$6,000	$9,000
33	Repairs and Maintenance	$0	$0	$0
34	Taxes and Licenses	$0	$0	$0
35	Telephone			
36	Business Line	$535	$900	$1,200
37	Toll-Free 800 Number	$630	$1,500	$2,100
38				
39	Travel (contract negotiations)	$6,863	$6,000	$6,000
40	Uniforms	$500	$1,000	$1,000
41	Utilities	$0	$0	$0
42	**Total Operating Expenses**	**$24,258**	**$50,750**	**$73,020**
43				
44	Other Expenses			
45	Equipment Purchases	$400	$2,400	$1,000
46	Miscellaneous	$0	$1,000	$2,000
47	Total Other Expenses	$400	$3,400	$3,000
48				
49	**Total Expenses**	**$24,658**	**$54,150**	**$76,020**
50				
51	**Net Profit before Taxes**	**$12,842**	**$20,850**	**$48,980**

WORLD BEAT TOURS
Cash Flow Projection, Year One

#	A	Nov. 1997 (B)	Dec. 1997 (C)	Jan. 1998 (D)	Feb. 1998 (E)	Mar. 1998 (F)	Apr. 1998 (G)	May 1998 (H)	Jun. 1998 (I)	Jul. 1998 (J)	Aug. 1998 (K)	Sept. 1998 (L)	Oct. 1998 (M)	Total Yr 1 (N)
2	Projected Sales	$0	$0	$25,000	$0	$25,000	$25,000	$25,000	$25,000	$25,000	$0	$0	$0	$150,000
3	Cost of Sales (75%)	$0	$2,000	$0	$16,750	$2,000	$2,000	$18,750	$18,750	$18,750	$16,750	$16,750	$0	$112,500
4	**Gross Profit**	$0	($2,000)	$25,000	($16,750)	$23,000	$23,000	$6,250	$6,250	$6,250	($16,750)	($16,750)	$0	$37,500
5														
6	Operating Expenses													
7	Bad Debts													
8	Bank Charges	$10	$10	$10	$10	$10	$10	$10	$10	$10	$10	$10	$10	$120
9	Commissions													$0
10	Consumable Supplies													$0
11	Donations													$0
12	Employee Benefits													$0
13	Equipment Leases													$0
14	Equipment Maintenance													$0
15	Insurance	$0	$0	$1,500	$0	$0	$0	$0	$0	$0	$0	$0	$0	$1,500
16	Interest													$0
17	Legal and Accounting	$0	$1,000	$1,000	$0	$0	$0	$0	$0	$0	$0	$0	$0	$2,000
18	Marketing													
19	Advertising	$0	$0	$500	$500	$500	$500	$500	$0	$0	$0	$0	$0	$2,500
20	Brochure Design		$1,000											$1,000
21	Internet Fees	$0	$200	$50	$50	$50	$50	$50	$50	$50	$50	$50	$50	$700
22	Mailing Lists	$0	$600											$600
23	Promotional Items	$0	$0	$0	$0	$1,500	$0	$0	$0	$0	$0	$0	$0	$1,500
24	Trade Shows													$0
25														
26	Memberships and Subscriptions	$85	$10	$10	$10	$10	$10	$10	$10	$10	$10	$10	$10	$195
27	Office Supplies	$25	$25	$25	$25	$25	$25	$25	$25	$25	$25	$25	$25	$300
28	Payroll Salaries													$0
29	Payroll Taxes													$0
30	Postage	$100	$1,875	$100	$100	$100	$100	$100	$100	$100	$100	$100	$100	$2,975
31	Printing	$200	$2,140	$0	$0	$0	$0	$0	$0	$0	$0	$0	$0	$2,340
32	Rent													$0
33	Repairs and Maintenance													$0
34	Taxes and Licenses													$0
35	Telephone													
36	Business Line	$95	$40	$40	$40	$40	$40	$40	$40	$40	$40	$40	$40	$535
37	Toll-Free 800 Number	$0	$105	$0	$0	$0	$105	$105	$105	$105	$105	$0	$0	$630
38														
39	Travel (contract negotiations)	$363	$500	$0	$1,000	$0	$0	$1,000	$1,000	$1,000	$1,000	$1,000	$0	$6,863
40	Uniforms	$0	$0	$0	$500	$500	$0	$0	$0	$0	$0	$0	$0	$500
41	Utilities													$0
42	**Total Operating Expenses**	$878	$7,505	$3,235	$1,735	$2,735	$840	$1,840	$1,340	$1,340	$1,340	$1,235	$235	$24,258
43														
44	**Net Income from Operations**	($878)	($9,505)	$21,765	($18,485)	$20,265	$22,160	$4,410	$4,910	$4,910	($18,090)	($17,985)	($235)	$13,242
45	Other Cash Disbursements													
46														
47	Equipment Purchases	$400	$0	$0	$0	$0	$0	$0	$0	$0	$0	$0	$0	$400
48	Principal Payments													$0
49	Miscellaneous													$0
50	**Total Other Disbursements**	$400	$0	$0	$0	$0	$0	$0	$0	$0	$0	$0	$0	$400
51														
52	Other Cash Inflows													
53	Investors/Loans													$0
54														
55	**Net Cash Flow**	($1,278)	($9,505)	$21,765	($18,485)	$20,265	$22,160	$4,410	$4,910	$4,910	($18,090)	($17,985)	($235)	$12,842
56														
57	Beginning Cash Balance	$200	($1,078)	($10,583)	$11,182	($7,303)	$12,962	$35,122	$39,532	$44,442	$49,352	$31,262	$13,277	
58	Projected Ending Balance	($1,078)	($10,583)	$11,182	($7,303)	$12,962	$35,122	$39,532	$44,442	$49,352	$31,262	$13,277	$13,042	

WORLD BEAT TOURS
Cash Flow Projection, Year One (with Investment)

#	A	B	C	D	E	F	G	H	I	J	K	L	M	N
1		Nov. 1997	Dec. 1997	Jan. 1998	Feb. 1998	Mar. 1998	Apr. 1998	May 1998	Jun. 1998	Jul. 1998	Aug. 1998	Sept. 1998	Oct. 1998	Total Yr 1
2	Projected Sales	$0	$0	$25,000	$0	$25,000	$25,000	$25,000	$25,000	$25,000	$0	$0	$0	$150,000
3	Cost of Sales (75%)	$0	$2,000		$16,750	$2,000	$2,000	$18,750	$18,750	$18,750	$16,750	$16,750	$0	$112,500
4	**Gross Profit**	**$0**	**($2,000)**	**$25,000**	**($16,750)**	**$23,000**	**$23,000**	**$6,250**	**$6,250**	**$6,250**	**($16,750)**	**($16,750)**	**$0**	**$37,500**
5	Operating Expenses													
6														
7	Bad Debts													$0
8	Bank Charges	$10	$10	$10	$10	$10	$10	$10	$10	$10	$10	$10	$10	$120
9	Commissions													$0
10	Consumable Supplies													$0
11	Donations													$0
12	Employee Benefits													$0
13	Equipment Leases													$0
14	Equipment Maintenance													$0
15	Insurance	$0	$0	$1,500	$0	$0	$0	$0	$0	$0	$0	$0	$0	$1,500
16	Interest													$0
17	Legal and Accounting	$0	$1,000	$1,000	$0	$0	$0	$0	$0	$0	$0	$0	$0	$2,000
18	Marketing													
19	Advertising	$0	$0	$500	$500	$500	$500	$500	$0	$0	$0	$0	$0	$2,500
20	Brochure Design	$0	$1,000	$0	$0	$0	$0	$0	$0	$0	$0	$0	$0	$1,000
21	Internet Fees	$0	$200	$50	$50	$50	$50	$50	$50	$50	$50	$50	$50	$700
22	Mailing Lists	$0	$600	$0	$0	$0	$0	$0	$0	$0	$0	$0	$0	$600
23	Promotional Items	$0	$0	$0	$0	$1,500	$0	$0	$0	$0	$0	$0	$0	$1,500
24	Trade Shows													$0
25														
26	Memberships and Subscriptions	$85	$10	$10	$10	$10	$10	$10	$10	$10	$10	$10	$10	$195
27	Office Supplies	$25	$25	$25	$25	$25	$25	$25	$25	$25	$25	$25	$25	$300
28	Payroll Salaries													$0
29	Payroll Taxes													$0
30	Postage	$100	$1,875	$100	$100	$100	$100	$100	$100	$100	$100	$100	$100	$2,975
31	Printing	$200	$2,140	$0	$0	$0	$0	$0	$0	$0	$0	$0	$0	$2,340
32	Rent													$0
33	Repairs and Maintenance													$0
34	Taxes and Licenses													$0
35	Telephone													
36	Business Line	$95	$40	$40	$40	$40	$40	$40	$40	$40	$40	$40	$40	$535
37	Toll-Free 800 Number	$0	$105	$0	$0	$0	$105	$105	$105	$105	$105	$0	$0	$630
38														
39	Travel (contract negotiations)	$363	$500	$0	$1,000	$0	$0	$1,000	$1,000	$1,000	$1,000	$1,000	$0	$6,863
40	Uniforms	$0	$0	$0	$0	$500	$0	$0	$0	$0	$0	$0	$0	$500
41	Utilities	$0	$0	$0	$0	$0	$0	$0	$0	$0	$0	$0	$0	$0
42	**Total Operating Expenses**	**$878**	**$7,505**	**$3,235**	**$1,735**	**$2,735**	**$840**	**$1,840**	**$1,340**	**$1,340**	**$1,340**	**$1,235**	**$235**	**$24,258**
43														
44	**Net Income from Operations**	**($878)**	**($9,505)**	**$21,765**	**($18,485)**	**$20,265**	**$22,160**	**$4,410**	**$4,910**	**$4,910**	**($18,090)**	**($17,985)**	**($235)**	**$13,242**
45														
46	Other Cash Disbursements													
47	Equipment Purchases	$400	$0	$0	$0	$0	$0	$0	$0	$0	$0	$0	$0	$400
48	Principal Payments													$0
49	Miscellaneous													$0
50	**Total Other Disbursements**	**$400**	**$0**	**$0**	**$0**	**$0**	**$0**	**$0**	**$0**	**$0**	**$0**	**$0**	**$0**	**$400**
51														
52	Other Cash Inflows													
53	Investors/Loans	$20,000	$0	$0	$0	$0	$0	$0	$0	$0	$0	$0	$0	$20,000
54														
55	**Net Cash Flow**	**$18,722**	**($9,505)**	**$21,765**	**($18,485)**	**$20,265**	**$22,160**	**$4,410**	**$4,910**	**$4,910**	**($18,090)**	**($17,985)**	**($235)**	**$32,842**
56														
57	Beginning Cash Balance	$200	$18,922	$9,417	$31,182	$12,697	$32,962	$55,122	$59,532	$64,442	$69,352	$51,262	$33,277	
58	Projected Ending Balance	$18,922	$9,417	$31,182	$12,697	$32,962	$55,122	$59,532	$64,442	$69,352	$51,262	$33,277	$33,042	

WORLD BEAT TOURS
Cash Flow Projection, Year Two

	A	B Nov. 1998	C Dec. 1998	D Jan. 1999	E Feb. 1999	F Mar. 1999	G Apr. 1999	H May 1999	I Jun. 1999	J Jul. 1999	K Aug. 1999	L Sept. 1999	M Oct. 1999	N Total Yr 2
2	Projected Sales	$0	$0	$50,000	$0	$50,000	$50,000	$50,000	$50,000	$50,000	$0	$0	$0	$300,000
3	Cost of Sales (75%)	$0	$2,000	$0	$35,500	$2,000	$2,000	$37,500	$37,500	$37,500	$35,500	$35,500	$0	$225,000
4	**Gross Profit**	**$0**	**($2,000)**	**$50,000**	**($35,500)**	**$48,000**	**$48,000**	**$12,500**	**$12,500**	**$12,500**	**($35,500)**	**($35,500)**	**$0**	**$75,000**
5														
6	Operating Expenses													
7	Bad Debts													
8	Bank Charges	$20	$20	$20	$20	$20	$20	$20	$20	$20	$20	$20	$20	$240
9	Commissions													
10	Consumable Supplies													
11	Donations													
12	Employee Benefits													
13	Equipment Leases													
14	Equipment Maintenance													
15	Insurance	$0	$0	$1,500	$0	$0	$0	$0	$0	$0	$0	$0	$0	$1,500
16	Interest													
17	Legal and Accounting	$1,000	$0	$1,000	$0	$0	$0	$0	$0	$0	$0	$0	$0	$2,000
18	Marketing													
19	Advertising	$500	$500	$500	$500	$500	$500	$500	$0	$0	$0	$0	$0	$3,500
20	Brochure Design	$1,250	$0	$0	$0	$0	$0	$0	$0	$0	$0	$0	$0	$1,250
21	Internet Fees	$50	$50	$50	$50	$50	$50	$50	$50	$50	$50	$50	$50	$600
22	Mailing Lists	$0	$600	$0	$0	$0	$0	$0	$0	$0	$0	$0	$0	$600
23	Promotional Items	$0	$0	$0	$0	$3,000	$0	$0	$0	$0	$0	$0	$0	$3,000
24	Trade Shows	$0	$0	$0	$1,500	$0	$0	$0	$0	$0	$0	$0	$0	$1,500
25														
26	Memberships and Subscriptions	$500	$10	$10	$10	$10	$10	$10	$10	$10	$10	$10	$10	$610
27	Office Supplies	$50	$50	$50	$50	$50	$50	$50	$50	$50	$50	$50	$50	$600
28	Payroll Salaries	$0	$0	$0	$1,000	$0	$0	$1,000	$1,000	$1,000	$1,000	$1,000	$0	$6,000
29	Payroll Taxes	$0	$0	$0	$100	$0	$0	$100	$100	$100	$100	$100	$0	$600
30	Postage	$100	$3,750	$100	$100	$100	$100	$100	$100	$100	$100	$100	$100	$4,850
31	Printing	$0	$4,500	$0	$0	$0	$0	$0	$0	$0	$0	$0	$0	$4,500
32	Rent	$500	$500	$500	$500	$500	$500	$500	$500	$500	$500	$500	$500	$6,000
33	Repairs and Maintenance													
34	Taxes and Licenses													
35	Telephone													
36	Business Line	$75	$75	$75	$75	$75	$75	$75	$75	$75	$75	$75	$75	$900
37	Toll-Free 800 Number	$50	$50	$200	$50	$50	$200	$200	$200	$200	$200	$50	$50	$1,500
38														
39	Travel (contract negotiations)	$0	$0	$1,000	$0	$0	$0	$1,000	$1,000	$1,000	$1,000	$1,000	$0	$6,000
40	Uniforms	$0	$0	$0	$0	$1,000	$0	$0	$0	$0	$0	$0	$0	$1,000
41	Utilities	$0	$0	$0	$0	$0	$0	$0	$0	$0	$0	$0	$0	$0
42	**Total Operating Expenses**	**$4,095**	**$10,105**	**$5,005**	**$3,955**	**$5,355**	**$1,505**	**$3,605**	**$3,105**	**$3,105**	**$3,105**	**$2,955**	**$855**	**$46,750**
43														
44	**Net Income from Operations**	**($4,095)**	**($12,105)**	**$44,995**	**($39,455)**	**$42,645**	**$46,495**	**$8,895**	**$9,395**	**$9,395**	**($38,605)**	**($38,455)**	**($855)**	**$28,250**
45														
46	Other Cash Disbursements													
47	Equipment Purchases													$0
48	Principal Payments													$0
49	Miscellaneous													$0
50	Total Other Disbursements	$0	$0	$0	$0	$0	$0	$0	$0	$0	$0	$0	$0	$0
51														
52	Other Cash Inflows													
53	Investors/Loans													$0
54														
55	**Net Cash Flow**	**($4,095)**	**($12,105)**	**$44,995**	**($39,455)**	**$42,645**	**$46,495**	**$8,895**	**$9,395**	**$9,395**	**($38,605)**	**($38,455)**	**($855)**	**$28,250**
56														
57	Beginning Cash Balance	$4,000	($95)	($12,200)	$32,795	($6,660)	$35,985	$82,480	$91,375	$100,770	$110,165	$71,560	$33,105	
58	Projected Ending Balance	($95)	($12,200)	$32,795	($6,660)	$35,985	$82,480	$91,375	$100,770	$110,165	$71,560	$33,105	$32,250	

14

WORLD BEAT TOURS
Cash Flow Projection, Year Two (with Investment)

#	A	B Nov. 1998	C Dec. 1998	D Jan. 1999	E Feb. 1999	F Mar. 1999	G Apr. 1999	H May 1999	I Jun. 1999	J Jul. 1999	K Aug. 1999	L Sept. 1999	M Oct. 1999	N Total Yr 2
1														
2	Projected Sales	$0	$0	$50,000	$35,500	$50,000	$50,000	$50,000	$50,000	$50,000	$35,500	$35,500	$0	$300,000
3	Cost of Sales (75%)	$0	$2,000	$0	$35,500	$2,000	$2,000	$37,500	$37,500	$37,500	$35,500	$35,500	$0	$225,000
4	**Gross Profit**	$0	($2,000)	$50,000	($35,500)	$48,000	$48,000	$12,500	$12,500	$12,500	($35,500)	($35,500)	$0	$75,000
5														
6	Operating Expenses													
7	Bad Debts													$0
8	Bank Charges	$20	$20	$20	$20	$20	$20	$20	$20	$20	$20	$20	$20	$240
9	Commissions													$0
10	Consumable Supplies													$0
11	Donations													$0
12	Employee Benefits													$0
13	Equipment Leases													$0
14	Equipment Maintenance	$0	$0	$1,500	$0	$0	$0	$0	$0	$0	$0	$0	$0	$1,500
15	Insurance	$0	$0	$0	$0	$0	$4,000	$0	$0	$0	$0	$0	$0	$4,000
16	Interest	$0	$0	$0	$0	$0	$0	$0	$0	$0	$0	$0	$0	$2,000
17	Legal and Accounting	$1,000		$1,000										
18	Marketing													
19	Advertising	$500	$500	$500	$500	$500	$500	$500	$0	$0	$0	$0	$0	$3,500
20	Brochure Design	$1,250	$0	$0	$0	$0	$0	$0	$0	$0	$0	$0	$0	$1,250
21	Internet Fees	$50	$50	$50	$50	$50	$50	$50	$50	$50	$50	$50	$50	$600
22	Mailing Lists	$0	$600	$0	$0	$0	$0	$0	$0	$0	$0	$0	$0	$600
23	Promotional Items	$0	$0	$0	$0	$3,000	$0	$0	$0	$0	$0	$0	$0	$3,000
24	Trade Shows	$0	$0	$0	$1,500	$0	$0	$0	$0	$0	$0	$0	$0	$1,500
25	Memberships and Subscriptions	$500	$10	$10	$10	$10	$10	$10	$10	$10	$10	$10	$10	$610
26	Office Supplies	$50	$50	$50	$50	$50	$50	$50	$50	$50	$50	$50	$50	$600
27	Payroll Salaries	$0	$0	$0	$1,000	$0	$0	$1,000	$1,000	$1,000	$1,000	$1,000	$0	$6,000
28	Payroll Taxes	$0	$0	$0	$100	$0	$0	$100	$100	$100	$100	$100	$0	$600
29	Postage	$100	$3,750	$100	$100	$100	$100	$100	$100	$100	$100	$100	$100	$4,850
30	Printing	$0	$4,500	$0	$0	$0	$0	$0	$0	$0	$0	$0	$0	$4,500
31	Rent	$500	$500	$500	$500	$500	$500	$500	$500	$500	$500	$500	$500	$6,000
32	Repairs and Maintenance													$0
33	Taxes and Licenses													$0
34														
35	Telephone													
36	Business Line	$75	$75	$75	$75	$75	$75	$75	$75	$75	$75	$75	$75	$900
37	Toll-Free 800 Number	$50	$50	$200	$50	$50	$200	$200	$200	$200	$200	$50	$50	$1,500
38														
39	Travel (contract negotiations)	$0	$0	$1,000	$0	$0	$0	$1,000	$1,000	$1,000	$1,000	$1,000	$0	$6,000
40	Uniforms	$0	$0	$0	$0	$1,000	$0	$0	$0	$0	$0	$0	$0	$1,000
41	Utilities	$0	$0	$0	$0	$0	$0	$0	$0	$0	$0	$0	$0	$0
42	**Total Operating Expenses**	$4,095	$10,105	$5,005	$3,955	$5,355	$5,505	$3,605	$3,105	$3,105	$3,105	$2,955	$855	$50,750
43														
44	**Net Income from Operations**	($4,095)	($12,105)	$44,995	($39,455)	$42,645	$42,495	$8,895	$9,395	$9,395	($38,605)	($38,455)	($855)	$24,250
45														
46	Other Cash Disbursements													
47	Equipment Purchases													$0
48	Principal Payments	$0					$20,000							$20,000
49	Miscellaneous													$0
50	**Total Other Disbursements**	$0					$20,000							$20,000
51														
52	Other Cash Inflows													
53	Investors/Loans													$0
54														
55	**Net Cash Flow**	($4,095)	($12,105)	$44,995	($39,455)	$42,645	$22,495	$8,895	$9,395	$9,395	($38,605)	($38,455)	($855)	$4,250
56														
57	Beginning Cash Balance	$24,000	$19,905	$7,800	$52,795	$13,340	$55,985	$78,480	$87,375	$96,770	$106,165	$67,560	$29,105	
58	Projected Ending Balance	$19,905	$7,800	$52,795	$13,340	$55,985	$78,480	$87,375	$96,770	$106,165	$67,560	$29,105	$28,250	

15

WORLD BEAT TOURS
Cash Flow Projection, Year Three

	Nov. 1999	Dec. 1999	Jan. 2000	Feb. 2000	Mar. 2000	Apr. 2000	May 2000	Jun. 2000	Jul. 2000	Aug. 2000	Sept. 2000	Oct. 2000	Total Yr 3
Projected Sales	$0	$0	$83,333	$0	$83,333	$83,333	$83,333	$83,333	$83,333	$0	$0	$0	$499,998
Cost of Sales (75%)	$0	$2,000	$0	$60,500	$2,000	$2,000	$62,500	$62,500	$62,500	$60,500	$60,500	$0	$375,000
Gross Profit	$0	($2,000)	$83,333	($60,500)	$81,333	$81,333	$20,833	$20,833	$20,833	($60,500)	($60,500)	$0	$124,998
Operating Expenses													
Bad Debts													$0
Bank Charges	$30	$30	$30	$30	$30	$30	$30	$30	$30	$30	$30	$30	$360
Commissions													$0
Consumable Supplies													$0
Donations													$0
Employee Benefits													$0
Equipment Leases													$0
Equipment Maintenance													$0
Insurance			$2,000										$2,000
Interest													$0
Legal and Accounting	$1,500		$2,000										$3,500
Marketing													
Advertising	$500	$500	$1,000	$1,000	$1,000	$1,000	$1,000	$500	$500	$500	$500	$500	$8,500
Brochure Design	$1,500												$1,500
Internet Fees	$50	$50	$50	$50	$50	$50	$50	$50	$50	$50	$50	$50	$600
Mailing Lists		$600											$600
Promotional Items					$5,000								$5,000
Trade Shows				$2,000									$2,000
Memberships and Subscriptions	$500	$10	$10	$10	$10	$10	$10	$10	$10	$10	$10	$10	$610
Office Supplies	$75	$75	$75	$75	$75	$75	$75	$75	$75	$75	$75	$75	$900
Payroll Salaries	$1,000	$1,000	$1,000	$1,000	$1,000	$1,000	$1,000	$1,000	$1,000	$1,000	$1,000	$1,000	$12,000
Payroll Taxes	$100	$100	$100	$100	$100	$100	$100	$100	$100	$100	$100	$100	$1,200
Postage	$150	$6,300	$150	$150	$150	$150	$150	$150	$150	$150	$150	$150	$7,950
Printing		$7,000											$7,000
Rent	$750	$750	$750	$750	$750	$750	$750	$750	$750	$750	$750	$750	$9,000
Repairs and Maintenance													$0
Taxes and Licenses													$0
Telephone													
Business Line	$100	$100	$100	$100	$100	$100	$100	$100	$100	$100	$100	$100	$1,200
Toll-Free 800 Number	$50	$50	$300	$50	$50	$300	$300	$300	$300	$300	$50	$50	$2,100
Travel (contract negotiations)	$0	$0	$1,000	$0	$0	$0	$1,000	$1,000	$1,000	$1,000	$1,000	$0	$6,000
Uniforms					$1,000								$1,000
Utilities													$0
Total Operating Expenses	$6,305	$16,565	$8,565	$5,315	$9,315	$3,565	$4,565	$4,065	$4,065	$4,065	$3,815	$2,815	$73,020
Net Income from Operations	($6,305)	($18,565)	$74,768	($65,815)	$72,018	$77,768	$16,268	$16,768	$16,768	($64,565)	($64,315)	($2,815)	$51,978
Other Cash Disbursements													
Equipment Purchases													$0
Principal Payments													$0
Miscellaneous													$0
Total Other Disbursements	$0	$0	$0	$0	$0	$0	$0	$0	$0	$0	$0	$0	$0
Other Cash Inflows													
Investors/Loans													$0
Net Cash Flow	($6,305)	($18,565)	$74,768	($65,815)	$72,018	$77,768	$16,268	$16,768	$16,768	($64,565)	($64,315)	($2,815)	$51,978
Beginning Cash Balance	$8,000	$1,695	($16,870)	$57,898	($7,917)	$64,101	$141,869	$158,137	$174,905	$191,673	$127,108	$62,793	
Projected Ending Balance	$1,695	($16,870)	$57,898	($7,917)	$64,101	$141,869	$158,137	$174,905	$191,673	$127,108	$62,793	$59,978	$51,978

SECTION THREE: SUPPORTING DOCUMENTS

Attachment A

Adventure Tourism

. . . According to Mallett, almost 50 percent of the $400 billion U.S. travel industry is based on outdoor active recreation, with the driving force consisting of women, families, and people over 50 years old. . . . "We've made hard adventure safer and easier," says Mallett, "bringing it within reach of the general traveler." . . . In other words, travelers are swapping their rest and relaxation time for good old-fashioned thrill-seeking. Says Strader, "We're seeking something more than sitting around a pool with a piña colada."

Source: Dec. 1995 *Entrepreneur,* p. 111

Attachment B

Trends for the New Millennium

Clanning

The inclination to join up, belong to, hang out with groups of like kinds, providing a secure feeling that our own belief systems will somehow be validated by consensus.

Implications/Examples: Need for community; power of special interest groups (e.g., militia?). Products/services related to this trend might be clubby megabookstores, planned communities, 12-step programs, membership badges.

Fantasy Adventure

As a break from modern tensions, we actively seek excitement in basically risk-free adventures, whether it be via travel, food, or virtual reality.

Implications/Examples: Peterman Catalog (fantasy adventure/romance-oriented copy); eating exotic (buffalo steak) food; wearing military clothing; mountain bikes; wildering; fascination with aliens; "utility" vehicles that go anywhere.

Pleasure Revenge

Consumers tired of all the rules and regulations want to cut loose and have secret bacchanals with a bevy of forbidden fruits.

Implications/Examples: We are fed up with self-deprivation in the name of health and correct behavior. This trend is the pursuit of pleasure with a hint of anger—pleasure as a reward for all we have suffered. Butter sales are back up again!

17

Small Indulgences

Stressed out from ever increasing expenses, consumers are finding ways to reward themselves with affordable luxuries. One of the key words here is *small.*

Implications/Examples: This is an excellent area for small business to concentrate on—a good fit. When the economy is booming, a small indulgence might mean selecting a BMW convertible instead of a sedan. When the economy is down, a small indulgence might mean the occasional bouquet of flowers. The size of the indulgence will follow the economy. Small indulgences include indulging one's pets (witness the success of pet superstores). Products/services include fountain pens (at an all-time high) instead of ballpoints; mini trips; small but chic hotels; literally smaller size of regular items (palm-size color TV, minibooks).

Source: Popcorn, Faith and Marigold, Lys: *Clicking,* HarperCollins, Inc.; New York, NY; 1996; pp. 29–31.

Attachment C

Six million Americans will make travel arrangements over the Internet or an online service this year, according to the Travel Industry Association.

Source: TravelAge East, November 17, 1997.

Attachment D

Christine Johnson
30 Mill Street
Dover, NH 03820
603-749-2533

QUALIFICATIONS

Excel in human relations, able to deal gracefully with the public. Outstanding problem solver, work well independently. Strong leadership qualities. Highly motivated. Possesses a variety of computer skills, including Web master certification on Microsoft FrontPage.

EXPERIENCE
Sept. 1995–June 1997

SKI 93 TRIPS, INC., Exeter, New Hampshire
Account Executive

Built group tour business and maintained key relationships (including annual contract negotiations) with ski resorts and properties throughout Vermont, New York, and Western states. Serviced a base of over 2,000 skiers. Increased profit margin by 10 percent in a zero growth industry. Researched and assisted in the development of several travel programs including the South America Ski Division, the Western Ski Division, and the Adventure Travel Division. Attended industry conferences and trade shows regularly. Completely designed and created the Web page http://www.Ski93Trips.com.

June 1993–June 1995

KCMU 90.3 FM, Seattle, Washington
Public Relations Director and Promotions Coordinator

Initiated and implemented a complete redesign of the station's short- and long-term marketing strategies. Secured several key media sponsorships as a result of cultivating positive, professional relationships with the music, arts, and entertainment communities. Welcomed many sold-out performances such as the *Cranberries* concert. Supported the local music scene by originating and promoting KCMU New Night Music at one of the most frequented venues in town. Increased club card participation by 25 percent. Revived the station's ticket giveaway program and increased the number of free tickets available to listeners by 50 percent. Achieved all of the above in the first nine months of employment.

EDUCATION

Babson College, Wellesley, Massachusetts

Awarded Bachelor of Science in Marketing Communications and Entrepreneurial Studies, December 1989.

19

▼▼▼▼▼▼▼▼▼▼▼▼▼▼▼▼▼▼▼▼▼▼▼▼▼▼▼▼▼

KEY TO URLINKS

▼▼▼▼▼

The earth to be spann'd, connected
by net-work,
The people to become brothers
and sisters, ...
The oceans to be cross'd, the
distant brought near,
The lands to be welded together.

—*Walt Whitman,* Passage to India

 *E*ach chapter in this book includes one or more links to relevant sites on the World Wide Web. All of the sites are free, or at least offer some free information, and none of them require you to provide any personal data. Many of the links listed here are to specific pages in a much larger site, and in each case it's usually a good idea to go to the site's homepage to see all the resources offered. Frequently, one site will provide you with links to many more, so there's a virtually limitless network of useful and current information right here for your use!

LEGAL NOTICE

These sites are provided to help you more efficiently access the Internet's enormous database of free and useful information. The links are offered for general informational purposes only. Many of these sites are operated by commercial interests: their inclusion here does not mean that the authors, Upstart, or Dearborn Financial Publishing endorse them in any way. We do not recommend any products or services by referring to their Web site or by referring to a Web site that advertises or endorses a product or service. We also cannot be responsible for the accuracy of the information included on any site referenced here, so use good judgment. Also remember that Web addresses and site

▼▼▼▼▼▼▼▼▼▼▼▼▼▼▼▼▼▼▼▼▼▼▼▼▼

content may change or become obsolete. These references are current and relevant at the time of publication.

If you're not yet on the Web, don't despair. The U.S. Small Business Administration has set up Business Information Centers (BICs) all over the country. Most centers are equipped with the latest computer technology (including Internet connection) and all have an extensive publications library. Call 800-827-5722 for the location nearest you.

Chapter 1

URL	Site	Content
http://microsoft.com/mscorp	Microsoft Corporation	Microsoft corporate homepage featuring facts about the company and its products, history, mission, and vision for the future.
http://www.research.apple.com	Apple Computer	Apple Computer corporate homepage featuring news, product information, corporate history, and facts about the company.
http://www.amazon.com	Amazon.com	The internationally famous online bookstore that pioneered e-commerce.
http://www.score.org	SCORE®	SCORE® Counselors to America's Small Business; SCORE® (Service Corps of Retired Executives) offers online resources, tips, workshops, and free e-mail counseling for small businesses on a wide range of topics.
http://www10.geocities.com/WallStreet/2172/sbdcnet.htm	Small Business Development Centers on the Internet	Personal Web site operated by Kent Campbell, a financial analyst who works for the SBA. This page is a list of links to local SBDC Web sites, but check out the homepage, too, which offers a wealth of links and resources.
http://www.sba.gov/hotlist/sbdc.html	SBA Small Business Development Centers (SBDCs) Hotlist	The Small Business Administration's state-by-state list of online SBDC resources.

Chapter 2

URL	Site	Content
http://www.sbaonline.sba.gov	United States Small Business Administration	Official SBA site includes a searchable database of SBA publications and information about SBA offices, services, and resources.

URL	Site	Content
http://www.doc.gov/eda	United States Department of Commerce, Economic Development Administration	Homepage of the Department of Commerce EDA includes relevant resources, information, regulations, and notices.
http://www.mbda.gov	United States Department of Commerce, Minority Business Development Agency	Provides information about MBDA opportunities and programs, as well as useful minority business-related links and an impressive database of online articles.
http://www.frbsf.org/econedu/indx.eced.html	Federal Reserve Bank of San Francisco: Economics Education	An online primer for economics and monetary theory designed for teachers, but many elements and all informational links are generally accessible. A highly active site, loads slowly, and some features require Quick-Time for Windows (free download).
http://www.toolkit.cch.com/text/P02_3431.stm	Business Owner's Toolkit™ (CCH): New Distribution Channel	CCH has created a highly useful site for small business developers, including searchable advice, interactive features, in-depth articles, and a wide range of valuable resources.
http://www.amazon.com	Amazon.com	The internationally famous online bookstore that pioneered e-commerce.

Chapter 3

URL	Site	Content
http://www.disney.com/Business_Info/index.html	The Walt Disney Company	Information about the business side of the Magic Kingdom, including products, services, and company history
http://tnt.turner.com/index.html	Turner Network Television	Information about TNT programming and schedules.
http://www.virgin.com	Virgin Group	Corporate Web site featuring information and news about the enormous Virgin empire.
http://microsoft.com/mscorp/	Microsoft Corporation	Microsoft corporate homepage, featuring facts about the company and its products, history, mission, and vision for the future.

URL	Site	Content
http://www.mcdonalds.com/corporate/history/index.html	McDonald's Corporation: The McDonald's Story	Part of McDonald's corporate Web site, this is a history of the origins, development, and growth of the global fast-food franchise. Check out the homepage for more information.
http://www.wal-mart.com/community/mrh/history.html	Wal-Mart: Our History: How It All Began	Part of the Wal-Mart Web site, this is the official history of the national discount retailer. Go to the homepage for more business information.
http://www.corporate-ir.net/ireye/ir_site.zhtml?ticker=aapl&script=100&layout=9	Apple Computer	Investor information, corporate history, and executive biographies.
http://www.hp.com/abouthp/history.htm	Hewlett Packard, About HP	Decade-by-decade history of one of the nation's leading high-tech companies.
http://www.benjerry.com/scoop/freeconehistory.html	Ben & Jerry's Homemade, Inc.	Lively corporate history of the unconventional ice cream company.
http://www.mot.com/General/Timeline/timeln24.html	Motorola, Inc., Timeline	Company history timeline with hyperlinks to products and biographies.
http://www.us.dell.com/corporate/access/dellstory/index.htm	Dell Computer Corporation	Historical timeline of the development of Dell Computers.
http://www10.geocities.com/WallStreet/2172/sbdcnet.htm	Small Business Development Centers on the Internet	Personal Web site operated by Kent Campbell, a financial analyst who works for the SBA. This page is a list of links to local SBDC Web sites, but check out the homepage, too, which offers a wealth of links and resources. *See also:* http://www.sba.gov/hotlist/sbdc.html (SBA Hotlist)

Chapter 4

URL	Site	Content
http://www.bec.com.au/becarm/assess.htm	Business Enterprise Centres: Assess Your Business Idea	An Australian site with checklists and interactive worksheets.
http://www.slu.edu/eweb/bplan1.htm	eWeb, Education for Entrepreneurship at Saint Louis University: Business Planning	Thorough educational site features many valuable links to relevant and authoritative pages.

Chapter 5

URL	Site	Content
http://poe.acc.virginia.edu/ ~sms3k/weblioorg.htm	University of Virginia, Batten Graduate School of Business: Entrepreneurship Organizations and Associations	Excellent links collection to a diverse array of public, private, government, and institutional sites containing valuable information for entrepreneurs.

Chapter 6

URL	Site	Content
http://www.business-plan.com/ automate.html	Automate Your Business Plan Software	Commercial page describing business planning software (created by one of this book's authors). Features a downloadable business plan outline.
http://bus.colorado.edu/centers/ entrep/publications/purpose.htm	University of Colorado at Boulder, Center for Entrepreneurship: Purpose of a Business Plan	Brief three-part statement of a business plan's purpose from an academic center for small business studies.
http://www.cbsc.org:4000/sbc-doc/ intro_bp.html	Canadian Business Service Centres: Interactive Business Planner	This is a general discussion of business plans, but the site also includes an interesting free interactive business planning program. Good to play with to see if you like working with business planning software. A nonidentifying password is required to access the planner.
http://www.azresource.com/ busplan.htm	Web Resource Marketing, Arizona Small Business Resource: Business Planning	Small business information site provided by a Web design and development firm specializing in small businesses. Offers general interest links, articles, and resources.
http://www.toolkit.cch.com/Text/ P01_4500.stm	Business Owner's Toolkit™ (CCH): Building a Business Plan	CCH has created a highly useful site for small business developers, including searchable advice, interactive features, in-depth articles, and a wide range of valuable resources.
http://www.fascination.com/pub/ bellis/bizplan.html	Fascinations: Bill's Small Business Links	Personal Web site containing descriptions of links to a variety of small business pages.

URL	Site	Content
http://guide.infoseek.com/Topic/ Business/Small_business/ Start_a_business/Business_plan	Infoseek Business Channel	Search results screen from Infoseek displaying business plan-related pages.
http://www.toolkit.cch.com/Tools/ buspln_m.stm	Business Owner's Toolkit™ (CCH): Business Plan Components: Sample Plans Illustrate Required Content	CCH has created a highly useful site for small business developers, including searchable advice, inter-active features, in-depth articles, and a wide range of valuable resources.

Chapter 7

URL	Site	Content
http://www.businessleader.com/ blsep96/shared.html	Business Leader Magazine: "A Shared Vision"	Article focusing on the importance of a mission statement in a small business context.
http://www.washingtonpost.com/ wp-srv/frompost/features/nov97/ stories/hoax17.htm	Washington Post: "Dilbert Creator Goes Undercover"	Amusing online newspaper story about Scott Adams, creator of the popular "Dilbert" comic strip, going undercover in a corporate mission statement meeting.

Chapter 8

URL	Site	Content
http://www.equitysecurities.com/ about_financing/about_financing.htm	American Capital Strategies: About Financing	Commercial service site offers valuable information about types of financing.
http://www.uacpa.org/smallbiz/ financin.htm	Business Financing	Article by Scott W. Pickett, CPA with Coopers & Lybrand.
http://www.kcilink.com:443/rbff/	Regional Business Financing Forum: Financing Guide	Collection of articles about small business financing issues, written by a variety of experts.
http://www.nvca.org/	National Venture Capital Association	Homepage includes membership information and events held around the country. The Industry Overview is an excellent "quick read" on venture capital.
http://www.aaeg.org/	American Entrepreneurs for Economic Growth	Provides information on legislation, education, and networking opportunities for emerging growth companies.

URL	Site	Content
http://www.nasbic.org/	National Association of Small Business Investment Companies	A well-maintained site that explains the role of an SBIC, and where to find one near you.

Chapter 9

URL	Site	Content
http://ewmdws003.ibm.net/smb/ smbusapub.nsf/DetailContacts/ 862566130059C0DC8525662100 66AB45?OpenDocument	IBM Business Center White Paper: Selecting the Right Accounting Information Systems and Financial Management	Article from IBM detailing issues faced by small businesses in choosing an accounting information system.
http://www.techweb.com:3040/ smallbiz/product1224a.html	CMPNet: The Business of Small Biz Accounting	Article providing a survey and links concerning small business accounting technologies.

Chapter 10

URL	Site	Content
http://www.edgeonline.com/main/ bizbuilders/index.shtm	Entrepreneurial Edge Online: Business Builders	Marketing site, for series of self-training modules for small business development, provides free interactive worksheets, search engines, and assessments.
http://www.toolkit.cch.com/tools/ tools.stm#DZ02	Business Owner's Toolkit™ (CCH): Business Tools	CCH has created a highly useful site for small business developers, including searchable advice, interactive features, in-depth articles, and a wide range of valuable resources.
http://www.edgeonline.com/main/ toolbox/pbalsht.shtml	Entrepreneurial Edge Business Toolbox: Balance Sheet	Marketing site, for series of self-training modules for small business development, provides free interactive worksheets, search engines, and assessments.
http://www.smalloffice.com/miser/ archive/mmsays44.htm	Smalloffice.com: "Money— Calculate Your P&L"	Online small business magazine article about calculating P&L. Site includes tips, news, reviews, and links.
http://www1.bigyellow.com/ ma/z_bz_971215.mat	The Biz Guru	Article about financing your small business start-up with little or no money. Site includes additional articles on small business, interactive features, and discussions of financing options.

URL	Site	Content
http://sbinformation.miningco.com/MSUB18.HTM	Mining Company	Links to accounting sites and information.

Chapter 11

URL	Site	Content
http://smallbizpartners.com/success/pricing.html	Small Business Success Magazine	Lengthy article about pricing for profitability.
http://www.sba.gov/opc/pubs/co28.html	Small Business Administration	Overview of the basic facts about starting a small business.

Chapter 12

URL	Site	Content
http://www.toolkit.cch.com/Text/P06_4244.stm	Business Owner's Toolkit™ (CCH): Credit Policy	CCH has created a highly useful site for small business developers, including searchable advice, interactive features, in-depth articles, and a wide range of valuable resources.
http://www.equifax.com/	Equifax	Corporate informational site including general information on business credit issues.
http://www.experian.com/	Experian	Corporate informational site including general information on business and consumer credit issues.

Chapter 13

URL	Site	Content
http://www.new-direction.com/NAME.HTM	New Direction Business Systems	Naming your business: issues and links.
http://www.namestormers.com/nameg.htm	Namestormers: The Naming Guide	Company and brand name developer offers naming tips, a checklist, relevant links, and product information.
http://www.entrepreneurmag.com	Entrepreneur Mag.com	Online version of *Entrepreneur Magazine* offers searchable tips, tools, and links on a wide range of small business issues.
http://thelogofactory.com/case/gallery1.html	The Logo Factory	Gallery of sample commercial logos created by a graphic design, marketing, and Internet services company.

URL	Site	Content
http://windows.microsoft.com/typography/links/link6.htm	Microsoft: Typography	Online typography magazine; this page features links to other typography-related Web sites

Chapter 14

URL	Site	Content
http://www.bea.doc.gov/	United States Department of Commerce: Bureau of Economic Affairs	Federal government homepage for the BEA; features information, statistics, and analysis of key national, international, and regional aspects of the United States economy.
http://www.census.gov/	United States Department of Commerce: Bureau of the Census	Federal government homepage for the Census Bureau, featuring a searchable database of facts and statistics about the United States population.
http://www.ita.doc.gov/	United States Department of Commerce: International Trade Administration	The ITA is a government agency dedicated to helping United States businesses compete internationally. This site includes data about foreign markets and information about international trade, news, and statistics.
http://www.state.ia.us/sbro/tools.htm	Iowa Department of Economic Development: Small Business Resource Office	State Web site featuring general interest information about marketing and market research for small businesses.

Chapter 15

URL	Site	Content
http://www.sbaer.uca.edu/docs/Publications/pub00028.txt	Small Business Advancement National Center	This site features an SBA white paper, "Planning Your Advertising: Focus on the Facts." The parent site, www.sbaer.uca.edu, is a Web site run by the University of Arkansas, and is one of the largest online searchable libraries of small business information in the world: try it!
http://www.whcsb.com/	White House Conference on Small Business: Delegates' Business and Communication Center	Links to resources, information, and networking opportunities

Chapter 16

URL	Site	Content
http://www.toolkit.cch.com/Text/P03_7020.stm	Business Owner's Toolkit™ (CCH): Advertising Ideas	CCH has created a highly useful site for small business developers, including searchable advice, interactive features, in-depth articles, and a wide range of valuable resources.
http://www.cba.neu.edu/alumni/molloy/art-32.html	Northeastern University College of Business Administration: "Advertising Plays a Critical Role in Firm's Success"	One of many articles on small business issues from an academic Web site.
http://www.toolkit.cch.com/text/P01_2240.stm	Business Owner's Toolkit™ (CCH): Advertising Ideas: Advertising and Marketing Costs	CCH has created a highly useful site for small business developers, including searchable advice, interactive features, in-depth articles, and a wide range of valuable resources.
http://sbinformation.miningco.com/msub19.htm	Mining Co. Guide to Small Business Information: Advertising and Promotion	Links to a wide variety of interesting and informative sites about advertising (for fun, look at the ones that feature advertising goofs and disasters).

Chapter 17

URL	Site	Content
http://www.net101.com/reasons.html	Net 101: The Original "20 Reasons to Put Your Business on the WWW"	Informative commercial site supporting a company that offers Internet solutions for businesses.
http://www.homeofficemag.com/page.hts?N=6475&Ad=S	Entrepreneur Mag.com: "The New Marketplace"	Online version of *Entrepreneur Magazine* offers searchable tips, tools, and links on a wide range of small business issues, including e-commerce.
http://microsoft.com/magazine/guides/internet/history.htm	Microsoft Personal Computing Internet Guide and Web Tutorial: A Brief History of the Internet	Interesting historical overview of the Internet's development and evolution.
http://www.icat.com/mall	iCat Corporation: iCat Shopping Mall	An example of the "virtual mall" approach to e-commerce.

Chapter 18

URL	Site	Content
http://www.irs.ustreas.gov/prod/bus_info/index.html	United States Department of the Treasury: Internal Revenue Service: Tax Info for Business	Links to official IRS information, news, bulletins, and assistance regarding small business tax issues, as well as other informational links.
http://www.irs.ustreas.gov/prod/cover.html	United States Department of the Treasury: Internal Revenue Service: The Digital Daily	Daily IRS online newsletter includes news, forms, information, bulletins, and assistance regarding small business tax issues.
http://www.irs.ustreas.gov/prod/tax_edu/teletax/tc408.html	United States Department of the Treasury: Internal Revenue Service: Sole Proprietorship	IRS "Tax Topic" discussion.
http://www.irs.ustreas.gov/prod/tax_edu/teletax/tc306.html	United States Department of the Treasury: Internal Revenue Service: Penalty for Underpayment of Estimated Tax	IRS "Tax Topic" discussion.
http://www.irs.ustreas.gov/prod/tax_edu/teletax/tc554.html	United States Department of the Treasury: Internal Revenue Service: Self-Employment Tax	IRS "Tax Topic" discussion.
http://www.irs.ustreas.gov/prod/forms_pubs/pubs/p54114.htm	United States Department of the Treasury: Internal Revenue Service: Form 1065 Example	IRS case study of a taxpayer's experience with Form 1065.

Chapter 19

URL	Site	Content
http://www.toolkit.cch.com/text/p06_4488.stm	Business Owner's Toolkit™ (CCH): Service Contracts	CCH has created a highly useful site for small business developers, including searchable advice, interactive features, in-depth articles, and a wide range of valuable resources.

Chapter 20

URL	Site	Content
http://www.uspto.gov/	United States Patent and Trademark Office	Official patent and trademark site provides forms, advice, guidance, and a searchable database of trademarks (try a search of "Upstart Publishing").
http://www.jonesaskew.com/patent.html	Jones & Askew: Patent-Related Articles by Jones & Askew Attorneys	This Web site, maintained by an Atlanta, Georgia, law firm, offers an array of informative articles on patent, copyright, and trademark law.

URL	Site	Content
http://lcweb.loc.gov/copyright/circs/	United States Copyright Office, Library of Congress: Copyright Basics	Detailed guide to copyright procedures, provided by the Copyright Office. The site also features numerous links and useful information.
http://rs.internic.net/domain-info/nic-rev03.html	InterNIC/Network Solutions: Network Solutions' Domain Name Dispute Policy	From the official domain name registry, an explanation of what happens when two or more entities claim the same URL.

Chapter 21

URL	Site	Content
http://www.onlinewbc.org/docs/starting/location.html	United States Small Business Administration: Online Women's Business Center: Choosing a Location for Your Business	Information and considerations to keep in mind when selecting a location for any small business.
http://www.entrepreneurmag.com/radio/tip155.hts	Entrepreneur Mag.com: Smart Tip of the Day	Considerations to keep in mind when selecting a location for your small business.

Chapter 22

URL	Site	Content
http://www.aahbb.org/	American Association of Home-Based Businesses	Homepage of national home-based business organization offers tips, links, resources, and membership info.
http://207.240.161.90/index2.html	American Home Business Association: Home-Based Business Resources	Tools, services, information, and resources from a national home-based business organization.
http://www.homeofficemag.com/	Entrepreneur Mag.com: Entrepreneur's Home Office On-Line	Articles, tips, resources, and technology reviews.
http://www.home-bus.com/	Micro Grafix Corporation: Home Business Guide	Online home-based business newsletter features articles and resources of interest to home-based businesses.
http://www.homebusinessmag.com/	Home Business Magazine	Online promotional version provides useful resources and articles.
http://www.irs.ustreas.gov/	United States Department of the Treasury: Internal Revenue Service	IRS homepage.

Chapter 23

URL	Site	Content
http://entrepreneurmag.com/homebiz/home200.hts	Entrepreneur Mag.com	242 home-based franchise opportunities.
http://www.bbbmbc.com/bbbtips/tip65.htm	Better Business Bureau of Mainland British Columbia	Canadian site provides a list of general-interest guidelines for considering any franchise opportunity.
http://www.entrepreneurmag.com/resource/buying_tips.hts	Entrepreneur Mag.com: Franchise 500	Magazine's ranking of the 500 best franchise opportunites includes a searchable database, tips, resources, and information.
http://www.ftc.gov/	United States Federal Trade Commission	Homepage of the FTC.
http://www.ftc.gov/bcp/conline/pubs/invest/buyfran.htm	United States Federal Trade Commission: A Consumer Guide to Buying a Franchise	Article featuring advice and guidance from the FTC for those considering a franchise.

Chapter 24

URL	Site	Content
http://www.smartbiz.com/sbs/cats/buysell.htm	Smart Business Supersite (SBS): Buying/Selling a Business	Articles, reviews, and other useful information.
http://www.bizbooksoftware.com/links.htm	Parker-Nelson Publishing	Links to informational sites about buying or selling a business.
http://www.moneyminded.com/worklife/uboss/c7stbu11.htm	Moneyminded: Worklife	Article about buying a business versus starting a new one, in an extensive collection of business-related materials.
http://www.toolkit.cch.com/columns/starting/buybiz.stm	Business Owner's Toolkit™ (CCH): Buying a Business	CCH has created a highly useful site for small business developers, including searchable advice, interactive features, in-depth articles, and a wide range of valuable resources.

Chapter 25

URL	Site	Content
http://www.toolkit.cch.com/text/P01_5450.STM	Business Owner's Toolkit™ (CCH)	CCH has created a highly useful site for small business developers, including searchable advice, interactive features, in-depth articles, and a wide range of valuable resources.

URL	Site	Content
http://www.toolkit.cch.com/text/P05_0005.stm	Business Owner's Toolkit™ (CCH): Should You Hire Someone?	CCH has created a highly useful site for small business developers, including searchable advice, interactive features, in-depth articles, and a wide range of valuable resources.
http://www.lawcrawler.com	FindLaw Internet Legal Resource	Searchable database is extremely valuable for researching employment law issues (and other small business legal topics).
http://www.irs.ustreas.gov/prod/tax_edu/teletax/tc751.html	United States Department of the Treasury, Internal Revenue Service: Social Security and Medicare Withholding Rates	IRS "Tax Topic" discussion.
http://www.irs.ustreas.gov/prod/tax_edu/teletax/tc752.html	United States Department of the Treasury, Internal Revenue Service: Where, When and How to File	IRS "Tax Topic" discussion on employment tax issues.
http://www.irs.ustreas.gov/prod/tax_edu/teletax/tc753.html	United States Department of the Treasury, Internal Revenue Service: Employee's Withholding Allowance Certificate	IRS "Tax Topic" discussion.
http://www.irs.ustreas.gov/prod/tax_edu/teletax/tc755.html	United States Department of the Treasury, Internal Revenue Service: Employer Identification Number (EIN)—How to Apply	IRS "Tax Topic" discussion.
http://www.irs.ustreas.gov/prod/tax_edu/teletax/tc757.html	United States Department of the Treasury, Internal Revenue Service: Form 941 Deposit Requirements	IRS "Tax Topic" discussion.
http://www.irs.ustreas.gov/prod/tax_edu/teletax/tc762.html	United States Department of the Treasury, Internal Revenue Service: Tips—Withholding and Reporting	IRS "Tax Topic" discussion.
http://www.irs.ustreas.gov/prod/tax_edu/teletax/tc750.html	United States Department of the Treasury, Internal Revenue Service: Employer Tax Information	IRS "Tax Topic" discussion.

Chapter 26

URL	Site	Content
http://www.toolkit.cch.com/ text/P02_3201.STM	Business Owner's Toolkit™ (CCH): Business Expansion	CCH has created a highly useful site for small business developers, including searchable advice, interactive features, in-depth articles, and a wide range of valuable resources.
http://www.vandoren.net/ default2.htm	Van Doren Consulting: Planning—A Primer	Personal Web site provides interesting information on business planning from a Florida-based consultant.
http://www.hp.com/sbso/tips/ tips.html	Hewlett-Packard: Small Business Tips & Tricks	Small business-related articles from three noted experts.

ADDITIONAL BIOGRAPHIES

James N. Holly

Dr. James N. Holly graduated from the U.S. Air Force Academy in 1960 and served as an Air Force pilot until 1969. In 1969, he started working in industry as a technical writer and editor where he developed considerable practical experience coordinating the efforts of proposal writing and planning teams.

Later, as Engineering Services Manager, he coordinated the day-to-day operations of a publication group, a design and drafting group, a model shop, and a technical library. In this position, Jim was responsible for coordinating marketing support, operations, and administrative activities in support of a research and design engineering department.

While working in industry, Jim earned a Master of Ocean Engineering degree and a Master of Business Administration degree from Florida Atlantic University and served on the university's faculty as an Adjunct Professor in the departments of Mechanical Engineering, Communication, Management, and Public Administration. In 1983, he completed a doctoral program in organization communication at the University of Illinois Institute of Communication Research. While studying for his Ph.D., he taught professional writing and speech communication courses at the University of Illinois.

Jim served as Director of the Business Development Center and as a member of the Professional Programs in Business faculty at the University of Wisconsin–Green Bay. He is currently a Lecturer on Master of Administrative Science faculty at the University of Wisconsin–Green Bay where he teaches project management, organizational, communication, systems, and processes courses. He also consults with and provides training to a variety of public and private sector organizations.

Dr. Holly has a unique combination of experience, training, and interests that are focused by the quality-oriented workplace. Prior to joining the UW–Green Bay staff he served as a training consultant to various federal and private clients including ARCO Metals, AT&T Technology, Chevron U.S.A., Department of Energy, Defense Contract Audit Agency, Environmental Protection Agency, Exxon, Kaiser-Jamaica, Los Angeles Water & Power, Martin-Marietta, Pacific Telesis, U.S. Coast Guard, Soil Conservation Service, U.S. Forest Service, Union Oil, White Sands Missile Range (U.S. Army), and many others.

Jill A. Rossiter

Jill Rossiter has been developing and delivering training throughout the Midwest for over ten years. She specializes in topics related to leadership development, strategic planning and goal setting, total quality transformation, human resources management, and personal and professional development.

Jill Rossiter has also worked as a consultant to small businesses and nonprofit organizations in Iowa, Minnesota, and Wisconsin, specializing in business planning, strategic planning, and general and total quality management.

Rossiter had two books published in 1996: *Human Resources: Mastering Your Small Business* and *Total Quality Management: Mastering Your Small Business*. Both books have become part of the University of Wisconsin Small Business Development Center (SBDC) Small Business Mastery Series.

Rossiter holds two master's degrees: one in education from Boston University and one in business administration from the University of Iowa. She is a certified trainer in Total Quality Transformation. Before starting her own business, MEI // Management Education Institute, Rossiter was an Assistant Professor of Management at Mankato State University; an Associate Dean and Assistant Professor of Management and Education at Simpson College; and Associate State Director for the Wisconsin Small Business Development Center.

Susan Stites

Susan Stites owns Management Allegories, a training and writing practice that specializes in leadership and employee development. Susan helps businesses and individuals focus on what is important to them, assists them in setting goals, then provides the necessary tools for them to achieve their goals. Susan has worked with organizations of all sizes in the service, nonprofit, manufacturing, and government sectors.

Her clients include Wisconsin Power & Light, the National Safety Council, EPIC Life Insurance, American Automobile Association, CUNA & Affiliates, the U.S. Navy, Wisconsin Department of Natural Resources, and FTD Florists.

Prior to starting her own business, Susan was the Director of Human Resources at Central Life Insurance, and, before that, she was Manager of Training for Lands' End, Inc., and Human Resources Manager for Montgomery Ward.

Susan has published nine books and numerous articles on a variety of human resources issues. She has also published seven professional training programs on a variety of safety and health topics. Susan holds a master's degree in Industrial Education from Northwestern University. She is a member of the American Society for Training and Development (ASTD) and is a former president of the ASTD's South Central Wisconsin Chapter. She is listed in the 1997 *Who's Who in America*.

Glossary

How forcible are right words!

Job, *vi. 25.*

acid test ratio Cash, plus other assets that can be immediately converted to cash, should equal or exceed current liabilities. The formula used to determine the ratio is as follows:

Cash + Receivables (net) + Marketable securities ÷ Current liabilities

The "acid test" ratio is one of the most important credit barometers used by lending institutions, as it indicates the abilities of a business enterprise to meet its current obligations.

account A record of a business transaction. A contract arrangement, written or unwritten, to purchase and take delivery with payment to be made later as arranged. A separate record showing the increases and decreases in each asset, liability, owner's equity, revenue, and expense item.

account balance The difference between the debit and the credit sides of an account.

accountant One who is skilled at keeping business records. Usually, a highly trained professional rather than one who keeps books. An accountant can set up the books needed for a business to operate and help the owner understand them.

accounting The process by which financial information about a business is recorded, classified, summarized, and interpreted by a business.

accounting method A set of rules used to determine when and how the taxpayer's income and expenses are reported. Important accounting methods include the cash method and the accrual method.

accounting period A time interval at the end of which an analysis is made of the information contained in the bookkeeping record to determine tax liability. Also the period of time covered by the profit and loss statement, income statement, and other financial statements that report operating results.

accounts payable Amounts owed by a business to its creditors on open account for goods purchased or services rendered that have been received but not yet paid for.

accounts receivable Amounts owed to the business on open account as a result of extending credit to a customer who purchases, but has not yet paid for, products or services.

accrual method of accounting A method of accounting where income is included when it is earned by the taxpayer, whether or not collected in the same period, and expenses are deducted when they are incurred by the taxpayer, whether or not paid in the same period.

accrued expenses Expenses that have been incurred but not paid (such as employee salaries, commissions, taxes, interest, etc.).

accrued income Income that has been earned but not received.

administrative expense Expenses chargeable to the managerial, general administrative, and policy phases of a business in contrast to sales, manufacturing, or cost of goods expense.

advertising The practice of bringing to the public's notice the good qualities of something in order to induce the public to buy or invest in it.

agent A person who is authorized to act for or represent another person in dealing with a third party.

aging receivables A scheduling of accounts receivable according to the length of time they have been outstanding. This shows which accounts are not being paid in a timely manner and may reveal any difficulty in collecting long overdue receivables. This may also be an important indicator of developing cash flow problems. An appropriate rate of loss can be applied to each age group in order to estimate probable loss from uncollectible accounts.

amortization To liquidate on an installment basis; the process of gradually paying off a liability over a period of time, i.e., a mortgage is amortized by periodically paying off part of the face amount of the mortgage.

annual report The yearly report made by a company at the close of the fiscal year, stating the company's receipts and disbursements, assets and liabilities.

appraisal Evaluation of a specific piece of personal or real property. The value placed on the property evaluated.

appreciation The increase in the value of an asset in excess of its depreciable cost due to economic and other conditions, as distinguished from increases in value due to improvements or additions made to it.

arrears Amounts past due and unpaid.

articles of incorporation A legal document filed with the state which sets forth the purposes and regulations for a corporation. Each state has different regulations.

assets Anything of worth (such as resources, inventory, or property rights) that is owned by an individual or business. Accounts receivable are assets.

audit An examination of accounting documents and of supporting evidence for the purpose of reaching an informed opinion concerning their propriety.

audit trail A chain of references that makes it possible to trace information about transactions through an accounting system.

bad debts Money owed to you that you cannot collect.

balance The amount of money remaining in an account.

balance sheet An itemized statement that lists the total assets, liabilities, and net worth of a given business to reflect its financial condition (net worth) at a given moment in time. It is usually done at the close of an accounting period by summarizing business assets, liabilities, and owner's equity.

bank statement A monthly statement of account which a bank renders to each of its depositors.

basis For income tax purposes, it is the acquisition cost of the property to the taxpayer. The basis is used to determine the gain or loss on the sale of property and when computing depreciation.

benchmarking Rating a company's products, services, and practices against those of the front runners in the industry.

bill of lading A document issued by a railroad or other carrier that acknowledges the receipt of specified goods for transportation to a certain place. It sets forth the contract between the shipper and the carrier, and it provides for proper delivery of the goods.

bill of sale Formal legal document that conveys title to or interest in specific personal property from the seller to the buyer.

board of directors Those individuals elected by the stockholders of a corporation to manage the business.

bookkeeping The process of recording business transactions into the accounting records. The "books" are the documents in which the records of transactions are kept.

bottom line The figure that reflects company profitability on the income statement. The bottom line is the profit after all expenses and taxes have been paid; the net profit or loss after taxes for a specific accounting period.

brand name A term, symbol, design, or combination thereof that identifies and differentiates a seller's products or service.

breakeven point The point of business activity when total revenue equals total expenses. Above the breakeven point, the business is making a profit. Below the breakeven point, the business is incurring a loss. At breakeven, the business no longer incurs a loss but has yet to make a profit. The breakeven point can be expressed in total dollars of revenue exactly offset by total expenses, or total units of production, the cost of which exactly equals the income derived from their sale.

budget An estimate of the income and expenditures for a future period of time, usually one year; the development of a set of financial goals. A business is then evaluated by measuring its performance in terms of these goals. The budget contains projections for cash inflow and outflow and other balance sheet items. Also known as cash flow statement.

business financial history A summary of financial information about a company from its start to the present.

business venture Taking financial risks in a commercial enterprise.

C corporation A regular corporation which is taxed under Subchapter C of the Internal Revenue Code.

capital Money available to invest or the total of accumulated assets available for production. Capital funds are those funds needed for the base of the business. Usually they are put into the business in a fairly permanent form such as in fixed assets, plant, and equipment, or are used in other ways that are not recoverable in the short run unless the entire business is sold. See also *owner's equity*.

capital equipment Equipment used to manufacture a product, provide a service, or to sell, store, or deliver merchandise. Such equipment will not be sold in the normal course of business, but will be used and worn out or consumed in the course of business.

capital expenditures An expenditure for a purchase of an item of property, plant, or equipment that has a useful life of more than one year (fixed assets).

capital gain A gain from the sale or exchange of a capital asset.

capital loss A loss from the sale or exchange of a capital asset.

cash method of accounting The method of accounting where income is reported only as it is received, either actually or constructively, and expenses are deducted only in the year that they are paid.

cash Money in hand or readily available.

cash discount A deduction given for prompt payment of a bill.

cash flow The actual movement of cash within a business: cash inflow minus cash outflow. A term used to designate the reported net income of a corporation plus amounts charged off for depreciation, depletion, amortization, and extraordinary charges to reserves, which are bookkeeping deductions and not actually paid out in cash. Used to offer a better indication of the ability of a firm to meet its own obligations and to pay dividends, rather than the conventional net income figure.

cash flow statement See *budget*.

cash position See *liquidity*.

cash receipts The money received by a business from customers.

certified public accountant An accountant to whom a state has given a certificate showing that he has met prescribed requirements designed to ensure competence on the part of the public practitioner in accounting and that he is permitted to use the designation Certified Public Accountant, commonly abbreviated as CPA.

chart of accounts A list of the numbers and titles of a business's general ledger accounts.

choice A decision to purchase based on an evaluation of alternatives.

closing entries Entries made at the end of an accounting period to reduce the balances of the revenue and expense accounts to zero. Most businesses close books at the end of each month and at the end of the year.

collateral Something of value given or held as a pledge that a debt or obligation will be fulfilled. An asset pledged to a lender in order to support the loan.

commission A percentage of the principal or of the income that an agent receives as compensation for services.

comparative financial statements Financial statements that include information for two or more periods or two or more companies.

contract An agreement regarding mutual responsibilities between two or more parties that is enforceable in court against parties who made the agreement.

controllable expenses Those expenses that can be controlled or restrained by the business person.

corporation A voluntary organization of persons, either actual individuals or legal entities, legally bound together to form a business enterprise; an artificial legal entity created by government grant and treated by law as an individual entity. A business structure that is granted separate legal status under state law and whose owners are stockholders of the corporation.

cosigners Joint signers of a loan agreement who pledge to meet the obligations of a business in case of default.

cost of good sold The direct cost to the business owner of those items that will be sold to customers. The cost of raw materials plus the cost of labor in the production of a product. Cost of goods sold reflects the cost of inventory sold during an accounting period. It is equal to the beginning inventory for the period, plus the cost of purchases made during the period, minus the ending inventory for the period.

counteroffer A proposal made in response to an offer in which the terms vary from the terms of the original offer.

credit An amount entered on the right side of an account in double-entry accounting. A decrease in asset and expense accounts. An increase in liability, capital, and income accounts. Another word for debt. A bank gives credit when it lends money.

credit line The maximum amount of credit or money a financial institution or trade firm will extend to a customer.

creditor A company or individual to whom a business owes money.

current assets Valuable resources or property owned by a company that will be turned into cash within one year or used up in the operations of the company within one year. Generally includes cash, accounts receivable, inventory, and prepaid expenses.

current liabilities Amounts owed that will ordinarily be paid by a firm within one year. Such items include accounts payable, wages payable, taxes payable, the current portion of a long-term debt, and interest and dividends payable.

current ratio A ratio of a firm's current assets to its current liabilities. A dependable indication of liquidity; a ratio of 2.0 is acceptable for most businesses. Because a current ratio includes the value of inventories that have not yet been sold, it does not offer the best evaluation of the firm's current status. The "acid test" ratio, covering the most liquid of current assets, produces a better evaluation (see *acid test ratio*).

debit An amount entered on the left side of an account in double-entry accounting. A decrease in liabilities, capital, and income accounts. An increase in asset and expense accounts.

debt Borrowed funds, whether from your own coffers or from other individuals, banks, or institutions. Debt is generally secured with a note, which in turn may be secured by a lien against property or other assets. Ordinarily, the note states repayment and interest provisions, which vary greatly in both amount and duration, depending upon the purpose, source, and terms of the loan. Some debt is convertible; that is, it may be changed into direct ownership of a portion of a business under certain stated conditions.

debt capital The part of the investment capital that must be borrowed.

debt ratio The key financial ratio used by creditors in determining how indebted a business is and how able it is to service the debts. The debt ratio is calculated by dividing total liabilities by total assets. This higher the ratio, the more risk of failure. The acceptable ratio is dependent upon the policies of your creditors and bankers.

declining-balance method An accelerated method of depreciation in which the book value of an asset at the beginning of the year is multiplied by an appropriate percentage to obtain the depreciation to be taken for that year.

default The failure to pay a debt or meet an obligation.

deficit The excess of liabilities over assets; a negative net worth.

demographics The statistical study of human populations, especially with reference to size, density, distribution, and vital statistics. Relating to the dynamic balance of a population, especially with regard to density and capacity for expansion or decline.

depreciable base of an asset The cost of an asset used in the computation of yearly depreciation expense.

depreciation A decrease in value through age, wear, or deterioration. Depreciation is a normal expense of doing business that must be taken into account. There are laws and regulations governing the manner and time periods that may be used for depreciation.

desktop publishing Commonly used term for computer-generated printed materials such as newsletters and brochures.

differentiated marketing Selecting and developing a number of offerings to meet the needs of a number of specific market segments.

direct expenses Those expenses that relate directly to your product or service.

direct mail Marketing goods or services directly to the consumer through the mail.

direct selling The process whereby the producer sells to the user, ultimate consumer, or retailer without intervening middlemen.

discount A deduction from the stated or list price of a product or service.

distribution The delivery or conveyance of a good or service to a market.

distribution channel All of the individuals and organizations involved in the process of moving products from producer to consumer. The route a product follows as it moves from the original grower, producer, or importer to the ultimate consumer. The chain of intermediaries linking the producer of a good to the consumer.

distributor Middleman, wholesaler, agent, or company distributing goods to dealers or companies.

double-entry accounting A system of accounting under which each transaction is recorded twice. This is based on the premise that every transaction has two sides. At least one account must be debited and one account must be credited and the debit and credit totals for each transaction must be equal.

downsize Term currently used to indicate employee reassignment, layoffs, and restructuring in order to make a business more competitive, efficient, and/or cost-effective.

entity An organization that is considered for tax purposes to have a separate existence. Examples of entities are corporations, partnerships, trusts, and estates.

entrepreneur An innovator of business enterprise who recognizes opportunities to introduce a new product, a new process, or an improved organization, and who assumes risk to raise the necessary money, assemble the factors for production, and organize an operation to exploit the opportunity.

equipment Physical property of a more or less permanent nature ordinarily useful in carrying on operations, other than land, buildings, or improvements to either of them. Examples are machinery, tools, trucks, cars, ships, furniture, and furnishings.

equity Equity is the owner's investment in the business. Unlike capital, equity is what remains after the liabilities of the company are subtracted from the assets: thus it may be greater than or less than the capital invested in the business. Equity investment carries with it a share of ownership and usually a share in profits, as well as some say in how the business is managed. Equity is calculated by subtracting the liabilities of the business from the assets of the business.

equity capital Money furnished by owners of the business.

expenses The costs of producing revenue through the sale of goods or services.

facsimile machine (fax) Machine capable of transmitting written input via telephone lines.

fair market value The amount at which property would change hands between a willing buyer and a willing seller, neither being under any compulsion to buy or to sell and both having reasonable knowledge of the relevant facts.

financial statements The periodic reports that summarize the financial affairs of a business.

first in, first out method (FIFO) A method of valuing inventory that assumes that the first items purchased are the first items to be sold. When ending inventory is computed the costs of the latest purchases are used.

fiscal year Twelve consecutive months ending on the last day of any month other than December or a 52–53 week year used by a business for accounting purposes.

fixed asset log A record used to keep track of the fixed assets purchased by a business during the current financial year. This record can be used by an accountant to determine depreciation expense to be taken for tax purposes.

fixed assets Items purchased for use in a business which are depreciable over a fixed period of time determined by the expected useful life of the purchase. Usually includes land, buildings, vehicles, and equipment not intended for resale. Land is not depreciable, but is listed as a fixed asset.

fixed costs Costs that do not vary in total during a period even though the volume of goods manufactured may be higher or lower than anticipated.

fixed expenses Those costs which don't vary from one period to the next. Generally, these expenses are not affected by the volume of business. Fixed expenses are the basic costs that every business will have each month.

foreign corporation Generally, a corporation that is not organized under the laws of one of the states or territories of the United States.

franchise Business that requires three elements: (1) franchise fee, (2) common trade name, and (3) continuous relationship with the parent company.

fringe benefits A form of compensation or other benefits received by an employee, such as health insurance and pension plans.

fundraising Events staged to raise revenue.

general journal Used to record all the transactions of a business. Transactions are listed in chronological order and transferred or posted to individual accounts in the general ledger.

general ledger In double-entry accounting, the master reference file for the accounting system. A permanent, classified record is kept for each business account. The forms used for the accounts are on separate sheets in a book or binder and are then referred to as the general ledger.

gross profit The difference between the selling price and the cost of an item. Gross profit is calculated by subtracting cost of goods sold from net sales.

gross profit margin An indicator of the percentage of each sales dollar remaining after a business has paid for its goods. It is computed by dividing the gross profit by the sales.

gross profit on sales The difference between net sales and the cost of goods sold.

guarantee (also guaranty) A pledge by a third party to repay a loan in the event that the borrower cannot.

homepage The "table of contents" to a Web site, detailing what information is on a particular site. The first page one sees when accessing a Web site.

horizontal analysis A percentage analysis of the increases and decreases on the items on comparative financial statements. A horizontal financial statement analysis involves comparison of data for the current period with the same data of a company for previous periods. The percentage of increase or decrease is listed.

income statement A statement of income and expenses for a given period of time. A financial document that shows how much money (revenue) came in and how much money (expense) was paid out.

indirect expenses Operating expenses that are not directly related to the sale of your product or service.

interest The price charged for the use of money or paid for the use of credit; the cost of borrowing money.

Internet The vast collection of interconnected networks that provide electronic mail and access to the World Wide Web.

inventory The stock of goods that a business has on hand for sale to its customers; a list of assets being held for sale. The materials owned and held by a business firm, including new materials, intermediate products and parts, work in progress and finished goods, intended either for internal consumption or for sale.

invest To lay out money for any purpose from which a profit is expected.

investment measures Ratios used to measure an owner's earnings for his or her investment in the company. See *return on investment (ROI)*.

invoice A bill for the sale of goods or services sent by the seller to the purchaser.

Keogh plans A retirement plan that is available to self-employed taxpayers.

keystone Setting a retail price at twice the wholesale price.

last in, first out method (LIFO) A method of valuing inventory that assumes that the last items purchased are the first items to be sold. The cost of the ending inventory is computed by using the cost of the earliest purchases.

lead The name and address of a possible customer.

lease A long-term rental agreement.

liability Amount owed by a business to its creditors; a debt of a business.

liability insurance Risk protection for actions for which a business is liable.

license Formal permission to conduct business.

lien A charge against an interest in property or an interest in property given to secure payment of a debt or performance of an obligation. It limits the property owner's right to sell the property.

lifestyle A pattern of living that comprises an individual's activities, interests, and opinions.

limited liability The liability of a business and its owners to other persons or businesses is limited to the assets of the business. Limited liability is a characteristic of a corporation. As a shareholder, you are generally not liable for the debts of the corporation, except to the extent of your investment in the business.

limited liability company An entity formed under state law by filing articles of organization as an LLC. Unlike a partnership, none of the members of an LLC are personally liable for its debts.

limited partner A partner in a partnership formed under a state limited partnership law, whose personal liability for partnership debts is limited to the amount of money or other property that the partner contributed or is required to contribute to the partnership.

limited partnership A limited partnership is formed under a state limited partnership law and composed of at least one general partner and one or more limited partners, where some owners are allowed to assume responsibility only up to the amount invested.

liquidity The ability of a company to meet its financial obligations. The degree of readiness with which assets can be converted into cash without loss. A liquidity analysis focuses on the balance sheet relationships for current assets and current liabilities. A term used to describe the solvency of a business, liquidity has special reference to the degree of readiness in which assets can be converted into cash without a loss. Also called *cash position*. If a firm's current assets cannot be converted into cash to meet current liabilities, the firm is said to be *illiquid*.

loan Money lent with interest. Debt money for private business is usually in the form of bank loans, which, in a sense, are personal because a private business can be harder to evaluate in terms of creditworthiness and degree of risk. A secured loan is a loan that is backed up by a claim against some asset or assets of a business. An unsecured loan is backed by the faith the bank has in the borrower's ability to pay back the money.

loan agreement A document that states what a business can and cannot do as long as it owes money to the lender. A loan agreement may place restrictions on the owner's salary, dividends, amount of other debt, working capital limits, sales, or the number of additional personnel.

long-term liabilities Liabilities that will not be due for more than a year in the future.

management The art of conducting and supervising a business.

market A set of potential or real buyers, or a place in which there is a demand for products or services. Actual or potential buyers of a product or service.

market demand Total volume purchased in a specific geographic area by a specific customer group in a specified time period under a specified marketing program.

market forecast An anticipated demand that results from a planned marketing expenditure.

market niche A well-defined group of customers for which what you have to offer is particularly suitable.

market positioning Finding a market niche that emphasizes the strengths of a product or service in relation to the weaknesses of the competition.

market share A company's percentage share of total sales within a given market.

marketing mix The set of product, place, promotion, price, and packaging variables that a marketing manager controls and orchestrates to bring a product or service into the marketplace.

marketing research The systematic design, collection, analysis, and reporting of data regarding a specific marketing situation.

mass marketing Selecting and developing a single offering for an entire market.

merchandise Goods bought and sold in a business. Merchandise or *stock* is a part of inventory.

microbusiness An owner-operated business with few employees and less than $250,000 in annual sales.

middleman A person or company who performs functions or renders services involved in the purchase and/or sale of goods in their flow from producer to consumer.

mileage log The recording of business miles traveled during an accounting period.

modified accelerated cost recovery system (MACRS) A method of depreciation or cost recovery used for federal income tax purposes for long-term assets purchased after January 1, 1987. Under MACRS, long-term assets fall automatically into certain classes, and the costs of all assets in a class are charged to expense through a standard formula.

multilevel sales Also known as network marketing. Rather than hiring sales staff, multilevel sales companies sell their products through thousands of independent distributors. Multilevel sales companies offer distributors commissions on both retail sales and the sales of their "downline" (the network of other distributors they sponsor).

need A state of perceived deprivation.

net What is left after deducting all expenses from the gross.

net income The amount by which revenue is greater than expenses. On an income statement this is usually expressed as both a pre-tax and after-tax figure.

net loss The amount by which expenses are greater than revenue. On an income statement this figure is usually listed as both a pre-tax and after-tax figure.

net profit margin The measure of a business's success with respect to earnings on sales. It is derived by dividing the net profit by sales. A higher margin means the firm is more profitable.

net sales Gross sales less returns and allowances and sales discounts.

net worth The owner's equity in a given business represented by the excess of the total assets over the total amounts owed to outside creditors (total liabilities) at a given moment in time. The total value of a business in financial terms. Also, the net worth of an individual. Net worth is calculated by subtracting total liabilities from total assets. Generally refers to tangible net worth (i.e., does not include goodwill, etc.). See *owner's equity*.

niche A well-defined group of customers for which the product or service you have to offer is particularly suitable.

nonrecurring One time, not repeating. Nonrecurring expenses are those involved in starting a business which only have to be paid once and will not occur again.

note A document that is recognized as legal evidence of a debt; a written promise with terms for payment of a debt. The basic business loan, a note represents a loan that will be repaid, or substantially reduced 30, 60, or 90 days later at a stated interest rate. These are short term, and unless they are made under a line of credit, a separate loan application is needed for each loan and each renewal.

operating costs Expenditures arising from current business activities. The costs incurred to do business such as salaries, electricity, and rent. Also may be called *overhead.*

operating expenses Normal expenses incurred in the running of a business.

operating profit margin The ratio representing the pure operations profits, ignoring interest and taxes. It is derived by dividing the income from operations by the sales. The higher the percentage of operating profit margin the better.

organizational market A marketplace made up of producers, trade industries, governments, and institutions.

other expenses Expenses that are not directly connected with the operation of a business. The most common is interest expense.

other income Income that is earned from nonoperating sources. The most common is interest income.

outsourcing Term used in business to identify the process of subcontracting work to outside vendors.

overhead A general term for costs of materials and services not directly adding to or readily identifiable with the product or service being sold.

owner's equity The financial interest of the owner of a business. The total of all owner equity is equal to the business's assets minus its liabilities. The owner's equity represents total investments in the business plus or minus any profits or losses the business has accrued to date.

partnership The relationship between two or more persons who join to carry on a trade or business, with each person contributing money, property, labor, or skill and each expecting to share in the profits and losses of the business whether or not a formal partnership agreement is made.

payable Ready to be paid. One of the standard accounts kept by a bookkeeper is *accounts payable.* This is a list of those bills that are current and due to be paid.

perception The process of selecting, organizing, and interpreting information received through the senses.

personal financial history A summary of personal financial information about the owner of a business. The personal financial history is often required by a potential lender or investor.

personal service corporation A corporation whose principal activity is the performance of personal services in the field of health, law, engineering, architecture, accounting, actuarial science, performing arts, or consulting.

petty cash fund A cash fund from which noncheck expenditures are reimbursed.

physical inventory The process of counting inventory on hand at the end of an accounting period. The number of units of each item is multiplied by the cost per item resulting in inventory value.

positioning A marketing method based on determining what market niche your business should fill and how it should promote its products or services in light of competitive and other forces.

posting The process of transferring data from a journal to a ledger.

prepaid expenses Expenditures that are paid in advance for items not yet received.

price The exchange value of a product or service from the perspective of both the buyer and the seller.

price ceiling The highest amount a customer will pay for a product or a service based upon perceived value.

price floor The lowest amount a business owner can charge for a product or service and still meet all expenses.

price planning The systematic process for establishing pricing objectives and policies.

principal The amount of money borrowed in a debt agreement and the amount upon which interest is calculated; the amount shown on the face of a note or a bond. Unpaid principal is the portion of the face amount remaining at any given time.

pro forma A projection or estimate of what may result in the future from actions in the present. A pro forma financial statement is one that shows how the actual operations of the business will turn out if certain assumptions are achieved.

producers The components of the organizational market that acquire products and services that enter into the production of products and services that are sold or supplied to others.

product Anything capable of satisfying needs, including tangible items, services, and ideas.

product life cycle The stages of development and decline through which a successful product typically moves. Often referred to as PLC.

product line A group of products related to each other by marketing, technical, or end-use considerations.

product mix All of the products in a seller's total product line.

profit Financial gain; returns over expenditures. The excess of the selling price over all costs and expenses incurred in making a sale. Also, the reward to the entrepreneur for the risks assumed by him or her in the establishment, operations, and management of a given enterprise or undertaking.

profit and loss statement (P&L) A list of the total amount of sales (revenues) and total costs (expenses). The difference between revenues and expenses is profit or loss. See *income statement*.

profit margin The difference between selling price and costs.

promotion The communication of information by a seller to influence the attitudes and behavior of potential buyers.

promotional pricing Temporarily pricing a product or service below list price or below cost in order to attract customers.

property, plant, and equipment (PP&E) Assets such as land, buildings, vehicles, and equipment that will be used for a number of years in the operation of a business and (with the exception of land) are subject to depreciation.

psychographics The system of explaining market behavior in terms of attitudes and lifestyles.

publicity Any nonpaid, news-oriented presentation of a product, service, or business entity in a mass media format.

quantitative forecasts Forecasts that are based on measurements of numerical quantities.

quarterly budget analysis A method used to measure actual income and expenditures against projections for the current quarter of the financial year and for the total quarters completed. The difference is usually expressed as the amount and percentage over or under budget.

questionnaire A data-gathering form used to collect information by a personal interview, with a telephone survey, or through the mail.

quick ratio A test of liquidity subtracting inventory from current assets and dividing the result by current liabilities. A quick ratio of 1.0 or greater is usually recommended.

ratio The relationship of one thing to another. A ratio is a short-cut way of comparing things, which can be expressed as numbers or degrees.

ratio analysis An analysis involving the comparison of two individual items on financial statements. One item is divided by the other and the relationship is expressed as a ratio.

real property Land, land improvements, buildings, and other structures attached to the land.

realized gain or loss The difference between the amount realized upon the sale or other disposition of property and the adjusted basis of such property.

receivable Ready for payment. When you sell on credit, you keep an accounts receivable ledger as a record of what is owed to you and who owes it. In accounting, a receivable is an asset.

recognized gain or loss The realized gain or loss which is subject to income taxation.

reconciling the bank statement The process used to bring the bank's records, the accounts, and the business's checkbook into agreement at the end of a banking period.

retail Selling directly to the consumer.

retail business A business that sells goods and services directly to individual consumers.

retailing Businesses and individuals engaged in the activity of selling products to final consumers.

retained earnings Earnings of a corporation that are kept in the business and not paid out in dividends. This amount represents the accumulated, undistributed profits of the corporation.

return on investment (ROI) The rate of profit an investment will earn. The ROI is equal to the annual net income divided by total assets. The higher the ROI, the better. Business owners should set a target ROI and decide what they want their investments to earn.

revenue Total sales during a stated period. The income that results from the sale of products or services or from the use of investments or property. Total sales during a stated period.

revenue and expense journal In single-entry accounting, the record used to keep track of all checks written by a business and all income received for the sale of goods or services.

S corporation A small business corporation that meets various requirements of the Internal Revenue Code and has validly elected not to be taxed as a regular corporation.

sales potential A company's expected share of a market as marketing expenditures increase in relation to the competition.

sales promotion Marketing activities that stimulate consumer purchasing in the short term.

sales representative An independent salesperson who directs efforts to selling your products or service to others but is not an employee of your company. Sales reps often represent more than one product line from more than one company and usually work on commission.

sales tax This is a state- or local-level tax on the sale of certain property. Generally, the buyer pays the tax, and the seller collects it, as an agent for the government.

salvage value The amount that an asset can be sold for at the end of its useful life.

sample A limited portion of the whole of a group.

security Collateral that is promised to a lender as protection in case the borrower defaults on a loan.

service business A business that provides services to customers, rather than selling goods. Examples include utilities providing telephone and transportation service as well as trades and professions such as laundry, repair, consulting, and maintenance help. A retail business that deals in activities for the benefit of others is a service business.

share One of the equal parts into which the ownership of a corporation is divided. A share represents part ownership in a corporation.

short-term notes Loans that come due in one year or less.

single-entry accounting The term referring to a recordkeeping system which uses only income and expense accounts. Now generally used by many smaller businesses, this system is easier to maintain and understand, extremely effective, and 100 percent verifiable.

sole proprietorship A legal structure of a business having one person as the owner. A type of business organization in which one individual owns the business. Legally, the owner is the business and personal assets are typically exposed to liabilities of the business.

stock An ownership share in a corporation; another name for a share. Another definition would be accumulated merchandise.

stockholders Owners of a corporation whose investment is represented by shares of stock.

stockholders' equity The stockholders' shares of stock in a corporation plus any retained earnings.

straight-line method of depreciation A method of depreciating assets by allocating an equal amount of depreciation for each year of their useful life.

sum-of-the-years'-digits method An accelerated method of depreciation in which a fractional part of the depreciable cost of an asset is charged to expense each year. The denominator of the fraction is the sum of the numbers representing the years of the asset's useful life. The numerator is the number of years remaining in the asset's useful life.

supplementary proceeding A court supervised questioning of the debtor. The purpose of a supplementary proceeding is to examine the debtor, under oath, in the presence of a court commissioner, as to the debtor's current financial status and to reveal the amount and location of all property owned by a judgment debtor.

suppliers Individuals or businesses that provide resources needed by a company in order to produce goods and services.

survey A research method in which people are asked questions.

takeover The acquisition of one company by another company.

tangible personal property Machinery, equipment, furniture, and fixtures not attached to the land.

target market The specific individuals, distinguished by socioeconomic, demographic, and/or interest characteristics, who are the most likely potential customers for the goods and/or services of a business.

target marketing Selecting and developing a number of offerings to meet the needs of a number of specific market segments, as determined by competitive strengths and marketplace realities.

tax year The annual accounting period upon the basis of which taxable income is computed.

telemarketing Marketing goods or services directly to the consumer via the telephone.

term loans Either secured or unsecured loans, usually for periods of more than a year to as many as ten years. Term loans are paid off like a mortgage: so many dollars per month for so many years. The most common uses of term loans are for equipment and other fixed asset purposes, for working capital, and for real estate.

terms of sale The conditions concerning payment for a purchase.

three-year income projection A pro forma (projected) income statement showing anticipated revenues and expenses for a business.

tort A legal wrong or injury caused by one against another.

trade credit Permission to buy from suppliers on open account.

travel record The record used to keep track of expenses for a business-related trip away from the home business area.

trial balance A listing of all the accounts in the general ledger and their balances used to prove the equality of debits and credits in accounts.

undifferentiated marketing Selecting and developing one offering for an entire market.

unearned income Revenue that has been received, but not yet earned.

use tax A sales tax that is collectible by the seller or paid by the buyer where the buyer resides in a different state than the seller.

variable costs Expenses that vary in relationship to the volume of activity of a business.

venture capital Money invested in enterprises that do not have access to traditional sources of capital.

venue The county in which a case or action will be heard and decided.

vertical analysis A percentage analysis used to show the relationship of the components in a single financial statement. In vertical analysis of an income statement each item on the statement is expressed as a percentage of net sales.

volume An amount or quantity of business; the volume of a business is the total it sells over a period of time.

wholesale Selling for resale.

wholesale business A business that sells its products to other wholesalers, retailers, or volume customers at a discount.

wholesaling Businesses and individuals engaged in the activity of selling products to retailers, organizational users, or other wholesalers. Selling for resale.

work in progress Manufactured products that are only partially completed at the end of the accounting cycle.

working capital The excess of current assets over current liabilities. The cash needed to keep the business running from day to day. Contrasted with capital, a permanent use of funds, working capital cycles through your business in a variety of forms: inventories, accounts and notes receivable, and cash and securities.

INDEX